W9-BOE-287

MANAGEMENT ACCOUNTING

A Decision Emphasis

MANAGEMENT ACCOUNTING
A Decision Emphasis

DON T. DeCOSTER
University of Washington, Seattle

ELDON L. SCHAFER
Pacific Lutheran University, Tacoma

A Wiley/Hamilton Publication
JOHN WILEY & SONS, INC.
Santa Barbara New York London Sydney Toronto

Library of Congress Cataloging in Publication Data:

DeCoster, Don T.
Management accounting.

"A Wiley/Hamilton publication."
Includes bibliographies and index.
1. Managerial accounting. 2. Decision-making.
I. Schafer, Eldon L., joint author. II. Title.
HF 5635.D3 658.1'51 7533743
ISBN 0-471-20500-1
Printed in the United States of America
10 9 8 7 6 5 4 3 2 1

About the Authors

DON T. DECOSTER, Ph.D., C.P.A. is Professor of Accounting at the University of Washington in Seattle. He holds a Ph.D. in Business Administration from The University of Texas and a Ph.D. in Counseling Psychology from the University of Oregon. He co-authored, with William J. Bruns, Jr., *Accounting and Its Behavioral Implications* (McGraw-Hill Book Company, 1969) and, with K. V. Ramanathan and Gary Sundem, *Accounting for Managerial Decision Making* (Melville Publishing Company, 1974). Articles by Dr. DeCoster have appeared in *The Accounting Review, Journal of Accounting Research, Cost and Management, The Journal of Accountancy, Business Budgeting, The Journal of Vocational Behavior,* and other professional journals. He is a member of the American Accounting Association, the AICPA, and the American Psychological Association. Currently, he is serving as editor of *The Accounting Review.*

ELDON L. SCHAFER, Ph.D., C.P.A. is Professor of Accounting at Pacific Lutheran University in Tacoma, Washington. He holds a Ph.D. in Business Organization and Management from the University of Nebraska. He taught previously at the University of Washington, Syracuse University, San Jose State University, and the University of Nebraska. A member of the American Accounting Association, the Washington Society of C.P.A.'s, and the National Association of Accountants, he has been active in professional development programs in management accounting throughout the United States.

Please return this book; I find though many of my friends are poor arithmeticians, they are nearly all good bookkeepers.

Sir Walter Scott
1771–1832

Preface

This book is an introductory text in management accounting. It integrates the generally accepted areas of management accounting with a focus on what the authors believe is a portent of the future in management accounting education. It is intended to meet the needs of students in a second or third course in accounting. The authors assume that students have had a rudimentary introduction to the basic accounting process of measuring and summarizing business transactions. However, it is not necessary that previous exposures to accounting theory and practice be extremely rigorous.

The authors intend that this book accomplish more than one pedagogical goal. First, they believe that the basic framework of the text recognizes the evolutionary nature of management accounting. Systematically, management accounting has moved from the more classical role of accumulating and reporting data to the more complicated role of communicating financial data for decision making. The purposes of data collection must necessarily converge at that crucial point when a decision is to be made. All past data and all projections seek to reduce uncertainty in making decisions. This trend in accounting is recognized by the organization of topics in this book, which focuses the student's attention upon the primary purpose of data—decisions by management.

Second, the authors stayed within the bounds of current management accounting techniques and theories. Since this book is intended for students studying management accounting for the first time, it would be inappropriate to plow new ground. The organization and the focus are new, not the theory and practice covered. Although some mathematical techniques and current thinking from the behavioral sciences are included, they are not overemphasized.

Finally, the authors intended to keep the content and explanations clear and understandable to undergraduate students who may or may not major in accounting. The topics in this book are important to any person who must make economic decisions. To deny the content to people who do not have a concentration in accounting courses would be unfortunate. However, an understanding of the subject must rest upon active involvement by the student. To achieve this involvement there are numerous problems, both simple and complex, at the end of each chapter. The authors hope that the student is challenged and his ability to use management accounting skills enhanced. At the same time it is not their intention to develop the strong procedural foundation required of professional cost accountants or CPAs.

There are 15 chapters organized into three broad parts. The first part is entitled "Accounting Data for Decision Making." The five chapters in this part introduce the student to the decision process and the current accounting methodologies of data gathering and selection. This is done with a minimum of accounting bookkeeping. The goal of this approach is to concentrate upon the concepts of accounting data without binding the student to any extant data-collection system.

Chapter 1 sets the stage by providing a planning and control framework through a review of the nature of the decision process and the types of decisions that business management must make. Chapter 2 discusses the determination of fixed and variable costs and their role in cost-volume-profit analysis. Chapter 3 concentrates upon how historical accounting creates the flow of costs necessary for measuring production costs. The flow of costs using an absorption costing system under both job and process costing is demonstrated. Chapter 4 deals with the problems of indirect overhead costs. Special emphasis is placed upon predetermined overhead rates and the analysis of overhead variances. Chapter 5 is concerned with variable costing for both internal and external reporting purposes. Chapters 1 through 5 are a basic skill package of concepts and terms necessary to enter into the study of management decision making.

The second part of the book is entitled "The Use of Data in Decision Making." The four chapters in this section focus upon the data needed for specific types of decisions. Chapters 6 and 7 deal with short-range decisions. Chapter 6 contains a discussion of both economic and accounting approaches to pricing decisions. Chapter 7 covers a number of short-range decisions that affect production output and costs.

Chapters 8 and 9 concentrate upon long-range decisions involving productive capacity and long-lived assets. The present-value model is taken as normative. Chapter 8 introduces long-range decisions and discusses the measurement of revenues and costs for long-range decisions, determination of an acceptable rate of return, and the effect of income taxes. The chapter closes with an introduction of present-value techniques. Chapter 9 presents the techniques of investment analysis. Various methods are compared and evaluated with emphasis upon those that consider the time value of money.

The third part of the book is entitled "Planning and Control Systems for Decision Implementation." The focus in this section is upon integrating decision data into a meaningful, coordinated package. The purpose of this integration is to allow the decision maker to test, before the fact, the implications of future decisions. Simultaneous with the integration of data, the opportunity for control is enhanced. Guidelines for action are determined to provide benchmarks for comparison with actual results, ensuring that the system and the decisions are "in control."

Chapter 10 introduces budgeting for planning and control with an emphasis upon the organizational and human side. Chapter 11 introduces standard cost systems. Emphasis is placed upon setting standards, operating a standard cost system, and understanding standard cost variances. Because of its relevance to decision making and control, variable standard costing is presented along with absorption standard costing.

Chapters 12, 13, and 14 develop the budgetary system, using a single company as an example. This approach allows the integration of the previous decision chapters into a coordinated whole. Chapter 12 covers profit planning in detail, starting with problems of revenue forecasting and cost estimating, then moving through the development of a profit plan. Chapter 13 continues to develop the budgetary system with a cash flow budget and projected position statement coordinated with the profit plan. These two chapters deal with budgetary theory as well as the procedural aspects of developing budget schedules. Chapter 14 relates the budgetary process to the budgetary reporting system. Throughout the budgetary reporting system, responsibility accounting is stressed.

Chapter 15 deals with problems that are unique to larger, decentralized organizations. Problems discussed in this chapter include divisional profits, intercompany transfer pricing, and divisional rates of return.

Every author wants to include every relevant and related topic, but finds space a real constraint. We have excluded some topics that others might consider important. Among these are psychological and organizational decision theory, statistical decision theory, and the theory of information economics. These topics are growing in recognized importance but at the current time they are not typically included in an introductory course.

Throughout the text the masculine pronoun is used generally to refer to accountants, economists, and other members of the financial community, simply to avoid the burdensome repetition of *he or she* and *him or her.* Unfortunately, no neuter pronoun has yet been formed. Although we use the traditional masculine reference, we fully acknowledge and respect the involvement of women in the business world—those currently employed and those preparing to enter.

We have been encouraged and supported in our writing by many people. Foremost are our families, who have sacrificed much to help us. We have also had the support of our colleagues and friends who have read and commented upon sections of the manuscript. Among these are Gary L. Sundem and Lois Etherington of the University of Washington, Howard O. Rockness of the University of North Carolina, Mary Longstaff of Highline Community College, Naomi Tsumagari of Tokyo University, Raymond M. Powell of the University of Notre Dame, Robert E. Bennett of Northern Illinois University, Samuel Frumer of Indiana University, Willis R. Greer, Jr. of the University of Oregon, Michael J. Barrett of the University of Minnesota, Harley Courtney of The University of Texas at Arlington, Joseph G. San Miguel of Harvard University, and Ronald Patten of the University of Connecticut. Finally, we would like to thank Mary T. Soulier who worked with us as a graduate research assistant.

Each of these reviewers made valuable comments and suggestions. We have given serious consideration to each suggestion. Beyond doubt they had a positive influence on our thinking and we believe their efforts strengthened the manuscript. Of course, we must take full responsibility for the text.

We are also indebted to the American Institute of Certified Public Accountants, the National Association of Accountants, the Society of Industrial Accountants of Canada, and many publishers and companies for their permission to quote from their publications and examinations. Problems from the Uniform CPA Examinations are designated *CPA adapted;* problems from the examinations administered by the Society of Industrial Accountants are designated *Canada SIA adapted;* and problems from the Certificate in Management Accountant examination given by the Institute of Management Accounting are designated *CMA adapted.*

The authors and the publisher will welcome comments from users.

Don T. DeCoster

Eldon L. Schafer

Contents

Preface **vii**

PART ONE Accounting Data for Decision Making **1**

1 The Planning and Control Process for Decision Making **2**

2 Cost Behavior Patterns and Cost-Volume-Profit Interactions **48**

3 Absorption Costing Systems for Product Costing **105**

4 A Further Look at Factory Overhead Costing **149**

5 Variable Product Costing and the Contribution Margin Approach **191**

PART TWO The Use of Data in Decision Making **243**

6 Revenue and Pricing Decisions **244**

7 Production Decisions **283**

8 Information for Long-range Decisions **332**

9 Techniques of Investment Analysis **372**

PART THREE Planning and Control Systems for Decision Implementation 419

10 Budgeting: A Systematic Approach to Planning 420

11 Cost Efficiency through Standard Costs 462

12 Budgeting: The Profit Plan 515

13 Budgeting for Resource Planning 571

14 Budgetary Reporting and Responsibility Accounting 620

15 Measuring Divisional Performance 675

Glossary 710

Appendix A–Present Value of $1 734

Appendix B–Present Value of an Annuity of $1 736

Index 738

PART ONE

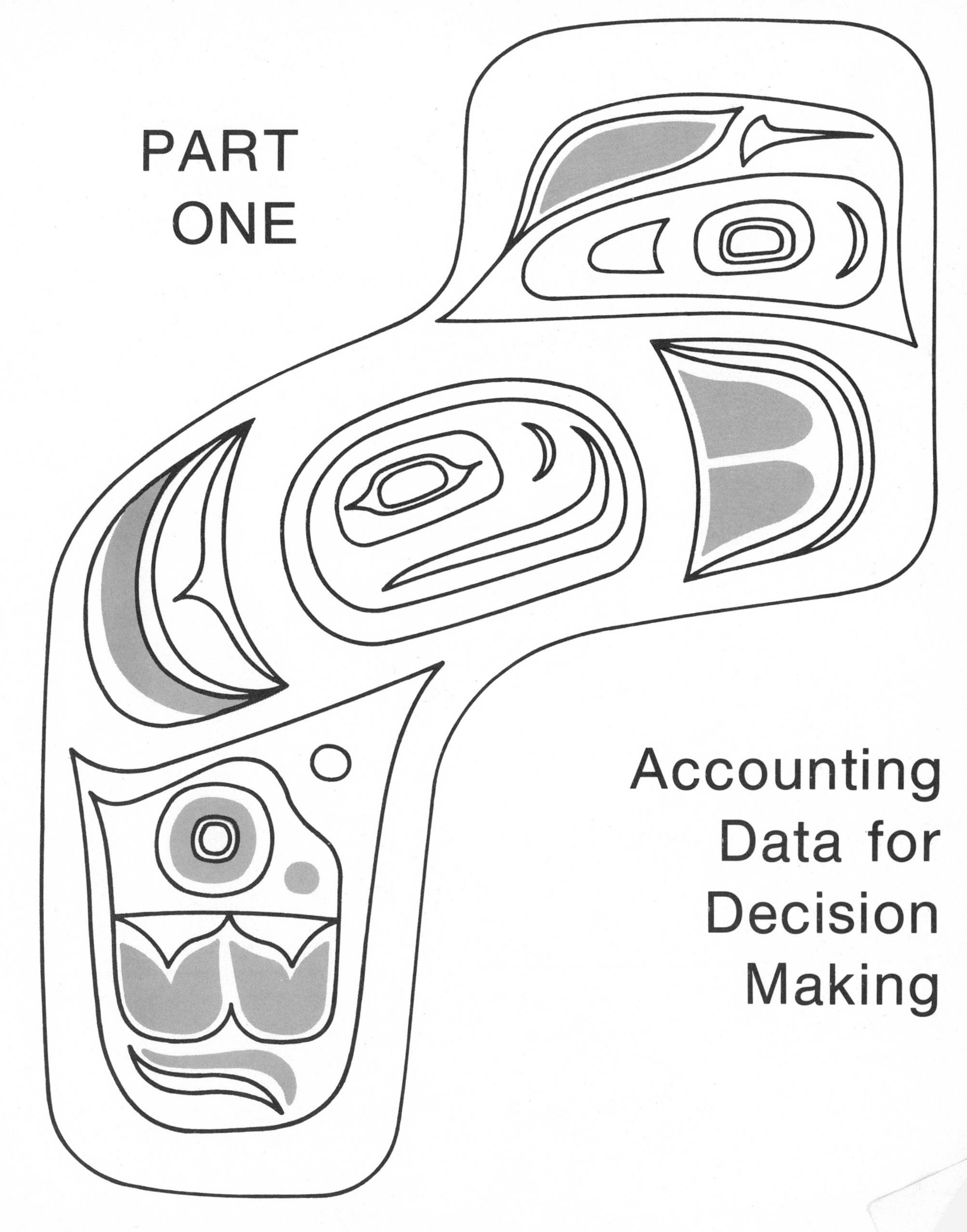

Accounting Data for Decision Making

1 The Planning and Control Process for Decision Making

ACCOUNTING FOR BUSINESS DECISIONS
- *Interfirm Allocation Decisions*
- *Intrafirm Allocation Decisions*

THE PLANNING STAGE
- *Organizational Goals*
- *Resource Utilization Decisions*
- *Types of Decisions*
- *Costs and Benefits Relevant to Decisions*
- *Relevant Costs and Benefits for Operating Decisions*
  - *The Accounting Approach to Operating Decisions*
  - *The Economic Approach to Operating Decisions*
  - *A Comparison of the Accounting and Economic Approaches*
- *Relevant Costs and Benefits for Capacity Decisions*
- *Decisions Expressed through Budgets*

POST-DECISIONAL CONTROL STAGE
- *Performance Data*
- *Nonfinancial Controls*

THE MANAGEMENT ACCOUNTANT'S RESPONSIBILITIES

SUMMARY

The primary purpose of an economic system is to satisfy the wants and needs of its members by allocating the resources available. In the not-for-profit segment of the economy, particularly governmental entities, the plans for resource allocation are made through the budgetary process. The legislative and executive branches, through their agencies, decide what resources will be used for national defense, maintenance of law and order, recreational and park activities, welfare benefits, and resource reclamation, among others. Once these needs are determined and budgeted, taxes are levied to support them. It is through the collection of taxes and subsequent governmental expenditures that economic resources are allocated in the public sector.

The decisions of business managers allocate resources in the profit-oriented segment of the economy. Business resource allocations take place at two levels. First, and most visible, are interfirm decisions made in the capital markets, such as the stock and bond exchanges. The flow of resources between firms is determined in part by these markets. Investors commit their resources (funds) to those firms where they believe they can earn an acceptable rate of return on their investment.[1] As the rate of return declines in one economic activity, its capital tends to flow to another that has a higher rate of return. Second, once resources are invested in a firm, its managers must make decisions about how best to use them. Efficient use of a firm's resources is necessary if the firm is to earn a satisfactory rate of return and maintain its capital investment.

The role of accounting is to provide meaningful information for both of these resource-allocation decisions. In the broadest sense, accounting is a vehicle for communicating the data necessary for making intelligent decisions. Its task is not the making of decisions. This job is the responsibility of the operating managers within a firm and the investors outside the firm.

ACCOUNTING FOR BUSINESS DECISIONS

Because accounting provides a data base for both types of economic decisions, interfirm and intrafirm, it is logical to assume that accounting data must be multipurpose. The focus of accounting data for *interfirm* resource allocations is termed **financial accounting.** The focus of accounting data for *intrafirm* allocations through the planning and control process is termed **management accounting.** There is much common ground between financial and management accounting. The development of a single system for both financial and management accounting involves overlapping data and common terminology. There are, however, important differences in both data requirements and philosophical approaches to these data.

[1]Rate of return on investment is measured by: Income ÷ Investment. A detailed discussion of rate of return for performance evaluation will be found in Chapter 15.

Interfirm Allocation Decisions

For interfirm decisions, where the focus is upon the flow of resources between firms, data needs are more general than for intrafirm decisions. Financial accounting directs its attention to the problems of generating and allocating the resources of industry through the capital markets. This application requires that accounting data be useful to people beyond the firm's management structure. Financial accounting data are used by people who do not have access to the data resources nor to the accounting system that accumulates, transposes, and reports the data. Thus, data published in the accounting reports must communicate to persons outside the firm. These people include past, present, and future stockholders, bondholders, bankers and creditors, labor unions, and any others interested in the firm's operations. When the stock of a corporation is publicly held, this information becomes available to anyone seeking it.

Financial accounting data serve two distinct purposes. First, these data serve as an information source for investors and creditors making their investing and lending decisions. Financial reports (statement of financial position, income statement, statement of retained earnings, and statement of changes in financial position) are used by the prudent investor in selecting his investments. They provide clues to the financial security and stability of a firm and point toward the possible result of future operations. Second, for society-at-large, financial data are used to ensure that a firm has complied with societal regulations and laws. Examples of the compliance function of accounting data are myriad. To the absentee owner it is important to know that management has acted to protect and conserve the firm's resources. He wants to be sure that the data he receives are fair and reliable and that management is not misusing the firm's assets. Compliance focuses upon the implicit and explicit duties corporate management owes to the owners. Compliance reporting also focuses on general societal needs. For example, financial accounting data are used to meet the legal requirements of federal, state, and city tax-collecting agencies; for registration with stock exchanges and the Securities and Exchange Commission; for reports to the Interstate Commerce Commission and the Department of Commerce; and, more recently, for compliance with Environmental Protection Agency regulations.

When financial accounting data are made available to the public, requisites are imposed. First, the users, whether they are stockholders, bondholders, or governmental agencies, typically use these data in their decision-making activities without access to the detailed transactions that are the basis of the summary reports. They must have assurance of a fair and objective presentation of facts. The independent auditor (Certified Public Accountant) serves the function of attesting to the general fairness of the data.

Second, because the financial data serve many diverse interests and people, there is a need for uniformity and standardization. Accounting data would create a variation of the Tower of Babel without some commonality of terms and language, accounting systems, and methods of presentation. This need for standardization and uniformity has generated many accounting activities seeking to develop a common base of knowledge and hence common communication. For example, the Financial Accounting Standards Board seeks to develop a common theory of measuring and reporting transactions and events to the public.

Intrafirm Allocation Decisions

Intrafirm operating decisions begin when resources have been committed to the firm. The goal of management accounting is to optimize the use of these financial resources. Typically, the focus of management accounting is specific rather than general. The data demands of the manager are more specific than the data demands of the investor. There must be allocations between products, asset structures, territories, departments, and management responsibility centers.[2] The nature of a specific decision is often well defined so that the data can be accurately pinpointed and decision rules developed. It should be pointed out that it may be relatively simple to determine what data are needed for a decision. This does not mean, however, that the gathering of this information is simple or easy. It may be difficult, and at times impossible, to isolate the data necessary for a particular decision. But management has one advantage that people outside the firm may not have. With access to the sources of events, management can modify the accounting system and reports to meet its unique specifications. This accessibility makes the data flexible and allows the development of specific data for specific decisions.

This text emphasizes management accounting; that is, information that management needs to make specific intrafirm resource allocations. Such emphasis assumes that accounting must perform the two separate, distinct functions of financial and management reporting and that the data needs for each are often different. However, there are common threads that run through both financial and management accounting. Moreover, the societal and legal requirements of financial accounting often act to limit the flexibility of management accounting.

THE PLANNING STAGE

As a philosopher once said, "To make no decision at all is to make a decision." Businessmen cannot avoid making decisions, even if the decision is to do nothing. They must choose whether to focus their decision making toward specific goals or merely to react to events as they take place. Without goals, and without data about these goals, decisions will lack purpose. A

[2]We will use the term *responsibility center* a few times in a general sense before we give a detailed definition. A responsibility center is an organizational unit where there is specific managerial responsibility for a specific activity and therefore for the related costs, revenues, or resources.

good management decision will be both effective and efficient. An **effective** decision accomplishes the goals management seeks. An **efficient** decision consumes the minimum amount of resources necessary to achieve the goal.

The following section discusses the nature of business decisions. Three assumptions are implicit in this discussion. First, it is assumed that the firm has scarce, but unallocated, resources at its disposal. These resources may be financial, such as cash; physical, such as material, equipment, and buildings; or human, such as the time, skill, and energy of people. Second, it is assumed that management desires to make decisions about how to use these resources in an effective and efficient way. Third, it is assumed that the planning process can be generalized for all types of economic entities. Each firm or organization will approach the steps in the process somewhat differently, but we can isolate and study the common thread running through the planning process. Exhibit 1-1 provides a generalized overview of the planning and decision process.

The first step in making a decision is **planning,** which involves the selection of enterprise goals and the development of programs to allocate resources to achieve these goals. Planning is the backbone of effective decision making. The total firm, including the principal segments that comprise it, must have a plan. It is through the planning process that management formulates courses of action that reduce uncertainty about the future and assimilate the many pressures that bear on the firm.

The planning process may be formal or informal. Formal planning is superior to informal planning, but informal planning is better than none at all. Formal planning should begin with the development of the firm's goals and a recognition of the individual and societal limitations the firm faces in accomplishing its goals.

Organizational Goals

During her adventures in Wonderland, Alice was walking down a path when she came to a fork in the road. There appeared before her a Cheshire Cat of whom Alice asked:

> "Would you tell me, please, which way I ought to go from here?"
> "That depends a good deal on where you want to get to," said the Cat.
> "I don't much care where—" said Alice.
> "Then it doesn't matter which way you go," said the Cat.
> "—so long as I get *somewhere,*" Alice added as an explanation.
> "Oh, you're sure to do that," said the Cat, "if you only walk long enough."[3]

Without a desired destination any decision will lack purpose—it makes no difference which path you take. Even the energy used in gathering data, such as the energy used by Alice in asking questions, is wasted if it provides no useful information.

[3]Lewis Carroll, *Alice's Adventures in Wonderland,* New Junior Classics, Ed. Mabel Williams and Marcia Dalphin (New York: P. F. Collier and Son Corporation, 1949), V, p. 51.

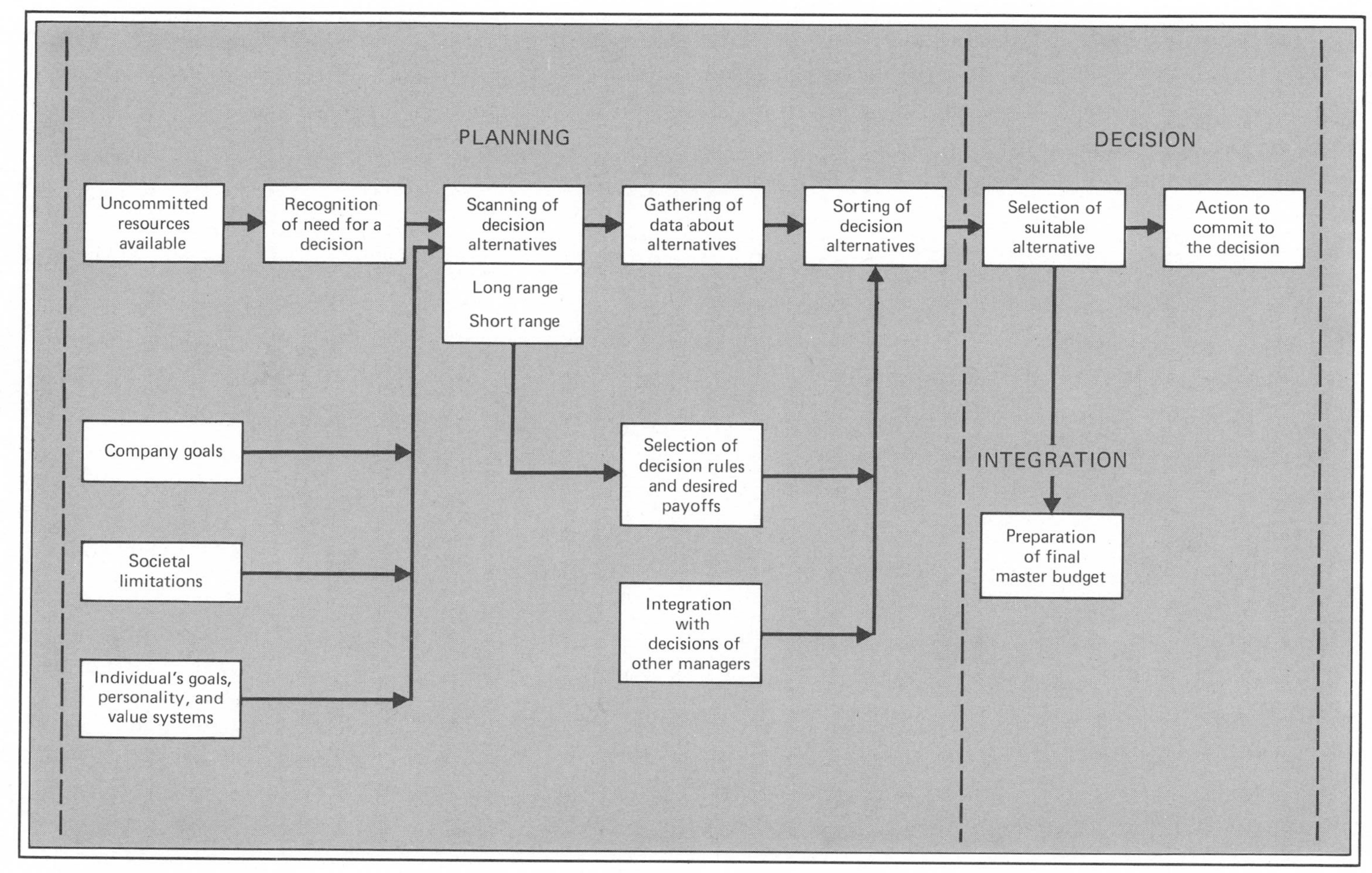

EXHIBIT 1-1
The planning and decision process

Before there can be purposeful decisions, there must be a goal—a direction. The **goal** is the basic aim of the decision maker. It is the direction toward which all decisions and activities are focused. In capitalistic countries such as the United States and Canada, it is generally held that business activity has the common goal of making a profit. Springing from traditional economic theory, this fundamental goal is often stated directly. At other times the profit goal is implied within broader statements such as "providing a public service" or "providing for the long-run existence of the firm." The assumption is that if a firm provides a useful sought-after service it will receive a fair price and profits will result. Similarly, the long-run existence of a firm is assured if it can continue to provide a desired service at an acceptable price. Certainly, the common element that links all business firms, from the smallest to the largest, is the profit motive.

It would be too simplistic to say that the *only* goal of a business firm is to *maximize* profits, however. There are many goals other than profit. Some managers seek to establish a power base and build an empire. Others seek social prestige and peer-group or public approval. Another goal is security. The removal of uncertainty or ambiguity about the future can often override the pure profit motive. Finally, many individuals and firms have humanitarian goals. Hiring disabled workers, providing a cure for a dread disease, maintaining a clean environment, providing an enjoyable place to work, and advancing social and cultural frontiers are examples of humanitarian goals.

For a particular firm many goals must be combined. Absentee stockholders commit their funds to the firm so they can earn dividends and capital gains. Management people, as representatives of the stockholders, also desire a profit. At the same time each manager and worker will have his own unique set of goals. Within the overriding limitation that the firm must earn a satisfactory profit to maintain its existence, each manager and worker strives to meet his own goals. These owners', managers', and workers' goals must be combined within the framework of the legal, political, and economic objectives of society.

The problems of combining many diverse yet separate goals into a unified whole should be apparent. Unless management is successful in blending the majority of goals together, the firm will operate at cross purposes with society or the workers or the owners. The firm must find a way to achieve adequate **goal congruence.** This need is complicated by the fact that most goals are subjective and unspoken. Further, they are broad and rarely capable of being quantified. Perhaps it is because of the vagueness of many goals that decision makers emphasize the most quantifiable objective—the profit motive.

Resource Utilization Decisions

When a firm has uncommitted resources, or resources that may be shifted from one use to another, a decision is necessary. The goals of the firm, as well as any external limitations, act as guides for the managers' decisions.

Beginning with these goals there are several planning steps that management will take to ensure an effective and efficient decision.

The first step shown in Exhibit 1-1, once the need for a decision is recognized, is to define the problem and list decision alternatives. J. Maurice Clark, in a classic book entitled *Studies in the Economics of Overhead Costs,* succinctly summarized the types of resource utilization decisions faced by a firm:

1. The plant is not yet built, and the problem is whether the building of a new plant is economically justified or not. . . .
2. The plant is not yet built, and the problem is how large to build it. . . .
3. The plant is built and in operation, and the problem is whether it is economical to change the methods of production. . . .
4. The plant is built and in operation, and the problem is: What income is available for dividends? . . .
5. It is estimated that a reduced price will make possible increased sales, and the problem is how cheaply it will pay to sell goods. . . .
6. Competition becomes increasingly keen and threatens to cut into the existing sales of the concern. The problem is how low the concern can afford to cut prices in order to hold its business. . . .
7. A depression occurs, and the problem arises whether the plant should be shut down temporarily, pending revival. . . .
8. It is proposed to develop a side line which can keep the plant and working force occupied during seasons when experience shows that the main product is in slack demand. The problem here is: What are the costs attributable to this side line for purposes of determining whether it is worth undertaking? . . .
9. Finally we come to the stage at which the question arises whether this plant is no longer needed, and should be permanently abandoned.[4]

Written over fifty years ago, this list of possible economic decisions is provocative and surprisingly complete.

Types of Decisions

The first three decisions listed by Clark call for the commitment of company resources to plant and equipment, whereas the last decision problem concerns disposing of plant and equipment. Usually these four decision problems are termed **long-range** or **capacity decisions.** Long-range decisions have two unique characteristics. First, they involve changes in the productive or service potential of the firm. Second, and equally important, they cover a relatively long time span so their effect on the firm is best measured in terms of cash flow, adjusted for the time value of money. The **time value of money** is a formal recognition of the simple fact that a dollar invested today will earn interest and be worth more later. Conversely, a dollar to be received in the future is worth less today.

[4]J. Maurice Clark, *Studies in the Economics of Overhead Costs* (Chicago: University of Chicago Press, 1923), pp. 177–180.

The decisions involving production output, competition pricing, additions to the product line, temporary shutdown, and distribution of profits as dividends are **short-range** or **operating decisions.** Each of these decisions spans a short enough time period so the time value of money is not considered significant, although it is present. Further, none involves adding to or reducing production facilities; rather, they involve obtaining the best results possible from existing facilities.

Costs and Benefits Relevant to Decisions

As shown in Exhibit 1-1, after the decision alternatives have been isolated, the next step in the planning process is the development of data on costs and benefits of the alternatives. The accounting system is a valuable source of data about the possible alternatives, although it is not the only source. The accounting system accumulates financial data resulting from past decisions. For it to be useful for subsequent decisions, management must be interested in data measured in dollars and believe that past results are useful in predicting the future.

To make an effective and efficient decision management requires estimates of all costs and benefits relevant to the alternatives being considered. A **relevant cost** or **benefit** is one affected by the decision. A cost or benefit not affected by the decision is **nonrelevant.** A nonrelevant cost or benefit can be ignored in making a decision because it will not change as a result of that decision. The ability to distinguish between which costs and benefits are relevant and which are nonrelevant underlies any efficient decision.

To illustrate the concept of relevant costs and benefits let's take a simple example. John is currently working in a lumberyard. He is considering returning to college. What data are relevant to his decision? Obviously the added costs of tuition, books, and school fees are relevant. How about his room and board? Since he is self-supporting he would incur room and board whether he went to school or continued working at the lumberyard. Only the difference, if any, in room and board between the two alternatives would be relevant. If he could continue to live in the same boardinghouse his costs of room and board would be nonrelevant. More difficult to estimate are the benefits of the two alternatives. If he goes to college he must forego the revenue he would earn at the lumberyard. Economists and accountants call this foregone revenue an **opportunity cost.** However, if he continues to work at the lumberyard he might earn less in later years than he would as a college graduate. It is the difference in income across time that is relevant to his decision.

To illustrate relevant and nonrelevant costs and benefits in a business setting, let's assume that the Bradford Company recently purchased a building for $100,000, with an estimated useful life of 10 years. The firm has two alternative uses for the building. One alternative is to lease it to another company for a flat monthly rental fee. The second alternative is to store inventory in the building. In this illustration, the depreciation charges are nonrelevant since they will not be affected by either choice. Only the differences in maintenance and operating costs are relevant costs to compare with the alternative benefits of a monthly rental fee or the value of the warehouse as storage space.

Another way of thinking about costs and benefits that is useful for decision making is that of differential cost or differential benefit. A **differential cost** is the difference in cost between any two available, acceptable alternatives. A **differential benefit** is the difference in benefits between any two available, acceptable alternatives. This approach compares the two alternatives directly by looking at the differences between them. Thus the difference in cost between operating a Cadillac and a Pinto is a differential cost. The difference in cost between leasing and purchasing a car is a differential cost. The difference in benefits between receiving a commission as opposed to a fixed salary is a differential benefit. Many accountants also call this process **incremental analysis,** since they are measuring the total "additional" costs or benefits of one alternative over another.

As shown in Exhibit 1-1, the next step in the planning process, after scanning the decision alternatives, is the sorting of alternatives by determining which costs and benefits are relevant. This sorting requires the development of decision criteria or rules. Because long-range decisions are conceptually different from short-range decisions, accountants have developed different decision rules for each. In the next section we will develop an overview of these two decision rules. Then, in later chapters, we will look at them in even more detail.

Relevant Costs and Benefits for Operating Decisions

THE ACCOUNTING APPROACH TO OPERATING DECISIONS

Operating decisions involve choosing the best use of existing capacity. Experience and study have shown that one of the best methods accountants have for determining which costs are relevant and which costs are nonrelevant in operating decisions is to view costs from a perspective of how they change as output changes. Some costs change with output changes; others do not change. Costs that change with variations in output (variable costs) are relevant to output decisions; costs that do not change (fixed costs) are not relevant.

Variable costs

Variable costs are those that vary in total dollar amount in direct proportion to changes in volume. Increases in production output result in parallel and proportionate increases in variable costs. Raw materials used in production typically represent variable costs. If raw materials cost $3 per unit of product,

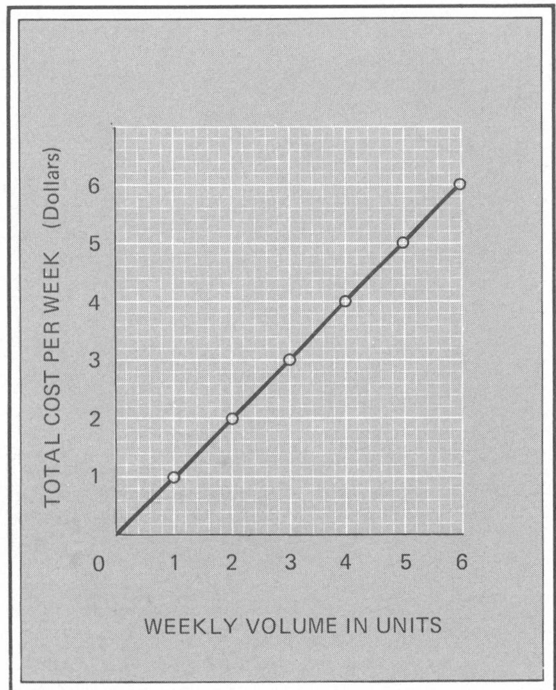

EXHIBIT 1-2
Total variable cost

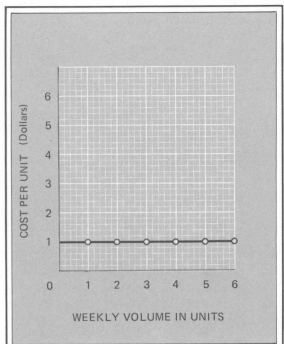

EXHIBIT 1-3
Variable cost per unit

it would take a total cost of $3 to produce one unit, $6 to produce two units, $18 to produce six units, and $36 to produce twelve units.

One of the apparent traits of a variable cost is that while the total variable cost increases proportionately to volume, the variable cost per unit of output is constant. Exhibit 1-2 is a graphic presentation of a completely variable cost that increases at the rate of $1 per unit of output. Exhibit 1-3 shows this same cost from a different perspective—that of cost per unit. If the total dollar amount of a cost varies in direct proportion to changes in volume, then it must be constant per unit of production.

Fixed costs

Fixed costs represent the costs of productive capacity that are unaffected by changes in volume. In the short run they remain the same regardless of changes in production output. For example, assume that plant maintenance is contracted with an outside firm at $24,000 per year, or $2,000 per month. Regardless of the plant output, this cost will not change. The greater the

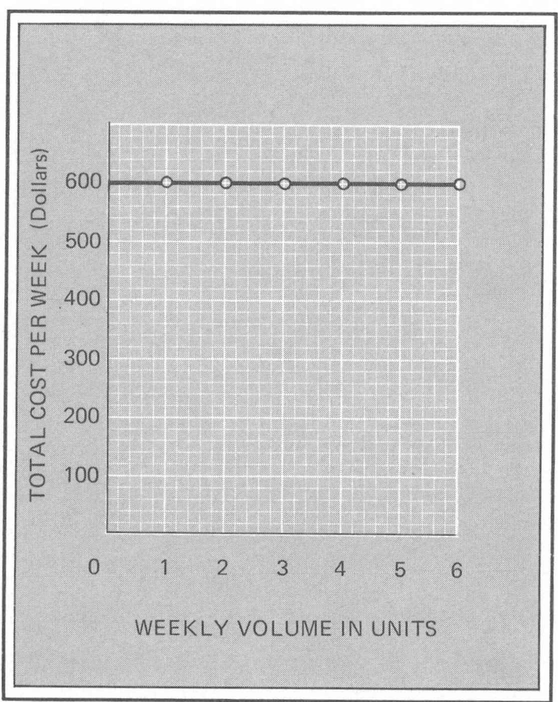

EXHIBIT 1-4
Total fixed cost

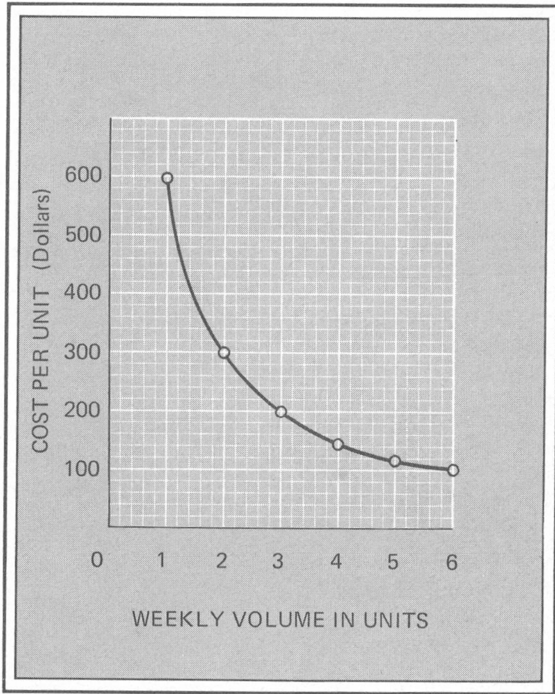

EXHIBIT 1-5
Fixed cost per unit

plant output, the lower the maintenance cost *per unit* of output. If the firm produces 2,000 units per month, maintenance cost will be $1 per unit. If the firm produces only 200 units, the cost per unit will be $10. Thus, fixed costs are constant in total as volume levels change, but vary per unit inversely with changes in volume. This effect is shown graphically in Exhibits 1-4 and 1-5. Exhibit 1-4 shows a fixed cost of $600 per week. Exhibit 1-5 shows the same fixed cost from a cost-per-unit perspective.

When looking at costs in terms of their behavior patterns (how they change with changes in volume), the time period is held constant. Ordinarily this time span is one year, although it could be any time period selected by management. This consideration puts definite limits on the interpretations of fixed and variable costs. Let's assume that a firm has a machine with a depreciable cost of $1,000 and a useful life of five years. We can see the effect of the assumption of a constant time period when considering cost variability. Management is considering the two alternative depreciation methods of straight-line and sum-of-the-years' digits in accounting for the machine. Exhibit 1-6 shows the annual depreciation charge for each of these assumptions.

	STRAIGHT-LINE DEPRECIATION		SUM-OF-THE-YEARS' DIGITS DEPRECIATION	
Year	Annual Proportion of Total Cost	Annual Depreciation	Annual Proportion of Total Cost	Annual Depreciation
1	1/5	$200	5/15	$333
2	1/5	$200	4/15	$267
3	1/5	$200	3/15	$200
4	1/5	$200	2/15	$133
5	1/5	$200	1/15	$ 67

EXHIBIT 1-6
Comparative depreciation schedules

In year 1 the *fixed cost* would be $200 under the straight-line depreciation method, whereas under the sum-of-the-years'-digits method it would be $333. Since the amount of depreciation is not related to the volume of production, the costs from either schedule would be fixed although they change from year to year. Thus, costs are fixed or variable only in relationship to volume changes within a given time period.

Semivariable costs

Of course not all costs are perfectly fixed or perfectly variable. Many costs change with changes in production volume, but not in direct proportion. These costs are called **semivariable costs.** They have both fixed and variable cost attributes. Some people call them **semifixed** although *semivariable* is more commonly used.

Among the reasons for semivariable costs are the following factors:

1. It is frequently necessary to have a minimum organization or to consume a minimum quantity of supplies or services in order to maintain productive readiness. Beyond this minimum cost, which is fixed, additional costs may vary with changes in volume.

2. The accounting classification system may group fixed and variable costs together. For example, by accumulating all insurance premiums into an account entitled "Insurance Expense," the accounting system may group together various types of policy premium costs having different behavior patterns.

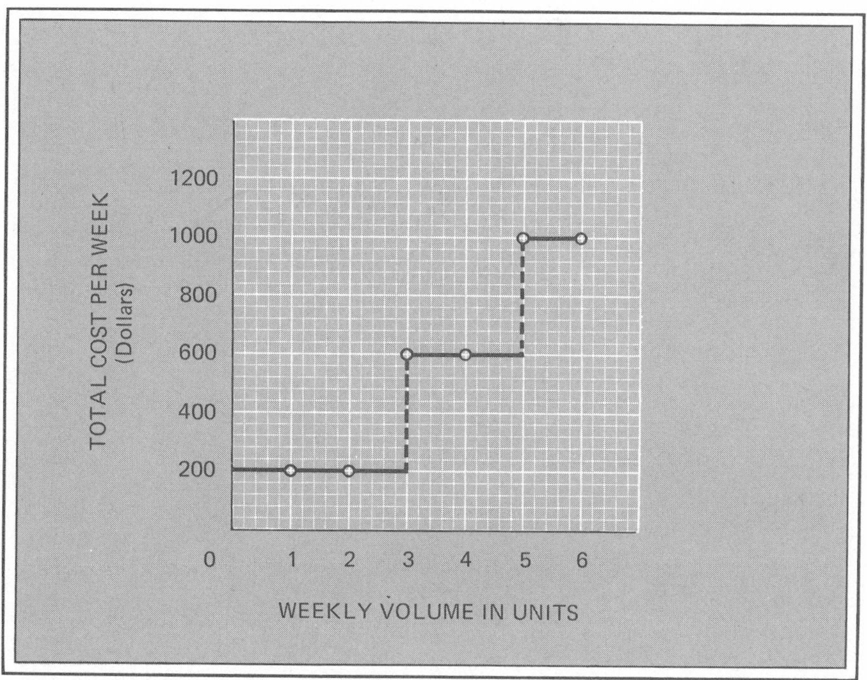

EXHIBIT 1-7
A stairstep cost

3. Often production factors are not divisible into infinitely small units. For example, moving from a single-shift to a double-shift production schedule will cause some costs to change in stairstep fashion.

In general, there are three broad classes of semivariable costs. Perhaps the easiest to visualize is the **stairstep cost** shown in Exhibit 1-7. Supervisory salaries often behave in this way. One supervisor may supervise ten production line workers. As the number of workers increases because of increased production volume, another supervisor is added.

Stairstep semivariable costs allow further exploration of the nature of fixed costs and how they differ from other cost behavior patterns. One way to think about fixed costs is that they are stairstepped costs. For example, assume a company has a machine with a maximum capacity of 1,000 units per year. The firm will have to buy a new machine to increase production to 1,001 units per year. In this sense all fixed costs are stairstepped.

Exhibit 1-8 shows two different cost patterns. Both Costs *A* and *B* vary with changes in volume. Cost *B*, however, varies over smaller incremental changes in volume than does Cost *A*. If during the coming year the company plans to produce between 2,000 and 6,000 units, Cost *A* would be considered fixed and Cost *B* would be semivariable. If the company's volume ranges

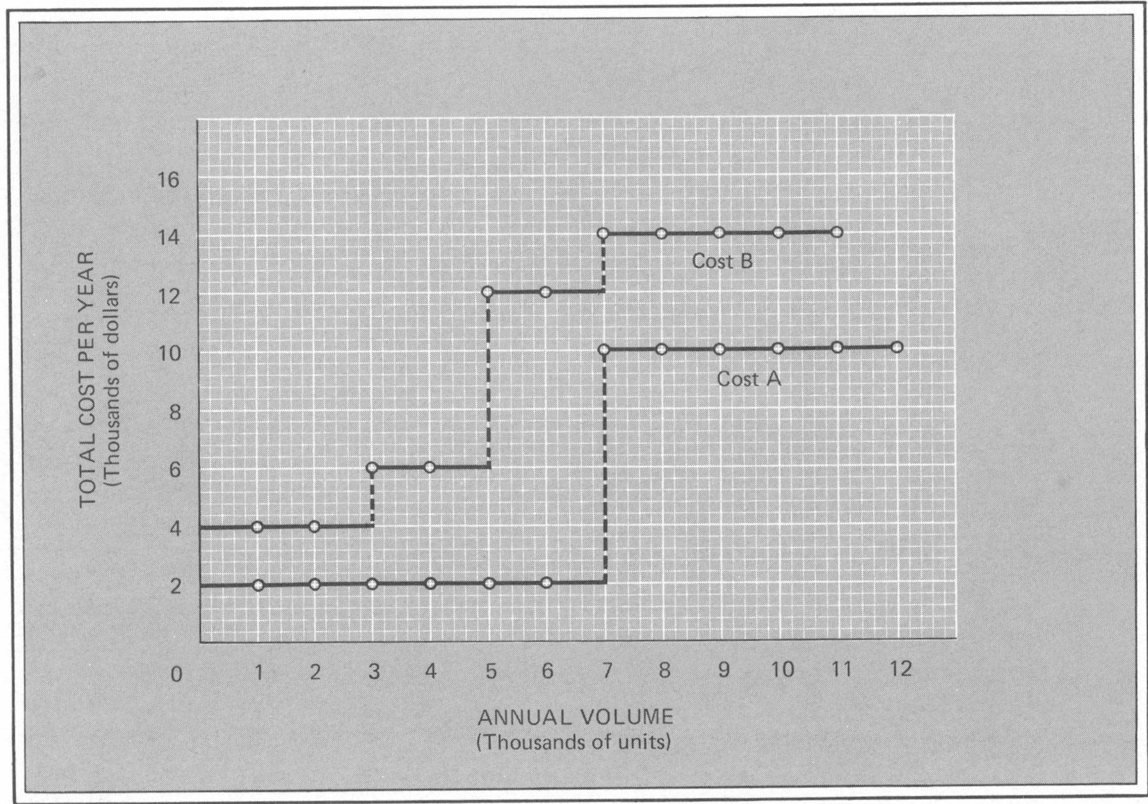

EXHIBIT 1-8
Comparison of two stair stepped costs

between 2,000 and 10,000 units, both costs would be semivariable. Both costs would be fixed if the production plans were between 3,001 and 5,000 units. This illustration shows that costs are fixed only in relationship to volume in the short range, and that all costs can change in the long range. An absurdly short time period, for example one hour, would make almost all costs fixed. A long time period, for example 20 years, would make almost all costs variable.

Another type of semivariable cost is that which includes both a fixed and a variable component. Maintenance is an example of such a cost. If the company produces nothing, maintenance will still be required. As the volume of production increases, the amount of required maintenance will increase. The common name of a cost with both fixed and variable cost attributes is **mixed cost.** A mixed cost is shown in Exhibit 1-9. In this illustration the fixed component is $200 and the variable costs increase at the rate of $.20 per unit of volume.

Other costs change with production volume, but in a nonlinear way. Costs such as utilities often increase at a decreasing rate. For example, assume that a manufacturing process requires one gallon of water per unit of

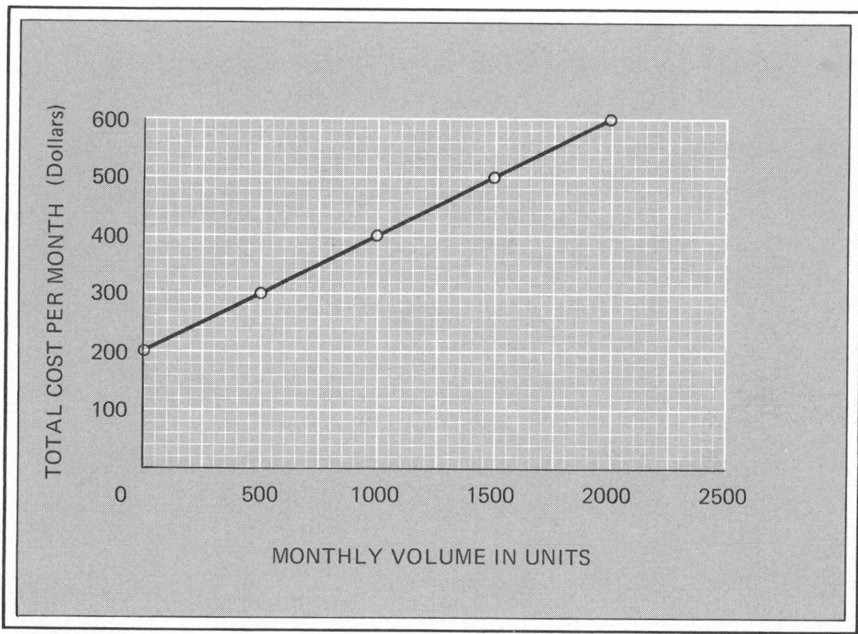

EXHIBIT 1-9
A mixed cost

output, and that the cost per gallon of water is $.03 for consumption between 1,000 and 3,000 gallons; $.02 for consumption between 3,001 and 5,000 gallons; $.01 for consumption between 5,001 and 10,000 gallons; and $.005 per gallon for consumption over 10,000 gallons. This cost is shown graphically in Exhibit 1-10.

A few costs increase at an increasing rate. These costs are really fines and penalties. Examples include demurrage charges on rail cars, pollution fines, and in some instances, the costs of labor. One effect of the energy crisis may be to shift the semivariable costs of energy from costs that decrease per unit with increased usage to costs that increase per unit as usage increases.

Accountants, through their measuring tools, normally convert semivariable costs into their fixed and variable components by using a straight-line assumption. We will examine these tools and their effects on semivariable costs in the following chapter. For now we will assume that fixed and variable costs have been determined and that all semivariable costs have been segregated into purely fixed and purely variable components.

When costs are identified by the accountant as fixed or variable, he is also implying another important concept—the relevant range of activity. The **relevant range** is the span of volume over which the cost behavior can reasonably be expected to remain valid. If raw material is a variable cost of $3 per unit under normal operating conditions, it is likely, because of quantity

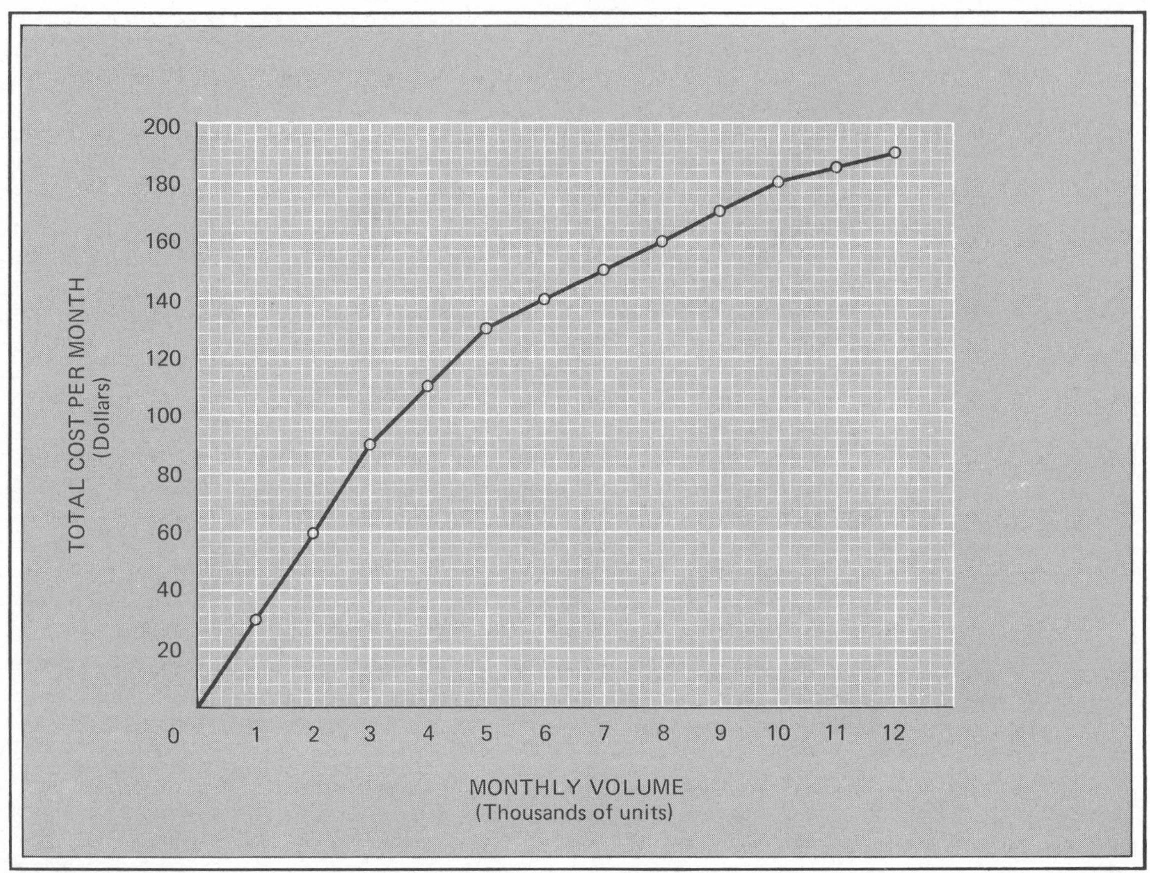

EXHIBIT 1-10
Curvilinear semivariable cost

discounts, that it would increase as volume declines sharply or decrease if production doubles or triples. Thus, costs are fixed or variable only over a relevant range of output.

The contribution margin approach

The understanding of a firm's fixed and variable costs facilitates the measurement of differential costs in operating decisions. In most differential production decisions the variable costs are relevant and the fixed costs are nonrelevant. The identification and reporting of fixed and variable cost behavior patterns is a major contribution that the management accountant can make to management decision making.

To measure benefits from operating decisions, the accountant uses the selling price of the items being produced. He assumes that the items can be sold at the average selling price per unit. The difference between the average revenue per unit and the variable cost per unit is the **contribution margin per**

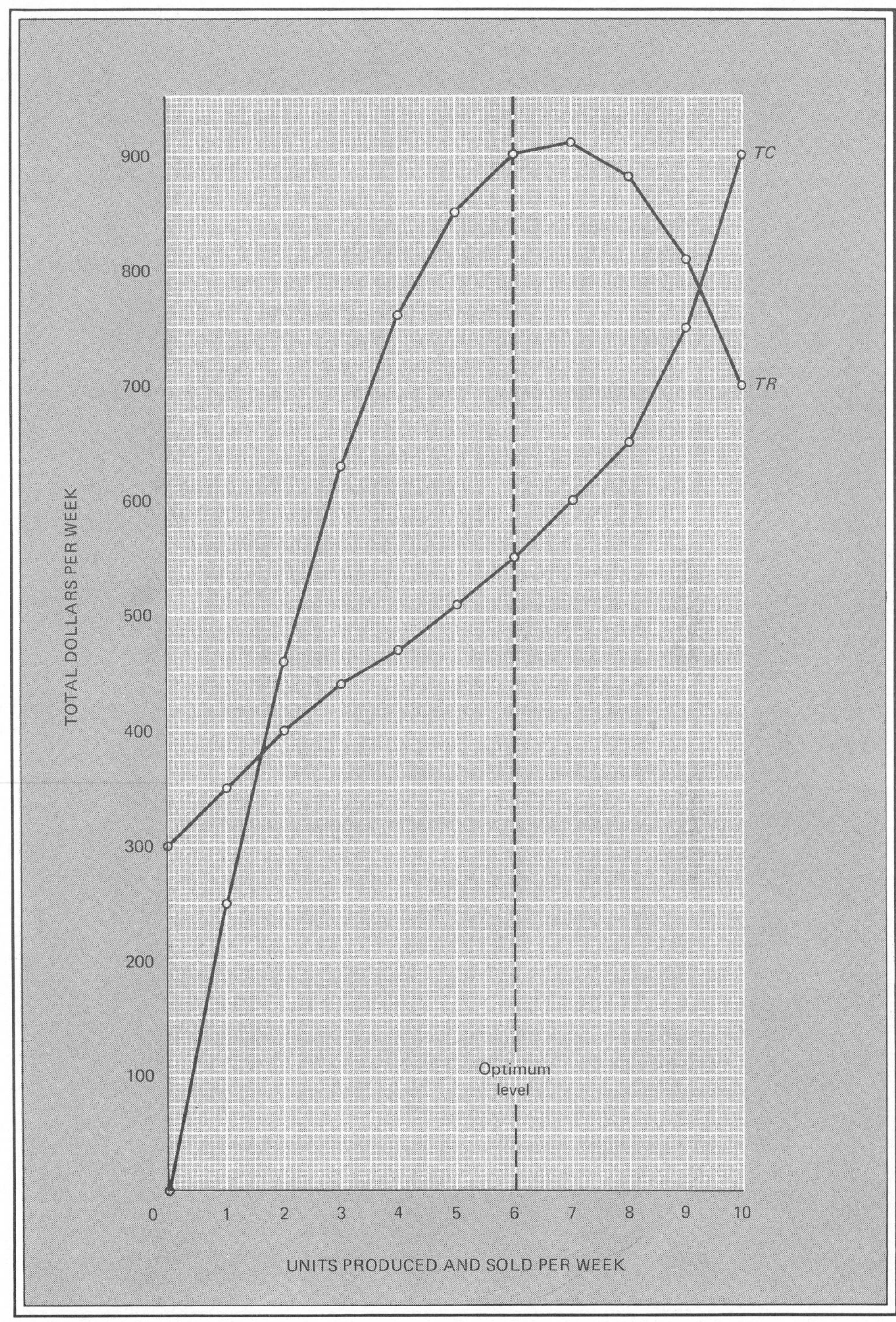

EXHIBIT 1-12
Economist's total cost and total revenue curves

unit the *rate* of increase is relatively constant. Production inefficiencies show up when more than eight units are produced per week. These inefficiencies cause the total cost line to rise sharply.

A revenue line is added to our illustration in Exhibit 1-12. **Total revenue** is the quantity sold times the price per unit. Economics assumes that the price per unit must be reduced to sell more units. The firm must offer price concessions to obtain increased sales volume.[5]

Total revenue minus total cost is total income. The effect of the decreasing price per unit, caused by price reductions necessary to increase demand, and the increasing cost per unit, caused by diminishing returns on the production facilities, is to have an income figure that increases to a point and then decreases until it becomes a loss. Thus, the optimum production level is where the total revenue line exceeds the total cost line by the largest amount. In our illustration the greatest income is earned when six units per week are produced and sold. Income, at each output level, may be computed as shown in the accompanying tabulation.

Quantity	*Total Revenue*	*Total Cost*	*Income (Loss)*	
0	$ 0	$300	$(300)	
1	$250	$350	$(100)	
2	$460	$400	$ (60)	
3	$630	$440	$ 190	
4	$760	$470	$ 290	
5	$850	$510	$ 340	
6	$900	$550	$ 350	← Optimum level
7	$910	$600	$ 310	
8	$880	$650	$ 230	
9	$810	$750	$ 60	
10	$700	$900	$(200)	

Earlier we indicated that the economist's decision model states that optimum output is where the marginal cost equals the marginal revenue. These are concepts that relate the changes in cost and revenue effected by adding *one* unit. Let's develop these concepts by examining the behavior of costs and revenue on a *per-unit* basis, rather than on a total cost and revenue basis.

The *per-unit* costs for average total costs *(ATC)* and marginal costs *(MC)* are shown graphically in Exhibit 1-13. **Marginal cost** is the change in

[5]This statement is true in all cases except pure competition. In pure competition the selling price per unit is assumed to be constant over the output range since the individual producer cannot offer a large enough amount to influence the price. Further discussion of this point is contained in Chapter 6, where pricing decisions are discussed.

total costs incurred by producing one additional unit. Stated differently: Marginal cost is the additional cost incurred in production of the last unit of output and, therefore, the cost that can be "saved" by reducing total output by the last unit. Marginal cost could also be determined by subtracting the total variable cost for a specific output from the total variable cost at the next highest level of output. This is true because only the variable cost changes with changes in output. The marginal costs are also plotted on Exhibit 1-13. The marginal cost curve is J- or U-shaped, first falling but ultimately rising, recognizing the effects of economies of scale and diminishing returns.

It can be seen in Exhibit 1-13 that the average total cost curve is pulled downward when the marginal cost is less than the average cost. When the marginal cost exceeds the average total cost, it acts to pull the average total cost up. When the marginal cost equals the average total cost, the average total cost is at its lowest point. Similarly, the marginal cost curve cuts through the average variable cost curve at its lowest point. On Exhibit 1-13 the marginal cost curve crosses the average total cost curve *slightly* above its lowest point. This is true because we are plotting discrete points rather than smooth, continuous curves.

Exhibit 1-14 adds average revenue *(AR)* and marginal revenue *(MR)* curves to the cost curves in Exhibit 1-13. Average revenue is the price *(P)* per unit at a specific output level. **Marginal revenue** is the increment in total revenue effected when volume is increased by an increment of one. Marginal revenue analysis assumes that the price will never be negative (producers would be paying customers to take their products), but that the marginal revenue may be negative, since the price of *all* units must be lowered to attain the added sales volume. In Exhibit 1-14 both revenue lines slope downward to the right, with the marginal revenue line below the average revenue line.

Examine only the marginal cost and marginal revenue lines. Marginal cost and marginal revenue, at each level of output, are as shown in the accompanying tabulation.

Quantity	*Average Total Cost*	*Marginal Revenue*	*Marginal Cost*	
1	$350	$ 250	$350	
2	$200	$ 210	$ 50	
3	$147	$ 170	$ 40	
4	$118	$ 130	$ 30	
5	$102	$ 90	$ 40	Optimum level
6	$ 92	$ 50	$ 40 ←	slightly over
7	$ 86	$ 10	$ 50	six units
8	$ 81	$ (30)	$ 50	
9	$ 83	$ (70)	$100	
10	$ 90	$(110)	$150	

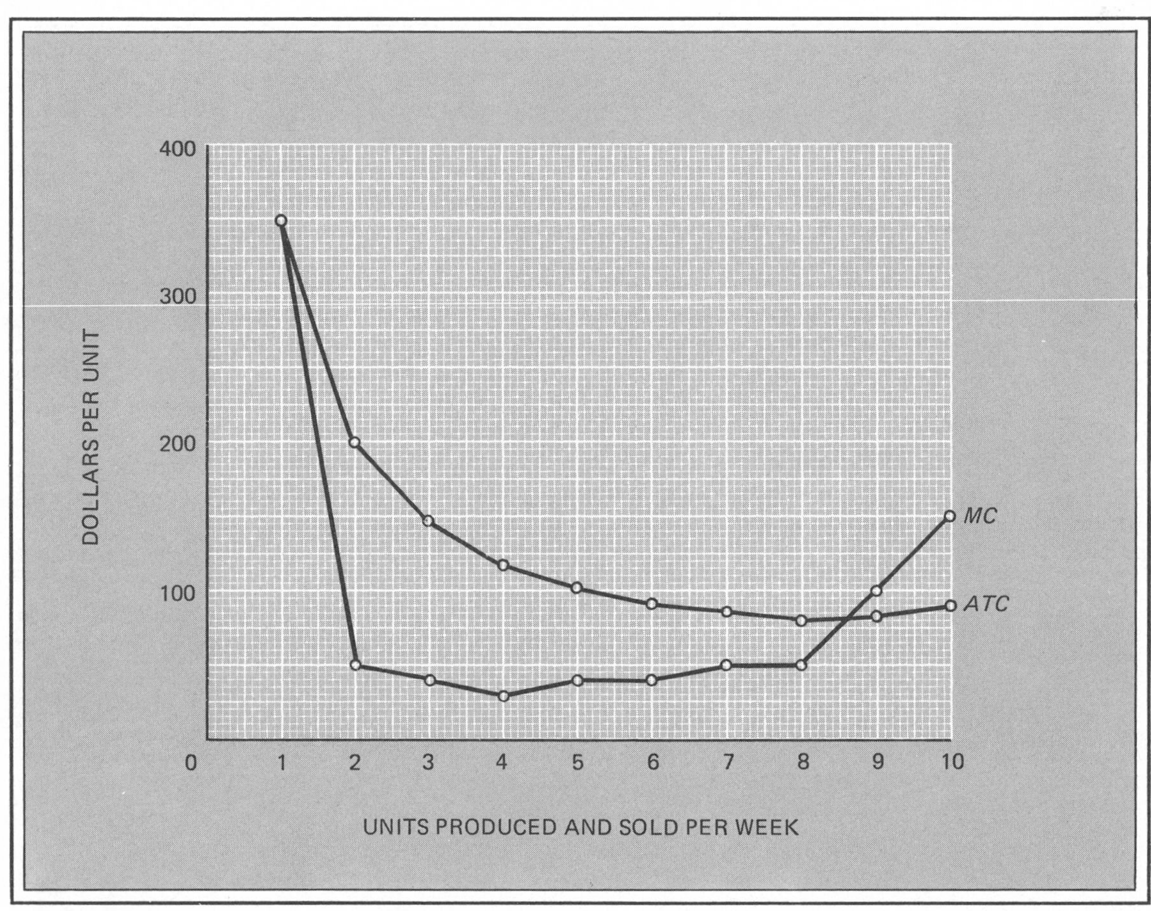

EXHIBIT 1-13
Economist's marginal and average cost curves

This is the same volume level that was determined to be the optimum level in Exhibit 1-12, using total cost and total revenue. Actually marginal cost and marginal revenue are the rates of change in total cost and total revenue respectively. When the rate of increase in the total cost line and the rate of decrease in the revenue line are equal, the difference between them will be maximum and therefore at the level of highest income.

Three additional points should be made about economic marginal analysis. First, the shape of a marginal cost curve will depend upon plant design. In many firms the marginal cost curve is relatively flat at the bottom. This flatness shows a relatively constant marginal cost over a wide range of activity. A curve of this type permits wide fluctuations in product demand or large forecasting errors while operations remain at an efficient level.

Second, output is restricted by plant capacity. In the short run this capacity cannot be changed. In the long run, however, plant capacity can be modified by changing the plant size or changing the number of plants in

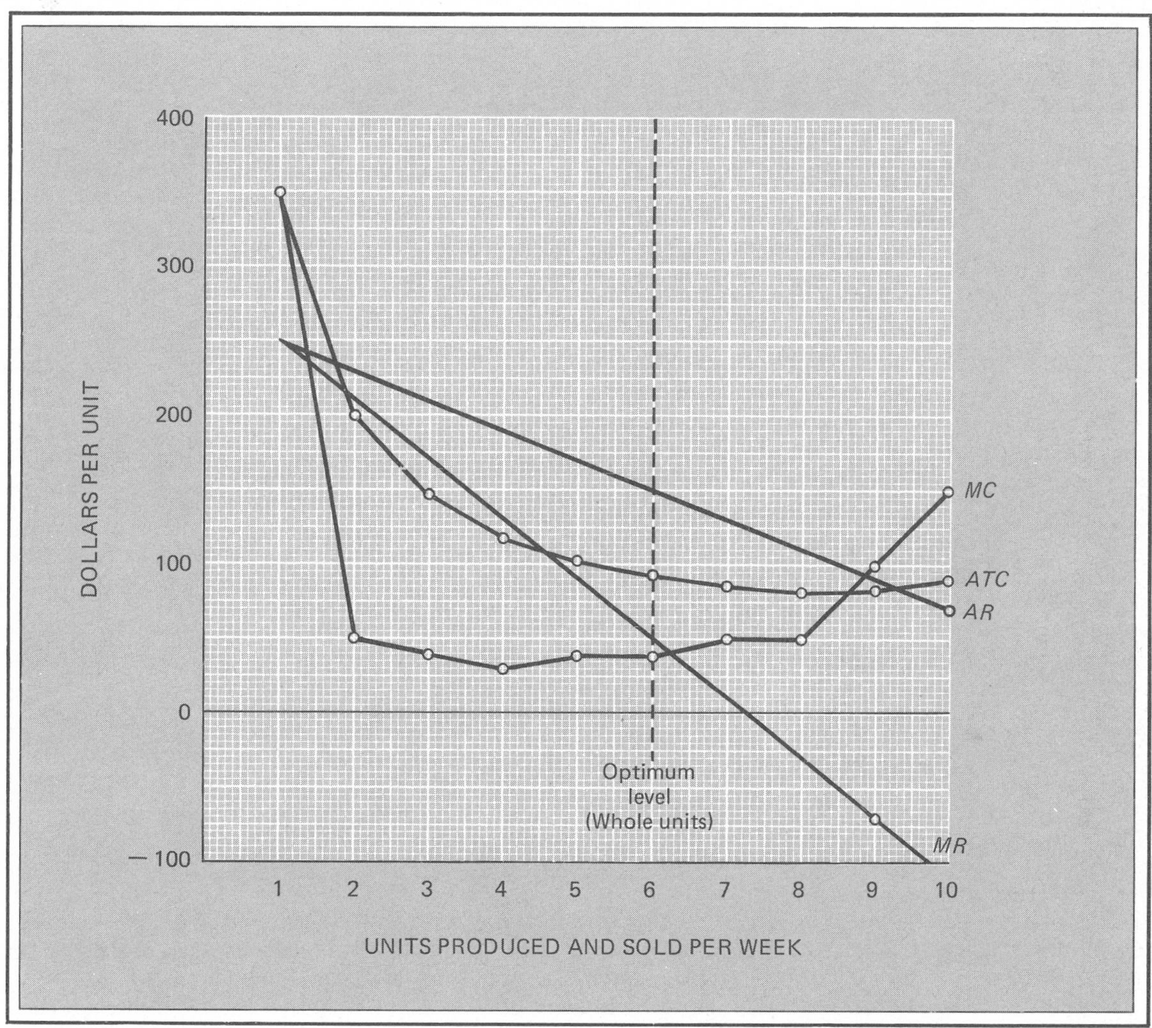

EXHIBIT 1-14
Economist's marginal cost and marginal revenue curves

operation. Thus, there are both long-run and short-run cost curves. Marginal analysis is, in essence, limited by a time constraint. Given more time the company could adjust its cost curves by adjusting its plant size. When we say that the marginal cost is the increased cost of adding another unit, there is an automatic assumption that the time span does not allow the firm to adjust productive capacity.

Third, the slope of marginal revenue and average revenue lines is dependent upon the type of marketplace. Average revenue and marginal revenue depend upon the market's supply and demand functions. In Chapter 6 we will examine supply and demand more closely.

At the optimum level of production (where marginal cost equals marginal revenue) profit maximization, or loss minimization, will occur. Marginal analysis does not automatically imply that the firm will make a profit. If there is no output, the fixed costs will be incurred anyway. However, if price is greater than average variable cost there will be a contribution toward the fixed costs which will reduce the loss. Economic analysis shows that the firm should operate only if total revenue exceeds total cost, or if total cost exceeds total revenue by some amount less than total fixed costs. This could also be expressed by saying that the firm should produce if the price is equal to or greater than average variable costs. A profit will result if total revenue exceeds total cost, and a loss will result if total cost exceeds total revenue. From a per-unit view, there will be a profit if the price exceeds average total cost, and there will be a loss if average total cost exceeds price.

A COMPARISON OF THE ACCOUNTING AND ECONOMIC APPROACHES

A comparison of the economist's and the accountant's assumptions is shown in Exhibit 1-15. The economist's marginal cost curve is J- or U-shaped; the accountant's per-unit variable cost is a constant, which, when plotted, is a flat, horizontal line. Similarly, the economist's marginal revenue curve for any marketplace except pure competition slopes downward to the right, while the accountant's per unit revenue line is horizontal. The horizontal revenue line of the accountant is the same as the economist's revenue line in a pure competition marketplace.

These differences can be examined another way. Exhibit 1-16 shows total revenue and total cost under both the accountant's and economist's assumptions. (Note that the vertical axis is total dollars, not dollars per unit as used in Exhibit 1-15.) The economic curve shows that optimum output is where the total revenue exceeds the total cost by the maximum amount. The accounting curves shows that the optimum output is at the maximum plant capacity.

Before leaving this comparison we should return to a very important concept—the relevant range. The accountant assumes that there is a relevant range of activity over which linear assumptions are valid. If production falls outside the relevant range of activity, the entire cost and revenue patterns must be reassessed. The economist, on the other hand, has developed a descriptive model for wide ranges of activity. Inside the relevant range of activity, the accountant's curves are often very similar to those of the economist. Over a limited volume range the economist's curves would appear as straight lines, which are what the accountant assumes.

Relevant Costs and Benefits for Capacity Decisions

As stated earlier, long-range decisions involve adding to or decreasing the productive capacity of the firm. Typically they involve long periods of time before the benefits of the decision are fully realized by the firm. This con-

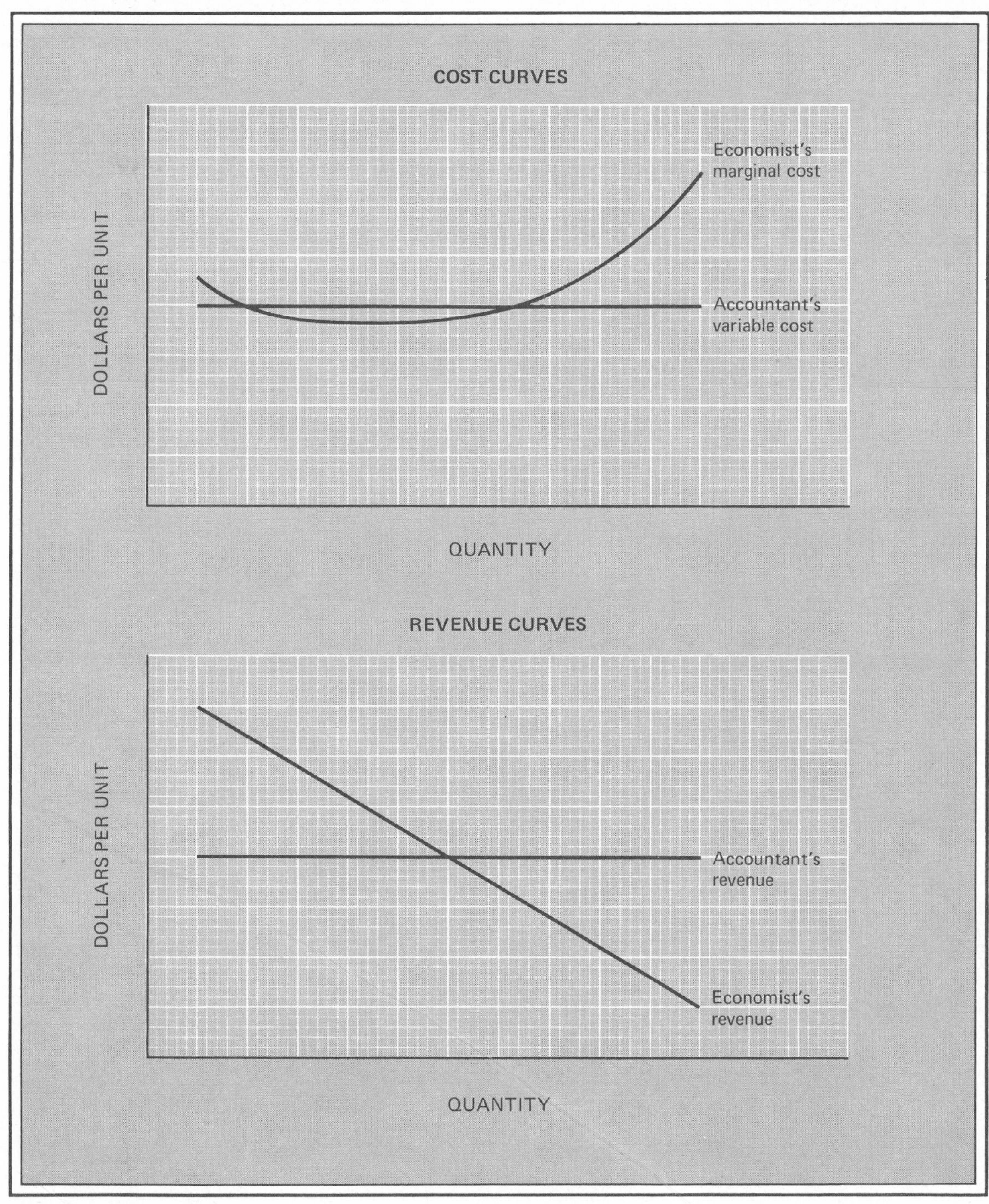

EXHIBIT 1-15
Contrast of accountant's and economist's cost per unit and revenue per unit curves

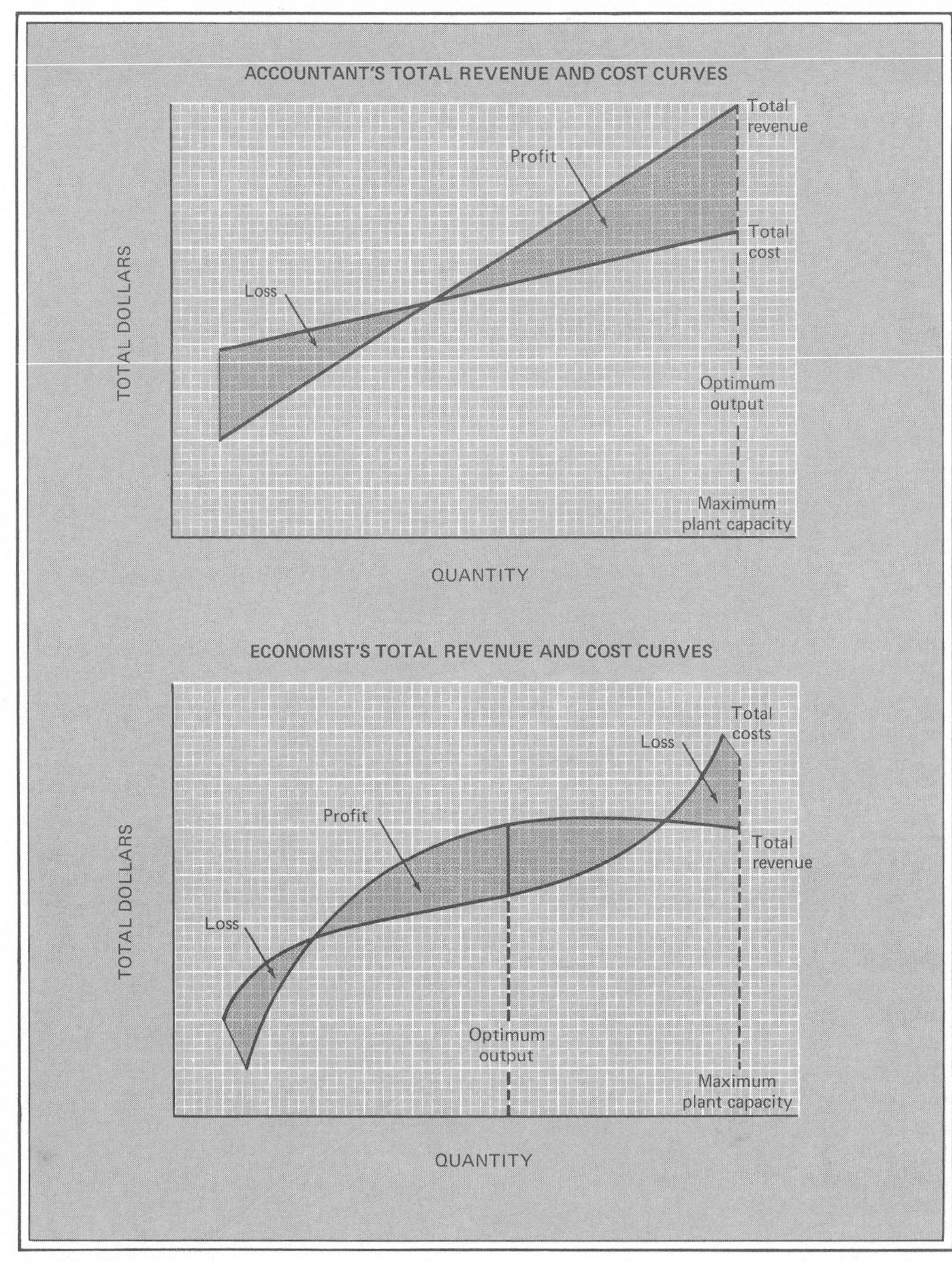

EXHIBIT 1-16
Contrast of accountant's and economist's total cost and revenue curves

sideration makes the time value of money a significant cost in long-range decisions. Money, like any other resource, has a cost. In long-range decisions this cost is significant. In short-range decisions the time value of money, while present, is not a significant factor.

The costs and benefits relevant to a capacity decision are different from the costs and benefits relevant to an operating decision. In the long run all costs and all cost behavior patterns can be changed because the firm can adjust its productive facilities. In the long run all costs are variable. Fixed and variable cost concepts are not meaningful in the long run.

Accountants use the more basic view of cash inflow and cash outflow to measure costs and benefits. In long-run decisions costs and benefits are measured in terms of their impact on cash.

From this perspective, out-of-pocket and sunk costs are meaningful. An **out-of-pocket cost** is one that requires an expenditure of cash as a result of a decision. The expenditure of cash has already been made for a **sunk cost**[6] and a current cash expenditure is not required. Out-of-pocket and sunk costs are opposite. A sunk cost is a prior investment of cash resources; an out-of-pocket cost is a current or near-future cash expenditure.

Some decision makers assume incorrectly that all variable costs are out-of-pocket costs and that all fixed costs are sunk costs. This is not so. The president's salary may be fixed, but it is still an out-of-pocket cost. The cost of petroleum to an oil company may be sunk since it has already expended cash resources in obtaining the oil, but it will be a variable cost per gallon of product produced. However, in most instances the costs of depreciation, depletion, and the amortization of intangibles are sunk costs. Likewise, in most instances the costs of material and labor are out-of-pocket costs and are also variable. It is imperative that the decision maker keep in mind that the perspective of fixed and variable costs is different than the perspective of out-of-pocket and sunk costs. While at times they may overlap and appear synonymous, they are not the same view of cost.

A long-range decision must consider both the time value of money and the timing of the investment and recovery of cash. The accountant's long-range decision rule is that an investment decision is favorable if incremental benefits, measured by cash inflows directly attributable to the decision and adjusted for the time value of money, are at least equal to incremental costs, measured by cash outflows directly attributable to the decision and adjusted for the time value of money.

Decisions Expressed through Budgets

As managers begin the selection of possible alternatives and collect data to facilitate their decisions, they are preparing a **tentative budget.** While they sort the decision alternatives (see Exhibit 1-1) leading to an ultimate selection,

[6]The economist often uses the terms *fixed costs* and *sunk costs* interchangeably. In accounting they have different meanings.

they rely upon a forecast of what they believe would happen if they made a decision. These forecasts are not final until there is a commitment to a specific decision. They are tentative budgets.

Budgets express management's plans in quantitative terms. Budgets show the probable impact upon the responsibility center and the firm if plans are committed to action. A budget may be limited to a particular activity, as is an advertising budget or a capital additions budget. It may deal with total operations including expected income, expenses, and assets, or it may be in terms of anticipated cash flow, as in a cash budget.

The budget begins to take final shape when all tentative budgets for the responsibility centers are integrated. Budgets for each individual decision ultimately must be combined into a coordinated whole called the **master budget.** The master budget expresses the anticipated total impact of all the responsibility centers' decisions upon revenues, expenses, assets, liabilities, and owners' equity. In this function the master budget is the principal coordinating vehicle for the firm's plans.

The master budget also serves another important role. By requiring a formal, written commitment to coordinated decisions, it serves as a benchmark against which actual performance can be compared. This control function acts to ensure that plans and performance are congruent.

POST-DECISIONAL CONTROL STAGE

Management control follows management planning. **Control** is the process of measuring and correcting actual performance to ensure that the firm's goals and plans are accomplished. Control presupposes the existence of plans. There is no way to know if the firm is meeting its goals without a previous statement of what is desirable and some feedback on operating results.

Performance Data

The old adage, It's too late to shut the barn door after the horse has run away, is particularly applicable to the control process. A manager cannot control what is past. He may study the effects of past actions, but his focus should be to find ways to avoid unwanted actions in the future. The best control process a manager can install is one that corrects deviations *before* they occur. The next best control process is one that detects deviations *as* they happen. The later the report of a need for correction after the actual event, the weaker the control system.

Exhibit 1-17 shows the sequence of the control process, which begins with selection of suitable alternatives, and expression of these plans in the form of a final budget. Comparing Exhibit 1-17 with Exhibit 1-1 we can see that the control process begins with the completion of the planning process. Once the desired alternatives have been chosen, there must be definitive

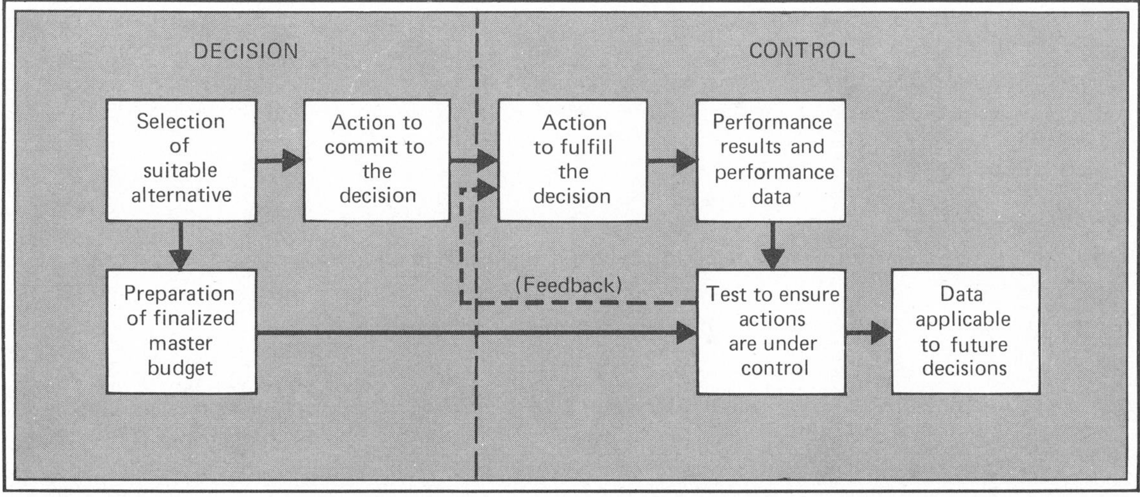

EXHIBIT 1-17
The control process

action to commit the firm to the decision. Contracts are signed, employees hired, production scheduled, and raw materials purchased.

As these actions are taken, the firm begins to build performance data. Accounting, as a data base, is a major source of performance data. The control process evaluates actual performance by comparing it to the plans. This comparison ensures that actions are under control. Any deviations are communicated to management for corrective action. Simultaneously, a comparison of planned and actual performance serves as the beginning of the next planning process, and the cycle starts again.

Nonfinancial Controls

The preceding discussion may be misleading since it focuses on quantified plans and controls. It is dangerous to assume that *all* plans are quantifiable into a master budget and that *all* performance data are financial in nature. Many activities are planned and controlled through nonfinancial data. The planning process (Exhibit 1-1) and the control process (Exhibit 1-17) are general statements applicable to both quantifiable and nonquantifiable control systems, although our discussion has concentrated upon the financial aspect.

One broad class of nonfinancial planning and control data is comprised of physical measures. These are particularly applicable at the lower organizational levels where materials are used, labor and services are consumed, machine hours are operated, ton-miles of freight are carried, kilowatt hours are consumed, units are produced per direct labor hour, customers are served, or employee turnover exists. The number of possible physical measures is almost infinite.

Many other aspects of crucial importance to the firm's long-run existence cannot be expressed in financial terms. How do you measure, in dollars, an employee's morale or the value of a "team" attitude within a department? How do you measure the competence of an accountant in minimizing the company's tax liability? What quantitative measures can be used to assess the goodwill customers feel toward salesmen? These questions show how difficult it is to establish quantitative plans and controls for *all* phases of business activites. There are many places where nonfinancial plans and controls are more useful than financial measures.

THE MANAGEMENT ACCOUNTANT'S RESPONSIBILITIES

The management accountant, often called the **controller,** is the manager of the data base used in decision planning and in the subsequent control of operations. As the manager of the data base, the management accountant must bear in mind that different decisions require different data. Short-run production decisions require different data than long-run decisions, and external reports require different data than internal reports. Decisions affecting the total company, such as product lines to be produced, require more aggregate data than decisions affecting the optimum use of a particular machine. The generation of different data for different decisions requires a high degree of flexibility.

The management accountant is a decision maker himself. Not only must he gather data applicable to others' decisions, he must also gather data for his own use. He must decide how best to structure the accounting system to meet both financial and management accounting requirements. The development of the data base consumes resources of the firm that could be used in other ways. Accounting is an economic activity requiring economic resources. As such, a good accounting system is one where the benefits of having the data exceed the cost of gathering it. Unless data generated by the accounting system is relevant, there should be no effort expended in gathering it. Unfortunately the determination of benefits from accounting data are vague and difficult to measure. An emerging area called **information economics** deals with this difficult topic of costs and benefits of accounting data.

SUMMARY

Management's role is to make decisions about how to use the firm's resources effectively and efficiently so the firm will have a satisfactory rate of return on its investment. These decisions can be classified as either long-range or short-range. Long-range decisions involve adding to or deducting from the firm's service potential. Because they span a long period of time, the time value of money is important. The manager's long-range decision rule is to add to productive capacity whenever the cash inflows resulting from the decision, adjusted for the time value of money, are at least equal to the cash outflows resulting from the decision, adjusted for the time value of money.

Short-range decisions are concerned with how best to use existing capacity, and span a short time period so that the time value of money need not be considered. The economist shows that optimum price and output exist when marginal cost equals marginal revenue. The accountant assumes that within the relevant range of activity both the revenue and variable cost curves are linear and that revenue minus variable costs is the contribution margin. Thus, the accountant's short-range decision rule of maximizing the total contribution margin of the firm is, within the relevant range of activity, comparable with the economist's theory.

The process of planning focuses management's attention on needed decisions. Planning involves the determination of the firm's goals and the selection of specific courses of action to achieve these goals. The summary of management's plans is the master budget. The master budget serves as a way of coordinating the firm's plans and as a benchmark to control the effectiveness and efficiency of actual performance.

SUPPLEMENTARY READING

Alex, Marcus, and Charles Z. Wilson. *Organization Decision Making.* Englewood Cliffs, NJ: Prentice-Hall, Inc., 1967.

Anthony, Robert N. *Planning and Control Systems: A Framework for Analysis.* Cambridge, Mass.: Harvard Business School, 1965.

Archer, Stephen H. "The Structure of Management Decision Theory." *Academy of Management Journal,* December, 1964.

Bruns, William J. Jr., "Accounting Information and Decision-Making: Some Behavioral Hypotheses." *The Accounting Review,* July, 1968.

DeCoster, Don T., Kavasseri V. Ramanathan, and Gary L. Sundem. *Accounting for Managerial Decision Making.* Los Angeles: Melville Publishing Company, 1974.

Ijiri, Yuji, Robert K. Jaedicke, and Kenneth E. Knight. "The Effects of Accounting Alternatives on Management Decisions." *Research in Accounting Measurement,* Ed. Robert Jaedicke, Yuji Ijiri, and Oswald Nielson. Evanston, Ill.: American Accounting Association, 1966.

Kemp, Patrick S. "Accounting Data for Planning, Motivation, and Control." *The Accounting Review,* January, 1962.

Killough, Larry N. "Does Management Accounting Have a Theoretical Structure?" *Management Accounting,* April, 1972.

Tersine, Richard J. "Organization Decision Theory—A Synthesis." *Managerial Planning,* July–August, 1972.

QUESTIONS

1-1 What purpose should a statement of goals serve in an organization? Does the purpose differ between a profit-seeking organization and a not-for-profit organization?

1-2 What is meant by goal congruence within a firm? Why is goal congruence essential to a successful, prospering organization?

1-3 While maximizing profit is the most commonly stated objective of business firms, there are other motivations. Discuss the more important nonprofit motivations.

1-4 Making an optimal decision requires careful planning. Outline the steps necessary to make a business decision.

1-5 Define both *long-range* and *short-range decisions,* distinguish between them, and discuss how the data needs between the two differ.

1-6 Joe is trying to decide whether to attend college or to accept a job as a store clerk. He views this decision as affecting his long-range plans and goals. What data would he need to make this long-range decision? What decision rule should he follow? What nonfinancial data are relevant to his decision?

1-7 What are the main functions of the master budget?

1-8 Discuss how the master budget provides flexibility and how it restricts flexibility in the planning and control process.

1-9 "While historical data may be suitable for external reporting, it is not suitable for management decisions." Do you agree or disagree? Why?

1-10 One of the most valuable resources a management accountant can bring to bear in his professional activities is a "questioning and flexible attitude." Discuss.

1-11 "Planning and control are interrelated." Discuss this statement.

1-12 Discuss how the concept of the relevant range of activity makes accounting data comparable with economic theory.

1-13 What is meant by *diminishing returns?* What effect, if any, does it have upon (a) marginal cost, (b) average fixed costs, (c) average variable costs, and (d) average total costs.

1-14 "The role of planning is to reduce uncertainty about the future." Discuss this statement. How does a budget help reduce uncertainty?

1-15 Distinguish between financial accounting activities and management accounting activities. Would it be correct to say that the financial accountant is primarily concerned with the control process, whereas the management accountant is primarily concerned with the planning process? Discuss.

PROBLEMS

1-16 Match the following terms and definitions

1. Goal congruence
2. Financial accounting
3. Responsibility center
4. Operating decisions
5. Management accounting
6. Master budget
7. Contribution margin approach
8. Capacity decisions
9. Goals
10. Interfirm decisions

a. Statements that provide broad direction for the decision makers.
b. Focus of accounting upon intrafirm resource allocations and optimizing use of firm's resources.
c. The matching and combining of diverse, separate goals into a unified whole.
d. Decisions involving productive capacity and spanning a period of time over which the time value of money is important.
e. Decisions involving allocation of resources in the capital markets.
f. Decisions concerning production volume and selling prices of the product.
g. Focus of accounting data necessary for interfirm allocations and for maintenance of capital markets.
h. Result of combining budgets of individual responsibility centers into a coordinated plan.
i. Analysis based upon a separation of costs into fixed and variable components.
j. The organization structure for the classification of costs and revenues to the department responsible for them.

1-17 Match the following terms and definitions.

1. Relevant range of activity
2. Marginal cost
3. Fixed cost
4. Variable cost
5. Marginal revenue
6. Time value of money
7. Average cost
8. Total cost
9. Average revenue
10. Data base

a. Costs incurred even when production is zero.
b. Sum of fixed and variable costs needed to produce at a certain level of output.
c. Costs that proportionally increase as output increases.
d. Increment in total cost obtained when production output is increased by an increment of one unit.
e. Fixed costs plus variable costs divided by total units produced.
f. Total revenue divided by total units produced and sold.
g. Range of production over which total fixed costs remain constant.
h. A dollar to be received in the future is worth less than a dollar received today.
i. Information gathered to support and facilitate decisions.
j. Increment in total revenue obtained when production output is increased by an increment of one unit.

1-18 Indicate whether the following are long-range or short-range decisions. Give the reasons for your decision.

1. A manufacturing company is trying to decide whether or not plant expansion is economically justifiable.

2. A wholesaler is considering a decrease in selling price to regain lost markets. Competitors have increased their share of the market.

3. The unemployment rate has increased substantially. The state legislature is trying to decide whether to create jobs through a park-renovation project.

4. Technological advancements in new equipment will drastically decrease production costs. A factory manager is trying to decide whether to purchase the new equipment and change production methods.

5. An analysis of last period's sales shows that some products are declining in sales volume while others are showing growth. The marketing manager is trying to decide which products should be advertised.

6. The price of feed grain has tripled in the past year. A chicken farmer is trying to decide whether to sell his flock or continue to produce eggs.
7. The profit picture looks good for the year. Sales have risen and costs have remained stable but the increased production has caused a drain on cash. The board of directors is trying to decide how much in cash dividends can be paid without placing the firm in a dangerously low cash position.
8. Demand for the company's product has fallen to almost zero. The president is trying to decide whether to shut down the plant until demand increases or another product is developed.
9. A research institute has found a cure for a dread disease. The board of trustees is now considering new goals and challenges.
10. The city council of a small town is attempting to decide whether to grant a permit for a new regional shopping center.

1-19 The president of the Major Toy Company was presented with the following statistics as a part of his review of the company's performance for the past year.

Net income	$45,000
Net income as a percent of sales	2%
Return on owner's equity	4%
Sales increased 1% over the past year while operating costs increased	15%

Industry averages showed a 4% return on sales and an 8% return on owner's equity. The president is concerned with the company's performance.

REQUIRED:

A. Suggest some goals that management might consider.
B. Develop some measurement criteria that management might adopt to measure its performance in achieving these goals.

1-20 You have just accepted a position as assistant manager of the Eastside Neighborhood Health Center. You will be responsible for nonmedical administration and financial management. The center was organized four months ago to serve the health needs of a low-income neighborhood including a public health project. About 75% of the family heads in the housing project are employed, but many have low incomes.

The center was started with a federal grant and has provided health care for slightly more than two months. The grant will reimburse the center for service provided to low-income families not covered by Medicaid or Medicare.

On your first day of work you are notified by the bank that the center's account is overdrawn. You find that the financial records are limited to a desk drawer full of documents supporting the transactions and a checkbook that has not been reconciled. The federal grant requires a financial report in two months, including cost and utilization data to support the billing rate.

REQUIRED:

A. What should you do? Your answer should cover actions aimed at both the short-range and long-range concerns of the center.

B. State the primary goal of the center as completely as you can.

1-21 Each Division Manager of the Brickbat Salvage Company prepares a report on his division for the corporate office. The report must include data on the past year's accomplishments as well as problems facing the division.

Agnes Snodgrass included the following items in her report for the scrap rubber division.

Division net income forecast for the next year.
Division sales for the past year.
Five-year sales forecast.
Operating expenses for the past year.
Progress report on the new milling plant under construction.
Efficiency study of processing facilities.
Proposed labor contract for the division.
Description of a campaign to reduce the use of paper and other supplies.
Proposal for installation of computer facilities.
Reevaluation of credit policies.

REQUIRED:

Indicate how each of the items selected by Agnes Snodgrass would be useful in planning, decision making, and control.

1-22 The Flue Company produces a line of fireplace accessories. A fuel oil shortage has increased the demand for its products. Most of the increased demand exceeds present productive capacity. To take advantage of this demand, management is considering building a new factory.

REQUIRED:

A. List some of the costs that might be relevant to the decision to build a new factory. Indicate whether these costs are likely to be fixed or variable if the decision is made to add to the plant.

B. What would be the relevant costs to the Flue Company of using any excess productive capacity obtained from the plant addition in part A above?

C. Suppose that instead of building a new plant the Flue Company decided to replace its outdated productive machinery. The new machinery would increase productive capacity by 50%. What would be the relevant costs? Would these costs probably be fixed or variable?

1-23 The Mayor of Swamp City formed a Citizens' Task Force to study the operations of the city and make suggestions for better service to the people. He was particularly interested in being able to show improvement in services.

The Citizens' Task Force suggested the following measures of accomplishment for the fire department.

Reduction of fires in the city.
Reduction of losses from fires.
Reduction of fire-related injuries or deaths.
Modernization of fire equipment.
Reduction of fire insurance rates in the city.
Improvement in fire-prevention programs in the area.
Presentation of fire-prevention programs through the schools.
Development of a first aid unit for the district.
Reduction of number of fund-raising events needed to supplement funding from taxes.
Intensification of training for fire-combat units.
Expansion of fire permit and inspection service.

The fire chief feels that the list is confusing, conflicting, and excessive. He has asked your help in ranking these performance measures and preparing a statement of objectives for the fire department.

REQUIRED:

A. Rank these performance measures in *your* order of priority.
B. State each performance measure as a goal that will provide specific targets for the fire department. (You will not be able to provide specific quantities or dates; therefore use "x" amount, etc.)

1-24 Billy and Bobby recently graduated from Skyking Vocational and Technical College. Billy studied diesel mechanics and Bobby studied commercial truck driving. They are considering forming a partnership to buy a large sleeper tractor. They plan on hauling the trailers of two moving companies on a contract basis. They know the dispatcher of one of the companies who told them that both he and the other moving company need tractors and drivers.

REQUIRED:

A. What specific data should the two men obtain to assist them in their decisions. Where would you go to get this needed data?
B. What governmental agencies would likely affect their planning and decisions?
C. What are Billy and Bobby's opportunity costs?

1-25 John graduated from high school last year. To earn money for his college education he took a job with a local bakery, delivering bread. When he took the job he thought that his salary of $600 per month would allow him to save from $150 to $200 per month, particularly if he lived frugally. After nine months of working he had been able to save only $300. He was quite disappointed and came to you for help. He had his checkbook, which showed all of his earnings and expenditures. The checkbook was in agreement with the bank and very complete.

REQUIRED:

A. Explain to John why he is "out of control."

B. What specific steps would you recommend to John to ensure that he save as much as possible?

C. What use will you make of John's excellent historical records in bringing John's activities "under control?"

1-26 The Bunny Corporation has the following sales volume at each selling price.

Selling Price	*Sales in Units*
$7	50,000
$6	140,000
$5	260,000

In addition, variable costs are $4 per unit and fixed costs are $125,000.

REQUIRED:

A. What price should be charged to maximize sales?

B. What price should be charged to maximize profits?

C. Why do the answers for parts A and B differ?

1-27 The Sandstorm Corporation prepared the following schedule.

Units	*Variable Costs*	*Fixed Costs*	*Total Costs*	*Total Revenue*
300	$300	$200	$ 500	$ 900
301	301	200	501	903
400	400	200	600	1,200
800	800	500	1,300	1,600

All units produced are sold.

REQUIRED:

A. At 300 units, what is the marginal revenue from selling one more unit? What is the marginal cost?

B. What is the difference in costs of a change from producing and selling 300 units to producing and selling 800 units? What is the difference in revenue? Is this an advantageous move to the firm? Explain.

C. As production increases to 800 units the fixed costs rise and the revenue per unit decreases. What might be the causes for each of these occurrences? If these fixed costs rise are they really fixed costs?

1-28 The Spencer Company has an idle production line after discontinuing a losing product. After careful study the company has narrowed potential new products to two: Zeon and Trion. Only one of the two products may be manufactured on the production line. Revenue and cost estimates for the two products are presented below. In addition to the variable costs for each product, fixed costs associated with the production line are $500.

Zeon			**Trion**		
Output in Units	*Total Revenue*	*Total Variable Costs*	*Output in Units*	*Total Revenue*	*Total Variable Costs*
50	$ 7,500	$ 6,000	2,000	$4,000	$3,000
60	8,400	6,600	2,100	4,200	2,520
70	9,100	7,000	2,200	4,400	2,200
80	9,600	7,200	2,300	4,600	2,990
90	9,900	9,000	2,400	4,800	3,840
100	10,000	11,000	2,500	5,000	4,750

REQUIRED:
Prepare a schedule that shows management the most profitable product and the optimum quantity of that product it should produce and sell.

1-29 The Nipper Company has forecast its potential demand and costs as follows:

Units	*Price per Unit*	*Total Variable Costs*
120	$80	$ 8,400
130	78	8,840
140	76	9,240
150	74	9,700
160	72	10,560
170	70	11,900
180	68	13,500
190	66	15,200
200	64	17,000
210	62	18,900

Fixed costs are $1,000.

REQUIRED:

A. Prepare a schedule showing the total revenue and marginal revenue amounts at each price. What operating level would give the company the largest total revenue?

B. Prepare a schedule showing the total cost and marginal cost at each operating level.

C. Prepare a schedule showing the profit potentials at each operating level. Show that the maximum profit potential is where the marginal cost equals the marginal revenue. What would the sales price be at that level?

1-30 Information concerning revenues and costs was gathered by the management accountant of the Sundance Beauty Corporation and presented in the following partially completed table. In addition, the Sundance Corporation has total fixed costs of $5 per month.

	Revenue			**Costs**			
Quantity	*Price*	*Total Revenue*	*Marginal Revenue*	*Total Variable*	*Total Costs*	*Marginal Costs*	*Income (Loss)*
0	$11			$ 0			
1	10			8			
2	9			15			
3	8			21			
4	7			26			
5	6			33			
6	5			42			
7	4			51			

REQUIRED:

A. Complete the table.

B. Prepare a graph showing marginal cost and marginal revenue.

C. At what price does the company maximize net income? What is the optimum level of production? Explain.

1-31 Samuel Johnson founded his business many years ago and through hard work has expanded it to include a manufacturing plant, three retail outlets, and a consulting branch. He now owns 75% of the outstanding stock and acts as general manager. Due to his many years of experience Sam has a "feel" for the business. He knows approximately how the firm is doing throughout the year. When he feels production is not acceptable he goes down to the manufacturing department and applies pressure on the employees. Sam believes that each time he purchases a new piece of equipment production should become more efficient and monthly output should increase. Unfortunately, these gains have not occurred.

As the firm has grown Sam has found it increasingly difficult to keep track of what everyone is doing and where everything is kept. Errors have begun to increase. To make matters worse, the lease on his main retail outlet is about to expire and it cannot be renewed. As a final straw, an economic slump has reduced sales by 20%. Sam obviously has several problems and is faced with some decisions, both long-run and short-run.

REQUIRED:

A. Discuss Sam's methods of managing the firm up to this point.

B. Discuss some decisions, both long-run and short-run, Sam should be concerned about.

C. What steps would you recommend that Sam take to ensure that his decisions are made wisely?

1-32 The Smog Flats Foundry is faced with the choice of installing pollution-control equipment or terminating operations. Two pollution-control processes are available and each will meet the clean-air requirements. Economic feasibility studies of the two processes provided the information that follows. (Assume that all data are adjusted for the time value of money.)

Scrubbing unit: A scrubbing unit would be installed in two stages. Stage one would be installed immediately, at a cost of $500,000; stage two would be installed in three years, at a cost of $1,500,000. Disposal of the sludge will cost an average of $50,000 per year.

Bag plant: A bag plant would be installed immediately, at a cost of $5,000,000. This process would capture the material previously passed through the smokestack. Approximately 100,000 tons of material per year could be recovered. By processing the emission material, at a cost of $5 per ton, it could be sold for $8 per ton as a soil conditioner. Assume the life of each process to be 10 years.

REQUIRED:

A. Which process should be installed? Explain.

B. How will the installation of the pollution-control equipment affect the goals of the company?

1-33 The Steppen On Sales Company had the financial statements shown here.

BALANCE SHEET
December 31, 19X6

Assets:		Liabilities:	
Cash	$ 5,000	Accounts payable	$10,000
Accounts receivable	20,000	Notes payable	15,000
Inventory	10,000		$25,000
Equipment (net)	15,000	Owner's equity:	
Building (net)	35,000	Common stock	$40,000
		Retained earnings	20,000
			$60,000
Total assets	$85,000	Total liabilities and owner's equity	$85,000

INCOME STATEMENT Year Ending December 31, 19X6		
Sales		$80,000
Cost of sales		20,000
Gross margin		$60,000
Operating expense:		
Administrative expense	$20,000	
Selling expense	5,000	
Depreciation	5,000	
Other	10,000	
Total operating expenses		40,000
Income before taxes		$20,000
Income tax (25%)		5,000
Net income after taxes		$15,000

Management is anticipating a 100% expansion of sales activity which would require an additional $30,000 in capital. This capital could be raised either through increased borrowing or through the sale of capital stock.

REQUIRED:

A. What data included in the financial statements might a bank loan officer use? What additional data would he be likely to want?

B. What data included in the financial statements might be used by an investor in the company's stock? What additional data would he be likely to want?

1-34 The Hungry People Eatery specializes in a limited line of hamburgers, hot dogs, french fries, shakes, soft drinks, and soft ice cream. Food is prepared on an assembly-line basis. One person cooks the meat, one person assembles the sandwiches, one person prepares the soft drinks and shakes, and one person takes orders and acts as cashier.

All transactions are for cash, including purchases and sales. Records of transactions are accumulated through the month and sent to an accountant for preparation of financial statements. At the end of each year, a detailed analysis of the restaurant's operations compared with industry averages is presented to management by the accountant.

In the report just received, cash and inventory shortages were excessive by industry standards. The president asked you for suggestions to improve his control over the operations.

REQUIRED:

A. Suggest methods for identifying shortages in a more timely manner.

B. Suggest controls that may be implemented by management.

1-35 The Black Asbestos Manufacturing Company achieved a technological breakthrough in one of its products. With a limited capital investment, it could double the productive capacity of the main plant while simultaneously reducing production costs by about one-fourth. The implementation of this breakthrough will require that the plant be closed for about three months. Since Black Asbestos exists in a highly competitive market, the sooner it starts this new process, the bigger the jump it will have on its competitors, who are also working to perfect the same technique.

At this time it is impossible to determine the long-run environmental impact, but there is some evidence to suggest that it may be substantial. To complicate matters further, if Black's competitors implement this new process and Black does not, many of Black's sales will be lost and it will have to lay off 350 to 400 workers. Because unemployment is already high in this area, the city fathers are pressuring Mr. Jason Fleece, Black's owner, to proceed with the new process and worry about the societal consequences later.

REQUIRED:

A. What quantitative and nonquantitative factors should Mr. Fleece consider in his decision?

B. Discuss what accounting data he might need to help him in his decision.

C. How would you go about helping Mr. Fleece in the selection of an alternative from among his possible courses of action?

1-36 Duval, Inc. is a large publicly held corporation that is well known throughout the United States for its products. The corporation has always had good profit margins and excellent earnings. However, Duval has experienced a leveling of sales and a reduced market share in the past two years resulting in a stabilization of profits rather than growth. Despite these trends, the firm has maintained an excellent cash and short-term investment position. The president has called a meeting of the treasurer and the vice-presidents for sales and production to develop alternative strategies for improving Duval's performance. The four individuals form the nucleus of a well organized management team that has worked together for several years to bring success to Duval, Inc.

The sales vice-president suggests that sales levels can be improved by presenting the company's product in a more attractive and appealing package. He also recommends that advertising be increased, and that the current price be maintained. This latter step would have the effect of a price decrease because the prices of most other competing products are rising.

The treasurer is skeptical of maintaining the present price when others are increasing prices since this will curtail revenues, unless this policy provides a competitive advantage. He also points out that the repackaging will increase costs in the near future, at least, because of the start-up costs of a new packing process. He does not favor increasing advertising outright because he is doubtful of the short-run benefit.

The sales vice-president replies that increased, or at least redirected, advertising is necessary to promote the price stability and to take advantage of the new packaging; the combination would provide the company with a competitive advantage. The president adds that the advertising should be studied closely to determine the type of advertising to be used—television, radio, newspaper, magazine. In addition if television is used, attention must be directed to the type of programs to be sponsored—children's, family, sporting events, news specials, etc.

The production vice-president suggests several possible production improvements, such as a systems study of the manufacturing process to identify changes in the work flow which would cut costs. He suggests operating costs could be further reduced by the purchase of new equipment. The product could be improved by employing a better grade of raw materials and by engineering changes in the fabrication of the product. When queried by the president on the impact of the proposed changes, the production vice-president indicated that the primary benefit would be product performance, but that appearance and safety would also be improved. The sales vice-president and treasurer commented that this would result in increased sales.

The treasurer notes that all the production proposals would increase immediate costs, and this could result in lower profits. If profit performance is going to be improved, the price structure should be examined closely. He recommends that the current level of capital expenditures be maintained unless substantial cost savings can be obtained.

The treasurer further believes that expenditures for research and development should be decreased since previous outlays have not prevented a decrease in Duval's share of the market. The production vice-president agrees that the research and development activities have not proven profitable, but thinks that this is because the research effort was applied in the wrong area. The sales vice-president cautions against any drastic reductions because the packaging change will only provide a temporary advantage in the market; consequently, more effort will have to be devoted to product development.

Focusing on the use of liquid assets and the present high yields on securities, the treasurer suggests that the firm's profitability can be improved by shifting funds from the presently held short-term marketable securities to longer-term, higher-yield securities. He further states that cost reductions would provide more funds for investments. He recognizes that the restructuring of the investments from short-term to long-term would hamper flexibility.

In his summarizing comments, the president observes that they have a good start and the ideas provide some excellent alternatives. He states, "I think we ought to develop these ideas further and consider other ramifications. For instance, what effect would new equipment and the systems study have on the labor force? Shouldn't we also consider the environmental impact of any plant and product change? We want to appear as a leader in our industry—not a follower.

"I note that none of you considered increased community involvement through such groups as the Chamber of Commerce and the United Fund.

"The factors you mentioned plus those additional points all should be considered as we reach a decision on the final course of action we will follow."

REQUIRED:

A. State explicitly the implied corporate goals being expressed by each of the following:
   1. Treasurer
   2. Sales vice-president
   3. Production vice-president
   4. President

B. Compare the type of goals discussed above with the corporate goal(s) postulated by the economic theory of the firm. *(CMA adapted)*

2 Cost Behavior Patterns and Cost-Volume-Profit Interactions

DETERMINING FIXED AND VARIABLE COSTS

Choosing a Volume Measure

Measuring Variations of Cost with Volume

Expressing Cost Behavior Patterns: The Flexible Budget

The Relevant Range of Activity

FIXED AND VARIABLE COSTS AND REVENUE

Cost-Volume-Profit Analysis through Graphs

Cost-Volume-Profit Analysis through Equations

Cost-Volume-Profit Analysis through the Contribution Margin

EFFECTS OF CHANGING FACTORS

Effects of Changes in Selling Price

Effects of Changes in Variable Costs

Effects of Changes in Fixed Costs

Volume Necessary to Achieve Desired Net Income

Effects of Multiple Changes

UNDERLYING ASSUMPTIONS OF COST-VOLUME-PROFIT RELATIONSHIPS

A Curvilinear Approach to Cost-Volume-Profit Analysis

Multiproduct Situations

Multidepartmental Comparisons

SUMMARY

Many factors cause changes in costs and hence in profits. Costs change because of inflationary trends in the economy, changes in the labor market, technological advances, or changes in size or quality of production facilities. Each of these represents a unique, sporadic change. Regular, recurring events also cause costs to change. One of the most significant causes of variations in costs is a change in the volume of activity. In the first section of this chapter we will study how the accountant determines which costs are variable and therefore change with volume, and which costs are fixed and therefore remain constant over volume changes. Later in the chapter we will study how knowledge of fixed and variable costs helps in understanding cost-volume-profit interrelationships.

DETERMINING FIXED AND VARIABLE COSTS

Fixed and *variable* are specific ways of classifying costs. The typical accounting system does not record costs as fixed or variable. Traditionally, accounting summarizes costs by the nature of the expenditure. For example, when an invoice for the purchase of insurance on the factory is received, the amount is recorded in factory overhead, not as a fixed or variable cost. In a very real sense the classification of costs into their fixed and variable components requires a special study above and beyond normal accounting procedures. It is a different perspective of costs that requires different measuring tools.

Choosing a Volume Measure

The first step in measuring the variability of costs is to find a suitable measure of volume or activity. When only one type of product is produced, it is possible to express volume in terms of physical units. However, when a company produces many different products, it may be difficult to find a single measure of volume. The following considerations are important when selecting a volume measure.

1. The unit of measurement must measure fluctuations in the activity level, or volume, which cause costs to vary. There must be a definite, positive relationship between the incurrence of costs and the activity measure.
2. The volume measure should be simple and easy to understand. Thus, measures such as sales dollars, labor hours, labor dollars, units of product, and machine hours are particularly attractive.
3. The activity figures should be attainable without undue additional clerical expense. The cost of gathering accounting information must be kept in mind.

Measuring Variations of Cost with Volume

There are three widely practiced ways of determining cost behavior patterns: inspection of contracts, engineering estimates, and inspection of past cost behavior patterns. The methods differ in the sources of data used. The first two are prospective in that they consider what cost patterns will be in the future. The last is retrospective in that it deals with past cost patterns.

INSPECTION OF CONTRACTS

The most intuitive method of determining whether a cost is fixed or variable is to examine the production activities and existing contracts. Some costs are fixed or variable by their nature, and their behavior patterns are readily determined. For example, depreciation by any method except the units-of-output basis would be fixed for any one year. Many salaries, such as the president's, are fixed. At the same time there are many costs that are inherently variable. Costs such as raw materials and production labor paid on a piecework wage plan are variable. For those situations where the subsequent analysis is not very sensitive to errors in classification of fixed and variable costs, this method may provide a quick and inexpensive measure of cost behavior. A special warning is necessary. The examination must cut beneath the surface and seek the basic contract. *All* depreciation charges are *not* necessarily fixed, and *all* workers' salaries are *not* necessarily variable.

ENGINEERING COST ESTIMATES

Where the contracts are unclear or where there is no past experience to use in estimating cost variability, there is no recourse but to make direct estimates. The technical expertise of industrial engineers can be drawn upon to estimate the quantities of materials, labor, and production facilities needed to produce a new product or to estimate the behavior patterns of many costs. Work measurement techniques can provide reliable estimates of some fixed and variable costs. As actual production takes place and a base of experience is developed, refinements can be made and more objective methods used to examine the cost behavior patterns. This process not only increases the reliability of the cost behavior patterns, but also allows an after-the-fact measure of the accuracy of engineering cost estimates. Estimates that have proven accurate in the past may provide a greater feeling of certainty about estimates that will be necessary in the future.

INSPECTION OF PAST COST BEHAVIOR PATTERNS

When past data are available they can provide empirical evidence of cost behavior patterns. While past experience may not always be the best guide, it can be useful. The analysis of experience inherently assumes that future cost behavior will be like past cost behavior. Where this assumption seems justified, there are systematic ways of determining how costs have varied with volume.

In Chapter 1, variable costs were defined as costs that vary proportionately with volume. Underlying this definition is a linear, or straight-line, assumption of the relationship between cost and volume. As long as this simplifying assumption is realistic, the relationship will apply to any volume level.

In order to measure the cost-volume relationship from past data, the accountant fits a straight line to the data. We may fit a straight line to any set of two or more points. The mathematical statement of a straight line is the equation $Y_c = a + b(x)$ where:

Y_c = Total cost at a specified volume

a = Amount of cost where the straight line intercepts the cost axis at the zero activity level (the fixed cost when activity is zero)

b = Amount of change in cost with a change in volume or the rate of slope in a straight line (average variable cost per unit of activity)

x = Measure of activity level (volume)

This equation may be illustrated as follows:

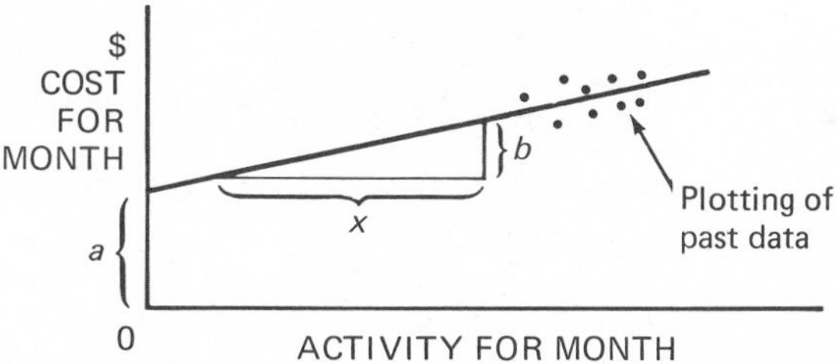

The equation allows us to describe the behavior of individual costs and sum them into one pattern of total costs. For example, a variable cost of \$1 per direct labor hour would be expressed by the formula Y_c = \$0 + \$1 (x), and graphed as:

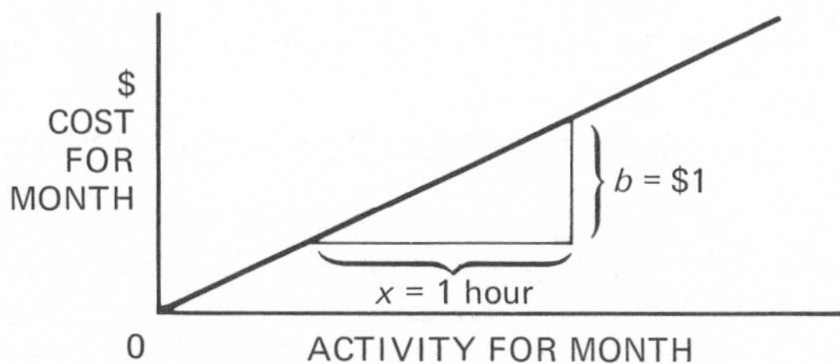

A fixed cost of \$100 per month would be expressed as Y_c = \$100 + \$0 (x), and graphed as:

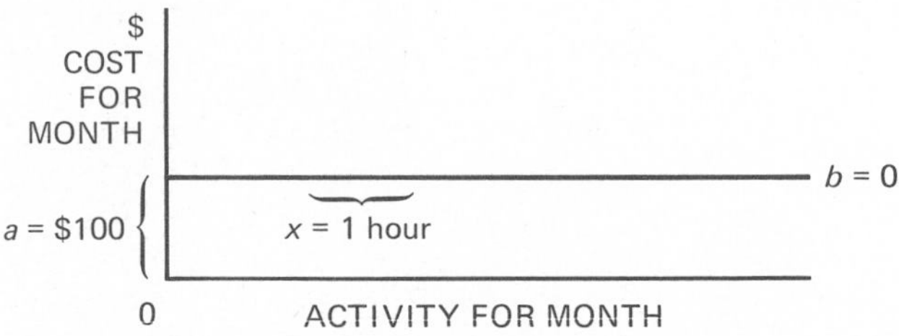

A mixed cost that includes both a fixed and a variable cost component, such as \$2,500 per month fixed cost and a variable cost of \$.20 per direct labor hour, would be expressed as Y_c = \$2,500 + \$.20(x) and graphed as:

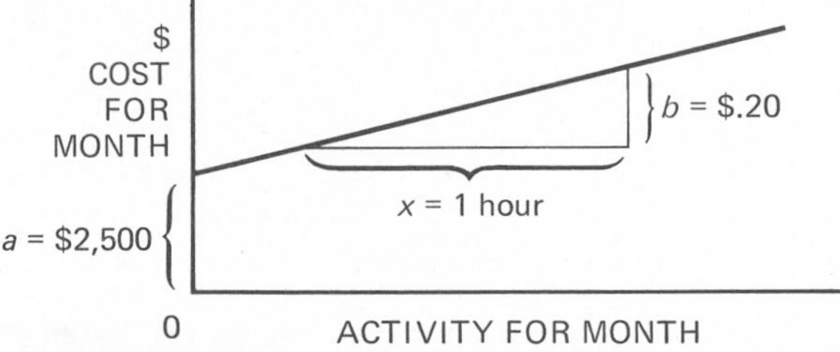

Since the volume measure on each of the three costs is direct labor hours, it is possible to add them together. The formula for the total of the individual costs is Y_c = \$2,600 + \$1.20(x). This can be used to estimate total costs at any volume level inside the relevant range of activity, that range over which the relationship expressed in the equation is valid.

To illustrate the separation of past cost data into fixed and variable costs, let's assume that an examination of the accounting records for the past year's maintenance costs of the Clark Manufacturing Company provides cost and volume information as shown in the accompanying tabulation.

	Hours of Activity	*Total Cost of Maintenance*
January	10,000	\$18,500
February	15,000	25,500
March	30,000	25,800
April	40,000	30,000
May	60,000	35,000
June	70,000	39,000
July	80,000	43,000
August	50,000	34,400
September	30,000	25,100
October	30,000	26,500
November	20,000	22,300
December	60,000	36,200

From this data we can see that maintenance costs increase as activity increases and fall as activity decreases. However, it is extremely difficult to draw an accurate mental image of this relationship when the data are presented in this form.

There are three general methods of fitting a straight line to this past data: the scattergraph, which relies upon a visual fitting; the high-low point method, which fits a line to two representative points of data; and regression analysis, which statistically fits a line to several observations.

Scattergraph estimates

Scattergraph estimates are made by plotting actual cost experiences at the various volume levels on graph paper and then fitting a line by visual inspection. The scattergraph allows us to draw a mental image of the relationship. Exhibit 2-1 shows the data for the Clark Manufacturing Company plotted on graph paper. The horizontal axis (*x* axis) represents the volume, measured by hours of activity, and the vertical axis (*y* axis) represents the total cost of maintenance. The graph shows the general relationship of the total cost of maintenance to the hours of activity. If the dots fall in a straight-line pattern over a significant range of activity, maintenance may be separated into its fixed and variable cost components with the scattergraph. The scattergraph also allows visual examination to reveal unusual observations as well as nonlinear patterns.

The simplest way to fit a line to the scattergraph plot is to draw a line from visual inspection so that about half the dots lie above the line and half lie below the line. The point where the "fitted" line intersects the cost axis (vertical axis) is the estimate of the fixed costs designated by *a*. In this case fixed costs are estimated at approximately $16,000. Variable costs may be determined at any given activity level by subtracting fixed costs from total costs on the line at that activity level. The variable cost per unit (*b*) of activity (*x*) is determined by dividing the total variable cost by the measure of activity at the selected level. For example, at 56,000 hours of activity the total cost estimate on the line is $35,000. Subtracting the fixed cost estimate of $16,000 from the $35,000 total cost provides a variable cost of $19,000. Dividing this $19,000 by the activity measure ($19,000 ÷ 56,000 hours) provides the variable cost of $.339 per hour.

A closer examination of the data on the scattergraph reveals that the February costs of $25,500 at the activity level of 15,000 hours seem somewhat out of line with the other costs. Something unusual may have happened that month. Perhaps extraordinary repairs were incurred, or the company made major repairs before the activity increase during summer months. Certainly, the unusually high cost calls for further analysis. If the $25,500 is considered abnormal, it could be excluded from the analysis of cost variability or adjusted by reflecting only "normal" activities of the same month. Then, when the company forecasts February costs, it can consider the "abnormality" as a separate issue.

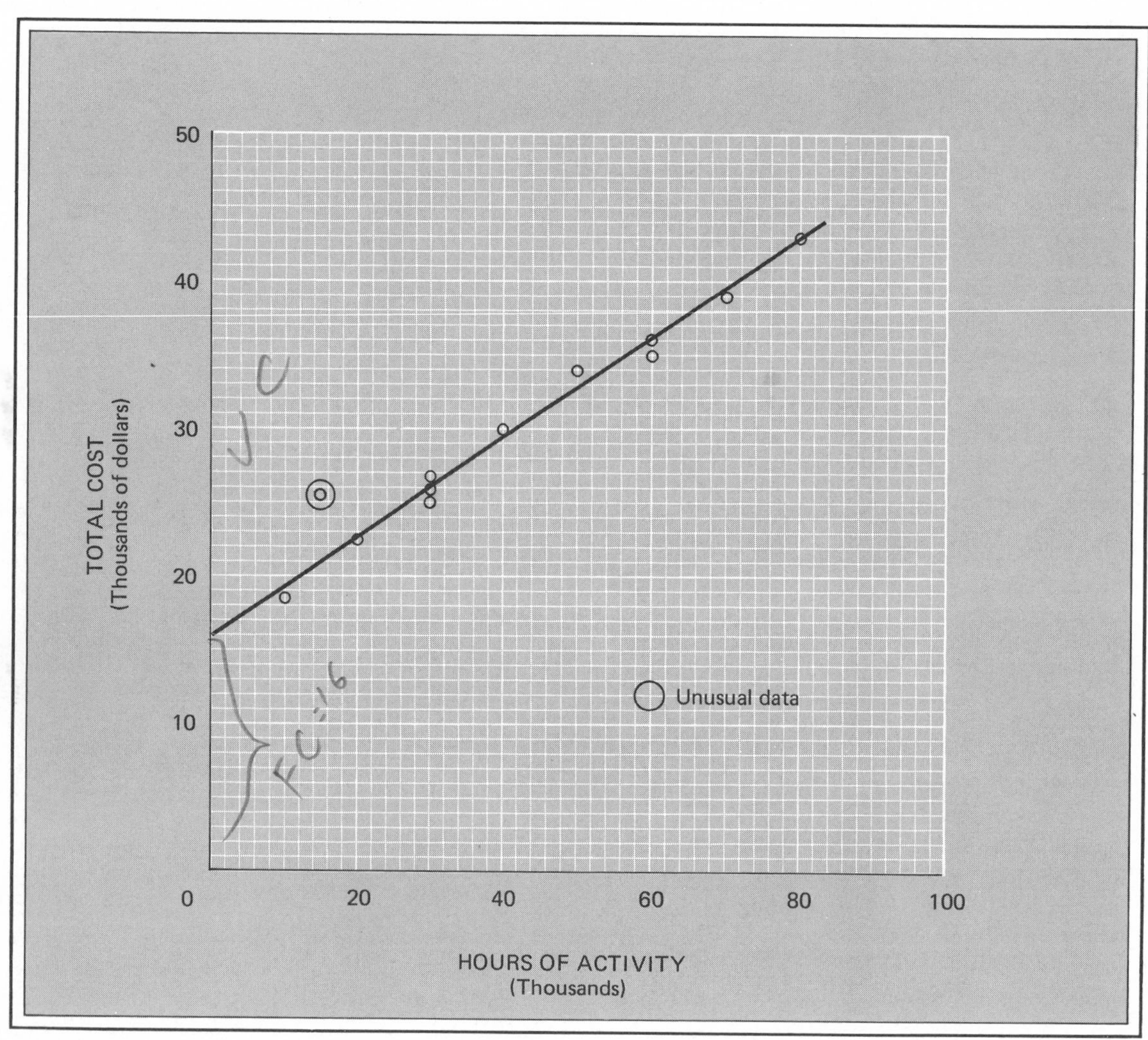

EXHIBIT 2-1
Scattergraph to determine fixed and variable cost components

A mistake in drawing the line could result in a large error. However, the error may not be significant in the relevant range of activity. For example, the following illustration shows an "estimated" pattern of cost behavior and a "correct" pattern of cost behavior. As long as the relationship is used to estimate costs *within the relevant range,* where the error in estimating costs may not be significant, the cost estimate should be useful in management decision making. However, most firms prefer the objectivity of the high-low point method or the least squares regression analysis.

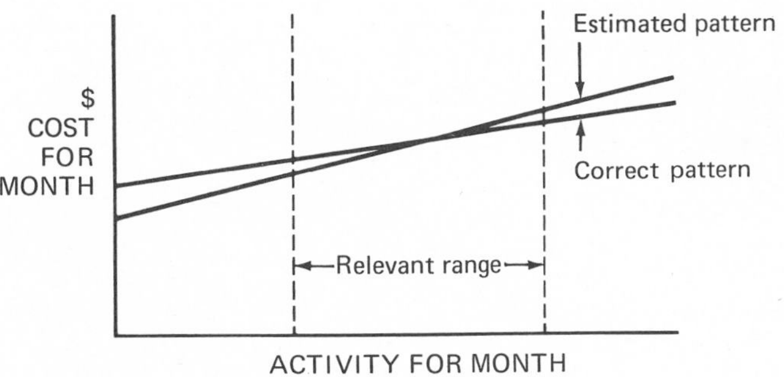

High-Low Point Estimates

The **high-low point** method of segregating fixed and variable costs uses only the highest and lowest volumes and their related costs to determine a straight-line relationship between costs and volume. It is the easiest way to objectively relate past cost patterns. The highest and lowest activity levels are isolated along with their related costs. The change between the high and low levels of activity is divided into the change in cost to provide the measure of variable cost per unit of activity. The variable rate is then used to determine the total variable costs at either the high or low activity level. Finally, the variable costs are subtracted from the total costs to arrive at fixed costs. For example, for the Clark Manufacturing Company the lowest activity level was 10,000 hours when the cost was $18,500; the highest activity level was 80,000 hours when the cost was $43,000. The differences in costs and volume for the high-low point method would be:

	Costs	*Activity*
Highest (July)	$43,000	80,000 hours
Lowest (January)	18,500	10,000 hours
Difference	$24,500	70,000 hours

The variable cost per hour is the change in costs divided by the change in volume ($24,500 ÷ 70,000 hours) or $.35 per hour. The fixed costs are then estimated by multiplying either the high or low activity, expressed in hours, by the variable rate ($.35 per hour) and subtracting this product from the total cost at that level. For example, multiplying the high level of 80,000 hours by $.35 variable cost per hour gives a total variable cost of $28,000. Subtracting this variable cost from the total cost of $43,000 provides a fixed cost estimate of $15,000. At the 10,000-hour level the variable costs are

\$3,500 (10,000 × \$.35), and the fixed costs are again \$15,000 (\$18,500 − \$3,500). Notice that fixed costs are determined by substituting the variable rate and activity level into the equation for the straight line and solving for fixed costs. For example:

$$
\begin{aligned}
Y_c &= a + b(x) \\
\$43{,}000 &= a + \$.35(80{,}000) \\
a &= \$43{,}000 - \$28{,}000 \\
a &= \$15{,}000
\end{aligned}
$$

The high-low point method of segregating fixed and variable costs is simple and easy to use. There are, however, some weaknesses in it. It assumes that the cost patterns at the highest and lowest points of activity are typical of other cost-volume experiences. In our example, the answer would differ considerably if the costs at the 15,000-hour activity level had been used in lieu of those at the 10,000-hour level. Judgment should be exercised to select a representative low and a representative high point. Also, the high-low point method, like the scattergraph, provides no objective way of estimating the accuracy of the fixed and variable cost measurement.

Statistical Regression Analysis

Statistical regression analysis is a more sophisticated and reliable method of estimating fixed and variable costs than either the scattergraph or the high-low method. **Regression analysis** is a systematic way of determining whether the *y* values (costs) are related to the *x* values (volume measures). The goal of regression analysis is twofold. First, the methodology fits a line that shows the average rate of variability.[1] In this respect it is similar to the hand-drawn line on the scattergraph and the line drawn from the high-low point method. Second, it provides the decision maker with a measure of how well the line actually fits the data.

The method of regression analysis using the least squares approach provides two mathematical properties that are missing in the lines drawn by inspection or high-low methods. First, the algebraic sums of the positive and negative deviations from the fitted line equal zero. Second, the sum of the squares of these deviations is less than the sum of the squared vertical deviations from any other line. The line determined by the least squares method provides assurance that it is an *average* line, free from *subjective* error; it is

[1]It should be pointed out that the accountant assigns a cause and effect relationship to regression analysis. He says, in essence, that the cost is the "effect" resulting from the "cause" of volume. The pure statistician, on the other hand, is not willing to assign cause and effect to regression analysis. He speaks only in terms of whether the *x* and *y* values are related.

the line of "best fit." The method of least squares uses two equations which must be solved simultaneously to determine the *a* value (fixed cost) and the *b* value (variable rate). These equations are:[2]

I. $\Sigma y = na + b\Sigma x$
II. $\Sigma xy = a\Sigma x + b\Sigma x^2$

where:

Σy = Total costs	a = Total fixed costs
Σx = Total volume	b = Variable cost per unit of volume
n = Number of time periods	Σxy = Costs times volume summed

Before calculating a regression line for the Clark Manufacturing Company using these equations, let's examine some of the underlying assumptions of regression analysis. Unless these assumptions are kept clearly in mind there is a danger of misinterpreting the results. First, the two normal equations stated above are based on the assumption that the relationship between costs and volume is linear. When this is not true, a straight line will not fit the actual data. (The assumption of nonlinearity and methods of coping with it will be discussed later in this chapter.) Second, it is assumed that the actual data are normally distributed (that is, bell-shaped) around the regression line. That is to say, all the differences between the actual costs at a given volume level and the estimates made by the regression line at the same volume level would create a normal, bell-shaped curve. Third, it is assumed that there is a uniform dispersion of actual costs around the regression line. At a high volume level the actual data are distributed around the regression line in the same way they are at lower volumes. Finally, it is assumed that the cost measures are independent of each other. For example, the costs reported in April are not dependent upon those reported in May.

Keeping these assumptions in mind and using the data given for the Clark Manufacturing Company, let's see how the normal equations are used to calculate a regression line. The first step is the development of the factors in the formulas, as shown in Exhibit 2-2. Substituting the values found in Exhibit 2-2 into the formulas provides:

I. $\Sigma y = na + b\Sigma x$
II. $\Sigma xy = a\Sigma x + b\Sigma x^2$

I. $362{,}300 = 12a + 495{,}000b$
II. $16{,}697{,}500{,}000 = 495{,}000a + 26{,}025{,}000{,}000b$

[2]It is beyond the scope of this book to show the mathematical proof of the equations. Students who are interested in the mathematical aspects of the least squares method should consult an introductory statistics book. For now, we will accept the mathematical validity of the normal equations.

MONTH	HOURS x	COSTS y	xy (Thousands)	x^2 (Thousands)
January	10,000	18,500	185,000	100,000
February	15,000	25,500	382,500	225,000
March	30,000	25,800	774,000	900,000
April	40,000	30,000	1,200,000	1,600,000
May	60,000	35,000	2,100,000	3,600,000
June	70,000	39,000	2,730,000	4,900,000
July	80,000	43,000	3,440,000	6,400,000
August	50,000	34,400	1,720,000	2,500,000
September	30,000	25,100	753,000	900,000
October	30,000	26,500	795,000	900,000
November	20,000	23,300	446,000	400,000
December	60,000	36,200	2,172,000	3,600,000
Total	495,000	362,300	16,697,500	26,025,000

$\Sigma x = 495{,}000$

$\Sigma y = 362{,}300$

$\Sigma xy = 16{,}697{,}500{,}000$

$\Sigma x^2 = 26{,}025{,}000{,}000$

EXHIBIT 2-2
Least squares regression line worksheet

To solve for b we must set the a factor in both equations equal to each other. We multiply the smallest coefficient of a (in our case 12) by a number that will make it equal to the largest coefficient (in our case 495,000). This number may be found by dividing the 495,000 in Equation II by the 12 in Equation I ($495{,}000 \div 12 = 41{,}250$). When we multiply Equation I by the 41,250 we modify Equation I to be:

$$\text{III.} \quad 14{,}944{,}875{,}000 = 495{,}000a + 20{,}418{,}750{,}000b$$

Subtracting Equation III from Equation II gives:

$$\text{IV.} \quad 1{,}752{,}625{,}000 = 5{,}606{,}250{,}000b$$

Solving for b gives:

V. $b = \$.313$ which is the variable cost per activity hour.

Substituting the value of b in Equation I and solving for a gives:

VI. $362{,}300 = 12a + 495{,}000\,(.313)$
VII. $12a = 207{,}365$
VIII. $a = \$17{,}280$

This solution differs slightly from the high-low point method. The high-low point method estimated the fixed costs at \$15,000 and the variable costs at \$.35 per hour. The regression method estimated the fixed costs at \$17,280 and the variable costs at \$.313 per hour. One reason for these differences is the effect of the month of February. The high-low point method excluded all months except January and July; the regression line method used all months. Inclusion of the unusual month of February acted to increase the fixed costs and reduce the slope of the line (variable rate). A regression line excluding February, to test for the effect of that month, provides a regression equation of $y_c = \$16{,}087 + .333x$. These values are nearly identical to the scattergraph estimate from Exhibit 2-1.

One of the distinct values of using the statistical regression model for determining cost variability is that it allows a test of the relationship between cost and volume. When the relationship is perfect, each point representing actual cost will fall exactly on the regression line and there will be no errors in prediction. Exhibit 2-3 shows a scattergraph where there is a perfect relationship. Each set of data in Exhibit 2-3 falls right on the regression line.

The statistician would describe this perfect relationship by saying there is no residual sum of squares. The **residual sum of squares** measures the remaining variation in y (cost) that cannot be accounted for by its relationship to x (volume). Where all actual costs fall directly on the regression line there is no remaining variation in y (cost). The calculation of the residual sum of squares is made by measuring the variation of each y value from the corresponding predicted value given by the regression equation. In formula form the residual sum of squares is $\Sigma(y - \tilde{y})^2$ where:

y = Observed value of cost (actual cost)
$\tilde{y}$ = Predicted value of cost obtained from the regression line

If we divide the residual sum of squares by $n - 2$ (number of observations $- 2$), we obtain a measure known as the *residual variance.* The square root of the residual variance is called the **standard error of the estimate.** The complete formula for the standard error of the estimate is:

$$SE_{y \cdot x} = \sqrt{\frac{\Sigma(y - \tilde{y})^2}{n - 2}}$$

The standard error of the estimate measures how far the actual observations are from the regression line. The farther the observations from the regression line, the larger will be the standard error. For example, including the month of February in the regression analysis will increase the standard error of the estimate for the Clark Manufacturing Company. Conversely, the closer the actual data are to the estimates of the regression line, the smaller the standard

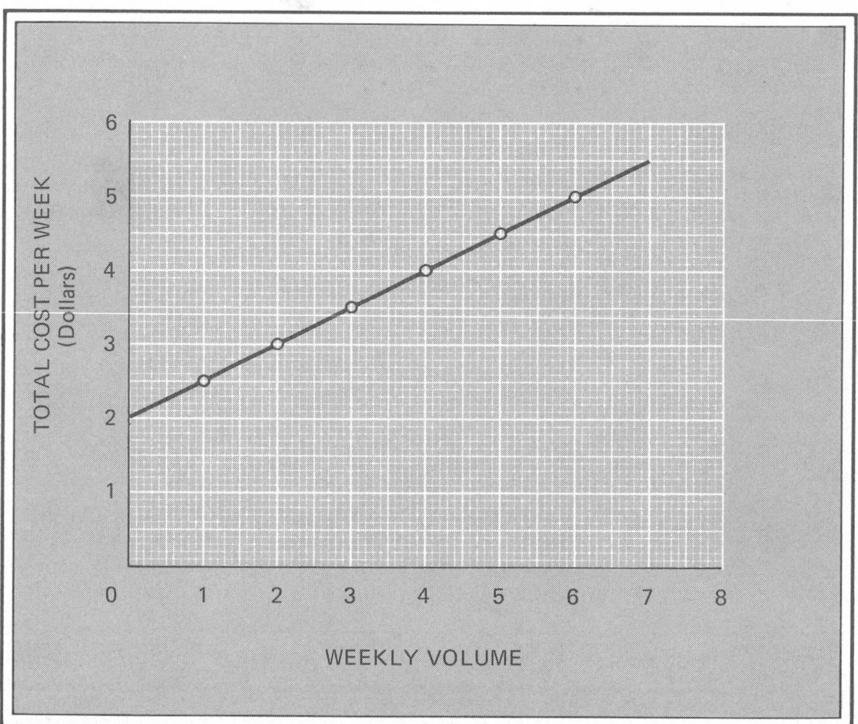

EXHIBIT 2-3
Scattergraph of a perfect cost-volume relationship

error of the estimate. The standard error permits the decision maker to determine the usefulness of his estimates. If the standard error is relatively large, the value of the equation in estimating costs may be limited.

The determination of the standard error of the estimate is shown in Exhibit 2-4. Using this standard error as a test, how accurate is our 12-month regression line for the Clark Manufacturing Company? Our regression line was \$17,280 + \$.313(x) and the standard error of the estimate was \$1,572. At the 40,000-hour level the company's estimate of maintenance cost from the regression line would be \$17,280 + \$.313(40,000), or \$29,800. Using a table of normal probabilities[3], 68.27% of all observations should fall between

[3]In statistics the normal distribution is the familiar bell-shaped curve. This curve has the property that 68.27% of all observations fall between the mean ($\bar{x}$) plus or minus one standard deviation; within the range of $\bar{x} \pm 2$ standard deviations, 95.45% are included; and with $\bar{x} \pm 3$ standard deviations, 99.73%, or nearly all of the items are included. It is beyond the scope of this text to discuss the normal distribution in depth. It is sufficient that the student know that it allows the manager to assess how well the regression line fits the observed data and to make probability statements about the fit to the data.

MONTH	HOURS OF ACTIVITY x	TOTAL COST y	REGRESSION LINE ESTIMATE* $\tilde{y}$	$y - \tilde{y}$	$(y - \tilde{y})^2$
January	10,000	18,500	20,410	−1,910	3,648,100
February	15,000	25,500	21,975	3,525	12,425,625
March	30,000	25,800	26,670	− 870	756,900
April	40,000	30,000	29,800	200	40,000
May	60,000	35,000	36,060	−1,060	1,123,600
June	70,000	39,000	39,190	− 190	36,100
July	80,000	43,000	42,320	680	462,400
August	50,000	34,400	32,930	1,470	2,160,900
September	30,000	25,100	26,670	−1,570	2,464,900
October	30,000	26,500	26,670	− 170	28,900
November	20,000	22,300	23,540	−1,240	1,537,600
December	60,000	36,200	36,060	140	19,600
Total					24,704,625

Then: $SE_{y \cdot x} = \sqrt{\dfrac{\Sigma(y - \tilde{y})^2}{n - 2}} = \sqrt{\dfrac{24,704,625}{12 - 2}} = 1,572$

*For example, for 10,000 hours the regression line would predict a cost of $17,280 + $.313 (10,000), or $20,410.

EXHIBIT 2-4
Standard error of the estimate worksheet

$y_c \pm$ $1,572. Thus, 68.27% of the time the actual cost should fall between $28,228 ($29,800 − $1,572) and $31,372 ($29,800 + $1,572). The smaller the standard error, the more confidence the decision maker can have in the regression line for prediction.

On the 11-month basis, i.e. excluding February, the regression line was $16,087 + $.333($x$). The standard error of the estimate for this regression line is $866. At the 40,000-hour level the company's estimate of maintenance cost would be $16,087 + $.333(40,000), or $29,407. The actual cost should fall between $28,541 and $30,273, 68.27% of the time. This interval is much tighter than that of the regression line based on the 12 months of data, but it is biased because it excludes an independent observation from the population.

A special warning seems appropriate here. Statistical decision-making methods are objective, yet they carry an aura of accuracy that must be approached with caution. Statistical methods do *not* remove the necessity for the decision maker to form his own judgments about the usefulness of the data. While we know the regression line and the standard error of the estimate for the Clark Manufacturing Company, subjective judgment is still required to determine whether or not we want to use the data.

There are occasions when it is impossible to fit a satisfactory regression line. Exhibits 2-5 and 2-6 illustrate two scattergraphs which defy a segregation

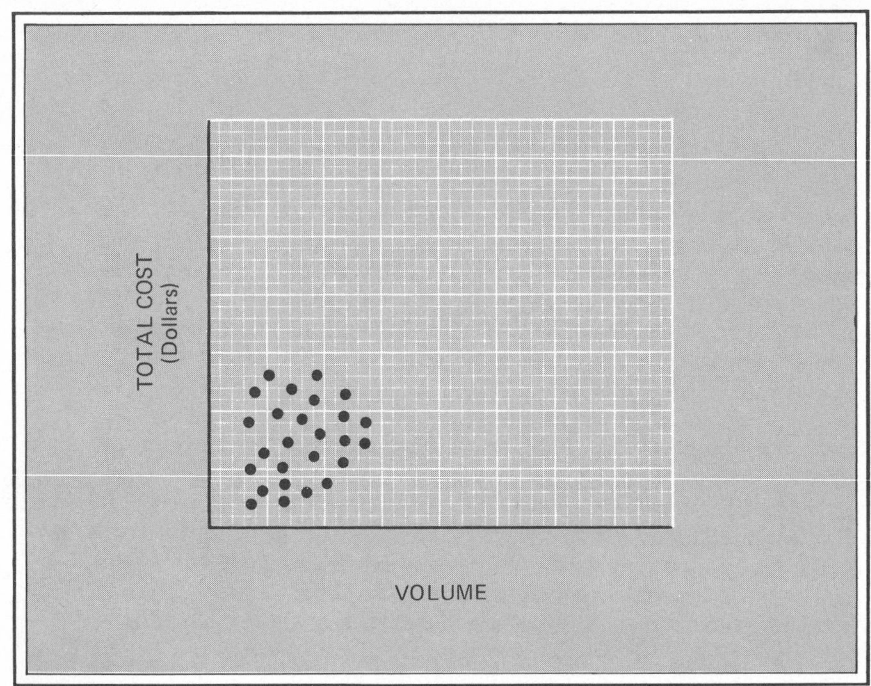

EXHIBIT 2-5
Scattergraph where no cost-volume relationship exists

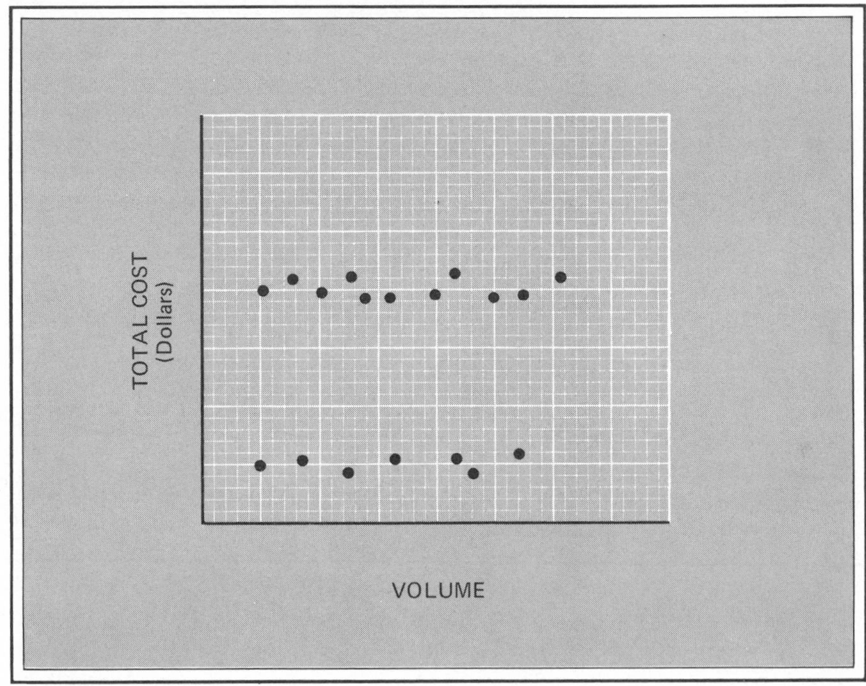

EXHIBIT 2-6
Scattergraph where cost-volume relationship is unclear

of the cost into its fixed and variable components. In both cases the regression line is not a good measure and the standard error of the estimate would be so large as to negate the meaning of the regression line. In both cases management has no recourse but to use its discretion in planning future costs. Usually the direct establishment of budgeted cost levels will result in treating the cost as fixed.

Advanced statistical techniques

The straight-line measure of cost variability is the method most widely used by accountants. It is not universally applicable however. There will be instances where a linear regression line will result in an unsatisfactory standard error of the estimate. In some instances the relationship may be curvilinear. As discussed in Chapter 1, some of the semivariable costs behave this way. To estimate this cost behavior pattern a second-degree curve, expressed by the following formula, would have to be used.

$$y_c = a + bx + cx^2$$

The solution of this formula requires three normal equations. With this and other higher-order curves the mathematics becomes quite complex. Without a computer these studies may not be feasible.

In addition to curvilinear patterns, the decision maker may find that the cost being studied is related to one or more factors in addition to volume, or that there are two or more different measures of volume. For some cost predictions there may be two or three independent measures, such as machine hours, labor hours, product dimensions, and labor skills. In this case the decision maker may find the techniques of multiple correlation useful. Multiple correlation measures the change in cost (y) for one of these variables, while holding all of the other variables constant. The formula to express the relationships among many variables is:

$$y_c = a + bx_1 + cx_2 + dx_3 \ldots$$

where: y_c is the cost to be predicted; x_1, x_2, and x_3 are the different volume measures; and a, b, and c are constants.

A detailed study of these two techniques is beyond the scope of this book. However, it is important that the student recognize some of the possible weaknesses in the single volume, straight-line model of cost variability. The search for a single volume base and the use of straight lines can limit the scope of inferences to be made by the decision maker about fixed and variable costs.

Expressing Cost Behavior Patterns: The Flexible Budget

Up to this point we have taken the view that management is studying each cost factor separately and individually. To make decisions involving the volume of production for the company as a whole, it must combine the behavior patterns of individual costs into a total cost picture. Accountants call the statement of fixed and variable costs, whether on an individual cost-by-cost basis or a total cost basis, the **flexible budget.** The flexible budget is a concise statement of how costs are related to changes in the chosen activity volume.

Assume that a company has only three costs: a fixed cost, a variable cost, and a mixed cost. The flexible budget for each individual cost and for total costs follows.

Cost	*Flexible Budget ($y_c = a + bx$)*
	a *b*
Fixed	\$500 + \$ 0 (*x*)
Variable	\$ 0 + \$.25 (*x*)
Semivariable	\$ 50 + \$.10 (*x*)
Total cost	\$550 + \$.35 (*x*)

For estimating and controlling individual costs, the company would use the flexible budget for each type of cost. For making decisions regarding the company as a whole, the flexible budget of \$550 + \$.35(*x*) would be used. In order to combine the individual cost elements, it is important to seek a single measure of volume that fits all costs. The volume measures must be the same if the individual flexible budget formulas are to be additive.

The Relevant Range of Activity

The purpose of determining cost behavior patterns and specifying costs as fixed and variable is to sharpen the decision data. Unless the concepts of cost variability allow the decision maker to be more precise and flexible in his decisions, the effort and money spent in developing fixed and variable cost patterns are wasted. The range of volume over which the cost behavior patterns can reasonably be expected to hold true is termed the **relevant range.** No analysis of fixed and variable costs should be made without specifying the relevant range of activity.

It would be a mistake to believe that the relevant range of activity extends from zero activity to maximum volume capacity. In the event of a drastic decrease in volume, management would take a different set of actions than if production continued at a normal pace. As volume declined, past policies and decisions would be reexamined. Perhaps executive salaries would be lowered, production lines closed, insurance policies cancelled or reduced, or products dropped from the production schedule. On the other end of the scale, as production increased to reach maximum capability, there would be "diminishing returns." Storerooms would become crowded and inefficient, machines would require additional maintenance, workers in the second shift or on overtime would be less productive, and production facilities would become overworked.

FIXED AND VARIABLE COSTS AND REVENUE

The study of cost-volume-profit relationships is most commonly called **breakeven analysis.** This term can be misleading. Firms do not seek to break even. They seek an acceptable rate of return on their investment. However, breakeven analysis need not be limited merely to seeking the point at which the firm's revenue equals its costs. It can span all volumes within the relevant range of activity. Central to cost-volume-profit studies is an understanding of which costs are fixed and which are variable, as developed in the previous section.

Cost-Volume-Profit Analysis through Graphs

The easiest way to see breakeven analysis is graphically. Exhibit 2-7 is a graphic presentation of cost-volume-profit relationships with the breakeven point indicated. This breakeven analysis of the Gordon Company was built upon a study of its cost behavior and revenue patterns. The Gordon Manufacturing Company produces a single product, a teak-handled can opener, which it sells to souvenir stores for $1.25 each. The firm's flexible budget shows that total fixed costs are estimated to be $30,000 per year and that variable costs per unit are estimated to be $.75. Management believes that the relevant range of activity is between 40,000 and 100,000 units per year. In constructing the graph, the fixed costs were plotted as a straight horizontal line at the $30,000 level. Variable costs were plotted at the rate of $.75 per unit of volume, providing the total cost line. The sales line was plotted at the rate of $1.25 per unit of volume. As a reminder of the constraints of the relevant range, two vertical lines were added to the graph. Beyond these lines the decision maker has little assurance that the cost-volume-profit relationships are valid.

The **breakeven point** is where the sales revenue line intersects the total cost line. At this volume, total revenues equal total expenses. When operations are at the breakeven point the firm will make neither a profit nor a loss. For the Gordon Manufacturing Company the breakeven point, determined from the vertical axis of the graph, is $75,000 in sales. This point occurs at a volume of 60,000 units, which is found on the horizontal axis. The area between the sales revenue line and the total cost line at a volume below the breakeven point represents the loss potential of the firm. If the company operates at a volume beyond the breakeven point, the area between the sales revenue line and the total cost line represents the profit potential of the firm.

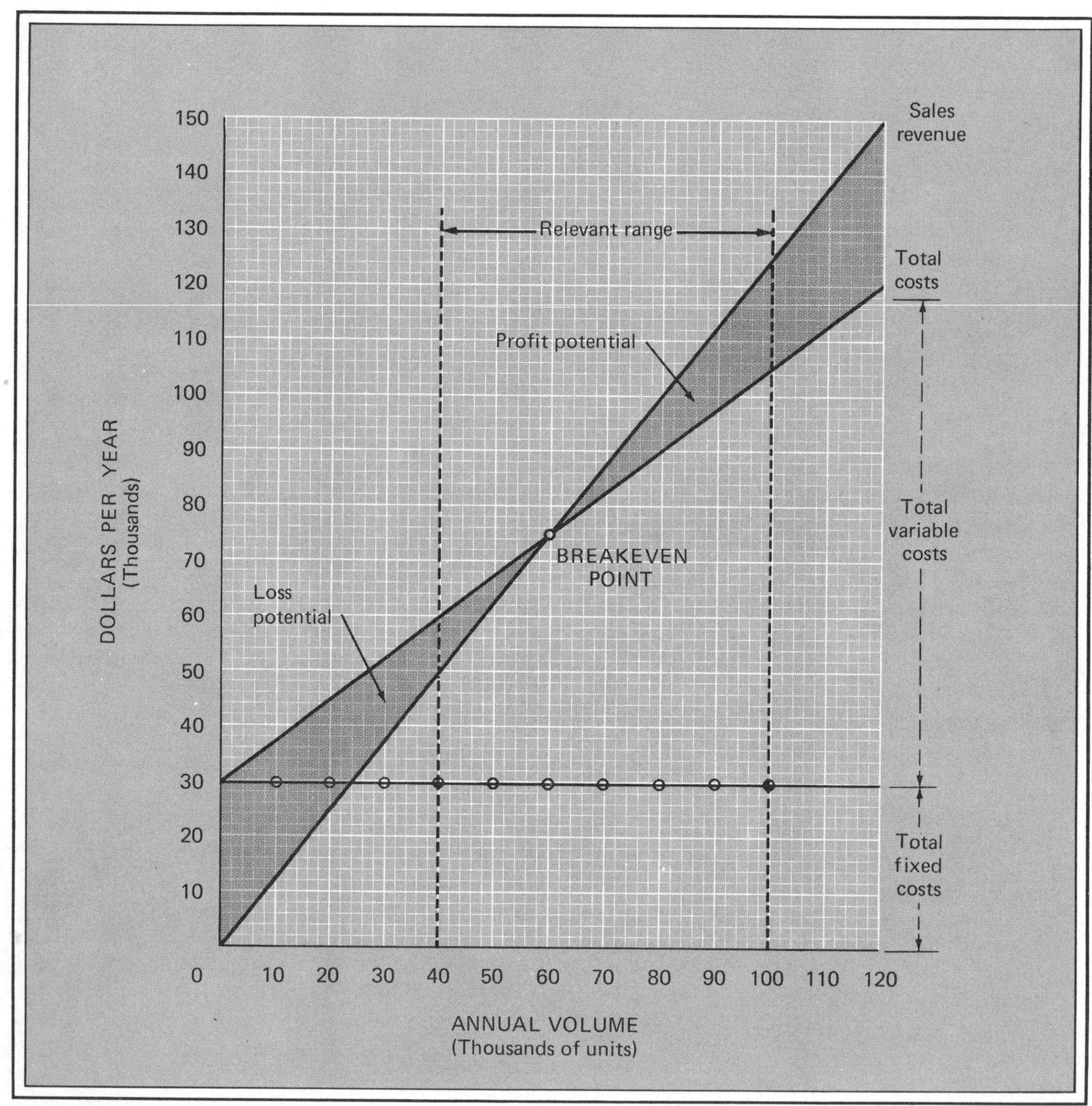

EXHIBIT 2-7
Breakeven graph for the Gordon Manufacturing Company

If the company sells 40,000 units, what will be their loss? Sales will be 40,000 units × \$1.25 per unit, or \$50,000. Variable costs will be 40,000 units × \$.75, or \$30,000. Fixed costs will be \$30,000. Combining these figures into an income statement, we can see that the loss will be \$10,000.

Sales (40,000 × \$1.25)	\$ 50,000
Variable costs (40,000 × \$.75)	30,000
Contribution margin (40,000 × \$.50)	\$ 20,000
Fixed costs	30,000
Net loss	\$(10,000)

The loss could also be found directly on the breakeven graph. Moving out the volume axis to 40,000 units, the loss of \$10,000 may be determined by taking the difference between the total cost line (\$60,000) and the total revenue line (\$50,000).

Cost-Volume-Profit Analysis through Equations

The graphic method is an easy way to see the implications of a cost-volume-profit relationship, but it is not the easiest way to calculate the breakeven point. Expressing the relationships in equation form is much more precise and rapid. A general form of expressing cost-volume-profit relationships that can be adapted to any situation is:

$$\text{Sales} - \text{Fixed costs} - \text{Variable costs} = \text{Net income}$$

or

$$\text{Sales} = \text{Fixed costs} + \text{Variable costs} + \text{Net income}$$

Since the amount of sales and variable costs are at the same level of activity, the equation must be restated as follows:

$$SP(x) = FC + VC(x) + NI$$

where:

SP = Selling price per unit
x = Number of units sold
FC = Fixed costs
VC = Variable cost per unit
NI = Net income

The Gordon Manufacturing Company's breakeven point, in number of units sold, may now be computed.

(1) $SP(x) = FC + VC(x) + NI$
(2) $\$1.25(x) = \$30,000 + \$.75(x) + 0$
(3) $\$.50x = \$30,000$
(4) $x = \$30,000 \div \$.50$
(5) $x =$ 60,000 units needed to break even

Notice that step (4) is the fixed costs divided by the contribution margin per unit. The breakeven equation could be stated as:

$$\text{Breakeven point in units} = \frac{\text{Fixed costs}}{\text{Contribution margin per unit}}$$

This equation underlies the contribution margin approach to breakeven.

Cost-Volume-Profit Analysis through the Contribution Margin

Many decision makers prefer to think in terms of an income statement for cost-volume-profit analysis. An income statement showing a contribution margin is well suited for this approach. If the selling price per unit is assumed to be constant, total revenue will be proportional to volume. We have already seen that the definition of variable costs is that they vary proportionally with volume. Thus, the difference between revenue and variable costs—the contribution margin—will also be proportional to volume. It is this relationship that makes the contribution margin income statement useful. For the Gordon Manufacturing Company the contribution margin is:

	Dollars	*Percentage*
Unit sales price	$1.25	100%
Unit variable cost	.75	60%
Unit contribution margin	$ .50	40%

Each unit generates a contribution margin which is available to cover fixed costs and, after they are covered, to contribute to profit. (It should be apparent that if there is a negative contribution margin, the firm will *never* break even since the variable costs will always exceed the sales revenue. In this case the more the company sells, the more it loses.) As shown earlier, dividing the fixed costs by the contribution margin per unit ($30,000 ÷ $.50) gives the breakeven point in units.

Alongside the income statement in dollars is a percentage analysis. If sales are considered 100%, then variable costs are 60% of each sales dollar. This relationship is called the **variable cost ratio.** The sales percentage minus the variable cost percentage is the **contribution margin ratio,** sometimes referred to as the **variable profit ratio.** For the Gordon Manufacturing Company this ratio is 40% (100% − 60%). The fixed costs divided by the contribution margin ratio ($30,000 ÷ 40%) is the breakeven point in dollars of sales ($75,000). This is the same as the formula:

$$\text{Breakeven in dollars} = \frac{\text{Fixed costs}}{1 - \dfrac{\text{Variable costs}}{\text{Sales}}}$$

The denominator, $1 - \dfrac{\text{Variable costs}}{\text{Sales}}$, is the contribution margin ratio.

In summary, the breakeven point is:

$$\text{Breakeven in units} = \frac{\text{Fixed costs}}{\text{Contribution margin per unit}}$$

or

$$\text{Breakeven in dollars} = \frac{\text{Fixed costs}}{\text{Contribution margin ratio}}$$

The contribution margin and the contribution margin ratio allow another useful graphic technique called the **profit-volume chart** (PV chart). Exhibit 2-8 shows the PV chart for the Gordon Manufacturing Company. Remember the question asked earlier about the amount of net loss if the company sold 40,000 units at $1.25? At sales of $50,000 (40,000 × $1.25), the net loss of $10,000 can be read directly from the PV chart. Note also that the PV chart shows that the loss at zero sales activity is equal to fixed costs. This relationship is also shown on the breakeven graph. In this illustration a sales level of 40,000 units is at the lower limit of the relevant range. In practice, most firms would aggressively reduce fixed costs as the volume began decreasing toward zero activity.

EFFECTS OF CHANGING FACTORS

A breakeven graph shows the relationship between four variables: sales price, fixed costs, variable costs, and volume. The study of these variables allows management to assess the potential profitability of the firm. In this section we will look at how changes in the three variables of sales revenue, fixed costs, and variable costs interact with volume to create a profit.

Effects of Changes in Selling Price

Let's assume that the management of the Gordon Manufacturing Company has the opportunity to increase the unit selling price of its can opener from $1.25 to $1.50. It believes that no other variable will change by a significant

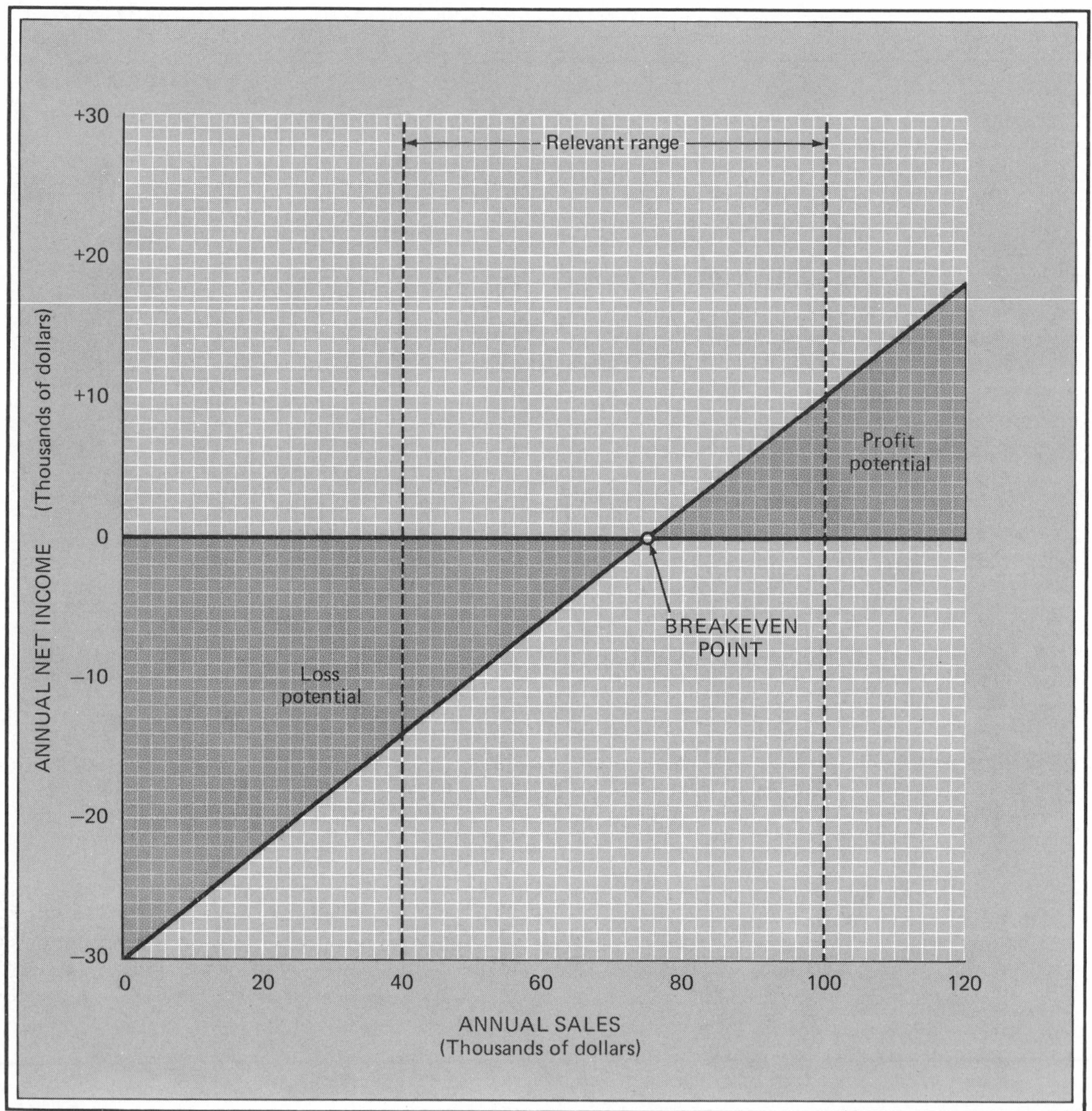

EXHIBIT 2-8
Profit-volume chart for the Gordon Manufacturing Company

amount. The immediate effect on the breakeven point is that it will be reached sooner. In this case the breakeven point in units would be:

$$\frac{\text{Fixed costs}}{\text{Contribution margin per unit}} = \frac{\$30{,}000}{\$1.50 - \$.75} = 40{,}000 \text{ units}$$

At the old selling price of $1.25 the breakeven point was 60,000 units. It is apparent that an increase in the selling price will raise the contribution margin if the variable costs are unchanged, and that an increase in the per-unit contribution margin will decrease the sales volume necessary to reach a desired goal.

What happens if the company has to lower the selling price to $1 per unit because of increased competition? The breakeven point will be increased to 120,000 units [$30,000 ÷ ($1.00 − $.75)]. At this output level the company will have to completely reassess its cost and revenue patterns since 120,000 units is beyond the relevant range of activity.

Effects of Changes in Variable Costs

Assume there have been changes in variable costs. The teak used in the product has increased in price by $.05 per unit. Teak has been in short supply; due to increased demand around the world, the price increased. Also, because of inflationary pressures, the wages of the production workers increased an average of $.20 per unit. These changes increased the total variable costs from $.75 per unit to $1 per unit. The new contribution margin becomes $.25 ($1.25 − $1.00), and the breakeven point in units would be:

$$\frac{\text{Fixed costs}}{\text{Contribution margin per unit}} = \frac{\$30{,}000}{\$.25} = 120{,}000 \text{ units}$$

Again, 120,000 units is beyond the relevant range.

Any time the selling price per unit decreases or the variable cost per unit increases, the contribution margin per unit will decline and the volume necessary to achieve breakeven will increase. Of course, increases in the selling prices or decreases in the variable costs will reduce the volume necessary to achieve the breakeven point.

Effects of Changes in Fixed Costs

Assume that the original fixed costs of $30,000 included only $3,000 for advertising, and that it is becoming clear to management that it will be necessary to add $6,000 for advertising if the company is to maintain its selling price of $1.25 per unit. The new breakeven point would be:

$$\frac{\text{Fixed costs} + \text{Additional fixed cost}}{\text{Contribution margin per unit}} = \frac{\$30{,}000 + \$6{,}000}{\$1.25 - \$.75}$$

$$= 72{,}000 \text{ units}$$

Notice that the one-fifth increase in fixed costs (from $30,000 to $36,000) resulted in a one-fifth increase in the breakeven point (from 60,000 to 72,000 units). Changes in fixed costs will always result in proportional changes in the breakeven point.

Volume Necessary to Achieve Desired Net Income

The examples so far have stressed the effect of changes in costs upon the breakeven point. Of course, management seeks a net income. What volume must the Gordon Manufacturing Company achieve to obtain a net income of $12,000 if it sells its can openers for $1.25 each, incurs $.75 per unit for variable costs, and has fixed costs of $30,000? The desired sales volume would be:

$$\text{Sales necessary for desired net income} = \frac{\text{Fixed costs} + \text{Desired net income}}{\text{Contribution margin per unit}}$$

$$= \frac{\$30{,}000 + \$12{,}000}{\$1.25 - \$.75} = 84{,}000 \text{ units}$$

There is another way to approach the same question. If management has already calculated the breakeven point, it can approach the volume needed to earn a desired income by determining the increment in sales beyond the breakeven point. In the Gordon Manufacturing Company the breakeven point is 60,000 units, or $75,000 of sales, assuming $30,000 of fixed costs and a contribution margin of $.50 per unit. At this level all fixed costs would be recovered. Beyond the breakeven point, the entire contribution margin per unit adds to the income. For each unit sold beyond 60,000, the net income would be increased by $.50, the contribution margin per unit. Thus, to achieve a net income of $12,000, the company would have to sell 24,000 units ($12,000 ÷ $.50) beyond breakeven, or a total of 84,000 units (60,000 + 24,000).

The net income in the previous illustrations has been the net income *before* income taxes. Management may want to state its net income objectives *after* income taxes. In this case the analysis must be expanded slightly. Assume that the company wants a net income after taxes of $14,000 and that its current tax rate is 30%. In this example the net income after taxes is 70% of the net income before taxes. The formula to calculate the sales *volume* necessary to earn $14,000 after taxes is:

$$\frac{\text{Fixed costs} + \dfrac{\text{Desired income after taxes}}{1 - \text{Tax rate}}}{\text{Contribution margin per unit}} = \frac{\$30{,}000 + \dfrac{\$14{,}000}{1 - .30}}{\$1.25 - \$.75}$$

$$= \frac{\$30{,}000 + \$20{,}000}{\$.50}$$

$$= 100{,}000 \text{ units}$$

To find the sales *dollars* needed to achieve an after-tax income of $14,000, the formula would be adjusted to divide by the contribution margin ratio (.40). This calculation is:

$$\frac{\$30{,}000 + \$20{,}000}{.40} = \$125{,}000$$

Effects of Multiple Changes

Let's assume that the management of the Gordon Manufacturing Company is bombarded by changes in its environment. It believes that by lowering the selling price from $1.25 to $1 per unit, it could increase the current sales volume by 30%. At the same time, some changes in production methods are planned. A new machine that would automate part of the production process has just come on the market. This machine would reduce the variable costs by $.25 per unit and would increase the fixed costs from $30,000 to $35,000 per year. What sales must the Gordon Manufacturing Company achieve for an after-tax net income of $7,500 if the current tax rate is 25%? A good way to bring these changes together simultaneously is with the formula:

$$\text{Needed sales volume} = \frac{\text{Fixed costs} + \dfrac{\text{Desired net income after taxes}}{1 - \text{Tax rate}}}{1 - \dfrac{\text{Variable costs per unit}}{\text{Sales per unit}}}$$

Taking into account the proposed changes, the data expressed in the formula would be:

$$\text{Needed sales volume} = \frac{\$30{,}000 + 5{,}000 + \dfrac{\$7{,}500}{1. - .25}}{1 - \dfrac{\$.75 \times 130\% \times 66\tfrac{2}{3}\%}{\$1.25 \times 130\% \times 80\%}}$$

$$= \frac{\$45{,}000}{.5}$$

$$= \$90{,}000 \text{ of sales, or } 90{,}000 \text{ units}$$

This formula shows the effect of the four proposed changes. First, the fixed costs have increased by $5,000. Second, the original price of $1.25 was lowered to $1. The new selling price is 80% of the original selling price. By multiplying the $1.25 by 80%, the formula reflects the new selling price of $1. (If this were the only change, the contribution margin ratio would decrease.) Third, the increase in sales volume will increase both total sales and total variable costs to 130% of their original level. Thus, changes in volume do not affect the contribution margin ratio since both sales and variable costs have been multiplied by 130%. Fourth, the decrease in the variable costs by $.25 per unit puts the variable costs at 66⅔% of their previous level ($.50 ÷ $.75). This decrease acts to increase the contribution margin ratio.

By thinking about the interaction of volume, selling price, variable costs, and fixed costs, the relevant variables and their effect upon income are considered simultaneously. Perhaps in this context a name for the breakeven graph that more clearly describes its function would be **profit planning chart.**

UNDERLYING ASSUMPTIONS OF COST-VOLUME-PROFIT RELATIONSHIPS

A thoughtful look at the breakeven graph provides insight into the underlying assumptions of cost-volume-profit analysis. Among them are the following considerations:

1. The breakeven graph shows costs separated into fixed and variable components. This classification implies that the decision maker has been successful in finding and using a method of segregating fixed and variable costs. Within this assumption lie the problems and limitations of cost-volume analysis.
2. The fixed costs are constant across the changes in volume and the variable costs change in direct proportion to volume. Inherent in this assumption is the concept of the relevant range. It is apparent that fixed costs will stairstep at some volume. Some variable costs are not linear. Labor will meet with diminishing returns at some activity level and raw materials may involve quantity discounts if used in large amounts. All these issues, and others like them, have been resolved within the assumption of a relevant range.
3. The revenue line is also linear. Throughout the relevant range it assumes that management is not granting price concessions to obtain higher sales volume. This is the economist's definition of pure competition.
4. When both costs and revenues are plotted on the same volume (x) axis, the assumption of a single volume measure is made. It is assumed that all production was sold or that there were no significant changes in the inventory levels.
5. Since the time implied by such a cost-volume-profit graph is an accounting period, for example, the fiscal year, the cost-volume-profit graph assumes no price level changes and no significant changes in production methods, products, or managerial policies during the accounting period.
6. Since the chart assumes a constant contribution margin, it implies that there is only one product or, if more than one, that the combination of products sold provides a constant contribution margin.

A Curvilinear Approach to Cost-Volume-Profit Analysis

Some accountants have called for a modified cost-volume-profit graph to compensate for some of these assumptions. The weakness of assuming a constant revenue line and the linearity of the fixed and variable costs have led some to prepare a graph as shown in Exhibit 2-9. On this graph the revenue line recognizes the necessity of price reductions to obtain higher volume. It also recognizes that as volume increases there will be "diminishing returns" in the production factors; that is, there will be fewer units of output

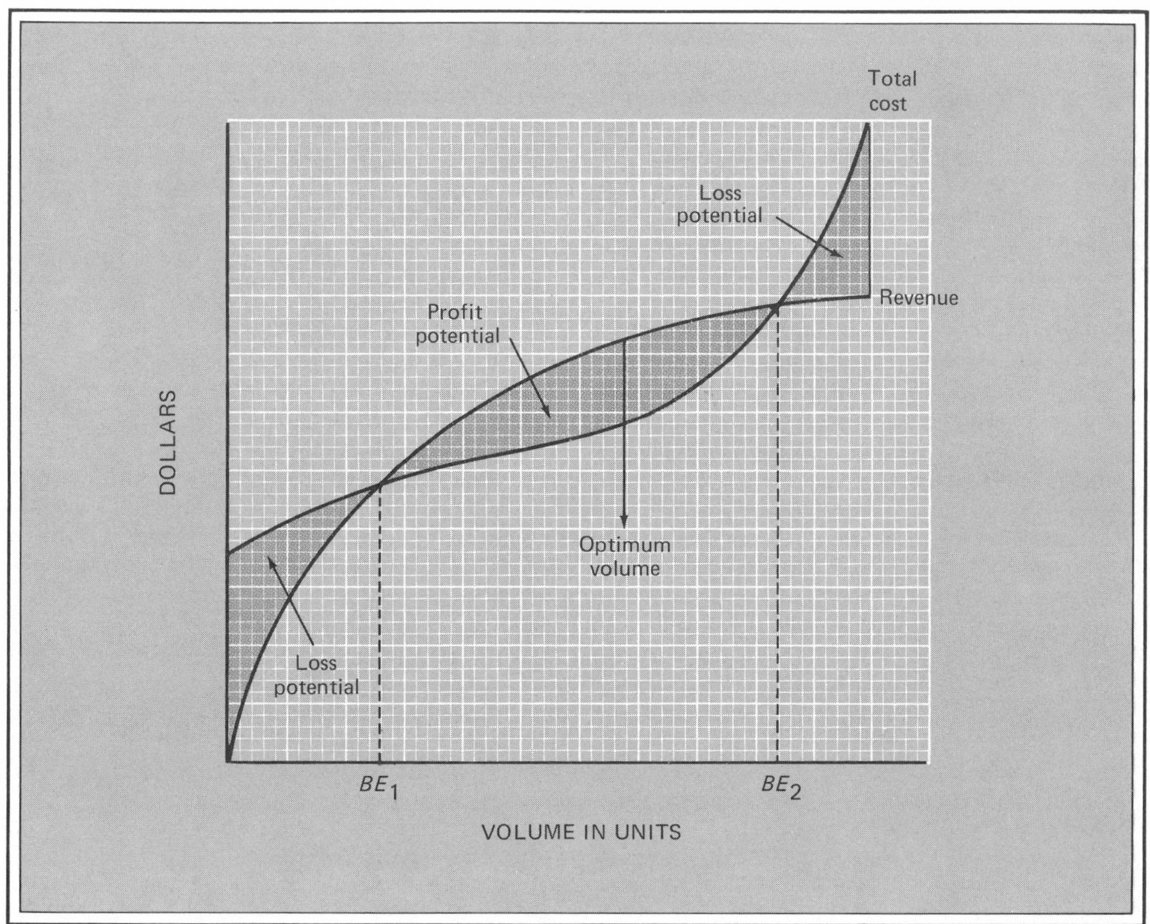

EXHIBIT 2-9
Economist's view of the breakeven graph

(production) for each unit of input (cost). The decreasing rate of the revenue line and the increasing rate of the cost line provide two breakeven points (BE_1 and BE_2). At a volume less than BE_1 and more than BE_2, the firm will have losses. There is one optimum production level where profits will be higher than at any other level. As shown in Chapter 1 this optimum level is where marginal costs equal marginal revenue.

Multiproduct Situations

The previous illustrations assumed that the Gordon Manufacturing Company produced only one product. However, many manufacturers make more than one type of product. The relative combination of the quantities of each product sold is called the **sales mix.** If each product has an identical contribution margin, changes in the product mix will not affect the breakeven point

	Can opener	Bottle opener	Corkscrew
Sales price per unit	$1.25	$2.00	$2.50
Variable cost per unit	.75	1.30	1.75
Contribution margin per unit	$ .50	$ .70	$ .75
Contribution margin ratio	40%	35%	30%
Fixed costs for total operations $36,000			
Projected units to be produced and sold	50,000	25,000	15,000

EXHIBIT 2-10
Projected cost and revenue data for the Gordon Company

nor the profit from operations. However, when the products have different contribution margins, changes in the product mix will affect the breakeven point and the results from operations.

To explore the effect of sales mix, let's assume that the management of the Gordon Manufacturing Company added two new items to its product line. In addition to the can opener, it decided to produce and sell a bottle opener and a corkscrew. Projected selling prices, cost patterns, and volume of sales are shown in Exhibit 2-10. Exhibit 2-11 shows the projected income statements for each product and for the company as a whole.

The breakeven point for the Gordon Manufacturing Company, given the sales mix of 50,000 can openers, 25,000 bottle openers, and 15,000 corkscrews, is $36,000 ÷ 35.8%, or $100,559. The 35.8% is the aggregate contribution margin ratio based upon the specific sales mix. At the bottom of Exhibit 2-11 the sales for each product are shown as a percent of total sales. Given the sales mix in Exhibit 2-11, the can openers account for 41.67% of the total sales of $150,000; the bottle openers, 33⅓%; and the corkscrews, 25%. Multiplying each product's percentage share of total sales by the contribution margin ratio for that product gives the total contribution margin *per sales dollar* for each product. Thus, the 16.67% for the can opener is its contribution margin per dollar of revenue.

Given this setting, and other things being equal, management should stress those products with the greatest contribution margins. Assume that during the year management had the opportunity to sell 25,000 additional

THE GORDON MANUFACTURING COMPANY
PROJECTED INCOME STATEMENT
For the Year Ended December 31, 19X6

	Can opener	Bottle opener	Corkscrew	Total	
Units sold	50,000	25,000	15,000		
Sales	$62,500	$50,000	$37,500	$150,000	100.00%
Variable cost	37,500	32,500	26,250	96,250	64.17%
Total contribution margin	$25,000	$17,500	$11,250	$ 53,750	35.83%
Fixed costs				36,000	
Net income before taxes				$ 17,750	
Sales as percentage of total sales	41.67%	33.33%	25.00%	100.00%	
times					
Contribution margin ratio	40.00%	35.00%	30.00%	35.83%	
equals					
Contribution margin of each product per dollar of revenue	16.67%	11.66%	7.50%	35.83%	

EXHIBIT 2-11
Projected income statements by product line for the Gordon Manufacturing Company

bottle openers in place of 25,000 can openers. The income statement for the year would be as shown in Exhibit 2-12. Based upon the sales of 25,000 can openers, 50,000 bottle openers, and 15,000 corkscrews, the breakeven point would be $36,000 ÷ 34.81%, or $103,419. The shift from selling 50,000 can openers and 25,000 bottle openers to selling 25,000 can openers and 50,000 bottle openers had a curious effect. It lowered the aggregate contribution margin ratio from 35.8% (Exhibit 2-11) to 34.81% (Exhibit 2-12) while simultaneously increasing the net profit by $5,000 ($22,750 − $17,750). The can opener has a higher contribution margin ratio (40%) than the bottle opener (35%), but the contribution margin per unit of the bottle opener is higher ($.70) than that of the can opener ($.50). The firm should move toward those products that provide the greatest *total contribution margin,* considering the product mix, rather than automatically choosing the product with the highest contribution margin ratio.

Exhibits 2-11 and 2-12 present income statements shown by product line. This arrangement presents problems in the handling of fixed costs. In

THE GORDON MANUFACTURING COMPANY
ACTUAL INCOME STATEMENT
For the Year Ended December 31, 19X6

	Can opener	Bottle opener	Corkscrew	Total	
Units sold	25,000	50,000	15,000		
Sales	$31,250	$100,000	$37,500	$168,750	100.00%
Variable cost	18,750	65,000	26,250	110,000	65.19%
Total contribution margin	$12,500	$35,000	$11,250	$ 58,750	34.81%
Fixed costs				36,000	
Net income before taxes				$ 22,750	
Sales as percentage of total sales	18.52%	59.26%	22.22%	100.00%	
times					
Contribution margin ratio	40.00%	35.00%	30.00%	34.81%	
equals					
Contribution margin of each product per dollar of revenue	7.40%	20.74%	6.67%	34.81%	

EXHIBIT 2-12
Actual income statements by product line for the Gordon Manufacturing Company

these two exhibits the fixed costs are shown as a lump-sum amount deducted from the total column. Fixed costs have not been allocated or apportioned to the individual product line income statements. It is not necessary to do so because for management decisions the question of which products to emphasize and the effect of cost-volume-revenue interactions on profits and break-even points do not depend upon allocation of fixed costs.

Multidepartmental Comparisons

The operating characteristics of different departments within a company, or of two different companies, can be examined through a closer study of their cost structures. Assume that a company has two decentralized departments with cost and revenue characteristics shown in the accompanying tabulation.

	Department A		*Department B*	
Sales	$50,000	100%	$50,000	100%
Variable costs	35,000	70%	10,000	20%
Contribution margin	$15,000	30%	$40,000	80%
Fixed costs	10,000		35,000	
Net income	$ 5,000		$ 5,000	
Breakeven points in sales dollars	$33,333		$43,750	

These two departments have the same net profit, although they have very different underlying economic characteristics. One way to examine these differences is through the **margin of safety,** which shows the difference between the actual (or budgeted) sales and the breakeven point. The two margins of safety are as follows:

	Department A	*Department B*
1. Margin of safety expressed in dollars		
($50,000 − $33,333)	$16,667	
($50,000 − $43,750)		$6,250
2. Margin of safety expressed as a percent of sales		
($16,667 ÷ $50,000)	33.33%	
($6,250 ÷ $50,000)		12.50%

Department B is operating closer to the breakeven point than is Department A. Department B has a narrower margin of safety. If the volume of Department B drops more than 12.50%, it will operate at a loss; Department A will not operate at a loss unless its volume drops 33.33%. In one sense the margin of safety is an inexact measure of the risks of investing in fixed costs rather than variable costs. A rise in the breakeven point reduces the margin of safety and increases managerial pressure to sustain a high sales volume.

SUMMARY

Basic to profit planning and control is the knowledge of how costs change with changes in volume. Fixed costs are costs that do not change with changes in volume; variable costs vary in direct proportion to changes in volume. Costs that change with changes in volume, but not in direct proportion, are semivariable costs. There are three types of semivariable costs: stair-stepped, mixed, and curvilinear. The flexible budget is the formal statement of how costs vary with volume.

The simplest and most straightforward way of determining fixed and variable costs is to examine the firm's contracts. Where there are no contracts, fixed and variable costs can be estimated directly through special studies. Historical costs, when available, can be used to estimate fixed and variable costs. One way to separate historical costs into their fixed and variable components is to plot the data on a scattergraph; volume is shown on the horizontal axis and costs are shown on the vertical axis.

A line is then drawn which bisects this plotted history. Fixed costs are determined where the line intersects the vertical axis; the variable cost rate is determined by measuring the slope of the line. Similar to the scattergraph approach is the high-low point method, which measures the variable cost rate between costs at the highest and lowest activity levels. A third method of analyzing historical costs is regression analysis. It is similar in effect to the scattergraph, but is more objective in separating costs into their fixed and variable components. An advantage of regression analysis is that the decision maker, through the standard error of the estimate, can assess the degree to which the flexible budget estimates fit the actual data.

The breakeven graph is a pictorial presentation of cost-volume-profit interactions. It clearly shows the point where total revenue equals total cost. More importantly, it shows how managerial decisions regarding revenues and volume affect the firm's profit. Inherent in cost-volume-profit analysis is the relevant range of activity. The relevant range is that volume over which the relationships can be assumed valid.

The breakeven point in dollars is the fixed costs divided by the contribution margin ratio. The breakeven point in units is the fixed costs divided by the contribution margin per unit. For firms with multiple products, the breakeven point must be built upon a specific product mix. Where there are separate departments within the firm, the effect of cost-volume changes can be seen by the margin of safety (budgeted or actual sales minus breakeven sales) and the margin of safety ratio (the difference between actual sales and breakeven sales divided by actual sales).

SUPPLEMENTARY READING

Bell, Albert L. "Break-Even Charts Versus Marginal Graphs." *Management Accounting,* February, 1969.

Dow, Alice S., and Orace Johnson. "The Break-Even Point Concept: Its Development and Expanding Implications." *Management Accounting,* February, 1969.

Gynther, R. S. "Improving Separation of Fixed and Variable Expenses." *N.A.A. Bulletin,* June, 1963.

Jenkins, David O. "Cost-Volume-Profit Analysis." *Management Services,* March–April, 1970.

Koehler, Robert W., and Charles A. Neyhart, Jr. "Difficulties in Flexible Budgeting." *Managerial Planning,* May–June, 1972.

National Association of Accountants. *Separating and Using Costs as Fixed and Variable.* New York: National Association of Accountants, 1960.

National Association of Accountants. *Analysis of Cost-Volume-Profit Relationships.* New York: National Association of Accountants, 1953.

Soldosky, Robert M. "Accountant's Versus Economist's Concepts of Breakeven Analysis." *N.A.A. Bulletin,* December, 1959.

Vickers, D. "On the Economics of Break-even." *The Accounting Review,* July, 1960.

Weiser, Herbert J. "Break-even Analysis: A Re-evaluation." *Management Accounting,* February, 1969.

QUESTIONS

2-1 "All costs are variable in the long run." Explain what is meant by this statement.

2-2 Some costs are fixed or variable because of management decisions, while others are fixed or variable because of accounting techniques. Explain why and give examples of each.

2-3 Three important constraints in relating cost variability to volume are: constant production methods, constant management policies, and a constant price level. Explain and discuss the importance of these constraints.

2-4 "One of the effects of the energy crisis is to shift the nature of any semi-variable costs of energy that a firm incurs." Do you agree or disagree? Defend your position. Explain some of the long-run consequences of the energy crisis upon costs.

2-5 Fixed and variable costs are based upon a straight-line assumption. Explain. What are some of the measuring tools used in classifying costs as fixed or variable?

2-6 Choosing an appropriate volume measure is essential to measuring the variability of costs. It becomes more critical in a multiproduct situation. Discuss. What are some of the factors that should be considered in selecting a volume base?

2-7 The inspection of contracts, engineering cost estimates, and past cost behavior patterns are different ways of separating costs into fixed and variable components. Explain how each method is used.

2-8 The calculation of a regression line depends upon several underlying assumptions. What are they? Why are they important?

2-9 Explain how the scattergraph, the high-low method, and statistical regression analysis are used to separate costs into fixed and variable patterns. Give examples where the use of each method would be appropriate.

2-10 Define and explain the following concepts: *variable costs, mixed costs, relevant range, contribution margin ratio, breakeven point,* and *margin of safety.*

2-11 One of the assumptions that must be made in breakeven analysis is that there are no significant changes in the inventory levels. Why is this assumption necessary?

2-12 "Fixed costs are *never* relevant to incremental production or output decisions." Do you agree or disagree? Discuss.

2-13 Would the allocation of fixed costs to product lines facilitate cost-volume-profit analysis? Discuss.

2-14 How do accountants' breakeven graphs differ from the breakeven graphs of the economists?

2-15 How are breakeven graphs and profit-volume charts similar? How are they dissimilar?

2-16 State whether the following costs are probably fixed, variable, or semivariable during a given accounting period.

a. Supplies used in the factory.
b. Supervisory salaries.
c. Costs of electrical power for the factory.
d. Advertising costs of purchasing a newspaper ad once a week.
e. Liability insurance premiums on a policy to protect the firm from lawsuits if a customer is injured.
f. A 10-year lease on the building where the rental is 1% of sales.
g. Depreciation of factory machinery based on a depreciation schedule calculated upon a machine-hour-used basis.
h. Maintenance on the physical facilities.
i. Depreciation determined by the sum-of-the-years'-digits method.
j. Telephone expense for factory telephones.
k. Cost accounting activities in the factory.
l. Flat monthly rental fee for the raw materials warehouse.
m. Costs of raw materials used in production.
n. Employer's share of Social Security taxes that are .0585% of the first $13,200 earned by the workers.
o. Rent on a factory building donated by the city. The agreement calls for rent of $50,000 less $.50 for each direct labor hour over 100,000 hours, a minimum rental payment of $20,000 must be paid.

PROBLEMS

2-17 Indicate whether the following statements are *true* or *false.*

1. All costs are fixed in the long run.

2. Fixed costs per unit vary with changes in volume.

3. Total variable costs remain constant with changes in volume.

4. Costs are fixed or variable only in relationship to volume changes within a given time period.

5. Statistical regression analysis is a more reliable and sophisticated method of estimating fixed and variable costs than is the high-low method.

6. The higher the standard error of the estimate, the more reliable the cost estimate.
7. Costs are fixed or variable in relationship to time.
8. Total variable costs increase proportionately with changes in volume but are constant per unit of output when viewed from a per-unit basis.
9. The use of a scattergraph in determining fixed and variable costs is more objective than the use of regression analysis.
10. The concept of diminishing returns will create a curvilinear semivariable cost.
11. The margin of safety is sales revenue less the variable costs.
12. In the formula form of the flexible budget, *b* is the fixed costs per unit.
13. Depreciation calculated on a straight-line basis is a good example of a semivariable cost.
14. Fixed costs per unit increase with increases in production volume.
15. In the formula form of the flexible budget, *x* is the volume measure.

2-18 Indicate whether the following statements are *true* or *false*.

1. If the selling price per unit is assumed to be constant, total revenue will be proportionate to number of units sold.
2. Decreasing the selling price decreases the breakeven point.
3. Fixed costs do not change with changes in production volume.
4. The contribution margin per unit is proportional to volume.
5. It is impossible to obtain a breakeven point with a negative contribution margin.
6. To obtain the breakeven point in units, the total fixed costs should be divided by the contribution margin ratio.
7. The margin of safety is found by subtracting fixed costs from sales.
8. If the variable costs per unit increase, the contribution margin ratio will increase.
9. As production volume increases, the contribution margin ratio increases.
10. Accountants usually assume that variable costs are linear.

2-19 REQUIRED:
Select the graph that matches the numbered factory cost or expense data.

The vertical axes of the graphs represent *total* dollars of expense and the horizontal axes represent production. In each case the zero point is at the intersection of the two axes. The graphs may be used more than once.

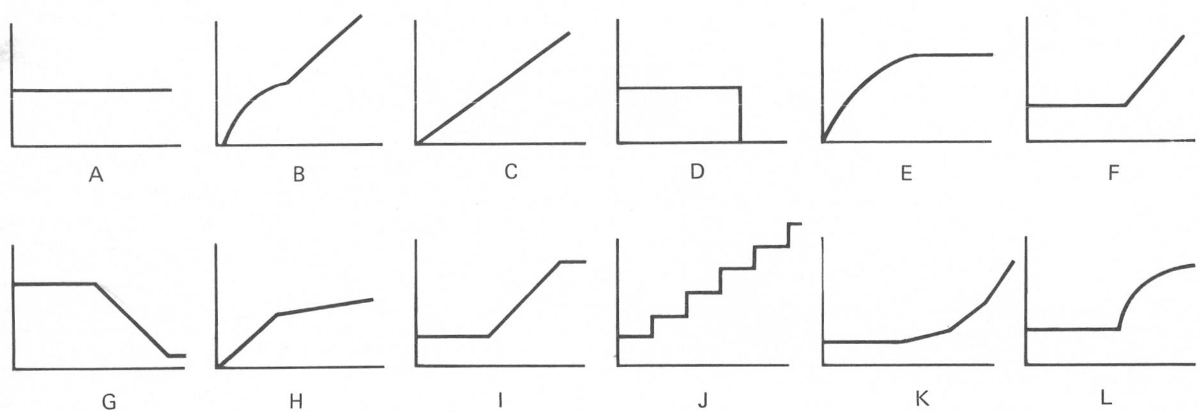

1. Depreciation of equipment, where the amount of depreciation charged is computed by the machine-hours method.
2. Electricity bill—a flat fixed charge, plus a variable cost after a certain number of kilowatt hours are used.
3. City water bill, which is computed as follows:

First 1,000,000 gallons or less	$1,000 flat fee
Next 10,000 gallons	.003 per gallon used
Next 10,000 gallons	.006 per gallon used
Next 10,000 gallons	.009 per gallon used
etc., etc., etc.	

4. Cost of lubricant for machines, where cost per unit decreases with each pound of lubricant used (for example, if one pound is used, the cost is $10.00; if two pounds are used, the cost is $19.98; if three pounds are used, the cost is $29.94; with a minimum cost per pound of $9.25).
5. Depreciation of equipment, where the amount is computed by the straight-line method. When the depreciation rate was established it was anticipated that the obsolescence factor would be greater than the wear and tear factor.
6. Rent on a factory building donated by the city, where the agreement calls for a fixed fee payment unless 200,000 man-hours are worked, in which case no rent need be paid.

7. Salaries of repairmen, where one repairman is needed for every 1,000 hours of machine hours or less (i.e. 0 to 1,000 hours requires one repairman, 1,001 to 2,000 hours requires two repairmen, etc.).
8. Federal unemployment compensation taxes for the year, where labor force is constant in number throughout year. Federal unemployment taxes are computed at .5% of the first $4,200 earned. Average annual salary is $6,000 per worker.
9. Cost of raw material used.
10. Rent on a factory building donated by county, where agreement calls for rent of $100,000 less $1 for each direct labor hour worked in excess of 200,000 hours, but minimum rental payment of $20,000 must be paid.

(CPA adapted)

2-20 The McLaine Company's cost accountant, in his study of four costs, made the following scattergraphs:

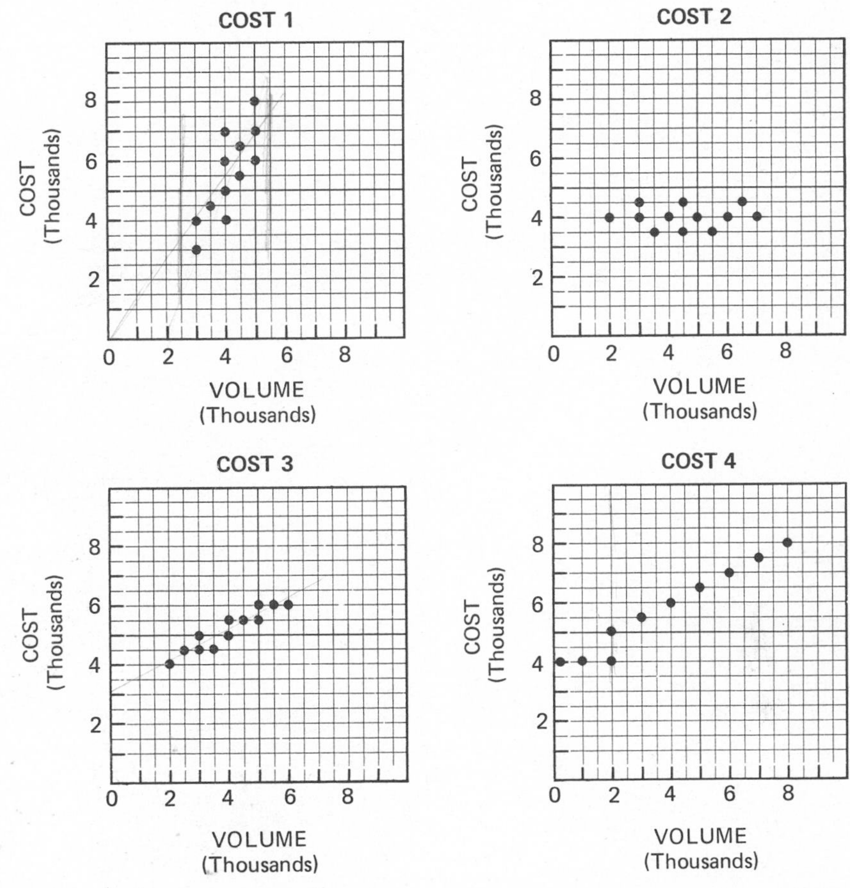

REQUIRED:
A. From the scattergraphs prepare flexible budget formulas for each individual cost.
B. Comment upon the reliability of your estimates. Which costs are the least reliable? Why?

2-21 The Sunny Sally Badminton Manufacturing Company experienced seasonal variation in its production and sales, from a low in January of 8,500 sets to a high in July of 23,000 sets. Production costs at the lowest activity level were $39,250 and at the highest level were $63,900.

REQUIRED:
A. Using the high-low method, determine the variable cost per unit and the total fixed costs per month. Express the flexible budget for production costs in formula form.
B. Using the flexible budget determined in part A above, calculate the budgeted costs at 10,000 units; at 28,000 units. How reliable do you believe these estimates are?
C. During the first month of the next year, 9,000 sets were produced at a cost of $42,000. How well did the firm control its costs?

2-22 A hospital has an average revenue of $100 per patient day. Variable costs are $20 per patient day, while fixed costs are $3,200,000 per year.

REQUIRED:
A. How many patient days does the hospital need to break even?
B. How many dollars in revenues are needed to earn $320,000 per year?
C. If variable costs drop to $18, what increase in fixed costs can be tolerated without changing the breakeven point determined in part A above?

2-23 Total average unit costs for the Sigma Company at output levels of 400 and 500 units are shown below:

	Total Average Unit Cost	
Cost	*400 units produced*	*500 units produced*
A	$3.75	$3.00
B	$2.90	$2.60
C	$1.75	$1.75
D	$ .50	$ .40
E	$4.15	$4.07

REQUIRED:
Prepare a table to show:
1. Per-unit variable cost
2. Total fixed cost
3. Type of cost (i.e. variable, fixed, semivariable, mixed)

2-24 *A.* Labor hours and production costs for four months, which you believe are representative for the year, were as follows:

Month	*Labor Hours*	*Total Production Costs*
September	2,500	$ 20,000
October	3,500	25,000
November	4,500	30,000
December	3,500	25,000
	14,000	$100,000

Based upon the above information and using the least squares method of computation with the letters listed below, select the best answers for each of questions 1 through 5.

Let a = Fixed production costs per month
b = Variable production costs per labor hour
n = Number of months
x = Labor hours per month
y = Total monthly production costs
Σ = Summation

1. The equation(s) required for applying the least squares method of computation of fixed and variable production costs could be expressed
   a. $\Sigma xy = a\Sigma x + b\Sigma x^2$
   b. $\Sigma y = na + b\Sigma x$
   c. $y = a + bx^2$
   $\Sigma y = na + b\Sigma x$
   d. $\Sigma xy = a\Sigma x + b\Sigma x^2$
   $\Sigma y = na + b\Sigma x$

2. The cost function derived by the least squares method
   a. Would be linear
   b. Must be tested for minima and maxima
   c. Would be parabolic
   d. Would indicate maximum costs at the point of the function's point of inflection

3. Monthly production costs could be expressed
   a. $y = ax + b$
   b. $y = a + bx$
   c. $y = b + ax$
   d. $y = \Sigma a + bx$

4. Using the least squares method of computation, the fixed monthly production cost is approximately
   a. $10,000
   b. $9,500
   c. $7,500
   d. $5,000

5. Using the least squares method of computation, the variable production cost per labor hour is
   a. $6.00
   b. $5.00
   c. $3.00
   d. $2.00

B. Maintenance expenses of a company are to be analyzed for purposes of constructing a flexible budget. Examination of past records disclosed the following costs and volume measures:

	Highest	*Lowest*
Cost per month	$39,200	$32,000
Machine hours	24,000	15,000

1. Using the high-low point method of analysis, the estimated variable cost per machine hour is
   a. $1.25
   b. $12.50
   c. $0.80
   d. $0.08

2. Using the high-low technique, the estimated annual fixed cost for maintenance expenditures is
   a. $447,360
   b. $240,000
   c. $230,400
   d. $384,000

C. Adams Corporation has developed the following flexible budget formula for annual indirect labor cost:

Total cost = $4,800 + $0.50 per machine hour

1. Operating budgets for the current month are based upon 20,000 hours of planned machine time. Indirect labor costs included in this planning budget are
   a. $14,800
   b. $10,000
   c. $14,400
   d. $10,400

(CPA adapted)

2-25 The Bloomingfield Company had the following costs and direct labor hours data applicable to the welding department.

	Hours	*Cost*
January	200	$ 3,200
February	100	1,900
March	300	4,100
April	700	7,700
May	800	9,200
June	800	9,000
July	900	10,500
August	600	7,100
September	200	2,500
October	300	3,800
November	400	4,900
December	500	6,400

Sum of the hours (Σx) = 5,800
Sum of the costs (Σy) = 70,300
Sum of hours times costs (Σxy) = 42,520,000
Sum of hours squared (Σx^2) = 3,620,000

REQUIRED:

A. Calculate the estimated total fixed costs and the estimated variable cost rate per hour using the regression method.

B. Using the high-low point method, test your answer obtained using the regression method. Why do they differ?

2-26 The Puget Foundry has prepared flexible budget equations for each cost. For maintenance the flexible budget is:

$$y_c = \$5{,}600 + \$.25(x)$$

where:

y_c is the estimate of total maintenance costs
x is direct machine-hours

REQUIRED:

A. Prepare a cost estimate for 6,000 machine hours; for 9,000 hours.

B. Management believes that there will be a general 10% price increase for maintenance costs that will affect both fixed and variable costs. Prepare a new flexible budget equation.

C. Prepare cost estimates for 6,000 and 9,000 machine-hours using the revised budget equation obtained in part B.

D. Using the original equation of $5,600 + $.25($x$), can you tell if management controlled costs effectively if actual costs of maintenance were $7,000 last year when the actual activity level was 4,000 machine hours?

E. Discuss the statement: "Fixed costs don't change with changes in volume, so it is impossible for management to control them." Do you agree or disagree? Why?

F. What would be the budget allowance if the department was in a "stand-by" position (zero activity but ready to produce if asked to do so)? Do you feel this allowance is realistic? Why?

2-27 REQUIRED:

A. List the assumptions that were made when the accompanying breakeven graph was prepared.

B. Determine the flexible budget formula for total costs.

C. Calculate total costs, revenue, and net income from the graph, assuming a production and sales level of 150 units.

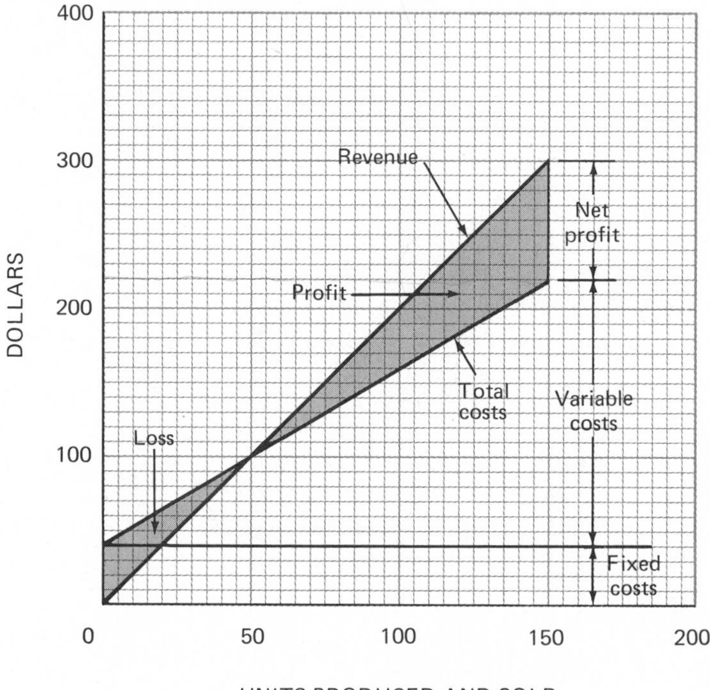

2-28 After reading an article you recommended on cost behavior, a friend asks you to explain the following excerpts from it:

1. "*Fixed costs* are variable per unit of output and *variable costs* are fixed per unit of output (though in the long run all costs are variable)."

2. "*Depreciation* may be either a fixed cost or a variable cost, depending on the method used to compute it."

REQUIRED:
For each excerpt:
A. Define the italicized terms. Give examples where appropriate.
B. Explain the meaning of the exerpts to your friend.

A breakeven graph as illustrated below, is a useful technique for showing relationships between costs, volume, and profits.

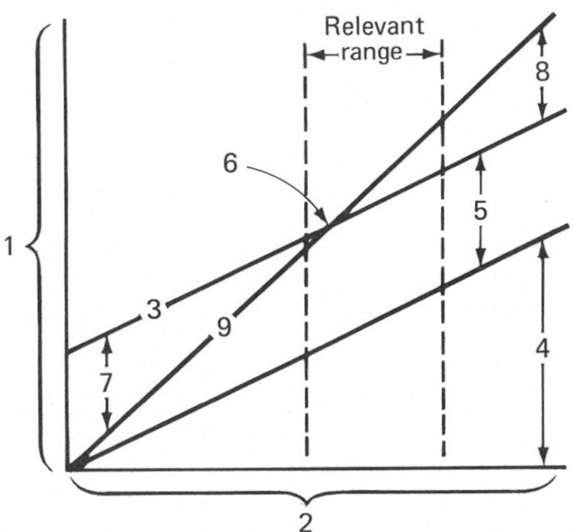

REQUIRED:
C. Identify the numbered components of the breakeven graph.
D. Discuss the significance of the concept of the "relevant range" to break-even analyses. *(CPA adapted)*

**2-29** The following are flexible budget equations for the Sundance Corporation.

Rent	\$4,700 + \$ 0 (x)
Indirect labor	\$ 0 + \$.40(x)
Repairs	\$1,800 + \$.25(x)

REQUIRED:
A. Develop flexible budget cost estimates for 5,000, 6,000, 7,000, 8,000, and 9,000 units. (Assume that the volume measure x is units.)
B. Calculate the per-unit cost for each level of activity. Why does the per-unit cost change as volume increases?
C. Graph the flexible budget for the sum of the three costs.

2-30 Carey Company sold 100,000 units of its product at \$20 per unit. Variable costs are \$14 per unit (manufacturing costs of \$11 and selling costs of \$3). Fixed costs are incurred uniformly throughout the year and amount to \$792,000 (manufacturing costs of \$500,000 and selling costs of \$292,000). There are no beginning or ending inventories.

REQUIRED:

1. The breakeven point for this product is
   - *a.* $3,640,000 or 182,000 units
   - *b.* $2,600,000 or 130,000 units
   - *c.* $1,800,000 or 90,000 units
   - *d.* $1,760,000 or 88,000 units
   - *e.* None of the above

2. The number of units that must be sold to earn a net income of $60,000 for the year before income taxes would be
   - *a.* 142,000
   - *b.* 132,000
   - *c.* 100,000
   - *d.* 88,000
   - *e.* None of the above

3. If the income tax rate is 40%, the number of units that must be sold to earn an after-tax income of $90,000 would be
   - *a.* 169,500
   - *b.* 157,000
   - *c.* 144,500
   - *d.* 104,777
   - *e.* None of the above

4. If the labor costs are 50% of variable costs and 20% of fixed costs, a 10% increase in wages and salaries would increase the number of units required to break even (in fraction form) to
   - *a.* 807,840/5.3
   - *b.* 831,600/5.78
   - *c.* 807,840/14.7
   - *d.* 831,600/14.28
   - *e.* None of the above

(CPA adapted)

2-31 The Plushy Purple Paper Company produces a line of quality napkins and paper table cloths. One particular product, a 72-inch round tablecloth, is causing disagreement between the sales department and the cost accounting department. The sales department believes that the product is selling well and contributing greatly to the profitability of the firm, stressing the fact that the product has a variable cost ratio of 55%. The cost accounting department, on the other hand, says that the yearly sales of 250,000 units at $1 per unit did not produce sufficient volume to cover the fixed costs of $130,000 per year.

REQUIRED:

A. What is the volume of sales necessary to break even?

B. What selling price per unit is necessary to break even at the present volume level?

C. Prepare a contribution margin income statement based upon the original data in the problem.
D. Prepare a PV chart for this product using the original data.
E. What actions could management take to correct the current situation?

2-32 Green Thumb Productions produces, among other products, a line of four-inch clay pots. Breakeven is currently at a sales volume of $18,000, or 36,000 clay pots. Each pot generates a contribution margin of $.20. The company desires a profit of $4,000 on the sale of these pots and is willing to increase advertising by $2,000 to obtain the needed volume increase.

REQUIRED: (Consider each case separately.)
A. How many pots beyond the breakeven point would the company have to sell to earn their desired profit without the advertising?
B. If fixed costs were to increase 10%, what volume of sales would be necessary to earn the desired profit of $4,000?
C. If the company decided to spend the $2,000 for advertising, what volume would be necessary to earn the $4,000 profit?
D. The company believes it can double sales by lowering the selling price to $.28 per unit. Would you advise doing this? Why or why not? Would your answer differ if the selling price were lowered to $.35 to achieve this volume increase?

2-33 The Woodchuck Chuck Manufacturing Company produces a line of fireplace logs that are packaged and sold in a container of 20 logs. During the past month it had the following revenue and cost patterns:

Selling price per unit	$ 4
Variable costs per unit	$ 2
Nonvariable costs	$1,000
Volume in units	1,000

REQUIRED: (Consider each case separately.)
A. Assume a 20% increase in production volume; what is the increase in profits?
B. Assume a decrease of 20% in the nonvariable costs; what is the new non-variable cost and the impact on profit?
C. Assume a 20% decrease in variable costs; what is the new variable cost and the new profit figure?
D. Assume a 20% increase in the selling price; what is the total revenue and the new profit figure?
E. Assume a 10% decrease in the selling price and a resultant 20% increase in production volume; what is the new profit figure?

2-34 REQUIRED:

A. List the assumptions that were made when the accompanying profit-volume chart was prepared.

B. Calculate contribution margin and net income from the chart, assuming a production and sales level of 150 units.

C. Are you able to determine total costs and revenue from the profit-volume chart? Why or why not?

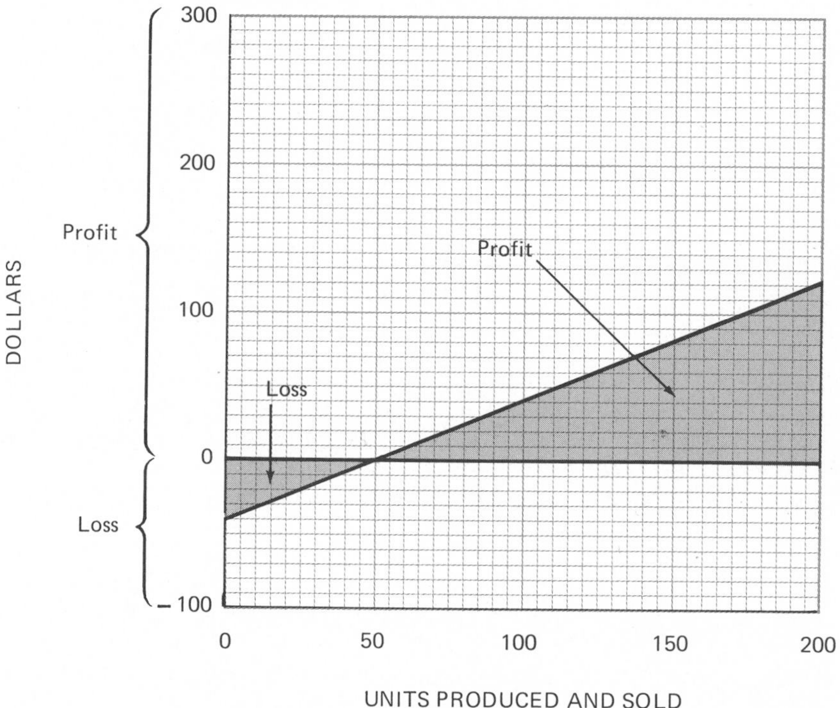

2-35 The Classic Company, a manufacturer of old pirate treasure chests for the modern collector, has two product sizes: a 48-inch chest and a 36-inch chest. Planned costs, revenue, and production data for the coming year are as follows:

	48-inch	*36-inch*
Selling price	$ 50	$ 36
Variable cost per unit	$ 30	$ 27
Sales volume in units	500	2,000
Fixed costs traceable to each product	$2,000	$6,000

REQUIRED:
A. Calculate the breakeven point for each product and for the company as a whole. What is the combined contribution margin ratio?
B. Calculate the margin of safety for each product.

2-36 REQUIRED:
A. Calculate the breakeven point for the following product:

Selling price per unit	$ 1.50
Variable costs per unit	$ .90
Total fixed costs	$15,000

B. Calculate the variable cost ratio and the contribution margin ratio.
C. Assuming that the company desires a profit of $10,000, what sales volume must it have? If sales were less than this by 10%, what would the profit or loss be?
D. If the selling price were increased to $1.80 and variable and fixed costs remained unchanged, what would the new breakeven point be?
E. If the sales price were increased by 15% and the variable costs by 25%, what would be the new variable cost ratio? The new contribution margin ratio?

2-37 Cost-volume-earnings analysis (breakeven analysis) is used to determine and express the interrelationships of different volumes of activity (sales), costs, sales prices, and sales mix to earnings. More specifically, the analysis is concerned with the effect on earnings of changes in sales volume, sales prices, sales mix, and costs.

REQUIRED:
A. Certain terms are fundamental to cost-volume-earnings analysis. Explain the meaning of each of the following terms:

1. Fixed costs
2. Variable costs
3. Relevant range
4. Breakeven point
5. Margin of safety
6. Sales mix

B. Several assumptions are implicit in cost-volume-earnings analysis. What are these assumptions?

C. In a recent period Zero Company had the following experience:

Sales (10,000 units @ $200)			$2,000,000
	Fixed	*Variable*	
Costs:			
Direct material	$ 0	$ 200,000	
Direct labor	0	400,000	
Factory overhead	160,000	600,000	
Administrative expenses	180,000	80,000	
Other expenses	200,000	120,000	
Total costs	$540,000	$1,400,000	1,940,000
Net income			$ 60,000

Each item below is independent.

1. Calculate the breakeven point for Zero in terms of units and sales dollars. Show your calculations.

2. What sales volume would be required to generate a net income of $96,000? Show your calculations.

3. What is the breakeven point if management makes a decision which increases fixed costs by $18,000? Show your calculations. *(CPA adapted)*

2-38 The controller of the Sellers Corporation is studying the cost behavior patterns of indirect labor in relationship to units produced. He believes that a knowledge of fixed and variable costs will help him budget future costs as well as control actual expenditures. Past cost and production data show the following:

Units Produced	*Cost*
10	$ 5,400
20	7,500
50	13,300
80	20,000
60	15,400
10	5,600
30	9,300
50	14,000
60	15,500

Sum of units (Σx) = 370
Sum of costs (Σy) = 106,000
Sum of units times cost (Σxy) = 5,358,000
Sum of units squared (Σx^2) = 20,100

REQUIRED:

A. Using the least squares regression technique, determine the flexible budget showing total fixed costs and the variable rate per unit.
B. Calculate and evaluate the standard error of the estimate.
C. Compare the flexible budget from the regression method with a cost estimate using the high-low method.

2-39 The Yellow Tractor Company had the following maintenance costs for the past six years.

	Total Maintenance Costs	*Hours of Activity*
Year 1	$122,500	65,000
Year 2	157,500	90,000
Year 3	159,000	165,000
Year 4	180,000	215,000
Year 5	205,000	315,000
Year 6	225,000	365,000

REQUIRED:

A. Determine the fixed and variable maintenance costs using the scatter-graph approach.
B. Determine the fixed and variable maintenance costs using the high-low method.
C. Determine the fixed and variable maintenance costs using the least squares regression method. Calculate the standard error of the estimate.
D. Which method do you feel is most accurate? Why?
E. What are some disadvantages in using the least squares regression method? Explain.

2-40 The Moosecall Company, in its annual review of the flexible budget, determined the following data about machinery repair costs.

Costs	*Volume in Hours*
$1,800	100
5,010	320
3,450	210
1,790	130
1,810	180
5,020	340
1,850	150
3,380	200
3,500	270
5,000	350
4,900	310
3,050	280

Sum of hours (Σx) = 2,840
Sum of costs (Σy) = 40,560
Sum of hours times costs (Σxy) = 10,794,500
Sum of hours squared (Σx^2) = 753,800

REQUIRED:

A. From the given data determine the total fixed costs and variable costs per hour using the regression method.

B. Calculate the standard error of the estimate.

C. Your management, while appreciating your effort, does not understand the least squares method. You are asked to plot the original data on a scattergraph. Does this scattergraph give you any insights into the cost behavior pattern of repair costs? Discuss.

2-41 The Evergreen Products Manufacturing Company has the following revenue and cost characteristics on their only product.

Selling price per unit	$ 3.00
Variable costs per unit	$ 2.10
Annual fixed costs	$180,000
Annual volume	270,000 units

REQUIRED:

A. Determine the following:

1. Variable cost ratio
2. Contribution margin ratio
3. Contribution margin per unit
4. Breakeven point in units and in dollars
5. Net profit at current operating level

B. For each of the following *independent* cases, determine the new contribution margin ratio, breakeven point in dollars, and net profit.

1. 5% increase in selling price
2. 20% increase in variable costs
3. 50% increase in fixed costs
4. 5% increase in sales and production volume
5. Decrease of $30,000 in fixed costs
6. Decrease in variable costs of $.10
7. Decrease in variable costs of $.30 and 20% increase in selling price
8. 20% decrease in fixed costs and 20% increase in variable costs.

2-42 The Acorn Manufacturing Company produces two main product lines made of oak: an old-fashioned bucket, which sells for $5, and a five-gallon decorative wine cask, which sells for $7.50. The variable cost for the bucket is $3.75 per unit; for the wine cask it is $5. The bucket department had sales of 50,000 units, while the wine cask department had sales of 30,000 units. Identifiable fixed costs are $50,000 and $55,000 for the bucket and cask departments respectively.

REQUIRED:

A. Prepare contribution margin income statements for each product line and for the company as a whole.

B. Calculate the breakeven point for each product and for the company as a whole.

C. Calculate the contribution margin ratio for the company as a whole.

D. For each product, and for the company as a whole, determine:

1. The margin of safety in dollars
2. The margin of safety expressed as a percent of sales

E. Which line offers the least risk? Why?

2-43 The Living End Poster Company has the following cost and revenue patterns. Sales range from 1,000 to 10,000 posters per month, depending upon demand. The manufacture of the posters is subcontracted to three suppliers. Each subcontractor produces from 1,000 to 4,000 posters per month, depending upon the orders placed by the Living End Poster Company. Each contractor is guaranteed a minimum of $300 per month plus $1.60 for each poster produced. The Poster Company's sales are all mail order. It maintains an office which costs $250 for rent, $180 for utilities, and $1,800 for salaries of the administrative personnel per month. Each mail clerk can package and ship 2,000 posters per month. There is a permanent staff of two mail clerks; each receives $400 per month. When demand exceeds 4,000 per month, additional clerks are hired and paid $.25 for each poster they mail. Packaging materials and postage cost $.35 per poster. The sales price is $3.50 per poster.

REQUIRED:

A. Develop a flexible budget for each principal cost incurred by the company. In a table, show cost estimates at 2,000, 4,000, 6,000, 8,000, and 10,000 units.

B. Identify the fixed, variable, and semivariable costs.

C. Prepare a flexible budget graph for the mail clerks' wages.

D. What appears to be the relevant range of the firm? Of what significance is the relevant range?

2-44 The Red Oscar Manufacturing Company has decided to make a study of its manufacturing overhead to see if it can determine what portion of overhead is variable and what portion is fixed. To begin this study, the accountant gathered the following cost and production data.

	Total Costs of Overhead	*Total Labor Hours of Production*
January	$1,950	500
February	$1,900	450
March	$2,150	600
April	$3,100	800
May	$3,450	900
June	$4,600	1,350
July	$3,750	1,100
August	$3,550	750
September	$2,300	550
October	$1,950	400
November	$2,400	3,000
December	$3,000	950

REQUIRED:

A. Prepare a scattergraph of this data. From this scattergraph develop an estimate of the flexible budget showing total fixed costs and the variable cost rate per hour of production.

B. Which month(s) might bear closer examination? Why? Could this be a normal occurrence? Why?

C. What are some of the assumptions made when this cost behavior pattern is used to forecast the future?

D. When using the scattergraph for forecasting, is there any way to remove the effects of unusual occurrences? Should this be done? Discuss some of the consequences.

2-45 REQUIRED:

A. Using the data of the Red Oscar Manufacturing Company shown in problem 2-44, determine the fixed and variable cost estimates using the high-low method.

B. Discuss some of the weaknesses in using this method of determining fixed and variable costs.
C. Using your estimates of fixed and variable costs prepared in part A above, what is your estimate of the overhead costs at 2,750 hours?

2-46 REQUIRED:
A. Using the data of the Red Oscar Manufacturing Company shown in problem 2-44, determine the fixed and variable costs using the least squares regression method.
B. Calculate the standard error of the estimate for this regression line.
C. Discuss why this method could be considered superior to the scattergraph or high-low method.

2-47 R. A. Ro and Company, maker of quality handmade pipes, has experienced a steady growth in sales for the past five years. However, increased competition has led Mr. Ro, the president, to believe that an aggressive advertising campaign will be necessary next year to maintain the company's present growth.

To prepare for next year's advertising campaign, the company's accountant has prepared and presented Mr. Ro with the following data for the current year, 1972:

Cost Schedule	
Variable costs:	
Direct labor	$ 8.00/pipe
Direct materials	3.25/pipe
Variable overhead	2.50/pipe
Total variable costs	$13.75/pipe
Fixed costs	
Manufacturing	$ 25,000
Selling	40,000
Administrative	70,000
Total fixed costs	$135,000
Selling price, per pipe:	$ 25.00
Expected sales, 1972 (20,000 units):	$500,000
Tax rate: 40%	

Mr. Ro has set the sales target for 1973 at a level of $550,000 (or 22,000 pipes).

REQUIRED:
A. What is the projected after-tax net income for 1972?; 1973?
B. What is the breakeven point in units for 1972?; 1973?

C. Mr. Ro believes an additional selling expense of $11,250 for advertising in 1973, with all other costs remaining constant, will be necessary to attain the sales target. What will be the after-tax net income for 1973 if the additional $11,250 is spent?

D. What will be the breakeven point in dollar sales for 1973 if the additional $11,250 is spent for advertising?

E. If the additional $11,250 is spent for advertising in 1973, what is the required sales level in dollar sales to equal 1972's after-tax net income?

F. At a sales level of 22,000 units, what is the maximum amount that can be spent on advertising if an after-tax net income of $60,000 is desired?

(CMA adapted)

2-48 Ahmul and Ashmir raise and sell camels. They acquire the camels they sell by two methods. Half they buy from other breeders at an average price of $100. The other half is taken from their own herd. They try to maintain a stable breeding herd of 500 camels by selling their one-year old camels. It costs them an average of $50 per camel per year to feed, watch, and maintain their herd. They have a reputation for fair dealing and quality merchandise so there is no problem selling their supply. They sell an average of 600 camels every year, at an average price of $175 each.

This year, however, due to unexpected circumstances, the slightly larger than normal crop of 340 calves consisted of 80% white camels—a most unfortunate occurrence. White camels cannot be bartered or sold as beasts of burden because of local taboos. They must keep the white camels until they are two years old and then transport them, at a cost of $72 per head, to another country. There they can receive only $27 for each.

To add to their troubles, their principal customer insists that they deliver their normal quantity. If they do not meet his demands their sales will fall to 250 camels this year. The other camel raisers, knowing Ahmul and Ashmir cannot afford to lower their breeding herd below 500, are taking advantage of the supply and demand situation by increasing their prices from $100 to $150 per head.

REQUIRED:

A. Prepare a contribution margin income statement for a normal year for Ahmul and Ashmir.

B. Prepare a contribution margin income statement for the current year, assuming they decide to supply their normal sales volume of 600 camels.

C. Would it be better to buy the extra camels they need at current prices or allow their sales to fall to 250 camels? Support your decision.

D. Calculate the breakeven point under normal conditions. Calculate the new breakeven point, assuming they decide to buy the needed camels.

E. Assume that several zoos are interested in the white camels. They have no money to buy the camels but have offered to take the camels at the end of the first year if Ahmul and Ashmir deliver them to the town of Abdul.

They estimate it will cost $120 per head for delivery. Should Ahmul and Ashmir keep the camels for two years and then sell them in another country, or should they ship them to the zoos at the end of the first year? Support your conclusions.

2-49 Dr. Harsch and Dr. Shields, two research physicians on the staff of University Hospital, have submitted a request for new equipment for the hematology laboratory. The lab is currently performing 60,000 blood tests per year—the capacity of the present equipment. Patients are charged $5 per test. Costs for 19X6 are expected to be as follows:

Research physicians' salaries	20% of gross receipts
Supplies	$1 per test
Technicians and clerical salaries	$80,000 per year
Depreciation of equipment	$40,000 per year

The proposed equipment will cost $500,000 and have an expected useful life of 10 years. An additional 30,000 tests can be performed on the new equipment. Because more complex tests will be performed on the new equipment, $3 of supplies will be required and the patients will be charged $10 per test. An additional technician with an annual salary of $22,500 will be needed to operate the new equipment.

REQUIRED:

A. Prepare a profit-volume chart for current operations. What is the breakeven point in number of tests? How much is the lab contributing to hospital overhead?

B. If operated at capacity, how much will the new equipment contribute to hospital overhead? Assuming both old and new equipment are operated and that one new test is performed for each two old tests, what is the breakeven point in dollars of revenue?

2-50 Mr. Calderone started a pizza restaurant in 1970. For this purpose a building was rented for $400 per month. Two ladies were hired to work full time at the restaurant and six college boys were hired to work 30 hours per week delivering pizza. An outside accountant was hired for tax and bookkeeping purposes. For this service Mr. Calderone pays $300 per month. The necessary restaurant equipment and delivery cars were purchased with cash. Mr. Calderone has noticed that expenses for utilities and supplies have been rather constant.

Mr. Calderone increased his business between 1970 and 1973. Profits have more than doubled since 1970. Mr. Calderone does not understand why his profits have increased faster than his volume.

A projected income statement for 1974 has been prepared by the accountant and is shown below:

CALDERONE COMPANY
PROJECTED INCOME STATEMENT
For the Year Ended December 31, 1974

Sales		$95,000
Cost of food sold	$28,500	
Wages & fringe benefits of restaurant help	8,150	
Wages & fringe benefits of delivery boys	17,300	
Rent	4,800	
Accounting services	3,600	
Depreciation of delivery equipment	5,000	
Depreciation of restaurant equipment	3,000	
Utilities	2,325	
Supplies (soap, floor wax, etc.)	1,200	73,875
Net income before taxes		$21,125
Income taxes		6,338
Net income		$14,787

Note: The average pizza sells for $2.50. Assume that Mr. Calderone pays out 30% of his income in income taxes.

REQUIRED:

A. What is the breakeven point in number of pizzas that must be sold?

B. What is the cash flow breakeven point in number of pizzas that must be sold?

C. Mr. Calderone would like an after-tax net income of $20,000. What volume must be reached in number of pizzas in order to obtain the desired income?

D. Briefly explain to Mr. Calderone why his profits have increased at a faster rate than his sales. *(CMA adapted)*

3 Absorption Costing Systems for Product Costing

COSTS FROM A FINANCIAL REPORTING PERSPECTIVE
Production Costs
Nonproduction Costs
METHODS OF CALCULATING THE UNIT COST OF PRODUCTION
JOB COSTING ILLUSTRATED
PROCESS COSTING ILLUSTRATED
SUMMARY

In the first two chapters we examined ways that the decision maker can look at costs relevant to his decisions. In this and the next two chapters we will look at the cost-accumulation systems accountants commonly use to gather data. For the decision maker to select the relevant costs, it is necessary that he understand the way costs are actually measured and reported in practice. Our emphasis will be upon a manufacturing concern. This emphasis is based on the premise that the physical flow, and hence the cost flow, of a manufacturing concern is more involved than that of a retailing or service concern. With an understanding of the more involved system, the student will be able to transfer his knowledge to less complicated situations.

COSTS FROM A FINANCIAL REPORTING PERSPECTIVE

Financial accounting entails the measurement and reporting of financial position and its changes due to operations. Central to measurement of financial position and net income are the concepts of expired and unexpired costs. As resources are acquired they are considered as **unexpired costs** (assets) on the statement of financial position. These costs are carried forward to future periods where they are expected to contribute to future revenues. When they have been consumed in the generation of revenue and have no future revenue-producing potential, they are considered as **expired costs** (expenses) on the income statement. For example, as a firm produces goods for resale, the costs incurred in production are carried in the inventory as unexpired costs on the statement of financial position. When the goods are sold, the inventory cost is matched with revenue as expired costs. Expired costs have already produced their share of revenue, or they have been consumed without providing a benefit to the firm. A cost that has been consumed in the production of revenue is called an **expense.** A cost that has been consumed without providing a benefit or revenue is termed a **loss.** An entire body of financial accounting theory is directed to the problem of measuring expired and unexpired costs, since they directly affect the reported net income and statement of financial position. The presentation in this chapter is in conformity with this body of accounting theory.

In a manufacturing concern materials flow through the factory where labor and other factory costs are expended to convert them into a finished, salable product. Production costs can be thought of as adhering or attaching to the unit of product so that cost flow in the books of account parallels physical flow in the factory. Costs incurred in one form, such as materials, workers' wages, heat, light, and power, are converted and transformed into the product. **Product costs** are costs that accountants attach to the unit of product and hold as an asset in the inventory until the goods to which they are attached are sold. They are matched with revenue when the sale is measured. Costs that are not inventoried and, as a result, are treated as expenses in the period they are considered consumed, are called **period costs.**

In a merchandising concern the goods are ready for sale when purchased. The merchandising firm performs no conversion function. In a manufacturing concern raw materials are purchased and then converted into a new product. Iron is converted into steel, aluminum into airplanes, logs into lumber, and lumber into boat hulls. The **Raw Materials Inventory** contains the raw materials on hand but not yet processed. The **Work-In-Process Inventory** contains the raw materials, labor, and factory overhead in the process of manufacture. The **Finished Goods Inventory** contains completed goods awaiting sale.

Most manufacturing firms use the three inventory accounts of Raw Materials, Work-in-Process, and Finished Goods to accumulate and hold the product costs. Each inventory account is an unexpired cost, an asset. Thus, when raw materials are issued to Work-in-Process and combined with labor and factory overhead, the cost of manufacturing is treated as a product cost and, therefore, an unexpired cost until the product is sold. At the point of sale these product costs move from an asset account, Finished Goods, to the expired cost account, Cost of Goods Sold.

Product and period costs provide a way of determining which costs are unexpired and which are expired. It is a generally accepted accounting principle for financial reporting that all production costs are treated as product costs and are unexpired until sold. Nonproduction costs are not treated as product costs; they are matched with revenue on a time-period basis. This operational definition of product cost and period cost is termed **absorption costing, full-absorption costing,** or **full costing.** The product "absorbs" all costs necessary to produce it and have it in salable form. Exhibit 3-1 shows the flow of costs in an absorption costing system. The white boxes represent product costs and the shaded areas period costs.

In Exhibit 3-1 we can see that to coordinate the cost flow with the physical activities, the costs must be divided between production and nonproduction activities. **Production costs** (also called **manufacturing costs**) include the costs of raw materials and all other costs necessary to convert these materials into a finished product, such as factory labor; factory heat, light, and power; machinery depreciation; factory insurance; and the factory superintendent's salary. **Nonproduction costs** include the costs of selling the final products, distributing them, general and administrative costs, and financing costs.

It is sometimes difficult to know whether a cost should be treated as a production or a nonproduction cost. Two examples should highlight this problem. The president, in his daily activities, supervises both production and distribution activities. Should his salary be allocated between the two activities, and if so, what basis of allocation should be used? To solve this dilemma most firms simply assign his salary to nonproduction costs. Another example is that of packaging the final product. Some firms wait until the item is sold and treat the packaging costs as selling costs; others assign packaging costs to production costs. Typically, cost assignment depends upon *when* the

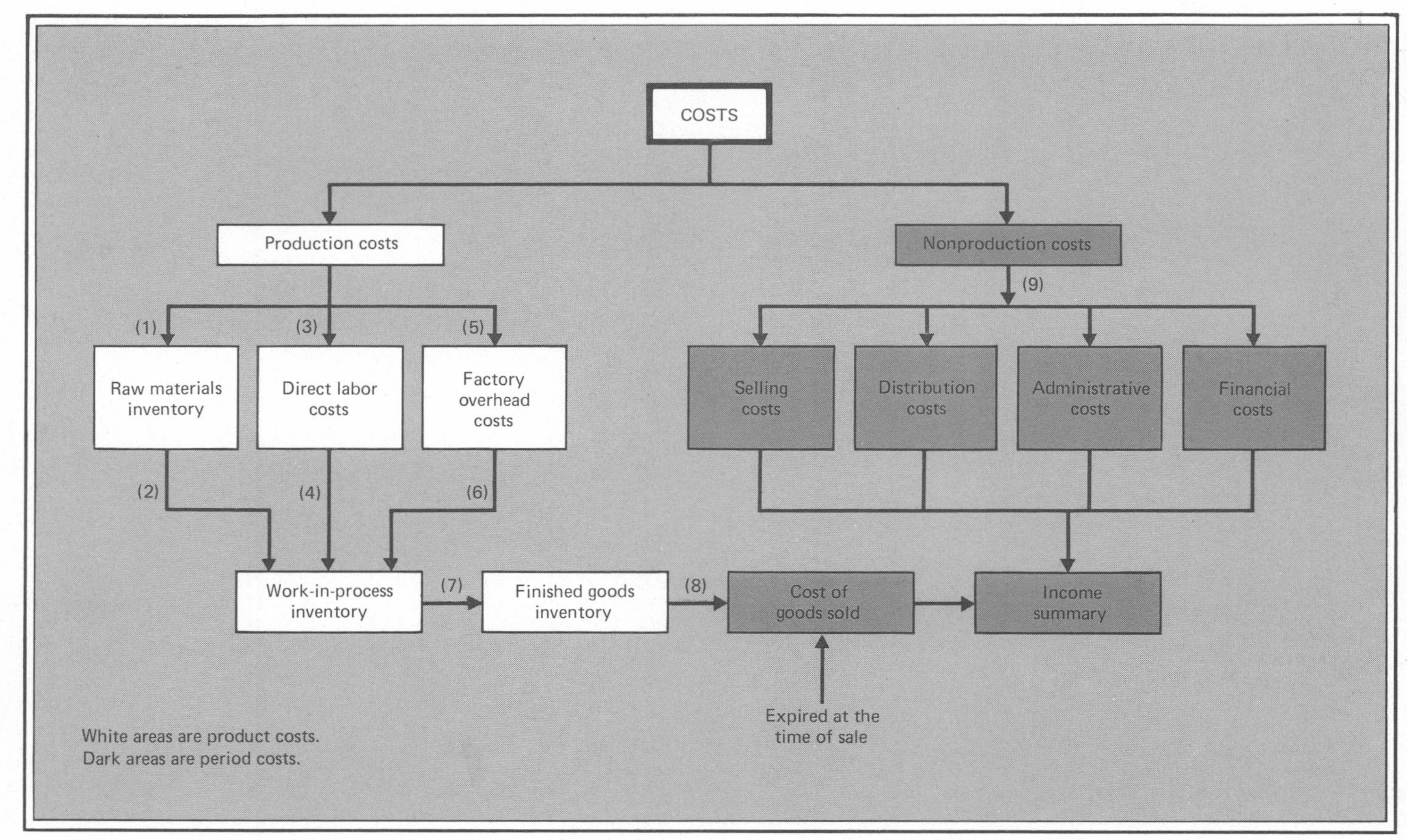

EXHIBIT 3-1
Cost flow with absorption costing

packaging is done. If the packaging is done in the warehouse, it will usually be treated as a selling expense; if it is done in the factory, it will probably be considered a production expense.

Production Costs

As shown in Exhibit 3-1, production costs are separated into three cost elements: raw materials, labor, and factory overhead. In this section we will look at each of these elements.

DIRECT AND INDIRECT MATERIALS

Raw materials include the physical commodities that are consumed in making the final product. Two views of materials seem prevalent. One view takes a physical approach. **Materials** are defined as all physical commodities that become a part of the final product. This approach is useful in the engineering design of the product but poses distinct accounting problems for commodities that are either physically small or of low cost. The other view is less physical and is oriented more toward the ease of accounting for costs. Only the major materials in terms of cost per unit or the materials that involve large physical quantities justify the record keeping necessary to trace them directly to the product. These are called **direct materials.** Minor materials are not traced to the product, although they may be vital to its production. Rather, these **indirect materials** are included in factory overhead. While the latter view is more practical, it does not completely describe the physical phenomenon.

DIRECT AND INDIRECT LABOR

Labor costs include the wages paid to factory workers who directly or indirectly aid in converting the raw materials into a finished product. **Direct labor** costs represent labor that is expended directly on the final product and traced directly to it. For example, through accounting records, the time of the machine operators, welders, grinders, and assemblers may be traced directly to the product they produce. Other employees, such as foremen, janitors, material handlers, and maintenance employees, do not work directly with the product. Their wages are considered **indirect labor** costs since there is no reasonable way to trace their activities directly to specific units of output. These costs are regarded as a part of factory overhead.

FACTORY OVERHEAD

Factory overhead includes all costs of operating the factory except those costs that have been designated as direct materials and direct labor. Included in factory overhead are indirect materials, indirect labor, and other costs such as depreciation of factory buildings and machinery, factory supplies, factory maintenance and repairs, insurance, property taxes, factory employees' fringe benefits, heat, light, and power. There is a diversity of terms used to describe these costs, including: **factory overhead, factory burden, manufacturing expenses, indirect factory costs, manufacturing overhead, indirect expenses,** and **indirect manufacturing costs.** Each firm seems to select a title that communicates best to its management.

Factory overhead is a potpourri of costs. It includes some material costs, some labor costs, and the costs of providing and maintaining productive capacity. The one thing these costs have in common is that they are difficult, if not impossible, to trace directly to the units of product. For this reason accountants typically use an averaging technique called a *factory overhead rate* to apply overhead to the product. We will explain this technique briefly in this chapter and examine it in detail in the following chapter.

Nonproduction Costs

Accountants have emphasized production costs in their cost studies. One reason for this emphasis has been the ability to find reliable cause and effect relationships between production costs and production volume. This relationship is more difficult to find in the nonproduction cost area. Another reason has been the rapid growth of industrialization and mechanization in the past century. This growth has required a close scrutiny of production cost patterns. As a practical matter, the concentration upon production activities has led to too little time and effort spent studying nonproduction costs. Yet in many firms the nonproduction costs are equal to or greater than production costs.

The elements of nonproduction costs are not as well defined as those of production costs. However, for our purposes they can be separated into four distinct categories: selling, distribution, general and administrative, and financial, as shown in Exhibit 3-1.

SELLING COSTS

Often called **order-getting costs,** selling costs are the result of marketing activities. They include, for example, the salespeople's salaries, commissions, and travel costs; advertising; catalog costs; and promotional costs.

DISTRIBUTION COSTS

At times called **order-filling costs,** distribution costs arise from ensuring that the proper goods are in the proper location, ready to sell. Distribution costs include outbound freight and transportation, warehousing, insurance, finished goods materials handling, packing, and shipping costs.

GENERAL AND ADMINISTRATIVE COSTS

There are a large number of costs that are not directly associated with production, selling, or distribution. Executive and clerical salaries, home office or headquarters costs, corporate legal costs, board of directors' fees, general accounting costs, and corporate public relation costs are all examples of general and administrative costs.

FINANCIAL COSTS

The costs of financing the organization's capital requirements often require special attention and are separated from administrative costs. Bank service charges, interest expense on both long-term and short-term borrowing, and the costs of underwriting stock issues comprise some of the financial costs.

METHODS OF CALCULATING THE UNIT COST OF PRODUCTION

Two systems have been developed to trace production costs to the product: job and process costing. Both systems have the same ultimate objective of determining the unit cost of the products produced. It is through this unit cost that the accountant determines the cost to hold in the inventory or the cost to match with revenue. Job and process costing are two methods of keeping the detailed records supporting the Work-in-Process Inventory and of determining the unit cost of production.

Job costing is used in factories where the products are manufactured in a series of identifiable and separate jobs, lots, or batches. Often the company has a firm sales order before it begins work on a job. Examples of industries where job costing is suitable include building construction, shipbuilding, printing, and aircraft manufacturing. In these plants each product unit is identifiable from the beginning of production. Costs are accumulated for each job, and the unit cost is the sum of all costs identified with the particular job. It is as if the product is sticky, like fly paper, and the costs cling to it. In these plants the **job cost sheet** serves as the focal point of costs. There is one job cost sheet for each unit or batch produced, and the sum of the costs on the job cost sheets must equal the dollars charged to the Work-in-Process Inventory.

In plants where the production is a continuous flow, or where one unit of product is indistinguishable from another, costs are assigned to the products through **process costing.** In a process cost system the costs are traced to departments during a specified time period, and the cost per unit of product is determined by:

$$\text{Unit cost} = \frac{\text{Production costs of process or department during time period}}{\text{Output produced by process or department during time period}}$$

The result is an average unit cost for all items produced. Industries that use process costing include steel mills, petroleum refineries, meat-packing plants, lumber mills, and aluminum manufacturers.

JOB COSTING ILLUSTRATED

In a job costing system the detailed record (subsidiary ledger) supporting the Work-in-Process Inventory is the **job cost sheet.** With a large product, such as an airplane or ship, there is usually one job cost sheet for each unit. With small units there could be a job cost sheet for a number of units; the cost of a single unit of product would be determined by dividing the total cost for the lot by the number of units in the lot.

Each job cost sheet is numbered so that each cost can be traced accurately. All product costs incurred must be traced to job cost sheets, either directly, through material requisitions and labor-time tickets, or indirectly, through an overhead rate. The total costs charged to Work-in-Process Inventory during any specific time period will be equal to the charges on the job cost sheets. When a product is completed, the job cost sheet for that product is totaled. The total of charges on the job cost sheet is the amount transferred to Finished Goods Inventory. Any jobs started but not completed represent the ending Work-in-Process Inventory. In a job costing system, accumulation of costs for a particular product is important. It may take two or more accounting periods before a particular job is finished and the unit cost determined.

To illustrate the flow of costs in a job costing system, let's examine the cost system for the Roving Jack Company, a manufacturer of mobile camper units. The journal entries illustrating the flow of costs for the Roving Jack Company are keyed to the cost flow diagram shown in Exhibit 3-1. Refer to Exhibit 3-1 occasionally to maintain an overall perspective of the flow of costs through the system. The job cost sheets are shown in Exhibit 3-2, and T-accounts summarizing the journal entries are presented in Exhibit 3-3.

At the beginning of October the Roving Jack Company had three units in the process of construction. Inventories at the beginning of the month included \$2,500 of materials in the Raw Materials Inventory, \$6,344 in the Work-in-Process Inventory for the three partially completed units, and no units in the Finished Goods Inventory. The job cost sheets in Exhibit 3-2 show the following detail for the three units in process.

	101-24′	*102-18′*	*103-20′*	*Total*
Direct materials	\$1,355	\$ 917	\$1,080	\$3,352
Direct labor	625	520	215	1,360
Factory overhead (\$3 per labor hour)	750	624	258	1,632
Total cost	\$2,730	\$2,061	\$1,553	\$6,344

The transactions of the Roving Jack Company for October follow.

ROVING JACK COMPANY

Job Cost Sheet No. 101-24'

Date	Material	Labor	Overhead	Total
Bal. 9-30	$1,355	$ 625	$ 750	$2,730
October	500	2,200	2,250	4,950
Total	$1,855	$2,825	$3,000	$7,680

ROVING JACK COMPANY

Job Cost Sheet No. 102-18'

Date	Material	Labor	Overhead	Total
Bal. 9-30	$ 917	$ 520	$ 624	$2,061
October	317	950	900	2,167
Total	$1,234	$1,470	$1,524	$4,228

ROVING JACK COMPANY

Job Cost Sheet No. 103-20'

Date	Material	Labor	Overhead	Total
Bal. 9-30	$1,080	$ 215	$ 258	$1,553
October	820	1,600	1,650	4,070
Total	$1,900	$1,815	$1,908	$5,623

ROVING JACK COMPANY

Job Cost Sheet No. 104-28'

Date	Material	Labor	Overhead	Total
October	$3,350	$3,100	$3,000	$9,450
Total				

EXHIBIT 3-2
Job cost sheets for the Roving Jack Company

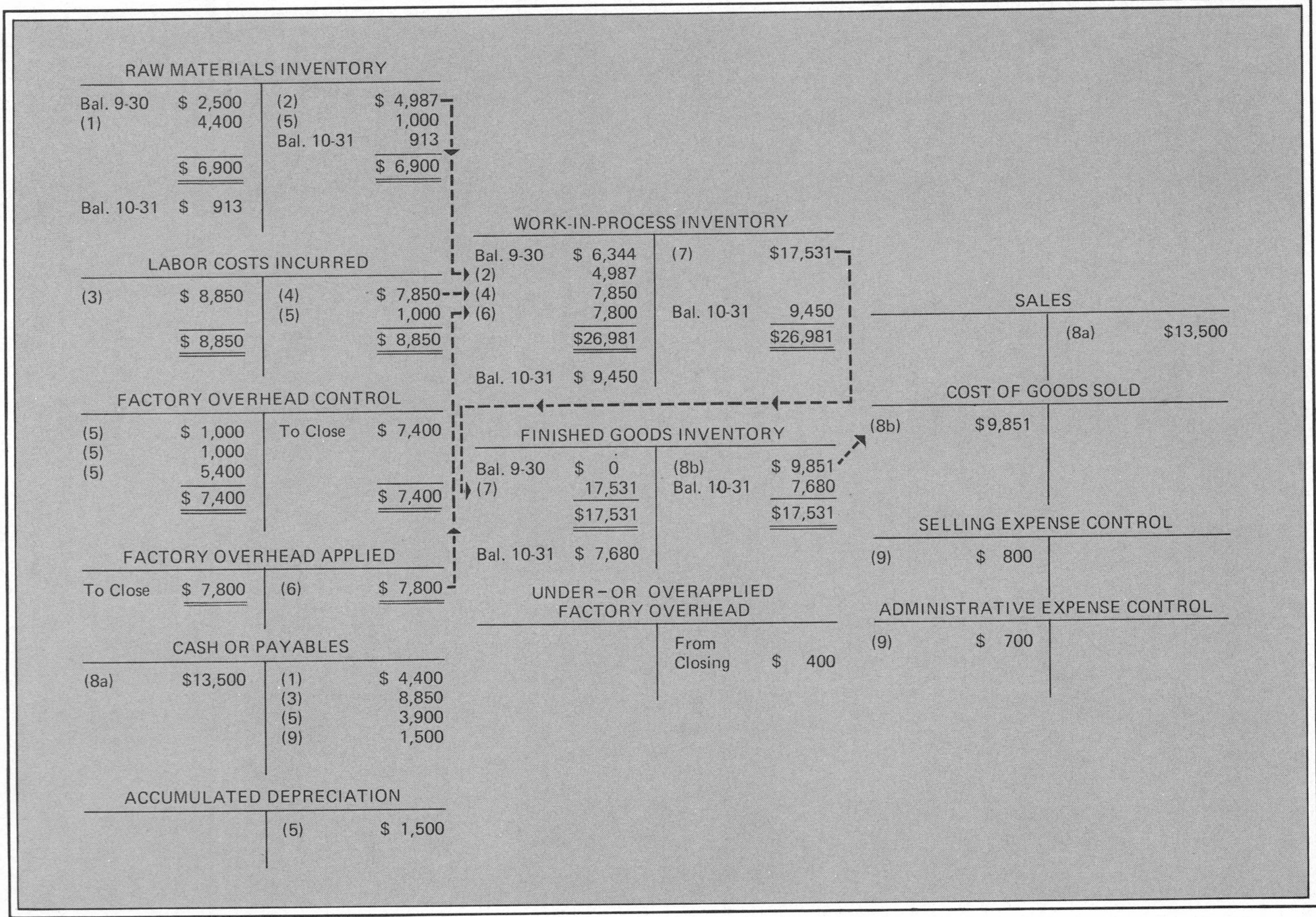

EXHIBIT 3-3
General ledger accounts for the Roving Jack Company

PURCHASE OF RAW MATERIALS

The storeroom records indicated that the company needed additional raw materials. The storekeeper sent a **purchase requisition** to the purchasing department to advise of the need for raw materials. Using the purchase requisition as authority, the purchasing agent issued a **purchase order** notifying his supplier of the material needs. No accounting entry was made for these two events, since no exchange with outside parties was completed.

When the supplier received the purchase order he shipped the materials. At the same time, he sent an **invoice** for the selling prices of the materials. After the goods were received, inspected, and accepted by the Roving Jack Company, the accountant made the following journal entry to record the purchase of raw materials.

(1)	Raw Materials Inventory	$4,400	
	Accounts Payable (or Cash)		$4,400

To record the purchase of raw materials.

The Raw Materials Inventory is a control account; that is, the aggregate total is kept in the general ledger and supported by detailed records in a subsidiary ledger. For each type of raw material a subsidiary ledger card is kept to show the quantity and price of the items received, issued, and on hand. (We have not included the subsidiary ledger records for the Raw Materials Inventory account.)

ISSUE OF RAW MATERIALS

The production schedules for October called for the completion of Jobs 101-24', 102-18', and 103-20' and for the start of one new job: 104-28'. On the basis of this production schedule, the production manager prepared **material requisitions** for the material necessary to perform the scheduled work.

Material requisitions serve as authority for the storeroom to release materials to the factory and as evidence to support the accounting entry. The following summation of these material requisitions for October showed direct materials issued to the jobs.

Job 101-24′	$ 500
Job 102-18′	317
Job 103-20′	820
Job 104-28′	3,350
Total direct materials	$4,987

Materials issued from the storeroom were removed from the raw materials ledger card (not shown) and were posted to the individual job cost sheets, as shown in Exhibit 3-2. The following journal entry records the issue of this direct material.

(2) Work-in-Process Inventory	$4,987	
Raw Materials Inventory		$4,987

To record the issue of direct materials.

The material requisitions showed that in addition to the direct materials previously listed, $1,000 of indirect materials were issued to the factory. The following journal entry records this issue.

(5) Factory Overhead Control	$1,000	
Raw Materials Inventory		$1,000

To record the issue of indirect materials.

PURCHASE AND CONSUMPTION OF LABOR

There are two distinct functions involved in labor accounting. First, the time for which the workers are to be paid is determined by their **clock cards.** From these cards the payroll department prepared their paychecks and distributed them on payday. The following journal entry reflects the payment of the labor payroll for the month.

(3) Labor Costs Incurred	$8,850	
Cash		$8,850

To record the payment of worker payroll.

The clock cards used in preparing the payroll show what the workers have earned but do not indicate the activities they performed while working. To determine these activities there must be a second document. At the end of each day employees prepare **time tickets** that list the amount of time spent on each job (treated as direct labor) and the amount of nonproduction time (treated as indirect labor). From the details of the time tickets, the Roving Jack Company's accountants found that of the $8,850 paid to the workers, $7,850 was direct labor that could be traced directly to the jobs, and $1,000 was indirect labor that was treated as overhead. The direct labor was used as follows:

Job 101-24′	750 hours	$2,200
Job 102-18′	300 hours	950
Job 103-20′	550 hours	1,600
Job 104-28′	1,000 hours	3,100
Total direct labor		$7,850

The following journal entry records the direct labor.

(4) Work-in-Process Inventory	$7,850	
Labor Costs Incurred		$7,850

To record the distribution of direct labor.

The amount of the direct labor was also posted to the individual job cost sheets shown in Exhibit 3-2.

The following journal entry records the indirect labor.

(5)	Factory Overhead Control	$1,000	
	Labor Costs Incurred		$1,000

To record the distribution of indirect labor.

The account, Labor Costs Incurred, deserves special mention. This is a temporary account used by the Roving Jack Company that allows the clock cards and time tickets to be prepared in different departments and at different times in the payroll cycle. However, by the end of the accounting period the balance of the Labor Costs Incurred account will be zero. Unlike Raw Materials Inventory, there is no inventoriable "residual" cost of labor because the workers are not paid until after they have completed their work. Labor Costs Incurred is an accounting convenience with no financial accounting implications.

PURCHASE OF FACTORY OVERHEAD

We have already recorded indirect materials of $1,000 and indirect labor of $1,000 as factory overhead. Assume that the Roving Jack Company's accountant processed the following other factory overhead costs.

Heat, light, and power	$ 700
Labor-related costs	1,300
Depreciation of building	1,500
Factory insurance	400
Miscellaneous (normally detailed)	1,500
Total	$5,400

The following journal entry records these actual overhead costs incurred.

(5)	Factory Overhead Control	$5,400	
	Accumulated Depreciation		$1,500
	Cash, or Payables or Prepaids		$3,900

To record the incurrence of factory overhead.

Factory Overhead Control is a control account; that is, the details of the individual costs are kept in a subsidiary ledger. The details of the subsidiary ledgers may be classified by a **natural classification**—by the nature of the expenses. Another way to classify overhead costs is by the purpose or function they perform. Most typical in practice of this **functional classification** is the recording of overhead costs by department or management responsibility center.

TRANSFER OF FACTORY OVERHEAD TO WORK-IN-PROCESS INVENTORY

As stated earlier, factory overhead costs are diverse and difficult, if not impossible, to trace directly to the jobs. Therefore, it is necessary to apportion or allocate them to the jobs. The **factory overhead rate** is the accountant's method of allocating these costs. Under absorption costing, all factory overhead costs are included in the overhead rate.

At the beginning of the year the management of the Roving Jack Company estimated that the units produced during the year would require 24,000 direct labor hours. The accountant for the Roving Jack Company had prepared an analysis of the cost behavior pattern for factory overhead costs and arrived at the flexible budget of:

Total factory overhead costs = \$48,000 + \$1(direct labor hours)

Factory overhead for the year was predicted at \$72,000 [\$48,000 + \$1(24,000 direct labor hours)], and a factory overhead rate was computed at \$3 per direct labor hour (\$72,000 ÷ 24,000 hours). The rate is composed of a fixed factory overhead rate of \$2 per direct labor hour (\$48,000 ÷ 24,000 hours) and a variable factory overhead rate of \$1 per direct labor hour.

The factory overhead rate of \$3 per direct labor hour was used during the previous months and will be used for the rest of the year. So far this year the incurrence of factory overhead costs and the actual direct labor hours worked have been exactly as planned.

The following journal entry applies factory overhead to individual jobs in the Work-in-Process Inventory for October.

		Debit	Credit
(6)	Work-in-Process Inventory	\$7,800	
	Factory Overhead Applied		\$7,800

To apply factory overhead to jobs at the rate of \$3 per direct labor hour.

The factory overhead is then applied to each job.

Job	Direct Labor Hours	×	Factory Overhead Rate per Labor Hour	=	Total Factory Overhead Applied
101-24′	750		\$3		\$2,250
102-18′	300		\$3		900
103-20′	550		\$3		1,650
104-28′	1,000		\$3		3,000
Total factory overhead applied to jobs					\$7,800

The two previous factory overhead entries used two accounts that require special comment. When actual factory overhead costs are incurred, accountants accumulate the amounts in Factory Overhead Control. Factory overhead is applied to the individual jobs with a factory overhead rate determined at the beginning of the year. The amount of factory overhead applied to the jobs is accumulated in the account, Factory Overhead Applied. The difference between the Factory Overhead Control account and the Factory Overhead Applied account resulted because of two factors. First, the actual costs were not incurred in conformity with the flexible budget equation for the year. The original flexible budget had predicted that costs would be incurred as: Total factory overhead costs = \$48,000 + \$1(direct labor hours). Second, the number of labor hours actually worked (2,600) was different than the planned hours of 2,000 (24,000 annual planned hours ÷ 12 months). An analysis of these differences will be shown in the next chapter.

COMPLETION OF THE JOBS

The costs of production shown on the job cost sheets are transferred from Work-in-Process Inventory to Finished Goods Inventory when the jobs are completed and moved from the factory to the warehouse. Factory records for the Roving Jack Company indicate that Jobs 101-24′, 102-18′, and 103-20′ were completed during the month and transferred to the showroom. Job cost sheets for the completed mobile units showed the following completed job costs.

Job 101-24′	\$ 7,680
Job 102-18′	4,228
Job 103-20′	5,623
Total cost of completed jobs	\$17,531

Job 104-28′ was uncompleted and remained in the factory. The following journal entry records the completed units.

(7) Finished Goods Inventory	\$17,531	
Work-in-Process Inventory		\$17,531

To record the completion of Jobs 101-24′, 102-18′, and 103-20′.

After this journal entry is posted to the Work-in-Process Inventory account, the balance will be \$9,450, the accumulated costs of Job 104-28′.

SALE OF FINISHED PRODUCTS

The **sales invoices** of the Roving Jack Company indicate that the salesmen sold Job 102-18′ for \$6,000 cash and Job 103-20′ for \$7,500 cash. Two entries are required to recognize the sale. First, the sales revenue must be recognized.

(8a) Cash $13,500
  Sales Revenue $13,500

To record the sales revenue ($6,000 + $7,500).

Second, the cost of the units sold must be transferred from Finished Goods Inventory to Cost of Goods Sold. The amounts shown on the completed job cost sheets associated with the units sold serve as the source of the amounts for this journal entry.

(8b) Cost of Goods Sold $9,851
  Finished Goods Inventory $9,851

To record the cost of goods sold of Jobs 102-18′ and 103-20′ ($4,228 + $5,623).

After this entry has been posted to the Finished Goods Inventory account, the balance will be $7,680. This is the cost of Job 101-24′, which is still unsold.

INCURRENCE OF NONPRODUCTION COSTS

For simplicity, we will assume that the Roving Jack Company incurred $800 of selling costs and $700 of administrative costs, and that it incurred no distribution or financial costs. The following journal entry records these costs.

(9) Selling Expense Control $800
 Administrative Expense Control $700
  Cash, or Payables, or Prepaids $1,500

To record the incurrence of actual selling and administrative expenses.

In an actual setting, detailed information about the selling and administrative costs would be recorded in subsidiary ledgers to the control accounts. This subsidiary ledger would be similar to the details kept for Factory Overhead Control. To simplify our example we have used only the total costs incurred and have omitted the details.

CLOSING THE OVERHEAD ACCOUNTS

At the end of the month, the Factory Overhead Control account, which shows the costs actually incurred, and the Factory Overhead Applied account, which shows the overhead charged to the jobs, are closed. The difference between the two accounts is computed and transferred to an account called *Under- or Overapplied Factory Overhead.* If the factory overhead applied to production during the month is larger than the actual factory overhead incurred (shown in Factory Overhead Control), overhead is *overapplied.* If the control balance is larger than the applied balance, the overhead is *underapplied.* This difference between the Factory Overhead Control and the Factory Overhead Applied accounts exists because actual factory overhead costs and actual direct labor hours differed from the planned factory overhead costs and the planned direct labor hours. The following journal entry closes the factory overhead accounts.

Factory Overhead Applied	$7,800	
Under- or Overapplied Factory Overhead		$ 400
Factory Overhead Control		$7,400

To close the factory overhead accounts.

In firms like the Roving Jack Company that use predetermined factory overhead rates based upon *annual* estimates, Factory Overhead Under- or Overapplied is closed to Cost of Goods Sold as a period cost at the end of the accounting period. During the year, when interim statements are prepared, the account is usually carried on the statement of financial position as a deferred charge or deferred credit. The account would not be closed until the end of the accounting period, since during the year there could be wide seasonal variations in activity or cost incurrences. In any one month the under- or overapplied factory overhead could be the result of these seasonal variations. Overapplied factory overhead in some months should offset underapplied factory overhead in other months. Thus, by the end of the accounting period, the balance due to seasonal variations would be insignificant.

In Exhibit 3-4 we have presented a monthly income statement for the Roving Jack Company. Although this is an interim, monthly statement we have included Factory Overhead Overapplied to illustrate how it would be handled at the end of the accounting period. The net income would be $400 less ($2,149) if the overapplied overhead had been carried forward on the statement of financial position.

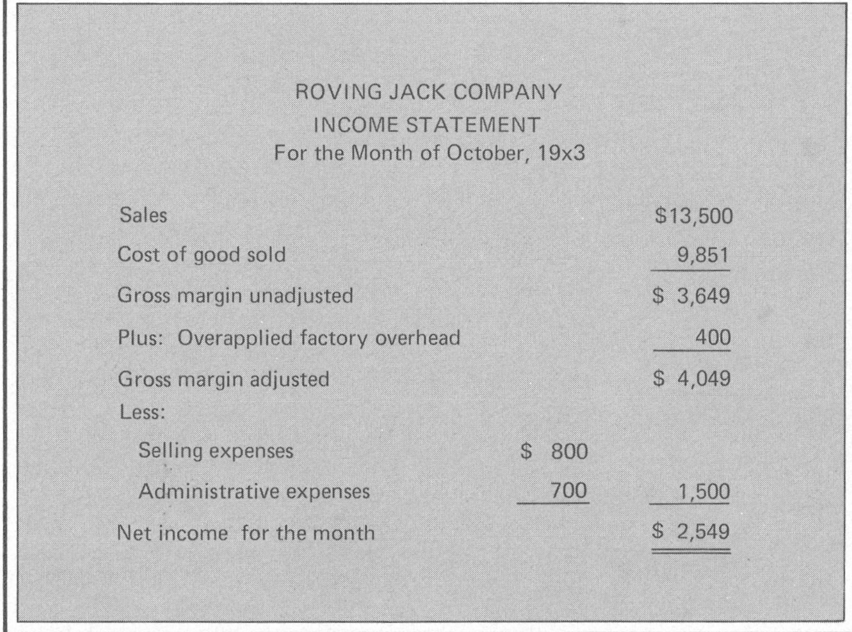
ROVING JACK COMPANY
INCOME STATEMENT
For the Month of October, 19x3

Sales		$13,500
Cost of good sold		9,851
Gross margin unadjusted		$ 3,649
Plus: Overapplied factory overhead		400
Gross margin adjusted		$ 4,049
Less:		
Selling expenses	$ 800	
Administrative expenses	700	1,500
Net income for the month		$ 2,549

EXHIBIT 3-4 Income statement for the Roving Jack Company

PROCESS COSTING ILLUSTRATED

Process costing differs from job costing by the way in which costs are focused into the factory and unit costs are determined. In a process costing system the costs are accumulated for departments or processes for a specified period of time, often one month. The unit cost of manufacturing the goods is found by dividing these departmental costs by the units produced during the time period. It should be apparent that process costing is used where similar units are produced over a long period of time.

To illustrate process costing, let's assume that the Supertronics Company manufacturers a computer circuit board in three departments: A, B, and C. In Department A the materials are issued at the beginning of the process and loosely attached to the board. These semifinished boards are then transferred to Department B, where the transistors are soldered to the board. In Department C the board is coated and completed through testing. Departments B and C use no new raw materials. Any supplies they use are included in factory overhead. Labor and factory overhead are added uniformly throughout the production process in the factory.

The Supertronics Company follows the policy of combining direct labor and factory overhead in its Work-in-Process Inventory accounts. Called **conversion costs,** the sum of direct labor and factory overhead is treated as a package, since overhead is charged to the departments on the basis of direct labor. Treating these two cost elements as a single cost allows the accountants of the Supertronics Company to simplify their calculation of unit costs.

Exhibit 3-5 shows the quantity and cost reports for the three departments for the month of March. These monthly production and cost reports are focused on the departments and serve as the data base for calculating the unit cost of units transferred out of the departments and of those left in the final inventories. The departmental production report shows the units and costs for which the department must account.

The first step in determining the unit cost is to recast the units found on the production report into a quantity report.

	Department A	*Department B*	*Department C*
Beginning units in process	0	0	15,000
New units started	60,000	60,000	40,000
Units available to finish	60,000	60,000	55,000
Ending units in process	0	20,000	12,000
Units transferred out	60,000	40,000	43,000

This report shows the flow of the units throughout the factory. The 40,000 units transferred from Department B become the "raw materials" for Department C, just as the 60,000 units transferred from Department A

THE SUPERTRONICS COMPANY
DEPARTMENTAL PRODUCTION AND COST REPORT
For the Month of March, 19X2

	DEPARTMENTS		
	A	B	C
QUANTITY DATA:			
Units in process, March 1			
Department A	None	—	—
Department B	—	None	—
Department C (100% complete as to prior department costs; 1/3 complete as to conversion costs)	—	—	15,000
New units started	60,000	—	—
Units received from prior departments	—	60,000	40,000
Units completed and transferred to:			
Department B	60,000	—	—
Department C	—	40,000	—
Finished goods inventory	—	—	43,000
Units in process, March 31			
Department A	None	—	—
Department B (100% complete as to prior department costs; 1/4 complete as to conversion costs)	—	20,000	—
Department C (100% complete as to prior department costs; 1/3 complete as to conversion costs)	—	—	12,000
COST DATA:			
Beginning inventory, March 1			
Prior department costs	None	None	$53,000
Conversion costs	None	None	$ 7,900
New costs incurred this period			
Raw materials	$60,000	None	None
Prior department costs	None	?	?
Conversion costs	$30,000	$58,500	$86,100

EXHIBIT 3-5
Departmental production and cost reports for the Supertronics Company

become the "raw materials" for Department B. The 43,000 units leaving Department C are transferred to Finished Goods Inventory, where they await sale.

We will proceed systematically through the successive departments to see how the unit cost of production is calculated and used as the basis of journal entries.

Department A—No Beginning or Ending Inventories

In Department A there was no beginning Work-in-Process Inventory. During the month of March, $60,000 of raw materials and $30,000 of direct labor and factory overhead were used in Department A. The following summary journal entry records the transfer of these costs to Department A, assuming that factory overhead was applied to Work-in-Process Inventory as 100% of direct labor cost.[1]

		Debit	Credit
(1)	Work-in-Process Inventory—Department A	$90,000	
	Raw Materials Inventory		$60,000
	Labor Costs Incurred		$15,000
	Factory Overhead Applied		$15,000

To record the issue of raw materials, the actual costs of direct labor, and the application of factory overhead to Department A.

There are no difficulties in accounting for Department A's costs. There were no beginning or ending inventories in Department A, so all costs charged there are transferred to the next department. The unit cost of the 60,000 units transferred is $1.50 ($90,000 ÷ 60,000 units). The following journal entry records the transfer.

		Debit	Credit
(2)	Work-in-Process Inventory—Department B	$90,000	
	Work-in-Process Inventory—Department A		$90,000

To transfer production costs from Department A to Department B.

After this entry is posted, the balance of the Work-in-Process Inventory of Department A is zero.

[1]The overhead rate was determined by dividing estimated direct labor cost for the year into estimated factory overhead cost for the year. Estimated factory overhead was determined by applying estimated direct labor cost to the flexible budget equation for the company. It would be possible to have both a fixed factory overhead rate and a variable factory overhead rate, allowing managment to separate variable costs relevant for several decisions. In addition, separate factory overhead rates could be determined for each department. These points are discussed in the next chapter.

Department B—No Beginning Inventories

The following summary entry of March's transactions records the transfer of costs to Department B.

(3) Work-in-Process Inventory—Department B	$58,500	
Labor Costs Incurred		$29,250
Factory Overhead Applied		$29,250

To record the issue of actual direct labor costs and the application of factory overhead to Department B.

In Department B there are units in the final inventory in addition to the units transferred out. To calculate the unit cost for the period, it is necessary to calculate **equivalent units of production,** the number of equivalent "whole" units of product that the department or cost center is actually accountable for during the time period. For example, two half-completed units are equivalent in cost to one totally complete unit. Equivalent units of production recognizes that not all of the units in process shown on the quantity report are fully completed. Equivalent units of production are measured as the sum of the units transferred out and that portion of the ending work-in-process inventory completed this period.[2] The equivalent units of production schedules for Department B for the month of March are as shown in the accompanying tabulation.

	Equivalent Units of Production	
	Prior Department Costs (100% Complete)	*Conversion Costs*
Transferred out to Department C (100% complete)	40,000	40,000
Ending inventory (25% of work in Department B completed)	20,000	5,000 (20,000 × 25%)
Equivalent units of production	60,000	45,000

The calculation of equivalent units of production is complicated by the fact that not all the cost factors in the department are at the same stage of

[2]In this text we show only the weighted average method of determining unit cost of manufacturing. This method averages the costs of the beginning inventory and current production to arrive at unit cost. There are other methods of determining the unit cost. However, these are topics more suited to an advanced course.

completion. The prior department costs transferred in from Department A represent raw materials to Department B. The ending inventory in Department B is 100% complete as far as these prior department costs are concerned. Conversion costs, on the other hand, are not 100% complete. Since the 20,000 units in the final inventory have progressed only one-fourth of the way through the process, and conversion costs are added uniformly throughout the process, the department "equivalently" completed only 5,000 of these 20,000 units. Next period the department will have to add sufficient conversion costs to finish the equivalent of 15,000 units. Of course, the 40,000 units transferred to Department C were 100% as to all cost factors, or they would not have been finished and suitable to transfer.

Because each cost factor can be at a separate stage of completion, most firms determine equivalent units of production and, subsequently, unit costs for each type of cost element. The total unit cost is then the sum of the unit costs for the individual cost factors. The total cost, equivalent units of production, and unit cost for each cost element in Department B are shown in the computations that follow.

Computation of Unit Cost—Department B

	Total Cost	÷	*Equivalent Units of Production*	=	*Unit Cost*
Prior department costs	$ 90,000		60,000		$1.50
Conversion costs	58,500		45,000		1.30
Total cost	$148,500				$2.80

The following computations show the inventory values and the costs transferred out.

Computation of Costs of Inventory and Transferred Out—Department B

Ending work-in-process Inventory of Department B, March 31:		
Prior department costs	(20,000 × $1.50)	$30,000
Conversion costs	(5,000 × $1.30)	6,500
Total ending work-in-process inventory		$ 36,500
Transferred to Department C (40,000 × $2.80)		112,000
Total costs of Department B accounted for		$148,500

The following journal entry records the transfer to Department C.

		Debit	Credit
(4)	Work-in-Process Inventory—Department C	$112,000	
	Work-in-Process Inventory—Department B		$112,000

To transfer production costs from Department B to Department C.

After this entry is posted, the Work-in-Process Inventory—Department B will have a $36,500 balance, which was the amount determined in the preceding computation as the value of the ending inventory.

Department C—Beginning and Ending Inventories

The following summary entry records the cost of direct labor and the application of factory overhead to Department C in March.

		Debit	Credit
(5)	Work-in-Process Inventory—Department C	$86,100	
	Direct Labor Incurred		$43,050
	Factory Overhead Applied		$43,050

To record the issue of actual direct labor and the application of factory overhead to Department C.

The equivalent units of production schedules for Department C are as shown in the accompanying tabulation.

Equivalent Units of Production

	Prior Department Costs (100% Complete)	*Conversion Costs*
Transferred out to finished goods inventory (100% complete)	43,000	43,000
Ending inventory ($33\frac{1}{3}$% of work in Department C completed)	12,000	4,000 ($12,000 \times 33\frac{1}{3}$%)
Equivalent units of production	55,000	47,000

Using these equivalent units of production figures, the unit costs are as shown in the computations that follow.

Computation of Unit Cost—Department C

	Total Costs	÷	Equivalent Units of Production	=	Unit Cost
Prior department costs:					
Beginning inventory	$ 53,000				
Current production	112,000				
Total	$165,000		55,000		$3.00
Conversion costs:					
Beginning inventory	$ 7,900				
Current production	86,100				
Total	$ 94,000		47,000		2.00
Total	$259,000				$5.00

The following computations show the inventory values and the costs transferred out.

Computation of Costs of Inventory and Transferred Out—Department C

Ending work-in-process inventory of Department C, March 31:		
Prior department costs	(12,000 × $3.00)	$ 36,000
Conversion costs	(4,000 × $2.00)	8,000
Total ending work-in-process inventory		$ 44,000
Transferred out to finished goods inventory	(43,000 × $5.00)	$215,000
Total costs of Department C accounted for		$259,000

The following journal entry transfers the 43,000 units to Finished Goods Inventory.

		Debit	Credit
(6)	Finished Goods Inventory	$215,000	
	Work-in-Process Inventory—Department C		$215,000
	To record the transfer of cost of completed units from Department C to Finished Goods Inventory.		

After this entry is posted, the balance of Work-in-Process Inventory—Department C will be $44,000.

To complete our illustration, let's assume that the Supertronics Company began the period with no finished goods inventory and that it sold 40,000 units this period at an average sales price of $8 each. The following entries would record this sale.

		Debit	Credit
(7a)	Accounts Receivable	$320,000	
	Sales		$320,000
	To record the sales revenue.		
(7b)	Cost of Goods Sold (40,000 × $5)	$200,000	
	Finished Goods Inventory		$200,000
	To record the cost of goods sold.		

To summarize our previous entries, Exhibit 3-6 shows the inventory and Cost of Goods Sold accounts for the Supertronics Company.

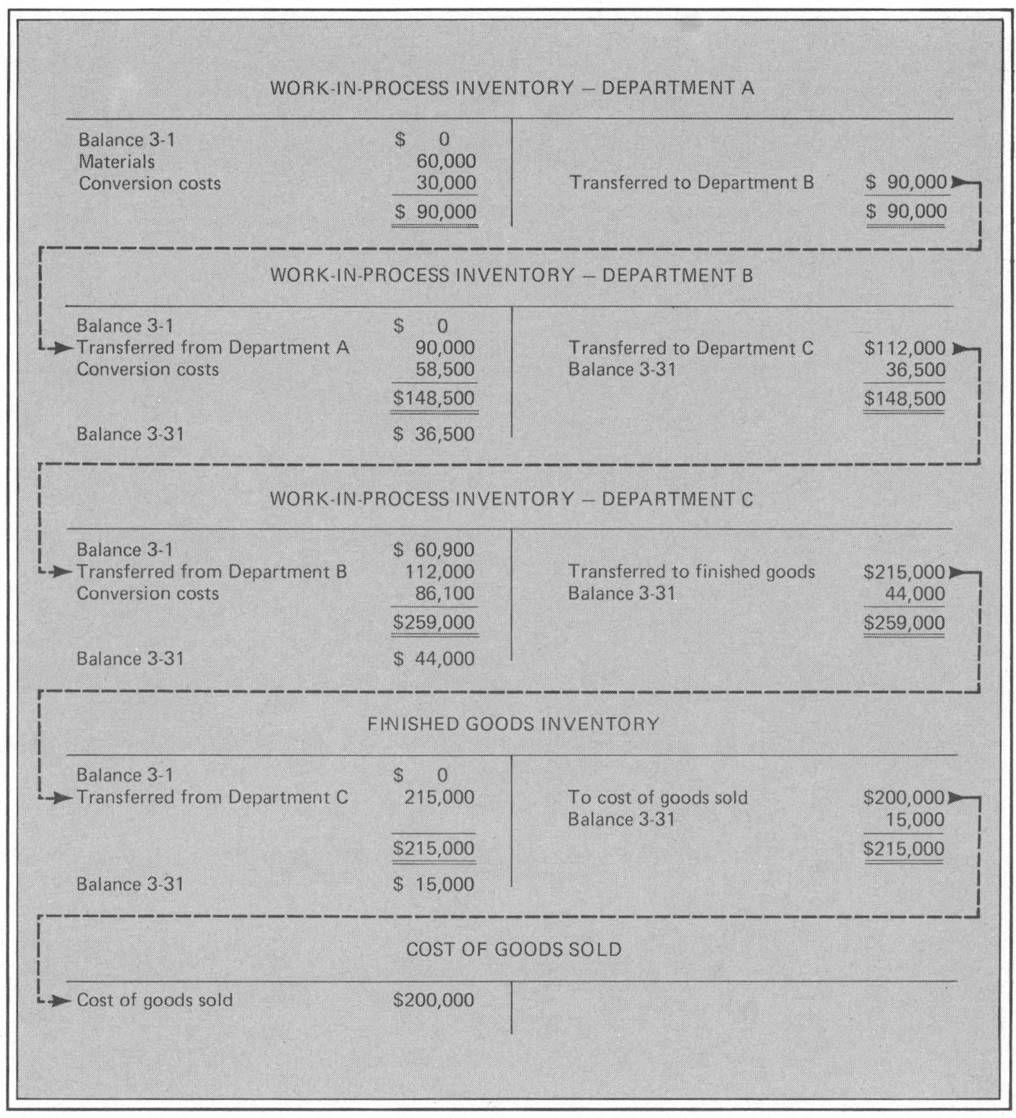

WORK-IN-PROCESS INVENTORY – DEPARTMENT A

Balance 3-1	$ 0		
Materials	60,000		
Conversion costs	30,000	Transferred to Department B	$ 90,000
	$ 90,000		$ 90,000

WORK-IN-PROCESS INVENTORY – DEPARTMENT B

Balance 3-1	$ 0		
Transferred from Department A	90,000	Transferred to Department C	$112,000
Conversion costs	58,500	Balance 3-31	36,500
	$148,500		$148,500
Balance 3-31	$ 36,500		

WORK-IN-PROCESS INVENTORY – DEPARTMENT C

Balance 3-1	$ 60,900		
Transferred from Department B	112,000	Transferred to finished goods	$215,000
Conversion costs	86,100	Balance 3-31	44,000
	$259,000		$259,000
Balance 3-31	$ 44,000		

FINISHED GOODS INVENTORY

Balance 3-1	$ 0		
Transferred from Department C	215,000	To cost of goods sold	$200,000
		Balance 3-31	15,000
	$215,000		$215,000
Balance 3-31	$ 15,000		

COST OF GOODS SOLD

Cost of goods sold	$200,000		

EXHIBIT 3-6
General ledger accounts for the Supertronics Company

SUMMARY

It is generally accepted by financial accountants that manufacturing inventories should include all costs of producing the product. This system of cost flow is called absorption costing or full costing. With absorption costing the costs of raw materials, direct labor, and factory overhead are combined in the Work-in-Process Inventory and are treated as product costs; that is, costs that are matched with revenue when the products are sold. All expired nonmanufacturing costs are treated as period costs.

There are two systems of combining the product costs to determine the inventory value. A job costing system is used in those industries where the product is large, identifiable, and often made to special order. In a job costing system the job cost sheet serves as the focal point of cost accumulation. The unit cost is determined by summing the costs that are recorded on the job cost sheets. In a process costing system the unit cost is determined by summing the costs of a department over a period of time and dividing by the number of equivalent units produced. A process system is used in industries where a large number of similar units are produced.

SUPPLEMENTARY READING

Anthony, Robert N. "Framework for Analysis." *Management Services,* March–April, 1964.

Anthony, Robert N., and James S. Hekimian. *Operations Cost Control.* Homewood, Ill.: Richard D. Irwin, Inc., 1967.

Benninger, L. J. "Accounting Theory and Cost Accounting." *The Accounting Review,* July, 1965.

Colbert, Bertram A. "Pathway to Profit: The Management Information System." *The Price Waterhouse Review,* Spring, 1967.

Davidson, H. Justin, and Robert M. Trueblood. "Accounting for Decision-Making." *The Accounting Review,* October, 1961.

Haseman, Wilber C. "An Interpretative Framework for Cost." *The Accounting Review,* October, 1968.

National Association of Accountants. "Costs Included in Inventories." *N. A. (C.) A. Bulletin,* August 15, 1947.

National Association of Accountants. *Accounting for Labor Related Costs.* New York: National Association of Accountants, 1957.

QUESTIONS

3-1 "Inventory accounts are really unexpired costs." Explain and discuss.

3-2 What costs are included in the following inventory accounts? Raw Materials, Work in Process, and Finished Goods.

3-3 "The distinction between production and nonproduction costs lies in their behavior as variable and fixed costs." Is this statement correct? Discuss these concepts.

3-4 The product "absorbs" all costs necessary to produce it and have it in salable form. Explain this term.

3-5 What costs are identified as product costs under absorption costing?

3-6 Distinguish between *actual* and *applied* overhead. What is meant by each?

3-7 What is the primary objective of job costing?

3-8 What is the primary objective of process costing?

3-9 What factors should the firm consider in the decision to use job costing or process costing?

3-10 "In process costing the distinction between direct and indirect costs may not be as significant as under job costing." Explain.

3-11 If the under- or overapplied factory overhead account has a debit balance at the end of the year, is the factory overhead underapplied or overapplied? Why?

3-12 Describe the purpose of each of the following documents.

a. Material requisition
b. Labor-time ticket
c. Overhead subsidiary ledger
d. Labor clock card
e. Purchase order
f. Purchase requisition

3-13 Explain the purpose of a job cost sheet. How could the data on a job cost sheet be useful to management?

3-14 Define the term *equivalent units of production* and indicate how it is determined.

3-15 Explain how the unit cost is determined under both job costing and process costing.

PROBLEMS

3-16 For the following companies indicate whether a job costing or process costing system would be used and briefly explain why.

a. Petroleum refiner
b. Meat-packing house
c. Highway construction firm
d. Automobile repair shop
e. Chocolate candy manufacturer
f. Food canning plant
g. Television set manufacturer
h. Soft drink bottler
i. Manufacturer of space vehicles
j. Custom furniture manufacturer

3-17 Match the following terms and definitions

1. Product cost
2. Period cost
3. Unexpired cost
4. Direct materials
5. Indirect labor
6. Job cost sheet
7. Material requisition
8. Time ticket
9. Equivalent production
10. Prior department costs

a. The wages of maintenance employees.
b. The denominator in computing average unit cost.
c. The record of costs traced to a specific lot of goods.
d. Factory costs related to goods transferred into a department.
e. A record of how an employee spent his time.
f. An asset.
g. Costs that accountants attach to the unit of product.
h. Materials that are traced to job cost sheets in a job cost system.
i. Costs that are treated as expenses in the period incurred.
j. The document used to authorize the withdrawal of materials from the storeroom.

3-18 Indicate whether the following statements are *true* or *false.*

1. Period costs are inventoried under absorption costing.

2. Financial accountants stress that only variable manufacturing costs should be included in the manufacturing inventory.

3. It is impossible to separate fixed and variable overhead costs when an absorption costing system is used.

4. Purchase requisitions are a source of accounting entries.
5. All nonproduction costs are treated as period costs.
6. Process costing differs from job costing by the fact that in process costing the unit of production is determined by tracing costs directly to the products produced.
7. A lumber mill would probably use process costing.
8. The Factory Overhead Applied account is used to record the amount of overhead that is recorded on the job cost sheets.
9. Job cost sheets are subsidiary ledgers for the Finished Goods Inventory.
10. Use of individual overhead items such as supplies are traced to the job cost sheets.

3-19 The following inventory data relate to the Shirley Company.

	Inventories	
	Ending	*Beginning*
Finished goods	$95,000	$110,000
Work in process	80,000	70,000
Direct materials	95,000	90,000
Costs Incurred During the Period		
Cost of goods available for sale		$684,000
Total manufacturing costs		584,000
Factory overhead		167,000
Direct materials used		193,000

1. Direct materials purchased during the year were
   a. $213,000
   b. $198,000
   c. $193,000
   d. $188,000
   e. None of the above or not determinable from the above facts
2. Direct labor costs incurred during the period were
   a. $250,000
   b. $234,000
   c. $230,000
   d. $224,000
   e. None of the above or not determinable from the above facts

3. The cost of goods sold during the period was
   a. $614,000
   b. $604,000
   c. $594,000
   d. $589,000
   e. None of the above or not determinable from the above facts

The Jorcano Manufacturing Company uses a process cost system to account for the costs of its only product, Product D. Production begins in the fabrication department, where units of raw material are molded into various connecting parts. After fabrication is complete, the units are transferred to the assembly department. There is no material added in the assembly department. After assembly is complete, the units are transferred to a packaging department where packing material is placed around the units. After the units are ready for shipping, they are sent to a shipping area.

At year-end, June 30, 19X3, the following inventory of Product D is on hand:

- No unused raw material or packing material.
- Fabrication department: 300 units, $\frac{1}{3}$ complete as to raw material and $\frac{1}{2}$ complete as to direct labor.
- Assembly department: 1,000 units, $\frac{2}{5}$ complete as to direct labor.
- Packaging department: 100 units, $\frac{3}{4}$ complete as to packing material and $\frac{1}{4}$ complete as to direct labor.
- Shipping area: 400 units.

4. The number of equivalent units of raw material in all inventories at June 30, 19X3, is
   a. 300
   b. 100
   c. 1,600
   d. 925

5. The number of equivalent units of fabrication department direct labor in all inventories at June 30, 19X3, is
   a. 1,650
   b. 150
   c. 300
   d. 975

6. The number of equivalent units of packing material in all inventories at June 30, 19X3, is
   a. 75
   b. 475
   c. 100
   d. 425

(CPA adapted)

3-20 The ABC Manufacturing Company has the following organization:

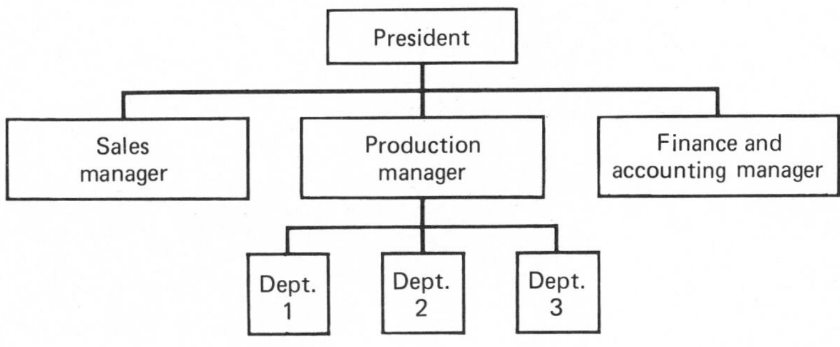

Some of the costs incurred by the firm include:
- Salary of factory production manager
- Salary of Department 1 manager
- Factory maintenance
- Machine repairs charged to Department 3
- Office supplies for the president's office
- Wages of production worker in Department 3
- Insurance on production plant
- Telephone bill for the company
- Annual audit bill
- Materials traced to Department 3
- Salesmen's automobile expense

REQUIRED:

A. Distinguish between direct and indirect expenses as far as (1) the factory as a whole and (2) Department 3.

B. In determining whether Department 3 is producing in an efficient manner, which of the above costs might be considered relevant? Nonrelevant? Why did you decide the way you did?

3-21 The Wolfe Company uses job costing to account for its products. It applies factory overhead to the jobs on the basis of machine hours. The predetermined overhead rate was estimated at the beginning of the year using the following data.

Fixed factory overhead	$ 36,000
Variable factory overhead	72,000
Total estimated factory overhead	$108,000
Total estimated machine hours	18,000

Job #411 was completed during the past month. Raw materials used on Job #411 were $68, direct labor was four hours at $5 per hour, and total machine hours were seven hours. Job #411 was a special order for the Sheep Company consisting of 65 machine-lathed candlesticks.

REQUIRED:

A. Prepare a job cost sheet for Job #411.
B. Calculate the cost per candlestick.
C. Prepare the journal entries for Job #411.
D. Assume that during the year the company actually worked 20,000 machine hours instead of the planned 18,000, and that it incurred actual overhead of $112,000, of which $80,000 was variable. Prepare the journal entry to close the factory overhead accounts.

3-22 The Monroe Publishing Company had the following information in its general ledger accounts at the beginning of the current month.

Raw Materials Inventory Balance	$ 6,500
Work-in-Process Inventory Balance	$25,000
Finished Goods Inventory Balance	$12,500

During the current month the following transactions took place.

a. Purchased raw materials of $24,000
b. Incurred and distributed direct labor of $42,000
c. Incurred factory utilities costs of $6,400
d. Recorded factory depreciation of $12,000
e. Incurred administrative expenses of $18,000
f. Requisitioned $22,000 of raw materials from the storeroom
g. Purchased and used $840 of factory supplies
h. Incurred miscellaneous factory overhead of $3,900
i. Applied overhead to work in the factory using an overhead rate of 45% of direct labor cost. The overhead rate was composed of a variable overhead rate of 20% and a fixed overhead rate of 25%.
j. Completed production of $94,000 of work in the factory
k. Sold $138,000 of products that cost $102,500

REQUIRED:

A. Prepare general journal entries assuming absorption costing.
B. Determine the inventory balances at the end of the month.
C. Prepare an income statement for the month.

3-23 The Lighter-than-Air Aircraft Company was in the process of manufacturing four planes—model 1230, model 1320, model 1023, and model 1032. During the month the following labor hours were used.

Model 1230	2,400 labor hours
Model 1320	3,600 labor hours
Model 1023	1,800 labor hours
Model 1032	8,400 labor hours

The firm's cost records show that actual factory overhead for the month was $20,250 variable costs and $12,150 fixed costs.

REQUIRED:

A. Determine the factory overhead rate based upon actual direct labor hours.

B. Determine the factory overhead costs of the four planes for the month using the overhead rate from part A.

C. Will there be any under- or overapplied factory overhead? Why?

3-24 The Hudson Company, a firm manufacturing gym equipment, uses absorption costing in its accounting system. A schedule of various general ledger accounts and other relevant data has been prepared and presented for analysis.

Schedule of Account Balances

Account	*Beginning Jan. 1, 19X6*	*Ending Dec. 31, 19X6*
Raw Material Inventory	$ 7,000	$ 10,000
Manufacturing Overhead Control	0	0
Manufacturing Overhead Applied	0	0
Work-in-Process Inventory	$25,000	$ 45,000
Finished Goods Inventory	$15,000	$ 35,000
Cost of Sales	0	$176,000

Other Data:

Raw materials purchased	$ 93,000
Raw materials issued to production	?
Direct labor cost incurred	$ 75,000
Variable factory overhead incurred	$ 35,600
Fixed factory overhead incurred	$ 15,400
General and administrative expenses	$ 5,200
Selling expenses	$ 7,300
Sales	$225,000

Manufacturing Overhead Applied for the year is $50,000. It is applied at a rate of two-thirds of direct labor cost. The firm's policy is to charge under- or overapplied factory overhead against cost of sales at the end of each year.

REQUIRED:

A. Make journal entries to summarize activities for year 19X6 that were recorded in the accounts shown.

B. Show T-accounts for the inventories, factory overhead accounts, and cost of sales.

3-25 The Work-in-Process Inventory for the Nelson Company at the beginning of the month showed a balance of $49,650, including $9,600 of fixed costs. At the beginning of the month 9,600 units were one-fourth completed. During the month the Nelson Company completed the beginning inventory and produced an additional 9,300 units, leaving no ending inventory of work in process. The following costs were incurred for the month.

Direct materials	$130,350
Direct labor	$ 82,500
Variable factory overhead	$ 49,500
Fixed factory overhead	$ 66,000

REQUIRED:

A. Determine the cost per unit of production. How much of this cost is variable cost?

B. Determine the cost of the ending Finished Goods Inventory assuming 18,600 units were sold.

3-26 The Randall Company uses a job cost system to determine the cost of its products. A predetermined factory overhead rate is used to apply overhead to individual jobs. The rate is based upon direct labor hours in Department A and machine hours in Department B. The following production and cost estimates were made at the start of the year.

	Department A	*Department B*
Direct material	$300,000	$100,000
Direct labor	$480,000	$ 80,000
Variable factory overhead	$240,000	$200,000
Fixed factory overhead	$240,000	$160,000
Machine hours	60,000	90,000
Direct labor hours	160,000	20,000

REQUIRED:

A. What are the predetermined overhead rates for both Departments A and B under absorption costing?

B. Assume that costs and production data for Job #1932 were as follows:

	Department A	*Department B*
Direct materials	$30	$20
Direct labor	$40	$15
Direct labor hours	14	4
Machine hours	2	5

How much factory overhead should be charged to Job #1932 under absorption costing?

C. What is the total cost per unit for Job #1932? What is the variable cost per unit for Job #1932?

3-27 The Ellis Company had the following transactions during the past year.

a. Purchased raw materials for cash	$150,000
b. Direct materials used in production	$135,000
c. Direct and indirect labor incurred	$165,000
d. Distributed direct labor to production	$115,000
e. Distributed indirect labor to factory overhead	$ 50,000
f. Recorded depreciation on plant and equipment	$ 60,000
g. Recorded other factory overhead (would normally be recorded in detail)	$100,000
h. Applied factory overhead to work in process at 200% of direct labor cost	?
i. Completed production	$430,000
j. Cost of goods sold	$400,000
k. Selling price of goods sold	$500,000
l. Administrative expenses incurred	$ 25,000

REQUIRED:

A. Give journal entries to record the transactions of the Ellis Company, assuming an absorption cost system is used.

B. Present T-accounts for the inventories assuming no beginning balances.

C. Show the journal entry to close the under- or overapplied factory overhead to Cost of Goods Sold.

3-28 The Reinsmith Company was formed on January 2 and has operated for a year. The owner's wife ran the office and kept the books. Because her experience was limited to keeping books for a restaurant, she set up a Work-in-Process account and recorded all "expenses" as debits and sales as a credit. The balance of the account was closed to Retained Earnings as income or loss for the month. The owner of the company was surprised that a loss was sustained. The company had received many orders, and goods were shipped the day they were finished. The owner asked you for help. The Work-in-Process account follows.

WORK-IN-PROCESS INVENTORY

Materials purchased	$120,000		
Payroll for year	250,000	Sales (60,000 @ $7)	$420,000
Depreciation expense	30,000		
Selling expense	50,000	Loss to Retained	
Other factory costs	60,000	Earnings	110,000
Advertising	20,000		
	$530,000		$530,000

An analysis of the items in Work-in-Process revealed the following:

1. There were $20,000 of raw materials in the storeroom at the end of the year.
2. Payroll included:

Owner's salary	$ 20,000
Direct labor payroll	$120,000
Other factory labor	$ 60,000
Selling and administrative payroll	$ 50,000

3. One-third of the fixed assets are used in selling and administrative activities.
4. During the year 100,000 units were started, 60,000 were finished and shipped, and 40,000 were in process three-fourths complete.

REQUIRED:

A. For each "expense" item recorded in Work-in-Process, indicate if it is properly recorded. If it is not properly recorded, determine the correct amount.

B. Determine the equivalent production and cost per unit for the year.

C. Determine the proper balances at the end of the year for:
   1. Raw Materials Inventory
   2. Work-in-Process Inventory
   3. Finished Goods Inventory

D. Prepare an income statement for the Reinsmith Company.

3-29 The following are partially completed T-accounts and additional information for the Adam Brooks Company for the month of November.

RAW MATERIALS INVENTORY

Bal. Nov. 1	$ 200	
	$1,000	

FINISHED GOODS INVENTORY

Bal. Nov. 1	$ 400	

FACTORY OVERHEAD APPLIED

WORK-IN-PROCESS INVENTORY

Bal. Nov. 1	$ 300	$1,200
Material requisition	$ 700	

COST OF GOODS SOLD

$1,500	

FACTORY OVERHEAD CONTROL

Additional information:

1. Labor-time tickets totaled 100 direct labor hours. Employees are paid at the rate of $4 per hour.

2. Factory overhead is applied at the rate of $2 per direct labor hour.

3. Actual factory overhead incurred during November amounted to $250.

4. Sales during the month were $2,500.

REQUIRED:

Determine the following amounts:

A. The balance of Raw Materials Inventory at November 30.

B. Direct labor cost for the month.

C. The amount of factory overhead applied to products during November.

D. The balance of Finished Goods Inventory on November 30.

E. The total of the job cost sheets at the beginning of November.

F. The total of the job cost sheets at the end of November.

G. The total of the costs added to the job cost sheets during November.

H. The amount of under- or overapplied factory overhead for November.

I. Gross margin for November before closing under- or overapplied factory overhead.

J. Assuming that selling and administrative expenses were $650, what was the net income for November?

3-30 In the four independent cases shown you are to compute and insert the missing information indicated by question marks. In each case all costs (material, labor, and overhead) are added uniformly throughout the process. Therefore, a single unit cost is computed for the process.

	A	B	C	D
Units in beginning inventory	0	100	500	?
Percent complete	?	80%	40%	50%
Cost of beginning inventory	0	$ 240	$ 200	$ 500
Units started in production	500	900	?	500
Units finished	300	?	2200	400
Equivalent production	?	?	2300	?
Costs incurred this period	$1000	?	$2100	$3700
Average unit cost	?	$ 4	?	?
Cost of units completed	?	$4000	$2200	?
Units in ending inventory	?	0	300	300
Percent complete	50%	?	?	$66\frac{2}{3}$%
Cost of units in ending inventory	?	0	$ 100	?

3-31 The RST Company uses a process costing system. The company's cost records showed the following:

		Amounts	
	Units	*Material*	*Conversion Costs*
Beginning inventory of work in process (material 100% complete, conversion $\frac{3}{4}$ complete)	200	$ 800	$ 900
Additional units started	700		
Material costs incurred		$2,800	
Conversion costs incurred			$4,700
Units completed and transferred to finished goods	600		
Ending inventory of work in process (material 100% complete, conversion $\frac{2}{3}$ complete)	300		

REQUIRED:

A. Prepare a schedule showing equivalent production for material and conversion costs.

B. Prepare a schedule showing the average unit cost for material and conversion costs.

C. Determine the total cost of the 600 units finished and transferred to Finished Goods Inventory.

D. Determine the cost of the ending Work-in-Process Inventory showing material cost, conversion cost, and total cost.

3-32 The White Company produces a single product and maintains a simple cost accounting system. Actual factory costs are accumulated in the Work-in-Process Inventory account during the year. At the end of the year physical counts of the goods on hand are used to determine the cost of the ending inventories.

The following data were recorded for the year's transactions.

(1) Factory costs:	
Materials	$ 30,000
Direct labor	$ 50,000
Other factory costs	$ 20,000
(2) Other expenses:	
Selling expenses	$ 22,000
Administrative expenses	$ 26,000
Depreciation (of which three-fourths relates to the factory)	$ 16,000
(3) Inventories:	
Beginning and ending raw materials inventories	$ 0
Beginning Work in Process	$ 10,000
Ending Work in Process	$ 20,000
Beginning Finished Goods	$ 25,000
Ending Finished Goods	$ 15,000
(4) Sales	$170,000

REQUIRED:

A. Record the data for the year in T-accounts.

B. Prepare an income statement for the year.

3-33 The Harvey S. Furniture Company produces wooden tables for schools. A process costing system is used to determine the product cost. At the beginning of October, inventories consisted of:

Raw Materials Inventory	$5,000
Work-in-Process Inventory (100 tables):	
Material (100% complete)	$1,000
Conversion Costs (60% complete)	2,400
	$3,400
Finished Goods Inventory	$ 0

During October, 1,000 tables were started and 900 were finished. The ending inventory of 200 units were 100% complete as to materials and 40% complete as to conversion costs (labor and overhead). Transactions during October were:

Raw materials purchased	$12,000
Raw materials issued to production	$10,000
Direct labor	$23,500
Factory overhead	$14,280
Units sold (800 @ $80)	$64,000
Selling and administrative expenses incurred	$20,000

REQUIRED:

A. Determine the equivalent production for (1) material and (2) conversion costs.

B. Determine the October average unit cost for (1) material and (2) conversion costs.

C. What was the average unit cost for a unit finished during October?

D. Prepare journal entries and post to T-accounts for the month's transactions. Assume the following T-accounts are used with balances as shown on October 1:

	dr.	*cr.*
Cash	$7,000	
Raw Materials Inventory	$5,000	
Work-in-Process Inventory	$3,400	
Finished Goods Inventory	$ 0	
Capital Stock		$10,000
Retained Earnings		$ 5,400
Sales		$ 0
Cost of Goods Sold	$ 0	
Selling and Administrative Expenses	$ 0	

(Note: For simplicity we have assumed all cash transactions. Because we are applying actual factory overhead, record the overhead directly into Work-in-Process Inventory.)

E. Prepare a statement of financial position at the end of October.

3-34 The Indestructible Tool Company produces a single product in two processes: machining and finishing. The following production and cost data were recorded for the month of February.

	Machining	*Finishing*
Quantity data:		
Units in process, February 1:		
Machining (material 100% complete, conversion 50% complete)	100	—
Finishing	—	0
Units started in machining	500	—
Units completed in machining	400	—
Units transferred into finishing	—	400
Units completed in finishing and transferred to finished goods	—	300
Units in process, Feburary 28:		
Machining (material 100% complete, conversion 75% complete)	200	—
Finishing (prior department cost 100% complete, conversion 60% complete)	—	100
Cost data:		
Beginning inventory, February 1:		
Material	$ 200	—
Conversion costs	$ 200	—
New costs incurred:		
Material	$1,000	—
Conversion costs	$2,000	$1,800

REQUIRED:

A. Without regard to the stage of completion, prepare a schedule for each department to show the following:

Units in beginning inventory	_______
Units started or transferred in	_______
Total	_______
Units completed and transferred out	_______
Units in ending inventory	_______
Total	_______

B. Prepare a schedule showing equivalent production for each department.

C. Compute the average unit cost for each department. Both the detail for material (or prior department cost in finishing) and conversion cost, as well as the total for the department, should be shown.

D. Determine the total cost of units transferred out in each department.

E. Determine the total cost of the ending inventory of Work-in-Process in each department.

3-35 The Dunbar Company had four orders in its Work-in-Process Inventory at the beginning of April. The following costs were assigned to these jobs during the previous accounting period.

	Jobs			
	A	*B*	*C*	*D*
Direct materials	$42.00	$118.00	$64.00	$289.00
Direct labor	32.50	42.00	21.00	112.00
Factory overhead*	16.25	21.00	10.50	56.00

*Factory overhead is applied to Work in Process at the rate of 50% of direct labor cost.

At the beginning of April the Raw Materials Inventory had a balance of $1,890, and there was no Finished Goods Inventory. During the month the company purchased $4,800 of raw materials. The following is a summary of the material requisitions and labor time tickets for the month.

	Jobs					
	A	*B*	*C*	*D*	*E*	*F*
Direct materials	$320.00	$256.00	$480.00	$124.00	$150.00	$385.00
Direct labor	366.00	496.00	790.00	60.00	175.00	290.00

The factory overhead rate remained the same in April as in the previous month. Jobs A, B, and C were completed this month and transferred to Finished Goods Inventory. The company uses absorption, job costing.

REQUIRED:

A. Develop job cost sheets for each job.
B. Make appropriate journal entries using totals for April.
C. Determine the cost of the ending Work-in-Process Inventory.
D. What was the gross margin for April, assuming the following sales were made?

Job A	$1,250
Job B	$1,600
Job C	$2,200

3-36 The Hytone Company had the following inventories on October 1.

Raw Materials	$ 5,500
Work-in-Process	$10,500
Finished Goods	$25,000

During the month of October the following transactions occurred. (Assume that all sales and purchases are on credit.)

October 1 Purchased $3,600 of raw materials, which were received and inspected.
3 Sold finished goods costing $5,000 for $7,500.
6 Material requisitions were issued for $6,500 of raw materials.
7 Paid the weekly factory payroll in the amount of $4,250.
10 Received a sales order for $15,000 of goods that will be completed during the month and will be shipped on October 31.
13 Purchased $225 of supplies for immediate use in the factory.
14 Paid the weekly factory payroll in the amount of $4,000.
14 Paid the semimonthly supervisory and maintenance payroll in the amount of $1,750.
15 Purchased $8,500 of raw materials.
18 Received the heat, light, and power bill in the amount of $650.
19 Issued raw materials in the amount of $9,000 determined from approved material requisitions.
19 The purchasing agent issued a purchase order in the amount of $2,300.
21 Paid the weekly factory payroll in the amount of $4,500.
22 Received and shipped an order for sales of $12,000; the units cost $9,000.
28 Paid the weekly factory payroll of $4,300.
28 Paid the semimonthly supervisory and maintenance payroll of $1,800.
29 Sold for immediate delivery goods that cost $10,000 for a sales price of $14,250.
30 Recorded monthly depreciation of $1,300 and factory insurance of $350.
30 Recorded the monthly summary of factory payroll from employee time tickets:

Direct labor	$15,000
Indirect labor	2,050
Total	$17,050

30 Applied factory overhead to Work-in-Process at $40 per unit for variable factory overhead and $25 for fixed factory overhead. Records indicate that 120 units were equivalently produced during the month.
30 Recorded completion of jobs in Work-in-Process Inventory and transferred them to Finished Goods Inventory in the amount of $40,000.
30 Shipped the order received on October 10. The cost of the order was $10,500.

30 Received $42,000 from customers in payment of accounts receivable.
30 Paid $10,000 to creditors in payment of accounts payable.
30 Incurred selling and administrative expenses of $5,500 for the month, on account.

REQUIRED:
A. Prepare journal entries for the month using absorption costing, and post the transactions to T-accounts.
B. Compute the end of the month inventory values.
C. Prepare an income statement for the month.

4 A Further Look at Factory Overhead Costing

DIRECT AND INDIRECT COSTS
Time Periods
Organizational Units
Products
ACCOUNTING FOR THE INDIRECT COSTS OF FACTORY OVERHEAD
Production Bases for Factory Overhead Rates
Historical and Predetermined Factory Overhead Rates
Different Factory Overhead Rates Illustrated
An Illustration of the Analysis of Under- or Overapplied Factory Overhead
A Second Illustration of the Analysis of Under- or Overapplied Factory Overhead
THE INTERRELATIONSHIP OF LONG-RANGE AND SHORT-RANGE CAPACITY UTILIZATION
DEPARTMENTALIZATION OF COSTS
Direct and Indirect Costs
Why Make Departmental Allocations?
SUMMARY

One of the more difficult problems facing the accountant is the allocation of indirect costs. Chapter 3 introduced the problems of allocating or apportioning the costs of factory overhead to the products. In this chapter we will look in detail at the problems and solutions of allocating factory overhead costs and the analysis of under- or overapplied factory overhead.

DIRECT AND INDIRECT COSTS

The concepts of direct and indirect costs become important as costs are classified, segregated, and transformed. During the grouping and regrouping of costs to achieve a particular measurement objective, some costs are capable of being traced and logically associated with the costing objective. These are **direct costs.** Others, **indirect costs,** are not logically assignable to the measurement objective without an arbitrary allocation process. Indirect costs have also been called **common** or **joint costs,** although many accountants restrict the use of these terms to specific situations where the costs of a single raw material or production process must be apportioned to more than one final product.

In accounting for direct and indirect costs, there are three measurement objectives: time periods, organizational units, and products.

Time Periods

For income determination purposes, the accrual system of accounting requires assignment of a cost to the time periods that are benefited. A cost is traceable to a particular time period and, therefore, direct to that time period if the benefits represented by the expenditure are realized in that particular period. For example, assume that on July 1 a company made the July lease payment on a salesman's car. This cost is direct to the month of July; there would be no need for cost allocation.

If the cost benefits more than one time period, it is an indirect cost with respect to any particular time period and must be apportioned to the periods benefited with some systematic and rational method of allocation. For example, when a machine that lasts five years is purchased, its cost is an indirect cost that must be assigned to five accounting periods. To determine an annual cost, this indirect cost must be allocated. The calculation of depreciation by some systematic method, such as the straight-line method or the sum-of-the-years'-digits method, is the process of allocating this cost.

Organizational Units

For the planning and control of costs by individual managers, it is desirable to assign costs to responsibility centers. A **responsibility center** is a segment of the organization in which an individual is held accountable only for those activities he directly affects. A responsibility center may be large, such as the Chevrolet division of General Motors, or small, such as the operation of a single machine. It may include any type of activity, such as a sales territory in the marketing area, a machining department in the factory, or a typing pool in the administration area.

There are different broad classes of responsibility centers. Accountants refer to organizational units to which only costs can be traced as **cost centers.** Responsibility centers where only revenues can be traced directly and costs cannot be traced directly are called **revenue centers.** Organizational units where both revenues and costs naturally come together are called **profit centers.** For larger segments of the firm, resources (assets), costs, and revenue are traced to **investment centers.** In investment centers it is possible to determine the return on investment. We will use the broader concept of responsibility center in this text unless it seems more appropriate to be specific at the time. By using the term *responsibility center,* we are implying that there is an organizational structure and, thus, a personal responsibility by some manager for the costs, revenues, and/or resources.

The planning of costs, the selection of proper methods of allocation, and the control of actual performance depend upon the ability to assign costs directly to responsibility centers. Costs that can be directly assigned are called **controllable costs** or **traceable costs.** These costs can be controlled by the individual manager. Costs that a specific manager cannot control are often called **noncontrollable costs.** Of course, all costs are controlled at some point by someone in the firm.

Products

When accountants deal with direct and indirect costs, their first inclination is to consider the process of assigning costs to the products. In Chapter 3 we discussed direct and indirect materials. Direct materials were defined as those which the accountant could trace to a specific unit of product; indirect materials were those which the accountant could not or did not trace to specific units of product. The whole concept of income determination is predicated upon the belief that costs must be assigned to products and held as unexpired costs until the products are sold. Here the role of factory overhead rates becomes significant.

No cost should be termed *direct* or *indirect* in a specific situation without first determining the objective of costing. A fine-line determination is often required. The plant manager's salary may be direct in terms of time periods and direct to his department, but it is indirect to the products produced. Depreciation accounting may result in a cost that is indirect to time periods and products, yet the same cost may be direct to a specific responsibility center.

ACCOUNTING FOR THE INDIRECT COSTS OF FACTORY OVERHEAD

As shown in the preceding chapter, absorption costing requires an allocation of total factory overhead costs to the individual products. An entire body of accounting literature deals with the unique problems of accounting for factory overhead. In this section we will examine some of the current methods of factory overhead costing.

Factory overhead costs are indirect costs relative to the products, but they may be direct to a responsibility center, making it necessary to apportion or allocate them to the products. This apportionment is made through the factory overhead rate. The following equation expresses the factory overhead rate in its simplest terms.

$$\text{Factory overhead Rate} = \frac{\text{Dollars of factory overhead}}{\text{A measurement of production output}}$$

The effect of the factory overhead rate is to create an average overhead cost per unit of production. Separate rates may be computed for fixed and variable costs. In this way, the benefits of separating fixed and variable costs may be carried through to the product costing system.

There are two issues involved in the development of factory overhead rates: (1) What is an acceptable measure of production? (2) When should the factory overhead rate be calculated and the factory overhead costs applied to Work-in-Process Inventory?

Production Bases for Factory Overhead Rates

The **production base** is a common denominator—a way to equate all of the units produced. If a firm produces only one product, such as a 12-ounce bottle of soft drink, the factory overhead rate can be determined quite simply by dividing the dollars of factory overhead by the number of bottles produced. This automatically results in a factory overhead cost per unit of product.

In firms where different items are produced, the production base must serve as a common denominator among products. Where the firm produces dissimilar products, the validity of the overhead rate rests upon the determination of a cause and effect relationship between the dollars spent for factory overhead and the base used to allocate the dollars to the product.

To clarify this point, we divide firms into two categories: those which are highly automated and those which are labor intensive. In highly automated firms the factory overhead costs are composed primarily of equipment costs such as power, maintenance, and depreciation charges. A measure of the time the machines are used to produce the product is a good basis for allocating factory overhead. These firms would typically use some form of machine-hour basis for applying factory overhead.

Other firms are labor intensive. The production process uses relatively few machines, and the majority of factory overhead dollars is composed of labor-oriented costs. In labor-oriented firms, the best common denominator among products is the amount of labor time or labor dollars spent on each product. The factory overhead rate in these firms is based upon direct labor hours or direct labor dollars. Of these, direct labor hours are more widely used. Most factory overhead costs are more closely related to the time workers spend in production than to the amount of pay workers receive. Only if labor wage rates are the same throughout the production process, or if higher-paid skills require proportionately less time, will the direct labor-hour basis and the direct labor-dollar basis of applying factory overhead yield approximately the same results. When this is not the case, the factory overhead rate based upon direct labor hours will probably describe more accurately a cause and effect relationship.

Historical and Predetermined Factory Overhead Rates

The second question involves the problem of *when* the factory overhead rate is calculated and the factory overhead costs are applied to the product. An **historical factory overhead rate** is applied to work in process *after* the production period is completed. To illustrate the application of factory overhead using an historical overhead rate, let's assume that the Alene Shipbuilding Company worked on three ships during the past accounting period. Cost records indicate that total factory overhead of $12,000 was incurred and that 9,600 direct labor hours were consumed. These 9,600 labor hours were used as follows:

Ship 90-1A	3,000 hours
Ship 110-4A	5,000 hours
Ship 30-3B	1,600 hours

The historical factory overhead rate, based on actual direct labor hours, is:

$$\frac{\$12{,}000}{9{,}600 \text{ hours}} = \$1.25 \text{ per direct labor hour}$$

This rate shows that, on the average, the firm spent $1.25 of factory overhead for each labor hour consumed. The following journal entry applies actual factory overhead to the Work-in-Process Inventory.[1]

Work-in-Process Inventory	$12,000	
Factory Overhead Control		$12,000

The factory overhead costs would be charged to the individual ships.

Ship 90-1A	3,000 hrs.	×	$1.25	=	$ 3,750
Ship 110-4A	5,000 hrs.	×	$1.25	=	6,250
Ship 30-3B	1,600 hrs.	×	$1.25	=	2,000
Total	9,600 hrs.	×	$1.25	=	$12,000

[1]We will omit explanations on all journal entries in this chapter.

Since actual overhead costs are charged to Work-in-Process Inventory, there will be no under- or overapplied factory overhead. For this reason, the Factory Overhead Applied account is not used. Factory Overhead Control is credited directly. At the end of each accounting period the balance of Factory Overhead Control will be zero.

The use of an historical factory overhead rate has distinct drawbacks. First, the unit costs of production cannot be calculated on a timely basis because overhead cannot be charged to Work-in-Process Inventory until all production for the period has been completed and measured. Second, there are problems of seasonality. Some of the factory overhead costs are fixed and do not change with changes in volume. Thus, when there are seasonal fluctuations in volume, the factory overhead rate will fluctuate. Remember that a fixed cost is constant in total dollar amount but varies per unit as the volume changes. As an illustration of the effect of seasonal variation on the factory overhead rate, let's assume that a firm has a monthly flexible factory overhead budget of: $y_c = \$36{,}000 + \$1.00(x)$, where x represents direct labor hours. The factory overhead rate would be computed as shown in the accompanying tabulation.

	January	*February*	*March*
Production output in terms of direct labor hours	18,000	24,000	12,000
Factory overhead:			
Fixed costs	$36,000	$36,000	$36,000
Variable costs	18,000	24,000	12,000
Total factory overhead costs	$54,000	$60,000	$48,000
Factory overhead rate per direct labor hour:			
Fixed factory overhead rate	$ 2.00	$ 1.50	$ 3.00
Variable factory overhead rate	1.00	1.00	1.00
Total factory overhead rate	$ 3.00	$ 2.50	$ 4.00

A close examination of this illustration shows that the factory overhead rate fluctuates because of the interaction of production volume with fixed costs. The variable rate of $1 per hour remains constant during the three months.

To overcome the deficiencies in the historical factory overhead rate, many firms adopt a predetermined factory overhead rate. Before the beginning of the accounting period the firm estimates the factory overhead and the volume base for the year and computes a predetermined rate.

$$\text{Predetermined factory overhead rate} = \frac{\text{Estimated dollars of factory overhead for the coming accounting period}}{\text{Estimated production measurement base for the coming accounting period}}$$

The product costs and, thus, the net income can be severely affected by the choice of the predetermined activity level for the denominator. The higher the proportion of fixed costs to variable costs in factory overhead, the more sensitive the choice of the denominator. It is the presence of fixed costs interacting with production output that creates fluctuations in the factory overhead rate.

The production output depends upon available plant capacity and customer demand for the product. Plant capacity exists because of previous decisions to buy and maintain it. At the time these decisions were made, management undoubtedly considered the capacity necessary to meet normal sales demands, given seasonal and cyclical variations.[2] Allowances were probably also made for anticipated growth. Thus, one way to view the predetermined activity level for computing a factory overhead rate is in light of the maximum output capability of the existing plant over a long period of time—the **practical capacity.** This upper level of capacity is not absolute. For example, it could be based upon a one-shift, 8-hour day or upon a two-shift, 16-hour day. In this case there would be two different maximum outputs possible. For our purposes we will consider practical capacity as the maximum output that can be achieved over an extended period of time, given the existing management policies of work week, shifts, and employee mix.

Most firms do not operate at practical capacity because it includes not only an allowance for output fluctuations because of changes in demand, but also an allowance for growth. A second measure of predetermined activity level for computing overhead rates is to use the capacity necessary to meet expected sales demand over a relatively long period of time, such as the next three to five years. This estimate would allow the averaging of seasonal, cyclical, and some long-run growth variations. Factory overhead rates based upon the capacity needed to meet relatively long-run sales demand are termed **normal** or **average rates.**

To illustrate one way firms can develop a normal factory overhead rate, let's assume the following production plan for the Sanford Company, based upon forecasts of sales for the next three years.

19X1	80,000	direct labor hours
19X2	60,000	
19X3	100,000	
Total	240,000	direct labor hours

On the average, over the next three years the company must work 80,000 hours per year to meet the long-run sales forecast. A factory overhead rate based upon 80,000 hours would be a normal overhead rate. Let's assume that the firm's annual flexible budget for factory overhead is y_c = \$160,000 + \$3(direct labor hours). The following factory overhead rate is based upon normal capacity.

[2]Seasonal variations are variations in output or customer demand within a fiscal or calendar year. Cyclical variations are variations in output or customer demand occurring over an economic business cycle.

$$\text{Normal factory overhead rate for 19X1 to 19X3} = \frac{\$160{,}000 + \$3(80{,}000 \text{ hours})}{80{,}000 \text{ hours}}$$

$$= \$5 \text{ per direct labor hour}$$

To see the effect of the normal factory overhead rate upon the absorption of factory overhead costs to the products, let's assume that in each of the three years the firm works exactly the hours forecasted and spends exactly the amount allowed by the flexible budget for factory overhead. The under- or overapplied factory overhead for each of the three years would be as shown in the accompanying tabulation.

	Hours Worked (x)	*Factory Overhead Incurred [$160,000 + $3(x)]*	*Factory Overhead Applied $5 × (x)*	*Annual (Under-) or Overapplied Factory Overhead*
19X1	80,000	$400,000	$400,000	$ 0
19X2	60,000	$340,000	$300,000	($40,000)
19X3	100,000	$460,000	$500,000	$40,000

In the first year there was no under- or overapplied factory overhead because the 80,000 hours worked were equal to the average for the three years. Factory overhead was underapplied in 19X2 because the company worked less than the average; factory overhead was overapplied in 19X3 because it worked more than the average. Over the three-year period, the underapplied and overapplied factory overhead cancel out, so the total amount of factory overhead incurred equals the amount applied to the products. The stability feature of a constant rate of $5 over time makes the normal overhead rate attractive.

It would be simplistic to assume that volume estimates and cost behavior patterns of the firm could be perfectly forecasted for a three-year period in a real-world setting. Some firms modify the previously shown approach by using a **rolling** or **moving average** in determining their normal capacity. Continuing with our illustration for the Sanford Company, assume that at the *end* of 19X1 a new projection of sales resulted in the following production forecasts.

19X2	61,000 direct labor hours
19X3	63,000
19X4	68,000
Total	192,000 direct labor hours

The new projected normal capacity is 64,000 hours (192,000 ÷ 3). The new factory overhead rate, assuming the flexible budget formula is unchanged, would be:

$$\text{Normal factory overhead rate for 19X2} = \frac{\$160{,}000 + \$3(64{,}000 \text{ hours})}{64{,}000 \text{ hours}}$$
$$= \$5.50 \text{ per direct labor hour}$$

In a real setting the flexible budget for factory overhead would probably also change because of changes in facilities, production processes, or price-level changes. The new factory overhead rate should reflect any changes in the flexible budget.

If the forecasts are accurate there will be underapplied factory overhead in 19X2 because the factory overhead rate of $5.50, based upon an average of 64,000 hours, will be applied to only 61,000 hours. In industries where the production volume increases, as in our illustration, the production costed with a rolling average will result in underapplied factory overhead. Across time, the rolling average approach to normal overhead will mean that the actual factory overhead incurred will not be equal to the costs applied to the products.

Instead of basing their rates on the long-run estimates implied in the practical and normal overhead rates, some firms use an expected rate. **Expected capacity** is the anticipated level of activity for the coming accounting period. It is also called **budgeted capacity.** Obviously the forecasting problems should be fewer than with a normal or practical rate. The use of the term *capacity* is somewhat misleading in the context of expected capacity; it does *not* imply either a maximum or an optimum output level. Expected capacity may be above or below normal capacity and may be well below practical capacity. It may be an efficient or inefficient level of operations.

Using the original Sanford Company illustration, the expected overhead rate for each year would be as shown in the accompanying tabulation.

Year	*Factory Overhead Rate*	*Estimated Factory Overhead [$160,000 + $3(x)]*	*Projected Hours (x)*
19X1	$5.00	$400,000	80,000
19X2	$5.67	$340,000	60,000
19X3	$4.60	$460,000	100,000

Different Factory Overhead Rates Illustrated

To illustrate the differences between the capacity estimates and their effects on overhead rates, let's assume that the Foilwing Aircraft Company uses a predetermined factory overhead rate. Before production begins it is estimated that total factory overhead will be composed of $48,000 of fixed costs and that variable factory overhead will be $1 per direct labor hour. A study of the plant indicates the following capacities:

Practical capacity	48,000 direct labor hours
Normal capacity	40,000 direct labor hours
Expected capacity	32,000 direct labor hours

Based on *practical capacity,* the factory overhead rate would be:

$$\text{Total factory overhead rate} = \text{Variable factory overhead rate} + \text{Fixed factory overhead rate}$$

$$\frac{\$96{,}000}{48{,}000\text{ hours}} = \frac{\$48{,}000}{48{,}000\text{ hours}} + \frac{\$48{,}000}{48{,}000\text{ hours}}$$

or

$$\$2.00\text{ per direct labor hour} = \$1.00 + \$1.00$$

Based on *normal capacity,* the factory overhead rate would be:

$$\frac{\$88{,}000}{40{,}000\text{ hours}} = \frac{\$40{,}000}{40{,}000\text{ hours}} + \frac{\$48{,}000}{40{,}000\text{ hours}}$$

or

$$\$2.20\text{ per direct labor hour} = \$1.00 + \$1.20$$

Based on *expected capacity,* the factory overhead rate would be:

$$\frac{\$80{,}000}{32{,}000\text{ hours}} = \frac{\$32{,}000}{32{,}000\text{ hours}} + \frac{\$48{,}000}{32{,}000\text{ hours}}$$

or

$$\$2.50\text{ per direct labor hour} = \$1.00 + \$1.50$$

From this illustration we can see that the variable factory overhead rate is a constant $1 regardless of the anticipated volume. The difference in the total overhead rates results solely from dividing the fixed costs by different production bases.

An Illustration of the Analysis of Under- or Overapplied Factory Overhead

When predetermined factory overhead rates are used to determine the product cost, it would be highly unusual for the Factory Overhead Control to agree exactly with Factory Overhead Applied. In this section we will analyze the causes of under- or overapplied factory overhead.

To continue our illustration of the Foilwing Aircraft Company, let's assume that management believed the expected factory overhead rate would satisfactorily measure product cost and so selected $2.50 per direct labor hour (variable $1.00 and fixed $1.50) as the factory overhead rate based upon 32,000 direct labor hours. Further, let's assume that only 30,000 actual labor hours were consumed during the year and that actual factory overhead incurred was $79,000 (including $47,000 fixed costs and $32,000 variable costs). The 30,000 hours were divided between two airplanes.

Plane 206-747	12,000 hours
Plane 207-747	18,000 hours

The following journal entry would record the incurrence of the actual factory overhead.

Factory Overhead Control	$79,000	
Payables, Cash		$79,000

The following entry applies factory overhead to the Work-in-Process Inventory.

Work-in-Process Inventory	$75,000	
Factory Overhead Applied (30,000 × $2.50)		$75,000

The job cost sheet for Plane 206-747 would receive factory overhead costs of 12,000 × $2.50, or $30,000, and the job cost sheet for plane 207-747 would receive overhead costs of 18,000 × $2.50, or $45,000. The Factory Overhead Applied account summarizes the amount of factory overhead transferred to Work-in-Process Inventory, whereas the Factory Overhead Control account accumulates what was actually spent. At the end of the accounting period the two accounts are closed with the following entry.

Factory Overhead Applied	$75,000	
Under- or Overapplied Factory Overhead	$ 4,000	
Factory Overhead Control		$79,000

In our example the Factory Overhead Control exceeds the Factory Overhead Applied. Accordingly, factory overhead is underapplied by $4,000. There are two reasons for this underapplied factory overhead. First, management anticipated spending $48,000 on fixed costs plus $1 for each labor hour worked. Actual costs did not meet this budget. According to the flexible budget allowances, $48,000 for fixed costs plus $30,000 for variable costs *should* have been spent to work 30,000 hours. Actual costs were $47,000 and $32,000 respectively. The **spending variance,** the deviation of actual costs from a budget allowance, is as shown in the following tabulation.

	Actual Factory Overhead	–	*Flexible Budget Allowance*	=	*Factory Overhead Spending Variance*
Fixed costs	$47,000		$48,000		$ 1,000 favorable
Variable costs	32,000		30,000		(2,000) unfavorable
Total factory overhead costs	$79,000		$78,000		$(1,000) unfavorable

Management did not control its variable cost expenditures and decided to spend less than the normal planned amount on fixed costs.

Second, when management selected the expected capacity to determine the factory overhead rate, it decided to absorb fixed costs over 32,000 direct labor hours. However, it absorbed the fixed costs over only 30,000 direct labor hours. As a result, only 30,000 × $1.50, or $45,000 of fixed costs were charged to the product, although the original plan was to charge $48,000 (32,000 × $1.50) to the Work-in-Process Inventory. This $3,000 difference is called the **volume variance.** The sum of the budget variance ($1,000 unfavorable) and the volume variance ($3,000 unfavorable) is equal to the underapplied overhead ($4,000).

To further explore the nature of the volume variance, let's make a different assumption. Instead of an expected factory overhead rate of $2.50 per hour, assume the company chose to use a normal overhead rate of $2.20 per direct labor hour (variable $1.00 and fixed $1.20). Also assume that the actual costs and activity levels are unchanged at $79,000 and 30,000 hours respectively. The Foilwing Aircraft Company would apply $66,000 of overhead to the Work-in-Process Inventory, and overhead would be underapplied by $13,000 ($79,000 – $66,000). The spending variances would be unchanged because the actual overhead is still $79,000 and the budget allowance is still $78,000. However, the volume variance would be different. By selecting a normal factory overhead rate, the firm planned to absorb the fixed costs of $48,000 over 40,000 direct labor hours, using a fixed overhead rate of $1.20 per hour. But because actual direct labor hours were 30,000, only $36,000 of fixed costs were absorbed. The difference between the budgeted fixed costs of $48,000 and the absorbed fixed costs of $36,000 results in a $12,000 unfavorable volume variance. When this unfavorable volume variance is added to the unfavorable spending variance of $1,000, the underapplied overhead is $13,000.

By comparing the two assumptions of an expected factory overhead rate and a normal factory overhead rate, we can see that the volume variance is the result of the difference between the fixed costs budgeted and the fixed costs absorbed. Further, the amount of fixed costs absorbed is dependent upon the volume measure chosen and the actual hours worked.

A Second Illustration of the Analysis of Under- or Overapplied Factory Overhead

As a final illustration of the analysis of under- or overapplied factory overhead, let's return to our example of the Roving Jack Company from Chapter 3. The firm had prepared a predetermined overhead rate of $3 per direct labor hour (variable $1 and fixed $2) based upon estimates of total factory overhead costs of $72,000 and 24,000 direct labor hours. Further, let's assume that the fixed costs are expected to be consumed uniformly throughout the year ($48,000 ÷ 12 months, or $4,000 per month) and that during the month of October the firm's plans called for 2,000 direct labor hours.

Finally, the accountant studied the actual overhead costs incurred and determined that the costs were fixed and variable as shown in the following tabulation. (The Roving Jack Company illustration in Chapter 3 shows how the actual overhead incurred was recorded.)

Variable Factory Overhead Costs		*Fixed Factory Overhead Costs*	
Indirect materials	$1,000	Indirect labor	$1,000
Heat, light, power	700	Depreciation	1,500
Labor related costs	1,300	Factory insurance	400
		Miscellaneous	1,500
Total	$3,000	Total	$4,400

During October the firm incurred actual factory overhead of $7,400 and applied factory overhead to Work-in-Process Inventory of $7,800 (2,600 hours × $3). As a result, the factory overhead was overapplied by $400.

First, the spending variance is computed.

	Actual Overhead	–	*Flexible Budget Allowance*	=	*Factory Overhead Spending Variance*
Fixed costs	$4,400		$4,000		$(400) Unfavorable
Variable costs	3,000		2,600		(400) Unfavorable
Total factory overhead costs	$7,400		$6,600		$(800) Unfavorable

During October actual fixed factory overhead costs exceeded budgeted fixed costs by $400. Management did not control the expenditure of fixed costs or perhaps made a decision to increase some fixed expenditures. Actual variable costs were $3,000. The flexible budget allowance for variable costs was $2,600, assuming the actual use of 2,600 labor hours (2,600 hours × $1 per hour). With an unfavorable variable overhead spending variance of $400, it also failed to control the rate of expenditure for variable costs. The total overhead spending variance is $800 ($400 + $400). Management must now decide if these variances are significant and deserve further detailed investigation. The company could analyze the spending variance further for each overhead item such as indirect materials, power, and labor-related costs.

Second, factory overhead was overapplied because work was at a higher activity level than originally planned. In the initial budget it was planned to work 2,000 direct labor hours in October, but 2,600 hours were actually worked. Fixed costs of $5,200 were applied to the Work-in-Process Inventory (2,600 hours × $2.00), although the plan was to absorb only $4,000. Thus, $1,200 of fixed costs were overapplied. This $1,200 volume variance is overabsorbed because the actual volume exceeded the expected volume. The net of the spending variance ($800 unfavorable) and the volume variance ($1,200 favorable) is the $400 overapplied overhead.

A summary worksheet of the total analysis of factory overhead of the Roving Jack Company is shown in Exhibit 4-1.

THE INTERRELATIONSHIP OF LONG-RANGE AND SHORT-RANGE CAPACITY UTILIZATION

In Chapter 1 we differentiated between long-range and short-range decisions using two criteria: (1) Long-range decisions span a long enough time period to make the time value of money a significant factor, whereas in short-range decisions the time value of money, while present, is not significant. (2) Long-range decisions involve modifying the productive capacity, whereas short-range decisions involve the use of existing capacity in the most effective and efficient way possible. Both long-range and short-range decisions have the same goal of providing an acceptable rate of return over the life of the enterprise.

To carry the analysis of capacity one step further, suppose that at the time of a capital investment decision, management decided to build a plant that could produce a maximum of 100,000 units per year over the long run. The designers of the plant felt that if maintenance was delayed and the plant was pushed to its upper limits, the firm could produce 120,000 units. The 120,000-unit capacity is generally called **rated capacity** or **ideal capacity.** This capacity meets the upper design specifications and generally could not be sustained over any extended period of time.

The 100,000-unit capacity is generally called the practical capacity, the output level that the firm can sustain in the long run. With two underlying

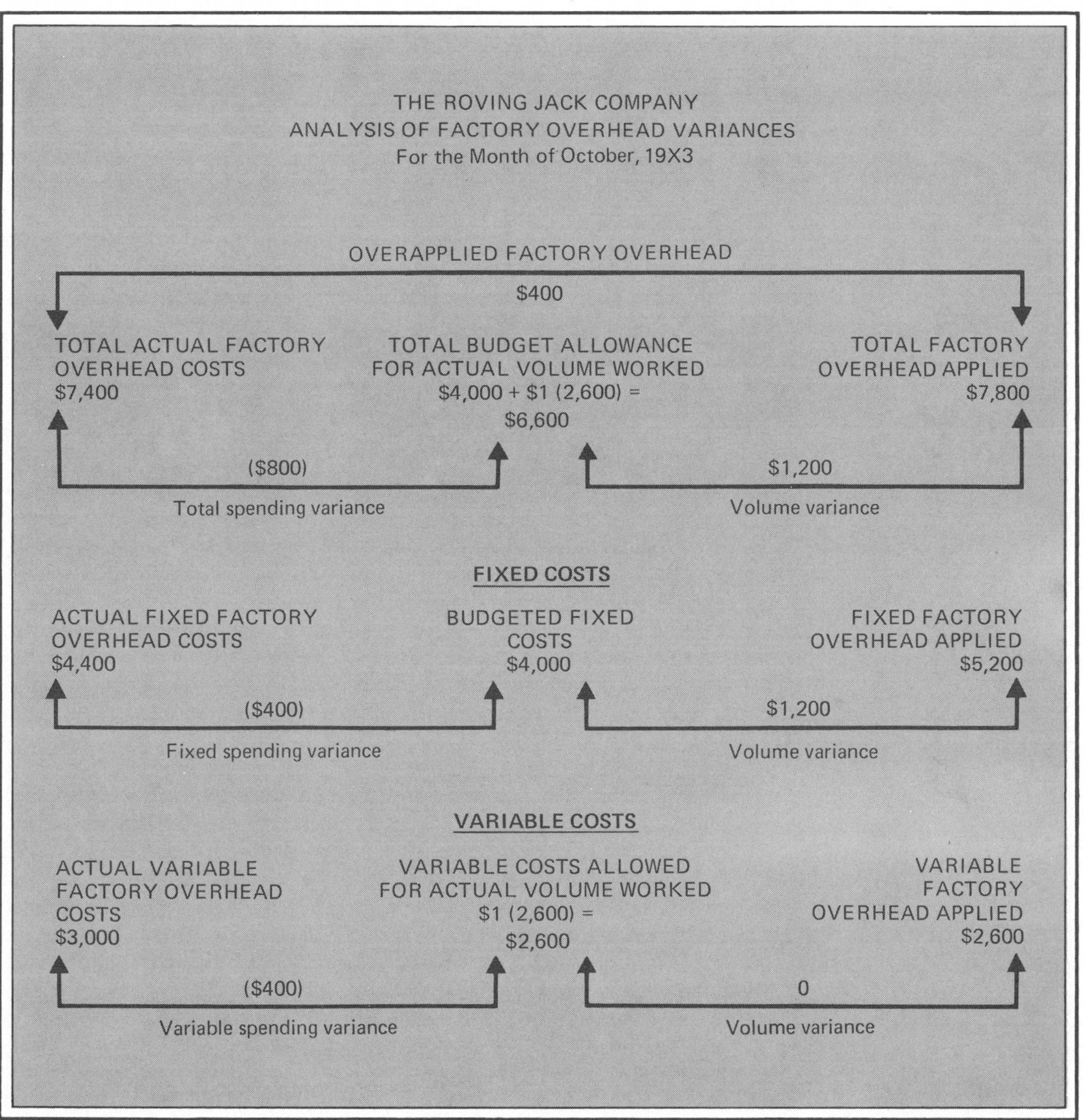

EXHIBIT 4-1
Analysis of under- or overapplied overhead

assumptions, the practical capacity takes on greater significance. If it is assumed that (1) the fixed costs remain constant over the total volume range and (2) the efficiency of effort does not diminish, then practical capacity can also mean that at this level the cost per unit will be at a minimum (see Chapter 1).

At the time the plant was built, management anticipated the average production to meet sales over the next five to ten years would be 80,000 units. This output, which is sufficient to meet sales demands over a period of time long enough to encompass seasonal and cyclical fluctuations, is called normal or average capacity. Management purchased a plant with a capacity of 100,000 units, although normal sales expectancies were about 80,000 units, in order to provide capacity to meet fluctuations in demand as well as to allow for growth.

Assume that for the coming year management anticipated an operating volume of 85,000 units, slightly above average. This expected volume would be used in short-range decisions. Finally, assume that the company actually produced only 75,000 units and that detailed reports show the reason it missed its budgeted volume was that the sales force obtained orders for only 78,000. Apparently, demand was not forecasted accurately or the salespeople did not work hard enough. Although orders were received for 78,000, only 75,000 were actually produced. These 3,000 units were not produced because of an unexpected plant breakdown.

The analysis in Exhibit 4-2 suggests the type of variations a manager can examine.[3] These variances are beyond the analysis of under- or over-applied overhead presented earlier, and show how the short run blends into the long run in capacity decisions. The measures shown in Exhibit 4-2 are in units. Many managers like to see variances expressed in dollars. The fixed factory overhead rate would be an inappropriate measure since it would be a function of the activity volume chosen to determine the fixed rate. The best measure of the dollar impact of capacity utilization variances is the foregone revenue from not using the capacity to its best advantage. If the company fails to use its capacity it will lose the *contribution margin* of the items not produced. Notice that the fixed costs do not change because of the capacity utilization decisions and thus are not relevant. The contribution margin is a realistic measure of the opportunity cost of not using the plant fully.

When a firm's growth pushes beyond the practical capacity, it will have to stop increasing production output or consider a plant addition. Conversely, if the sales demand and plant output fall so that the efficiency of plant scale can no longer provide a positive contribution margin, the plant should be shut down. The increase or decrease of plant activity beyond the short-range implications of the relevant range of activity opens the door for the long-range decisions. A subjective line separates the long run from the short run—a distinction that requires executive judgment. Human judgment will always be the crucial and final factor.

[3]This analysis is based on "A Contribution Margin Approach to the Analysis of Capacity Utilization," Charles T. Horngren, *The Accounting Review* (April, 1967), pp. 254–264.

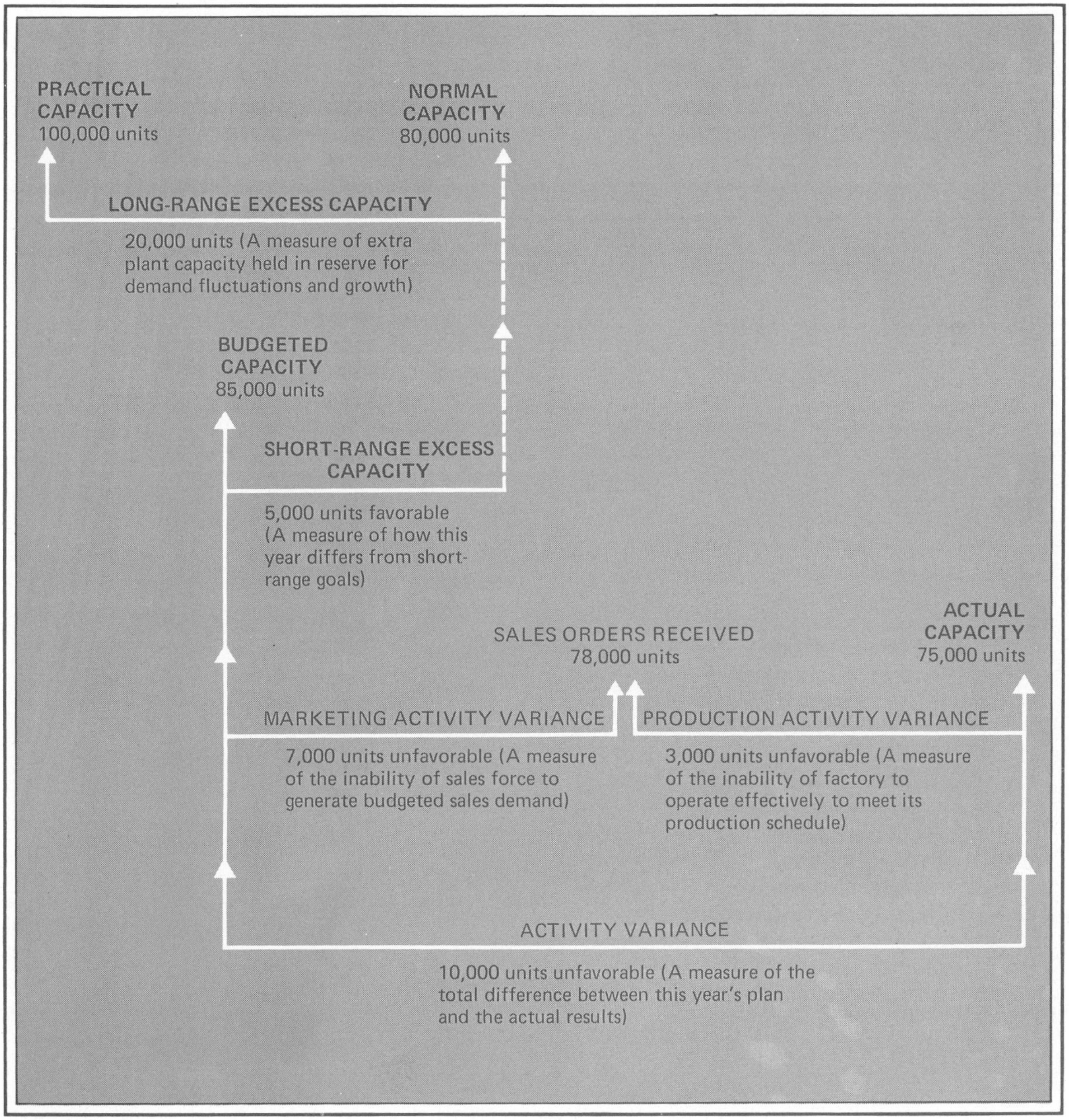

PRACTICAL CAPACITY
100,000 units

NORMAL CAPACITY
80,000 units

LONG-RANGE EXCESS CAPACITY

20,000 units (A measure of extra plant capacity held in reserve for demand fluctuations and growth)

BUDGETED CAPACITY
85,000 units

SHORT-RANGE EXCESS CAPACITY

5,000 units favorable (A measure of how this year differs from short-range goals)

SALES ORDERS RECEIVED
78,000 units

ACTUAL CAPACITY
75,000 units

MARKETING ACTIVITY VARIANCE

7,000 units unfavorable (A measure of the inability of sales force to generate budgeted sales demand)

PRODUCTION ACTIVITY VARIANCE

3,000 units unfavorable (A measure of the inability of factory to operate effectively to meet its production schedule)

ACTIVITY VARIANCE

10,000 units unfavorable (A measure of the total difference between this year's plan and the actual results)

EXHIBIT 4-2
The interrelationship of long-range and short-range capacity utilization

DEPARTMENTALIZATION OF COSTS

Effective planning and control require that responsibility for costs be established. By organizing the company into logical operations, by tracing costs to these departments, and by placing each department under the supervision of a manager, the company can assign management responsibility for the planning and control of costs.

Under absorption costing it is necessary to develop factory overhead rates that include a fair share of all factory overhead costs, direct as well as indirect. The departmental cost structure provides a vehicle for accumulating costs into cost centers and allocating indirect costs to the cost centers that work directly on the products. In this section we will see how costs can be apportioned to departments for the purposes of facilitating planning and control by departments and for the development of departmental factory overhead rates.

Direct and Indirect Costs

In the factory there are two broad classes of departments. **Producing departments** actually work on the product. They modify and convert the raw materials, by adding labor and overhead, into a finished product. Examples of producing departments are machining, fabricating, painting, plating, stamping, and assembly departments. Departments that support the producing departments but do not work directly on the final product are called **service departments.** Their purpose is to make the producing departments more efficient and effective. Examples of service departments include toolrooms, storerooms, timekeeping, cafeterias, maintenance, production scheduling, personnel, medical services, power generating plants, and materials handling.

In the development of a factory overhead rate all factory overhead costs must be related to the products in the producing departments—the only departments that come in contact with the products. Therefore, service department costs must be allocated to the producing departments in order for the producing departments' factory overhead rates to include all production costs.

The determination of departmental overhead rates requires a multistep sequence of apportioning costs. First, all direct factory costs are *traced* to individual producing or service departments. Then, all indirect factory costs are *apportioned* to the individual departments. Next, the service departments must be *allocated* to the producing departments. Finally, the producing departments' fully allocated costs must be *applied* to the products via the overhead rate. Costs traced to a department, whether a producing department or a service department, are direct costs. They do not require allocation. The costs that cannot be traced to a particular department, but are necessary to the department's activities, are indirect costs.

The allocation of service department costs to producing departments requires an allocation base. To explore allocation bases, let's assume that we are distributing the medical services department costs of $12,000 between the two producing departments: A and B. The most important criterion in choosing an allocation base is the discovery of an existing cause and effect relationship. The best allocation base taps this relationship. To find the cause and effect relationship in our example, the accountant should ask himself: "Why do medical service costs rise and fall? Are fluctuations attributable to the number of employees in the producing departments, the nature of work performed in the producing departments, the number of hours employees work, or some other cause?"

The ability to measure the allocation base is a practical constraint. For this reason physical measures are often best. For example, the number of employees in each department is a measure that is easily obtained and makes logical, intuitive sense as a cause of incurring medical services. Even more logical is the development of a direct measure such as a record-keeping system in the medical service department; actual services rendered would be recorded and billed directly to the departments. Where a direct measure is not available the accountant must resort to either selecting the base on a logical assumption or using some analytical method such as regression analysis, as shown in Chapter 2, to test for significant relationships.

For our purposes let's assume that the following measurements have been made.

	Plant Total	*Department A*	*Department B*
Direct labor hours	6,000	4,000	2,000
Number of employees	50	30	20
Number of office calls in medical service department	240	120	120

Based upon direct labor hours, the allocation to Department A would be $8,000 [(4,000 ÷ 6,000) × $12,000]. Based upon the number of employees, the allocation would be $7,200 [(30 ÷ 50) × $12,000]. Based upon the number of office calls, it would be $6,000 [(120 ÷ 240) × $12,000]. Which of these allocations is the best? It is difficult to say. However, given that the principal aim of cost allocation is to associate the cost with its causal factor, the company would probably choose the number of office calls. This choice is not completely clear and, in fact, requires management discretion. The less clear the relationship, the more uncertainty there will be in making the cost allocations.

For a complete illustration of the development of departmental factory overhead rates, let's assume that the Donnell Company has two producing

Departmental Statistics	Total	SERVICE DEPARTMENTS Maintenance	Medical	PRODUCING DEPARTMENTS Fabrication	Assembly
Machine hours	6,000	None	None	4,000	2,000
Total labor hours	8,000	1,500	500	2,000	4,000
Value of equipment	$ 120,000	$ 10,000	$ 20,000	$ 50,000	$ 40,000
Square feet occupied	50,000	8,000	2,000	20,000	20,000
Number of telephones	35	7	8	10	10
Maintenance man hours used	2,900	100	50	1,750	1,000
Number of employees	97	10	7	30	50

EXHIBIT 4-3
Departmental statistics of the Donnell Company

departments, fabrication and assembly, and two service departments, maintenance and medical services. The various parts going into the final products are machined in the fabrication department and assembled in the assembly department. Factory overhead costs in the factory overhead control subsidiary ledger are: indirect labor, employee fringe benefits, indirect materials, depreciation of machinery, depreciation of building, factory supervision, and telephone expense. The nature of the production activities caused management to use machine hours in the fabrication department and direct labor hours in the assembly department to apply factory overhead to the Work-in-Process Inventory. Statistical data necessary to allocate the indirect costs were gathered by the company and are shown in Exhibit 4-3,.

Exhibit 4-4 shows the allocation of the costs to the producing departments through a worksheet. When the worksheet is completed *all* factory overhead costs will be allocated to the two producing departments for the computation of departmental factory overhead rates. Through the departmental factory overhead rates, each unit of product will receive its share of factory overhead. In this worksheet the four departments are shown in the column headings and the factory overhead costs are listed on the left. Taking the four sequential steps one at a time, let's develop the worksheet.

Step 1. All direct factory costs are *traced* to individual producing or service departments. Indirect labor, employee fringe benefits, and indirect materials were traced to the two service and producing departments when the costs were originally recorded by department as direct costs incurred.

Step 2. Costs that are indirect to the service or producing departments must be *apportioned* to them before service department costs are reallocated to the producing departments. The Donnell Company could not trace depreciation of machinery, depreciation of building, factory supervision,

THE DONNELL COMPANY
DEPARTMENTAL COST WORKSHEET
For the Year 19X4

Step	Cost	Allocation Base	Total	SERVICE DEPTS.		PRODUCING DEPTS.	
				Maintenance	Medical	Fabrication	Assembly
1	Indirect labor	Direct	$28,500	$2,000	$1,500	$10,000	$15,000
1	Employee fringe benefits	Direct	12,900	500	300	5,000	7,100
1	Supplies/indirect materials	Direct	6,700	1,000	700	3,000	2,000
2	Depreciation of machinery	Value of machinery	4,800	400	800	2,000	1,600
2	Depreciation of building	Square feet occupied	6,000	960	240	2,400	2,400
2	Factory supervision	Total labor hours	3,200	600	200	800	1,600
2	Telephone expense	Number of phones	700	140	160	200	200
	Total overhead costs		$62,800	$5,600	$ 3,900	$23,400	$29,900
3	Distribute maintenance department	Maintenance man hours used		($5,600)	100	3,500	2,000
	Subtotal				$4,000	$26,900	$31,900
3	Distribute medical department	Number of employees			($4,000)	1,500	2,500
	Total overhead costs					$28,400	$34,400
	Basis of overhead rate					4,000 machine hours	4,000 labor hours
4	Departmental overhead rate					$7.10 per machine hour	$8.60 per labor hour

EXHIBIT 4-4
Worksheet for the departmental allocation of costs of the Donnell Company

and telephone expense directly to any departments. Therefore, these costs must be apportioned. Depreciation of machinery was apportioned on the basis of machinery value. Since the maintenance department had $10,000 in equipment, out of a total equipment base of $120,000, it received $400 [($10,000 ÷ $120,000) × $4,800] as its share. In a similar manner, building depreciation was apportioned on the basis of square feet occupied, factory supervision on the basis of direct labor hours, and telephone expense on the number of instruments.

The total overhead costs of operating each of the four departments can now be determined. The sum of the direct and indirect costs of operating the maintenance department is $5,600; medical service, $3,900; fabrication, $23,400; and assembly, $29,900.

Step 3. The next step is the *allocation* of the service department costs to the producing departments. The method chosen by the Donnell Company was to allocate maintenance department costs first on the basis of maintenance man hours used by other departments. The maintenance department serviced the medical department as well as the two producing departments. Thus, the medical department received an allocated share of maintenance costs. After the allocation of maintenance department costs was completed, medical department costs were allocated to the producing departments. This particular sequence was chosen because the maintenance department provided relatively more service to the medical department than the medical department provided to the maintenance department. As a general rule, the sequence should begin with the department that renders the greatest service to the greatest number of departments and continue stepwise to the departments giving the least service to other departments.[4]

The maintenance department costs in Exhibit 4-4 were allocated on the basis of maintenance man hours used. The fabrication department used 1,750 hours of maintenance time, resulting in an allocation of $3,500 [(1,750 ÷ 2,800) × $5,600]. Notice that the allocation is based upon 2,800 hours. Excluded are the 100 hours used by the maintenance department to take care of its own equipment. If these hours were included in the allocation base, the maintenance department would be apportioned some of its own costs. These would have to be reallocated, and the reallocations would continue indefinitely.

The medical services department costs were allocated on the basis of the number of employees. The assembly department received $2,500 of medical services costs [(50 ÷ 80) × $4,000]. Only 80 employees were used

[4]It should be observed that the medical department also provided services to the maintenance department, although the allocation procedure in this example does not take this into account. Our choice of allocating the maintenance department first and then allocating the medical department is not the only possibility. An alternative is to allocate the service departments directly to the producing departments without going through the sequential allocation of the service departments. A study of the many possible methods of allocating these costs is beyond the scope of our study in this text.

in the allocation, not the full 97; once the costs of a service department are allocated to the producing departments, no subsequent service department costs are reallocated to it.

Step 4. The final step involves the computation of departmental overhead rates so the fully allocated costs can be *applied* to the products. The total, fully allocated costs of the fabrication department are $28,400. Since the department used 4,000 machine hours, the overhead rate is $7.10 per machine hour ($28,400 ÷ 4,000 machine hours). The overhead rate for the assembly department is $8.60 per direct labor hour ($34,400 ÷ 4,000 direct labor hours).

The Donnell Company could have chosen to use a single, **plant-wide** (**blanket**) overhead rate for the entire company. If a plant-wide rate had been used, the allocation of indirect costs and service department costs would not have been necessary. The single rate would have been computed by dividing total factory overhead by some activity base. For the Donnell Company, a plant-wide rate based upon machine hours would have been $10.47 per machine hour ($62,800 ÷ 6,000 machine hours).

Why Make Departmental Allocations?

The steps necessary to prepare departmental factory overhead rates are complex and require many cost allocations. Notice in our simple illustration that the telephone expense, for example, was first allocated to the four departments, subsequently reallocated as part of the service department allocations, and, finally, averaged in the calculation of the overhead rates.

There are inherent weaknesses in allocating these indirect costs. First, the operating managers of the producing departments often have little influence over the allocation process. The effect of the allocation process is to imply that the managers are responsible for total costs. Yet they have had no control over the costs incurred or the efficiency of the service departments. If the service departments are inefficient their excess costs are transferred to the producing departments. Thus, allocation can easily disguise or hide operating inefficiencies.

Second, any allocation process will be imperfect. We search for cause and effect relationships, but they are not always apparent and clear. The result is a series of only partially accurate allocations. Each allocation in the sequence further hides the inaccuracies of the allocation process.

Finally, and most important, the allocation process ignores a basic rule of management decision making: Examine and consider only costs that differ between alternatives. The allocation process glosses over the facts that some costs are fixed and others variable and that some costs are controllable and others noncontrollable by a particular manager. The fully allocated costs are not useful in assessing a manager's performance and, on occasion, may distract management attention from the relevant costs.

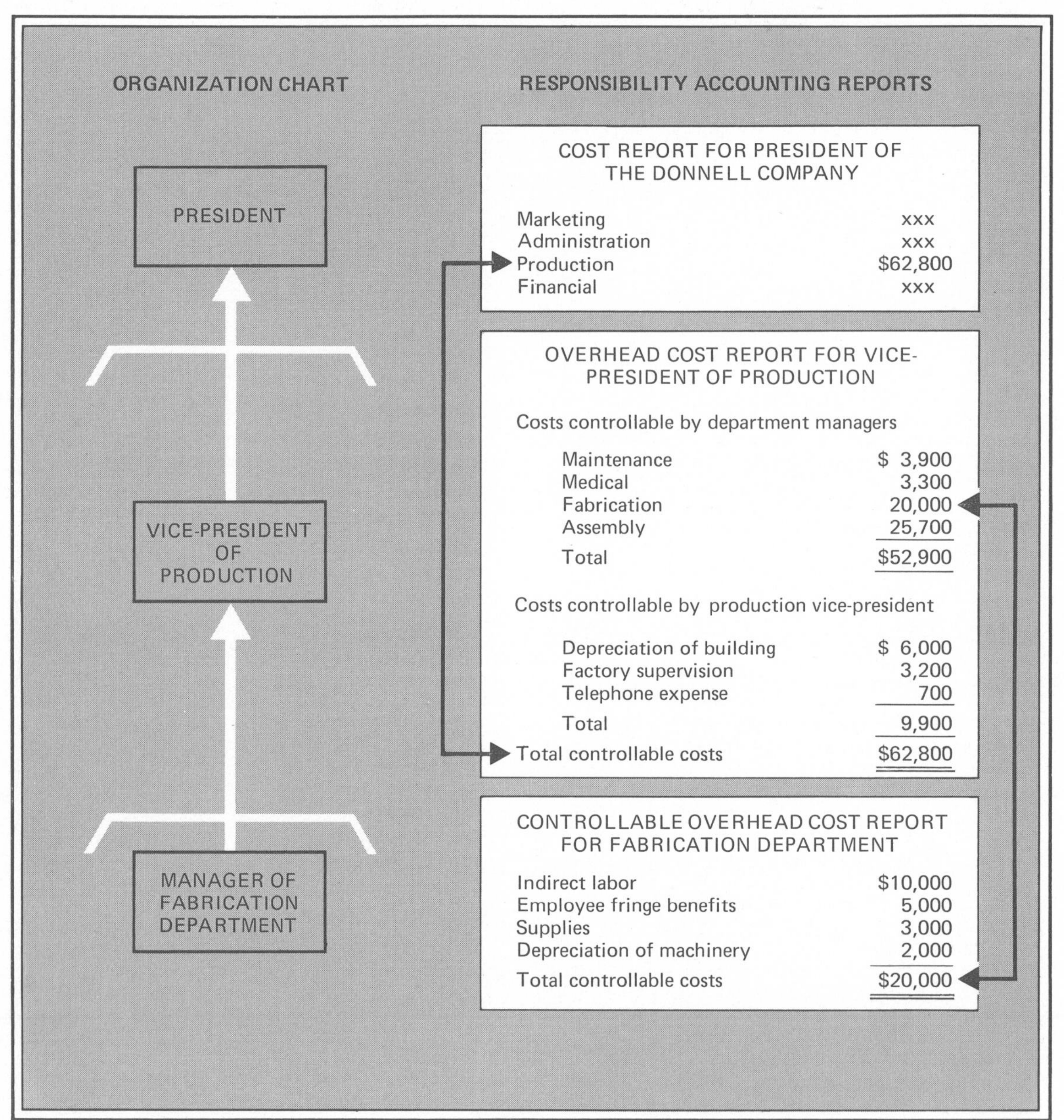

EXHIBIT 4-5
Responsibility reports of the Donnell Company

Because of these problems many firms follow the practice of preparing two sets of reports. A worksheet similar to Exhibit 4-4 would be prepared within the accounting department when the factory overhead rates are determined. Then, when reports are prepared for the operating managers, these costs are recombined into controllable and noncontrollable costs, as shown in Exhibit 4-5. The use of two reports allows the development of factory overhead rates within departments and alleviates the conflict of holding managers responsible for costs over which they have no control. Later in the text we will examine in greater detail the concept of responsibility reporting.

SUMMARY

Factory overhead is an indirect cost to the products. The factory overhead rate, factory overhead dollars divided by some measure of production output, is the accountant's method of allocating these costs to the product. The application of factory overhead to products requires the accountant to select a measure, such as units of output (machine hours, direct labor hours, or direct labor dollars), that best describes a cause and effect relationship between the factory overhead cost and the production output.

There are two types of factory overhead rates. The first is an historical factory overhead rate, where actual factory overhead cost is applied to the Work-in-Process Inventory after the production for the accounting period is completed. There will be no under- or overapplied factory overhead with historical factory overhead rates since actual factory overhead is applied using an actual activity measure. The second is a predetermined factory overhead rate that requires the accountant to estimate both factory overhead costs and production output before actual production begins. When a predetermined factory overhead rate is used, the actual overhead costs incurred are recorded in the Factory Overhead Control account. Factory overhead applied to Work-in-Process Inventory is recorded in the Factory Overhead Applied account. The difference between the two accounts is the under- or overapplied factory overhead.

Under- or overapplied factory overhead is the result of two factors: the spending variance and the volume variance. The spending variance measures how well the managers controlled their rate of expenditure. It is computed as the difference between the actual factory overhead costs incurred and the flexible budget adjusted to the actual activity level. The volume variance occurs because the volume used in calculating the predetermined fixed factory overhead rate differs from the actual volume attained. The volume variance measures the under- or overapplied fixed costs because the volume used in determining the fixed factory overhead rate differs from the actual volume used to apply factory overhead. The volume variance relates only to fixed costs; variable costs are constant per unit.

The selection of the predetermined factory overhead volume measure is important because the fixed costs in factory overhead will vary per unit of output with changes in output. Overhead rates may be based on three different capacity measures: first, practical capacity, the maximum capacity sustainable in the long run; second, normal capacity, the capacity necessary to meet sales demand in the long run; and third, expected or budgeted capacity, the volume planned for the coming accounting period.

In firms that have a departmental organization, it is often useful to calculate departmental factory overhead rates. This process requires the apportionment of indirect costs to the departments and the allocation of service department costs to producing departments. Separate factory overhead rates are then calculated for each producing department. The departmentalization of factory overhead costs is useful in determining departmental factory overhead rates, but it does not identify controllable and noncontrollable costs. For this reason, many firms recast their costs for management reports into a responsibility accounting format that identifies costs with the responsibility centers exercising control over them.

SUPPLEMENTARY READING

Beckett, John A. "A Study of the Principles of Allocating Costs." *The Accounting Review,* July, 1951.

Bergquist, Richard E. "Direct Labor v. Machine Hour Costing." *Management Accounting,* May, 1971.

Copeland, Ben R. "Analyzing Burden Variance for Profit Planning and Control." *Management Services,* January–February, 1965.

DeCoster, Don T. "Measurement of the Idle-Capacity Variance." *The Accounting Review,* April, 1966.

Horngren, Charles T. "A Contribution Margin Approach to the Analysis of Capacity Utilization." *The Accounting Review,* April, 1967.

National Association of Accountants. *Accounting for Costing of Capacity.* New York: National Association of Accountants, 1963.

Sharp, Harold E. "Control and Management of Indirect Expenses." *Management Accounting,* February, 1973.

Shwayder, K. "A Note on a Contribution Margin Approach to the Analysis of Capacity Utilization." *The Accounting Review,* January, 1968.

QUESTIONS

4-1 Factory overhead comprises a much larger part of total production costs than in the past. Why is this so? Should we expect the trend to continue?

4-2 In accounting for indirect costs there are three measurement objectives. Identify them and discuss.

4-3 "Only direct costs of a responsibility center are controllable by that responsibility center." Do you agree? Explain the concept of controllability in relation to direct and indirect costs.

4-4 What criteria can be used to determine an acceptable measure of production for allocating overhead to the products?

4-5 Compare the advantages and disadvantages of predetermined overhead rates and historical overhead rates. When are the effects of the two overhead rates identical?

4-6 Define the following bases for the determination of overhead rates: *unit of product, machine hours, direct labor hours,* and *direct labor dollars.* Under what circumstances should each be used? Name an industry that might use each type of overhead base.

4-7 What is the difference between departmental overhead rates and a blanket overhead rate? What are the major disadvantages of a blanket overhead rate? Major advantages?

4-8 The establishment of departmental overhead rates requires a four-step sequential process. What are these steps? Give examples.

4-9 Define and explain the differences among *practical capacity, normal capacity,* and *expected (budgeted) capacity.*

4-10 "The budget variance indicates to management how well costs were controlled in comparison to the firm's plans. The volume variance has little management usefulness." Do you agree or disagree? Why?

4-11 Explain the difference between the volume variance and the activity variance as they were developed in this chapter. Is either useful for performance measurement?

4-12 The most important criterion in choosing an allocation base for apportioning expenses to departments is the discovery of any cause and effect relationships that exist. Why is this so? How can cause and effect relationships be determined?

4-13 What is a *service department?* Name a few in a manufacturing setting. Name a few in a university setting.

4-14 "The basic rule of decision making is to examine only those costs that differ between alternatives." This statement seems to be contradictory with the cost allocation procedures. Is it? Why or why not?

4-15 The allocation of indirect costs can disguise or hide operating inefficiencies. Why is this so? What effect might this have on the operating manager of the producing department?

PROBLEMS

4-16 Indicate whether the following statements are *true* or *false.*

1. The machine-hour basis of applying overhead is appropriate where direct labor costs are relatively low and machine costs are relatively high.
2. The historical overhead rate is generally preferred over the predetermined overhead rate because it is precise and the predetermined overhead rate is only an estimate.
3. If activity fluctuates widely during a year due to seasonal variations, the historical overhead rate will provide more constant unit costs from month to month than will a predetermined overhead rate.

4. The overhead budget variance is the difference between actual overhead costs and the flexible budget adjusted for actual hours.

5. The volume variance is the difference between fixed overhead applied and the flexible budget allowance for fixed costs.

6. The volume variance will usually be larger if overhead is applied with an historical overhead rate than with a predetermined overhead rate.

7. The distinction between direct and indirect costs is their traceability to cost objectives.

8. Allocation of overhead costs to producing departments is necessary to identify operating inefficiencies in service departments.

9. Overhead rates fluctuate because of the presence of fixed costs interacting with changes in production volume.

10. Practical capacity is the capacity necessary to meet sales needs for the coming year.

4-17 Match the following terms and descriptions.

1. Direct costs
2. Responsibility center
3. Joint costs
4. Predetermined factory overhead rates
5. Practical capacity
6. Expected capacity
7. Normal capacity
8. Budget variance
9. Activity variance
10. Volume variance

a. Capacity needed to meet sales over a three- to five-year period.
b. Estimated factory overhead divided by estimated direct labor hours.
c. Output capability of the existing plant in sustained operations over a long period of time.
d. Segment of the organization in which an individual manager is held accountable for those activities he can directly affect.
e. Costs that can logically be associated with some costing objective.
f. Common costs.
g. Absorption costing variance due to producing more or less units than planned.
h. Variance due to selling more or less units than planned.
i. Planned level of operations.
j. Deviation of actual costs from a budget allowance.

4-18 The Allocate-all Company has ten service departments, as shown in the following list. It is company policy to allocate the costs of all service departments to the four producing departments in order to compute department overhead rates.

a. Building and grounds
b. Factory personnel department
c. General factory administration
d. Inventory storeroom
e. Cafeteria (operating loss)
f. Product engineering
g. Quality control
h. First aid
i. Cost accounting
j. Standby power generation plant

REQUIRED:
For each service department:
A. Indicate an order of allocation and state your reasons for choosing this order.
B. Indicate the basis of allocation (i.e. square feet, number of employees, etc.) and why this allocation basis was selected.

4-19 The Family Health Clinic, a not-for-profit clinic serving a low-income neighborhood, recorded a loss last year. In order to adjust the billing rates it is necessary to allocate the costs of the seven support departments to the seven mission departments.

The service department that provides the greatest service to other departments and draws the least from other departments is the first allocated, and so on, until the costs of all support departments are allocated. The seven mission departments, each of which bills its patients, are: social service, mental health, dental health, nutrition, pediatrics, internal medicine, and nursing.

REQUIRED:
For each of the following support departments, indicate your order of allocation and the preferable basis of allocation, and briefly explain why you chose the order and bases.

Support Department	*Service Rendered*
Eye clinic	(Services patients from pediatrics, internal medicine, and nursing)
Laboratory	(Services patients from pediatrics, internal medicine, and nursing)
Radiology	(Services patients from pediatrics, internal medicine, and nursing)
Accounting and medical records	(Maintains medical and financial records for entire center)
Administration	(Clinic director and his staff)
Evaluation	(Reviews activities of mission departments to maintain quality)
Building	(Provides space and maintenance of facilities)

4-20 The Bennett Corporation is a manufacturing concern with three separate production departments. The following statistics have been kept concerning these departments.

	Department 1	*Department 2*	*Department 3*
Direct labor hours	40,000	25,000	22,000
Number of employees	450	220	240
Factory floor space (square feet)	12,000	6,000	4,000
Machine hours worked	3,000	8,000	5,000

The firm is trying to determine the most appropriate base with which to allocate the following costs.

Factory maintenance	$24,200
Depreciation of factory building	$33,000
Employee cafeteria	$24,300
Depreciation of machinery	$32,000
Supervisory salaries	$65,520

REQUIRED:

A. What method of allocation would you recommend for each indirect cost? Why?

B. Does the order of allocation matter in this situation (i.e. depreciation of building allocated before factory maintenance, etc.)? Why or why not?

C. Prepare a schedule that shows your allocations and the total costs charged to each of the three producing departments.
D. Would your allocation change for factory maintenance if you discovered that it was incurred almost entirely to service the factory machinery? How?

4-21 The Raintree Manufacturing Company uses an absorption costing system with a predetermined rate for the application of factory overhead to production. Factory overhead is applied on a machine-hour basis in Department A and a direct labor-hour basis in Department B. The firm made the following projections at the beginning of the year.

	Department A	*Department B*
Direct labor cost	$32,000	$48,750
Factory overhead	$36,000	$37,500
Direct labor hours	1,000	5,000
Machine hours	250	1,250

REQUIRED:
A. Compute the predetermined factory overhead rate for each department.
B. The cost sheet for Job #125 shows actual costs and activity as follows:

	Department A	*Department B*
Direct materials	$18	$32
Direct labor	$24	$16
Direct labor hours	3	2
Machine hours	1	12

1. How much overhead should be applied to Job #125?
2. What is the total cost of Job #125?

C. At the end of the year the actual overhead data were as follows:

	Department A	*Department B*
Direct labor cost	$36,000	$42,000
Factory overhead	$42,000	$36,000
Direct labor hours	1,200	4,800
Machine hours	300	1,100

Determine the amount of under- or overapplied factory overhead by department, and indicate if it was overapplied or underapplied.

D. What would be the historical factory overhead rate based upon a plant-wide factory overhead rate using direct labor cost as basis of application? If this historical rate is used, how much factory overhead would be applied to Job #125?

4-22 Stove Manufacturing Company estimated the following factory overhead costs for 19X8.

Variable factory overhead:	
Indirect labor	$ 3,600
Factory supplies	1,800
Fixed factory overhead:	
Heat and light	800
Factory depreciation	4,700
Factory administration	8,900
	$19,800

The Stove Company planned to produce 600 units using a total of 1800 direct labor hours. Cost behavior studies have shown that changes in variable factory overhead costs relate closely to changes in direct labor hours.

REQUIRED:

A. Calculate the predetermined rate based upon:
   1. The number of units produced
   2. Direct labor hours

B. What is the motivation in calculating these factory overhead rates? Explain.

C. Assume that actual production for 19X8 was 500 units requiring 1600 direct labor hours. Calculate the applied factory overhead based upon (1) units and (2) labor hours.

D. Assume that actual factory overhead costs were:

Indirect labor	$3,000
Factory supplies	$1,700
Heat and light	$ 850
Factory depreciation	$4,100
Factory administration	$8,900

Determine the amount of under- or overapplied factory overhead if factory overhead was applied on (1) units and (2) labor hours.

E. Prepare a report to the factory manager that indicates how well he controlled his factory overhead costs during 19X8.

4-23 The Speedy Service Company produces a line of ball bearings with the following cost structure.

Direct materials	$65,000
Direct labor	$18,900
Variable factory overhead	$24,000
Fixed factory overhead	$32,700

During the year production required 2,100 direct labor hours and 6,300 machine hours.

REQUIRED:

A. Determine the factory overhead rate under absorption costing using (1) direct labor hours, (2) direct labor dollars, and (3) machine hours.

B. Which method of applying factory overhead to the products seems most appropriate? Why?

4-24 The White Circle Corporation produces a line of black cubes. For the coming year management anticipates the following activity level.

Sales (80,000 cubes)	$160,000
Estimated factory overhead	$ 24,000

Since all the products are the same, the unit of product method is used to calculate the predetermined factory overhead rate. Management is considering expanding its product line to include red triangles. Estimated sales are 40,000 black cubes and 40,000 red triangles.

REQUIRED:

A. Would the total units produced still be an appropriate base to determine the factory overhead rate after the new products are added? (Give the factors that might affect your decision.)

B. What data would you like to gather to select an appropriate application base?

4-25 The new accountant for the Cheepee Calculator Company recorded the following costs in the Factory Overhead Control account.

FACTORY OVERHEAD CONTROL

Factory supervision	$ 2,500	
Indirect labor	4,250	
Depreciation of building	12,000	
Repairs	3,000	
Heat, light, and power	4,200	
Supplies	2,500	
Company president	2,000	
Shipping expense	6,000	
Company cafeteria (loss)	800	

During the month 12,000 direct labor hours were used. An examination of the accounts revealed the following:

a. The entire depreciation on the building was charged to factory overhead. One-sixth of the building is devoted to selling and administrative areas.

b. Property tax of $600 and insurance of $300 applicable to the factory were charged to administration costs.

c. The president spends about two-thirds of his time in the factory. The accountant, therefore, charged two-thirds of his salary to factory overhead.
d. Two-thirds of the repairs represent the cost of renovating the president's office. The balance applies to factory equipment.
e. The flexible budget for heat, light, and power is $1,800 plus $.20 per direct labor hour. The fixed portion represents heat and light for the entire building.
f. Supplies included $500 of selling supplies.
g. Finished units are shipped directly from the factory.
h. The company employs 100 people, 80 of which are factory personnel.

REQUIRED:
A. Correct the Factory Overhead account to include the proper costs.
B. Assuming that the predetermined factory overhead rate is $2.20 per direct labor hour, compute the under- or overapplied factory overhead.

4-26 The management of the Leadbottom Clipper Ship Corporation was trying to develop predetermined factory overhead rates for the coming year. Engineering studies indicated the following:

Practical capacity	125,000 direct labor hours
Normal capacity	115,000 direct labor hours
Expected capacity	108,000 direct labor hours

The cost accounting department estimated fixed costs to be $66,000 and variable costs to be $.75 per direct labor hour.

REQUIRED:
A. Determine the factory overhead rate under absorption costing for each capacity.
B. Which activity level would you recommend that management adopt? Why?
C. Assume that the company adopted the normal capacity for determining its factory overhead rate and that through a severe strike the volume dropped to only 72,000 direct labor hours. What will be the amount of under- or overapplied fixed costs because of this volume decline? Will it affect net income under absorption costing?

4-27 The Weldone Drapery Company uses an absorption costing system with a predetermined factory overhead rate. The rate in use this month was based upon the following estimates.

Estimated fixed factory overhead	$ 7,480
Estimated variable factory overhead	23,800
Estimated total factory overhead	$31,280
Estimated direct labor cost	$68,000

During the accounting period the direct labor cost was actually $66,000. Actual factory overhead was $33,000, of which $7,350 was fixed factory overhead.

REQUIRED:

A. Determine the factory overhead rate the company would use if it based the rate upon direct labor cost.

B. Determine the actual factory overhead applied to Work-in-Process Inventory and the amount of factory overhead under- or overapplied.

C. Calculate (1) the total budget variance, (2) the fixed budget variance, and (3) the variable budget variance.

D. How do the variances in requirement C aid management in controlling costs? What might be some of the causes for these variances?

E. Determine the amount of factory overhead under- or overapplied because the actual direct labor cost was different than the predetermined labor cost. What does this tell management?

4-28 The following data were taken from the cost records of the Checkered Shirt Company.

Practical capacity	500,000 direct labor hours
Normal capacity	400,000 direct labor hours
Expected capacity	350,000 direct labor hours
Actual production level	300,000 direct labor hours
Salesmen's sales orders	340,000 direct labor hours
Production scheduled	310,000 direct labor hours

The company produces a single product, which it sells for $5 each. Variable production costs are $3 per unit and include a variable factory overhead cost of $.50 per unit. Budgeted fixed costs at normal capacity are $2,400,000. It takes, on the average, one-fourth of a direct labor hour to produce one unit of product.

REQUIRED:

A. Prepare an analysis of the utilization of capacity in terms of direct labor hours.

B. Prepare an analysis of the utilization of capacity in terms of lost contribution margin.

C. Prepare an analysis of the utilization of capacity in terms of the fixed factory overhead rate, assuming the rate is based on normal capacity.

D. Which of the three schedules do you believe would have the most meaning to management? Why?

4-29 The Penny Pen Company manufactures two styles of ball-point pens. The most popular style sells for $.20. The more expensive pen sells for $1.20. Over the years it has sold four $.20 pens for each $1.20 pen. The company has an *overall* contribution margin of 40%. A highly automated process can produce 100 popular and 25 expensive pens per machine hour. The plant is designed to operate 20,000 machine hours at practical plant capacity, although it has some excess capability. Normally the company operates only 18,000 hours to meet its sales demand. This particular year it has experienced some setback in the marketplace since a competitor started business. Management felt that 15,000 hours would meet this year's sales demand. However, the sales staff worked extra hard and gained orders for 17,000 hours worth of product. Unfortunately the production control department achieved only 16,000 hours of production because of poor scheduling of machine repairs. Actual factory overhead costs amounted to $240,000.

REQUIRED:
Prepare a schedule setting forth how well the company utilized its capacity. Use the lost contribution margin to quantify your report.

4-30 Five independent situations involving overhead follow. In each case you are to determine the amount where the question mark appears.

	A	*B*	*C*	*D*	*E*
Flexible budget for factory overhead:					
Fixed	$ 1,000	$2,000	$?	$ 4,000	$ 5,000
Variable (per direct labor hour)	$ 5	$?	$ 3	$?	$ 1
Planned hours	1,000	500	2,000	1,000	?
Budgeted factory overhead for year	$?	$4,000	$9,000	$ 6,000	$ 9,000
Factory overhead rate per direct labor hour	$?	$?	$ 4.50	$?	$ 2.25
Actual direct labor hours worked	500	1,000	?	1,000	2,000
Factory overhead applied to production	$?	$8,000	$9,000	$?	$?
Budget allowance based on actual hours	$ 3,500	$?	$?	$ 6,000	$ 7,000
Actual factory overhead	$ 3,800	$6,000	$9,000	$?	$?
Volume variance*	$?	$?	$?	$ 0	$(2,500)
Budget variance*	$ (300)	$?	$?	$(1,000)	$ 1,000

*Parentheses indicate the variance is unfavorable.

4-31 The Crown Company uses predetermined departmental factory overhead rates to apply factory overhead to its products. The firm has two production departments (Departments P-1 and P-2) and two service departments (Departments S-1 and S-2). The following factory overhead data are for the month of March.

	S-1	*S-2*	*P-1*	*P-2*
Indirect labor	$ 9,000	$3,000	$ 40,000	$ 50,000
Indirect materials	1,000	800	15,000	22,900
Insurance	100	200	2,000	2,150
Heat, light, power	1,700	500	13,250	11,450
Supervision	1,640	660	1,850	3,800
Total costs	$13,440	$5,160	$ 72,100	$ 90,300
Number of employees	20	10	100	50
Square feet occupied	2,000	1,000	7,000	5,000
Direct labor hours			42,000	48,000
Direct labor dollars			$160,000	$194,000
Machine hours			5,000	10,000

The company follows the policy of allocating the costs of Department S-1 first, using the number of employees in the departments as a basis of allocation. The costs of Department S-2 are apportioned next on the basis of square-footage occupied by the departments.

REQUIRED:

A. Prepare a worksheet to determine the fully allocated costs of Departments P-1 and P-2.

B. Assuming that Department P-1 uses direct labor hours to apply factory overhead and Department P-2 uses direct labor cost, determine the departmental factory overhead rates.

4-32 Your client recently purchased an engineering consulting practice from James Dider, who wishes to retire, and agreed to employ Mr. Dider and all of his employees for one year. You have been engaged to determine an estimate of the total cost of operations per chargeable man hour, for each member of the professional staff, in order that suitable billing rates may be established.

Your estimates of the hours for which the professional staff will be paid, their annual salaries, and the proportions of their working hours that will not be directly chargeable to any specific client follow.

Employee	*Total Hours*	*Annual Salary*	*Percentage of Time Devoted to Firm Overhead*
Able	1,200	$ 2,400	40%
Briscol	2,400	$12,000	10%
Case	2,000	$ 8,000	20%
Dider	800	$10,000	40%
Emel	2,400	$ 7,200	5%

Mr. Dider's other costs of operating his firm, including clerical wages, have averaged about $39,100 per year for the last three years.

REQUIRED:

A. Prepare schedules computing the following for the year subsequent to the acquisition of Dider's engineering consulting practice:
   1. Total indirect cost, including the nonbillable time of the professional employees.
   2. Total employees' salaries directly billable to clients.
   3. A billing rate per hour of billable time for each member of the professional staff.

B. A number of independent situations are listed below. State whether each situation, without considering other possible changes, would result in indirect costs being (1) overapplied, (2) applied as planned or having no effect, or (3) underapplied. Also state the reason for this result.

1. Able spends 50% of his time in nonproductive functions.
2. Briscol works 100 hours less than expected during the year and his salary is reduced accordingly.
3. Case works 100 hours more than expected during the year and his salary is increased accordingly.
4. Dider works 200 hours more than expected during the year and his salary is unchanged.
5. Emel received a salary increase, but his billing rate is not changed.

(CPA adapted)

4-33 Thrift-Shops, Inc. operates a chain of three food stores in a state that recently enacted legislation permitting municipalities within the state to levy an income tax on corporations operating within their respective municipalities. The legislation establishes a uniform tax rate, which the municipalities may levy, and regulations which provide that the tax is to be computed on income derived within the taxing municipality after a reasonable and consistent allocation of general overhead expenses. General overhead expenses have not been allocated to individual stores previously and include warehouse, general office, advertising, and delivery expenses.

Each of the municipalities in which Thrift-Shops, Inc. operates a store has levied the corporate income tax as provided by state legislation, and management is considering two plans for allocating general overhead expenses to the stores. The 19X9 operating results before general overhead and taxes for each store were as shown in the accompanying statement.

	Store			
	Ashville	*Burns*	*Clinton*	*Total*
Sales (net)	$416,000	$353,600	$270,400	$1,040,000
Less: Cost of sales	215,700	183,300	140,200	539,200
Gross margin	$200,300	$170,300	$130,200	$ 500,800
Less local operating expenses:				
Fixed	$ 60,800	$ 48,750	$ 50,200	$ 159,750
Variable	54,700	64,220	27,448	146,368
Total	$115,500	$112,970	$ 77,648	$ 306,118
Income before general overhead and taxes	$ 84,800	$ 57,330	$ 52,552	$ 194,682

General overhead expenses were as follows:		
Warehousing and delivery expenses:		
Warehouse depreciation	$ 20,000	
Warehouse operations	30,000	
Delivery expenses	40,000	$ 90,000
Central office expenses:		
Advertising	$ 18,000	
Central office salaries	37,000	
Other central office expenses	28,000	83,000
Total general overhead		$ 173,000

Additional information includes the following:

1. One-fifth of the warehouse space is used to house the central office, and depreciation on this space is included in other central office expenses. Warehouse operating expenses vary with quantity of merchandise sold.

2. Delivery expenses vary with distance and number of deliveries. The distances from the warehouse to each store and the number of deliveries made in 19X9 are illustrated in the following tabulation.

Store	*Miles*	*Number of Deliveries*
Ashville	120	140
Burns	200	64
Clinton	100	104

3. All advertising is prepared by the central office and is distributed in the areas in which stores are located.

4. As each store was opened, the fixed portion of central office salaries increased $7,000 and other central office expenses increased $2,500. Basic fixed central office salaries amount to $10,000 and basic fixed other central office expenses amount to $12,000. The remainder of central office salaries and the remainder of other central office expenses vary with sales.

REQUIRED:

A. For each of the following plans for allocating general overhead expenses, compute the income of each store that would be subject to the municipal levy on corporation income.

Plan 1. Allocate all general overhead expenses on the basis of sales volume.

Plan 2. First, allocate central office salaries and other central office expenses evenly to warehouse operations and each store. Second, allocate the resulting warehouse operations expenses, warehouse depreciation, and advertising to each store on the basis of sales volume. Third, allocate delivery expenses to each store on the basis of delivery miles times number of deliveries.

B. Management has decided to expand one of the three stores to increase sales by $50,000. The expansion will increase local fixed operating expenses by $7,500 and require ten additional deliveries from the warehouse. Determine which store management should select for expansion to maximize corporate profits. *(CPA adapted)*

4-34 The Parker Manufacturing Company has two production departments (fabrication and assembly) and three service departments (general factory administration, factory maintenance, and factory cafeteria). The following is a summary of costs and other data for each department prior to allocation of service department costs for the year ended June 30, 19X3.

	Fabrication	Assembly	General Factory Administration	Factory Maintenance	Factory Cafeteria
Direct labor costs	$1,950,000	$2,050,000	$90,000	$82,100	$87,000
Direct material costs	$3,130,000	$ 950,000	—	$65,000	$91,000
Manufacturing overhead costs	$1,650,000	$1,850,000	$70,000	$56,100	$62,000
Direct labor hours	562,500	437,500	31,000	27,000	42,000
Number of employees	280	200	12	8	20
Square-footage occupied	88,000	72,000	1,750	2,000	4,800

The costs of the general factory administration department, factory maintenance department, and factory cafeteria are allocated on the basis of direct labor hours, square footage occupied, and number of employees, respectively.

REQUIRED:
Round all final calculations to the nearest dollar.

1. Assuming that Parker elects to distribute service department costs directly to production departments without inter-service department cost allocation, the amount of factory maintenance department costs that would be allocated to the fabrication department would be
   a. $0
   b. $111,760
   c. $106,091
   d. $91,440
2. Assuming the same method of allocation as in item 1, the amount of general factory administration department costs allocated to the assembly department would be
   a. $0
   b. $63,636
   c. $70,000
   d. $90,000
3. Assume that Parker elects to distribute service department costs to other service departments (starting with the service department with the greatest total costs) as well as the production departments. (Note: Once a service department's costs have been reallocated, no subsequent service department costs are recirculated back to it.) The amount of factory cafeteria department costs allocated to the factory maintenance department would be
   a. $0
   b. $96,000
   c. $3,840
   d. $6,124

4. Assuming the same method of allocation as in item 3, the amount of factory maintenance department costs allocated to the factory cafeteria would be
a. $0
b. $5,787
c. $5,856
d. $148,910

(CPA adapted)

4-35 The Cox Company, manufacturer of a single product, operated at 80% of normal capacity in 19X8. Since Cox bases its factory overhead rate on normal capacity, the company had a substantial amount of underapplied factory overhead for the period.

Early in 19X9 Cox receives an order for a substantial number of units, at 30% off the regular $7 sales price. The controller wants to accept the order because $.80 of the total manufacturing cost of $5 per unit is fixed factory overhead and because the additional units can be produced within the company's practical capacity.

The president of Cox Company wants to know if you agree with the controller.

REQUIRED:

A. Differentiate among practical capacity, normal capacity, and expected capacity.
B. Discuss the financial considerations that the president should review before accepting or rejecting the order.
C. Because of this order, the financial statements of the Cox Company as of December 31, 19X9 are likely to show overapplied factory overhead.
1. What is overapplied factory overhead?
2. What are likely to be the major causes of overapplied factory overhead in 19X9?
3. How, if at all, should overapplied factory overhead be treated in the financial statements as of December 31, 19X9?

(CPA adapted)

5 Variable Product Costing and the Contribution Margin Approach

PRODUCT COSTING WITH ABSORPTION AND VARIABLE COSTING
VARIABLE AND ABSORPTION COSTING ILLUSTRATED
VARIABLE AND ABSORPTION COSTING ACROSS TIME PERIODS
EXTERNAL REPORTING AND VARIABLE COSTING
INTERNAL REPORTING AND THE CONTRIBUTION MARGIN APPROACH
Variable Costing and the Contribution Margin Approach
Contribution Margin Approach and Cost-Volume-Profit Analysis
Contribution Margin Approach in Nonmanufacturing Activities
Contribution Margin Approach and Product Line Contributions
Limitations of the Contribution Margin Approach
ALTERNATIVE PROPOSALS
SUMMARY

Before the advent of industrialization, with its concurrent heavy equipment investments, production costs consisted primarily of material and labor costs. These **prime costs,** the sum of direct materials and direct labor, were the only production costs of any significance to be inventoried. When industrialization began requiring large investments in capacity, the growth of factory overhead costs was rapid. For the first time the differences between fixed and variable costs became relevant because many of the costs of providing the productive capacity were fixed. Accountants have long measured the cost of an asset as the amount expended to bring it to a proper condition and location to use. It made intuitive sense to include in the unit cost of inventory *all* the costs necessary to make it salable, including the costs of capacity. Until recently accountants did not think of costs as fixed and variable, only as production and nonproduction costs.

By the turn of the twentieth century, accounting in the United States was solidified in the use of absorption product costing. Absorption product costing related the accounting cost flow system with physical activity in the plant. Until recently most accounting activity focused upon stewardship reporting via income measurement; little attention was paid to the specific problems of information for management decision making. Absorption costing became generally accepted practice in external, financial reporting.

Independent of accounting, however, economists were using the nature of fixed and variable cost behavior patterns in their marginal analysis. In the 1930s economic theory became more widely integrated with accounting thought, and an alternative to absorption costing was proposed. This alternative, which we call **variable costing,**[1] revolved around cost analysis from a fixed and variable viewpoint, rather than from a production and nonproduction viewpoint. The 1940s added impetus to the study of fixed and variable costs in accounting. World War II brought an urgency to make efficient economic allocation decisions, and many of our current scientific decision-making theories and models were born during this period. By the 1950s there was considerable discussion among accountants regarding alternative methods of presenting cost data for both internal and external purposes.

In this chapter we will look at the two alternatives most widely proposed for reporting inventory values: absorption costing and variable costing.

PRODUCT COSTING WITH ABSORPTION AND VARIABLE COSTING

Important differences exist between absorption and variable costing methods. One way to see these differences is to compare the way in which each system affects inventory values and income determination. From this financial re-

[1]It is also called **direct costing** by many accountants in the United States, although this term is a misnomer. In England it is called **marginal costing.** We will use the more descriptive term, *variable costing,* in this text.

porting view, product and period costs are relevant because they are defined differently by each costing method.

You will remember that product costs are costs that are held in the Work-in-Process Inventory until production is complete, and in the Finished Goods Inventory until the products with which they are associated are sold. Product costs are matched with revenue on a sales basis. Period costs, on the other hand, are not included in the inventory. They are matched with revenue on a time-period basis.

Absorption costing defines product costs as including *all* costs of production, and period costs as *all* nonproduction costs. The product "absorbs" all costs necessary to produce it and have it in salable form. Exhibit 5-1 shows the flow of costs in an absorption costing system. The white boxes represent product costs; the dark boxes are period costs. The production cost flow with absorption costing results in a unit cost that can be described as the *average unit cost to produce.*

Variable costing stems from an entirely different premise than absorption costing. Beginning with the idea that the separation of costs into their fixed and variable components provides management with information relevant for differential pricing and production decisions, variable costers redefine product and period costs. Variable costing defines the product costs as the variable costs to produce the product. Fixed production costs and all nonproduction costs are treated as period costs. The cost flow pattern for variable costing is shown in Exhibit 5-2. The white boxes represent product costs under the variable costing method; the dark boxes are period costs. A close examination of this diagram shows that the unit cost of the Work-in-Process Inventory and the Finished Goods Inventory can be described as the *variable cost to produce.*

VARIABLE AND ABSORPTION COSTING ILLUSTRATED

To illustrate the differences between variable and absorption costing in measuring inventory values and net income, let's assume that the McKay Manufacturing Company manufactures toy rocking horses. During the past year it manufactured 200,000 horses, but sold only 190,000 of them. The final inventory was 10,000 horses, since the period was started with no beginning inventory. The 190,000 horses were sold for $25 each, and the following production costs were incurred: direct materials $1,000,000; direct labor $1,200,000; variable factory overhead $800,000; and fixed factory overhead $600,000. The nonproduction costs were $700,000, of which $320,000 were fixed costs. Production costs per unit included: direct materials $5 ($1,000,000 ÷ 200,000 units); direct labor $6 ($1,200,000 ÷ 200,000 units); variable factory overhead $4 ($800,000 ÷ 200,000 units); and fixed factory overhead $3 ($600,000 ÷ 200,000 units).

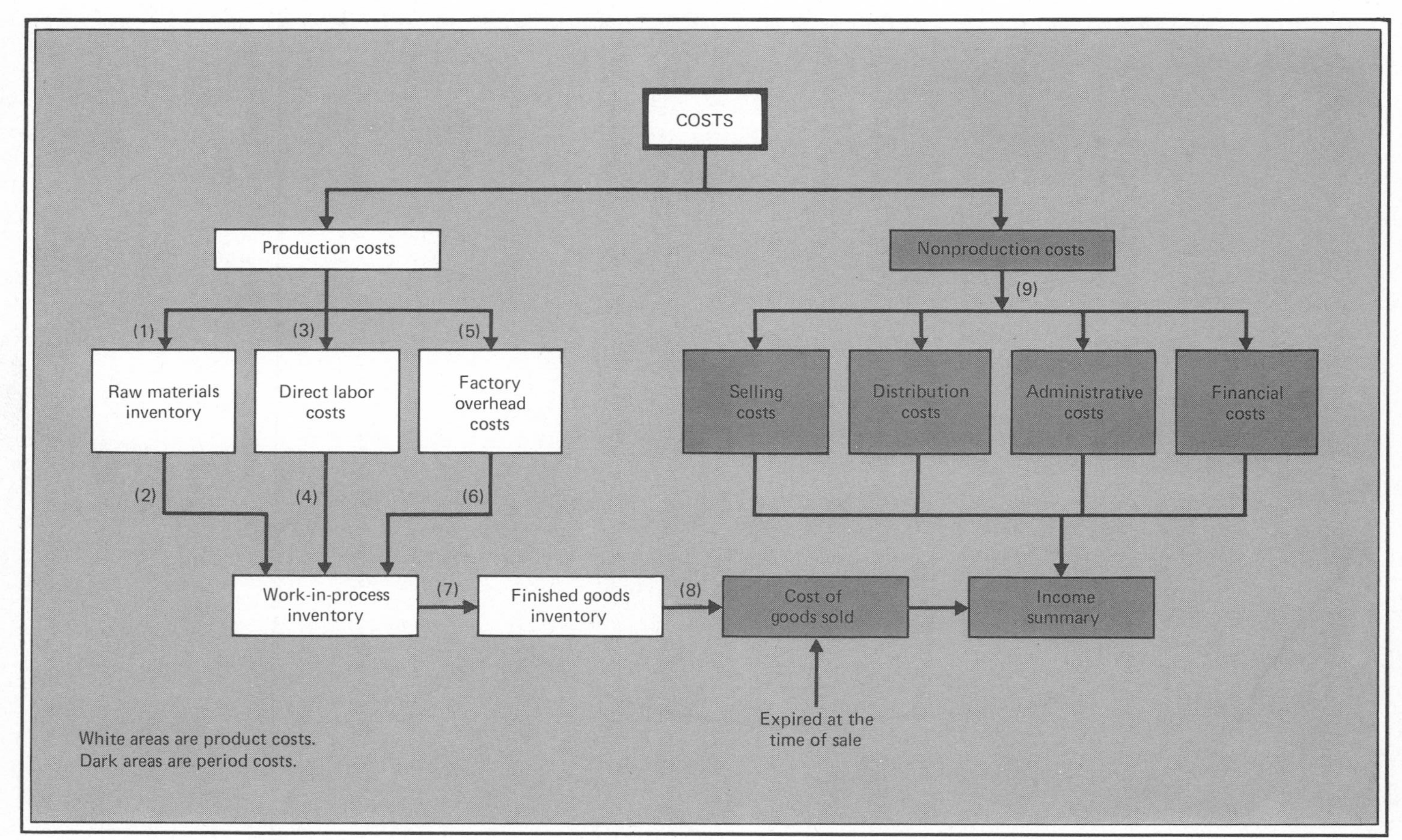

EXHIBIT 5-1
Cost flow with absorption costing

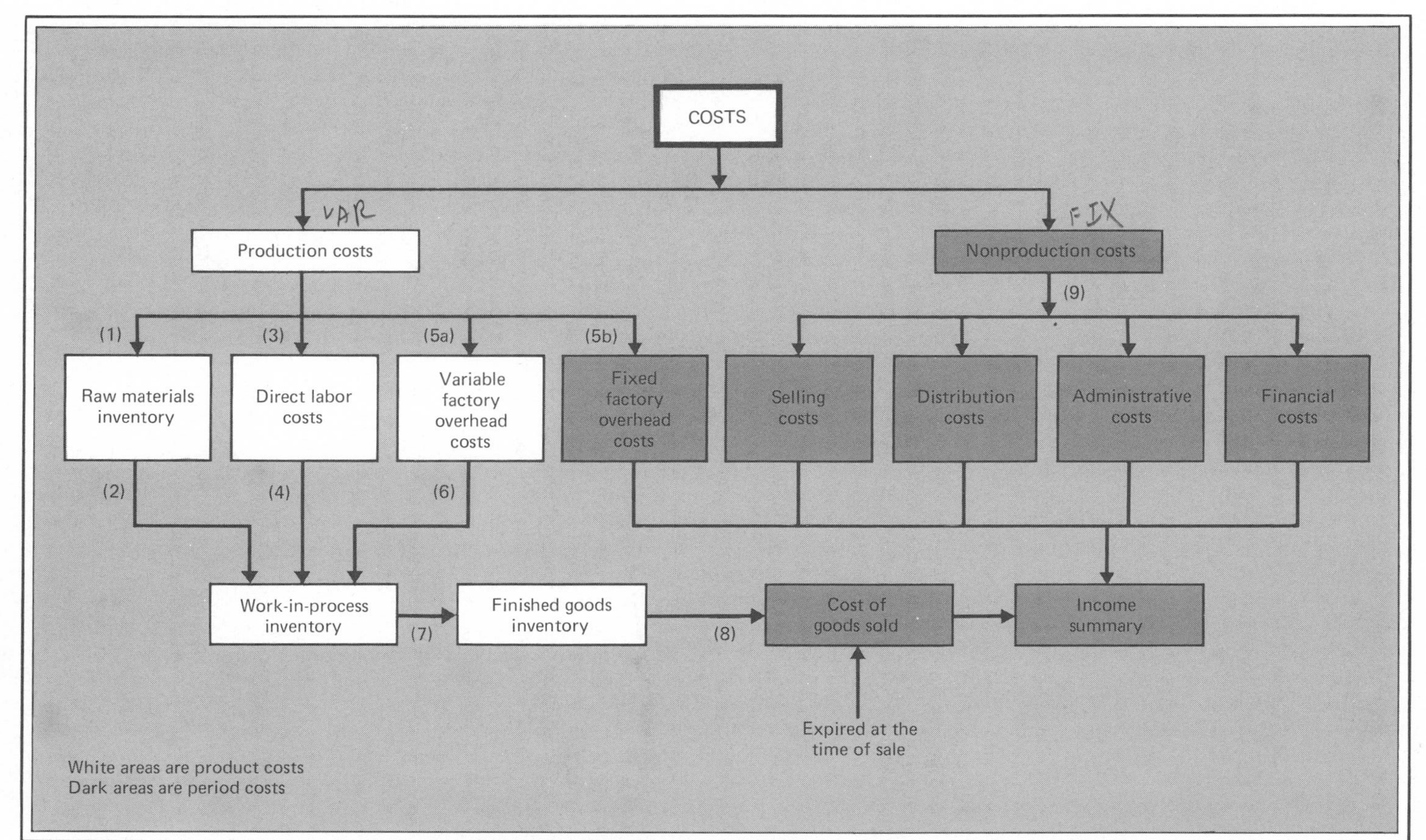

EXHIBIT 5-2
Cost flow with variable costing

The product unit costs to be inventoried under the two costing systems are as follows:

	Absorption Costing	*Variable Costing*
Direct material	$ 5	$ 5
Direct labor	6	6
Variable factory overhead	4	4
Fixed factory overhead	3	0
Total product cost	$18	$15

If the firm adopted variable costing, the unit cost of production, including only variable product costs, would be $15. If the firm adopted absorption costing, the unit cost of production would be $18. Obviously the difference between the two costing systems is the inclusion of the $3 per unit of fixed factory overhead in the product under absorption costing. Fixed factory overhead is treated as a product cost in absorption costing, whereas in variable costing it is treated as a period cost and is not allocated to the individual products.

Comparative income statements in Exhibit 5-3 show the effects of these two costing systems upon net income. The net income shown on the absorption costing income statement is $30,000 larger than the net income shown on the variable costing income statement. In variable costing the total fixed production costs of $600,000 were treated as a period cost; that is, all $600,000 was deducted in the current accounting period when the costs were incurred. In absorption costing only $570,000 of the fixed costs are included in the cost of goods sold, which was matched with revenue; the other $30,000 was retained in the final inventory of horses. The company produced 200,000 horses, but it sold only 190,000. Thus, the final inventory increased by 10,000 units. Under variable costing the final inventory would be $150,000 (10,000 units × $15); under absorption costing the final inventory would be $180,000 (10,000 units × $18). If the beginning and ending inventories of unsold horses had been zero, the net income under both systems would have been the same.

VARIABLE AND ABSORPTION COSTING ACROSS TIME PERIODS

Some accountants have argued that variable costing should be used in external reporting in lieu of absorption costing. One argument used to support this view is that fixed costs are the result of providing capacity in general, and that this productive capacity does not relate to any one specific unit. Another argument for variable costing is that fixed costs are more closely related to the passage of time than to production and thus are properly

VARIABLE COSTING

MC KAY MANUFACTURING COMPANY
INCOME STATEMENT
For the Year Ended December 31, 19X5

Sales (190,000 x $25)		$4,750,000	100%
Less variable costs:			
Production costs (200,000 x $15)	$3,000,000		
Less: Cost of units in ending inventory (10,000 x $15)	150,000		
Variable production costs of units sold (190,000 x $15)	$2,850,000		
Variable nonproduction costs (190,000 x $2)	380,000	3,230,000	68%
Contribution margin (190,000 x $8)		$1,520,000	32%
Less fixed costs:			
Fixed production costs	$ 600,000		
Fixed nonproduction costs	320,000	920,000	
Net income		$ 600,000	

ABSORPTION COSTING

MC KAY MANUFACTURING COMPANY
INCOME STATEMENT
For the Year Ended December 31, 19X5

Sales (190,000 x $25)		$4,750,000	100%
Less cost of goods sold:			
Production costs (200,000 x $18)	$3,600,000		
Less: Cost of units in ending inventory (10,000 x $18)	180,000	3,420,000	72%
Gross margin		$1,330,000	28%
Less: Nonproduction costs		700,000	
Net income		$ 630,000	

EXHIBIT 5-3
Comparative income statements of the McKay Manufacturing Company

treated as period costs. A third argument for the adoption of variable costing for income measurement is that the profits increase or decrease in direct relationship to increases or decreases in sales. With absorption costing the effects upon net income of increases or decreases in sales are intermingled with the effects of increases or decreases in production output.

Exhibit 5-4 compares the net income under variable and absorption costing for the same company over a four-year time span. In the first year more units are produced than sold. In the second and fourth years more units are sold than produced. In the third year production and sales are equal. The selling price and cost structure remain unchanged throughout the example. For simplicity, the only costs are production costs.

Selling price	$ 10 per unit
Variable production costs	$ 6 per unit
Fixed production costs	$270 per year

In this illustration we have assumed a LIFO (last-in, first-out), flow of inventory costs. Other methods, such as FIFO or average, would also illustrate the difference between absorption and variable costing, but income and inventory values would differ. LIFO was chosen because it presents a clearer flow of costs. With LIFO, cost of goods sold includes costs from the previous year only when the inventory level is decreased.

We have assumed that the cost behavior patterns remain unchanged throughout the four years. Under variable costing all units are costed at $6 per unit throughout the illustration. Because we are using an historical overhead rate, the unit cost under absorption costing is $8.70 [$6 variable + $2.70 fixed ($270 ÷ 100 units)] when 100 units are produced. When production is 90 units the unit cost will increase to $9.00 [$6 variable + $3 fixed ($270 ÷ 90 units)].

In the first year, production exceeded sales and the finished goods inventory increased by 20 units. The income under variable costing is lower than under absorption costing because all fixed costs are treated as period costs. Under absorption costing each of the 20 units in inventory includes $2.70 of fixed costs.

In the second year, sales exceeded production. In addition to current fixed costs for that year, the income statement for absorption costing includes the additional fixed costs applicable to the 10 units produced in the first year. Therefore, income under variable costing in the second year exceeds income under absorption costing by $27 (10 × $2.70).

During the third year, income is the same under the two costing systems. Since production and sales were equal, only current costs were included in the income statements.

The last year is comparable to the second year. Sales exceeded production, and the income statement for absorption costing included extra fixed costs from the beginning inventory.

Let's look at the differences in income determination for these four years.

	FIRST YEAR		SECOND YEAR		THIRD YEAR		FOURTH YEAR		TOTAL FOR FOUR YEARS	
	Variable	Absorption	Variable	Absorption	Variable	Absorption	Variable	Absorption	Variable	Absorption
Units sold	80	80	100	100	100	100	110	110	390	390
Units produced	100	100	90	90	100	100	100	100	390	390
Sales	$800	$800	$1,000	$1,000	$1,000	$1,000	$1,100	$1,100	$3,900	$3,900
Cost of goods sold										
Current production costs:										
Variable costs	$600	$600	$ 540	$ 540	$ 600	$ 600	$ 600	$ 600	$2,340	$2,340
Fixed costs	270	270	270	270	270	270	270	270	1,080	1,080
Total costs	$870	$870	$ 810	$ 810	$ 870	$ 870	$ 870	870	$3,420	$3,420
Change in inventory										
(Increase)	(120)	(174)							(120)	(174)
Decrease			60	87	–	–	60	87	120	174
Cost of goods sold	750	696	870	897	870	870	930	957	3,420	3,420
Net income	$ 50	$104	$ 130	$ 103	$ 130	$ 130	$ 170	$ 143	$ 480	$ 480
Beginning inventory:										
Units	0	0	20	20	10	10	10	10	0	0
Cost	–	–	$ 120	$ 174	$ 60	$ 87	$ 60	$ 87	–	–
Ending inventory:										
Units	20	20	10	10	10	10	0	0	0	0
Cost	$120	$174	$ 60	$ 87	$ 60	$ 87	–	–	–	–

EXHIBIT 5-4
Comparative income statements across four time periods

1. In years where production exceeds sales, the net income reported by absorption costing is greater than that reported by variable costing. This is true because some of the fixed costs remain in inventory under absorption costing.

2. In years where sales exceed production, variable costing reports a higher net income than absorption costing. This is true because absorption costing matches both current and some previously deferred fixed costs against revenue, whereas variable costing matches only current fixed costs against revenue.

3. In years where sales and production are equal, the two methods produce the same net income.

4. Comparing the second and third years we can see that in years where sales volume is constant but production fluctuates, variable costing gives identical net incomes. This is so because net income under variable costing is not affected by inventory changes. In absorption costing, net income fluctuates with changes in the inventories as well as with changes in sales because fixed costs are spread over a different number of units.

5. When the total production output over the years equals total sales, the total net income will be the same under either costing method.

In most industries, production will tend to equal sales over a long period of time. Therefore, over the long run the two procedures will produce similar results. Any controversy between the advocates of absorption costing and those who favor variable costing, in terms of income determination, is a matter of timing in the matching of fixed costs with revenue.

EXTERNAL REPORTING AND VARIABLE COSTING

The controversy over the proper reporting of cost data can be examined from two perspectives: external financial statements for investors and internal reports for management. A particular reporting method may be generally accepted for one purpose and rejected as nonrelevant in another. In this and the following section we will look at the use of variable costing for external reports and internal reports respectively.

For external reporting purposes, generally accepted accounting principles view absorption costing as the proper way to account for production costs. Professional and governmental accounting groups have approved absorption costing and rejected variable costing as a generally acceptable method of inventory valuation for external reports. The American Institute of Certified Public Accountants (AICPA), the professional organization primarily concerned with attesting to published financial data, stated its opinion in *Accounting Research Bulletin No. 43,* issued in 1953:

> The primary basis of accounting for inventories is cost, which has been defined generally as the price paid or consideration given to acquire the asset. As applied to inventories, cost means in principle the sum of the applicable expenditures and charges directly or indirectly incurred in bringing an article to its existing condition and location. . . . Although principles for the determination of inventory costs may be easily stated, the application, particularly to such inventory items as work in process and finished goods, is difficult because of the variety of problems encountered in the allocation of costs and charges. For example, under some circumstances, items such as idle facility expense, excessive spoilage, double freight, and rehandling costs may be so abnormal as to require treatment as current period charges rather than as a portion of the inventory cost. Also, general and administrative expenses should be included as period charges, except for the portion of such expenses that may be clearly related to production and thus constitute a part of inventory costs (product charges). Selling expenses constitute no part of inventory costs. It should also be recognized that the exclusion of all overheads from inventory costs does not constitute an accepted accounting procedure.[2]

A careful reading of the AICPA's statement can be confusing. It says that *all* overhead costs may not be excluded, but it does not say that *all* overhead costs must be included. This is a moot point, however. Most accountants in public practice have interpreted the statement to support absorption costing and reject variable costing for costing of inventories.

An American Accounting Association (AAA) committee took a firm position against variable costing in 1957. The committee report stated:

> Thus the cost of a manufactured product is the sum of the acquisition costs reasonably traceable to the product and should include both direct and indirect factors. The omission of any element of manufacturing cost is not acceptable.[3]

Unlike Research Bulletin No. 43 of the AICPA, the AAA committee report does not constitute binding, generally accepted accounting principles and does not represent an official position of the association. Committee members who dissented to the committee report stated:

> . . . Direct costing (variable costing) is at least as acceptable in accounting theory as is the conventional "full costing" concept. Moreover, they believe that use of direct costing (variable costing) procedures will, in many cases, yield results more useful to investors as well as management.[4]

[2]Committee on Accounting Procedure, *Accounting Research Bulletin No. 43* (New York: American Institute of Certified Public Accountants, 1953), pp. 28–29.

[3]*The Accounting Review* (October, 1957), p. 539.

[4]Ibid.

Another accounting organization, the National Association of Accountants (NAA), does not issue *official* pronouncements upon accounting practice, but has issued a number of research reports and published a number of journal articles in support of variable costing for external, as well as internal, reports. The NAA actively advocates variable costing. Since the members of this organization are primarily management accountants, their position is not too surprising.

In the governmental sphere there are three organizations concerned with costing of inventories for external reports. The most dominant has been the Securities and Exchange Commission (SEC). With responsibility for administering the federal securities acts, the SEC requires, among other reports, financial statements. The commission has refused to accept variable costing unless it is permitted by generally accepted accounting principles. Thus, any firms that use variable costing for internal purposes must adjust their inventory values and net income to absorption costing when filing with the SEC.

The Internal Revenue Service (IRS) has also refused to sanction variable costing until the method is a generally accepted accounting procedure. Overall, the IRS has held that any inventory accounting method must conform as nearly as possible to the best accounting practice in the trade or business and that the cost of inventory produced should include the cost of raw materials and supplies consumed, expenditures for direct labor, and indirect expenses as a reasonable proportion of management expenses. Recently the IRS specifically prohibited the use of variable costing, although some firms have reported this way for many years.

The newest governmental agency concerned with the costing of manufactured inventories is the Cost Accounting Standards Board (CASB). Established in 1970 as an agent of Congress, the CASB is responsible for establishing uniform cost accounting standards for contractors that sell to the federal government. It has been common practice in cost accounting for negotiated government contracts to use a full allocation of costs. The CASB indicated in its first standards that it intends to adhere to the concept of full costing wherever it is appropriate.

From this discussion we can see that variable costing has not been accepted by the accounting profession *for external reporting.* Determination of acceptable reporting practice revolves around the question: "What is a product cost?" Inherent in this question is another: "What is the proper timing in matching fixed costs with revenue?" Absorption costers hold that fixed costs are necessary to produce the product and cannot be excluded from inventories. As a consequence, they believe that fixed costs should be matched with revenue on a sales basis. For external reports they hold that the users of the financial statements are taking a more global, long-range view and that for this view the "averaging" of all costs is relevant to their decisions. Absorption costing meets these criteria and thus is considered the appropriate method for external reports.

INTERNAL REPORTING AND THE CONTRIBUTION MARGIN APPROACH

There is no question among accountants that the separation of costs into their fixed and variable components is useful and necessary in management decision making. This knowledge can help management decide which products to emphasize or de-emphasize, what prices to charge on special orders, the effects of price-cost-volume changes, and when to increase or decrease output. It can also serve as input to other decision models. In this section we will see how fixed and variable costs are used in variable costing for management.

Variable Costing and the Contribution Margin Approach

At the heart of variable costing is the contribution margin, which may be measured simply as revenue minus variable costs. However, there are two ways of viewing variable costing and the contribution margin.

The first view is from the standpoint of what costs are considered product costs and thus are included in the inventory, and what costs are considered period costs. This is essentially a question of income measurement. We will call this view **variable costing.** With both variable and absorption costing methods, accountants exclude all nonproduction costs from inventory. Under variable costing, fixed production costs are also excluded from the inventory; the contribution margin is sales revenue less variable production costs. This format is relevant when management is concerned with cost-volume relationships from production activities only.

The second view of contribution margin is much broader. Here the contribution margin is the amount of net revenue remaining after deducting *all* variable costs, both production and selling. It must cover fixed costs and provide a satisfactory profit. We will call this perspective the **contribution margin approach.** When management is concerned with the firm's total cost-volume relationships, the variable nonproduction costs become relevant, as well as the variable production costs.

Actually, variable costing should be considered a subset of the contribution margin approach. In this text, when we are dealing with only the production area and therefore variable costing, the contribution margin will be called **contribution margin from production,** to exclude nonproduction variable costs. However, when we are concerned with cost-volume-profit relationships for the entire firm, we will use the term **contribution margin from total operations** or simply **contribution margin.**

Let's return to the McKay Manufacturing Company illustration to examine these two views of the contribution margin. Remember that the McKay Company manufactured 200,000 rocking horses during the past accounting period. It sold 190,000 horses at $25 each and incurred the following variable production costs per unit: direct materials $5; direct labor $6; and variable factory overhead $4. The fixed production costs totaled $600,000; the nonproduction costs were $700,000, of which $320,000 were fixed.

To arrive at an inventory cost for income determination purposes, the product cost with variable costing flow would be:

Direct materials	$ 5
Direct labor	6
Variable factory overhead	4
Total inventoriable cost	$15

Using the inventoriable cost, the **unit contribution margin from production** is $10 (the selling price of $25 less the variable production cost per unit of $15). The **total contribution margin from production** is the excess of total sales revenue over total variable production costs, which in our case is $1,900,000 (190,000 units × $10), and the **contribution margin ratio from production** is 40% ($10 ÷ $25). These contribution margins from production do not include the variable nonproduction costs.

The broader view of contribution margin includes the total variable costs of the company. Total variable costs per unit of product for the McKay Company are:

Direct materials	$ 5
Direct labor	6
Variable factory overhead	4
Variable nonproduction costs	2
Total variable costs	$17

The variable nonproduction costs per unit were determined by dividing the variable nonproduction costs of $380,000 ($700,000 − $320,000) by the number of units sold, 190,000. No variable nonproduction costs were incurred for the units produced but not sold.

Using the total variable costs of the firm, not just the variable production costs, the **unit contribution margin from total operations** is the selling price of $25 less the variable cost per unit of $17, or $8. The **total contribution margin from total operations** is $1,520,000 (190,000 units × $8) and the **contribution margin ratio from total operations** is 32% ($8 ÷ $25).

The variable costing approach is useful in making incremental production decisions. The contribution margin approach is useful in making both incremental production *and* incremental selling decisions, in addition to its value in the study of cost-volume-profit relationships for the firm as a whole.

Contribution Margin Approach and Cost-Volume-Profit Analysis

Underlying the contribution margin's relevance to management decisions are two assumptions. First, the contribution margin approach assumes that the sales revenue per unit is constant. Second, it assumes that the variable costs per unit are also constant. These assumptions of a linear relationship of revenue and variable costs with volume imply that the contribution margin will also change linearly with changes in volume. Because the assumptions of linearity may not be valid over the full range of production and sales volume levels, the accountant specifies a relevant range of activity. The relevant range of activity is that span of volume over which the assumptions concerning cost behavior patterns and revenue flows are valid.

Since the contribution margin relates variable costs to sales, changes in profit caused by changes in sales volume are pinpointed. Fixed costs do not change with changes in volume and therefore are not relevant in measuring changes in profit arising from changes in volume. The higher the contribution margin ratio, the greater effect volume increases will have on profits. On the other hand, if the company is operating at a loss, the greater the unit contribution margin, the greater the loss will be if volume declines. The larger the contribution margin ratio, the larger the change in profit, given a change in volume; the smaller the contribution margin ratio, the smaller the change in profit, given a change in volume.

The breakeven graph, which was shown in Chapter 2, has been described as a graphic contribution margin income statement. To see the implications of this statement, let's use the McKay Manufacturing Company illustration again. An income statement based upon the contribution margin approach is shown in Exhibit 5-5. Using that information, let's determine the breakeven point by both formula and graph to show how the contribution margin approach facilitates cost-volume-profit decisions. The following calculations show the breakeven point for the McKay Company, in dollars and in units.

$$\text{Breakeven point in dollars} = \frac{\text{Fixed costs}}{\text{Contribution margin ratio}} = \frac{\$920{,}000}{.32}$$

$$= \$2{,}875{,}000$$

$$\text{Breakeven point in units} = \frac{\text{Fixed costs}}{\text{Unit contribution margin}} = \frac{\$920{,}000}{\$8}$$

$$= 115{,}000 \text{ units}$$

For a net income of $600,000, which was the firm's actual net income, the following sales would be needed.

MC KAY MANUFACTURING COMPANY
INCOME STATEMENT
For the Year Ended December 31, 19X5

Sales (190,000 x $25)		$4,750,000	100%
Less variable costs:			
Direct material (190,000 x $5)	$ 950,000		
Direct labor (190,000 x $6)	1,140,000		
Factory overhead (190,000 x $4)	760,000		
Nonproduction costs (190,000 x $2)	380,000		
Total variable costs (190,000 x $17)		3,230,000	68%
Contribution margin (190,000 x $8)		$1,520,000	32%
Less fixed costs:			
Factory overhead	$ 600,000		
Nonproduction costs	320,000		
Total fixed costs		920,000	
Net income		$ 600,000	

EXHIBIT 5-5
Contribution margin income statement of the McKay Manufacturing Company

$$\text{Dollars of sales needed for desired profit} = \frac{\text{Fixed costs} + \text{Desired net income}}{\text{Contribution margin ratio}}$$

$$= \frac{\$920{,}000 + \$600{,}000}{.32}$$

$$= \$4{,}750{,}000$$

The needed sales volume could also be expressed in units.

$$\text{Units of sales needed for desired profit} = \frac{\$920{,}000 + \$600{,}000}{\$8}$$

$$= 190{,}000 \text{ units}$$

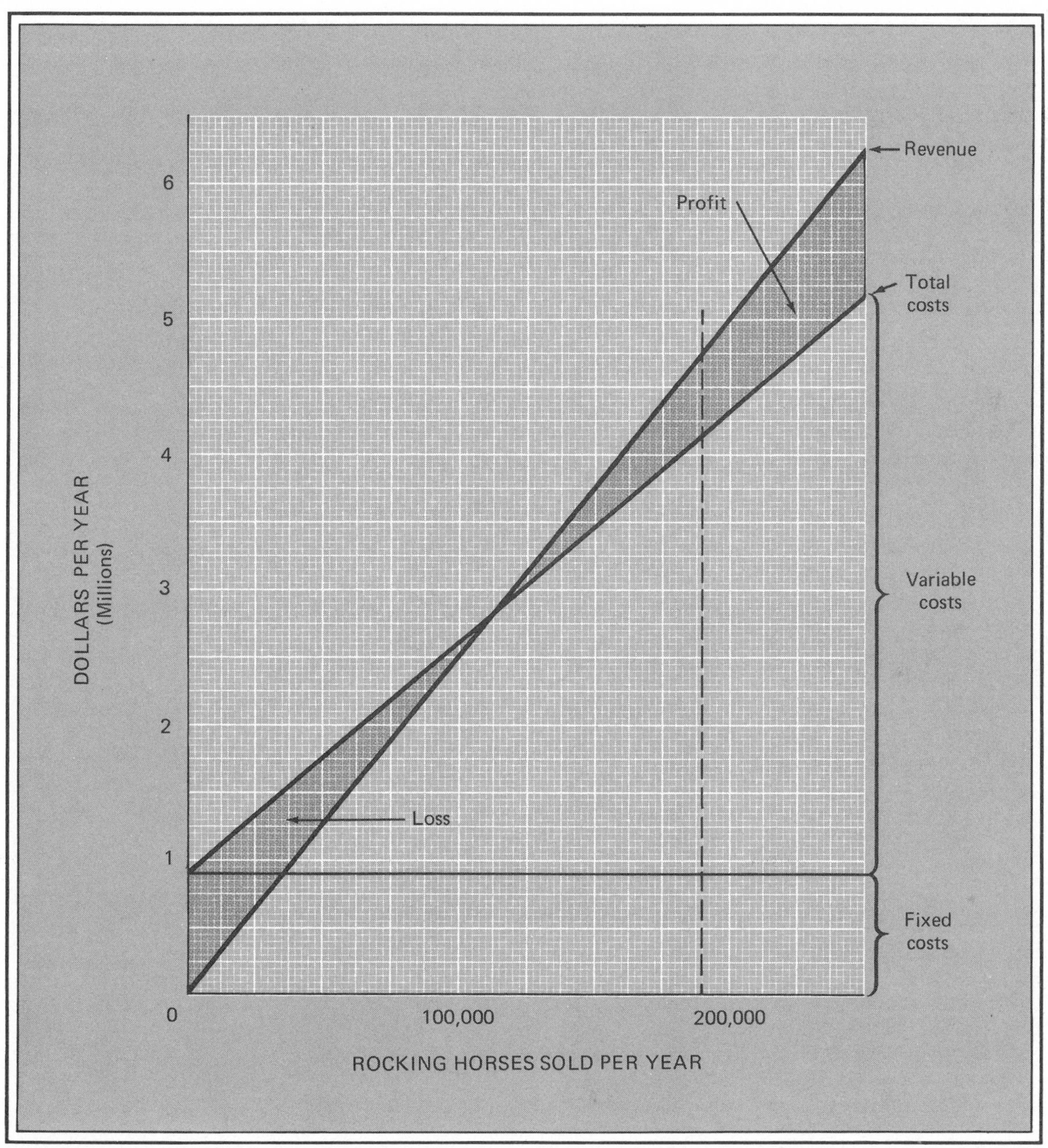

EXHIBIT 5-6
Breakeven chart of the McKay Manufacturing Company

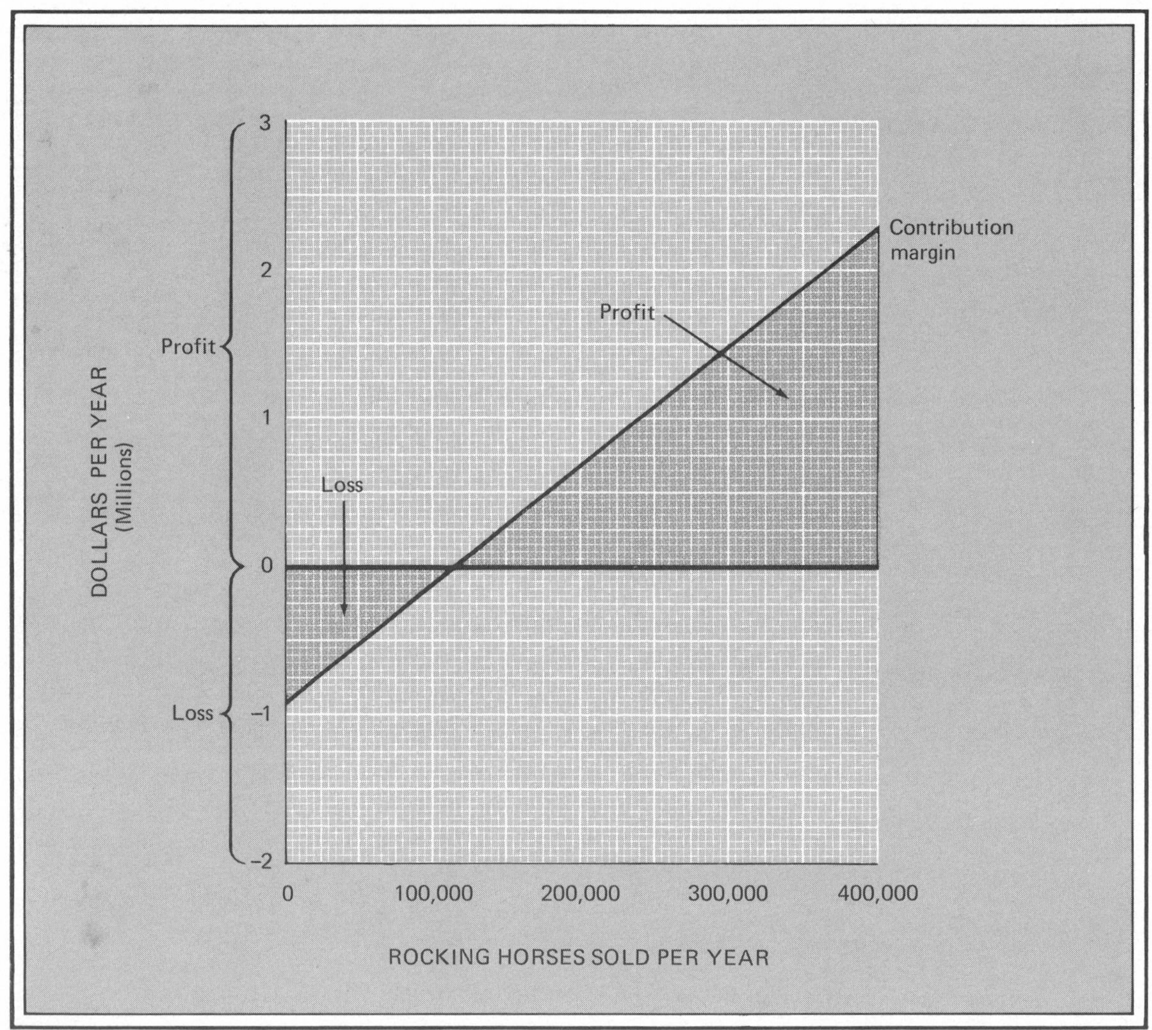

EXHIBIT 5-7
Profit-volume chart of the McKay Manufacturing Company

Exhibit 5-6 shows the same data plotted on a breakeven graph. From this graph we can read directly the breakeven point and the net income earned under actual operations. The contribution margin income statement is, in fact, another mode of presenting cost-volume-profit relationships. It lends itself directly, without reinterpretation, to cost-volume-profit analysis.

A second graphic representation of breakeven analysis discussed in Chapter 2 is the profit-volume (PV) chart. Only the contribution margin from operations is plotted on the chart. At zero activity there is no contribution margin and the loss is equal to the fixed costs. A profit-volume chart for the McKay Manufacturing Company is presented in Exhibit 5-7. Note that the same breakeven point and profit are determined from the two graphs.

Returning to Exhibit 5-3 for a moment, we can see that the gross margin using absorption costing does not lend itself to cost-volume-profit analysis. The gross profit percentage of 28% was predicated on the fact that the McKay Manufacturing Company allocated the fixed costs of production over 200,000 units ($600,000 ÷ 200,000 units = $3.00 per unit). What would have happened if the volume had increased to 250,000 units? With the same sales of 190,000 units, the inventory would have increased by 60,000 units instead of 10,000. The fixed costs of production would have been apportioned to the units at $2.40 per unit ($600,000 ÷ 250,000 units), and the total inventoriable cost per unit would have been $17.40 ($5.00 + $6.00 + $4.00 + $2.40). The new gross margin, as follows, uses absorption costing.

Sales (190,000 × $25)	$4,750,000	100.0%
Cost of goods sold (190,000 × $17.40)	3,306,000	69.6%
Gross margin (190,000 × $7.60)	$1,444,000	30.4%

The gross margin does not fulfill the same information role as does the contribution margin. Under absorption costing, the per-unit cost changes with changes in volume because the fixed costs must be spread over the production volume. In variable costing, changes in volume do not affect the contribution margin ratio or the unit contribution margin because both sales and variable costs are assumed to be linear over a relevant range.

Contribution Margin Approach in Nonmanufacturing Activities

The majority of the discussion in this text assumes a manufacturing setting. However, the contribution margin approach is valid in any setting. In fact, the contribution margin is easier to apply in a nonmanufacturing setting, where inventory consists of purchased goods—all of which are variable costs. There are no fixed costs associated with inventory in nonmanufacturing activities.

To illustrate the contribution approach for a retail firm, let's assume the following traditional income statement for a florist's shop.

ROSIE'S FLOWER SHOP
INCOME STATEMENT

Sales		$200,000
Cost of goods sold		120,000
Gross margin		$ 80,000
Operating expenses:		
Salaries	$30,000	
Supplies	10,000	
Utilities	5,000	
Depreciation	13,000	
Other	2,000	60,000
Net income		$ 20,000

Assume that a study of the cost-volume relationships supplied the following cost behavior patterns for the shop.

Variable costs		*Fixed costs*	
Cost of goods sold	$120,000	Salaries	$10,000
Salaries	20,000	Utilities	5,000
Supplies	10,000	Depreciation	13,000
Other	2,000		

The income statement that follows uses the contribution margin format.

ROSIE'S FLOWER SHOP
INCOME STATEMENT

Sales		$200,000	100%
Cost of goods sold		120,000	60%
Contribution margin from trading		$ 80,000	40%
Variable operating costs:			
Salaries	$20,000		
Supplies	10,000		
Other	2,000	32,000	16%
Contribution margin		$ 48,000	24%
Fixed operating costs:			
Salaries	$10,000		
Utilities	5,000		
Depreciation	13,000	28,000	
Net income		$ 20,000	

By identifying the contribution margin, questions that concern change in volume, such as the following, may be answered.

1. How much additional income will result from a 10% increase in volume? Revenue and variable costs will each increase by 10%. Since fixed costs will remain unchanged, the increased contribution margin of $4,800 ($48,000 × 10%) will increase income by $4,800. This question cannot be answered from the traditional income statement.

2. What is the volume of sales at breakeven?

$$\text{Sales at breakeven} = \frac{\text{Fixed costs}}{\text{Contribution margin ratio}} = \frac{\$28{,}000}{24\%} = \$116{,}667$$

Sales would have to decrease by 42% before the breakeven point is reached.

The contribution margin approach is not limited to the private, profit-seeking sector of the economy. There are many situations where not-for-profit organizations will find the contribution margin approach useful. For example, consider the following income statement for the Eastside Community Health Center, a not-for-profit health center.

EASTSIDE COMMUNITY HEALTH CENTER
INCOME STATEMENT

	August	*September*
Revenue from patients	$20,000	$22,500
Operating costs:		
Personnel costs:		
Consulting physicians	$ 8,000	$ 9,000
Nurses and lab technicians	6,500	6,500
Administration	3,200	3,200
Medical supplies	4,000	4,500
Rent and occupancy costs	1,800	1,800
Service bureau (medical records)	500	550
Total operating costs	$24,000	$25,550
Loss from operations	$ (4,000)	$ (3,050)

The following study of cost behavior patterns assumes 4,000 patient visits in August and 4,500 visits in September.

Variable cost per visit		*Fixed costs per month*	
Consulting physicians	$2.00	Nurses and lab technicians	$ 6,500
Medical supplies	1.00	Administrative salaries	3,200
Service bureau (medical records)	.10	Occupancy costs	1,800
		Service bureau (medical records)	100
Total	$3.10	Total	$11,600

The service bureau fee for maintenance of medical records is a mixed cost that includes a fixed monthly charge of $100 plus a variable charge of $.10 per patient visit.

The monthly income statements may now be recast to a contribution margin approach. The amount of loss does not change, but the income statements are much more useful. Contribution margin approach income statements are presented in Exhibit 5-8. The director of the health center now has the financial information to answer a number of questions.

EASTSIDE COMMUNITY HEALTH CENTER
INCOME STATEMENT

	AUGUST		SEPTEMBER	
	Amount	Per Patient Visit	Amount	Per Patient Visit
Revenue from patients	$20,000	$5.00	$22,500	$5.00
Variable operating costs:				
Consulting physicians	$ 8,000	$2.00	$ 9,000	$2.00
Medical supplies	4,000	1.00	4,500	1.00
Medical records	400	.10	450	.10
Total variable costs	12,400	3.10	13,950	3.10
Contribution margin	$ 7,600	$1.90	$ 8,550	$1.90
Fixed costs:				
Nurses and lab technicians	$ 6,500		$ 6,500	
Administration	3,200		3,200	
Occupancy costs	1,800		1,800	
Medical records	100		100	
Total fixed costs	11,600		11,600	
Loss from operations	$ (4,000)		$ (3,050)	

EXHIBIT 5-8
Contribution margin income statement of the Eastside Community Health Center

1. One of the goals of the health center is to become financially self-sufficient. Assuming that the cost-volume relationships do not change, how many patients must the center serve in order to break even?

$$\text{Breakeven in number of patients} = \frac{\text{Fixed costs}}{\text{Contribution margin per patient}}$$

$$= \frac{\$11{,}600}{\$1.90}$$

$$= 6{,}106 \text{ patient visits}$$

2. Assuming the health center considers a volume of 5,000 patient visits per month to be a normal level that can be served within the present cost structure, what billing rate per patient visit must be charged to break even?

   Revenue = Fixed costs + Variable costs
   $5{,}000(x) = \$11{,}600 + \$3.10\,(5{,}000)$

   where: x is the desired billing rate to break even.

   $5{,}000(x) = \$11{,}600 + \$15{,}500$
   $5{,}000(x) = \$27{,}100$
   $x = \$5.42$

   If the health center is to breakeven at a level of 5,000 patients with the present cost structure, the billing rate must be raised to $5.42 per patient visit.

The contribution margin approach can be useful in any setting where the impact of change on revenue and costs is needed for management decisions. Although most of our applications in this text relate to manufacturing settings, the contribution margin approach will provide useful information for decisions in other cases as well.

Contribution Margin Approach and Product Line Contributions

The contribution margin approach allows an examination of the way in which each class of products contributes toward the recovery of fixed costs and profit contribution. Exhibit 5-9 shows a contribution margin income statement by product line. A study of this exhibit helps extend our views of the contribution margin.

Since the fixed costs do not change with changes in volume, the important data are those which show the product that contributes most to the company's profits. Product A has a zero contribution margin; Product B has a contribution margin of $50 per unit and a contribution margin ratio of 25% ($1,000 ÷ $4,000); Product C has a contribution margin of $30 per unit and a contribution margin ratio of 30% ($1,500 ÷ $5,000). Product A is not contributing to company profits, and the company appears no better off for having produced it. Both Products B and C are profitable, although Product B returns the highest contribution margin per unit.

This exhibit also shows another important point. Certain fixed costs, shown on the statement as **separable fixed costs,** have been specifically identified with the product line. Other fixed costs, shown on the statement as **apportioned fixed costs,** have been allocated. The separable fixed costs are fixed costs that would be avoided if the product line were dropped. Sometimes they are called **avoidable costs.** Where there are separable fixed costs, a better measure of the product line's contribution is the **product margin,** determined after deducting separable fixed costs from the product's contribution margin.

	PRODUCT A (10 Units)	PRODUCT B (20 Units)	PRODUCT C (50 Units)	TOTAL
Sales	$3,000	$4,000	$5,000	$12,000
Variable production costs	2,500	2,400	2,500	7,400
Contribution margin from production	$ 500	$1,600	$2,500	$ 4,600
Variable nonproduction costs	500	600	1,000	2,100
Contribution margin	$ 0	$1,000	$1,500	$ 2,500
Separable (direct) fixed costs	300	400	300	1,000
Product margin	$ (300)	$ 600	$1,200	$ 1,500
Apportioned fixed costs	200	400	400	1,000
Net income (loss)	$ (500)	$ 200	$ 800	$ 500

EXHIBIT 5-9
Contribution margin income statements by product line

Where the company is already committed to the separable fixed costs or to retention of the product line, the fixed costs directly associated with the product line are not relevant, and the decision maker should look to the contribution margin of the product. In those instances where the company is not yet committed to the product line or the separable fixed costs, the product margin after separable costs is more appropriate for the decision maker. The apportioned fixed costs would not be relevant in either case.

If there is unused capacity, the firm can realize additional profits by increasing the sales of products with a positive contribution margin (Products B and C) and by decreasing the sales of any products with a negative or zero contribution margin (Product A). Which product in Exhibit 5-9 should the company emphasize? While Product C has the highest contribution margin ratio (30%), Product B has the highest unit contribution margin ($50). The firm should produce and sell in such a way as to maximize the *total contribution margin in dollars*—not the contribution margin ratio. This issue will be examined again in Chapter 7.

Limitations of the Contribution Margin Approach

The contribution margin approach is useful in making incremental production and distribution decisions, but it has limitations. First, it is based upon the cost-volume analysis used in determining fixed and variable costs. It assumes that the accountant has determined which costs are fixed and which are variable. As we discussed in Chapter 2, this analysis requires special tools also based on certain underlying assumptions.

Second, many accountants have felt that an overemphasis on the contribution margin may mislead the decision maker into assuming *only* a short-range decision attitude. They argue that the contribution margin approach may underemphasize the importance of the fixed costs. Proponents of the contribution margin approach counter that it actually highlights the fixed costs, since it does not "lose" them in the unit cost but instead keeps them intact.

Third, opponents of the contribution margin approach argue that heavy reliance upon variable costing may lead management to mistakenly overlook the need to maintain an adequate production volume. If the total contribution margin is allowed to fall too low it will not cover the fixed costs, even though the unit contribution margin is good. That is to say, the contribution margin approach may lead management to adopt only a short-range viewpoint. In the long run the firm may go broke with a good unit contribution margin. Proponents of the contribution margin approach argue that it reports profits and operating data in a way easily understood by management, and that this understanding leads to better short- and long-range decisions.

Fourth, even the best kept records of *past* costs are not useful in decision making unless they help predict future costs. This point applies to absorption costing as well as to the contribution margin approach. Since decisions are future oriented, past data is useful only if it is believed that the future will be similar to the past. Changes in operations, cost behavior classifications, and organizational structures cause the exact fixed and variable costs to change from year to year. If there are significant changes, neither absorption costing nor the contribution margin approach will be relevant. Decision data would have to come from special studies, not from the accounting records.

Allowing for its limitations, most accountants concerned with decision making believe that the knowledge of fixed and variable costs and the resultant contribution margin are of significant value to management, although they might advocate the use of absorption costing in external reports.

ALTERNATIVE PROPOSALS

It should be obvious to the reader that we cannot solve the controversy over variable costing versus absorption costing for external reporting, nor can we ignore the value that the contribution margin provides to management. There are at least two ways that a firm can reconcile the internal needs for the contribution margin and the external needs for absorption costing. One way combines both sets of data into a single set of records. Exhibit 5-10 shows a product cost sheet that gives both pieces of information. This example uses the product costs of the McKay Manufacturing Company used earlier in this chapter. The variable production costs are shown separately from the fixed costs. (Note the variable nonproduction costs are not shown because they are not used in inventory costing.) This approach allows the decision maker

PRODUCT COST SHEET

Variable costs:	
Direct material	\$ 5.00
Direct labor	6.00
Factory overhead	4.00
Total variable production costs for use in contribution margin	\$15.00
Fixed factory overhead (\$600,000 ÷ 200,000 units)	3.00
Total inventoriable cost for external reports	\$18.00

EXHIBIT 5-10
Dual purpose product cost sheet

to use \$15 in making differential production decisions and the accountant to use \$18 in inventory costing.

In those cases where the accountant believes that two types of data on the same report are confusing, an acceptable alternative is to provide each group with its data needs. Internally, the firm can use the contribution margin approach. When external reports are prepared, the accountant can make a simple adjustment to convert the financial statements to absorption costing. The adjustment of the inventories at the end of the year is a **supplementary fixed factory overhead rate.**

$$\text{Supplementary fixed factory overhead rate per unit of production activity} = \frac{\text{Total fixed factory overhead dollars}}{\text{Total production activity}}$$

To illustrate this point, we return to the McKay Manufacturing Company. If variable costing is used to account for production costs, the end of the accounting period will show a Finished Goods Inventory of \$150,000 (10,000 units × \$15), a Cost of Goods Sold of \$2,850,000 (190,000 units × \$15), and unapportioned fixed factory overhead of \$600,000. Fixed factory overhead costs can then be apportioned.

Finished Goods Inventory (shown on the statement of financial position) $\frac{10{,}000 \text{ units}}{200{,}000 \text{ units}} \times \$600{,}000 = \$30{,}000$

Cost of Goods Sold (shown on the income statement) $\frac{190{,}000 \text{ units}}{200{,}000 \text{ units}} \times \$600{,}000 = \$170{,}000$

This allocation would result in the inventory valuation and net profit figures that would have been measured using an historical factory overhead rate under absorption costing.

The amount of the adjustment must take into account the fact that there could be fixed factory overhead costs in the beginning inventory already recorded as a result of an adjustment in the previous period. In our McKay Manufacturing Company illustration there was no beginning inventory. The adjustment amount where there are fixed costs already assigned to the beginning inventory would be:

Net change in the inventory = Fixed factory overhead costs allocable to the ending inventories less any fixed factory overhead costs already apportioned to the beginning inventories

If the fixed factory overhead costs in the ending inventories exceed the fixed factory overhead costs in the beginning inventories, the adjustment will increase profits. If the fixed factory overhead costs in the beginning inventories exceed the fixed factory overhead costs apportioned to the final inventories, the adjustment will reduce profits.

SUMMARY

There are two major costing systems for determining product and period costs. Absorption costing classifies all production costs as product costs and all nonproduction costs as period costs. Variable costing treats the variable costs to produce the product as product costs; fixed production costs and nonproduction costs are treated as period costs. It is generally accepted accounting practice to use absorption costing for external reports. This practice has the support of most major accounting and governmental agencies.

There is wide agreement that the contribution margin is useful for management decision making. The contribution margin is sales revenue less variable costs; the contribution margin ratio is the contribution margin divided by the sales revenue. The contribution margin is particularly useful in cost-volume-profit analysis. As a matter of fact, the breakeven graph has been called a graphic variable costing income statement. The contribution margin from the variable cost flow system used in income determination can be different from that of the contribution margin approach; a contribution margin approach will include variable nonproduction costs.

To compromise between the two data needs of internal and external reports, it is possible to use the contribution margin approach within the firm, but to report externally using absorption costing. The accountant has the opportunity to present different costs for different purposes.

SUPPLEMENTARY READING

Broster, E. J. "The Dynamics of Marginal Costing." *The Accountant,* March 26, 1970.

Fremgen, James H. "The Direct Costing Controversy—An Identification of Issues." *The Accounting Review,* January, 1964.

Frye, Delbert J. "Combined Costing Method: Absorption and Direct." *Management Accounting,* January, 1971.

Largay, James A., III. "Microeconomic Foundations of Variable Costing." *The Accounting Review,* January, 1973.

Marple, Raymond P. (Ed.) *National Association of Accountants on Direct Costing: Selected Papers.* New York: The Ronald Press Company, 1965.

Moss, Morton F., and Wilber C. Haseman. "Some Comments on the Applicability of Direct Costing to Decision Making." *The Accounting Review,* April, 1957.

National Association of Accountants. *Current Application of Direct Costing.* New York: National Association of Accountants, 1961.

National Association of Accountants. *Direct Costing.* New York: National Association of Accountants, 1953.

Swalley, Richard W. "The Benefits of Direct Costing." *Management Accounting,* September, 1974.

QUESTIONS

5-1 Variable costing begins with an entirely different premise than absorption costing. What is this basic difference and why is it important?

5-2 How does an increase in Work-in-Process or Finished Goods Inventories affect the measurement of income when variable costing is used?

5-3 Why does the variable costing advocate state that fixed costs should not be included in the cost of inventories?

5-4 When a company sells the same number of units it produces, the net income under variable costing and absorption costing tends to be the same. Explain.

5-5 Some accountants consider variable costing as a short-run view of costs and absorption costing as a long-run view of costs. Do you agree? Explain.

5-6 When will an income statement under the contribution margin approach provide the same net income shown as on a breakeven chart? When will it not?

5-7 When will the income statement under absorption costing provide the same net income as shown on a breakeven chart? When will it not?

5-8 Why is there no volume variance under variable costing?

5-9 Is variable costing acceptable for reporting to stockholders? Why or why not?

5-10 Explain the position of the following organizations concerning the use of variable costing for external reporting.

a. Financial Accounting Standards Board
b. Securities and Exchange Commission
c. Internal Revenue Service
d. American Institute of Certified Public Accountants
e. National Association of Accountants

5-11 Should management use accounting techniques that are not acceptable for public reporting? Explain your position.

5-12 How can the manager of a profit center increase his reported net income without changing his price or cost structure or selling more units? Explain.

5-13 Variable costing is a subset of the contribution margin approach. Contrast the two concepts and illustrate their relationship.

5-14 "The contribution margin approach is useful in a manufacturing setting but cannot be used for other types of firms, such as retailing." Do you agree? Explain.

5-15 What are the significant limitations of the contribution margin approach?

PROBLEMS

5-16 Match the following terms and descriptions.

1. Prime costs
2. Period costs
3. Variable costs
4. Variable costing
5. Contribution margin
6. Net income
7. Contribution margin ratio
8. Product margin
9. Separable fixed costs
10. Apportioned fixed costs

a. Costs that change with activity.
b. Total of direct materials and direct labor.
c. Sales minus variable costs.
d. Sales minus variable costs and separable fixed costs.
e. Sales minus variable costs, separable fixed costs, and apportioned fixed costs.
f. Contribution margin divided by sales.
g. Common fixed costs.
h. Inclusion of only variable production costs in inventory.
i. Direct costs that do not change with activity.
j. Costs that are expensed when incurred.

5-17 Gyro Gear Company produces a special gear used in automatic transmissions. Each gear sells for $28. The company sells approximately 500,000 gears each year. Unit cost data for 19X3 follow.

Direct material	$6	
Direct labor	$5	
	Variable	*Fixed*
Other costs:		
Manufacturing	$2	$7
Distribution	$4	$3

A. The unit cost of gears for inventory purposes with variable costing is

a. $13
b. $20
c. $17
d. $27
e. $11
f. None of the above

B. Gyro has received an offer from a foreign manufacturer to purchase 25,000 gears. Domestic sales would be unaffected by this transaction. If the offer is accepted, variable distribution costs will increase $1.50 per gear for insurance, shipping, and import duties. The relevant unit cost to a pricing decision on this offer is

a. $17.00
b. $14.50
c. $28.50
d. $18.50
e. $12.50
f. None of the above

C. The unit cost of gears for inventory purposes with absorption costing is

a. $13
b. $20
c. $17
d. $27
e. $11
f. None of the above

D. The prime cost of the gears is

a. $13
b. $20
c. $17
d. $27
e. $11
f. None of the above

E. The conversion cost of the gears under absorption costing is

a. $11
b. $14
c. $13
d. $17
e. $20
f. None of the above *(CPA adapted)*

5-18 Supporters of variable costing contend that it provides management with more useful accounting information. Critics of variable costing believe that its negative features outweigh its contributions.

REQUIRED:

A. Describe variable costing. How does it differ from conventional absorption costing?
B. List the arguments for and against the use of variable costing.
C. Indicate how each of the following conditions would affect the amounts of net income reported under conventional absorption costing and variable costing.

1. Sales and production are in balance at normal volume.
2. Sales exceed production.
3. Production exceeds sales. *(CPA adapted)*

5-19 The Seth-Beth Company had the following production and sales quantities during the past year.

	1st Quarter	*2nd Quarter*	*3rd Quarter*	*4th Quarter*
Units produced	50	45	50	50
Units sold	40	50	50	55

During the year the selling price was constant at $10 per unit, variable production costs were $6 per unit, and fixed production costs were $135 per quarter. Assume a LIFO inventory flow.

REQUIRED:

A. Prepare income statements that set forth sales, variable and fixed costs, and net income for each quarter under both absorption and variable costing approaches.

B. Calculate the ending inventory values for each quarter under both absorption and variable costing.

C. Prepare a schedule that compares the ending inventory values showing why they differ under absorption and variable costing.

5-20 The Jensen Pottery Company manufactures a line of pots and dishes. During the past year it produced 10,000 sets of coffee cups, but sold only 9,500 sets. The selling price of the sets was $25. Production and distribution costs for the year were:

Materials	$50,000
Labor	$60,000
Variable factory overhead	$40,000
Fixed factory overhead	$30,000
Selling costs	$35,000

REQUIRED:

A. Develop the cost per unit under (1) absorption costing and (2) variable costing.

B. Develop income statements under (1) absorption costing and (2) variable costing.

C. Prepare a schedule showing the inventory values at the end of the year under both absorption and variable costing. What is the total difference in the ending inventory values? What causes this difference?

D. What would be the effect upon net income under absorption costing if the sales volume decreased to 6,000 units, assuming that the cost structures remained unchanged? What would be the effect upon net income under variable costing at the 6,000-unit sales level?

5-21 The following annual flexible budget has been prepared for use in making decisions relating to Product X.

	100,000 Units	*150,000 Units*	*200,000 Units*
Sales volume	$800,000	$1,200,000	$1,600,000
Manufacturing costs:			
Variable	$300,000	$ 450,000	$ 600,000
Fixed	200,000	200,000	200,000
	500,000	650,000	800,000
Selling and other expenses:			
Variable	$200,000	$ 300,000	$ 400,000
Fixed	160,000	160,000	160,000
	360,000	460,000	560,000
Income (or loss)	$ (60,000)	$ 90,000	$ 240,000

The 200,000-unit budget has been adopted and will be used for allocating fixed manufacturing costs to units of Product X. At the end of the first six months the following information is available.

	Units
Production completed	120,000
Sales	60,000

All fixed costs are budgeted and incurred uniformly throughout the year and all costs incurred coincide with the budget.

Under- and overapplied fixed manufacturing costs are deferred until yearend. Annual sales have the following seasonal pattern.

	Portion of Annual Sales
First quarter	10%
Second quarter	20
Third quarter	30
Fourth quarter	40
	100%

1. The amount of fixed factory costs applied to product during the first six months under absorption costing would be

a. Overapplied by $20,000
b. Equal to the fixed costs incurred
c. Underapplied by $40,000
d. Underapplied by $80,000
e. None of the above

2. Reported net income (or loss) for the first six months under absorption costing would be
   a. $160,000
   b. $80,000
   c. $40,000
   d. ($40,000)
   e. None of the above

3. Reported net income (or loss) for the first six months under variable costing would be
   a. $144,000
   b. $72,000
   c. $0
   d. ($36,000)
   e. None of the above

4. Assuming that 90,000 units of Product X were sold during the first six months and that this is to be used as a basis, the revised budget estimate for the total number of units to be sold during this year would be
   a. 360,000
   b. 240,000
   c. 200,000
   d. 120,000
   e. None of the above

(CPA adapted)

5-22 The Rhode Island Company was recently formed and is about to start production. The directors are trying to decide whether to use variable or absorption costing. The following projections were made for the first year of operations.

Production	10,000 units
Sales	7,000 units
Direct materials	$30,000
Direct labor	$20,000
Variable factory overhead	$10,000
Fixed factory overhead	$40,000

REQUIRED:

A. Compute the cost to be assigned to the inventory under variable costing and under absorption costing.

B. What is the difference between net income determined under variable costing and under absorption costing during the first year?

C. What considerations are important in deciding which method of inventory costing to use?

5-23 The Idaho Company produced 36,000 units of its product during 19X6. There were no beginning inventories. Ending inventories consisted of 6,000 units in Finished Goods Inventory. The selling price is $10 per unit.

Costs for the year were as follows:

	Fixed Costs	*Variable Costs*
Direct materials		$72,000
Direct labor		$54,000
Factory overhead	$36,000	$36,000
Selling expenses	$39,000	10% of sales
Administrative expenses	$31,600	$12,000

REQUIRED:

Compute the following:

A. Sales for the year.
B. Contribution margin from production.
C. Contribution margin from total operations.
D. Contribution margin ratio.
E. Net income under variable costing.
F. Breakeven point in dollars of sales.
G. Cost of ending inventory under variable costing.

5-24 The Vermont Company produced 36,000 units of its product during 19X6. There were no beginning inventories. Ending inventories consisted of 6,000 units in Finished Goods Inventory. The selling price is $10 per unit.

Costs for the year were as follows:

	Fixed Costs	*Variable Costs*
Direct materials		$72,000
Direct labor		$54,000
Factory overhead	$36,000	$36,000
Selling expenses	$39,000	10% of sales
Administrative expenses	$31,600	$12,000

REQUIRED:

Compute the following:

A. Sales for the year.
B. Gross margin.
C. Gross margin ratio.
D. Net income under absorption costing.
E. Breakeven point in units.
F. Cost of ending inventory under absorption costing.

5-25 The Cool Cube Manufacturing Company produces a line of small portable freezers. During the past year the following costs were incurred.

Direct materials	$270,000–variable
Direct labor	$540,000–variable
Compensation insurance (7% of direct and indirect labor)	$ 60,900–variable
Power	$ 8,700–variable
Factory supplies	$ 2,400–variable
Indirect factory labor	$330,000–variable
Repairs and maintenance	$ 39,000–variable
Light and heat	$ 4,800–variable
Property taxes	$ 4,200–fixed
Rent	$ 7,200–fixed
Depreciation on factory	$ 8,400–fixed
Insurance on factory	$ 2,400–fixed
Selling expenses	$120,000–fixed
Administrative expenses	$340,000–fixed

There were no beginning inventories in Raw Materials, Work-in-Process, or Finished Goods. At the end of the accounting period there were no ending inventories in Raw Materials or Work-in-Process. The firm manufactured 4,500 units during the year and sold 4,100 units.

REQUIRED:

A. What is the cost of the Finished Goods Inventory under absorption costing? Under variable costing?

B. Assuming sales were $1,700,000 for the year, how would the net income differ under the two systems? Why?

5-26 The Fredricks Company manufactures three principal products. During the past year it had the following cost, revenue, and production experiences.

	Product A	*Product B*	*Product C*
Units produced	5,000	10,000	1,000
Units sold	5,000	9,000	900
Unit sales price	$ 20	$ 15	$ 50
Direct material per unit	$ 5	$ 5	$ 20
Direct labor per unit	$ 6	$ 4	$ 10
Variable factory overhead per unit	$ 2	$ 1	$ 5
Fixed factory overhead per year	$2,500	$10,000	$5,000
Fixed selling expenses	$5,000	$10,000	$1,000

REQUIRED:

A. Prepare income statements for each product using the contribution margin approach.

B. Calculate for each product the contribution margin per unit and the contribution margin ratio per unit.
C. Prepare a schedule showing the ending inventory values for each product under both absorption costing and variable costing.
D. Discuss the value of the contribution margin in making incremental production decisions.

5-27 The following information applies to the Ace Manufacturing Company.

Total fixed costs	$15,000
Maximum capacity in sales	$70,000
Point where total costs equal revenue	$35,000

REQUIRED:
A. Prepare a PV (profit-volume) chart.
B. Calculate the variable costs, net income, and return on sales when the plant operates at full capacity.
C. Calculate the variable costs, sales revenue, net income, and return on sales when the company operates at 70% of capacity.
D. If the selling price is $1.75 per unit, what would be the breakeven point in units? What sales revenue would be necessary to achieve a net profit of $10,000?
E. If the selling price per unit was increased from $1.75 to $2.00 per unit without a change in volume, how would this shift the lines on your graph? Explain. What is the new breakeven point?

5-28 The following cost structure was developed for the Carson Company, a producer of a single product.

Direct materials	$ 6 per unit
Direct labor	$ 9 per unit
Variable factory overhead	$ 1 per unit
Fixed factory overhead	$10,000 per year
Selling expenses	$12,000 per year

The product sells for $21 per unit. In an average year 10,000 units are produced and sold.

REQUIRED:
A. What is the net income under absorption costing, assuming that 10,000 units are produced and sold? What is the cost per unit?
B. What is the net income under variable costing, assuming that 10,000 units are produced and sold? What is the cost per unit?
C. Assuming that production and sales dropped to 8,000 units, what would be the net income under absorption costing? What would be the net income under variable costing?
D. What factors affect the cost per unit under absorption costing between the two production levels?

5-29 The Kozy Komfy Patchy Quilt Company manufactures a line of fine quality patchwork quilts. Due to increased demand, the manager is faced with the decision of adding productive capacity. During the analysis of past costs, revenues, and net incomes, a question was raised in staff meeting about the definition of product cost. The company is presently using absorption costing, but the manager has heard that a variable costing system might prove more informative to management. The following information was developed to facilitate a comparison between the two systems.

	19X1	*19X2*	*19X3*	*19X4*
Units produced	1,200	1,500	1,200	1,200
Units sold	1,000	1,200	1,300	1,600

Cost and revenue information:

Variable costs:		
Raw materials	$30	
Direct labor	40	
Variable factory overhead	20	
Total variable costs	$90	
Other costs:		
Fixed production costs		$18,000 per year
Administrative costs		$14,000 per year
Selling costs		5% of sales revenue
Sales price		$150 per unit

Assume no beginning inventory and a LIFO inventory flow.

REQUIRED:

A. Prepare a schedule that shows net income for each year using both variable and absorption costing.

B. For each year reconcile the differences in net income between variable and absorption costing. As a part of your reconciliation show the ending Finished Goods Inventory under both variable and absorption costing.

5-30 The president of Wholesale Products Company is not satisfied with the following income statement that was prepared by his bookkeeper. Net income is lower than he thinks it should be. He doubts that all product lines are generating the income they should but does not have the information to evaluate individual product lines.

WHOLESALE PRODUCTS COMPANY INCOME STATEMENT For the Year 19X7		
Sales		$600,000
Cost of goods sold	$365,000	
Sales commissions	49,000	
Delivery costs	20,000	
Salaries	70,000	
Advertising	40,000	
Rent	24,000	
Other	6,000	574,000
Net income		$ 26,000

The president asks you to prepare an income statement that shows "how well he is doing" on each of his three product lines.

Additional information:

Sales for the three product lines:

Product A	$100,000
Product B	$300,000
Product C	$200,000

Cost of goods sold by product line:

Product A	60% of sales
Product B	55% of sales
Product C	70% of sales

Commissions by product line: Product A 10% of sales; Product B 5% of sales; Product C 12% of sales.

Salesmen's salaries: $20,000 for Product A and $30,000 for Product B.

Delivery Expense: 5% of sales for Products A and B.

Advertising: Product A $10,000; Product B $20,000; Product C $10,000.

The balance of the salaries are sales management and administration.

Rent and other expenses cannot be traced to product lines.

REQUIRED:

A. Prepare an income statement by product line using the contribution margin approach.

B. What can you tell from the contribution margin income statement that you could not tell from the income statement prepared by the bookkeeper?

C. Other firms in the industry have a return on sales of 8%. Were the president's suspicions correct? Explain.

5-31 The Leaky Tank Company presents a Plant Manager of the Month Award to the plant manager with the highest monthly income. The award is very important to the plant managers; it carries peer-group approval. Because of the high freight costs of the finished tanks, the company has several plants in strategic locations. The plants are of approximately the same size and have about the same cost structures, so top management believes that net income is a fair measure to use in presenting the monthly incentive award.

The plant manager of the Mud Flats Plant distrusts the accounting system because the manager of the Green River Plant has won the award for the past two months. The Green River Plant has sold fewer units in the past month and has had labor problems. Income statements follow for the two plants.

MUD FLATS PLANT
INCOME STATEMENT

	June	*July*
Sales (@ $400)	$40,000	$40,000
Cost of goods sold	30,000	30,000
Gross margin	$10,000	$10,000
Operating expense	5,000	5,000
Net income	$ 5,000	$ 5,000

GREEN RIVER PLANT
INCOME STATEMENT

	June	*July*
Sales (@ $400)	$40,000	$36,000
Cost of goods sold	25,000	20,250
Gross margin	$15,000	$15,750
Operating expense	5,000	5,000
Net income	$10,000	$10,750

You were asked to study the income statements of the two plants. The entire company uses a full-absorption costing system to measure unit cost and a LIFO cost flow method to match inventory cost with revenue. In the process of your investigation you discover the following additional information.

MUD FLATS PLANT		
	June	*July*
Variable production costs (per unit)	$ 150	$ 150
Fixed production costs (per month)	$15,000	$15,000
Beginning inventory	0	0
Units sold	100	100
Units produced	100	100

GREEN RIVER PLANT		
	June	*July*
Variable production costs (per unit)	$ 150	$ 180
Fixed production costs (per month)	$15,000	$15,000
Beginning inventory	0	0
Units sold	100	90
Units produced	150	200

REQUIRED:

A. Explain to the Mud Flats Plant manager why the award was won by the Green River Plant manager.

B. Prepare revised income statements under variable costing.

C. To whom would you give the award? Why?

5-32 The accounting firm of Coe, Roe, and Low is considering a number of changes including expansion and an increase of billing rates to clients. The following income statement does not provide the information needed by the partners.

COE, ROE, AND LOW INCOME STATEMENT For the Year 19X7		
Revenue		$200,000
Operating expenses:		
Salaries of employees	$64,000	
Salaries of partners	75,000	
Supplies	6,000	
Equipment depreciation	2,000	
Rent and utilities	12,000	
Travel	20,000	
Other	16,000	195,000
Net income		$ 5,000

A study of operating expenses revealed the following cost behavior patterns.

Salaries of employees	$2,000 per month plus 20% of revenue
Salaries of partners	$25,000 per year for each of three partners
Supplies	3% of revenue
Equipment depreciation	$2,000 per year
Rent and utilities	$1,000 per month
Travel	10% of revenue
Other	$1,000 per month plus 2% of revenue

REQUIRED:

A. Prepare an income statement using the contribution margin approach showing revenue and costs when revenue is $200,000, $220,000, and $250,000.

B. Prepare a profit-volume chart.

C. Does the income statement in part A and the profit-volume chart in part B show the same income at each of the three levels of revenue? Why or why not?

D. What kind of decisions will the income statement in part A and profit-volume chart in part B help the partners answer? Explain.

5-33 The voters of Happy Hollow rejected the $50,000 supplemental operating levy for the city's school system. As a result, the school board must reduce budgeted expenses by $50,000. The budget proposed to the voters is presented on the next page.

CITY OF HAPPY HOLLOW
PROPOSED BUDGET
For the Year 19X7–19X8

Revenues:	
Property taxes (regular levy)	$454,000
Property taxes (special levy)	50,000
Admission to athletic events	40,000
School lunch revenue	48,000
Total budgeted revenues	$592,000
Expenses:	
Salaries	$432,000
Material and supplies	76,000
Building repairs and utilities	36,000
Other	48,000
Total budgeted expenses	$592,000

An examination of expenses shows the following:

Salaries:		
Classroom teachers	(fixed)	$363,000
Coaching staff	(fixed)	10,000
School administration	(fixed)	40,000
Cafeteria personnel	(fixed)	15,000
Ticket takers for athletic events	(10% of revenue)	4,000
		$432,000
Material and supplies:		
Classroom materials	(variable)	$ 24,000
Athletic supplies	(variable)	10,000
Food	(variable)	42,000
		$ 76,000
Building repairs and utilities	(fixed)	$ 36,000
Other	($12,000 fixed; balance variable)	$ 48,000

Some members of the school board want to eliminate the athletic program and school lunch program because "they are a financial drain on the basic education resources."

REQUIRED:

A. The chairman of the school board wants you to prepare a revised budget that will show the impact of changes on the school. Recast the budget into a contribution margin approach and show the identifiable revenues and expenses for (1) basic education, (2) athletics, and (3) school lunch program.

B. How does your revised budget in part A assist the school board in its decisions? Explain.

5-34 The controller of the newly formed Barabas Company was asked to prepare a recommendation to the board of directors concerning the inventory costing method to be adopted by the company. One member of the board is also a director of another company that uses the contribution margin approach for internal reporting. He thinks the Barabas Company should prepare reports for the board of directors using the contribution margin approach. Another member of the board thinks it is wrong for the company "to keep two sets of books."

Data for the first year of operations follow.

Units produced	100,000, of which 80,000 were sold at $11 per unit.
Direct materials	$240,000
Direct labor	$320,000
Factory overhead:	
Variable costs	$ 80,000
Fixed costs	$160,000
Selling and administrative expenses:	
Variable costs	$ 48,000
Fixed costs	$180,000

REQUIRED:

A. Indicate the cost to be assigned to the inventory using:
   1. Variable costing
   2. Absorption costing

B. Prepare an income statement for the member of the board of directors who wants the company to use the contribution margin approach.

C. Prepare an income statement that will meet the requirements for reporting to the stockholders.

D. Prepare a recommendation to the board of directors concerning the costing method to be used for inventory costing. Your recommendation should consider the concerns of both directors.

5-35 At the end of its first year of business the following income statement was prepared by a Certified Public Accountant for the Francis Company.

FRANCIS COMPANY
INCOME STATEMENT
For the Year 19X7

Sales	(20,000 units × $12)		$240,000
Cost of goods sold:			
Production costs	(25,000 units × $ 8)	$200,000	
Ending inventory	(5,000 units × $ 8)	40,000	160,000
Gross margin			$ 80,000
Selling and administrative expenses			76,000
Net income			$ 4,000

Mr. Francis showed the income statement to his daughter, Wendy, who was home from college during the semester break. He was pleased that the company had shown a profit for the first year.

Wendy had just completed a course in management accounting and eagerly set about to apply the concepts from the course. From the accountant's report and other information about the company, Wendy found that the unit product cost of $8 included fixed costs of $2, and that fixed selling and administrative expenses amounted to $16,000.

After preparing a breakeven chart, Wendy said, "Sorry pops, but my breakeven chart shows that you lost about $6,000."

REQUIRED:

A. Prepare a breakeven chart for the Francis Company. What income or loss do you show at the 20,000-unit sales level?

B. Mr. Francis is confused about whether or not his company earned a profit last year. Is either his income statement or the breakeven chart wrong? Explain.

C. Prepare an income statement using variable costing and the contribution margin approach. Does your income or loss agree with the income statement or breakeven chart? Why?

D. What is the breakeven point in units? In sales dollars?

5-36 The president of Beth Corporation, which manufactures tape decks and sells them to producers of sound reproduction systems, anticipates a 10% wage increase on January 1 of next year to the manufacturing employees (variable labor). He expects no other changes in costs. Overhead will not change as a result of the wage increase. The president has asked you to assist him in developing the information he needs to formulate a reasonable product strategy for next year.

You are satisfied by regression analysis that volume is the primary factor affecting costs and have separated the semivariable costs into their fixed and variable segments by means of the least squares criterion. You also observe that the beginning and ending inventories are never materially different.

The following data for the current year are assembled for your analysis.

Current selling price per unit	$80
Variable cost per unit:	
Material	$30
Labor	12
Factory overhead	6
Total	$48
Annual volume of sales	5,000 units
Fixed costs	$51,000

REQUIRED:

Provide the following information for the president, using cost-volume-profit analysis.

A. What increase in the selling price is necessary to cover the 10% wage increase and still maintain the current contribution margin ratio?

B. How many tape decks must be sold to maintain the current net income if the sales price remains at $80 and the 10% wage increase goes into effect?

C. The president believes that an additional $190,000 of machinery (to be depreciated at 10% annually) will increase present capacity (5,300 units) by 30%. If all tape decks produced can be sold at the present price, and the wage increase goes into effect, how would the estimated net income before capacity is increased compare with the estimated net income after capacity is increased? Prepare income statements under the contribution margin approach *before* and *after* the expansion. *(CPA adapted)*

5-37 Flear Company has a maximum productive capacity of 210,000 units per year. Normal capacity is 180,000 units per year. Fixed factory overhead is $360,000 per year and variable production costs are $11 per unit. Variable selling expenses are $3 per unit and fixed selling expenses are $242,000 per year. The unit sales price is $20.

During 19X1 the company produced 160,000 units and sold 150,000. The beginning inventory consisted of 10,000 units. Cost of the beginning inventory was $130,000 under absorption costing ($11 variable and $2 fixed cost per unit) and $110,000 under variable costing ($11 variable cost per unit).

REQUIRED:

A. What is the breakeven point expressed in dollar sales?

B. How many units must be sold to earn a net income of $60,000 per year?

C. How many units must be sold to earn a net income of 10% on sales?

D. Assuming that the predetermined factory overhead rate of $2 per unit was based upon normal capacity, compute the cost of production under absorption costing in 19X1. Compute the volume variance under absorption costing.

E. Compute the cost of production under variable costing in 19X1. Why is there no volume variance under variable costing?

F. Assuming that the volume variance under absorption costing is added to Cost of Goods Sold, prepare income statements for 19X1 under:

1. Absorption costing

2. Variable costing

G. Briefly account for the difference in net income between the two income statements. *(CPA adapted)*

5-38 The Soggy Company has sales of $500,000 in both May and June (100,000 units at $5 per unit). The following production costs apply to each of the two months.

Fixed costs per month	$300,000
Variable costs per unit	$ 1.10

Production for May was 100,000 units. Production for June was 300,000 units, the output at 100% of practical capacity. The May 1 finished goods inventory was zero.

REQUIRED:

A. Compute the cost of the ending inventory at the end of June, assuming the company used historical (actual) absorption costing to cost the inventory.

B. Compute the cost of the ending inventory at the end of June, assuming the company used variable costing.

C. Compute the unit cost of production during the month of May, assuming the company used absorption costing with a predetermined overhead rate based upon practical capacity.

D. Compute the contribution margin of the Soggy Company.

E. Compute the net income for the month of May, assuming the company used variable costing.

F. Compute the net income for the month of June, assuming the company used absorption costing with a ''normal'' overhead rate based upon a normal activity level of 200,000 units.

5-39 Joe Bottler was a successful farmer who had, on his farm, a spring that was famous throughout the state. It had an ever-flowing supply of mineral water that tasted like sparkling burgundy and was reported to cure all manner of ailments. Joe's friends had often urged him to bottle and sell this as a beverage. One year, when his crops were poor, Joe decided to look into the matter.

Joe checked with the general store and found that he could buy jugs for $.25 each. Joe talked about his project with a neighbor named Sally Fuller, who was an amateur artist. She offered to fill the jugs at the spring and paint labels on them for $.25 each. He then approached Oscar Deal, the soda fountain operator. Oscar said he could sell this drink for $1.50 a jug and that he was willing to pay Joe $1 a jug and pick them up at the farm. This looked like a sound venture, so Joe decided to start operations.

After a short time, Joe had a nice little business. Sally was bottling, and Deal was selling, 40 jugs a day. Joe was receiving $1 each, or $40 a day. He was paying Sally $.25 each, or $10 a day. His jugs were costing him $.25 each, or another $10 a day. He was making a profit of $.50 each, or $20 a day.

Joe soon found, however, that the soft drink business was not so simple as it seemed. One morning the local board of health ordered Joe to stop bottling and selling his beverage because the jugs were not being sterilized. He finally found a washer that could be rented for $10 a day. Steam could be piped from a geyser close to his spring. The board inspected this arrangement and gave Joe permission to resume operations.

Joe's business was getting more complex. He now could figure his profit in two ways. If he continued to sell 40 jugs a day, his additional cost per jug would be: $10 ÷ 40 = $.25 per jug. Thus, his profit would be reduced $.25 per jug, or $10 a day. This is the conventional accounting method.

However, Joe was not an accountant and he preferred to figure it in a simpler way. His basic profit (or profit contribution) was still $.50 a jug. That is, the difference between his sales price of $1 and his variable expense per unit (often termed fixed unit costs) for jugs and labor was still $.50 each, no matter how many jugs he sold. The first 20 jugs he sold paid the rent on his washer and he made a profit of $.50 each on all over 20 he sold. In other words, his breakeven point was 20 jugs per day. If he should sell less than that, he would fail to cover his constant washer rent and would lose money. If he continued to sell 40 jugs a day he would make his profit of $.50 each on the second 20 jugs, or $10 a day. By figuring it this way, Joe could easily see just how he was coming out on any volume of business.

But Joe was not satisfied with $10 a day. He talked to Deal about increasing the sales. Deal told Joe that if he could supply 7 oz. bottles for his cooler, he could sell 1,000 bottles a day at $.10 a bottle. He was willing to pay $.06 a bottle. Joe could buy bottles for $.03 each and Sally's sister, Suzie, was willing to wash and fill the bottles for $.01 each. No labels were needed, but Sally was to furnish a new hand-painted poster to Deal each day to put over his cooler. Sally was willing to paint these posters for $2 each. Joe looked at this proposition in the following way.

Income per bottle		$ .06
Cost of bottle	$.03	
Labor cost	.01	
Total		.04
Basic profit per bottle		$ .02
Added constant cost		$2.00 per day

Thus Joe figured that he only needed to sell 100 bottles a day to cover his added constant cost. It sounded like a good proposition so he decided to go ahead with it. His overall situation was now as follows:

Washer rent	$10.00 per day
Posters	2.00 per day
Total constant cost	$12.00 per day
Basic profit per jug = $.50	
Basic profit per bottle = $.02	

Now the value of Joe's simple method of figuring his profit by thinking of total constant cost per day and basic profit or "profit contribution" per unit rather than allocating fixed charges to each product on a unit basis really began to show up. He could easily figure his profit on any combination of sales. If he continued to sell 40 jugs a day and also sold 1,000 7 oz. bottles, his profit would be as follows:

Basic profit on jugs	40 × $.50 =	$20.00
Basic profit on bottles	1,000 × $.02 =	20.00
Total basic profit		$40.00
Total constant cost		12.00
Net profit		$28.00

However, after a short time he found that he was selling 30 jugs and 1,500 bottles per day.

Basic profit on jugs	30 × $.50 =	$15.00
Basic profit on bottles	1,500 × $.02 =	30.00
Total basic profit		$45.00
Total constant cost		12.00
Net profit		$33.00

If Joe had been trained in accounting, he no doubt would have figured his costs by allocating the washer rental to each product on an estimate of the portion of washer time used by each. He then would have divided this allocated amount by his assumed quantities. When his actual sales differed from his assumed sales, he would have had an overabsorbed or underabsorbed burden. All very complex. But since Joe kept his constant costs separate, and thought in terms of basic profit per unit, he could figure his profit picture for any assortment or volume by simple arithmetic.

The beverage business went along smoothly for some time. Joe was making a profit of $33 a day, Sally was making $9.50 a day and Suzie was making $15 a day. One day Sally came to Joe and told him she was tired of getting the short end of the deal while Joe and Suzie were making big money. She demanded $.50 per jug and $3 per poster, or she would quit painting labels and posters. Joe blustered and squirmed, but since Sally was the only capable artist in the community he was forced to agree to her demands. Joe figured his profit under the new circumstances.

Income per jug		$ 1.00
Cost of jug	$.25	
Labor cost	.50	.75
Basic profit per jug		$ .25
Basic profit on jugs	30 × $.25 =	$ 7.50
Basic profit on bottles	1,500 × $.02 =	30.00
Total basic profit or *profit contribution*		$37.50
Constant cost of washer	$10.00	
Constant cost of posters	3.00	
Total constant cost		13.00
Net profit per day		$24.50

Again, Joe was dissatisfied with his profit. He told Deal he would have to get $.25 more per jug because of his increased labor cost. Deal agreed to pay $1.25 per jug, but said he would raise the retail price to $1.75 and this might reduce the volume of sales to as low as 20 a day. He checked with a number of Deal's customers and convinced himself that this was a good estimate of the maximum loss of volume he could expect. Joe figured his profit picture this way.

Basic profit on $1.00 jugs = 30 × $.25 = $ 7.50
Basic profit on $1.25 jugs = 20 × $.50 = $10.00
Increased net profit per day = $2.50

He decided to take the gamble and make the change.

REQUIRED:
Comment upon Joe's use of accounting data in making his decisions.

5-40 *Al:* Joe, you said you put in these peanuts because some people ask for them, but do you realize that this rack of peanuts is *costing* you?

Joe: It ain't gonna cost. 'Sgonna be a profit. Sure, I hadda pay $25 for a fancy rack to holda bags, but the peanuts cost $.06 a bag and I sell 'em for $.10. Figger I sell 50 bags a week to start. It'll take $12\frac{1}{2}$ weeks to cover the cost of the rack. After that I gotta clear profit of $.04 a bag. The more I sell, the more I make.

Al: That is an antiquated and completely unrealistic approach, Joe. Fortunately, modern accounting procedures permit a more accurate picture which reveals the complexities involved.

Joe: Huh?

Al: To be precise, those peanuts must be integrated into your entire operation and be allocated their appropriate share of business overhead. They must share a proportionate part of your expenditures for rent, heat, light, equipment depreciation, decorating, salaries for your waitresses, cook,—

Joe: The *cook?* What'sa he gotta do wit'a peanuts? He don' even know I got 'em!

Al: Look, Joe, the cook is in the kitchen, the kitchen prepares the food, the food is what brings people in here, and the people ask to buy peanuts. *That's* why you must charge a portion of the cook's wages, as well as a part of your own salary, to peanut sales. This sheet contains a carefully calculated cost analysis which indicates the peanut operation should pay exactly $1,278 per year toward these general overhead costs.

Joe: The peanuts? $1,278 a year for overhead? The nuts?

Al: It's really a little more than that. You also spend money each week to have the windows washed, to have the place swept out in the mornings, keep soap in the washroom and provide free sodas to the police. That raises the total to $1,313 per year.

Joe: (Thoughtfully) But the peanut salesman said I'd make money—put 'em on the end of the counter, he said—and get $.04 a bag profit.

Al: (With a sniff) He's not an accountant. Do you actually know what the portion of the counter occupied by the peanut rack is worth to you?

Joe: Ain't worth nothing—no stool there—just a dead spot at the end.

Al: The modern cost picture permits no dead spots. Your counter contains 60 square feet and your counter business grosses $15,000 a year. Consequently, the square foot of space occupied by the peanut rack is worth $250 per year. Since you have taken that area away from general counter use, you must charge the value of the space to the occupant.

Joe: You mean I gotta add *$250 a year more* to the *peanuts?*

Al: Right. That raises their share of the general operating costs to a grand total of $1,563 per year. Now then, if you sell 50 bags of peanuts per week, these allocated costs will amount to $.60 per bag.

Joe: WHAT?

Al: Obviously, to that must be added your purchase price of $.06 per bag, which brings the total to $.66. So you see, by selling peanuts at $.10 per bag, you are losing $.56 on every sale.

Joe: Somethin's crazy!

Al: Not at all! Here are the *figures.* They *prove* your peanut operation cannot stand on its own feet.

Joe: (Brightening) Suppose I sell *lotsa* peanuts—thousand bags a week 'stead of fifty?

Al: (Tolerantly) Joe, you don't understand the problem. If the volume of peanut sales increases, our operating costs will go up—you'll have to handle more bags, with more time, more depreciation, more everything. The basic principle of accounting is firm on that subject: "The bigger the operation, the more general overhead costs that must be allocated." No. Increasing the volume of sales won't help.

Joe: Okay. You so smart, *you* tell *me* what I gotta do.

Al: (Condescendingly) Well—you could first reduce operating expenses.

Joe: How?

Al: Move to a building with cheaper rent. Cut salaries. Wash the windows biweekly. Have the floor swept only on Thursday. Remove the soap from the washrooms. Decrease the square-foot value of your counter. For example, if you can cut your expenses 50 percent, that will reduce the amount allocated to peanuts from $1,563 to $781.50 per year, reducing the cost to $.36 per bag.

Joe: (Slowly) That's better?

Al: Much, much better. However, even then you would lose $.26 per bag if you charge only $.10. Therefore, you must also raise your selling price. If you want a net profit of $.04 per bag you would have to charge $.40.

Joe: (Flabbergasted) You mean even after I cut operating costs 50 percent I still gotta charge $.40 for a $.10 bag of peanuts? Nobody's that nuts about nuts! Who'd buy 'em?

Al: That's a secondary consideration. The point is, at $.40 you'd be selling at a price based upon a true and proper evaluation of your then reduced costs.

Joe: (Eagerly) Look! I gotta better idea. Why don't I just throw the nuts out—put 'em in a ash can?

Al: Can you afford it?

Joe: Sure. All I got is about 50 bags of peanuts—cost about three bucks—so I lose $25 on the rack, but I'm outa this nutsy business and no more grief.

Al: (Shaking head) Joe it isn't that simple. You are *in* the peanut business! The minute you throw those peanuts out you are adding $1,563 of annual overhead to the *rest* of your operation. Joe—be realistic—*can you afford to do that?*

Joe: (Completely crushed) It'sa unbelievable! Last week I was a make money. Now I'm in a trouble—justa because I think peanuts on a counter is a gonna bring me some extra profit—justa because I believe 50 bags of peanuts a week is a easy.

Al: (With raised eyebrow) That is the object of modern cost studies, Joe—to dispel those false illusions.

REQUIRED:

A. Discuss the accounting concepts in this case as they relate to financial and managerial accounting.

PART TWO

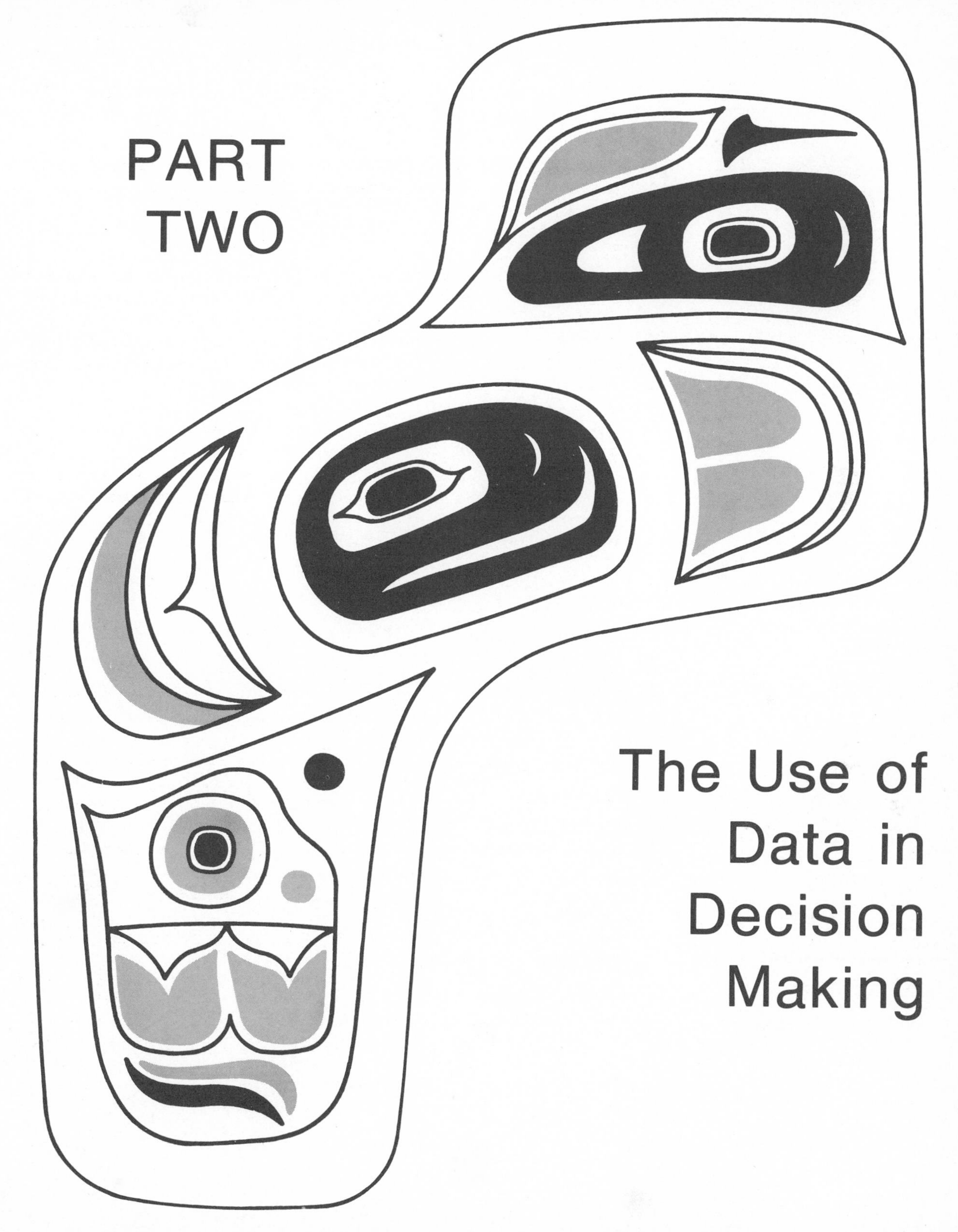

The Use of Data in Decision Making

6 Revenue and Pricing Decisions

OPEN MARKET PRICING

The Economic Theory of Price

Pricing: An Art or a Science?

FULL COST-BASED PRICING

Problems in Apportioning Fixed Costs

Problems in Apportioning Joint Costs

Pricing Nonstandard Products with Cost-based Formulas

CONTRIBUTION MARGIN-BASED PRICING FOR SHORT RANGE AND SPECIAL ORDERS

PRICE DISCRIMINATION

SUMMARY

The most important operating decisions management must make are those establishing the selling prices for its products and services. A company's long-range survival depends upon its pricing decisions. In the long run the firm's prices must be sufficient to cover all costs and leave a profit margin adequate to reward the financial investors for the use of their funds. If the firm's revenue consistently fails to cover costs and provide a satisfactory profit, the investors will seek new opportunities and the firm will fail.

In this chapter we will look at how accounting and economic data can be used by management to make pricing decisions. We will study pricing from three different perspectives. First, we will examine pricing where there is an established marketplace. The economic theory of pricing, as shown by the supply and demand curves, is relevant here. Second, we will examine pricing decisions where the marketplace is not well established and prices are often determined by accounting costs plus a profit percentage. Third, we will look at unusual situations where the firm must make nonroutine, distress pricing decisions.

OPEN MARKET PRICING

A large segment of microeconomic theory is devoted to pricing and the resultant volume decision. Economic theory assumes there is a known, open, and free marketplace for the goods and services being offered for sale. There are two key elements in assessing the market structure. The first concerns the number of buyers and sellers in the marketplace. Typically, the larger the number of buyers and sellers, the more competitive the market.

Second, the market structure is influenced by the extent the product is standardized. If other products are reasonable substitutes for the ones offered for sale, there will be increased competition. For example, in the transportation industry a plane, a bus, and a railroad may be in competition to provide service between two points. The more easily one mode of transportation can be substituted for another, the greater the competition. Also, the nature of the product can determine the market structure. For example, with a highly perishable product, such as fresh strawberries, it is impossible to compete in many geographic markets without incurring excessive transportation and distribution costs.

The Economic Theory of Price

The basic factors in economic theory are the supply of the product and the demand for it. It makes intuitive sense that the quantity of the product that customers will buy over a period of time depends upon the price. The higher the price, the fewer the units of product customers will be willing to buy; the lower the price, the more units of product they will buy. A typical demand curve (*dd*) is shown in Exhibit 6-1. The **demand curve** relates the market

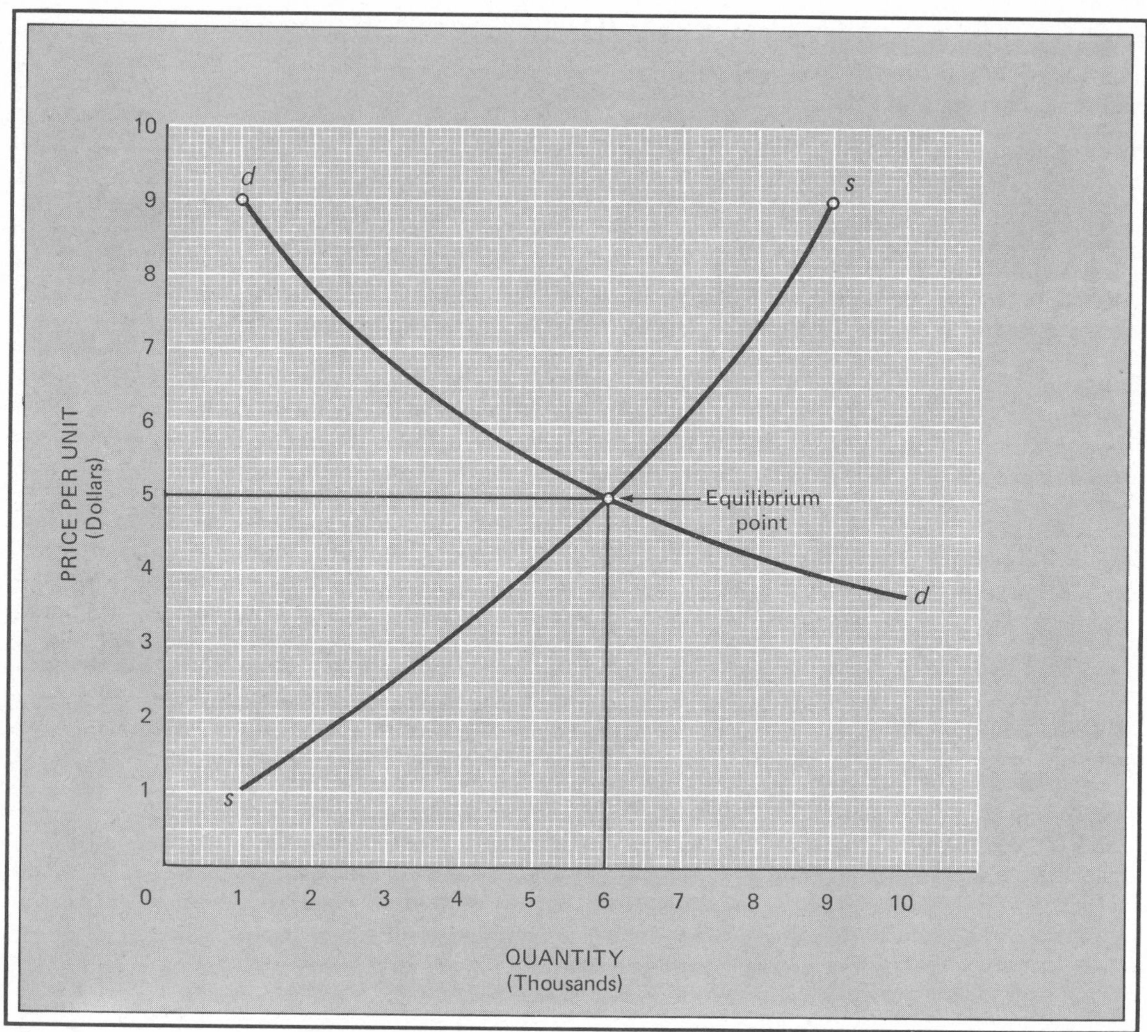

EXHIBIT 6-1
Supply and demand curves

prices and the quantity of the product the *customers* want to buy. The demand curve slopes downward and to the right, showing that when the price is increased customers will be willing to buy a smaller quantity, and when prices are lowered customers will buy a larger quantity.

The **supply curve** relates the market prices and the quantity of product that the *suppliers* or *producers* are willing to supply. As shown in Exhibit 6-1, the supply curve (*ss*) rises upward to the right. At a higher price the supplier will increase output. However, as production increases, the supplier ultimately faces diminishing returns on the productive facilities. **Diminishing returns** recognizes that as the use of production facilities increases, it takes more productive energy per unit to produce one additional unit. Workers become tired and inefficient, machines break down more often, factories become crowded, and premium prices must be paid to get material and labor.

How do supply and demand interact to determine the market price? The demand schedule shows us the quantities demanded by the customers combined with the prices they are willing to pay. We can then say, "If customers demand so much, the price will be thus and so." The supply schedule shows us how much the producers are willing to produce at various prices. We can then say, "If so much product is available, the price is thus and so, and the producers will provide so much product." However, neither schedule alone tells what the price will be or how much will be produced by the suppliers or purchased by the customers.

The market price will be determined at the intersection point of the supply and demand curves. At exactly this **equilibrium point** the amount the producers will provide equals the amount the customers demand, and the market is cleared. This point is shown on Exhibit 6-1, where the equilibrium price is $5 and the equilibrium quantity is 6,000 units. If the market price were to increase, to $9 for example, the quantity supplied would increase to 9,000 units. The increased price would cause the quantity demanded to decrease to 3,000 units. At $9 the quantity supplied would exceed the quantity demanded. At a point lower than the equilibrium price, say $4 per unit, the quantity demanded would exceed the quantity supplied, and the buyers would "bid" the price up.

The previous discussion has assumed that the changes taking place were in the quantity supplied or the quantity demanded. The difference in the quantity demanded is shown in the graph on the left. The movement is along a single demand curve.

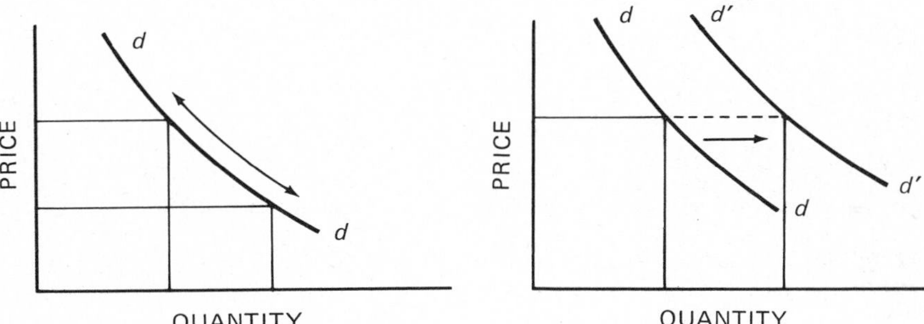

It is also possible that the supply or demand curve might shift. For example, the graph on the right shows a difference in the customer demand that is independent of price differences. The demand curve could shift because of changes in consumer tastes, consumer income, or the prices of related products that could be substituted. In the same way, the supply curve could shift because of changes in the factors of production or the cost of the inputs.

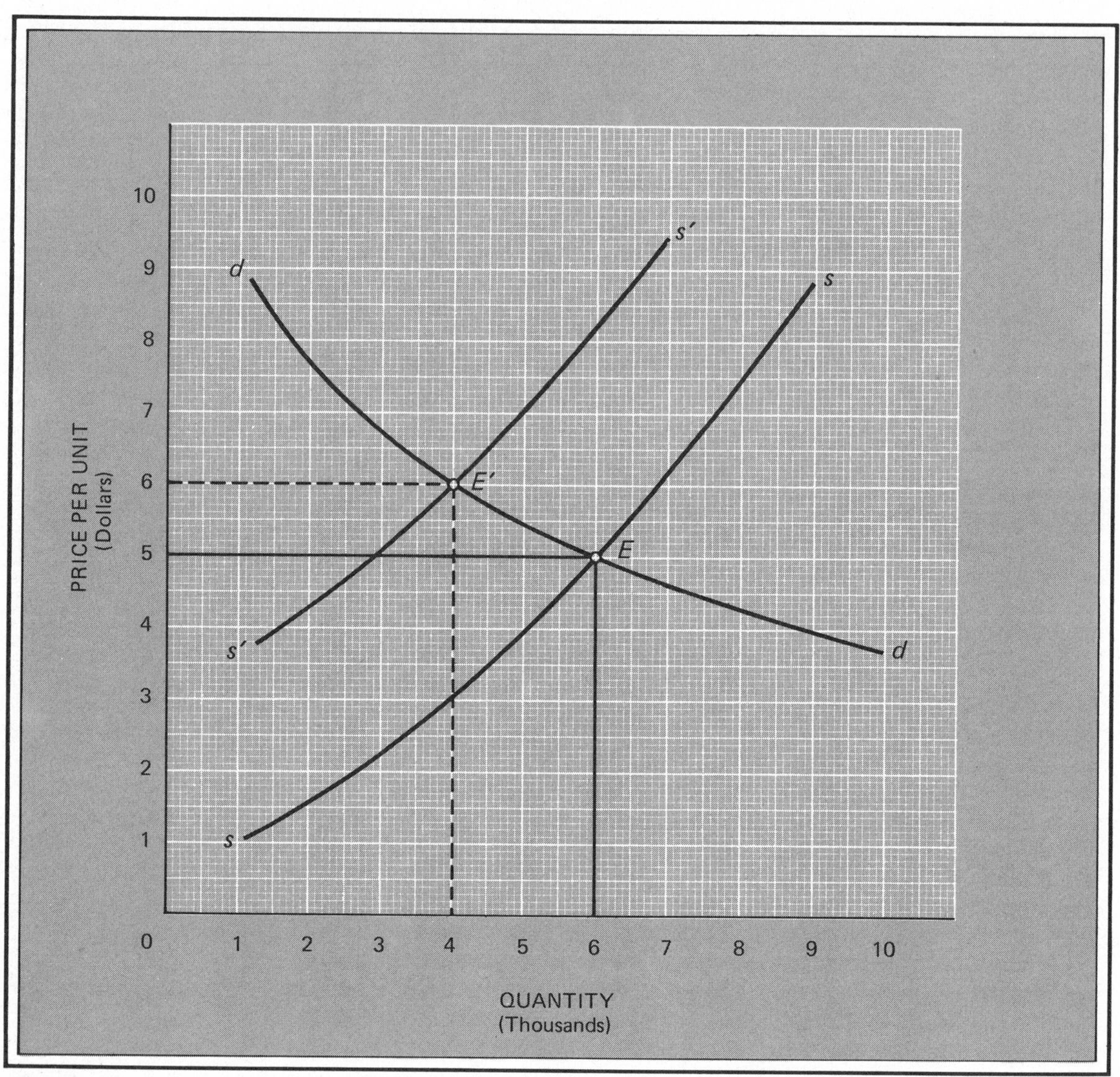

EXHIBIT 6-2
Effects of shift in supply curve

What happens if the producers decrease the supply of the product available? Exhibit 6-2 shows how the original supply curve *ss* has shifted to the left and become supply curve *s′s′*. The demand has not changed, but the equilibrium price has moved from $5 at point *E* to $6 at point *E′*. This new price would bring the supply and demand into equilibrium again at 4,000 units. What would happen if the demand for the product increases and the supply curve stays the same? Exhibit 6-3 shows the demand curve shifting to

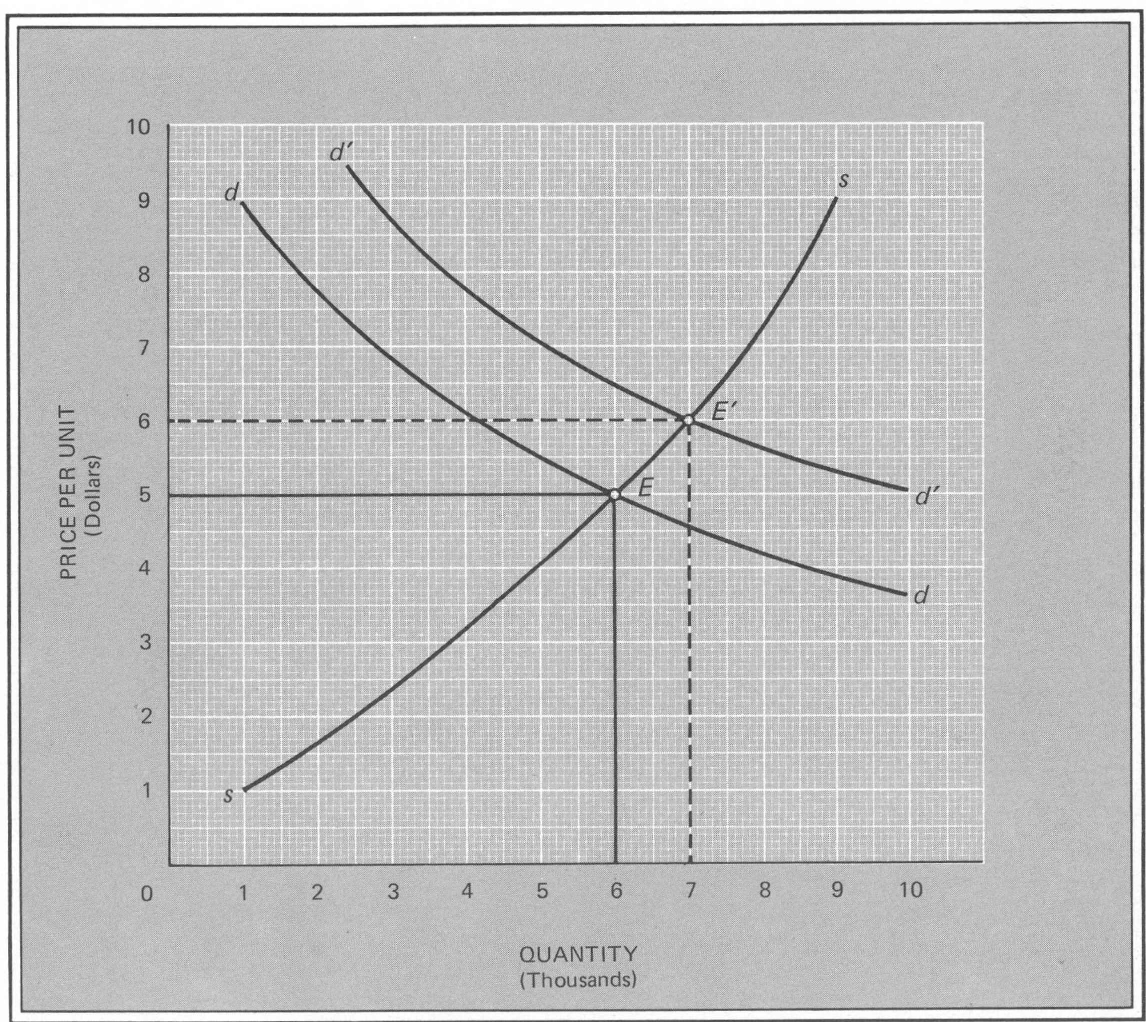

EXHIBIT 6-3
Effects of shift in demand curve

the right from *dd* to *d′d′*. The increased demand and the constant supply curve have forced an increase in the price needed for equilibrium from the original $5 price at point *E* to $6 at point *E′*.[1]

The slope of the demand curve for a particular firm will depend upon its market structure; that is, the degree of competition in the market for the product. There are four broad classes of market structures: pure competition, pure monopoly, monopolistic competition, and oligopoly.

[1]The way in which a change in price affects the demand is called **price elasticity.** If a small decrease in price creates a larger increase in quantity sold, the demand is called *elastic.* If a substantial decrease in price is required to increase quantity sold, demand is called *inelastic.* A study of price elasticity is beyond the scope of this book.

PURE COMPETITION

In a purely competitive market there are a large number of buyers and sellers; each firm's transactions are so small in relation to the total market that they do not affect the price.[2] The price is determined in the marketplace. The firm can sell as much as it wishes if it sells at the market price. More importantly, it cannot sell *any* product at a higher price. The firm's demand curve is horizontal. The price is constant and the average revenue and the marginal revenue are equal. However, the industry demand curve will be shaped like the curve in Exhibit 6-1. A purely competitive firm (1) can sell nothing above the equilibrium price, (2) can sell all it produces at exactly that price, and (3) would have no reason to lower its price below the existing market price. Management's decision in a purely competitive market is to select the output (volume) level that maximizes the firm's profits, it must accept the going price.

PURE MONOPOLY

In a pure monopoly there is only one producer. The industry consists of one firm. In a monopoly the industry demand curve is the same as the demand curve for the firm. Since the industry demand curves are downward-sloping, the demand curve of the monopolist will slope downward to the right. For profit maximization the firm should operate at the output level where its marginal cost equals the marginal revenue. This point will simultaneously determine the optimum price and output level. The monopolistic firm can determine either the price or the quantity, but not both. Given one, the other is automatically determined by the market.

MONOPOLISTIC COMPETITION

It is very rare to find pure competition or pure monopoly. Most firms have some competition, although not pure competition. In the monopolistic competitive market structure the customers believe there are differences between the products of different firms. These firms have a number of competitors producing substitutable products. Nevertheless, they have some control over their pricing policies. These firms face downward-sloping demand curves, in contrast to the horizontal demand curve in a purely competitive market.

If a firm is successful in differentiating its product from the products of other firms, it will have greater flexibility in pricing and output decisions. A firm with strong product differentiation and loyal customers has greater

[2]Other assumptions of pure competition include: perfect homogeneity of the products; free entry and exits to the market; and perfect information about price, cost, and quality by the buyers and sellers in the market.

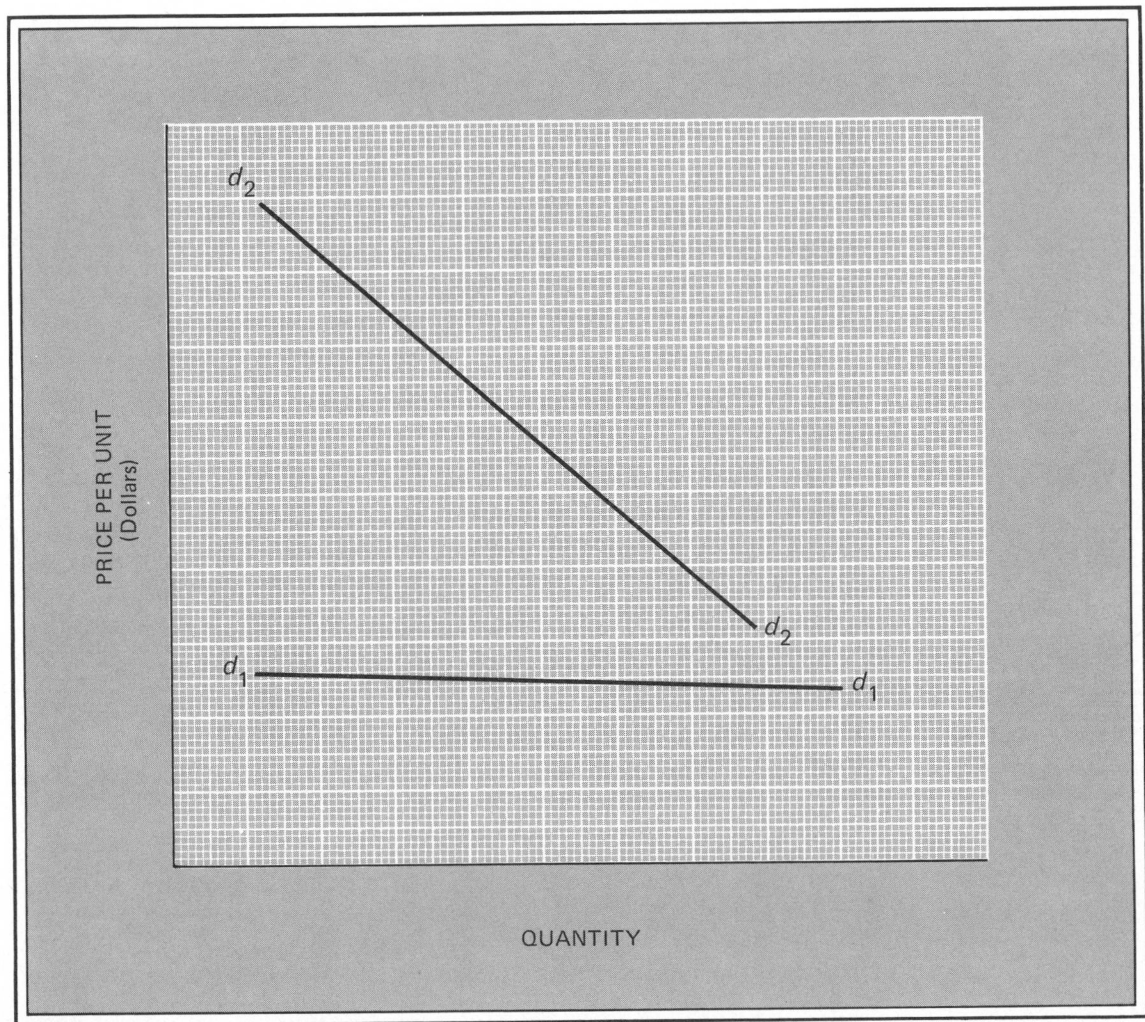

EXHIBIT 6-4
Demand curves for two firms in monopolistic competition

control over its prices. Exhibit 6-4 shows the demand curves for two firms. The demand curve d_1 shows a firm whose customers differentiate its product only slightly from those of competitors. The demand curve is almost horizontal, indicating active competition. Demand curve d_2 shows a firm that has been successful in differentiating its products from other products available, with a resulting decrease in the competition from other firms.

OLIGOPOLY

In most markets firms have some control over price (unlike the pure competitive market), are in competition with some firms (unlike the pure monopoly), and are limited in some way by close substitutes for their products. In an oligopoly there are a few large sellers, each with a large share of the market. These firms interact with each other. The revenue of a given seller depends upon the reactions of his competitiors to changes in his selling prices. An action taken by one firm will cause a reaction by others. If an oligopolistic seller raises his prices and his competitors raise theirs, or if he lowers his and they lower theirs, his demand curve will have the same general shape as the demand curve for the whole market. In the oligopoly marketplace, the optimal price and output decision depends upon how competing firms react.

Firms joined together in a cartel could set a price to maximize the industry's profits. If the cartel is successful it can create a monopolistic market. Because of this possibility, formal or informal agreements that restrict prices and outputs have been made illegal in the United States. Also, cartels are difficult to establish for there is often disagreement among the members about how to share the profits; one firm can subvert the cartel to maximize its own profit at the expense of the other firms. An acceptable means of reducing uncertainty in an oligopoly is for one firm to establish itself as the leader and price setter. Because of the leader's strength, all other firms must then accept its pricing policy. A firm may become dominant because of its relative size to others, its cost efficiency, its products offered, or because of revenue and cost forecasting accuracy.

Pricing: An Art or a Science?

Economic theory provides a relatively clear and straightforward approach to establishing price and volume for pure monopoly, pure competition, and monopolistic competition. Under an oligopolistic market, the approach is more complex and often impossible to specify, since a firm can interact in many ways. Because of this complexity, price leadership by the dominant firm, or firms, is common, and stable prices develop. Also, oligopolistic firms actively engage in nonprice competition such as service improvement, style differences, and advertising.

While the theoretical pricing model developed by the economists is sound, it is difficult to apply directly in practice. First, it assumes that the firm's demand curve is known. Generally management does not have available data that is accurate and reliable enough to give more than a rough picture of the demand curve. Therefore, while firms may consider the shape of the demand curve, they may not be able to do so in an exacting way.

Second, economics assumes that firms are profit maximizers. Many legal and societal goals and constraints influence management's desire for profits. Certainly stability, growth, and security are important to managers, and these can be obtained short of total profit maximization.

Third, there are many factors besides price that affect a firm's demand function. For example, there is a necessary interaction between marketing and distribution policies, promotional and advertising policies, sales staff deployment, customer services offered, and the types of products sold. All these factors have a heavy influence upon the amount of product that can be sold at a specific price.

In a very real sense pricing is an art rather than a science. Economics provides a sound theoretical background that may be difficult to apply in practice. These difficulties in determining the demand functions have led management to adopt a trial and error (**heuristic**) approach to pricing.

FULL COST-BASED PRICING

One method of establishing price, particularly where the firm lacks knowledge of the demand curve, is to calculate the cost of the product and then add a percentage markup for net income. This method has been called **cost-based pricing, cost-plus pricing,** or **average cost pricing.** Each term implies that an addition for net income is made to some suitable cost base. The net income markup can be stated as either a percentage of cost or selling price.

The following formula expresses the full cost-based price.

$$\text{Price per unit} = \frac{\text{Total cost} + \text{Desired net income}}{\text{Quantity}}$$

For firms that think of net income as a return on investment, the formula would be modified.

$$\text{Price per unit} = \frac{\text{Total cost} + (\text{Desired rate of return} \times \text{Investment})}{\text{Quantity}}$$

As an example, assume that a firm has budgeted production of 150,000 units requiring the following costs: direct materials \$150,000; direct labor \$250,000; variable factory overhead \$125,000; fixed factory overhead \$75,000; and fixed selling and administrative costs \$300,000. Management would also like to earn a 15% rate of return on the stockholders' equity of \$1,000,000. The following equation shows the desired price based on full cost.

$$\begin{aligned}\text{Price per unit} &= \frac{(\$150{,}000 + \$250{,}000 + \$125{,}000 + \$75{,}000 + \$300{,}000) + (.15 \times \$1{,}000{,}000)}{150{,}000 \text{ units}} \\ &= \frac{\$900{,}000 + \$150{,}000}{150{,}000 \text{ units}} \\ &= \$7 \text{ per unit}\end{aligned}$$

In this illustration with only one product, the \$900,000 includes all costs incurred by the firm. In a multiproduct firm the cost per unit is considered to be the total of variable costs for the product and some apportioned or allocated share of fixed costs.

Problems in Apportioning Fixed Costs

The proper treatment of the fixed costs presents a problem. As discussed in Chapters 3 and 4, the determination of a total cost per unit requires that the fixed costs be apportioned over a specific number of units. The fixed factory overhead costs in the previous example were $75,000, and the fixed selling and administrative expenses were $300,000. At a production and sales output of 150,000 units, the fixed costs per unit are $2.50 ($375,000 ÷ 150,000 units). If the company's volume increased to 300,000 units, the per-unit fixed cost would drop to $1.25 ($375,000 ÷ 300,000). The per-unit fixed cost would increase to $5.00 ($375,000 ÷ 75,000) if the volume dropped to 75,000 units. Unlike the fixed costs, the variable costs will remain at $3.50 per unit at all levels [($150,000 + $250,000 + $125,000) ÷ 150,000 units].

Assuming that the firm has a policy of adding to its full cost a 10% profit margin, it could have the following prices, depending upon its volume decision.

Number of units	*75,000*	*100,000*	*150,000*	*300,000*
Variable costs per unit	$3.50	$3.50	$3.50	$3.50
Fixed costs per unit	5.00	3.75	2.50	1.25
Total costs per unit	$8.50	$7.25	$6.00	$4.75
10% markup on cost	.85	.73	.60	.48
Selling price	$9.35	$7.98	$6.60	$5.23

When the decision maker selects 150,000 units as the most likely sales volume, he anticipates that the net income per unit will be $.60. Let's assume that based upon this budget a selling price of $6.60 is established and, because of an unexpected market penetration, actual sales were 200,000 units. The actual net income and the budgeted net income are shown in Exhibit 6-5.

	Budgeted		Actual	
Sales	(150,000 x $6.60)	$990,000	(200,000 x $6.60)	$1,320,000
Variable costs	(150,000 x $3.50)	525,000	(200,000 x $3.50)	700,000
Contribution margin	(150,000 x $3.10)	$465,000	(200,000 x $3.10)	$ 620,000
Fixed costs		375,000		375,000
Net income before taxes		$ 90,000		$ 245,000

EXHIBIT 6-5
Effects of volume changes upon net income

There is a difference between the budgeted net income per unit of \$.60 and the actual net income per unit of \$1.225 (\$245,000 ÷ 200,000 units) because the actual fixed cost per unit at 200,000 units is \$1.875 (\$375,000 ÷ 200,000 units); it was originally budgeted at \$2.50. The difference between the \$2.50 budgeted fixed costs per unit and the \$1.875 actual fixed costs per unit is \$.625, which is also the difference between the actual net income per unit of \$1.225 and the budgeted net income of \$.60.

Problems in Apportioning Joint Costs

There is a major problem with firms that have multiple products. The price based upon full cost assumes that there is a satisfactory way to allocate all manufacturing and, in most cases, selling and administrative costs among the several products. There are no absolute criteria for the allocation of these **joint** costs. Joint costs are not inherently traceable to individual products or product lines, and some method must be found to apportion them. To examine this problem of joint costs, let's assume that a firm manufactures two products with the following cost and production data.

	Product A		*Product B*
Variable costs per unit	\$ 4		\$ 9
Labor hours per unit	1		3
Units produced per year	15,000		10,000
Joint costs of production		\$120,000	

The joint costs represent costs incurred that are applicable to both products. To arrive at a full cost for each product, the joint costs must be allocated. The variable costs per unit of product, the labor hours used per unit of product, or the quantity of each product manufactured are all possible bases of allocating the joint costs. The method chosen should be simple, easy to measure, and relate the "cause" (activity base used to apportion) with the "effect" (cost).

The joint costs could be apportioned on the basis of variable costs.

	Variable Costs	*Ratio*	*Joint Costs*
Product A (15,000 × \$4)	\$ 60,000	60/150	\$ 48,000
Product B (10,000 × \$9)	90,000	90/150	72,000
Total	\$150,000	150/150	\$120,000

The joint costs could also be allocated on the basis of total labor hours as shown below.

	Total Labor Hours	*Ratio*	*Joint Costs*
Product A (15,000 × 1)	15,000	15/45	$ 40,000
Product B (10,000 × 3)	30,000	30/45	80,000
Total	45,000	45/45	$120,000

An allocation based upon the number of units produced would assign the following joint costs.

	Total Units Produced	*Ratio*	*Joint Costs*
Product A	15,000	15/25	$ 72,000
Product B	10,000	10/25	48,000
Total	25,000	25/25	$120,000

If the joint costs were apportioned on the basis of variable costs, Product A would receive two-fifths of the $120,000 joint costs, or $48,000. Since 15,000 units of Product A were produced, the full cost would be [$4.00 + ($48,000 ÷ 15,000 units)], or $7.20. If the joint costs had been apportioned on the basis of total labor hours, Product A would receive one-third of the $120,000 joint costs, and the full cost would be [$4.00 + ($40,000 ÷ 15,000 units)], or $6.67. The full cost and hence the price will be affected by the joint fixed-cost allocation base chosen.

A word of caution is necessary. The joint costs often will include a large proportion of fixed costs. There is a danger that the unit cost *after* the allocation of joint costs will be viewed by the decision maker as a variable cost. He must be careful not to treat allocated fixed costs as variable costs.

While the cost-based pricing formula is simple, it does not agree with economic theory because it ignores the relationships between demand and price and between price and volume. The price determined by full cost plus a markup may be so high that there are no customers. If so, some of the volume potential of the firm will be idle. There is a circularity problem. Volume is used to determine price in the cost-based pricing formula, yet the number of units the company sells and, therefore, the firm's volume may depend upon price.

Nevertheless, pricing policies based on full cost are widely used. Why? Certainly a principal reason is the inability of the decision maker to quantify the demand curve. This inability to apply economic theory leads the businessman to apply intuitive judgement coupled with trial and error methods. Many decision makers begin with a full-cost approach and then, based upon the buyers' reception of their price, adjust the price. In this way the full cost-based price represents a first approximation—a target price whose markup must be adjusted to meet the actual marketplace.

Another reason for the adoption of full cost-based prices is the belief that they represent a "floor" or "safe" price that will prevent losses. This safety factor is more illusory than real. While the per-unit sales price will cover the per-unit full cost, losses may still be incurred if the sales volume is miscalculated. The higher the proportion of fixed costs, the more the profit is influenced by sales volume. If the full cost-based price is so high that it drives customers away, the sales volume can be reduced to the extent that actual average cost is greater than the price.

Perhaps the most convincing reason for the use of full cost-based prices is that the costs of a particular firm will be comparable with costs of other firms in the industry. One firm's costs are reasonable estimates of its competitors' costs, and hence its prices will be comparable to those of its competitors. This would be particularly true in oligopolistic industries. If most companies use similar facilities to perform similar activities, they will have similar full costs and thus similar prices.

Pricing Nonstandard Products With Cost-based Formulas

The best way for a buyer or seller to ensure a fair price is to rely upon a competitive marketplace. Unfortunately this is not always possible. Where there is demand for a product that does not currently exist, such as the space program's lunar vehicle, competition in price cannot take place. Here, competition is based upon scientific and technical competence, management skills, and past experience, not upon price alone. In these situations price is determined by negotiation and contract commitments.

While a large number of different contract types are available, two broad classes are typical:

1. In a **fixed price contract** both parties agree to a price that remains unchanged for the life of the contract. A fixed price contract requires past experience with the product or relatively low risk for both the buyer and seller.

2. In a **cost reimbursable contract** the seller is reimbursed all reasonable (allowable) costs incurred in fulfilling the contract plus an agreed upon fee. The buyer assumes a large portion of the risk, since he must reimburse the seller for all allowable costs. The seller should not suffer a loss, although he could fail to make an acceptable rate of return on his productive assets.

Three broad types of cost reimbursable contracts have been widely used. In the **cost-plus-percentage contract** (CPP), the fee is a percentage of the actual costs incurred. If the contract is cost-plus-10%, and the supplier incurred costs of $100,000, the supplier would earn profits of $10,000 on the contract and $110,000 would be the price to the buyer. If the costs were

$200,000, the fee would be $20,000 and the total price, $220,000. This contract is potentially dangerous for the buyer because the supplier can indiscriminately incur costs to increase his fee. It was widely used for government contracting in World War II, but it is not widely used today.

In the **cost-plus-fixed-fee contract** (CPFF) the buyer and the seller negotiate a fee based upon budgeted costs. Suppose, for example, that both the supplier and the buyer believe that costs of $500,000 are reasonable to design and manufacture a new lunar lander, and that a fee of 15% of this cost, or $75,000, is fair and adequate. The contract would be for $575,000. If, because of cost overruns, the actual costs were $600,000, the buyer would reimburse the supplier $675,000—the original fee of $75,000 plus all costs allowed in the contract. The actual profit return, based on cost is 12.5% ($75,000 ÷ $600,000) rather than the planned 15%. Since the extra costs probably consumed company capacity, the lower return on costs may mean that the overall rate of return for the seller will fall below an acceptable rate to maintain his investment.

An **incentive contract** can be used to encourage a supplier to conserve costs. For example, an incentive contract may call for cost-plus-fixed-fee if the company meets or exceeds the original budgeted costs and include a predetermined way for the buyer and seller to share in cost savings when costs are below budget. Assume that a firm has an incentive contract that calls for sharing with the buyer all cost savings in a 50:50 ratio. The original contract was for $500,000 costs and a $75,000 fee. If the firm incurs allowable costs of $460,000 to complete the job, it will be reimbursed $555,000 ($460,000 costs + $75,000 fee + ½ of $40,000 savings). The firm's profit percentage would be raised to 20.7% ($95,000 ÷ $460,000), considerably higher than the 15% originally planned. If the seller is unsuccessful in reducing costs and his actual costs are $600,000, he would receive $675,000 ($600,000 costs + $75,000 fee), and his return would fall to 12.5% ($75,000 ÷ $600,000).

In those situations where the price is determined by a contractual cost-based formula, cost accounting plays a vital role. Because the contract calls for the reimbursement of all allowable costs, both the buyer and the seller have a stake in how costs are defined, measured, and accumulated. For suppliers to the Department of Defense, *Armed Services Procurement Regulations* (ASPR) has been the authoritative guidebook. It specifies which costs are allowable for reimbursement and how costs should be accumulated and apportioned to products.

Difficulties that arose in interpreting and applying ASPR caused Congress to establish the Cost Accounting Standards Board (CASB) in 1970. The CASB is charged with assisting governmental agencies as buyers of goods and services in understanding and negotiating cost-based prices. To accomplish this task, the board has issued standards of cost accounting to which government suppliers must conform. These cost standards are to ensure that the government pays a fair price for the goods it buys on a cost-based contract. It must be recognized that the intent of the CASB is *not* to develop cost data for managerial decision making, but to simplify the pricing and auditing problems of the U.S. government.

CONTRIBUTION MARGIN-BASED PRICING FOR SHORT RANGE AND SPECIAL ORDERS

The previous discussion of economic theory and full cost-based prices has assumed a relatively stable, recurring marketplace. Management must also make price decisions for special, nonrecurring events. These decisions include pricing for special orders and distress pricing.

The contribution margin provides a good analytical tool in pricing special orders. It does not require the allocation of joint costs nor the determination of an expected volume to allocate the fixed costs. From an incremental view of costing, the only relevant costs to pricing decisions are those costs that would be avoided if the order were not accepted. Ordinarily these are the variable production and distribution costs.

To illustrate how pricing decisions can be made with a contribution margin approach, let's assume that the C.M. Manufacturing Company has excess productive capacity. Normal plant capacity is 150,000 units per year; current operations are 100,000 units per year. At this level it is operating at two-thirds of capacity. The current production of 100,000 units is sold in the regular markets for $2 each. Variable costs are $1.20 per unit and annual fixed costs are $60,000. The following income statement is based upon current production and sales.

C.M. MANUFACTURING COMPANY CONTRIBUTION MARGIN INCOME STATEMENT For the Year Ended December 31, 19X6	
Sales (100,000 × $2.00)	$200,000
Variable costs (100,000 × $1.20)	120,000
Contribution margin (100,000 × $.80)	$ 80,000
Fixed costs	60,000
Net income	$ 20,000

The firm's full cost is [$1.20 + ($60,000 ÷ 100,000 units)], or $1.80 per unit. Now assume that it receives an offer from a foreign buyer to manufacture and sell an additional 20,000 units at $1.50. Should it accept the order? The price of $1.50 is below the full cost of $1.80 but above the $1.20 variable cost. If the additional order does not affect the regular market price of $2, only the variable costs are relevant to the decision. The additional order would affect the net income favorably. The following income statement assumes that the special order was accepted.

C.M. MANUFACTURING COMPANY
CONTRIBUTION MARGIN INCOME STATEMENT
For the Year Ended December 31, 19X6

	Regular	*Special*	*Total*
Sales: Regular (100,000 × \$2.00)	\$200,000		
Special (20,000 × \$1.50)		\$30,000	\$230,000
Variable costs:			
Regular (100,000 × \$1.20)	120,000		
Special (20,000 × \$1.20)		24,000	144,000
Contribution margin	\$ 80,000	\$ 6,000	\$ 86,000
Fixed costs			60,000
Net income			\$ 26,000

The special order increased the net income by \$6,000. A contribution margin approach shows this effect. The unit contribution margin on the special order is \$.30 (\$1.50 − \$1.20) and the total contribution margin on the additional order is \$6,000 (\$.30 × 20,000 units).

What would happen to the firm if the special order affected its current market? Assuming that the demand curve was such that *all* products had to be offered at the special-order price, the income statement would then show a loss.

C.M. MANUFACTURING COMPANY
CONTRIBUTION MARGIN INCOME STATEMENT
For the Year Ended December 31, 19X6

Sales (120,000 × \$1.50)	\$180,000
Variable costs (120,000 × \$1.20)	144,000
Contribution margin (120,000 × \$.30)	\$ 36,000
Fixed costs	60,000
Net loss for the year	\$ (24,000)

If the special order infiltrates the regular market, it could jeopardize the firm's profit structure. If special-order pricing dominates, the lower price will increase demand but could, at the same time, reduce net income. This possible effect has caused many people to reject variable cost-based pricing for both long-run and short-run decisions in favor of full cost-based prices. Obviously, before any decision is made to sell a regular product at a special price, serious consideration must be given to the potential effect of this decision on regular sales.

The contribution margin approach holds that the short-run objective of a pricing decision is to maximize the firm's total contribution margin. The contribution margin—the excess of revenues over variable costs—is to cover fixed costs and then to provide a net income. If the contribution margin is maximized, net income will be maximized. It accepts the view that any unit providing a positive contribution margin will enhance the firm's profit picture. To illustrate this view further, let's assume that a firm has the following cost and revenue structure.

Normal selling price at 100% of normal capacity of 100,000 units	$5 per unit
Variable production costs	$3 per unit
Variable selling costs	$1 per unit
Fixed production costs	$30,000 per year
Fixed selling costs	$20,000 per year

It has received an offer to sell 10,000 units per year for the next five years to a special buyer at a special price of $3.50. Once the contract is consummated, the buyer will take delivery of the goods at the factory; no variable selling costs will be required on these 10,000 units. Should the firm accept the offer? Comparative income statements are shown in Exhibit 6-6. According to these income statements the answer is no. To accept the order would reduce profits by $5,000. What is the minimum price acceptable for this order to maintain current profits? For this decision the fixed costs are not relevant; they do not change as a result of the decision. To maintain the current profit rate there must be an average contribution margin of $1 per unit, the current contribution margin. In order for the remaining 90,000 units to achieve this contribution margin, the 10,000-unit special order must also achieve a contribution margin of $1. The variable production costs of $3 will be the only relevant costs for the special order. The minimum price would be $4 ($3 variable cost + $1 contribution margin). At a price of $4 or above the special order would be acceptable; below $4 it would be unacceptable.

To carry the contribution margin approach one step further, let's assume that the company has an excess inventory of 500 units that it cannot sell in its normal market because of a style change. What is the minimum price it can accept for these units and be better off than by merely scrapping them? A full cost-based approach might respond $4.50 [($300,000 + $100,000 + $30,000 + $20,000) ÷ 100,000 units]. A deeper analysis shows that the fixed costs remain unchanged. Further, the variable costs to produce the

	Without Special Order		With Special Order	
Sales	(100,000 x $5.00)	$500,000	(90,000 x $5.00)	$450,000
			(10,000 x $3.50)	35,000
		$500,000		$485,000
Variable costs:				
Production	(100,000 x $3.00)	$300,000	(100,000 x $3.00)	$300,000
Selling	(100,000 x $1.00)	100,000	(90,000 x $1.00)	90,000
		400,000		390,000
Contribution margin	(100,000 x $1.00)	$100,000		$ 95,000
Fixed costs:				
Production	$30,000		$30,000	
Selling	20,000		20,000	
Total		50,000		50,000
Net income		$ 50,000		$ 45,000

EXHIBIT 6-6
Effects of special order upon net income

products are not relevant because the units have already been produced. The only relevant cost is the variable selling cost. If the firm could sell the 500 units for $1.10 they would be $50 [($1.10 − $1.00) × 500 units] better off than if it did not sell them. If it sold the units for $.80 each, it would lose an additional $.20 per unit ($1.00 − $.80).

PRICE DISCRIMINATION

Because of their size, cost structure, large customer base, or favorable market position, some firms can price their products low enough to drive competitors out of business. However, Congress has passed a number of antitrust laws in order to protect and encourage wholesome competition. In 1914 passage of the Clayton Act created the Federal Trade Commission, an administrative and semijudicial agency empowered to restrict unfair methods of competition and deceptive practices by competitors.

In 1936 the Clayton Act was amended by the Robinson-Patman Act. Among the principal subsections of this law are limitations on unfair price discrimination. When a seller is charged by a buyer with discriminating in price between customers, the seller must show that the different prices were the result of cost differentials. However, a seller can justify his lower price by showing that it was made to meet an equally low offer by a competitor.

If a firm is considered to have discriminated in price, the Federal Trade Commission can issue an order for it to stop selling at that price.

Since the Robinson-Patman Act deals with price differences to buyers of the same product, it is relevant only to standard products. In a case where the nature of a contract between a buyer and seller allows the seller to effect a cost savings that he shares with the buyer, there would not be price discrimination. Discrimination can exist only where the *same* products and services are provided to different buyers at different prices.

Although prices differ between buyers, there may not be price discrimination. In defense of charges brought under the Robinson-Patman Act, the comparison of cost differences is potentially important. While not the only defense,[3] it is a crucial one; the seller may justify actual differences in price by showing that costs were different. Cost differences are readily justified when the price depends upon the quantity of an individual order or shipment. In these instances the differences in cost must be shown to result from the quantity sold or the method of selling. For example, simply showing that there are differences in the costs of shipping carload lots, as opposed to partial carload lots, may be all that is necessary to justify differences in costs and hence prices between two orders sizes.

Generally the cost differences are more readily traced to selling and distribution costs than to production costs. Where the goods are produced for warehouse stock, the costs of manufacturing goods for specific customers are indistinguishable. In these cases, production costs are not relevant because they are not differential costs. However, whether a particular product was identified with a particular customer before it was manufactured or afterward, differences in costs of distribution may be attributed to differences in quantities sold, shipping methods, or modes of selling. Here the Robinson-Patman Act has a positive impact upon management accounting since it has necessitated that accounting effort be spent upon understanding and evaluating the firm's distribution costs.

It would be misleading to imply that all firms must constantly be on the defense against price discrimination charges. Most pricing and cost decisions lie outside the scope of the Robinson-Patman Act. A charge of unfair price discrimination must be brought by an injured party stating that the seller discriminated in price between different purchases of goods of like grade and quality in an attempt to lessen competition. While cost defenses under the Robinson-Patman Act do happen, they are not an everyday event for most firms.

[3]Other defenses could include proving that the price differences were not discriminatory; that in consideration of discounts, allowances, and rebates, the prices were similar; that all business was intrastate; that the goods were not of similar grade or quality; or that the customers had different functional status, such as retailer and wholesaler.

SUMMARY

From several approaches to the problem of setting prices, we can make some general statements and conclusions. In economic theory the price and output quantity where the market is in equilibrium is at the intersection of the demand curve and the supply curve. This is true whether the market structure is pure competition, pure monopoly, monopolistic competition, or oligopoly. Market structures affect the shape and slope of the demand curve but do not change the underlying principle that the intersection of the supply and demand curves determines the equilibrium price and output.

While theoretically sound, economic pricing theory is difficult to apply in practice. Because the exact shape of the demand curve is very difficult to measure, many firms rely upon full cost-based prices, although they are less sound theoretically. This approach can best be thought of as a first estimate of price. The actual obtainable price will be found by trial and error.

The contribution margin approach offers some insights into the pricing dilemma. In special-order and distress pricing situations, the contribution margin offers a decision attitude that is more relevant than full cost-based prices. Nevertheless, in the long run all revenue must cover all costs and provide an adequate net income to give the investors a reasonable return on their investment. It is not enough to use only full cost or only the contribution margin in pricing decisions. The decision maker should choose the best approach for specific circumstances.

In today's complicated business world there are many influences besides demand that determine price. There are governmental and political factors operating to stop unfair price discrimination, inpart because the U.S. economic system is based upon the assumption that price competition is desirable. Another cause of the political and legal constraints is the need to protect the consumer from unfair pricing practices. As a result, most pricing decisions of influential monopolies and some oligopolies, such as the railroads, airlines, electric utilities, and telephone companies, are regulated. Their prices are determined by governmental agencies and controlled to provide only a reasonable, normal return on investment.

We began this chapter by saying that pricing decisions comprise the most important class of decisions a firm must make. We can close the chapter with one additional comment. Not only is it the most important decision, it is also the most difficult when considering the problems of gathering reliable data and integrating the decision with broad societal constraints and pressures.

SUPPLEMENTARY READING

Brenner, Vincent C. "An Evaluation of Product Pricing Models." *Managerial Planning,* July–August, 1971.

Herson, Richard J. L., and Ronald S. Hertz. "Direct Costing in Pricing: A Critical Reappraisal." *Management Services,* March–April, 1968.

Oxenfeldt, Alfred R., and William T. Baxter. "Approaches to Pricing: Economist versus Accountant." *Business Horizons,* Winter, 1961.

National Association of Accountants. *Product Costs for Pricing Purposes.* New York: National Association of Accountants, 1953.

National Association of Accountants. *Cost Control for Marketing Operations.* New York: National Association of Accountants, 1954.

Taylor, Otto F. "Cost Accounting Under the Robinson-Patman Act." *The New York Certified Public Accountant,* June, 1957.

Wright, Howard W. "Uniform Cost Accounting Standards: Past, Present, and Future." *Financial Executive,* May, 1971.

QUESTIONS

6-1 "Short-run pricing decisions determine the long-run survival of the firm." Discuss the validity of this statement.

6-2 While economic pricing models are theoretically sound, they are difficult to apply in practice. Discuss why this is true.

6-3 "Unit cost after the allocation of joint costs should not be viewed by the decision maker as a variable cost." Do you agree or disagree? Explain. Give examples of joint costs.

6-4 While cost-based pricing formulas are simple to use, they may not be valid in theory. Why or why not? What are some of the reasons this pricing method is so widely used?

6-5 Joint costs are not relevant to production and distribution decisions subsequent to the allocation. Discuss why this is so.

6-6 "The adoption of full cost-based prices prevents losses and ensures the recovery of all costs." Do you agree or disagree? Discuss.

6-7 Explain the difference between *cost-plus-percentage contracts, cost-plus-fixed-fee contracts,* and *incentive contracts.* Which is most advantageous to the seller? To the buyer?

6-8 Discuss the concepts: *cost-based pricing, heuristic (trial and error) pricing, common costs in pricing decisions, fixed-price contracts,* and *cost reimbursable contracts.*

6-9 What are the areas of management accounting where the Robinson-Patman Act has had the most impact?

6-10 A good cost defense under the Robinson-Patman Act focuses upon those costs that are relevant. Explain and give examples.

6-11 "Different costs are relevant to different situations." What effect might this statement have on the effectiveness of the Robinson-Patman Act? Explain.

6-12 Define and differentiate among *pure competition, pure monopoly, monopolistic competition,* and oligopoly. Give examples of industries that might belong in each classification.

6-13 Although a special order contributed $50,000 to profits, and excess capacity was available, management rejected the order. Give several possible reasons for management's action.

6-14 In today's marketplace there are many influences that determine the price of a product. Name some of these influences and give examples.

6-15 There are two key elements in assessing the market structure: (1) the number of buyers and sellers in the marketplace and (2) the extent to which products are standardized. Explain why these elements have such an impact on the market structure.

PROBLEMS

6-16 *1.* In an oligopolistic market there are
a. Many buyers
b. Few buyers
c. Many sellers
d. Few sellers

2. The automobile industry could be described as
a. A pure monopoly
b. Pure competition
c. Monopolistic competition
d. Oligopoly

3. If Products A and B are close substitutes, a substantial reduction in the price of A will
a. Reduce the demand for B
b. Increase the price of B
c. Reduce the supply of A
d. Increase the demand for B

4. In monopolistic competition there are
a. A very few firms producing identical products
b. A large number of firms producing identical products
c. Many firms producing differentiated products
d. A few firms producing identical products and competing through advertising

5. In which of the following market situations are prices likely to be under the control of an individual firm?
a. Pure competition
b. Pure monopoly
c. Monopolistic competition
d. Oligopoly

6. In a competitive industry the demand curve of the individual firm
a. Slopes downward to the right
b. Slopes upward to the right
c. Is the same as the demand curve for the industry
d. Is horizontal
e. Is vertical

7. Which of the following firms is correctly described as a monopolist?
   a. General Motors Corporation, with more than a 50% market share in the automobile industry
   b. British Airways, the only British airline serving the Atlantic air route
   c. A penicillin producer who possesses an expired patent right to produce the product
   d. A jeweler who holds an exclusive right to sell jewelry in the only regional shopping mall for a particular market area
   e. An independent gasoline dealer during a period of gasoline shortage

8. The pricing behavior in an oligopolistic industry is best described by which of the following statements?
   a. An individual firm is not likely to adjust its price to changes in cost immediately because the firm is not certain about the reaction of competitors to its price change. The industry's price, therefore, is likely to be rigid.
   b. Price is likely to rise or fall continuously because each firm possesses substantial market power to manipulate market price.
   c. Cutthroat price competition is the normal feature because competitors try to squeeze each other out until one finally survives and becomes the monopoly.
   d. There is a tendency for the competitors to fix price by explicit price-fixing agreement.
   e. The smallest firm in the industry always leads the price change for the industry.

9. An increase in demand for a particular item will generally cause its demand curve to shift
   a. Downward and leftward
   b. Upward and rightward
   c. Only if supply shifts
   d. Only if the price changes
   e. None of the above

10. Which of the following is the clearest statement of the law of demand?
    a. As income rises, people buy more of all goods and services.
    b. As price increases, the quantity of a good demanded will fall, assuming all other things are equal.
    c. As price decreases, the quantity of a good demanded will fall.
    d. Demand can never exceed supply.
    e. The higher a person's income, the greater the percentage of income saved.

(Some questions CMA adapted)

6-17 Indicate whether the following statements are *true* or *false.*

1. Close substitutes for a product cause increased competition.
2. With a typical downward-sloping demand curve, as prices increase less quantity will be demanded.
3. The upward slope of the supply curve is caused by diminishing returns.
4. In a purely competitive market, if the seller raises his price he will not sell as much of his product, but his profit will increase because of higher profit margins.
5. One danger in using the contribution margin approach to pricing is that the company might not foresee the need for the sales volume necessary to cover fixed costs.
6. The greater the degree of product differentiation, the greater the slope of the demand curve.
7. It is best to use full cost-based prices in establishing distressful and special-order pricing policies.
8. Full cost-based prices are theoretically more sound than prices based upon supply and demand curve analysis.
9. With a downward-sloping demand curve, if there is an increase in supply with no change in the demand, price will decrease.
10. The Robinson-Patman Act is based upon the assumption that competition is healthy for the U.S. economy.

6-18 The Jack Summers Dress Company, a manufacturer of high-fashion dresses, still has 10,000 units of one line of dresses in stock at the end of the year. Unfortunately styles have changed and these units are no longer desired as fashion items. The following costs are associated with these dresses.

Variable costs to produce, per unit	$40
Variable costs to sell, per unit	$ 5
Fixed production costs, per unit	$10
Fixed selling costs, per unit	$15

The dresses are stored in a public warehouse and have accumulated storage charges of $5,000.

A discount store has offered $30,000 for the lot and will pick up the dresses immediately.

REQUIRED:

A. Should Jack Summers accept the offer? Explain.

B. What costs are relevant to the decision? If Jack Summers dresses are sold only through selected specialty shops, are there nonfinancial costs involved in accepting this order? Explain.

C. What is the minimum amount that Jack Summers could charge on the order and be as well off as if the dresses were given away to be shredded and used in the production of paper for greeting cards?

6-19 The Ace Manufacturing Company produces a single product. Its cost estimates for the coming year at a production level of 80,000 units are: direct materials \$60,000; direct labor \$80,000; total manufacturing overhead \$120,000; and selling and administrative costs \$120,000. Management has set a profit objective at \$60,000 for the year. Only direct materials and direct labor costs are variable.

REQUIRED:

A. What price per unit must management set to obtain its profit objective?

B. What would the price per unit be for an expected production level of 120,000 units? 50,000 units?

C. What is the percentage return on sales if 80,000 units are produced and sold?

6-20 The Jiffy Zipper Company has been asked to bid on a government contract to supply 1,000 of a specialty product for use in the space program. An estimate of the costs per unit are:

Direct materials	\$25.00
Direct labor (1 hour)	\$12.50
Variable factory overhead	120% of direct labor cost
Fixed factory overhead	\$22.50 per direct labor hour

In addition to the above costs, special equipment costing \$5,000 would be required to produce the special order. This equipment would have no resale value.

REQUIRED:

A. Determine the amount of revenue required to make the company no worse off than if it did not receive the bid. The company has adequate production facilities available.

B. What is the minimum price the firm should bid per unit? Explain.

C. What would be the differential cost if the government increased its order from 1,000 units to 1,500 units?

6-21 The Wilson Company wants to determine the best sales price for a new appliance with a variable cost of $4 per unit. The sales manager has estimated probabilities of achieving annual sales levels for various selling prices, as shown in the following chart.

Sales Level	*Selling Price*			
(Units)	*$4*	*$5*	*$6*	*$7*
20,000	—	—	20%	80%
30,000	—	10%	40%	20%
40,000	50%	50%	20%	—
50,000	50%	40%	20%	—

The division's current profit rate is 5% on annual sales of $1,200,000; an investment of $400,000 is needed to finance these sales.

REQUIRED:

A. Prepare a schedule computing the expected incremental income for each of the sales prices proposed for the new product. The schedule should include the expected sales levels in units (weighted according to the sales manager's estimated probabilities), the expected total monetary sales, expected variable costs, and the expected incremental income.

B. What price should be charged to maximize income? Explain.

(CPA adapted)

6-22 The Wright Corporation has fixed costs of $200,000 and variable costs of $3 per unit. The company is attempting to choose the best of three possible prices. The expected volume of sales at each price is as follows:

Prices	$3.50	$4.00	$4.50
Expected sales (in units)	500,000	300,000	180,000

REQUIRED:

What price should be charged? Show your work.

6-23 The Jet Pack Manufacturing Company is developing a backpack for the government that would enable individuals to cross rivers and small lakes without boats or bridges. The company is working under a cost-plus-fixed-fee contract that includes a cost incentive provision with a 50:50 ratio. The contract also contains a clause for noncompletion that assesses a penalty of 5% of total cost per month if the delivery date is not met.

Up to this point, actual costs are 20% below the estimated costs of $300,000. However, there have been developmental problems that could postpone the completion date several months. An accelerated work program would finish the job on time, thus avoiding the penalty for late delivery, but it would result in a 20% overrun on costs. If the completion date is not accelerated, but the job is finished one month late (which is best current estimate), costs will exceed the original budget by 10%. The original profit was a fixed fee based on 15% of estimated costs.

REQUIRED:

A. What are your recommendations to management? You should be concerned with the recommendations that will reduce costs and maximize the return to the company.

B. Would your answer differ if you were the government negotiator charged with administering this contract?

6-24 The Slippery Sno-sled Company has been in a bidding competition to supply to the government a special sled with the ability to traverse all terrains and to perform many specialized jobs in the snow. It was agreed upon by management and the government negotiators that the cost of designing and manufacturing five prototypes for experimental purposes should be $800,000. They agreed upon a fee of 12% of cost to be included in the contract price.

REQUIRED:

A. Determine the net income and the income as a percentage of costs, assuming a cost overrun of $120,000 on a cost-plus-fixed-fee contract.

B. Determine the net income and the income as a percentage of costs, assuming a cost incentive contract with a 50:50 ratio and actual costs that were 15% below budgeted costs.

C. Which contract in part A or B would you prefer if you were the management of the Slippery Sno-sled Company? If you were a government negotiator? Why?

6-25 The Seuss Juice Company has recently leased manufacturing facilities for production of a new product. Based on studies made by the controller, the following data have been made available to you.

Estimated annual sales	24,000 units	
	Amount	*Per Unit*
Estimated costs:		
Material	$ 96,000	$4.00
Labor	14,400	.60
Factory overhead	24,000	1.00
Administrative expense	28,800	1.20
Total	$163,200	$6.80

Selling expenses are expected to be 15% of sales and net income is to amount to $1.02 per unit.

REQUIRED:

A. Compute the selling price per unit.

B. Prepare a projected income statement for the year.

C. Compute a breakeven point expressed in dollars and in units, assuming that all factory overhead and administrative expenses are fixed but that other costs are fully variable. *(CPA adapted)*

6-26 The Weaver Manufacturing Company manufactures a single product that sells for $20. The contribution margin ratio is 40% and total fixed costs are $240,000 per year. The estimate of sales volume for 19X8 was 40,000 units. Based upon these estimates, the following budgeted income statement was prepared.

Sales	$800,000
Variable costs	480,000
Contribution margin	$320,000
Fixed costs	240,000
Budgeted net income	$ 80,000

Actual sales were 36,000 units and the profit was only $48,000. The president cannot understand why the profit was so low. The budget showed a net profit of $2.00 per unit ($80,000 ÷ 40,000 units), but the actual profit was only $1.33 per unit ($48,000 ÷ 36,000 units).

REQUIRED:

Prepare an explanation to the president showing why the actual profit was $1.33 per unit instead of the planned profit of $2.00 per unit.

6-27 The Lenny Company produces two products for which the following cost and production data are estimated.

	Product A	*Product B*
Units produced and sold	10,000	20,000
Direct materials cost, per unit	$4	$ 9
Direct labor cost, per unit	$6	$15
Direct labor hours, per unit	2 hours	5 hours
Variable factory overhead, per unit	$2	$ 6
Fixed factory overhead, per month	$240,000	

The Lenny Company prices are set by adding a 20% markup to the full production cost.

REQUIRED:

A. Compute the selling prices of the two products, assuming the fixed costs are allocated to the products on the basis of total labor hours.

B. Compute the selling prices of the two products, assuming the fixed costs are allocated to the products on the basis of quantity of units produced.

6-28 The Seahorse Manufacturing Corporation has the following cost structure.

Direct materials	$10
Direct labor	15
Variable factory overhead	6
Fixed factory overhead	9
Total unit cost	$40

Fixed selling and administrative costs are $120,000; the budgeted production of the firm for the coming year is 60,000 units. In addition, stockholders' equity is $4,500,000, and management feels that a minimum return of 12% on stockholders' equity is necessary to satisfy investors.

REQUIRED:

A. What is the price that must be charged for the product to meet this required return on investment, assuming that all production is sold?

B. Assume that instead of a 12% return on investment, management wanted to earn a profit of $150,000. What price should it charge for the product?

C. Would your answer to part A change if the budgeted production volume was 90,000 units instead of 60,000 units? Why or why not?

6-29 The Acme Shoe Company produces high-fashion shoes. For one particular shoe variable production costs were $5.50 and variable selling costs were $1.75. There are identifiable fixed production costs of $34,000 and fixed selling costs of $25,000. At the selling price of $12 per pair, the firm has been able to sell the entire 20,000 pairs it can produce with available capacity. Acme has been requested to supply a one-time only order of 10,000 pairs of shoes to the Nickel Department Store Chain at a price of $10 per pair. Management estimates that the variable costs of selling these 10,000 pairs will be cut to $.75 per pair and that the fixed identifiable selling costs will be $20,000 instead of $25,000.

REQUIRED:

A. Should management accept this order? Why or why not? Support your conclusions.

B. Assume that fashions have changed to the point where one style of shoe, currently produced and in the inventory, is no longer marketable. Given the above costs, what is the least amount management should ask for these 3,000 pairs of shoes. Why? Will the firm make a profit or sustain a loss? What will be the amount of the profit or loss?

C. Given the original cost data, what is the quantity of shoes that must be sold to break even?

6-30 The Cross Corporation produces a line of cast iron urns. The variable production costs of one model of urn are $6.75 and fixed production costs are $36,000 per year. Management has followed the policy of determining the selling price by applying a 30% markup to full production cost. Depending upon the market conditions, the Cross Corporation could sell between 9,000 and 18,000 units during the coming year. While management anticipates sales of 12,000 units, it feels that there is a large degree of uncertainty in these predictions and wants information on the other possible sales levels.

REQUIRED:

A. Assuming that production volume and sales volume are equal, determine the fixed cost per unit, the dollar markup per unit, and the selling price per unit at each level of 9,000, 12,000, 15,000, and 18,000 urns.

B. What is the net income at each level of production in part A? What is the return on sales at each level?

C. Assuming that management priced its product on an anticipated sales volume of 15,000, what would be the differences between budgeted and actual income if actual sales reached 20,000 units? 9,000 units?

6-31 In its production process the Harmon Company incurs joint costs of $36,000. The following data concerning possible allocation bases were compiled.

	Variable Production Costs	*Labor Hours*	*Machine Hours*	*Units Produced*	*Selling Price*
Product A	$45	3	1	1,200	$ 55
Product B	$90	5	4	1,500	$110

REQUIRED:

A. What is the full cost for each product under each of the following allocation bases?

1. Variable costs
2. Labor hours
3. Machine hours
4. Units produced
5. Proportionate to the selling price times the number of units (sometimes called *relative sales-value method*)

B. Which allocation base do you prefer? Why?

C. Should this full cost be used for pricing decisions? Why or why not?

6-32 The Edwards Company is planning to establish a Canadian subsidiary corporation to produce its product in Canada. Production from the Canadian factory will be sold through manufacturer's representatives, who will receive a commission of 8% of the sales price. No central corporate expenses will be allocated to the Canadian subsidiary.

Based upon estimated annual sales of 50,000 units, the following costs and cost behavior patterns are estimated for the Canadian subsidiary.

	Estimated Annual Cost	*Percentage of Total Annual Cost That Is Variable*
Material	$180,000	100%
Labor	$120,000	75%
Factory overhead	$100,000	60%
Administration	$ 40,000	40%

REQUIRED:

A. Management wants to price its Canadian product to realize a 12% profit on selling price. Compute the selling price per unit necessary to provide the desired profit.

B. Compute the breakeven point in sales for the Canadian subsidiary.

C. Subsidiary companies in the United States are charged with a share of central corporate costs. Should central corporate costs be allocated to all subsidiaries including the Canadian subsidiary? Why or why not? The Canadian subsidiary's share of central office cost would amount to $22,000. Recompute the selling price to reflect its share of central office costs.

6-33 The Espana Jewelry Corporation manufactures a line of pendants featuring a flying sea gull. The demand for these pendants has been strong; anticipated sales are 50,000 units. The firm has excess capacity, so production could be increased by 50% without running into the problem of diminishing returns. These pendants sell for $6.50, which allows a contribution margin of 40% on sales. Fixed costs are $2 per unit. The firm has been approached by a European distributor requesting a one-time shipment of 10,000 units at a price of $4.50. The Espana Corporation would have to pay packaging and shipping charges of $2,500 on the order.

REQUIRED:

A. Compare the effect of the special order by preparing income statements assuming (1) the order is accepted and (2) the order is rejected. Would you recommend that the Espana Corporation accept this special order?

B. What other possibilities might management consider before making a decision? Discuss these possibilities.

6-34 Using the information regarding the Espana Jewelry Corporation in problem 6-33, assume that the company accepted the European order. The customer was very pleased with the product. He requested yearly shipments of 10,000 units at the same price and insisted upon a five-year contract. Before making a decision, management asks you to assist in an analysis of future costs, expected sales volume, and productive capacity. The following are the results of your analysis.

a. Estimated sales volume at home will increase 5,000 units each year, provided the selling price remains constant.
b. Beginning in the second year, variable costs are estimated to increase each year by $.20 per unit over the original cost.
c. The selling price cannot increase without a decline in sales volume by 5000 units for every $.10 increase in the selling price.
d. While equipment is available to increase capacity, management has made the decision not to do so. They are content with the current size of the plant and believe that a larger plant would interfere with their life style.

REQUIRED:
Present your findings to management along with your recommendations as to whether the firm should accept the special order. Support your recommendations with estimated income statements.

6-35 In July 19X7, the Comfortair Heating and Cooling Company sold 100 air-conditioning units for $250 each. Production costs included:

Materials	$75
Direct labor	$40
Factory overhead (90% of direct labor)	$36

Bank loans were used to finance production. Interest expense on an 8% bank loan was equivalent to $2 per unit. Federal income taxes at a 40% rate were equivalent to $16 per unit.

On July 1, 19X7, suppliers announced a materials price increase of 20%, and direct labor costs increased $10. On the same day the interest rate increased from 8% to 10%.

REQUIRED:
A. Assuming no change in the rate of factory overhead in relation to direct labor costs, compute the sales price per unit that will produce the same ratio of gross profit.
B. Assuming that 50% of the factory overhead consists of fixed costs, compute the sales price per unit that will produce the same ratio of gross profit.

(CPA adapted)

6-36 E. Berg and Sons build custom-made pleasure boats ranging in price from $10,000 to $250,000. For the past 30 years, the senior Mr. Berg has determined the selling price of each boat by estimating the costs of material and labor, prorating a portion of estimated overhead, and adding 20% to these estimated costs.

For example, a recent price quotation was determined as follows:

Direct materials	$ 5,000
Direct labor	8,000
Overhead (25% of labor)	2,000
Total estimated costs	$15,000
Plus 20%	3,000
Selling price	$18,000

If the customer rejected the price and business was slack, Mr. Berg would often reduce his markup to as little as 5% over estimated costs. Thus, average markup for the year is estimated at 15%.

Ed Berg, Jr. has just completed a course on pricing and believes the firm could use some of the techniques discussed in the course. The course emphasized the contribution margin approach to pricing and Ed feels such an approach would be helpful in determining the selling prices of their custom-made boats.

At the beginning of each year the overhead rate is established by dividing total estimated overhead by estimated direct labor cost. This year's total overhead, which includes selling and administrative expenses, was estimated at $150,000, of which $90,000 is fixed and the remainder is variable. Direct labor was estimated at $600,000 for the year.

REQUIRED:

A. Assume the customer in the example rejected the $18,000 quotation and also rejected a $15,750 quotation (5% markup) during a slack period. The customer countered with a $15,000 offer.
   1. What is the difference in net income for the year between accepting or rejecting the customer's offer?
   2. What is the minimum selling price Ed Berg, Jr. could have quoted without reducing or increasing net income?

B. What advantages does the contribution margin approach to pricing have over the approach used by the senior Mr. Berg?

C. What pitfalls are there, if any, to contribution margin pricing?

(CMA adapted)

6-37 The Red Hen House produces three types of chicken feed that are marketed regionally. The same grains and other supplements are used for each mixture, but in different combinations. The following materials costs apply to each type of feed.

Type of Feed	*Variable Costs for Materials per Hundred Weight*	*Estimated Sales*
Lay-a-lot	$5.70	240 tons*
Quickgro	$5.10	900 tons
Shurgro	$4.25	1,200 tons

*Assume 2,000 pounds per ton.

The joint production costs, which consist primarily of mixing tanks and indirect labor, are $93,600. In the past management has based its pricing policies on full cost, but the sales department has recently complained that Red Hen is being underpriced by competitors and that the firm's share of the market is declining. Management has been using a 20% markup on the full cost determined by apportioning the joint costs on the basis of the quantity produced.

REQUIRED:

A. Determine the selling price per 100-pound bag for each type of feed, assuming full-cost pricing.

B. With additional variable costs of $1 per 100-pound bag, Shurgro sales can be increased to 2,400 tons without affecting the sales of Lay-a-lot and Quickgro. However, management believes that the price of Shurgro cannot be raised more than $1.10 per bag over its current cost-based price. If this additional output is produced, the total joint costs will increase from $93,600 to $97,000. Assuming capacity is sufficient to allow the additional sales, what would you recommend? Explain fully.

6-38 The Justa Corporation produces and sells three products. The three products, A, B, and C, are sold in both a local market and in a regional market. At the end of the first quarter of the current year, the following income statement, showing income by market, was prepared.

	Total	*Local*	*Regional*
Sales	$1,300,000	$1,000,000	$300,000
Cost of goods sold	1,010,000	775,000	235,000
Gross margin	$ 290,000	$ 225,000	$ 65,000
Selling expenses	$ 105,000	$ 60,000	$ 45,000
Administrative expenses	52,000	40,000	12,000
Total expenses	157,000	100,000	57,000
Net income	$ 133,000	$ 125,000	$ 8,000

Management has expressed special concern with the regional market because of the extremely poor return on sales. This market was entered a year ago because of excess capacity. It was originally believed that the return on sales would improve with time, but after a year no noticeable improvement can be seen from the results as reported in the quarterly income statement.

In attempting to decide whether to eliminate the regional market, the following information was gathered.

SALES BY PRODUCTS

	Products		
	A	*B*	*C*
Sales	$500,000	$400,000	$400,000
Variable manufacturing expenses as a percentage of sales	60%	70%	60%
Variable selling expenses as a percentage of sales	3%	2%	2%

SALES BY MARKET FOR EACH PRODUCT

Product	*Local*	*Regional*
A	$400,000	$100,000
B	$300,000	$100,000
C	$300,000	$100,000

The selling expenses in the income statement are for local and regional sales offices and include both variable and fixed costs. If a market is dropped, the sales office will be closed. All administrative expenses are fixed for the period.

Cost of goods sold in the income statement includes both variable costs and fixed costs. Administrative costs and fixed manufacturing costs were allocated to the two markets to develop a full-cost income statement.

REQUIRED:

A. Prepare a quarterly income statement showing contribution margins by region.

B. Assuming there are no alternative uses for the Justa Corporation's present capacity, would you recommend dropping the regional market? Why or why not?

C. Prepare a quarterly income statement showing contribution margins by products.

D. It is believed that a new product can be ready for sale next year if the Justa Corporation decides to go ahead with continued research. The new product can be produced by simply converting equipment presently used in producing Product C. This conversion will increase fixed costs by $10,000 per quarter. What must be the minimum contribution margin per quarter for the new product to make the changeover financially feasible?

(CMA adapted)

6-39 The Largo Manufacturing Company makes and sells a single product, VOSTEX, through normal marketing channels. You have been asked by its president to assist in determining the proper bid to submit for a special manufacturing job for the Aztec Sales Company. You have collected the following information.

1. The special job is for MOFAC, a product unlike VOSTEX, even though the manufacturing processes are similar.
2. Additional sales of MOFAC to the Aztec Sales Company are not expected.
3. The bid is for 20,000 pounds of MOFAC. Each 1,000 pounds of MOFAC requires 500 pounds of Material A, 250 pounds of Material B, and 250 pounds of Material C.
4. Largo's materials inventory data follow.

Material	*Pounds in Inventory*	*Acquisition Cost per Pound*	*Current Replacement Cost per Pound*
A	24,000	$.40	$.48
B	4,000	$.25	$.27
C	17,500	$.90	$.97
X	7,000	$.80	$.85

Material X may be substituted for Material A in MOFAC. Material X, made especially for Largo under a patent owned by Largo, is left over from the manufacture of a discontinued product, is not usable in VOSTEX, and has a current salvage value of $180.

5. Each 1,000 pounds of MOFAC requires 180 direct labor hours at $3 per hour (overtime is charged at time and a half). However, Largo is working near its two-shift capacity and has only 1,600 hours of regular time available. The production manager indicates that he can keep the special job on regular time by shifting the production of VOSTEX to overtime if necessary.
6. Largo's cost clerk informs you that the factory overhead rate at normal production is as follows:

Fixed element	$ .20 per direct labor hour
Variable element	.80 per direct labor hour
Total factory overhead rate	$1.00 per direct labor hour

7. The bid invitation states that a performance bond must be submitted with the bid. A local agent will bond Largo's performance for 1% of the total bid.

REQUIRED:

A. The Largo Manufacturing Company has a net income objective of a 10% return on sales. Compute the bid that will allow Largo to meet this objective if regular sales presently satisfy this objective.

B. Compute the minimum bid (i.e. the bid that would neither increase nor decrease total net income) that Largo Manufacturing Company may submit.

C. Largo's president also wants to know what his new competitor, Melton Manufacturing Company, probably will bid. You assume that Melton's materials inventory has been acquired very recently and that Melton's cost behavior is similar to Largo's. You know that Melton has ample productive capacity to handle the special job on regular time. Compute the minimum bid (i.e. the bid that would neither increase nor decrease total net income) that Melton Manufacturing Company might submit.

(CPA adapted)

6-40 The management of the Southern Cottonseed Company has engaged you to assist in the development of information to be used for management's decisions. The company has the capacity to process 20,000 tons of cottonseed per year. The yield of a ton (2,000 pounds) of cottonseed is as follows:

Product	*Average Yield Per Ton of Cottonseed*	*Average Selling Price Per Trade Unit*
Oil	300 pounds	$ .15 per pound
Meal	600 pounds	$50.00 per ton
Hulls	800 pounds	$20.00 per ton
Lint	100 pounds	$ 3.00 per cwt.

A special marketing study revealed that the company can expect to sell its entire output for the coming year at the listed average selling prices. The study also indicated that cottonseed prices will vary widely in the next few years. At the present time Southern Cottonseed Company is paying $12 per ton.

You have determined the following costs for the company.

Processing costs:

Variable: $9 per ton of cottonseed put into process

Fixed: $108,000 per year

Marketing costs:

All variable: $20 per ton sold

Administrative costs:

All fixed: $90,000 per year

Management would like to know the average maximum amount that the company can afford to pay for a ton of cottonseed. The average maximum amount is the amount that would result in the company's having losses no greater when operating than when closed down, under the existing cost and revenue structure. Assume that the fixed costs will continue unchanged even when the operations are shut down.

REQUIRED:

A. Compute the revenue for the products produced from a ton of cottonseed.

B. What is the breakeven point in tons of cottonseed?

C. Compute the average maximum amount that the company can afford to pay for a ton of cottonseed.

D. Identify and discuss the factors other than costs that the company should consider in deciding whether to shut down a plant.

E. The stockholders consider the minimum satisfactory return on their investment in the business to be 25% before corporate income taxes. The stockholders' equity in the company is $968,000. Compute the maximum average amount that the company can pay for a ton of cottonseed to realize the minimum satisfactory return on the stockholders' investment in the business. *(CPA adapted)*

7 Production Decisions

CRITERIA FOR DECISION DATA
THE CONTRIBUTION MARGIN AND PRODUCTION DECISIONS
Adding a New Product
Sell or Process Further: A Single Product
Sell or Process Further: Multiple Products
Make or Buy Component Parts
Dropping a Product Line
Manufacturing the Optimum Product Combination
Production Lot Sizes
SUMMARY

In this chapter we explore how the decision maker uses accounting data to make production decisions. It is assumed that previous long-range decisions have provided a productive capacity; short-range decisions must be made concerning its use. The topics in this chapter focus upon how best to use existing productive capacity. Questions asked include: "How many units should the firm produce?" "Should it produce more of Product X than Product Y, or more of Product Y than Product X?" "Should a product be dropped?"

CRITERIA FOR DECISION DATA

Each decision made by management is unique. Different decisions call for different data. The overriding concepts of every decision are **relevant benefits and costs.** To be relevant, data must exhibit the characteristics of **futurity** and **differentiality.** Relevant data must be future data. Past benefits and costs are the results of a prior decision that cannot be changed. No future decision can change what has already happened. The role of the past in decision making lies in what can be learned from it. Through knowledge of the results of past decisions, future decisions can be more intelligent and reliable. In this way the past can be used to forecast or predict the future.

A future benefit or cost is not automatically relevant. A benefit or cost that is identical among the available alternatives will not affect the choice and, therefore, is not relevant to the decision.

Crucial to any measure of differential data is the **opportunity cost,** defined earlier as the foregone income that would have been earned had another alternative been chosen. For example, the opportunity cost of burying money in a glass jar in the backyard is the interest that could be earned if the money were put in a savings account at the bank. This is not the only possibility and, therefore, not the only opportunity cost. The money could be invested in high-grade government bonds, $.10 mining stocks, or blue chip stocks. Each would provide a different opportunity cost. The prudent manager will use the *next most likely possibility* to measure opportunity cost, not a highly unlikely possibility. When we examine the possible income that a firm could earn or costs that a firm could save in the selection of one alternative over another, we are viewing these as opportunity costs. We don't often use the term *opportunity cost,* but it is implied. When we use the contribution margin to measure the impact of production output decisions, we are treating the contribution margin as an opportunity cost.

THE CONTRIBUTION MARGIN AND PRODUCTION DECISIONS

Earlier in the text we emphasized the value of the contribution margin in making differential decisions. In Chapters 2 and 5 we stressed the role of fixed and variable costs in determining the contribution margin and in assessing cost-volume-profit interactions. In Chapter 6 we showed how the contribution margin facilitates nonroutine pricing decisions. Now let's turn our attention to how the contribution margin can be used in making production output decisions. As output is changed, within the relevant range, both variable costs and revenue will change. The contribution margin measures the combined effect of changes in revenue and variable costs, allowing a direct measure of the impact of output variations. Fixed costs, on the other hand, will not change and, therefore, are not relevant to production decisions as long as the firm stays inside the relevant range or does not change productive capacity.

Adding a New Product

Assume that Product A of the Sultan Company has not achieved the customer acceptance expected and that the company has excess productive capacity. In its search for new products to produce with existing facilities, the Sultan Company narrowed its study to two: Product B and Product C. The following tabulation shows estimated selling prices and costs directly associated with these new products.

	Product B	*Product C*
Selling price per unit	$20 per unit	$2.50 per unit
Costs:		
Direct materials	$10 per unit	$ .80 per unit
Direct labor	$ 3 per unit	$ .45 per unit
Variable factory overhead	$ 1 per unit	$ .15 per unit
Variable selling costs	$ 2 per unit	$ .50 per unit
Fixed selling costs	$6,000 per year	$10,000 per year

The current fixed factory overhead of $15,000 per year and fixed selling costs of $5,000 per year would not be affected and are not relevant. The Sultan Company has sufficient excess capacity to produce 4,000 units of Product B or 30,000 units of Product C. Market studies indicate that these units may be sold at the planned market prices.

Which product should be added? Projected income statements show the contribution margin and product margin for the two new products.

	PRODUCT B		PRODUCT C	
Number of units	4,000		30,000	
	Per Unit	*Amount*	*Per Unit*	*Amount*
Sales	$20.00	$80,000	$2.50	$75,000
Direct materials	$10.00	$40,000	$ .80	$24,000
Direct labor	3.00	12,000	.45	13,500
Variable factory overhead	1.00	4,000	.15	4,500
Variable selling costs	2.00	8,000	.50	15,000
Total variable costs	16.00	64,000	1.90	57,000
Contribution margin	$ 4.00	$16,000	$ .60	$18,000
Identifiable fixed selling costs		6,000		10,000
Product margin		$10,000		$ 8,000

Product C has the highest contribution margin; if there were no additional fixed costs Product C would be produced. However, these products involve new markets, so additional fixed selling costs are necessary. After subtracting the directly identifiable fixed selling costs from the contribution margin, the result is the **product margin,** the amount that net income will be increased by producing and selling the product. Product B, with a product margin of $10,000, should be produced and sold. Product C will provide only an $8,000 product margin and should be rejected in favor of Product B.

Sell or Process Further: A Single Product

The Sultan Company currently manufactures only Product A, which is sold to other firms who process it further. During normal operations 10,000 units of Product A are produced per year; they sell for $10 each. The following costs are incurred to produce and sell these 10,000 units.

	Product A	
	Per Unit	*Total*
Direct materials	$2.00	$20,000
Direct labor	3.00	30,000
Variable factory overhead costs	1.00	10,000
Variable selling costs	.25	2,500
Fixed factory overhead costs	1.50	15,000
Fixed selling costs	.50	5,000
Total unit cost	$8.25	$82,500

As an alternative to producing Product B, the managers of the Sultan Company are considering using their excess capacity to process Product A further. After additional processing, Product A could be sold for $14 per unit. The following are estimates of the *additional* costs of processing 10,000 units of Product A further.

Direct labor	$1.25 per unit
Variable factory overhead costs	$ .75 per unit
Variable selling costs	$ .50 per unit
Fixed factory overhead costs	$8,000 per year
Fixed selling costs	$5,000 per year

The following tabulation shows the contribution margin and the product margin of Product A, both with and without the additional processing.

	PRODUCT A					
	Without Further Processing		**With Further Processing**		**Difference**	
	Per Unit	*Total*	*Per Unit*	*Total*	*Per Unit*	*Total*
Sales	$10.00	$100,000	$14.00	$140,000	$4.00	$40,000
Variable costs:						
Direct material	$ 2.00	$ 20,000	$ 2.00	$ 20,000	—	—
Direct labor	3.00	30,000	4.25	42,500	$1.25	$12,500
Variable factory overhead	1.00	10,000	1.75	17,500	.75	7,500
Variable selling costs	.25	2,500	.75	7,500	.50	5,000
Total variable costs	6.25	62,500	8.75	87,500	2.50	25,000
Contribution margin	$ 3.75	$ 37,500	$ 5.25	$ 52,500	$1.50	$15,000
Identifiable fixed costs		—		13,000		13,000
Product margin		$ 37,500		$ 39,500		$ 2,000

The contribution margin would increase if the Sultan Company decided to process the product further. Would the net income increase? The added contribution margin per unit would be $1.50 ($5.25 − $3.75) and the total contribution margin would be increased by $15,000 ($1.50 × 10,000 units). Since the increase in fixed costs is $13,000 ($8,000 + $5,000) and the incremental contribution margin is $15,000, $2,000 would be added to the net income. In this case the product should be processed further.

Let's examine the firm's fixed cost structure. The original per-unit cost included fixed factory overhead costs of $1.50 and fixed selling expenses of $.50. These were calculated by dividing the total fixed costs of factory overhead and selling expenses by the number of units normally produced and sold. Therefore, the fixed factory overhead is $15,000 ($1.50 × 10,000 units) and the fixed selling expenses are $5,000 ($.50 × 10,000 units). The decision to process further does not change this fixed cost structure; these fixed costs are nonrelevant. The practice of studying fixed costs on a per-unit basis is potentially misleading and should be avoided in making differential decisions.

The Sultan Company has considered two different uses for its excess capacity. One alternative was to add a new product. Of those products considered, Product B would make the greatest contribution to income. Another desirable choice was to process Product A further. Which of the two alternatives should be chosen?

	PRODUCE PRODUCT B		PROCESS PRODUCT A FURTHER	
Number of units	4,000		10,000	
	Per Unit	*Amount*	*Per Unit*	*Amount*
Sales	$20.00	$80,000	$4.00	$40,000
Variable costs:				
Direct materials	$10.00	$40,000	—	—
Direct labor	3.00	12,000	$1.25	$12,500
Variable factory overhead	1.00	4,000	.75	7,500
Variable selling costs	2.00	8,000	.50	5,000
Total variable costs	16.00	64,000	2.50	25,000
Contribution margin	$ 4.00	$16,000	$1.50	$15,000
Identifiable fixed costs		6,000		13,000
Product margin		$10,000		$ 2,000

An income statement comparing the two alternatives shows that the new product will contribute $10,000 toward net income, whereas processing Product A further will contribute only $2,000 toward net income. The excess capacity should be used to produce Product B.

Sell or Process Further: Multiple Products

In many industries the production process consists of taking a single material input and producing more than one final product. In the petroleum industry a barrel of crude oil is refined into fuel oil, premium gasoline, regular gasoline, and many other types of petroleum products. The meat-packing industry produces hamburger, roasts, steaks, and many other products from a single steer. In the lumber industry a single log produces 2 × 4s, 4 × 4s, and 1 × 4s. These production processes are called **joint processes.**

The costs of the barrel of crude oil, the steer, or the log are **joint costs**—costs that are incurred to process a single raw material into more than one manufactured product. At the time joint costs are introduced into the production process, it is impossible to identify one finished product from another. Joint costs represent the costs of a single material, a single production process, or a series of production processes that simultaneously produce two or more finished products.

Assume that the Sprock Manufacturing Company produces three products: D, E, and F. Raw Material X enters the process in Department 1 of the factory. Department 1 separates Material X into Products D, E, and F. During the past year $260,000 of Material X was issued to Department 1. Other costs of operating Department 1 were $140,000. Department 1 output was 100,000 pounds of Product D, 50,000 pounds of Product E, and 200,000 pounds of Product F. The end of the production process in Department 1 is called the **split-off point,** where a single raw material yields two or more different products. Each product has a ready market at this point of split-off. At the point of split-off Product D sells for $2 per pound, Product E for $4 per pound, and Product F for $.50 per pound.

After the split-off Product D could be processed further in Department 2, with the additional cost of $200,000. After the additional processing Product D would sell for $4.50 per pound. After the split-off Product E could be processed further in Department 3 for $60,000 additional costs. After this additional processing Product E would sell for $5 per pound. Product F is not suitable for further processing and must be sold at the point of split-off. These production possibilities can be shown diagrammatically:

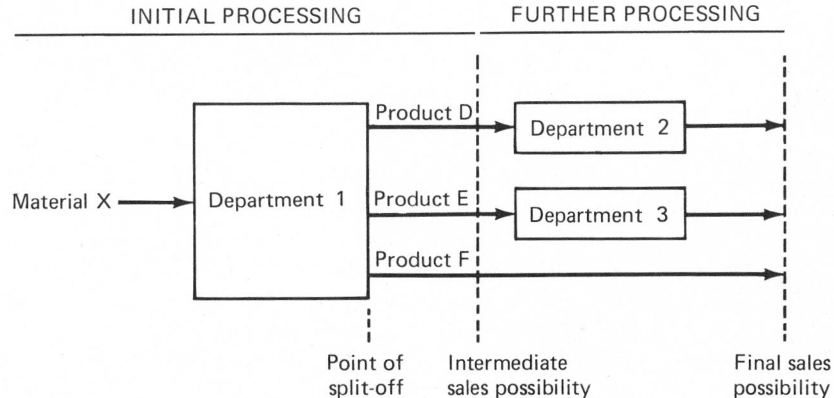

SPROCK MANUFACTURING COMPANY
INCOME STATEMENTS BY PRODUCT LINE
For the Year Ended December 31, 19X8

	PRODUCT D		PRODUCT E		PRODUCT F	
	Sell Now	Process Further	Sell Now	Process Further	Sell Now	Process Further
Sales	$200,000	$450,000	$200,000	$250,000	$100,000	–
Separable costs	–	200,000	–	60,000	–	–
Joint costs of $400,000 from Department 1	Not relevant because they will not change as a result of the decision					
Contribution margin	$200,000	$250,000 ↑	$200,000 ↑	$190,000	$100,000 ↑	–

EXHIBIT 7-1
Sell-or-process-further analysis

What actions should management take? A comparison of the contribution margins for the products under the possible alternatives is shown in Exhibit 7-1. For Product D the maximum contribution margin is attained when the product is processed further. For Product E the maximum contribution margin is $200,000 when it is sold without further processing. The optimum choice is to process Product D and sell Products E and F at the point of split-off. The following net income figure is based on these choices.

Sales ($450,000 + $200,000 + $100,000)	
Separable costs of additional processing	200,000
Separable margin	$550,000
Joint costs ($260,000 + $140,000)	400,000
Net income	$150,000

The incremental income from a decision to process a product further is equal to the *additional* revenue gained from selling the product at an advanced state of manufacture minus the *additional* processing costs traceable to the product. If this difference is positive, the decision to process further would be profitable in the short run. For example, the incremental revenue of Product D is $250,000; the incremental costs are $200,000; and the incremental income is $50,000. The joint costs ($400,000) are not relevant to the decision; they will not change because of subsequent decisions. In any incremental analysis joint costs such as these are not relevant. Costs incurred before the point of split-off are common to all products and cannot be treated incrementally to the individual products, even if allocated.

A second observation should be made. The decision was made without consideration of alternative uses for Departments 2 and 3. It was assumed that the only choice was to process the products further and that no other opportunity costs were applicable.

You may have noticed an accounting conflict. Joint costs are irrelevant for incremental production decisions because the joint costs do not change as a result of the decision to sell or process further. Yet for inventory costing and income-determination purposes, the financial accountant must allocate joint costs to the products. Where the selling prices of the products are similar, the joint costs can be allocated on the basis of the quantity of products produced. Where the selling prices of the product differ widely, the most common basis of allocating joint costs is the **relative sales-value basis** at either the point of split-off or after further processing. The following allocation assumes that the Sprock Company uses the relative sales-value basis at the point of split-off.

Product	*Units Produced*	*Selling Price at Split-off*	*Total Market Value at Split-off*		*Allocation of Joint Costs*
D	100,000	$2.00	$200,000	2/5	$160,000
E	50,000	$4.00	200,000	2/5	160,000
F	200,000	$ .50	100,000	1/5	80,000
Total	350,000		$500,000	5/5	$400,000

The gross margin percentages of the products at the point of split-off are as follows:

	Product D		*Product E*		*Product F*	
Sales at split-off	$200,000	100%	$200,000	100%	$100,000	100%
Less: Apportioned joint costs	160,000	80%	160,000	80%	80,000	80%
Gross margin	$ 40,000	20%	$ 40,000	20%	$ 20,000	20%

Notice that the effect of this allocation method is to provide a constant gross margin percentage for each product at the point of split-off. This fact makes the relative sales-value method unsuitable for management decisions, although it is useful in inventory costing.

After the allocation of the joint costs, the per-unit cost for inclusion in the inventory would be $3.60 for Product D [($160,000 + $200,000) ÷ 100,000 units], assuming the product was processed further. For Product E, assuming that it was to be sold at the point of split-off, the inventory value would be $3.20 ($160,000 ÷ 50,000 units). For Product F the inventoriable cost would be $.40 ($80,000 ÷ 200,000 units). These unit costs are applicable to inventory costing.

It may seem inadequate to talk about incremental income for the products rather than net income. To speak of "net" income by product line requires the allocation of joint costs to the various products. Incremental income, on the other hand, is the contribution of the individual products to the firm's joint costs and income. The allocation of joint costs, regardless of how they are allocated, will not change the net income of the firm over time and can mislead the decision maker into believing that the allocated joint costs are relevant in measuring incremental income.

Make or Buy Component Parts

Another important production decision is whether to make or buy component parts. This decision can involve both quantitative and qualitative factors. Many firms, to ensure their flow of finished products, control the total production flow from extraction or manufacture of the raw materials to the completion of the final product. This control creates an operation much less dependent upon suppliers and allows the firm to earn profits from manufacturing its subcomponents. However, the manufacture of subcomponents requires that skilled labor and productive facilities be available. A firm that follows the policy of manufacturing its parts when activity on the final product is slack, and purchasing them when its production facilities are busy on the final product, may find its suppliers less than willing to fill orders on a sporadic basis.

The economic effects of the make-or-buy decision are best seen through the contribution margin approach of measuring incremental income. The purchase price of the parts plus other incremental costs of procurement, such as ordering and receiving, can be compared with the additional costs of producing the part. As long as the incremental costs of making the part are less than the purchase costs of buying it, the firm should manufacture the part. When the incremental manufacturing costs exceed the purchase costs, the part should be purchased from the supplier.

To illustrate, assume that a firm has prepared the following cost estimate for the manufacture of a subcomponent—a motor casting—based upon an annual production of 5,000 parts.

	Per Unit	*Total*
Direct materials	$ 5	$ 25,000
Direct labor	8	40,000
Variable factory overhead	4	20,000
Fixed factory overhead (37.5% of direct labor cost)	3	15,000
Total cost per motor casting	$20	$100,000

A supplier has offered to provide the motor casting at a price of $16.50; the firm estimates that costs of ordering, receiving, and inspecting each part will be $1.50. The key to the decision lies in the examination of those costs that will change between the alternatives. Assuming that the productive capacity will be idle if not used to manufacture the part, the incremental analysis follows.

	Per Unit		**Total of 5,000 Units**	
	Make	*Buy*	*Make*	*Buy*
Direct material	$ 5	—	$25,000	—
Direct labor	8	—	40,000	—
Variable factory overhead	4	—	20,000	—
Purchase price plus ordering, receiving, and inspection costs	—	$18	—	$90,000
Total relevant costs	$17	$18	$85,000	$90,000

In this case the company should make the product rather than purchase it from the supplier. The variable costs to produce the part are $17; the purchase costs are $18. The fixed overhead is not relevant to the decision.

Let's carry the illustration one step further. Assume that management can choose to make the motor casting or buy it from the supplier, using the excess capacity to make 5,000 pump housings. Cost and revenue estimates for the pump housing follow.

Pump Housing		
Selling price		$25.00
Direct material	$ 8.00	
Direct labor	10.00	
Variable factory overhead	4.00	
Fixed factory overhead (37.5% of direct labor cost)	3.75	
Total costs		25.75
Net loss per unit		($ .75)

At first glance it would seem unprofitable to produce the pump housing; total costs exceed total revenue by $.75 per unit. Closer examination shows that the variable costs per unit of producing the pump housing are $22 ($8 + $10 + $4) and the contribution margin per unit is $3 ($25 − $22). If the motor castings are sold for $26, the total contribution margin for producing and selling motor castings will be $45,000 [($26 − $17) × 5,000 units]. However, if motor castings are purchased and pump housing produced, the total contribution margin will increase to $55,000.

	Motor Castings		Pump Housings		Total
Sales	$26	$130,000	$25	$125,000	$255,000
Variable costs	18	90,000	22	110,000	200,000
Contribution margin	$ 8	$ 40,000	$ 3	$ 15,000	$ 55,000

Management's optimum decision would be to produce the pump housing and buy the motor casting. The fixed costs of the factory are not relevant to the make-or-buy decision, although they must be covered before the firm makes a profit.

The previous discussion assumed that the firm did not need additional plant facilities to produce the unit. If the plant had to be enlarged or new equipment purchased, the firm would need to make a long-range capacity decision. The savings from producing the part would have to be compared to the additional investment to ensure an adequate rate of return on the investment. In this situation the make-or-buy alternatives would be an integral input to the capital investment decision shown in Chapters 8 and 9.

As a final example of a make-or-buy decision, suppose that a firm uses a specifically machined gear in its final product. The manager can manufacture the gear or buy it from an outside supplier for $10 each. To manufacture the gear he would incur variable costs of $5 per unit, but he would have additional relevant fixed costs specifically identified with the manufacture of the gears of $20,000 per year. Exhibit 7-2 shows that the firm should buy the part if volume is under 4,000 gears per year, but should make the gear if volume is over 4,000 gears per year.

Dropping a Product Line

Assume that the Wagner Company manufactures and sells three products: G, H, and I. Income statements for the three products and for the total firm are shown in Exhibit 7-3. Management is considering dropping Product G because it is apparently not contributing to the income of the firm. Recasting the product income statements into a contribution margin format allows us to examine the products according to their respective incremental contribution margins. As shown in the recasted income statements in Exhibit 7-4, the joint costs are common to all products and hence are irrelevant to the decision.

From Exhibit 7-4 the role of the three products in contributing to net income is clearer. Product G has a positive contribution margin to help cover the joint costs, although it is not as large as the contribution margins of the other two products. If Product G were discontinued, the net income would decline.

A customer offered to purchase 2,000 units of Product J at $30 per unit if the Wagner Company would produce them. To produce Product J the variable costs are estimated at $24,000; the fixed costs specifically identifiable

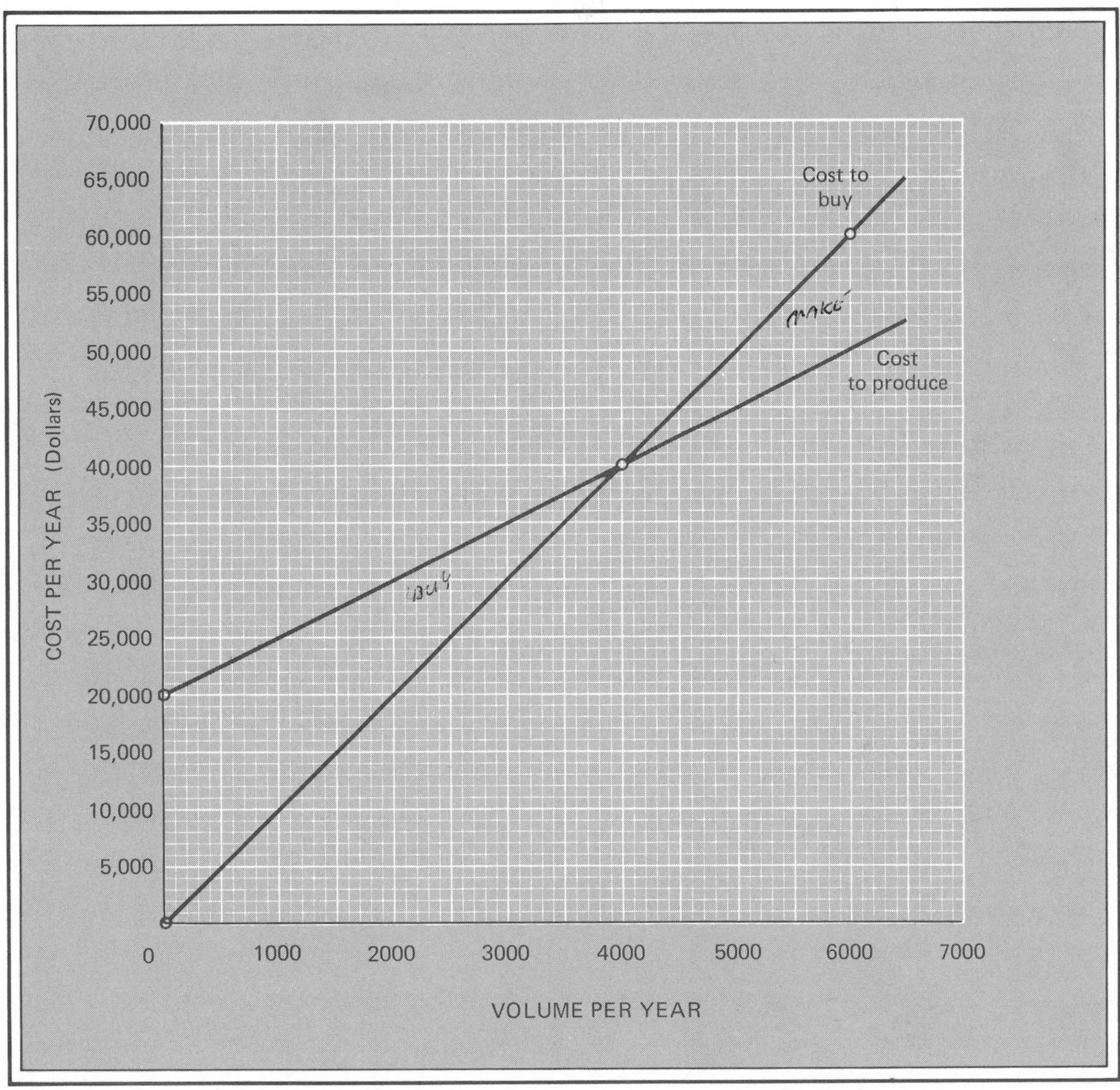

EXHIBIT 7-2
Make-or-buy decisions

with Product J are $20,000. Because the plant has no idle capacity, one of the existing products would have to be dropped. Would this be profitable? Let's look at the product margin of Product J.

Sales (2,000 × $30)	$60,000
Variable costs (2,000 × $12)	24,000
Contribution margin (2,000 × $18)	$36,000
Identifiable fixed costs	20,000
Product margin before joint costs	$16,000

THE WAGNER COMPANY
INCOME STATEMENT
For the Year Ended December 31, 19X7

	Product G	Product H	Product I	Total
Sales	$100,000	$300,000	$200,000	$600,000
Variable costs	60,000	210,000	150,000	420,000
Contribution margin	$ 40,000	$ 90,000	$ 50,000	$180,000
Fixed costs:				
Identifiable to products	$ 30,000	$ 30,000	$ 20,000	$ 80,000
Joint costs allocated on sales basis	10,000	30,000	20,000	60,000
Total fixed costs	40,000	60,000	40,000	140,000
Net income	$ 0	$ 30,000	$ 10,000	$ 40,000

EXHIBIT 7-3
Income statements by product line with apportioned joint costs

If Product J can be produced in the void left by dropping Product G, it would be economically sound to do so. If, on the other hand, the production of Product J would require the productive time, space, and energy devoted to either Product H or Product I, it would be an unwise choice.

Suppose that management was considering producing one-third more of Product H instead of accepting the offer to produce Product J. The productive facilities used in Product G could be used for this increase. The identifiable fixed costs currently associated with Product G would be associated with the additional units of Product H. The product margin of the incremental quantity of Product H follows.

Sales	$100,000
Variable costs	70,000
Contribution margin	$ 30,000
Identifiable joint costs	30,000
Product margin before joint costs	$ 0

THE WAGNER COMPANY
INCOME STATEMENT
For the Year Ended December 31, 19X7

	Product G	Product H	Product I	Total
Sales	$100,000	$300,000	$200,000	$600,000
Variable costs	60,000	210,000	150,000	420,000
Contribution margin	$ 40,000	$ 90,000	$ 50,000	$180,000
Fixed costs identifiable to products	30,000	30,000	20,000	80,000
Product margin	$ 10,000	$ 60,000	$ 30,000	$100,000
Joint costs				60,000
Net Income				$ 40,000

EXHIBIT 7-4
Income statements by product line

Given these three alternatives, the decision hierarchy should be to produce Product J and, if this is not possible, to produce Product G. The choice to produce an additional one-third of Product H would not be profitable.

Manufacturing the Optimum Product Combination

In assessing production decisions, management is confronted with how best to allocate the firm's limited production resources. If facilities are not limited, management can produce all it wants of any product. In previous examples we have assumed that the firm was not fully utilizing its productive facilities. With this assumption of idle capacity we were not faced with resource limitations. However, all resources are limited in some way. The maximum amount of resources that can be committed to production is a restriction or **constraint.**

TWO OR MORE PRODUCTS WITH ONLY ONE CONSTRAINT

Assume that a company produces two products, K and L, with the following contribution margins per unit.

	Product K		*Product L*	
Sales	$6.00	100%	$20.00	100%
Variable costs	4.00	67%	16.00	80%
Contribution margin	$2.00	33%	$ 4.00	20%

The annual fixed costs of production are $36,000, which remain unchanged regardless of the combination of products produced. If there are no production constraints, the product with the highest contribution margin per unit should be produced until demand is satisfied. In our illustration the firm should emphasize Product L, which has a contribution margin per unit of $4. When there are no market or production limitations the decision rule can be stated simply: "Choose the product with the highest contribution margin per unit until the demand is satisfied; then choose the product with the next highest contribution margin per unit." This decision will maximize net income.

Where demand for the product is greater than the production capabilities of the firm, and the production is subject to a single constraint, the firm should maximize the total contribution margin per unit subject to the single production constraint. To illustrate, let's assume that the firm has a production constraint of 100,000 machine hours; the machine capacity is the scarce resource. Further, assume that Product K requires two machine hours to produce and Product L requires five machine hours. One way to express this constraint is to determine the contribution margin per machine hour.

	Product K	*Product L*
Selling price	$6.00	$20.00
Variable costs	4.00	16.00
Contribution margin	$2.00	$ 4.00
Divided by machine hours required per unit	2	5
Contribution margin per machine hour	$1.00	$ .80

Since Product K returns the highest contribution margin per machine hour, it is the preferred product. The firm should limit its production to Product K as long as the market demand and cost structure is unchanged. There is no benefit from selling Product L over Product K.

	Product K	Product L
Sales:		
Product K (50,000 x $6)	$300,000	
Product L (20,000 x $20)		$400,000
Variable costs:		
Product K (50,000 x $4)	200,000	
Product L (20,000 x $16)		320,000
Contribution margin:		
Product K (50,000 x $2)	$100,000	
Product L (20,000 x $4)		$ 80,000
Fixed costs	36,000	36,000
Net income	$ 64,000	$ 44,000

EXHIBIT 7-5
Comparative product income statements

Another way to view the same data is to prepare comparative income statements assuming only one product is produced, as shown in Exhibit 7-5. This solution is simple because there is only one constraint that affects both products. In the next section we will examine more complex situations.

TWO OR MORE PRODUCTS AND TWO OR MORE CONSTRAINTS

A mathematical technique called **linear programming** provides a solution to the problem where there are limited resources and two or more products and/or constraints. Let's assume that the George Sank Company manufactures two styles of lamps: a table lamp and a floor lamp. There are two departments, each with production limitations. Management is considering the use of linear programming to determine the optimum quantity of each product to produce.

A number of requirements must be met if the George Sank Company is to use linear programming appropriately. First, there must be limited resources. For example, the number of machine hours or employee workbenches might be limited. The more time that is spent to manufacture floor lamps, the less time there will be to make table lamps. Second, there must be alternative courses of action available. The production facilities and the market demand must be flexible enough to allow different outputs of floor and table lamps. Third, there must be an objective that the firm is striving to achieve. The most commonly stated objective is to maximize dollar profits. For linear programming the dollar profit is stated as the contribution margin per unit because it is linear to sales volume. Fourth, the variables in the model must be interrelated. Total profit, for example, must reflect profit from the table lamps plus profit from the floor lamps. Finally, the firm's objectives and limitations or constraints must be expressible as linear mathematical equations or inequalities. For example, the firm's dollar contribution margin, stated in linear equation form, would be:

$$\text{Firm's contribution margin} = \begin{bmatrix}\text{Contribution margin per floor lamp} \times \text{Number of floor lamps}\end{bmatrix} + \begin{bmatrix}\text{Contribution margin per table lamp} \times \text{Number of table lamps}\end{bmatrix}$$

To develop the theory of linear programming, let's assume the following cost and production estimates.

Department	Hours Required to Make 1 Unit		Total Production Hours Available
	Floor Lamp	*Table Lamp*	
A	3	4	72
B	6	2	66
Contribution margin per unit	\$12	\$8	

From this data we can see that to manufacture a floor lamp takes 3 hours in Department A and 6 hours in Department B, for a total of 9 hours. The table lamp requires 4 hours in Department A and 2 hours in Department B, for a total of 6 hours. Department A has a maximum production capability (constraint) of 72 hours; Department B has a constraint of 66 hours. The decision maker must determine the best possible combination of floor and table lamps to realize the maximum total contribution margin, assuming that the contribution margin is \$12 for the floor lamp and \$8 for the table lamp.

Graphic solution

In this section we will show a graphic solution. In the following section we will show a simple algebraic solution.

Step 1. Restate the data in mathematical form. We will use the symbol Q_1 to represent the optimum number of floor lamps and Q_2 to represent the optimum number of table lamps. If P is the maximized contribution margin, the **objective function** that relates output to profit is:

$$P = \$12(Q_1) + \$8(Q_2)$$

The incremental profit of one floor lamp is \$12, measured by the contribution margin; the total profit from floor lamps will be \$12 times the number produced and sold (Q_1).

The time available to produce the lamps is a production constraint. Certainly, the time used to make the two products cannot exceed the total time available in each of the two departments. The hours available to make one floor lamp times the number of floor lamps produced, plus the hours to make one table lamp times the number of table lamps produced, must be equal to or less than the time available in each department. Expressed mathematically:

$3(Q_1) + 4(Q_2) \leq 72$ for Department A
$6(Q_1) + 2(Q_2) \leq 66$ for Department B

The sign $\leq$ in this inequality statement means *is less than or equal to.* The first statement shows that the hours required in Department A to produce one floor lamp (3) times the number of floor lamps made (Q_1), plus the number of hours needed to make one table lamp (4) times the number of table lamps made (Q_2), must be equal to or less than the total of 72 hours available. These inequalities are capacity constraints on output and hence on profits.

If the answers are to be meaningful they must be positive. It is not conceptually possible to "unmake" a lamp. Thus, all variables in the linear programming model must be equal to or greater than zero. This can be expressed mathematically:

$Q_1 \geq 0$ and $Q_2 \geq 0$

The symbol $\geq$ means *greater than or equal to.* Thus, the solution must be where the values of Q_1 and Q_2 are positive.

The mathematical expressions can now be summarized.

Maximize $P = \$12(Q_1) + \$8(Q_2)$
subject to the constraints of:

$$3(Q_1) + 4(Q_2) \leq 72$$
$$6(Q_1) + 2(Q_2) \leq 66$$
$$Q_1 \geq 0$$
$$Q_2 \geq 0$$

Step 2. Plot the constraints on a graph such as the one shown in Exhibit 7-6. The number of units of Product Q_1 is shown on the x axis and the number of units of Product Q_2 is shown on the y axis. The inequality $3(Q_1) + 4(Q_2) \leq 72$ was plotted by locating the two terminal points, setting Q_1 and then Q_2 equal to zero, and then joining them by a straight line. These terminal points were determined by the following equations.

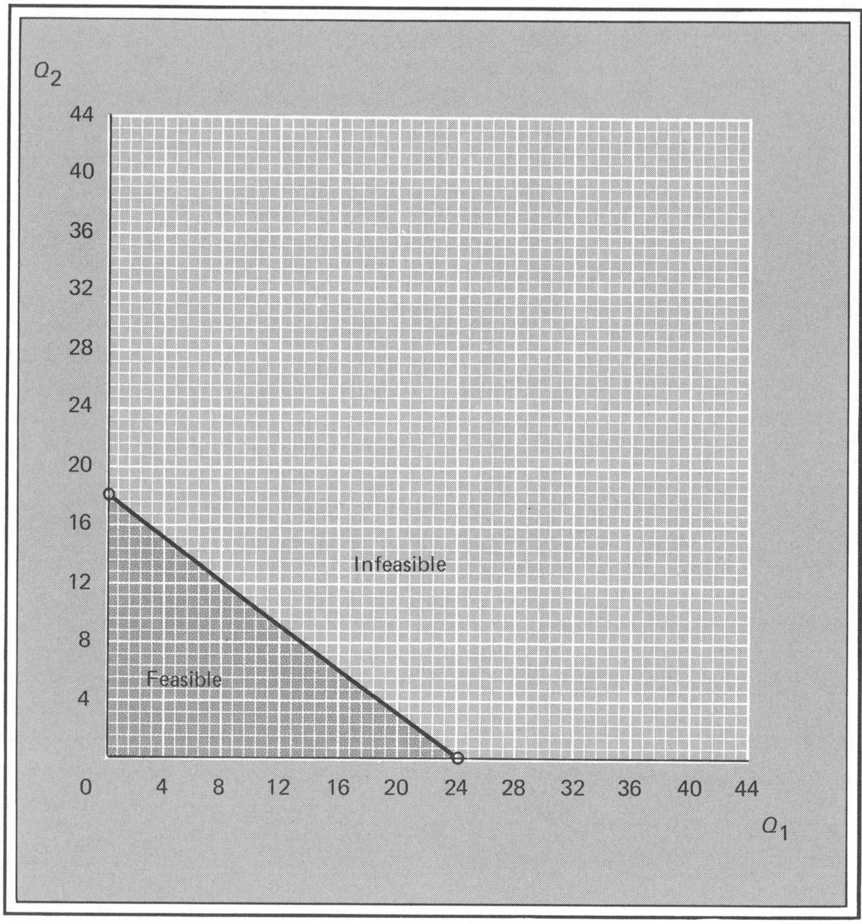

EXHIBIT 7-6
Graphic plot of Department A constraints

If all the capacity available were used to make only Product Q_1:

$$3(Q_1) + 4(0) \leq 72$$
$$Q_1 \leq 24$$ (Maximum number of floor lamps the department could produce)

If all the capacity available were used to make only Product Q_2:

$$3(0) + 4(Q_2) \leq 72$$
$$Q_2 \leq 18$$ (Maximum number of table lamps the department could produce)

On Exhibit 7-6 the first point is where Q_1 is 24 and Q_2 is zero. The second point is where Q_1 is zero and Q_2 is 18. These points were then joined by a straight line. The dark area under the line represents feasible combinations of different production outputs. For example, it is feasible to produce the following combinations from the many possibilities.

$$12(Q_1) + 9(Q_2) = 72 \text{ hours}$$
$$3(Q_1) + 12(Q_2) = 57 \text{ hours}$$
$$17(Q_1) + 4(Q_2) = 67 \text{ hours}$$

Step 3. Plot the constraints for the second department with the same procedures used in step 2. The plot is shown in Exhibit 7-7. The terminal points are:

$$6(Q_1) + 2(0) = 66 \text{ hours}$$
$$Q_1 = 11 \text{ floor lamps}$$

$$6(0) + 2(Q_2) = 66 \text{ hours}$$
$$Q_2 = 33 \text{ table lamps}$$

Step 4. Combine the two graphs determined in steps 2 and 3 to show the feasible alternatives for the whole plant. The two inequalities are plotted in Exhibit 7-8. The dark area, included within the points *A–B–C–D*, contains all possible combinations of products that satisfy the two original inequalities.

Reading the graph in Exhibit 7-8 for point *D* we can see that the quantity at point *D* is 6 floor lamps (Q_1) and 13 table lamps (Q_2). Actually, point *D* falls somewhat beyond 6 floor lamps and short of 7. We are assuming that the firm wants to produce only completed lamps; it should produce 6. At point *D* the combination of floor and table lamps does not use all the time available in each department.

Steps 1 through 4 have defined the technical constraints of the plant.

Step 5. Determine the particular combination of products that will maximize total profits. The profit function, previously defined, was:

$$P = \$12(Q_1) + \$8(Q_2)$$

With this objective function the total contribution margin (P) at points *A, B, C,* and *D* would be:

$$P_A \quad (0,0) = \$12(0) + \$8(0) = \$0$$
$$P_B \quad (11,0) = \$12(11) + \$8(0) = \$132$$
$$P_C \quad (0,18) = \$12(0) + \$8(18) = \$144$$
$$P_D \quad (6,13) = \$12(6) + \$8(13) = \$176$$

The greatest contribution margin is found at point *D*.

To further explore the impact of the objective function, let's assume that the objective function, due to changes in demand, becomes:

$$P = \$12(Q_1) + \$3(Q_2)$$

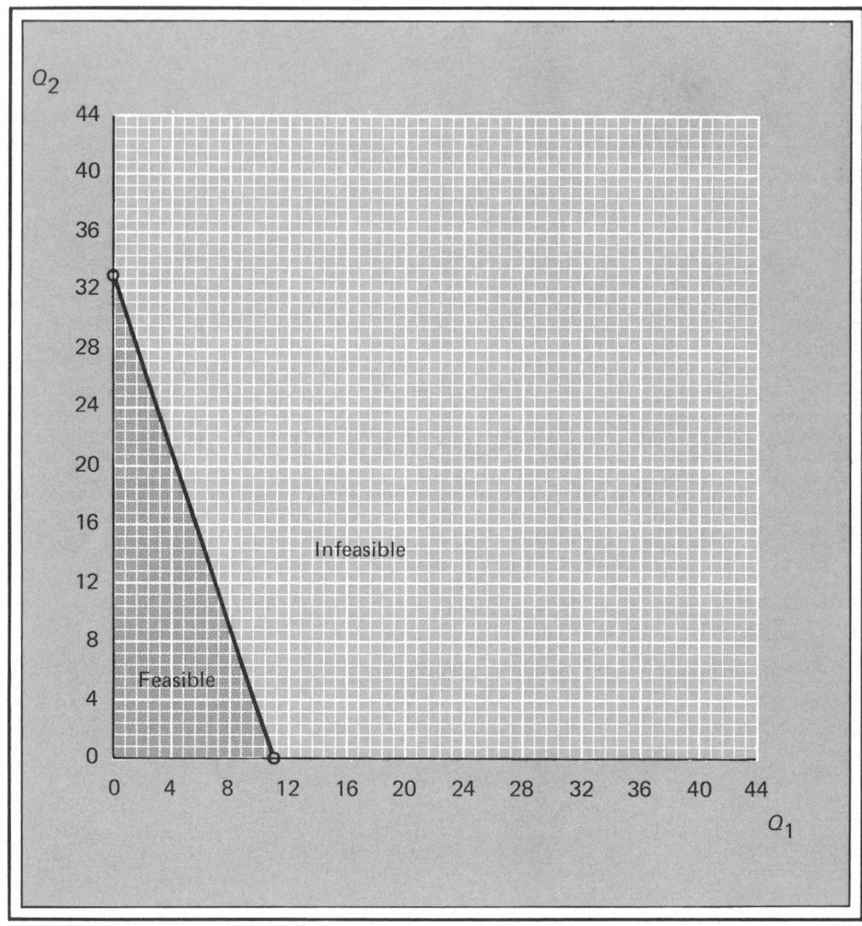

EXHIBIT 7-7
Graphic plot of Department B constraints

The total contribution margin at each point becomes:

$$
\begin{array}{llllll}
P_A & (0,0) & = \$12(0) & + \$3(0) & = \$0 \\
P_B & (11,0) & = \$12(11) & + \$3(0) & = \$132 \\
P_C & (0,18) & = \$12(0) & + \$3(18) & = \$54 \\
P_D & (6,13) & = \$12(6) & + \$3(13) & = \$111
\end{array}
$$

In this case the greatest contribution margin is found at point *B*. The maximum profit line can be found by calculating the profit for each particular combination of products. Then, the feasible point that yields the highest profit is the optimum choice.

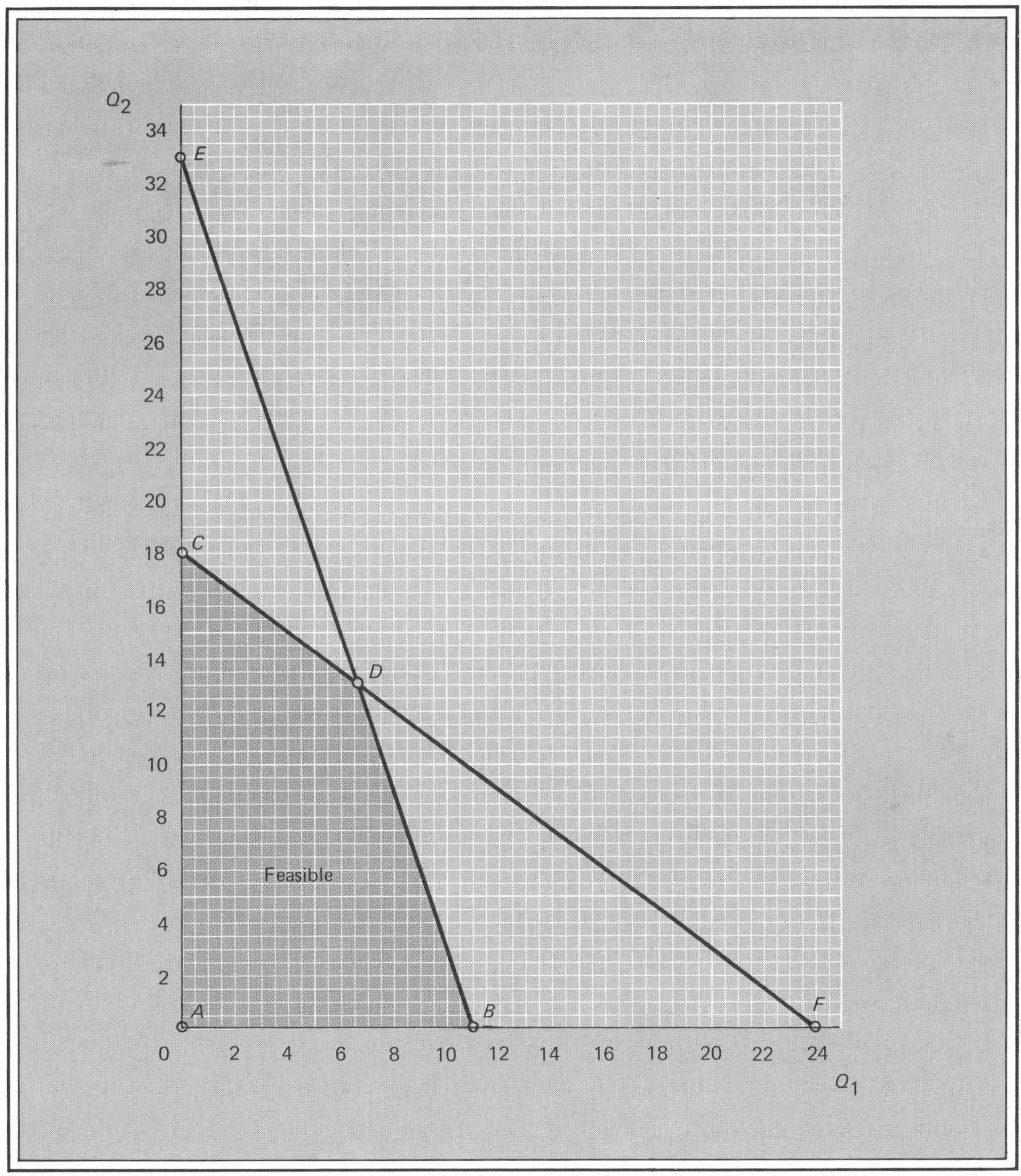

EXHIBIT 7-8
Graphic plot of Departments A and B constraints

Algebraic solution

An alternate method of determining the optimum product mix is through the use of simultaneous equations. By solving the original equations of the two inequalities, point *D* can be found. The equations are:

$$(1) \quad 3(Q_1) + 4(Q_2) = 72$$
$$(2) \quad 6(Q_1) + 2(Q_2) = 66$$

Multiplying the first equation by +2 so that the Q_1 values are equal, we get:

$$(3)\quad 6(Q_1) + 8(Q_2) = 144$$
$$(2)\quad 6(Q_1) + 2(Q_2) = 66$$

Subtracting equation (2) from equation (3) we get:

$$(4)\quad 6(Q_2) = 78$$
$$Q_2 = 13$$

Substituting 13 for Q_2 in one of the original equations we can solve for Q_1. For example, substituting 13 into equation (1) we get:

$$(1)\quad 3(Q_1) + 4(13) = 72$$
$$Q_1 = 6+$$

The simultaneous equations arrive at point *D*. With this point step 5 can now be completed.

More complex solutions

In most firms there are more than two products, several departments, and many constraints. Visualize a company with 15 products manufactured in various combinations through 20 departments. The graphic method would be completely inadequate and the algebraic method of simultaneous equations would be impractical because of the size of the problem. A procedure widely used in these complex cases is the **simplex method.** Using matrix algebra, the simplex method works toward the optimal solution by repeating the computational routine over and over until the best solution is reached. A study of the simplex method is far beyond the scope of this book, although the informed decision maker should know that a solution method is available for multiproduct and multiconstraint situations.

Production Lot Sizes

Once the desired quantities of product have been determined, management is still faced with choosing the quantities to be made on each production run. There are many companies that produce items in lots or batches rather than in a continuous, uninterrupted flow. Where products are produced in batches, a firm must incur a **setup cost** each time a batch is produced. These setup costs include the additional costs of preparing and realigning the machines; installing dies, jigs, and templates; necessary paperwork to prepare the production run; and reorienting the workers to their jobs.

To minimize setup costs the firm could manufacture the entire year's needs at one time, incurring only one setup cost per year. However, the manufacture of a year's supply in one production run would incur other costs. The products would have to be stored in the inventory, increasing **carrying costs**—the incremental costs incurred to keep the inventory until it is sold. They include all incremental costs of storage facilities, insurance, interest

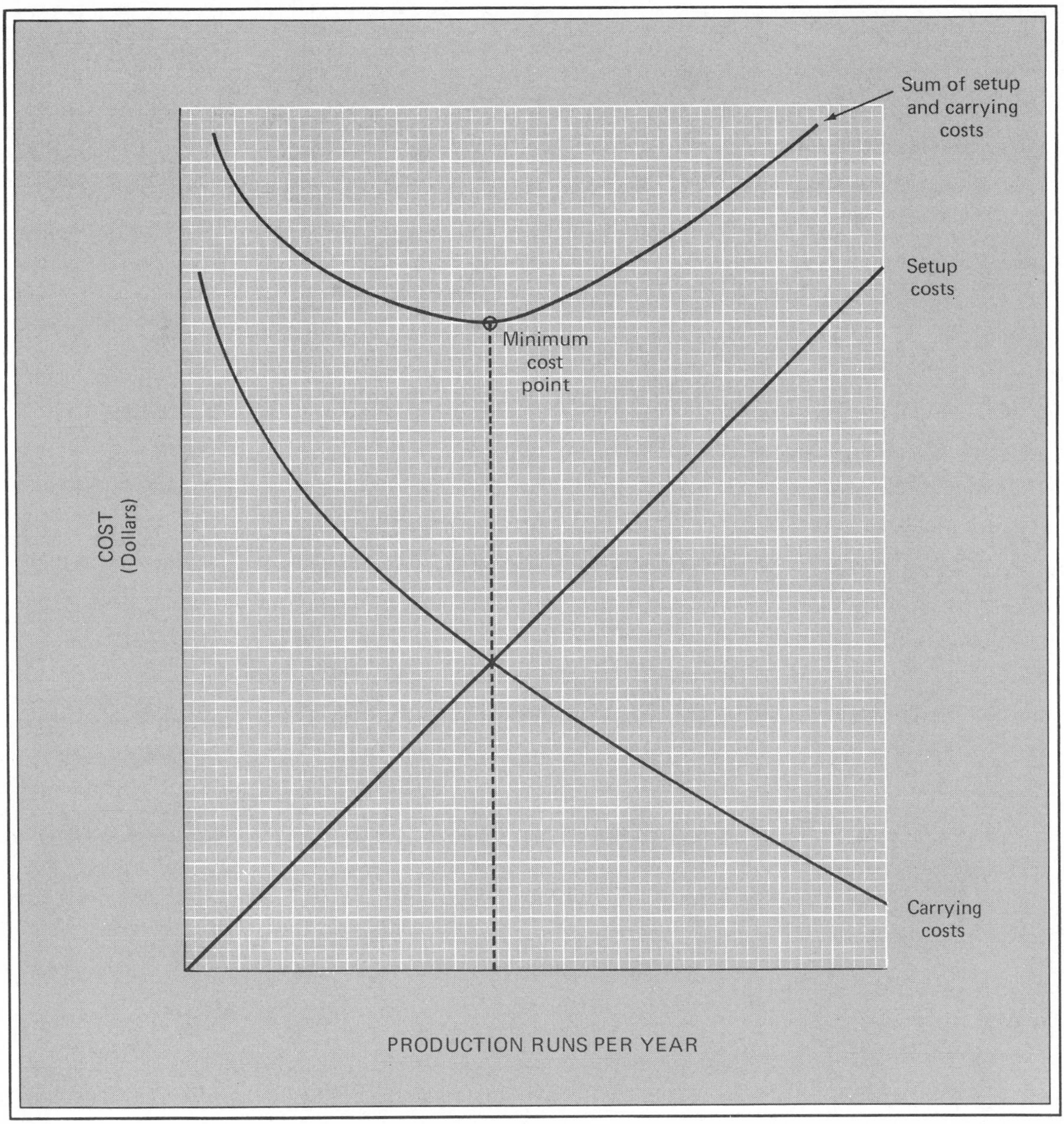

EXHIBIT 7-9
Economic production-run graph

on the investment in the inventory, salaries of the storeroom personnel, and losses from spoilage and obsolescence.

The interrelationship of carrying costs and setup costs is shown in Exhibit 7-9. The setup costs are only incurred when a separate production run is made. This cost increases linearly with each production run. Conversely, carrying costs are high when the inventory is produced in a single run, and grow smaller with each additional production run because there is a smaller average inventory on hand. The minimum "total cost" (the sum of carrying costs and setup costs) is where the carrying costs equal the setup costs.

The optimum number of production runs per year can be determined by the formula:[1]

$$N = \sqrt{\frac{A \times C}{2 \times S}}$$

where:

N = Optimum number of runs per year
A = Annual production cost of product
C = Carrying costs expressed as a percentage of inventory cost
S = Setup cost per production run (ORDERING COSTS)

This formula is based upon the assumption that the goods are withdrawn from the inventory at a constant rate and that the next production run is delivered to the warehouse just as the last item is withdrawn.

[1]The first step in the development of an **economic order quantity** (EOQ) formula, for the minimization of procurement or setup costs and carrying costs, is to state the costs in symbol form. The manager has the option of one, two, five, or N purchase orders or production runs per year. Each purchase order or setup incurs a cost, which we will term S. Annual procurement or setup costs will be:

$$N \times S \tag{1}$$

The manager also knows that the fewer purchase orders or setups per year, the larger average quantity he will have on hand. If he chooses one purchase order or setup per year, his average inventory will be:

$$\frac{A}{2} \tag{2}$$

where A is the annual usage in dollars. If the choice of two purchase orders or setups per year is chosen, the average inventory on hand will be:

$$\frac{A}{2 \times 2} \tag{3}$$

and hence the possibility of the average inventory on hand is:

$$\frac{A}{N \times 2} \tag{4}$$

As the inventory increases, the costs of carrying the inventory will increase. As the number of Ns increase, the amount of carrying costs will decrease. If C is the cost of carrying the inventory, the cost of possessing an inventory with N purchase orders or setups will be:

$$\frac{A \times C}{N \times 2} \tag{5}$$

Since the minimum cost is where the carrying costs equal the procurement or setup costs, we can then say that the following will present minimum costs:

$$\frac{A \times C}{N \times 2} = N \times S \tag{6}$$

To illustrate the use of the EOQ formula, let's assume that the ABC Company produces and sells \$100,000 of small boat propellors per year in addition to other products, that its differential costs of carrying the finished goods are 20% of the inventory value per year, and that the setup cost per production run is \$200. The optimum number of production runs per year is:

$$N = \sqrt{\frac{A \times C}{2 \times S}} = \sqrt{\frac{\$100{,}000 \times .20}{2 \times \$200}} = \sqrt{\frac{\$20{,}000}{\$400}} = \sqrt{50}$$

$N = 7$ production runs per year

Seven runs will minimize the costs for the ABC Company, but a special word of caution is warranted. The fact that the sum of the differential costs is minimized does not mean the production system that causes the costs is optimal. The setup procedures, warehouse operations, and factory methods may be efficient, grossly inefficient, or (more likely) somewhere in between. However, even in an inefficient system this decision mode offers a means of minimizing costs.

By solving for N we find:

$$A \times C = 2N^2 \times S \quad (7)$$

and

$$N^2 = \frac{A \times C}{2 \times S} \quad (8)$$

and

$$N = \sqrt{\frac{A \times C}{2 \times S}} \quad (9)$$

This formula shows the number of purchase orders or setups that will minimize carrying costs and procurement or setup costs. When a firm wants the economic order quantity in dollars of purchases (Q) rather than number of purchase orders (N), the formula can be modified to:

$$N = \frac{A}{Q} \quad (10)$$

and

$$NS = \frac{AC}{2N} \text{ (see formula 6)}$$

then

$$\frac{AC}{2A/Q} = \frac{AS}{Q} \quad (11)$$

and

$$\frac{CQ}{2} = \frac{AS}{Q} \quad (12)$$

$$CQ^2 = 2AS \quad (13)$$

$$Q^2 = \frac{2AS}{C} \quad (14)$$

$$Q = \sqrt{\frac{2AS}{C}} \quad (15)$$

SUMMARY

The accountant has a large role to play in management's production decisions by providing data on relevant costs. Relevant costs are future costs—estimates of what the decision maker believes *will* happen. They are also differential costs. To be relevant, a future cost must differ among alternatives. For this reason, many fixed costs are not relevant to production decisions. All historical costs are nonrelevant. Joint costs are also nonrelevant for all decisions subsequent to their incurrence.

The contribution margin plays a vital role in short-range production decisions as an estimate of incremental, future revenue. To obtain the maximum profit from an existing plant, the decision should be to maximize the total contribution margin of the firm. All decisions on whether to make or buy a component part, to add or drop a product, or to sell a product or process it further hinge upon an analysis of differential contribution margins.

Where there are multiproduct and plant production constraints, linear programming facilitates choosing an optimum product mix. It recognizes the constraints of the departments to determine which outputs are feasible. The objective function, to maximize the product contribution margins, allows the selection of the product mix that will maximize total contribution margin.

SUPPLEMENTARY READING

Doney, Lloyd D. "Coping with Uncertainty in the Make or Buy Decision." *Management Accounting,* October, 1968.

Harris, William T., Jr., and Wayne R. Chapin. "Joint Product Costing." *Management Accounting,* April, 1973.

Jaedicke, Robert K. "Some Notes on Product Combination Decisions." *The Accounting Review,* October, 1958.

National Association of Accountants. *Costing Joint Products.* New York: National Association of Accountants, 1957.

National Association of Accountants. *Analysis of Manufacturing Cost Variances.* New York: National Association of Accountants, 1952.

Palmer, B. Thomas. "Management Reports for Multiproduct Plants." *Management Accounting,* August, 1970.

Rinehard, Jack R. "Economic Purchase Quantity Calculations." *Management Accounting,* September, 1970.

Schuba, Kenneth E. "Make-or-Buy Decisions—Cost and Non-Cost Considerations." *N.A.A. Bulletin,* March, 1960.

QUESTIONS

7-1 The only relevant benefits and costs for decision making are future benefits and costs. Discuss. Of what value are past benefits and costs for decision making? Explain.

7-2 Discuss the concepts of *futurity* and *differentiality* in determining the relevance of benefits and costs for decision making.

7-3 Some decisions are new and unique, whereas others occur at regular intervals. How should this affect the accountant's task in accumulating, measuring, and reporting data to management? How might the data needs, both quantitative and qualitative, differ?

7-4 "It is potentially misleading to examine fixed costs on a per-unit basis." Do you agree or disagree? Defend your position.

7-5 "Unit costs determined through the allocation of joint costs are applicable to inventory costing but are not useful for decision making." Do you agree or disagree? Explain.

7-6 "The method chosen to allocate joint costs to individual products can change the net profit of the firm." Do you agree or disagree? Explain.

7-7 Define *contribution margin* and *product margin* and indicate the difference in the concepts.

7-8 Identify the benefits and costs relevant to the short-run decisions of (a) adding a new product and (b) dropping a product.

7-9 Why might management decide to produce a product internally at a higher cost than to buy the same product in the open market? Give some possible examples.

7-10 There are a number of requirements that must be met before linear programming can be used appropriately. List these requirements and explain the importance of each.

7-11 "To minimize production costs, setup costs should be decreased to the lowest amount possible." Do you agree or disagree? Explain.

7-12 Explain the role of the objective function in linear programming. How is the objective function usually measured?

7-13 The relative sales-value method is a common method of allocating joint costs to individual products. Describe the method and indicate when it should be used.

7-14 Define the term *opportunity cost.* Is contribution margin a valid measure of opportunity cost? Is net income by product a valid measure of opportunity cost? Explain.

7-15 List some of the costs management should consider in trying to decide upon the optimum number of units to produce in a given production run.

PROBLEMS

7-16 Indicate whether the following statements are *true* or *false.*

1. If the firm is producing at the optimum output, the sales revenue of one more unit of production will be greater than the additional costs.
2. Only future costs that differ between alternatives are relevant to decisions.
3. The opportunity cost should be measured by the *best* available opportunity rather than by the *next best* available opportunity.
4. Fixed costs, since they do not change with production decisions, can *never* be relevant.
5. Joint costs can be directly traced to individual products.
6. Where the decision is to hold production facilities constant and to increase or decrease production output, variable costs are not relevant.
7. A widely used basis for joint cost allocations where products differ widely is the relative sales value basis.
8. The principal reason for allocating joint costs is to enhance management's ability to make decisions.
9. A product should be processed further only if the net income from the product is increased.

10. The optimum output quantity in a production run is where the costs of carrying the inventory exactly equal the cost of setup.

7-17 List some of the opportunity costs and the relevant costs associated with the following situations.

1. Continuing your education by working toward a graduate degree or taking your bachelor's degree and going to work.
2. Changing your field of study in your junior year from premedicine to prelaw.
3. Purchasing a scientific-business calculator for $400 or purchasing an inexpensive $60 four-function calculator.
4. Taking a part-time job at $3.50 per hour near your home, as opposed to taking a part-time job that pays $4.00 per hour and is one-half hour travel time from your home.
5. Quitting your present salaried position and starting your own business or maintaining your current job.
6. Depositing a $1,000 gift in a savings and loan institution or investing it in a government savings bond.
7. Going to the mountains for a weekend of skiing or staying home and studying.
8. Developing your film in your own darkroom or having it processed by a commercial developer.
9. Hiring only college graduates or hiring only high school graduates in your office.
10. Using a $1,000 gift to buy a car or using it to buy a new stereo system.

7-18 The Loadstone Company produces a line of ball and chains. Management is trying to determine the production schedule for the coming year. It estimates that annual demand will be $75,000. It costs the firm $250 to set up the machinery for each production run. The cost of carrying the inventory is estimated at 15% of the inventory value.

REQUIRED:

A. How many production runs should be made in the coming year?
B. If setup costs increased to $400, would you change your answer? How?
C. What if the carrying costs climbed to 20% and the setup costs remained at $250?

7-19 Nature's Best Cereal Company produces three granola cereals. A two-month sales promotion is being planned, during which a premium costing $.20 will be given away with the purchase of a box of one of the cereals. The cereal to be promoted is to be selected on the basis of the following figures.

	Crunchy Granola	*Nutty Granola*	*Fruity Granola*
Regular selling price per box	$.80	$1.20	$1.10
Cost per box of cereal	$.69	$ .84	$ .91
Contribution margin ratio	40%	20%	30%
Expected increase in number of boxes sold because of premium	200,000	400,000	300,000

REQUIRED:
Which product should be chosen? Present appropriate figures to support your answer.

7-20 The Springerville General Hospital currently employs its own janitorial staff, which incurs the following costs per year.

Labor	$ 80,000
Supplies	60,000
Overhead	130,000
	$270,000

The hospital employees are asking for a 25% wage increase and it appears that an increase of at least 20% will be necessary. An outside contractor has approached the hospital and offered a three-year contract to do the job for $210,000 per year. Overhead includes depreciation of $20,000, allocated administrative and other fixed costs of $100,000, and variable indirect costs of $10,000.

REQUIRED:
A. Should the Springerville General Hospital accept the offer? Show your analysis.
B. If a 25% wage increase is granted to the hospital employees, what is the highest contract price the hospital could pay the outside contractor without increasing total hospital costs? Explain fully.

7-21 The Judson Company produces two products. The selling prices, costs, and other relevant data follow.

	Product J	*Product K*
Selling price	$33	$50
Direct material	$ 4	$24
Direct labor	15	10
Variable overhead (20% of labor)	3	2
Fixed overhead (40% of labor)	6	4
Net income	$ 5	$10
Materials used	4 pounds	24 pounds
Labor hours	3 hours	2 hours
Power consumed	11 kwh.	14 kwh.
Demand for products	10,000 units	8,000 units

REQUIRED:

A. How much of each product should be produced if adequate resources are available?

B. How much of each product should be produced if capacity is limited to 40,000 labor hours?

C. How much of each product should be produced if only 100,000 pounds of material are available?

D. How much of each product should be produced if only 111,000 kwh. of power are available?

7-22 The following costs and other data apply to two component parts used by Griffon Electronics.

	Part A	*Part B*
Direct material	$ .40	$ 8.00
Direct labor	1.00	4.70
Factory overhead	4.00	2.00
Unit cost	$5.40	$14.70
Units needed per year	6,000	8,000
Machine hours per unit	4	2
Unit cost if purchased	$5.00	$15.00

In the past years, Griffon has manufactured all its required components. However, in 1974 only 30,000 hours of otherwise idle machine time can be devoted to the production of components. Accordingly, some of the parts must be purchased from outside suppliers. In producing parts, factory overhead is applied at $1 per machine hour. Fixed capacity costs, which will not be affected by any make-buy decision, represent 60% of the applied overhead.

REQUIRED:

A. Assuming that the 30,000 hours of available machine time are to be scheduled so that Griffon realizes maximum potential cost savings, determine the relevant production costs that should be considered in the decision to schedule machine time.

B. Compute the number of units that Griffon should produce if it allocates the machine time based upon the potential cost savings per machine hour.

(CPA adapted)

7-23 From a particular joint process, Watkins Company produces three products: X, Y, and Z. Each product may be sold at the point of split-off or processed further. Additional processing requires no special facilities, and production costs of further processing are entirely variable and traceable to the products involved. In 19X3 all three products were processed beyond split-off. Joint production costs for the year were $60,000. Sales values and costs needed to evaluate Watkins' 19X3 production policy follow.

			Additional Costs and Sales Values if Processed Further	
Product	*Units Produced*	*Sales Values at Split-Off*	*Sales Values*	*Added Cost*
X	6,000	$25,000	$42,000	$9,000
Y	4,000	$41,000	$45,000	$7,000
Z	2,000	$24,000	$32,000	$8,000

Joint costs are allocated to the products in proportion to the relative physical volume of output.

REQUIRED:

A. Prepare a production schedule that will maximize firm profits.

B. Prepare an income statement at the maximum profit level.

(CPA adapted)

7-24 Harry Huntley is a traveling salesman for the Silver Spoon Company. He is considering expanding his sales territory to two new towns. The following record shows last year's automobile expenses for traveling 30,000 miles.

Gasoline	$1,200
Oil and lubrication	500
Parking and toll fees	50
Tires (1 set per year)	250
Insurance	300
Licenses and taxes	150
Tune-ups and maintenance	350
Depreciation based upon straight-line depreciation	1,100
Total costs	$3,900

If Harry includes the two new towns, he will have to travel an additional 5,000 miles per year.

REQUIRED:

A. Indicate which of these costs are likely to be fixed and which are likely to be variable.
B. Which costs are relevant to his decision to expand the sales territory?
C. Prepare a schedule showing the estimated differential costs between traveling the old territory compared with the new one.
D. Discuss any nonfinancial factors Harry should consider.

7-25 Central Area Community Health Center performs a certain lab test with the following average costs per test.

Labor	$1.50
Material	1.00
Overhead items	2.50
	$5.00

The center is attempting to reduce costs. An outside source offers to do the tests for $3 each. If the center accepts the offer, it will release the appropriate technician. Lab overhead is composed of depreciation of lab equipment calculated on a straight-line basis and an apportioned share of administrative costs.

REQUIRED:

Prepare an analysis to show whether the center should do the test itself or accept the offer.

7-26 The obstetrics unit of the Westside Hospital collects an average revenue of $105 per patient day. Variable costs are $25 per patient day. The unit averages 5,000 patient days per year. Fixed costs of operating the unit are as follows:

Salaries	$270,000
Equipment depreciation	90,000
Building depreciation	45,000
Administrative overhead	45,000
	$450,000

One of the goals of the not-for-profit hospital is to be financially self-sufficient. Losses in the obstetrics unit have been increasing. If obstetrics is dropped, the space can be used for other services expected to contribute $100,000 per year to joint costs.

REQUIRED:

Prepare an analysis showing whether Westside Hospital should drop its obstetrics unit.

7-27 Bill owns a fishing boat that he uses in a salmon fleet off the coast of Alaska. Due to a 10% increase in the price the cannery is willing to pay for salmon, he is considering the purchase of a second boat. The following estimated costs are for the coming season for his current boat.

Diesel fuel	$ 6,000	(variable)
Crew wages	10,000	(variable)
Maintenance	2,500	(fixed)
Depreciation	3,250	(fixed)
Insurance	1,500	(fixed)
Fishing permits	750	(fixed)
Total	$24,000	

Bill feels that he could decrease the time spent fishing by 60% with the use of two boats and still catch 80% of the original amount of fish in each boat. His revenue from last season's catch was $60,000. In addition to his crew's wages, Bill pays his crew 20% of the season's revenue as part of their compensation. The new boat would cost $75,000 and have an estimated useful life of 10 years with no residual value.

REQUIRED:

A. What are the relevant costs that Bill should consider?

B. What would be the differences in net income for the next fishing season between (1) using only the original boat and (2) using two boats at 60% of capacity. Support your answers with comparative income statements.

7-28 The Little People Company manufactures two styles of little dolls for little people. The following cost, revenue, and production data apply to the manufacture of the dolls.

	Production Time Tiny Tina Doll	*Production Time Wee Willie Doll*	*Capacity in Machine Hours*
Molding department	6	4	60
Assembly department	4	2	40

REQUIRED:

A. State the production constraints in algebraic form.

B. Show graphically the production constraints and the feasible region of production.

C. What production output would you recommend to management if the contribution margin of Tiny Tina is $4 and of Wee Willie, $6?

7-29 The Longbranch Company manufactures two products in two departments. It estimates that the following production and cost data are relevant for the coming year.

	Product G	*Product H*	*Available Machine Hours per Week*
Department A	2 hours	4 hours	48 hours
Department B	5 hours	3 hours	60 hours
Contribution margin per unit	$10	$24	

REQUIRED:

A. Summarize the above data with mathematical equations.

B. Solve for the optimum production quantity of each product, using the graphic method.

C. Solve for the optimum production quantity of each product, using the algebraic method.

7-30 Girth, Inc. makes two kinds of men's suede leather belts, with the following revenue and costs for each product.

	Belt A	*Belt B*
Selling price per unit	$19.50	$5.75
Direct material	$ 5.00	$1.00
Direct labor	6.00	3.00
Variable overhead	1.50	.75
Fixed overhead	2.00	1.00
Allocated general and selling expense	1.00	.30
Net income per belt (loss)	$ 4.00	$ (.30)

Girth, Inc. is able to sell all the belts it can make. Constraints are:

1. Belt A requires a fancy buckle, of which only 400 are available per day.

2. Girth, Inc. has the capacity to make 1,000 units of B per day. Each A belt requires twice as much manufacturing time as a B belt.

3. Belt B requires a plain buckle, of which 700 are available per day.

4. Only enough suede is available to produce 800 belts per day.

REQUIRED:

A. Prepare a graph, labeling each of the constraints by using their corresponding numbers.

B. From the graph determine how many units of Belt A and Belt B should be produced to maximize daily sales.

C. From the graph determine how many units of Belt A and Belt B should be produced to maximize net income.

D. The supplier of fancy buckles (for Belt A) informs Girth, Inc. that it cannot supply more than 100 fancy buckles a day. Other facts remain the same.

   1. Reflect this new information on the graph.

   2. Determine the number of each of the two belts that should be produced to maximize net income. *(CMA adapted)*

7-31 The Redwood Lumber Company produces 2 × 2s, 2 × 4s, and 4 × 4s in its first process. Normal capacity is 10 million board feet, which requires an input of $1,250,000 of timber. Total operating costs for labor and factory overhead in the first process are $350,000 per year. After they emerge from the first process, the products could be processed further. The three products, if processed further, would enter the second process, where additional costs of production are $80,000. Finally, the 2 × 2s could enter process 3, where they could be turned into decorative spindles. The costs of operating process 3 are $160,000. Revenue and production data are:

	2 × 2s	*2 × 4s*	*4 × 4s*
Selling price at end of process 1 (per 1,000 board feet)	$150	$200	$250
Selling price at end of process 2 (per 1,000 board feet)	$160	$210	$270
Selling price at end of process 3 (per 1,000 board feet)	$220		
Normal production (in 1,000 board feet)	2,500	5,000	2,500

REQUIRED:

A. Prepare a schedule that highlights the effects of the possible alternatives. Your schedule should show estimated contribution margins and net incomes.

B. What actions would you recommend to management?

7-32 Brownstone Manufacturing Company produces a line of building blocks that it markets through lumberyards and building supply stores for $.10 each. Currently, 500,000 blocks are produced per year using only 50% of plant capacity. The following costs per block were incurred last year.

Direct material	$.025
Direct labor	.005
Variable factory overhead costs	.010
Variable selling costs	.003
Fixed factory overhead costs	.023
Fixed selling costs	.009
Total unit cost	$.075

Management would like to use the excess capacity and has several possibilities:

1. It could produce additional units of the same block and ship the additional production out of the present market area, which is saturated. Management estimates that it could market 300,000 blocks this way. Additional freight charges would be $.01 per block and fixed overhead would increase by $8,000 per year. There would be no other changes in the cost structure.

2. It could process the original block further, making it into a decorative block. Management believes that it could sell 150,000 decorative blocks at a price of \$.25 each, in addition to current sales of 500,000 blocks. The following cost estimates are for processing 150,000 blocks further.

Direct materials	\$.001
Direct labor	.065
Variable factory overhead costs	.030
Variable selling costs	.014
Total variable costs per unit	\$.110
Fixed factory overhead costs	\$4,000 per year
Fixed selling costs	\$1,000 per year

REQUIRED:
Prepare income statements setting forth the contribution margin and net income for the following atlernatives:

1. Current production of 500,000 blocks continues unchanged.
2. The firm adds the 300,000 blocks in alternative 1.
3. The firm adds the 150,000 decorative blocks in alternative 2.

7-33 Using the information in problem 7-32, management has recently discovered it could use the excess capacity to produce and market a new and unrelated product. The capacity could be used to produce 50,000 units per year at a price of \$10 per unit with the following cost estimates.

Direct materials	\$2.00
Direct labor	4.50
Variable factory overhead costs	1.30
Total costs per unit	\$7.80

This new product would require *additional* fixed selling costs of \$40,000 and fixed factory overhead costs of \$60,000.

REQUIRED:

A. Present an income statement for the company with the new product.
B. Which of the alternatives in Problem 7-32 and this problem would you recommend to management? Explain.

7-34 The Vernom Corporation, which produces and sells to wholesalers a highly successful line of summer lotions and insect repellents, has decided to diversify in order to stabilize sales throughout the year. A natural area for the company to consider is the production of winter lotions and creams to prevent dry and chapped skin.

After considerable research, a winter products line has been developed. However, because of the conservative nature of the company management, Vernom's president has decided to introduce only one of the new products for this coming winter. If the product is a success, further expansion in future years will be initiated.

The product selected (called *Chap-off*) is a lip balm that will be sold in a lipstick-type tube. The product will be sold to wholesalers in boxes of 24 tubes for $8 per box. Because of available capacity, no additional fixed charges will be incurred to produce the product. However, a $100,000 fixed charge will be absorbed by the product to allocate a fair share of the company's present fixed costs to the new product.

Using the estimated sales and production of 100,000 boxes of Chap-off as the standard volume, the accounting department has developed the following costs.

Direct labor	$2.00 per box
Direct materials	3.00 per box
Total overhead	1.50 per box
Total	$6.50 per box

Vernom has approached a cosmetics manufacturer to discuss the possibility of purchasing the tubes for Chap-off. The purchase price of the empty tubes from the cosmetics manufacturer would be $.90 per 24 tubes. If the Vernom Corporation accepts the purchase proposal, it is estimated that direct labor and variable overhead costs would be reduced by 10% and direct material costs would be reduced by 20%.

REQUIRED:

A. Should the Vernom Corporation make or buy the tubes? Show calculations to support your answer.

B. What would be the minimum purchase price acceptable to the Vernom Corporation for the tubes? Support your answer with an appropriate explanation.

C. Instead of sales of 100,000 boxes, revised estimates show sales volume at 125,000 boxes. At this new volume additional equipment, at an annual rental of $10,000, must be acquired to manufacture the tubes. However, this incremental cost would be the only additional fixed cost required even if sales increased to 300,000 boxes. (The 300,000 level is the goal for third year of production.) Under these circumstances, should the Vernom Corporation make or buy the tubes? Show calculations to support your answer.

D. The company has the option of making and buying at the same time. What would be your answer to part C if this alternative were considered? Show calculations to support your answer.

E. What nonquantifiable factors should the Vernom Corporation consider in determining whether to make or buy the lipstick tubes?

(CMA adapted)

7-35 The Red Baron Manufacturing Company produces three styles of refrigerated display cases: 18′ chill, 12′ frozen, and 18′ frozen. The following income statements are for the three products and for the company.

	18′ Chill	*12′ Frozen*	*18′ Frozen*	*Total*
Sales	$250,000	$225,000	$375,000	$850,000
Variable costs	195,000	150,000	230,000	575,000
Contribution margin	$ 55,000	$ 75,000	$145,000	$275,000
Fixed costs:				
Identifiable to the product	$ 30,000	$ 30,000	$ 55,000	$115,000
Joint costs allocated on sales basis	35,000	31,500	52,500	119,000
Total fixed costs	65,000	61,500	107,500	234,000
Net income (loss)	$ (10,000)	$ 13,500	$ 37,500	$ 41,000

REQUIRED:
Each part is independent.

A. Management is concerned with the low income of the firm and is considering the elimination of the 18′ chill unit. Should the 18′ chill unit be eliminated? Support your decision with appropriate analysis.

B. The company is now operating at practical capacity. Management has the opportunity to produce a walk-in refrigerated unit with estimated sales of $630,000, a contribution margin ratio of 18%, and identifiable fixed costs of $66,000. To produce this product the 18′ chill box would have to be eliminated. Prepare an income statement including the new product. Should Red Baron produce the new product?

7-36 The cost accountant of the Stangren Corporation, your client, wants your opinion of a technique suggested to him by a young accounting graduate he employed as a cost analyst. The following information was furnished you for the corporation's two products, trinkets and gadgets.

EXHIBIT A

	Daily Capacities in Units			
	Cutting Department	*Finishing Department*	*Sales Price per Unit*	*Variable Cost per Unit*
Trinkets	400	240	$50	$30
Gadgets	200	320	$70	$40

1. The daily capacities of each department represent the maximum production for *either* trinkets *or* gadgets. However, any combination of trinkets and gadgets can be produced as long as the maximum capacity of the department is not exceeded. For example, two trinkets can be produced in the cutting department for each gadget not produced, and three trinkets can be produced in the finishing department for every four gadgets not produced.

2. Material shortages prohibit the production of more than 180 gadgets per day.

3. Exhibit B is a graphic expression of simultaneous linear equations developed from the production information above.

EXHIBIT B
GRAPH OF PRODUCTION RELATIONSHIPS

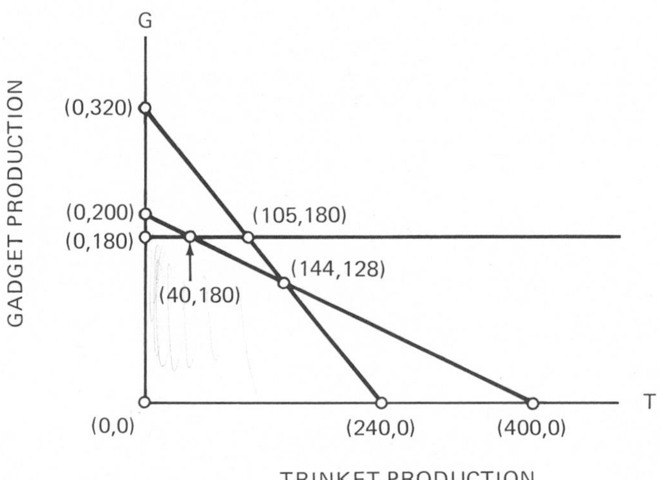

REQUIRED:

A. For what kinds of decisions are contribution margin data (revenue in excess of variable cost) useful?

B. Comparing the information in Exhibit A with the graph in Exhibit B, identify and list the graphic location (coordinates) of the following:
   1. Cutting departments capacity
   2. Production limitation for gadgets because of the materials shortage
   3. Area of feasible (possible) production combinations

C. Compute the contribution margin per unit for trinkets and gadgets.

D. Compute the total contribution margin of each of the points of intersections of lines bounding the feasible (possible) production area.

E. Identify the best production alternative. *(CPA adapted)*

7-37 The Lamptown Restaurant Supply Company produces internally a disposable grease-vat strainer, which it markets to restaurants. In a normal year it produces 12,000 units that sell for $14.00 each at the following unit cost:

Direct materials	$ 3.00
Direct labor	3.00
Variable factory overhead	1.50
Fixed factory overhead (150% of direct labor)	4.50
	$12.00

An outside supplier has offered to supply this component to the Lamptown Company for a price of $10.50 per unit.

REQUIRED:

A. Should management accept the offer? Show your analysis.

B. Assume that if management bought the strainer from the outside supplier, the productive capacity used for strainers could now be used to produce a sheet metal garbage can with the following cost and revenue characteristics:

Selling price		$7.00
Material costs	$2.40	
Labor costs	1.20	
Variable factory overhead	1.80	
Fixed factory overhead (150% of direct labor)	1.80	
Total		7.20
Net profit per unit		$ (.20)

What would be your recommendation to management? Support your conclusions with comparative variable income statements.

7-38 The Robney Company is a restaurant supplier that sells a number of products to various restaurants in the area. One of its products is a special meat cutter with a disposable blade.

The blades are sold in packages of 12 for $20 per package. After a number of years, it has been determined that the demand for the replacement blades is at a constant rate of 2,000 packages per month. The packages cost the Robney Company $10 each from the manufacturer and require a three-day lead time from date of order to date of delivery. The ordering cost is $1.20 per order and the carrying cost is 10% per annum.

Robney is going to use the economic order quantity formula:

$$\text{EOQ} = \sqrt{\frac{2(\text{Annual requirements})(\text{Cost per order})}{(\text{Price per unit})(\text{Carrying cost})}}$$

REQUIRED:

A. Calculate:
   1. The economic order quantity
   2. The number of orders needed per year
   3. The total cost of buying and carrying blades for the year

B. Assuming there is no reserve (e.g. safety stock) and that the present inventory level is 200 packages, when should the next order be placed? (Use 360 days equals one year.)

C. Discuss the problems that most firms would have in attempting to apply this formula to their inventory problems. *(CMA adapted)*

7-39 Management of the Scoopa Company has asked your assistance in arriving at a decision to continue manufacturing a part or buy it from an outside supplier. The part, Faktron, is a component used in some of the finished goods of the company. The following data is typical of the company's operations.

1. The annual requirement for Faktrons is 5,000 units. The lowest quotation from a supplier was $8 per unit.

2. Faktrons have been manufactured in the precision machinery department. If Faktrons are purchased from an outside supplier, certain machinery will be sold and would realize its book value.

3. Following are the total costs of the precision machinery department during the year when 5,000 Faktrons were made.

Materials	$67,500
Direct labor	$50,000
Indirect labor	$20,000
Light and heat	$ 5,500
Power	$ 3,000
Depreciation	$10,000
Property taxes and insurance	$ 8,000
Payroll taxes and other benefits	$ 9,800
Other	$ 5,000

4. The following precision machinery department costs apply to the manufacture of Faktrons: material, $17,500; direct labor, $28,000; indirect labor, $6,000; power, $300; other, $500. The sale of the equipment used for Faktrons would reduce the following costs by the amounts indicated: depreciation $2,000; property taxes and insurance $1,000.

6. The following additional precision machinery department costs would be incurred if Faktrons were purchased from an outside supplier: freight, $.50 per unit; indirect labor for receiving, materials handling, inspection, etc., $5,000. The cost of the purchased Faktrons would be considered a precision machinery department cost.

REQUIRED:

A. Prepare a schedule showing a comparison of the total costs of the precision machinery department (1) when Faktrons are made and (2) when Faktrons are bought from an outside supplier.

B. Discuss the considerations in addition to the cost factors that you would bring to the attention of management in assisting them to arrive at a decision whether to make or buy Faktrons. Include in your discussion the considerations that might be applied to the evaluation of the outside supplier. *(CPA adapted)*

7-40 George Jackson operates a small machine shop. He manufactures one standard product available from many other similar businesses and he also manufactures products to customer order. His accountant prepared the following annual income statement.

	Custom Sales	*Standard Sales*	*Total*
Sales	$50,000	$25,000	$75,000
Material	$10,000	$ 8,000	$18,000
Labor	20,000	9,000	29,000
Depreciation	6,300	3,600	9,900
Power	700	400	1,100
Rent	6,000	1,000	7,000
Heat and light	600	100	700
Other	400	900	1,300
	44,000	23,000	67,000
	$ 6,000	$ 2,000	$ 8,000

The depreciation charges are for machines used in the respective product lines. The power charge is apportioned on the estimate of power consumed. The rent is for the building space which has been leased for 10 years at $7,000 per year. The rent and heat and lights are apportioned to the product lines based on amount of floor space occupied. All other costs are current expenses identified with the product line causing them.

A valued custom parts customer has asked Mr. Jackson to manufacture 5,000 special units for him. Mr. Jackson is working at capacity and would have to give up some other business in order to take this order. He can't renege on custom orders already agreed to, but he could reduce the output of his standard product by about one-half for one year while producing the specially requested custom part. The customer is willing to pay $7.00 for each part. The material cost will be about $2.00 per unit and the labor will be $3.60 per unit. Mr. Jackson will have to spend $2,000 for a special device that will be discarded when the job is done.

A. Calculate and present the following costs related to the 5000 unit custom order:
   1. The incremental cost of the order
   2. The full cost of the order
   3. The opportunity cost of taking the order
   4. The sunk costs related to the order

B. Should Mr. Jackson take the order? Explain your answer.

(CMA adapted)

7-41 The officers of Bradshaw Company are reviewing the profitability of the company's four products and the potential effect of several proposals for varying the product mix. An excerpt from the income statement and other data follow.

	Total	*Product P*	*Product Q*	*Product R*	*Product S*
Sales	$62,600	$10,000	$18,000	$12,600	$22,000
Cost of goods sold	44,274	4,750	7,056	13,968	18,500
Gross profit	$18,326	$ 5,250	$10,944	$ (1,368)	$ 3,500
Operating expenses	12,012	1,990	2,976	2,826	4,220
Income before income taxes	$ 6,314	$ 3,260	$ 7,968	$ (4,194)	$ (720)
Units sold		1,000	1,200	1,800	2,000
Sales price per unit		$ 10.00	$ 15.00	$ 7.00	$ 11.00
Variable cost of goods sold per unit		$ 2.50	$ 3.00	$ 6.50	$ 6.00
Variable operating expenses per unit		$ 1.17	$ 1.25	$ 1.00	$ 1.20

REQUIRED:

Each of the following proposals is to be considered independently of the other proposals. Consider only the product changes stated in each proposal; the activity of other products remains stable. Ignore income taxes.

1. If Product R is discontinued, the effect on income will be
   a. $900 increase
   b. $4,194 increase
   c. $12,600 decrease
   d. $1,368 increase
   e. None of the above

2. If Product R is discontinued and a consequent loss of customers causes a decrease of 200 units in sales of Q, the total effect on income will be
   a. $15,600 decrease
   b. $2,866 increase
   c. $2,044 increase
   d. $1,250 decrease
   e. None of the above

3. If the sales price of R is increased to $8, with a decrease in the number of units sold to 1,500, the effect on income will be
   a. $2,199 decrease
   b. $600 decrease
   c. $750 increase
   d. $2,199 increase
   e. None of the above

4. The plant in which R is produced can be utilized to produce a new product, T. The total variable costs and expenses per unit of T are $8.05; 1,600 units can be sold at $9.50 each. If T is introduced and R is discontinued, the total effect on income will be
   a. $2,600 increase
   b. $2,320 increase
   c. $3,220 increase
   d. $1,420 increase
   e. None of the above

5. Part of the plant in which P is produced can easily be adapted to the production of S, but changes in quantities may make changes in sales prices advisable. If production of P is reduced to 500 units (to be sold at $12.00 each) and production of S is increased to 2,500 units (to be sold at $10.50 each), the total effect on income will be
   a. $1,765 decrease
   b. $250 increase
   c. $2,060 decrease
   d. $1,515 decrease
   e. None of the above

6. Production of P can be doubled by adding a second shift, but higher wages must be paid, increasing variable cost of goods sold to $3.50 for each of the additional units. If the 1,000 additional units of P can be sold at $10.00 each, the total effect on income will be
   a. $10,000 increase
   b. $5,330 increase
   c. $6,500 increase
   d. $2,260 increase
   e. None of the above

(CPA adapted)

7-42 You have been engaged to assist management of the Stenger Corporation in arriving at certain decisions. The Stenger Corporation has its home office in Philadelphia and leases factory buildings in Rhode Island, Georgia, and Illinois. The same single product is manufactured in all three factories. The following information is available regarding 19X4 operations.

	Total	*Rhode Island*	*Illinois*	*Georgia*
Sales	$900,000	$200,000	$400,000	$300,000
Fixed costs:				
Factory	$180,000	$ 50,000	$ 55,000	$ 75,000
Administration	59,000	16,000	21,000	22,000
Variable costs	500,000	100,000	220,000	180,000
Allocated home office expense	63,000	14,000	28,000	21,000
Total	802,000	180,000	324,000	298,000
Net profit from operations	$ 98,000	$ 20,000	$ 76,000	$ 2,000

Home office expense is allocated to the plants on the basis of units sold. The sales price per unit is $10.

The management of Stenger Corporation is displeased with the poor performance of the Georgia factory. The lease on the Georgia factory expires at the end of 19X5. If the lease is renewed, the annual rental will increase by $15,000. If the Georgia factory is shut down, proceeds from the sale of equipment will just cover termination expenses.

If the Georgia factory is shut down, Stenger Corporation will continue to serve the customers of the Georgia factory by one of the following methods:

1. Expand the Rhode Island factory. This would increase fixed expenses of the Rhode Island factory by 15%. In addition, shipping expenses of $2 per unit will be incurred on the increased production.

2. Enter into a contract with a competitor who will serve the customers of the Georgia factory. The competitor will pay Stenger Corporation a commission of $1.60 per unit.

REQUIRED:
A. What will be the net incomes of Stenger Corporation under each alternative?
B. Prepare a recommendation to the management of Stenger Corporation.

(CPA adapted)

7-43 Nubo Manufacturing, Inc. is presently operating at 50% of practical capacity producing about 50,000 units annually of a patented electronic component. Nubo recently received an offer from a company in Yokohama, Japan, to purchase 30,000 components at $6 per unit. Nubo has not previously sold components in Japan. Budgeted production costs for 50,000 and 80,000 units of output follow.

Units	50,000	80,000
Costs:		
Direct material	$ 75,000	$120,000
Direct labor	75,000	120,000
Factory overhead	200,000	260,000
Total costs	350,000	500,000
Cost per unit	$ 7.00	$ 6.25

The sales manager thinks the order should be accepted, even if it results in a loss of $1 per unit. The production manager does not wish to have the order accepted primarily because the order would show a loss of $.25 per unit when computed on the new average unit cost. The treasurer has made a quick computation indicating that accepting the order will actually increase gross margin.

REQUIRED:

A. Explain the apparent cause of the drop in cost from $7.00 per unit to $6.25 per unit when budgeted production increases from 50,000 to 80,000 units. Show supporting computations.

B. Explain whether (either or both) the production manager or the treasurer is correct in his reasoning.

C. Explain why the conclusions of the production manager and the treasurer differ.

D. Explain why each of the following may affect the decision to accept or reject the special order.

1. The likelihood of repeat special sales and/or all sales to be made at $6 per unit
2. Whether the sales are made to customers operating in two separate, isolated markets or whether the sales are made to customers competing in the same market *(CPA adapted)*

8 Information for Long-Range Decisions

LONG-RANGE DECISION RULE
MEASUREMENT OF BENEFITS AND COSTS
Measurement of Cash Outflows
Measurement of Cash Inflows
Effect of Income Taxes on Cash Flows
Rate of Return
THE CONCEPT OF PRESENT VALUE
LONG-RANGE DECISIONS IN THE PUBLIC SECTOR
Long-Range Decision Rule
Measurement of Social Costs
Measurement of Social Benefits
Present Value
SUMMARY

In Chapter 1 management decisions were divided into long-range capacity decisions and short-range operating decisions. Long-range decisions have two unique characteristics. First, they involve *change* in the productive or service potential of the firm. A change in the firm's capacity requires investments of resources, usually large in amount, where each decision is unique and affects the firm's operations over long periods of time. Once a change is initiated it may be difficult and costly to reverse.

Second, there is typically a long span of time before benefits from a long-range investment are wholly realized. The use of any resource, including capital or money, has a cost. The cost of obtaining and maintaining this capital must be considered in long-range investment analysis. The purchase of a machine, for example, will usually require several years of operations to recover the investment. During this period of time the company has incurred a cost to its creditors and owners for the use of capital. This cost must be included in the decision to acquire the machine.

LONG-RANGE DECISION RULE

The critical factor in a long-range decision is time. The time factor is recognized formally through present-value calculations.[1] In long-range decisions an investment is favorable if the incremental benefits, measured by cash inflows directly attributable to the investment and adjusted for the time value of money, are at least equal to the incremental costs, measured by cash outflows directly attributable to the investment and adjusted for the time value of money. Any investment that provides discounted benefits equal to discounted costs will earn exactly the desired rate of return and will contribute to maintaining the wealth of the enterprise. Any investment that provides greater discounted benefits than discounted costs will contribute to an increase in the wealth of the firm. The basic assumption of any long-range decision is that the firm is trying to maximize its wealth.

MEASUREMENT OF BENEFITS AND COSTS

The conventional accounting measurement of income for a particular period of time involves the matching of revenues, as realized through sale transactions, with the expired costs incurred to produce the revenues. A proper measure of income necessitates the assignment of costs to the period during

[1]An explanation of present value will be made later in this chapter. The terms *discounting* or *discounted* will be used several times prior to that explanation. *Discounting* is the process of adjusting cash flows by an interest rate for the time the money is in use. The interest rate used should relate to the cost the company incurs to obtain capital (cost of capital).

which revenues are earned. In this way, effort is matched with accomplishment; the resulting income is a measure of the past earning power. The cost of a long-lived asset, such as a building or piece of equipment, enters the matching process by a systematic but arbitrary method of allocating cost over the economic useful life of the asset. For example, consider a firm that purchases a single asset for $12,000. This asset will produce revenues (cash inflows) of $5,000 per year for three years, at which time it will be worn out and have no further value. During the lifetime of the asset, revenues will be $15,000, costs will be $12,000, and income will be $3,000. It is necessary, however, to provide a periodic measurement of income. Assuming that the $12,000 cost will be spread evenly over the economic useful life of the asset, annual cost will be $4,000 and annual income will be $1,000. Income for the three years is presented in Exhibit 8-1. If any other method of depreciation is used the pattern of income will differ. For example, accelerated depreciation, such as sum-of-the-years' digits, will provide an increasing trend of income. *Regardless of the method of depreciation chosen,* the total revenue is $15,000, the total cost is $12,000, and total income is $3,000 over the three-year span.

For investment analysis the recognition of income, as measured by accounting, is not important. Rather, it is necessary to know *when capital is invested,* and therefore not available for other investments, and *when capital is recovered,* and therefore available for reinvestment elsewhere. Invested and recovered capital is determined by *cash flows* directly traceable to the investment. Both the amounts of cash flows and the timing of the cash flows must be estimated accurately if a proper investment decision is to be made. Allocations of cost are necessary for annual accounting measurements of income but are not relevant in investment decisions.

Year	Revenue	Expired* Cost	Income
1	$5,000	$4,000	$1,000
2	5,000	4,000	1,000
3	5,000	4,000	1,000

*Investment of $12,000 amortized on straight-line basis over three years with no salvage value.

EXHIBIT 8-1
Accounting income for selected investment

The informational needs for long-range decisions are:

1. The amount and timing of cash outflows
2. The amount and timing of cash inflows
3. A measure of the time value of money

We will examine these data needs in detail.

Measurement of Cash Outflows

In any investment decision the relevant cash outflows are the incremental cash outflows that are directly traceable to the investment. In most decisions there will be substantial initial cash outflows. An investment in a new building would involve an initial outlay for its purchase or construction. In the case of construction, the initial outlay may be spread over several years. In addition, all cash outflows must be identified subsequent to acquisition. For a building this would include maintenance, repairs, property taxes, and similar cash outflows directly related to the building over its useful life.

All additional resources required for the higher level of activity must be considered in the decision. In most cases, additional productive facilities also require additional working capital to support the increased level of activity. **Working capital** is the excess of current assets over current liabilities. It will be necessary for the firm to have larger amounts of raw materials, work in process, and finished goods; increased sales will necessitate additional accounts receivable; and additional funds will be needed to pay the additional wages and other production costs. The amount of working capital needed to support a plant can often be greater than the cost of the plant facilities. While the entire amount of working capital should be recovered by the end of the venture, there is a cost associated with the resources invested in the working capital. When the plant is discontinued and the working capital may be used for other purposes, the reduction of working capital should be considered as a recovery of cash.

When an investment decision involves any nonmonetary resource presently owned by the firm, such as a building or equipment, the relevant "cost" is the cash value of the asset, not the book value in the accounting records. For example, assume that a division manager is deciding whether to sell an idle plant or use it to produce a new product. If the plant is retained, the investment amount relevant to the decision is the sale price foregone, not the undepreciated cost shown in the accounting records.

Measurement of Cash Inflows

Like cash outflows, the relevant cash inflows are the *incremental cash inflows* to be received in the future and directly related to the decision. In most long-range decisions the cash inflows are spread over the life of the investment.

A new plant generates cash inflows in the form of increased contribution margin (increased sales less increased variable costs).

The distinction between revenue and expense transactions is *not* carried over into cash flows. A cash inflow directly attributable to the investment, *regardless of the reason,* should be considered. Therefore, a dollar of cost saved is equivalent to a dollar of revenue received from the sale of a product and should be considered cash inflow. For example, if a new labor-saving machine is installed, the cash inflow could include the savings in expenses, such as labor and fringe benefits, that required cash. There is also no distinction between cash inflow from revenue during the life of an investment and cash inflow from sale or salvage of the productive asset at the end of the project.

Effect of Income Taxes on Cash Flows

We have stressed that the relevant cash flows in long-range decisions are the incremental cash flows, to be received or paid in the future, that are directly attributable to that decision. The income taxes paid by the company must be considered as a cash outflow. In general, income taxes are assessed as a percentage of the income determined by the conventional accounting system. The amount of taxes to be paid in a particular year is determined by the deduction of depreciation as well as operating cash inflows and outflows. The tax code is complex; there are many provisions enacted by Congress to encourage or discourage investment in productive assets. Among these provisions are accelerated depreciation (for example, sum-of-the-years' digits method), capital gains taxes on gains from the sale of long-lived assets, and the investment credit. Corporate tax rates[2] and other provisions of the code relating to investments in long-lived productive assets are changed by Congress as governmental fiscal policy changes. We may well see extra deductions and subsidies granted through the tax system to provide solutions to environmental and energy problems.

In this chapter we are dealing with investment in productive assets with long lives. Income taxes have a significant impact on the timing and amount of cash flows from long-lived assets. From the many provisions of the tax code we will examine topics that have the greatest impact on investment decisions. These are:

1. Depreciation for purposes of computing taxable income
2. Carryback and carryforward of operating losses
3. Capital gains tax arising from the sale of long-lived assets
4. The investment credit

[2]Corporate tax rates in 1975 were 20% on the first $25,000 of taxable income, 22% on the next $25,000, and 48% on taxable income over $50,000. The maximum rate on capital gains is 30%. For simplicity we will use a rate of 40%.

DEPRECIATION

When a long-lived asset is acquired, the accounting concept of income, as well as the Internal Revenue Code, requires that the cost of the asset be amortized over its useful life in a systematic and rational manner. The cash outflow from purchase takes place in the year the asset is acquired, but the cost is matched with revenue over the life of the asset to determine income. Therefore, depreciation expense will reduce the taxable income during the lifetime of the asset, not just in the year of acquisition. The cost of an asset to be depreciated is often called a **tax shield** because it shields income of future years against tax, to the extent that depreciation may be taken. The federal tax code allows lives for tax purposes that, in general, are shorter than the economic useful lives of long-lived assets. For example, a building with an economic useful life of 40 to 50 years may be depreciated over 25 to 30 years. Three methods of computing depreciation are commonly used for tax purposes: *straight-line,* which spreads the cost equally over the life, and *sum-of-the-years' digits* and *double-declining balance,* which provide for a large amount of depreciation in the first year and declining amounts in each succeeding year.[3] A firm will often use straight-line depreciation in the external financial statements and sum-of-the-years' digits or double-declining balance depreciation in the tax return. For purposes of investment analysis, we are interested in determining the impact of taxes on cash flows. Therefore, we are concerned with the life and method of depreciation used to determine tax payments, not necessarily net income.

The cash outflow due to taxes can be illustrated by referring to our previous example involving the purchase of an asset for $12,000 with a three-year life and annual cash operating income of $5,000. If we use straight-line depreciation and a three-year life with no salvage value, taxable income for each year would be:

Cash operating income	$5,000
Less: Depreciation ($12,000 ÷ 3)	4,000
Taxable income	$1,000

Assuming a corporate income tax rate for this firm of 40%, the tax payment each year will be $400 ($1,000 × 40%). The same result could be obtained by applying the tax rate to each item separately.

Tax on annual operating income of $5,000 at 40%	$2,000
Less: Tax *savings* from deduction of annual depreciation expense ($4,000 × 40%)	1,600
Net tax payment per year	$ 400

[3]The sum-of-the-years' digits method will be used in this text to illustrate accelerated depreciation. The declining balance method is more complex and will not be used. It applies a constant percentage to the declining asset balance.

We want to know the cash outflow due to taxes. Both procedures provide identical results. However, the second method has an advantage because it allows us to consider the tax impact on each cash flow item separately. Thus, one tax rate may be used for some cash flows, such as proceeds from the sale of a long-lived asset, while a different rate is used for cash flows from other sources, such as operating income.

The method of depreciation chosen will have an impact on cash flows. For example, we may postpone part of the tax payments by adopting the sum-of-the-years' digits method for tax purposes. To illustrate the impact of sum-of-the-years' digits depreciation on tax payments, let's assume the facts presented in our previous illustration, but depreciation will be computed by the sum-of-the-years' digits method rather than by straight-line depreciation. Taxable income and tax payments (or refund) are shown in Exhibit 8-2. Note that the *total* taxable income and taxes paid are the same, regardless of the

	Year 1	Year 2	Year 3
Cash operating income	$ 5,000	$ 5,000	$ 5,000
Depreciation deduction:			
Year 1 3/6 x $12,000*	6,000		
Year 2 2/6 x $12,000		4,000	
Year 3 1/6 x $12,000			2,000
Taxable income (loss)	$(1,000)	$ 1,000	$ 3,000
Tax payment (refund) assuming 40% rate	$ (400)	$ 400	$ 1,200

Cost of asset	$12,000
Cash operating income	$ 5,000 per year
Life of investment	3 years
Salvage value	$ 0
Depreciation method	Sum-of-the-years' digits
Tax rate	40%

*Sum-of-the-years' digits is 6 (1+2+3); first-year depreciation is 3/6 of cost to be depreciated. Sum-of-the-years' digits for long periods may be computed by the following formula: $S = n\left(\frac{n+1}{2}\right)$ where n is number of years.

EXHIBIT 8-2
Tax payments using sum-of-the-years' digits depreciation

method of depreciation. Total taxable income for the three years is $3,000 and the taxes paid are $1,200. The timing, however, is different and thus affects the cash flows in the investment decision. The differences in cash flows may be illustrated by using a schedule of inflows and outflows for each year, or *cash flow time line,* as presented in Exhibit 8-3. In the first year, assuming the loss produced a tax refund, the cash flow using sum-of-the-years' digits is $800 higher than with the use of straight-line. Again, it is not depreciation that causes the change in cash flows, it is the *difference in taxes paid* by deducting different amounts of depreciation in particular years.

CARRYBACK AND CARRYFORWARD OF OPERATING LOSSES

The tax code allows a corporation with an operating loss to receive a refund for taxes paid in past years or to reduce tax payments in the future. An operating loss may be carried back to each of the previous three years and forward to each of the succeeding five years as an offset to operating income in those years. This provision affects cash flows for a particular investment decision because an operating loss may result in a cash inflow from a tax refund. For example, in our illustration involving sum-of-the-years' digits depreciation, an operating loss of $1,000 was sustained in the first year. If the firm had had taxable operating income of at least $1,000 in the preceeding three years and had paid taxes of at least $400, a tax refund of $400 would be available in year 1 of the investment project. If this were a new company in its first year of operation, the loss of $1,000 would be carried forward to offset operating income of $1,000 in year 2. In either case, the net tax payment for the three-year period of the investment would be $1,200. However, the cash flows in individual years would be different. Differences in timing of cash flows may make a significant difference in the attractiveness of the investment.

For a more complete example, assume the following income (loss) and tax payments (refund) for Mad Henry's Pub.

Year	Income (Loss)	Tax Payment (Refund) (40% Rate)
19X1	$ 30,000	$ 12,000
19X2	20,000	8,000
19X3	10,000	4,000
19X4	(100,000)	(24,000)
19X5	10,000	0
19X6	20,000	0
19X7	20,000	4,000
19X8	30,000	12,000
19X9	30,000	12,000
Total	$ 70,000	$ 28,000

	Cash Flow Time Line — Years			
	0 (Now)	1	2	3
STRAIGHT-LINE DEPRECIATION				
Cash outflow:				
Initial investment	$(12,000)			
Cash inflow:				
Cash operating income net of tax ($5,000 x 60%)*		$3,000	$3,000	$3,000
Tax savings from depreciation deduction ($4,000 x 40%)		1,600	1,600	1,600
Net annual cash flows	$(12,000)	$4,600	$4,600	$4,600
SUM-OF-THE-YEARS' DIGITS DEPRECIATION				
Cash outflow:				
Initial investment	$(12,000)			
Cash inflow:				
Cash operating income net of tax ($5,000 x 60%)		$3,000	$3,000	$3,000
Tax savings from depreciation deduction:				
Year 1 ($6,000 x 40%)		2,400		
Year 2 ($4,000 x 40%)			1,600	
Year 3 ($2,000 x 40%)				800
Net annual cash flows	$(12,000)	$5,400	$4,600	$3,800

Cost of asset	$12,000
Cash operating income	$ 5,000 per year
Life of investment	3 years
Salvage value	$ 0
Tax rate	40%

*After tax income may be computed by multiplying the before-tax income by (1 − tax rate). In this case it is 1 − .40, or .60.

EXHIBIT 8-3
Comparison of after-tax cash flows between straight-line depreciation and sum-of-the-years' digits depreciation

Income taxes of $24,000 were paid during 19X1 through 19X3. The loss in 19X4 was first carried back to 19X3, then to 19X2, and finally to 19X1, with $60,000 of the 19X4 loss offset by income in those three past years. A tax refund of $24,000 (the taxes paid during 19X1 through 19X3) was collected in 19X4. The remaining loss ($40,000) was carried forward: $10,000 to 19X5, $20,000 to 19X6, and $10,000 to 19X7. No tax was paid in 19X5 and 19X6, and only $4,000 [($20,000 − $10,000) × 40%] in 19X7. Note that a total of $28,000 tax was paid on a total income of $70,000 during the nine-year period.

CAPITAL GAINS

The capital gains provisions of the tax code, concerning gains and losses from the sale of long-lived assets, are very complex. In general, gains on the sale of long-lived assets not held for resale as inventory may be taxed at approximately half the tax rate on ordinary income if the assets were held at least six months. The tax code requires different treatment for gains and losses from the sale of (1) land and other nondepreciable assets, (2) depreciable equipment, and (3) buildings.

The entire gain on the sale of land and other nondepreciable assets not held for resale as inventory is taxed at the capital gains rate.

Any gain on the sale of depreciable equipment is taxed at ordinary income tax rates, to the extent that depreciation was taken in the past. For example, assume that a firm sold a piece of equipment that cost $10,000 and on which $7,000 of depreciation had been taken. Any selling price over the remaining cost of $3,000 ($10,000 − $7,000) results in a gain. The gain up to $7,000 is treated as ordinary income. Any gain over $7,000 is treated as a capital gain. Therefore, a piece of depreciable equipment must be sold for more than its original cost before any of the gain is treated as a capital gain.

In the case of a depreciable building, the entire gain is treated as a capital gain unless an accelerated depreciation method (such as sum-of-the-years' digits) were used. If the taxpayer used an accelerated depreciation method, the gain equal to the *excess* of accelerated depreciation over straight-line depreciation is taxed as ordinary income. The balance of the gain is taxed as a capital gain.

A corporation cannot offset a capital loss against ordinary income, only against capital gains. The tax effect of a capital loss is lost to the corporation unless there are capital gains at least equal to the capital losses during the carryback-carryforward period.

There are many exceptions to these provisions. This discussion is a brief introduction to capital gains. For our purposes, it is sufficient to know that capital gains exist and that they may have a significant impact upon cash flows.

INVESTMENT CREDIT

Congress devised the **investment credit** as a stimulus for investment in productive assets. The taxpayer is entitled to a credit against his income tax of 7% of the investment in certain productive assets, excluding land and buildings. If the assets have a life of less than seven years, or the assets are held less than seven years, only a portion of the investment credit may be taken. To the extent that taxes are reduced, the investment credit represents a subsidy to encourage investment in productive assets.

The combination of the investment credit and accelerated depreciation can have a significant impact on timing of cash flows. Projects that are otherwise unfavorable can become attractive when tax incentives are considered. As we shall see later, any act that speeds up cash inflows or slows down cash outflows of a particular investment will enhance the investment's attractiveness.

Rate of Return

The minimum rate of return on a particular investment should not be less than the cost of acquiring and maintaining the corporation's capital resources. The cost of capital (from the standpoint of the user of the funds) or return on investment (from the standpoint of the provider of the funds) is determined by the general formula:

$$\text{Cost of capital} = \frac{\text{Annual payment to investor}}{\text{Market value of securities}}$$

The cost is different for different sources of capital (bonds versus common stock, for example) because each capital source involves a different set of rights and privileges. The bondholder accepts a lower rate of return in exchange for lower risk; he will receive a fixed return over the life of the bond and the face amount of his bond at maturity. The common stockholder has the greatest risk if the enterprise fails and the greatest opportunity for gain if it succeeds. He will receive dividends only if earned and declared, and he is last in line to receive assets when the company is liquidated.

The financing decision (how the capital is raised) should not be confused with the investment decision (how the capital is used). If the cost of a particular source of capital, the **specific cost of capital,** is used to justify a particular investment, the firm would be encouraged to issue excessive amounts of long-term debt because the cost is usually lower than for other sources. A more correct approach would be to use an overall cost of capital, the **weighted average cost of capital,** as the minimum acceptable return for all projects. A weighted average cost of capital is computed, first, by determining the specific cost of capital for each source of long-term capital (long-term debt, preferred stock, and common stock equity) and, then, by computing an average rate—weighting the cost for each source of capital by its market value.

To illustrate the computation of the weighted average cost of capital, let's start with a simple setting of a company with only common stock and then expand the analysis to include long-term debt. The method we propose is not the only method available; agreement among authorities is far from unanimous on how the cost of capital should be computed. However, the method advanced here is sound and has support among accountants.

COST OF COMMON STOCK

If all earnings are paid out in dividends to common stockholders, the previously shown formula, where annual payments are divided by the market value of the common stock, can be used to compute the specific cost of capital for common stock. However, very few companies pay out all their earnings in dividends. Some pay none, and the majority pay less than half their earnings in dividends. When earnings are retained, the corporation should grow and be able to pay larger dividends in the future.

We can compute a specific cost of capital for common stock equity by adding a growth factor representing management's objectives for growth in dividends. Thus, $k = d/M + g$, where: k is the specific cost of capital for common stock; d is the current annual dividend; M is the current market value of the common stock; and g is the expected rate of growth in dividends. Assume that the Karl Company has the following capital structure.

Common stock, 10,000 shares, \$10 par value, current annual dividend \$1 per share, current market price \$18 per share	\$100,000
Retained earnings	50,000
Total owners' equity	\$150,000

If we assume that a corporate objective is an 8% growth rate in dividends, the specific cost of capital is:

$$\begin{aligned} k &= \frac{d}{M} + g \\ &= \frac{\$1}{\$18} + 8\% \\ &= 5.6\% + 8\% \\ &= 13.6\% \end{aligned}$$

If this 13.6% cost of capital is accepted as the minimum desired rate of return, we are saying that any new investment must have a minimum rate of return of 13.6% after taxes, to provide for the cost of capital and maintain the value of the company.

COST OF LONG-TERM DEBT

Let's assume that the Karl Company has issued long-term debt and now has the following capital structure.

6% long-term debt, 8-year life, market quotation 90, yield to maturity 8%[4]	$100,000
Common stock	100,000
Retained earnings	50,000
Total long-term debt and owners' equity	$250,000

Interest on long-term debt is fixed in amount and is deductible for tax purposes. The specific cost of capital for long-term debt is computed as $k = (1 - t)r$, where: k is the specific cost of capital for long-term debt; t is the tax rate; and r is the yield to maturity. In our illustration:

$$
\begin{aligned}
k &= (1 - t)r \\
&= (1 - .40)8\% \\
&= 4.8\%
\end{aligned}
$$

WEIGHTED AVERAGE COST OF CAPITAL

We may now compute the weighted average using market values of each element in the capital structure.[5] As shown in the following calculations, long-term debt comprises one-third of the total market value and common stock comprises two-thirds. These proportions are multiplied times the specific cost of capital for each element; the products are summed to arrive at the weighted average cost of capital.

	Market Value	*Proportion*		*Specific Cost of Capital*		*Weighted Average Cost of Capital*
Long-term debt ($100,000 × 90%)	$ 90,000	1/3	×	4.8%	=	1.6%
Common stock (10,000 shares × $18)	180,000	2/3	×	13.6%	=	9.1%
Total	$270,000	3/3				10.7%

The weighted average cost of capital dropped from 13.6% with only common stock to 10.7% with stock and long-term debt. The use of debt with a lower cost of capital is called **leverage,** or **trading on the equity.** The return to

[4]The price of bonds is always quoted as a percentage of the face value of a bond. In this case a $1,000 bond would sell for $900 ($1,000 × 90%). Yield to maturity is the rate the investor will earn on the money he actually invests ($900 for the $1,000 bond) to the maturity of the bond.

[5]To simplify the illustration we have omitted preferred stock from the example. The preferred stockholders have given up their right to vote for a preference as to dividends and assets in the act of liquidation over common. Usually their dividends are limited, and the general formula applies in measuring their specific cost of capital.

the common stockholder is potentially greater because of the low specific cost of debt capital. To illustrate this point further, let's assume that the amount of long-term debt is doubled. If the interest rate and other terms are not changed, the 4.8% specific cost of capital for long-term debt will continue but will occupy a larger share of the weighted average cost of capital.

Long-term debt	$180,000	1/2	× 4.8%	=	2.4%
Common stock	180,000	1/2	× 13.6%	=	6.8%
	$360,000	2/2			9.2%

The weighted average cost of capital will continue to fall as more debt is added until the investment market recognizes the higher risk due to excess debt and raises the interest rates to the company.[6] Ideally, a firm would continue to increase the use of debt in the capital structure until the cost of capital begins to increase. When the cost of capital is at its lowest point, the firm will have achieved the optimum balance between the use of debt and equity securities.

A TARGET RATE OF RETURN

The weighted average cost of capital should be the *minimum* rate of return used by the firm in long-range decisions. However, the use of a single rate of return in investment analysis is appropriate only if the same degree of risk exists in all projects considered. One way to deal with risk is to rank the projects by risk classes, such as high-risk projects, moderate-risk projects, and low-risk projects. Low-risk projects would be expected to earn at least the weighted average cost of capital. Moderate-risk projects would be expected to earn a higher return (in the Karl Company example, somewhere between 12% and 15%). High-risk projects would be expected to earn an even higher rate, between 18% and 20%. To illustrate techniques of investment analysis in this chapter, we will use only one rate of return, the weighted average cost of capital. Risk and uncertainty will be discussed later.

THE CONCEPT OF PRESENT VALUE

The time factor of long-range decisions is formally recognized by consideration of the **time value of money.** The timing of cash flows as well as the amount of cash flows affects value. Because a dollar in hand today can be invested to earn a return, it has a greater value than a dollar to be received one year from today. For example, $100 invested in a savings account at 6%

[6]Financial investment services place a risk grading on long-term debt. One service uses the ratings *Aaa, Aa, . . . C; Aaa* is the rating for the highest quality of long-term debt. A typical difference in interest rates between *Aaa* bonds and *Aa* bonds is about .4%. A change in debt ratings to a higher risk class for a large city may cost the taxpayers millions of dollars in additional interest on future borrowings.

compounded quarterly will grow to $106.13 at the end of one year and will double in slightly under twelve years. The difference between a dollar invested now and the dollar received at some future time is the time value of money. This difference is the rate of return you must receive to be indifferent about receiving a dollar today or waiting for a year to receive a dollar. For a business, the weighted average cost of capital is usually the minimum measure of the time value of money.

To make the time value of money concept useful, we must have a way of applying it to a cash flow at any point in time and of comparing it with a cash flow at any other point in time. This is done through the use of present-value calculations.

Assume that a firm invests a lump sum of $1,000 for a period of three years and that the investment pays a 10% return compounded at the end of each year. The growth of the investment is presented in Exhibit 8-4. The value to which the $1,000 will grow at the end of the three years, at 10% compounded annually, is $1,331. The amount to which a given investment will grow at the end of a given period of time, compounded at a given annual rate of interest, is its **future value.** If you are satisfied with a 10% rate of return on your money, you should be indifferent toward receiving $1,000 now, $1,100 one year from now, $1,210 two years from now, or $1,331 three years from now.

In a long-range decision we want to compare a series of cash inflows and a series of cash outflows at different times over the life of the investment to determine if a satisfactory rate of return is achieved. To do this, the cash flows must be converted to their discounted values at the *same* point of time. Any point in time could be used. We could state all cash flows in future values at the end of the life of the investment. However, since the decision is being made now (in the present time period), it is more logical to state the cash

Year	Investment at Beginning of Period	Interest at 10% for Period	Investment at End of Period	Formula $I(1+r)^n$
0 (Now)			$1,000	I
1	$1,000	$100	1,100	$I(1+r)$
2	1,100	110	1,210	$I(1+r)(1+r)$
3	1,210	121	1,331	$I(1+r)(1+r)(1+r)$

EXHIBIT 8-4
Future value—$1,000 compounded at 10% annually

flows in the **present value** of the investment. The present value is the amount that must be invested now to reach a given amount at a given point of time in the future, assuming it is compounded periodically at a specified rate of interest.

In our illustration, $1,000 invested now will accumulate to $1,331 three years from now, when compounded annually at 10%. The present value of $1,331 to be received three years from now is $1,000. It would be useful to develop a set of present-value factors that show the time value of money between given points of time and at given rates of interest. Such a set of values would allow us to determine the present value of any amount at any future date for any rate of interest. Continuing the illustration begun in Exhibit 8-4, we have prepared a portion of a present-value table in Exhibit 8-5 by dividing $1,000 (the present value) by each future value. The present-value factor for $1 to be received one year from now, assuming a 10% rate, is .909; two years from now it is .826; and three years from now it is .751. To illustrate the use of present-value factors, assume an investment is to be made now in the amount of $2,500 and that it will result in a single cash inflow of $3,000 two years from now. Is it a wise investment if the cost of capital is 10%? The present value of the initial investment is $2,500 ($2,500 × 1.000). A dollar today is worth one dollar. The present value of the cash inflow is

Period	Investment* at End of Period (Future Value) at 10%	Present Value / Future Value	General Formula
0 (Now)	$1,000	$\frac{\$1,000}{\$1,000} = 1.000$	$\frac{I}{I}$
1	1,100	$\frac{\$1,000}{\$1,100} = .909$	$\frac{I}{I(1+r)}$
2	1,210	$\frac{\$1,000}{\$1,210} = .826$	$\frac{I}{I(1+r)^2}$
3	1,331	$\frac{\$1,000}{\$1,331} = .751$	$\frac{I}{I(1+r)^3}$

**Developed in Exhibit 8-4.*

EXHIBIT 8-5
Development of present-value factors

	Cash Flow Time Line				PRESENT-VALUE COMPUTATIONS
Time	0	1	2	3	Amount × P.V.F.* = Present value $S_{\overline{n}\rceil r}$
Cash outflow:					
Initial investment	$(12,000)				$(12,000) × 1.000 ($S_{\overline{0}\rceil 10\%}$) = $(12,000)
Cash inflows:					
Cash operating income:					
Year 1		$ 5,000			$ 5,000 × .909 ($S_{\overline{1}\rceil 10\%}$) = $ 4,545
Year 2			$ 5,000		$ 5,000 × .826 ($S_{\overline{2}\rceil 10\%}$) = $ 4,130
Year 3				$ 5,000	$ 5,000 × .751 ($S_{\overline{3}\rceil 10\%}$) = $ 3,755
Total cash inflows					$12,430
Net present value					$ 430

Amount of investment	$12,000
Cash operating income	$ 5,000 per year
Life of investment	3 years
Salvage value	$ 0
Desired rate of return	10%

*P.V.F. – The exhibits in Chapters 8 and 9 identify the present-value factor utilized in computation of present value with the following notations: $S_{\overline{n}\rceil r}$ and $A_{\overline{n}\rceil r}$ where: S is a single sum; A is an annuity; n is the number of periods; and r is the rate of return.

EXHIBIT 8-6
Present-value computations for a selected investment

$2,478 ($3,000 × .826). The cash inflow, adjusted for the time value of money, is not equal to or greater than the cost, adjusted for the time value of money; the project should be rejected.

Let's return to the first example in this chapter. A firm had an opportunity to invest $12,000 now in an asset, with the expectation of a $5,000 cash inflow at the end of each of the next three years. Assume the cost of capital is 10%. Computation of the present value of cash flows for this investment opportunity is presented in Exhibit 8-6. The present value of the cash outflow (the initial investment) is $12,000. It is not necessary to use a present-value factor of 1.00 for initial payments or receipts ($12,000 × 1.000

	Cash Flow Time Line				Present-Value Computations		
Time	0	1	2	3	Amount	× P.V.F. $S_{\overline{n}\rvert r}$	= Present value
Cash outflow:							
Initial investment	$(12,000)				$(12,000)	× 1.000 $S_{\overline{0}\rvert 10\%}$	= $(12,000)
Cash inflows:							
Cash operating income:							
Year 1		$ 4,600			$ 4,600	× .909 $S_{\overline{1}\rvert 10\%}$	= $ 4,181
Year 2			$ 4,600		$ 4,600	× .826 $S_{\overline{2}\rvert 10\%}$	= $ 3,800
Year 3				$ 4,600	$ 4,600	× .751 $S_{\overline{3}\rvert 10\%}$	= $ 3,455
Total cash inflows							$11,436
Net present value							$ (564)

Amount of investment	$12,000
Cash operating income	$ 5,000 per year
Life of investment	3 years
Salvage value	$ 0
Depreciation method	Straight-line
Tax rate	40%
Desired rate of return	10%

EXHIBIT 8-7
Present-value computations for a selected investment using after-tax cash flows

= $12,000). We do it in this text only for emphasis. The present value of the $5,000 to be received at the end of year 1 is $4,545 (5,000 × .909); the next $5,000 is $4,130 (5,000 × .826); and the last is $3,755 (5,000 × .751). If we sum the present values of the cash inflows ($4,545 + $4,130 + $3,755) and compare the total ($12,430) with the present value of the cash outflow ($12,000), we find the investment should be made if income taxes are ignored. However, if we consider income taxes at a 40% rate and use straight-line depreciation, the cash inflows are reduced by $400 each year. Refer to Exhibit 8-7 for a complete explanation. The sum of the present value of the cash inflows is reduced to $11,436 ($4,181 + $3,800 + $3,455) and the firm should reject the project. In this illustration, as in many long-range decisions, exclusion of income taxes leads to an incorrect decision.

Note that in our illustration the stream of cash inflows is equal and the time intervals are equal. We could sum the present-value factors (.909 + .826 + .751), apply the sum (2.486) to the amount of a receipt ($5,000 before tax or $4,600 after tax), and determine the present value of the entire stream.

2.486 × $5,000 = $12,430
2.486 × $4,600 = $11,436

An equal stream of payments made at equal intervals of time is called an **annuity.** The present value of an annuity is equal to the sum of the present values of each of the individual payments in the stream. A table showing the present value of an annuity of $1 may be constructed by adding the present-value factors from the table of present value of $1, as illustrated in Exhibit 8-8. More extensive tables and the general formula for the present value of an annuity of $1 per period are presented in the appendix at the end of the text.

Availability of present-value tables greatly simplifies the calculation of present values. For most uses the tables in Appendix A, Present value of $1, and Appendix B, Present value of an annuity of $1, provide sufficient accuracy. If a given interest rate is not presented in the table, interpolation between two present-value factors can be made. Interpolation involves the estimation of a present-value factor for a rate or time period between two factors in the table. For example, what is the present-value factor applicable to a sum to be received three years from now with interest computed at 9%? The table in Appendix A shows present-value factors for 8% in three years (.794) and 10% in three years (.751) but does not include the factor for 9%. You want a factor that is approximately halfway between .751 and .794. The

Period	Present Value of $1 (10% Rate)	Cumulative Present Value (Present Value of an Annuity of $1)
1	.909	.909
2	.826	1.735 (.909 + .826)
3	.751	2.486 (1.735 + .751)
4	.683	3.169 (2.486 + .683)
5	.621	3.790 (3.169 + .621)
6	.564	4.354 (3.790 + .564)

EXHIBIT 8-8
Development of table for present value of an annuity of $1 at 10% received annually

amount may be computed as [.751 + $\frac{1}{2}$ × (.794 − .751)], or .7725. This amount differs slightly from the amount calculated by the formula, .7722, because the present-value formula is not linear. However, for most purposes interpolation is sufficiently accurate.

LONG-RANGE DECISIONS IN THE PUBLIC SECTOR

Many enterprises in the public sector face the same decisions as private enterprise. For example, government-owned utilities and transportation systems face the same long-range decisions as investor-owned utilities and transportation companies. The tremendous growth in economic activity by government and other not-for-profit organizations has led to a search for systematic methods of analyzing public expenditures. Decision making in the public sector has been highly qualitative. Often it has been influenced more by funds available than by economic efficiency. Measures of economic efficiency must be used to ensure that decisions are economically sound, as well as politically expedient.

Every decision should have at its core the relationship between benefits and costs of the particular project. In the private sector the primary goal of long-range decisions is the maximization of the wealth of the enterprise. In the public sector the concept is much broader; the goal of **benefit-cost analysis** is to maximize the welfare of society. We are asking, "Will society be better off by engaging in a particular act?" In place of cash inflows to the organization, the public sector is concerned with social benefits. In place of cost, the public sector is concerned with social cost or social value foregone.

Long-range Decision Rule

In the public sector an investment decision is favorable if the discounted social benefits attributable to the decision exceed the discounted social costs attributable to the decision. The welfare of society is increased when the ratio of discounted social benefits to discounted social costs is greater than one.

Measurement of Social Costs

The cost side of benefit-cost analysis should include all unfavorable effects of a decision on society for the entire life of the project. This concept of social costs is a much broader view than the concept of discounted cash flow analysis for the private sector, which we examined earlier in this chapter. In addition to the incremental cash outflows for a project, consideration must also be given to any indirect side effects (**externalities**) of a decision that inflict harm on others without compensation.

For example, the construction of a dam for hydroelectric power will flood the river valley above the dam, destroying natural landscape and wildlife refuges and preventing fish from returning to their spawning grounds. A value should be attributed to these externalities to arrive at a comprehensive cost.

The requirement for environmental impact studies, whether for a public or private project, now brings long-range project planning by private enterprise closer to benefit-cost analysis used in the public sector, at least on the cost side of the calculation. Impact on the environment does not enter investment analysis directly in the private sector unless a cash flow is involved. However, the social cost to the environment (much broader than just cash flow) will be a qualitative factor that *must* be satisfied. Unless environmental quality is maintained, the project cannot be undertaken. In the public sector these social costs are included whether or not cash flow is involved.

Measurement of Social Benefits

The selection and measurement of social benefits constitute an identification of those services we want from government action. Ideally, we want to maximize welfare in the public sector. However, welfare in the broad sense eludes measurement; we usually settle for some measure of per capita income as a surrogate for welfare. If a chronically unemployed person or a disabled person is trained and later employed, one measure of the benefits is the added income to society over the lifetime of the individual.

Social benefits are the favorable impacts of any decision, regardless of their recipient. Once the favorable impacts of a project are determined, they should be valued at the prices that a competitive market system would assign to them. This valuation is difficult because in many cases a project is undertaken by the public sector due to market failures in the private sector.

All favorable side effects of a decision should be considered in the calculations. To continue with our earlier example of a dam, the benefits from its construction should include the value of averting potential flood damage and providing recreation possibilities, as well as the power that will be produced and sold.

In many cases measurement of benefits is very difficult. When a single objective criterion dominates, such as deaths averted, it may be satisfactory to use a nonfinancial measure of benefits. This type of analysis, labeled **cost effectiveness,** relates costs to some nonfinancial measure such as cost per death averted or cost per pupil educated. The analysis may seek to maximize benefits for a given level of costs or to minimize the cost per increment of benefits. In cost effectiveness analysis it is important to identify the correct measure of benefits. Maximizing the teacher/pupil ratio does not necessarily maximize education.

Present Value

With the exception of projects involving water resources, it is only recently that present-value considerations have been utilized in the public sector. Most capital expenditure decisions, to the extent that economic efficiency was even considered, were made on the basis of costs in the first year of the project.

In the private sector we have suggested that the desired rate of return should be based upon the weighted average cost of capital. In the few cases where present-value analysis has been used in the public sector, the desired rate of return was based upon the average rate of interest paid on long-term government bonds, usually 3% to 5%. To illustrate the effect of a very low rate, assume that a flood-control project is proposed. The project will cost $50 million at the outset and will provide benefits averaging $4 million per year for 40 years. The present value of benefits and costs at different rates follow.

Benefits			*Costs*
4% rate ($4,000,000 × 19.793) $A_{\overline{40}\rceil 4\%}$	=	$79,172,000	$50,000,000
6% rate ($4,000,000 × 15.046) $A_{\overline{40}\rceil 6\%}$	=	$60,184,000	$50,000,000
8% rate ($4,000,000 × 11.925) $A_{\overline{40}\rceil 8\%}$	=	$47,700,000	$50,000,000
10% rate ($4,000,000 × 9.779) $A_{\overline{40}\rceil 10\%}$	=	$39,116,000	$50,000,000
15% rate ($4,000,000 × 6.642) $A_{\overline{40}\rceil 15\%}$	×	$26,568,000	$50,000,000

By using a rate below 8% (7.57% to be precise), the project will be favorable; by using a higher rate, the costs exceed the benefits. You can justify a very large dam at a 4% rate, in this case about $79,000,000 worth of dam.

Most economists now agree that the appropriate rate of return for the public sector is the opportunity cost rate in the private sector from which those funds were removed. The removal of funds from the private sector prevents their investment in the private sector. Unless these funds are better used by the public sector, economists argue that the funds should remain in the private sector and the project should not be undertaken.

An appropriate rate of return in the private sector appears to be somewhere between 10% and 15%. This return, however, has not been achieved in the public sector in many cases. One researcher found that a majority of the 53 Bureau of Reclamation and Corps of Engineers projects that he examined would have been rejected at a 10% rate.[7] The position that funds used in the public sector should carry the same cost as funds in the private sector may seem cold and antisocial unless it is remembered that public sector analysis should include *all* social benefits.

SUMMARY

The critical factor in any long-range decision is time. The time factor raises two problems in long-range decisions. First, because all resources have a cost, the time value of money must be reflected when there is a long period of time between investment and a full realization of the benefits. The practice of discounting all benefits and costs to their present value is an adjustment for the time value of money. The weighted average cost of capital is an appropriate discount rate.

Second, accounting's measurement of net income includes allocations of cost in order to match costs with revenue. For long-range decisions it is important to know when resources are committed and therefore not available for investment elsewhere, and when they are recovered and therefore available for reinvestment. Cash flows provide the relevant measures of costs and benefits for long-range decisions. Allocations of cost, such as those involved in income measurement, should not be allowed to distort the decision information. Income taxes affect the cash flow of the company and, therefore, must be considered in investment decisions.

The most significant practical problem in long-range decision making is the development of estimates of future cash flows relevant to each alternative. Even the most sophisticated model will not yield reliable results if the cash flow estimates are unreliable. The uniqueness of long-range decisions and the fact that these decisions require predictions of future cash flows place most long-range decision data beyond the capacity of the accounting data base.

In the public sector investment decisions are often based upon availability of funds rather than economic efficiency. The goal of investments in the public sector should be welfare maximization. This goal requires a broadened definition of costs and benefits to include all social costs and social benefits. The decision approach should reflect all favorable and unfavorable impacts of the action to society, adjusted for the time value of money.

SUPPLEMENTARY READING

Berezi, Andrew, and Jose Ventura. "A Proposal of Risk Analysis." *The Canadian Chartered Accountant,* August, 1969.

Edwards, James W. *Effects of Federal Income Taxes on Capital Budgeting.* New York: National Association of Accountants, 1969.

Estes, Ralph W. *Accounting and Society.* Los Angeles: Melville Publishing Company, 1973.

[7]Arnold C. Horberger, "The Interest Rate in Cost-Benefit Analysis," *Federal Expenditure Policy for Economic Growth and Stability* (U.S. Government Printing Office, 1957), p. 241.

Hertz, David B. "Risk Analysis in Capital Investment." *Harvard Business Review,* January–February, 1964.

King, Barry G. "Cost-Effectiveness Analysis: Implications for Accountants." *The Journal of Accountancy,* March, 1970.

Livingstone, John Leslie, and Sanford C. Gunn. *Accounting for Social Goals.* New York: Harper & Row Pubs., Inc., 1974.

National Association of Accountants. *Return on Capital as a Guide to Managerial Decisions.* New York: National Association of Accountants, 1965.

National Association of Accountants. *Long Range Profit Planning.* New York: National Association of Accountants, 1964.

National Association of Accountants. *Financial Analysis to Guide Capital Expenditure Decisions.* New York: National Association of Accountants, 1967.

QUESTIONS

8-1 List the informational needs of long-range decisions. How do they compare with the informational needs of short-range decisions?

8-2 "It is most important, when analyzing an investment opportunity, that the accounting measurement of income be considered." Do you agree? Discuss.

8-3 Why are cash flows, rather than income flows, used in long-range decisions?

8-4 An increase in working capital may be considered to be an investment in long-range decisions. Explain why this is so.

8-5 Explain the difference in benefit and cost measurements between private and public sector long-range decisions.

8-6 Define the following terms: *discounting, contribution margin, cash flow, future value of money, present value of money,* and *annuity.*

8-7 Explain: *tax shield, capital gains, investment credit, carryback* and *carryforward,* and *ordinary income.*

8-8 Explain the role of depreciation in long-range decisions.

8-9 Explain two of the most commonly used methods of depreciation. What is the impact of each on income and cash flow?

8-10 Projects that are otherwise marginal or unfavorable may become attractive when tax incentives are considered. Discuss.

8-11 What is the main problem with using specific cost of capital to justify a particular investment?

8-12 Show how to determine the following, either by formula or example.

a. Specific cost of capital for long-term debt
b. Specific cost of capital for common stock

8-13 "The weighted average cost of capital may be the most useful measure for the analysis of all long-range investment decisions." Do you agree? Discuss.

8-14 A single rate of return should not be utilized for *all* long-range investment decisions. Explain.

8-15 How do the theoretically appropriate rates differ between public and private sector long-range decisions?

PROBLEMS

8-16 The Julie Company is considering an investment proposal that has a three-year life. The owner has asked you to organize the data so that she may make the decision. The company is profitable and pays taxes at a 30% rate.

REQUIRED:
For each of the following transactions determine the before-tax and after-tax cash flows for each of the years. Consider each transaction independently.

A. The investment project will increase revenues by $10,000 per year.
B. Equipment will be leased for three years at an annual rental of $6,000.
C. Repairs of $1,000 must be made to the equipment in year 2.
D. The investment project will decrease the contribution margin from other products of the company by $3,000 per year.
E. Production for the new project will be carried on in an unused part of the plant that the company has been trying, unsuccessfully to rent for $2,000 per year.
F. The company paid $9,000 at the beginning of year 1 for a patent. The cost is expensed immediately for tax purposes but amortized on a straight-line basis over three years for financial accounting purposes.

8-17 The Harold Company has asked you to develop the data for an investment proposal. The project has a five-year life. The Harold Company is very profitable and is subject to a 60% tax rate on additional income.

REQUIRED:
For each of the following transactions determine the before-tax and after-tax cash flows for each of the five years. Consider each transaction independently.

A. A change in the production process resulting in a savings of $20,000 per year for materials.
B. Purchase of a new machine for $60,000 cash. The machine will have a five-year life and no salvage value. Depreciation is computed on a straight-line basis.
C. Use the same facts in part B, except that depreciation is computed on the sum-of-the-years' digits basis.
D. Investment of $60,000 in working capital in year 1.
E. Reduction of working capital by $30,000 in year 3.
F. Issuance of a $10,000 note payable for cash. Interest at 9% is paid at the end of each year. The note is repaid at the end of the third year.

8-18 Compute the present value of each of the following cash inflows. Use a 6% rate for discounting.

A. $50,000 received in a single sum five years from now.
B. $10,000 received at the end of each of the next five years.
C. $5,000 received at the end of each of the next ten years.
D. $10,000 received at the end of each of the next three years and $20,000 four years from now.
E. $10,000 now and $40,000 four years from now.
F. $10,000 now and $10,000 at the end of each of the next four years.

8-19 Compute the present value of the following cash outflows. Use an 8% rate of interest for discounting.

A. $5,000 paid now.
B. $5,000 paid at the end of five years.
C. $1,000 paid now and $1,000 at the end of each of the next five years.
D. $1,000 paid now, $2,000 paid at the end of year 2, and $2,000 paid at the end of year 3.
E. $500 paid at the end of each year for ten years, beginning five years from now.

8-20 Five different cash inflows are listed below.

a. $10,000 now
b. $20,000 in five years
c. $30,000 in ten years
d. $1,000 annually for twenty years
e. $1,000,000 in forty years

REQUIRED:

A. Without reference to the other requirements of this problem, rank the cash inflows listed above as to *your* personal preferences.

B. Rank the proposals in order of desirability, using a zero discount rate.

C. Rank the proposals in order of desirability, using a 10% discount rate.

D. Rank the proposals in order of desirability, using a 20% discount rate.

E. How does your ranking in part A compare with the subsequent three rankings in parts B, C, and D?

8-21 The Brunswick Company must acquire a new delivery truck. After careful investigation it has narrowed the alternatives to three.

1. A light import truck has low operating costs but a short life. The truck costs $4,000 but must be replaced every two years. Annual operating costs will be $2,000 and the trade-in allowance will be $1,000.

2. A heavier truck costs $6,000 but must be replaced after three years. Annual operating costs will be $3,000. The trade-in allowance will be $2,000.

3. A heavy-duty truck has a six-year life. The truck costs $10,000 and will have a salvage value of $2,000. Annual operating costs will be $3,000 with a special overhaul at the end of the fourth year costing $3,000.

To make the alternatives comparable, the company has selected a six-year life for the investment.

REQUIRED:

A. Prepare a cash flow time line for each alternative, identifying the before-tax cash flows over the six-year period.

B. Prepare a cash flow time line for each alternative, showing after-tax cash flows for the six-year period. Use straight-line depreciation but do not consider the investment credit. Assume a 40% tax rate.

C. What additional difficulties are involved if a life span of less than six years is used?

8-22 On your return to your alma mater for the 20-year reunion of your graduation class, you and several members of your class who have been unusually successful look up the old accounting professor who had such an impact upon your careers. You are shocked to find that his salary is not significantly higher than it was 20 years earlier. With pledges from other members of your class, you go to the trust department of your bank to create a trust that will provide a "chair" for the professor. The trust fund will add $10,000 per year to his income until he retires at the end of 10 years. The bank's trust officer will guarantee a 6% return on the trust. Payments will be made at the end of each year. You may assume that there will be no taxes on the trust or the donors.

REQUIRED:

A. What are the cash outflows during the life of the trust?

B. How much must you deposit with your banker to provide for the "chair."

8-23 Recently one type of used jet airliner has been in demand by small airfreight companies. The jet plane cost $6 million new, slightly over eight years ago. A major airline that owns several of the planes is offering one for sale. The plane was purchased over eight years ago and has been depreciated over an eight-year life with no salvage value. An airfreight company has offered to pay $6,500,000 for the plane.

REQUIRED:
Assuming a 50% tax rate on ordinary income, a 30% capital gains rate, and no unusual tax provisions related to airlines or jet aircraft, what is the after-tax cash flow to the major airline from the sale of this plane?

8-24 The Smith Publishing Company has a warehouse that is currently being used at 25% of capacity for storage of its inventory. The company has adequate space at other storage sites for the inventory currently stored in the warehouse. It has decided to move the inventory and seek alternative uses for the warehouse. The following possibilities are available.

a. Selling the warehouse now for $55,000.
b. Leasing the warehouse on a 10-year lease for the annual sum of $5,500. At the end of the lease the estimated selling price of the warehouse is $35,000.
c. Leasing the warehouse to an equipment contractor for $15,000 per year for the next two years. After two years it can be sold for only $30,000 because the equipment would heavily damage the floor.

The Smith Publishing Company is a young firm with good growth potential; a 10% return on their investment is one of the major goals of management and the stockholders.

REQUIRED:
A. What are your recommendations to management? Explain fully.
B. What are the opportunity costs of each alternative?
C. What are some of the nonquantifiable costs relevant to the decision?

8-25 You are preparing an analysis for a group of investors who wish to purchase a professional football team. Two franchises are available: (1) a franchise in the United States Football League, a strong and profitable league, for $15 million and (2) a franchise in the new International Football League for $250,000. The investors have raised the entire $15 million. If the franchise in the IFL is purchased, the money saved can be utilized to pay bonuses over the next five years to attract stars from the USFL. If this course of action is followed it is believed that the two leagues would be equal in quality and value by the end of the fifth year. Assume that the funds may be invested at 10% until needed for the bonus.

REQUIRED:
If the bonuses are paid in equal amounts at the end of each of the next five years, what is the maximum annual bonus that may be paid to recruit USFL players? Ignore taxes.

8-26 J. C. Peoples, Inc. is considering the purchase of a new machine. The machine will cost $48,000 and produce a contribution margin of $9,000 annually for six years. Assume no salvage value and a 40% tax rate.

REQUIRED:
A. Compute the accounting income for each year using:
   1. Straight-line depreciation
   2. Sum-of-the-years' digits depreciation
B. Compute the cash flow for each year for each method under part A above.

8-27 Continue with the illustration for J. C. Peoples, Inc. in problem 8-26 and assume that the desired rate of return is 10%.

REQUIRED:
A. Compute the present value of the cash flows from problem 8-26, part B.
B. Does the proposal satisfy the long-range decision rule advanced in Chapter 8? Explain.
C. If the required rate of return is decreased to 8%, would this change the attractiveness of this proposal? If so, how much?

8-28 The Graingerville Town Council has decided to acquire snow-removal equipment and is trying to decide whether to buy or lease. In either case, the equipment will be used for five years. If the town buys, the cost will be $20,000 payable at delivery, with an estimated salvage value of $2,000. If it leases, the rental payments will be made on the first day of each year in the following amounts:

Year 1	$6,000
2	$5,000
3	$4,000
4	$3,000
5	$2,000

Operating and maintenance costs will be the same in either case. The town is currently paying 8% on its long-term debt.

REQUIRED:
A. Prepare a recommendation to the town council. Your recommendation should be well written and supported by a proper analysis of the data.
B. What are some of the nonquantitative factors that may affect the decision?

8-29 Madisons, Inc. has decided to acquire a new piece of equipment. It may do so by an outright cash purchase at $25,000 or by a leasing alternative of $6,000 per year for the life of the machine. Other relevant information follows.

Purchase price due at time of purchase	$25,000
Estimated useful life	5 years
Estimated salvage value if purchased	$ 3,000
Annual cost of maintenance contract to be acquired with either lease or purchase	$ 500

The full purchase price of $25,000 could be borrowed from the bank at 10% annual interest and could be repaid in one payment at the end of the fifth year. Additional information:

- Assume a 40% income tax rate and use of the straight-line method of depreciation.
- The yearly lease rental and maintenance contract fees would be paid at the beginning of each year.
- The minimum desired rate of return on investment is 10%.
- All cash flows, unless otherwise stated, are assumed to occur at the end of the year.

1. The present value of the purchase price of the machine is
a. $25,000
b. $22,725
c. $22,500
d. $2,500
e. None of the above

2. Under the purchase alternative the present value of the estimated salvage value is
a. $3,000
b. $2,049
c. $1,863
d. $0
e. None of the above

3. Under the purchase alternative the annual cash inflow (tax reduction) related to depreciation is
a. $5,000
b. $4,400
c. $2,640
d. $1,760
e. None of the above

4. Under the purchase alternative the annual after-tax cash outflow for interest and maintenance would be
   a. $3,000
   b. $2,500
   c. $1,800
   d. $1,200
   e. None of the above

5. The after-tax present value of the leasing alternative is
   a. $14,785
   b. $16,263
   c. $24,652
   d. $27,105
   e. None of the above

6. The after-tax present value of the purchase alternative is
   a. $17,716
   b. $20,540
   c. $23,137
   d. $25,000
   e. None of the above

7. The after-tax present value of the purchase and borrow alternative is
   a. $13,927
   b. $15,525
   c. $22,040
   d. $25,000
   e. None of the above

8. Which alternative should the company select if the choice is based upon the *lowest* present value?
   a. Lease
   b. Purchase
   c. Purchase and borrow
   d. All should be rejected

(CPA adapted)

8-30 The top two business graduates of Red Rock University met two years after graduation and compared positions. John went to work with National Consolidated Foods immediately after graduation. Marcia received an MBA from Stamvard University before taking a job with National Consolidated Foods. Both were impressed with the future NCF offered them. Marcia's starting salary was equal to John's salary, even though he had been with the company for two years.

In comparing financial positions, John had saved $4,000, including the increased equity in the home he purchased upon starting to work for NCF. Marcia, on the other hand, was $8,000 in debt. John indicated that although they were in approximately equal positions in the company (in terms of income), he had avoided the $12,000 investment. Marcia countered with the point that her MBA should provide her with an annuity in the form of added income that should be worth more than a $12,000 investment. She estimated the annuity to average about $3,000 per year and expected to work for the company at least 30 years. In addition, with her MBA she should be in a better position for advancement in the company.

REQUIRED:

A. Assuming Marcia has a desired rate of return of 12% (before taxes), what is the minimum additional income she would have to earn to be financially equal to John?

B. What actual rate of return will make her estimate of $3,000 financially equal to an investment of $12,000?

C. Suppose, instead of an average $3,000 per year of additional income, Marcia had additional income, above John, of $1,000 for her first 10 years with NCF, $3,000 for the next 10 years, and $5,000 for her last 10 years. How would the comparison change?

8-31 The Mount Pleasant Ramblers, a professional football team that has been in last place for several years, plans to build a team that will be in the playoffs in three years. The team has drafted a Heisman Trophy winner, Y. A. Knute Simpson, and is about to begin contract negotiations. The team will play 16 games during the season.

Attendance has been very poor for the past several years. If Simpson joins the team, ticket sales will increase by at least 10,000 tickets per game. The manager believes that Simpson will have an impact upon ticket sales for 10 years or less. A study of cost-volume-revenue relationships shows that the contribution margin of each additional ticket sold is $5.

REQUIRED:

A. Prepare a projection of cash flows that should result if Simpson signs with the Ramblers.

B. How would you describe the risk of this "investment"? What rate would you use to discount the cash flows if the team had the following desired rates of return?

Low risk	10%
Medium risk	15%
High risk	20%

C. What would you recommend as a maximum bonus for the team to offer Simpson?

8-32 The most recent balance sheet for the K. Walsch Company contained the following information.

Current liabilities	$ 375,000
8% long-term notes payable	100,000
Common stock, $100 par, 5,000 shares authorized, issued and outstanding	500,000
Retained earnings	25,000
Total	$1,000,000

Other information:

Common stock:	
Current market price of common stock	$125 per share
Current annual dividend	$ 5 per share
Growth rate of dividends	5%
Long-term notes payable:	
Current market price	100% of face value
Yield to maturity	8%
Current tax rate	40%

REQUIRED:

A. Calculate the weighted average cost of capital for the K. Walsch Company.

B. Indicate how this rate should be used in long-range decisions.

8-33 Shortly after Chris Anson was appointed president of the Cheyenne Machine Company he reviewed the long-range decision policy of the company. He was surprised to find proposals rejected that would have been accepted in his previous company, a very successful machine tool company. Anson found that the company had been using a 20% required rate of return. The rate was adopted by the board of directors several years ago, after a president of the company purchased a company airplane. The plane was subsequently sold at a large loss. In spite of limiting investments to those producing the required rate of return, recent earnings and the price of common stock have declined. The company has large amounts of marketable securities earning an average of 6%. The securities will be sold and the funds invested in any project that will earn 20% or better.

The capital structure of the Cheyenne Machine Company follows.

6% long-term debt (current market price $90, yield to maturity 8.5%)	$100,000
7% preferred stock, par $100, 1,000 shares outstanding (current market price per share $95)	100,000
Common stock, par $10, 20,000 shares outstanding, (current market price $12 per share)	200,000
Retained earnings	100,000
Total	$500,000

The company has paid $1 per share dividends on common stock for the past few years in addition to the required dividends on preferred stock. The common stockholders of the company expect a long-term growth rate in dividends of 8%. Assume a 40% tax rate.

REQUIRED:

A. Based upon the limited information available, evaluate the use of the 20% required rate of return by Cheyenne Machine Company.

B. Prepare a recommendation to the new president of the company for a revision of the company's long-range decision policy. Your recommendation should include a suggested rate of return with adequate justification.

8-34 The price an investor pays for a bond is determined by computing the present value of the cash flows the investor will receive during the lifetime of the bond. Assume the following facts about a bond the James Company wants to purchase with some of the company's pension funds. The pension fund requires purchase of bonds with a rating of *Aa* or better. (One financial service rates bonds from *Aaa* to *C,* with *Aaa* the highest quality and therefore the lowest risk.)

The bond selected will mature in three years on January 1, 19X4. Interest is paid on January 1 and July 1 of each year. Additional data follow.

Face value of bond (This amount will be paid to the bondholder on January 1, 19X4.)	$10,000
Coupon rate (Attached to the bond is a page of six coupons. Each coupon is for $300, the amount of cash the investor will receive every six months when he clips a coupon and sends it to the company.)	6%
Market rate or yield to maturity (On January 1, 19X1, the investment market is insisting that investors earn 8% per year on their investment in bonds of *Aa* quality. Bonds of lower quality will earn higher rates.)	8%

REQUIRED:

A. Prepare a schedule showing the cash flows the pension fund will receive from the bond.

B. Compute the price the James Company should pay for the bond on January 1, 19X1.
(Note that the bond pays interest for periods of one-half year. This is the appropriate period for discounting and the rate should be adjusted by using one-half of the annual rate.)

8-35 The City of Pleasant Hill must install a new sewer system to meet federal pollution-control requirements. The city covers a large area including several hills. Consultants have proposed two alternatives that will meet all requirements:

a. Build two small treatment plants. *Each* plant would cost $5 million and have current operating costs of $175,000 per year.
b. Build one large treatment plant. The system would cost $12 million but would have annual operating costs of $200,000.

Either system will have a useful life of 25 years. Assume that construction costs must be paid as the plants are completed and that operating costs are paid at the end of each year.

REQUIRED:
A. Prepare a schedule of cash flows for each alternative.
B. Determine the present value of each alternative under each of the following assumptions:
  1. A discount rate of 4%, based upon long-term cost of capital, is used.
  2. A discount rate of 10%, based upon opportunity cost in the private sector, is used.
C. Are there any other costs or benefits you think should be considered?
D. Which alternative would you recommend if the decision must be placed before the voters?

8-36 Thorne Transit, Inc. has decided to inaugurate express bus service between its headquarters city and a nearby suburb (one-way fare $.50) and is considering the purchase of either 32- or 52-passenger buses, on which pertinent estimates are as follows:

	32-Passenger Bus	*52-Passenger Bus*
Number of each to purchased	6	4
Useful life	8 years	8 years
Purchase price of each (paid on delivery)	$80,000	$110,000
Mileage per gallon	10	7.5
Salvage value per bus	$ 6,000	$ 7,000
Drivers' hourly wage	$ 3.50	$ 4.20
Price per gallon of gasoline	$ .30	$ .30
Other annual cash expenses	$ 4,000	$ 3,000

During the four daily rush hours all buses would be in service and are expected to operate at full capacity (state law prohibits standees) in both directions of the route, each bus covering the route 12 times (six round trips) during that period. During the remainder of the 16-hour day, 500 passengers would be carried and Thorne would operate only four buses on the route. Part-time drivers would be employed to drive the extra hours during the rush hours. A bus traveling the route all day would go 480 miles and one traveling only during rush hours would go 120 miles a day during the 260-day year.

REQUIRED:

A. Prepare a schedule showing the computation of estimated annual revenue of the new route for both alternatives.

B. Prepare a schedule showing the computation of estimated annual drivers' wages for both alternatives.

C. Prepare a schedule showing the computation of estimated annual cost of gasoline for both alternatives.

D. Assume that your computations in parts A, B, and C are as follows:

	32-Passenger Bus	*52-Passenger Bus*
Estimated revenues	$365,000	$390,000
Estimated drivers' wages	$ 67,000	$ 68,000
Estimated cost of gasoline	$ 16,000	$ 18,000

Assuming that a minimum rate of return of 12% before income taxes is desired and that all annual cash flows occur at the end of the year, prepare a schedule showing the computation of the present values of net cash flows for the eight-year period. Include the cost of buses and the proceeds from their disposition under both alternatives, but disregard the effect of income taxes. *(CPA adapted)*

8-37 The Conner Company has the following capital structure.

Mortgage bonds 6%	$ 20,000,000
Common stock (one million shares)	25,000,000
Retained earnings	55,000,000
	$100,000,000

a. Mortgage bonds of similar quality are selling at 95 (95% of face amount) to yield $6\frac{1}{2}$%.

b. The common stock has been selling for $100 per share. The company has paid 50% of earnings in dividends for several years and intends to continue the policy. The current dividend is $4 per share. Earnings are growing at 5% per year.

c. If the company sold a new equity issue, it would expect to net $94 per share after all costs.

d. The tax rate is 50%.

Conner wants to determine a cost of capital to use in capital budgeting. Additional projects would be financed to maintain the same relationship between debt and equity. Additional debt would consist of mortgage bonds and additional equity would consist of retained earnings.

REQUIRED:

A. Calculate the firm's weighted average cost of capital.

B. Explain why you used the weighting system you used.

C. How should the Connor Company use the cost of capital computed in part A? *(CMA adapted)*

8-38 In 1969 the Archibald Freight Company negotiated and closed a long-term lease contract for newly constructed truck terminals and freight storage facilities. The buildings were erected to the company's specifications on land owned by the company. On January 1, 1970, Archibald Freight Company took possession of the leased properties. On January 1, 1970 and 1971, the company made cash payments of $1,200,000, which were recorded as rental expenses.

Although the terminals have a useful life of 40 years, the noncancelable lease runs for 20 years from January 1, 1970, with a favorable purchase option available upon expiration of the lease. The company should have recorded the transaction as the purchase of terminal facilities and a related issue of long-term debt.

The 20-year lease is effective for the period January 1, 1970, through December 31, 1989. Advance rental payments of $1,000,000 are payable to the lessor on January 1 of each of the first 10 years of the lease term. Advance rental payments of $300,000 are due on January 1 for each of the last 10 years of the lease. The company has an option to purchase all of these leased facilities for $1 on December 31, 1989. It also must make annual payments to the lessor of $75,000 for property taxes and $125,000 for insurance. The lease was negotiated to assure the lessor a 6% rate of return.

REQUIRED: (Round all computations to the nearest dollar.)

A. Compute the cost of the terminal facilities on January 1, 1970. Cost should be measured as the present value of cash payments to acquire the terminal facilities. Do not include insurance or property taxes as part of the cost of acquiring the terminal facilities.

B. Compute the amount of long-term debt the company issued to purchase the building. The long-term debt should be the present value of the cash payments *remaining* on the lease. Do not include insurance or property taxes as part of the liability.

C. Compute the depreciation expense for 1970 using the straight-line method and assuming zero salvage value.

D. How much of the lease payment on January 1, 1971, should have been accounted for as interest expense? *(CPA adapted)*

8-39 The Baxter Company manufactures toys and other short-lived fad type items.

The research and development department came up with an item that would make a good promotional gift for office equipment dealers. Aggressive and effective effort by Baxter's sales personnel has resulted in almost firm commitments for this product for the next three years. It is expected that the product's value will be exhausted by that time.

In order to produce the quantity demanded, Baxter will need to buy additional machinery and rent some additional space. It appears that about 25,000 square feet will be needed. 12,500 square feet of presently unused but leased space is available now. (Baxter's present lease with 10 years to run costs $3 a foot.) There are another 12,500 square feet adjoining the Baxter facility, which Baxter will rent for three years at $4 per square foot per year if it decides to make this product.

The equipment will be purchased for about $900,000. It will require $30,000 in modifications, $60,000 for installation, and $90,000 for testing; all of these activities will be done by a firm of engineers hired by Baxter. All of the expenditures will be paid for on January 1, 1973.

The equipment should have a salvage value of about $180,000 at the end of the third year. No additional general overhead costs are expected to be incurred.

The following estimates of revenues and expenses for this product for the three years have been developed.

	1973	*1974*	*1975*
Sales	$1,000,000	$1,600,000	$800,000
Material, labor, and factory overhead	$ 400,000	$ 750,000	$350,000
Allocated general expenses	40,000	75,000	35,000
Rent	87,500	87,500	87,500
Depreciation	450,000	300,000	150,000
Total costs	977,500	1,212,500	622,500
Income before tax	$ 22,500	$ 387,500	$177,500
Income tax (40%)	9,000	155,000	71,000
Income after tax	$ 13,500	$ 232,500	$106,500

REQUIRED:

A. Prepare a schedule that shows the incremental, after-tax, cash flows for this project.

B. Prepare a schedule showing the present value of the cash flows in part A.

(CMA adapted)

8-40 The Beta Corporation manufactures office equipment and distributes its products through wholesale distributors.

Beta Corporation recently learned of a patent on the production of a semiautomatic paper collator that can be obtained at a cost of $60,000 cash. The semiautomatic model is vastly superior to the manual model that the corporation now produces. At a cost of $40,000, present equipment could be modified to accommodate the production of the new semiautomatic model. Such modifications would not affect the remaining useful life of four years nor the salvage value of $10,000 that the equipment now has. Variable costs, however, would increase by one dollar per unit. Fixed costs, other than relevant amortization charges, would not be affected. If the equipment is modified, the manual model cannot be produced.

The current income statement relative to the manual collator appears as follows:

Sales (100,000 units @ $4)		$400,000
Variable costs	$180,000	
Fixed costs*	120,000	
Total costs		300,000
Net income before income taxes		$100,000
Income taxes (40%)		40,000
Net income after income taxes		$ 60,000

*All fixed costs are directly allocable to the production of the manual collator and include depreciation on equipment of $20,000, calculated on the straight-line basis with a useful life of 10 years.

Market research has disclosed three important findings relative to the new semiautomatic model. First, a particular competitor will certainly purchase the patent if Beta Corporation does not. If this were to happen, Beta Corporation's sales of the manual collator would fall to 70,000 units per year. Second, if no increase in the selling price is made, Beta Corporation could sell approximately 190,000 units per year of the semiautomatic model. Third, because of the advances being made in this area, the patent will be completely worthless at the end of four years.

Because of the uncertainty of the current situation, the raw materials inventory has been almost completely exhausted. Regardless of the decision reached, substantial and immediate inventory replenishment will be required. The engineering department estimates that if the new model is to be produced, the average monthly raw materials inventory will be $20,000. If the old model is continued, the inventory balance will average $12,000 per month.

REQUIRED:

A. Prepare a schedule that shows the incremental after-tax cash flows for the comparison of the two alternatives. Assume that the corporation will use the sum-of-the-years' digits method for depreciating the costs of modifying the equipment.

B. Assuming that the incremental after-tax cash flows calculated in part A and the annual incomes for the two alternatives are as given below, should Beta Corporation, if it has a cost of capital of 18%, decide to manufacture the semiautomatic collator? Assume all operating revenues and expenses occur at the end of the year.

Year	*Incremental Cash Flow (000 Omitted)*	**Annual Income (000 Omitted)**	
		Manual	*Semiautomatic*
1 Beginning	− $110		
1 End	+ $ 40	$24	$39
2 End	+ $ 40	$24	$39
3 End	+ $ 40	$24	$39
4 End	+ $ 50	$24	$39

(CMA adapted)

9 Techniques of Investment Analysis

TECHNIQUES THAT SATISFY THE LONG-RANGE DECISION RULE
- *Net Present Value*
- *Discounted Benefit/Cost Ratio*
- *Adjusted Rate of Return*
- *Problems of Comparison*

TECHNIQUES THAT DO NOT CONSIDER THE TIME VALUE OF MONEY
- *Payback Period*
- *Unadjusted Rate of Return*

RISK AND UNCERTAINTY

DECISION MAKING IN THE PUBLIC SECTOR: BENEFIT-COST ANALYSIS
- *Illustration of Benefit-Cost Analysis*
- *Political and Other Non-efficiency Considerations*

INVESTMENT TECHNIQUES IN PRACTICE

SUMMARY

A long-range investment opportunity is favorable if its discounted benefits are at least equal to its discounted costs. This approach to long-range decisions measures benefits and costs as the cash inflow and outflow directly attributable to the investment opportunity. These cash flows are discounted by some acceptable rate of return to reflect the time value of money. The minimum acceptable rate of return should be based upon the weighted average cost of capital to the firm.

The information needed for long-range decisions was discussed in Chapter 8. Techniques for using this data in investment analyses are examined in this chapter. We have separated the techniques into two types: those which satisfy the long-range decision rule and those which do not. Investment techniques that do not satisfy the long-range decision rule are deficient in theory, although they are often used with some success.

Each of the techniques examined in this chapter provides a criterion for ranking investment proposals. However, a ranking is necessary only if the firm has a shortage of capital; it then acts as a **capital rationing** device. If sufficient capital is available to finance all proposed long-term projects that are consistent with company goals, *all* projects that meet the criteria of the long-range decision rule should be selected.

TECHNIQUES THAT SATISFY THE LONG-RANGE DECISION RULE

Three techniques satisfy the long-range decision rule, varying only in the way the decision criteria are stated. The first two, net present value and discounted benefit/cost ratio, apply a desired or predefined discount rate and permit a ranking of the alternatives by their net present value or their ratio of discounted benefits to discounted costs. The third method, adjusted rate of return, computes the rate actually earned from each investment opportunity and ranks the investments by their adjusted rate of return.

Net Present Value

The **net present value** of a particular investment is the difference between the present value of future cash inflows and the present value of future cash outflows. All future cash inflows and outflows are discounted to their present values by the use of a predetermined discount rate. We will use the weighted average cost of capital as our minimum predefined rate of return. When the net present value is zero (discounted cash inflows are equal to discounted cash outflows), the investment will earn a rate of return equal to the weighted average cost of capital. If the net present value is positive (discounted cash inflows exceed discounted cash outflows), the investment will earn a rate of return greater than that needed to maintain the capital investment. If the net present value is negative (discounted cash inflows are less than discounted

	Cash Flow Time Line				Present-Value Computations
Time	0	1	2	3	Amount × P.V.F. $S_{\overline{n}\rvert r}$ = Present value
Cash outflow:					
Initial investment	$(12,000)				$(12,000) × 1.000 $S_{\overline{0}\rvert 10\%}$ = $(12,000)
Cash inflows:					
Cash operating income:					
Year 1		$ 5,000			$ 5,000 × .909 $S_{\overline{1}\rvert 10\%}$ = $ 4,545
Year 2			$ 5,000		$ 5,000 × .826 $S_{\overline{2}\rvert 10\%}$ = $ 4,130
Year 3				$ 5,000	$ 5,000 × .751 $S_{\overline{3}\rvert 10\%}$ = $ 3,755
Total cash inflows					$12,430
Net present value					$ 430

Amount of investment	$12,000
Cash operating income	$ 5,000 per year
Life of investment	3 years
Salvage value	$ 0
Desired rate of return	10%

EXHIBIT 9-1
Present-value computations for a selected investment

cash outflows), the investment's return will be less than necessary to maintain the capital investment.

Let's return to the illustration used in Chapter 8. In this example a firm was considering purchasing an asset for $12,000. The asset is expected to produce cash inflows of $5,000 per year at the end of each of the next three years. In Exhibit 8-6 (repeated here in Exhibit 9-1) we found the present value of the before-tax cash outflows for this investment to be $12,000, and the present value of before-tax cash inflows to be $12,430. The positive net present value of $430 ($12,430 − $12,000) indicates the investment is favorable because the actual rate of return exceeds the desired rate of 10%. Taxes are a cash flow and must be considered in any investment analysis. In Exhibit

	Cash Flow Time Line				Present-Value Computations		
Time	0	1	2	3	Amount	× P.V.F. $S_{\overline{n}\rvert r}$	= Present value
Cash outflow:							
Initial investment	$(12,000)				$(12,000)	× 1.000 $S_{\overline{0}\rvert 10\%}$	= $(12,000)
Cash inflows:							
Cash operating income:							
Year 1		$ 4,600			$ 4,600	× .909 $S_{\overline{1}\rvert 10\%}$	= $ 4,181
Year 2			$ 4,600		$ 4,600	× .826 $S_{\overline{2}\rvert 10\%}$	= $ 3,800
Year 3				$ 4,600	$ 4,600	× .751 $S_{\overline{3}\rvert 10\%}$	= $ 3,455
Total cash inflows							$11,436
Net present value							$ (564)

Amount of investment	$12,000
Cash operating income	$ 5,000 per year
Life of investment	3 years
Salvage value	$ 0
Depreciation method	Straight-line
Tax rate	40%
Desired rate of return	10%

EXHIBIT 9-2
Present-value computations for a selected investment using after-tax cash flows

8-7 (repeated here in Exhibit 9-2) the present value of after-tax cash outflows for this investment was $12,000, and the present value of after-tax cash inflows was $11,436. The negative net present value of $564 ($11,436 − $12,000) shows the investment to be unfavorable because the actual rate of return after taxes is less than the desired rate of 10%.

Suppose the firm elects to use the sum-of-the-years'-digits method of depreciation. Will the delay in tax payments increase the present value? In Exhibit 9-3 depreciation is computed by the sum-of-the-years'-digits method for tax purposes. The present value of after-tax cash outflows continues to be $12,000. However, the present value of after-tax cash inflows

	Cash Flow Time Line				Present-Value Computations		
Time	0	1	2	3	Amount	× P.V.F. $S_{\overline{n}\rceil\, r}$	= Present value
Cash outflow:							
Initial investment	$(12,000)				$(12,000)	× 1.000 $S_{\overline{0}\rceil\, 10\%}$	= $(12,000)
Cash inflows:							
Before-tax cash operating income:		$ 5,000	$ 5,000	$ 5,000			
Income tax*		400	$ (400)	(1,200)			
After-tax cash operating income:							
Year 1		$ 5,400			$ 5,400	× .909 $S_{\overline{1}\rceil\, 10\%}$	= $ 4,909
Year 2			$ 4,600		$ 4,600	× .826 $S_{\overline{2}\rceil\, 10\%}$	= $ 3,800
Year 3				$ 3,800	$ 3,800	× .751 $S_{\overline{3}\rceil\, 10\%}$	= $ 2,854
Total cash inflows							$11,563
Net present value							$ (437)

*Refer to Exhibit 8-2.

EXHIBIT 9-3
After-tax net present value of selected investment—Depreciation for tax purposes on sum-of-the-years' digits

increases to $11,563, leaving a negative net present value of $437. The investment is still unfavorable.

Suppose that, instead of having no salvage value at the end of its useful life to this firm, the asset may be sold for $3,000. The net present value of the investment is computed in Exhibit 9-4, where a salvage value of $3,000 and straight-line depreciation are used. The annual tax payments are greater because the annual depreciation is lower ($12,000 cost − $3,000 salvage = $9,000 to be depreciated in three years). There is no gain on the sale of the asset and therefore no tax because the cash received is equal to the book value of the asset (cost less accumulated depreciation) at the date of the sale. The investment is now favorable, showing a net present value of $694.

In the remainder of this chapter all illustrations will involve *after-tax* cash flows. We will assume that the firm has had income during the previous

	Cash Flow Time Line				Present-Value Computations		
Time	0	1	2	3	Amount	× P.V.F. $S_{\overline{n}\rceil r}$	= Present value
Cash outflow:							
Initial investment	$(12,000)				$(12,000)	× 1.000 $S_{\overline{0}\rceil 10\%}$	= $(12,000)
Cash inflows:							
Cash operating income:		$ 5,000	$ 5,000	$ 5,000			
Tax payments*		(800)	(800)	(800)			
Net annual inflow		$ 4,200	$ 4,200	$ 4,200	$ 4,200	× 2.486 $A_{\overline{3}\rceil 10\%}$	= $10,441
Sale of asset at end of life (salvage value)				$ 3,000	$ 3,000	× .751 $S_{\overline{3}\rceil 10\%}$	= $ 2,253
Total cash inflows							$12,694
Net present value							$ 694

Amount of investment	$12,000
Cash operating income	$ 5,000 per year
Life of investment	3 years
Salvage value	$ 3,000
Depreciation method	Straight-line
Tax rate	40%
Desired rate of return	10%

*Cash operating income	$ 5,000
Annual depreciation [($12,000 − $3,000) ÷ 3]	3,000
Annual taxable income	$ 2,000
Annual tax (40%)	$ 800

EXHIBIT 9-4
Net present value of selected investment

three years. Therefore, any loss may be carried back against income of the past three years with the result of a tax refund in the year of the loss. Depreciation for tax purposes will be computed on a straight-line basis for simplicity. A tax rate of 40% will be assumed.

If, instead of one investment opportunity, we examine several and attempt to determine the best, we need a ranking criterion. Assuming the investment opportunities are independent (none is related to any other; we may invest in one, all, or any combination), the net present-value method ranks investment opportunities by the net present value of each alternative. The investment with the greatest positive net present value would be the most desirable. If the firm has capital to make more than one investment, they would be selected, in order, down to the cutoff of zero net present value. An investment with a negative net present value will not be a desirable investment and should be rejected.

A summary of the financial data applicable to three investment opportunities follows. Assume the applicable cost of capital is 10% and all cash flows occur at the end of the period.

			Cash Operating Income at End of Year		
Investment	*Initial Investment*	*Productive Lite*	*1*	*2*	*3*
A	$20,000	2	$13,000	$15,400	—
B	$ 9,000	3	$ 0	$ 8,000	$8,000
C	$12,000	3	$ 5,000	$ 5,000	$5,000

Investment A has a life of only two years, beginning in year 1. Investment B has no income in the first year of its three-year life. Investment C is the previous illustration.

The after-tax cash flows of the three investment opportunities are presented in Exhibit 9-5. This data will be used as the relevant cash flows for the remainder of the chapter. There is one unusual cash flow. In the first year, depreciation expense for Investment B produces a loss for tax purposes and generates a tax refund of $1,200.

Computation of net present value for each of the investment opportunities is presented in Exhibit 9-6. Investments A and B have positive net present values and are therefore acceptable at the desired rate of return of 10%. Investment C has a negative net present value and is unacceptable. The net present values and ranking of the three investments are:

Investment	*Net Present Value*	*Ranking*
A	$1,662	1
B	$1,553	2
C	$ (564)	Not ranked

By the criterion of net present value, Investment A has the highest ranking, followed by B; C is unfavorable and is rejected.

Discounted Benefit/Cost Ratio

The **discounted benefit/cost ratio** is a ratio of discounted benefits (in the form of cash inflows) to discounted costs (in the form of cash outflows). The technique is identical to the net present-value method through the discounting step. However, instead of netting the discounted inflows and discounted outflows and arriving at a net present value, the ratio of discounted benefits to discounted costs is computed.

COMPUTATION OF TAXES (40% RATE)	Year 1	Year 2	Year 3
INVESTMENT A			
Revenues	$ 13,000	$ 15,400	
Depreciation expense*	10,000	10,000	
Taxable income	$ 3,000	5,400	
Tax (payment) refund	$ (1,200)	$ (2,160)	
INVESTMENT B			
Revenues	$ 0	$ 8,000	$ 8,000
Depreciation expense†	3,000	3,000	3,000
Taxable income (loss)	$ (3,000)	$ 5,000	$ 5,000
Tax (payment) refund	$ 1,200	$ (2,000)	$(2,000)
INVESTMENT C			
Revenues	$ 5,000	$ 5,000	$ 5,000
Depreciation expense §	4,000	4,000	4,000
Taxable income	$ 1,000	$ 1,000	$ 1,000
Tax (payment) refund	$ (400)	(400)	(400)

AFTER-TAX CASH INFLOWS	Year 1	Year 2	Year 3
INVESTMENT A			
Revenues	$ 13,000	$ 15,400	
Tax	(1,200)	(2,160)	
Cash inflows net of tax	$ 11,800	$ 13,240	
INVESTMENT B			
Revenues	$ 0	$ 8,000	$ 8,000
Tax	1,200	(2,000)	(2,000)
Cash inflows net of tax	$ 1,200	$ 6,000	$ 6,000
INVESTMENT C			
Revenues	$ 5,000	$ 5,000	$ 5,000
Tax	(400)	(400)	(400)
Cash inflows net of tax	$ 4,600	$ 4,600	$ 4,600

*$20,000 cost ÷ 2-year life = $10,000 annual depreciation expense
†$ 9,000 cost ÷ 3-year life = $ 3,000 annual depreciation expense
§$12,000 cost ÷ 3-year life = $ 4,000 annual depreciation expense

EXHIBIT 9-5
After-tax cash inflows for selected investments

	Cash Flow Time Line				Present-Value Computations		
Time	0	1	2	3	Amount	x P.V.F. $S_{\overline{n}\rceil r}$	= Present value
INVESTMENT A							
Cash outflow:							
Initial investment	$(20,000)				$(20,000)	x 1.000 $S_{\overline{0}\rceil 10\%}$	= $(20,000)
Cash inflows:							
Year 1		$11,800			$11,800	x .909 $S_{\overline{1}\rceil 10\%}$	= $10,726
Year 2			$13,240		$13,240	x .826 $S_{\overline{2}\rceil 10\%}$	= $10,936
Total cash inflows							$21,662
Net present value							$ 1,662
INVESTMENT B							
Cash outflow:							
Initial investment	$ (9,000)				$ (9,000)	x 1.000 $S_{\overline{0}\rceil 10\%}$	= $ (9,000)
Cash inflows:							
Year 1		$ 1,200			$ 1,200	x .909 $S_{\overline{1}\rceil 10\%}$	= $ 1,091
Years 2 and 3			$ 6,000	$ 6,000	$ 6,000	x 1.577 $A_{\overline{3-1}\rceil 10\%}$	= $ 9,462
Total cash inflows							$ 10,553
Net present value							$ 1,553
INVESTMENT C							
Cash outflow:							
Initial investment	$(12,000)				$(12,000)	x 1.000 $S_{\overline{0}\rceil 10\%}$	= $(12,000)
Cash inflows:							
Years 1, 2, and 3		$ 4,600	$ 4,600	$ 4,600	$ 4,600	x 2.486 $A_{\overline{3}\rceil 10\%}$	= $ 11,436
Net present value							$ (564)

EXHIBIT 9-6
Net present value of selected investments

A ratio of 1.00 indicates that discounted benefits and discounted costs are exactly equal and that the actual return on the investment is equal to the desired rate of return. If the ratio is greater than 1.00, the benefits exceed the costs and the investment should be accepted. If the ratio is less than 1.00, the investment provides less than the desired rate of return and should not be accepted. Exhibit 9-7 shows the calculations of the discounted benefit/cost ratios for the three investment opportunities shown in Exhibit 9-6. Investments A and B show discounted benefit/cost ratios of 1.08 and 1.17 respectively, indicating favorable investment opportunities. Investment C shows a ratio of .95, indicating an unfavorable investment. The ranking, however, differs from that determined by the net present-value method. The discounted benefit/cost ratio ranks Investment B as the best choice, whereas the net present-value method ranks A as the best choice.

A word of caution about the use of ratios: The ratio of two numbers depends, in part, upon the array of data used to arrive at the two numbers. It is possible that the rankings of the various proposals may change if the ratios are based upon *gross* operating cash flows rather than on *net* operating cash flows. Although the use of different data bases may cause the ratio to change, it cannot cause a favorable investment opportunity to appear unfavorable, nor an unfavorable investment opportunity to appear favorable. As a general rule, revenue and costs from operations for each year should be netted to arrive at a single cash inflow from operations figure. Nonoperating cash flows should be shown separately. These include original investments, additional working capital requirements, invested proceeds from the sale of the asset, and recovery of working capital when the project is terminated.

Investment	Discounted* Benefits (Discounted Cash Inflows)	Discounted* Costs (Discounted Cash Outflows)	Discounted Benefit/Cost Ratio	Ranking
A	$21,662	$20,000	1.08	2
B	10,553	9,000	1.17	1
C	11,436	12,000	.95	3

*Data from Exhibit 9-6.

EXHIBIT 9-7
Discounted benefit/cost ratio for selected investments

Adjusted Rate of Return

The net present-value and discounted benefit/cost ratio methods use a preestablished rate of return. The **adjusted rate-of-return** method, or **discounted rate-of-return** method as it is often called, determines the actual rate of return of an investment opportunity. This method determines the rate necessary to make the discounted cash inflows equal to the discounted cash outflows. Remember that with the net present-value method, if the net present value was zero, the actual rate of return was exactly equal to the predefined rate of return. With the adjusted rate-of-return method, a predefined rate is not used; instead, the actual rate of return is computed.

Unless the cash inflows are equal over the life of the project and begin in the first year of the project, a trial and error process is necessary. Initially, the net present value is calculated at an arbitrary rate of return. If the net present value at this rate is positive, a higher rate is tried. If the net present value is negative, a lower rate is tested. New rates are tested until a net present value of zero is reached. The actual discounted rate of return for the investment is where there is a zero net present value.

When cash inflows are equal over the life of the project, as in the case of Investment C, it is not necessary to use a trial and error approach. Instead, the actual rate may be determined directly from the present-value tables, as shown later in the chapter.

Because we chose a 10% rate in computing the net present value of each investment, we know that the actual rates of return are higher than 10% for Investments A and B, but less than 10% for Investment C. Let's accept the determination of the net present value at 10% for our first trial. Then, through a process of subsequent trials, we can determine the actual rates of return expected from Investments A and B. For our second trial we will compute the net present value of Investments A and B at 18%. If the net present value is not at or very near zero, we'll try again at higher or lower rates, depending on whether the net present value is positive or negative.

In Exhibit 9-8, using an 18% rate, Investment A shows a negative net present value of $(499); Investment B shows a very small negative net present value of $(22). We will accept 18% as the actual rate for Investment B. However, we must make another trial for Investment A at a rate of return less than 18%. The next trial for Investment A, using a 16% rate of return, is presented in Exhibit 9-9. The net present value on this last trial is so near zero, $9, we can say that the discounted rate of return for Investment A is 16%.

The adjusted rate of return for Investment C is easier to compute because the cash inflows are equal over the three-year life and the cash outflows are made at the beginning of the investment. The following formula may be used to find the actual rate of return at which the present value of the cash inflows is equal to the present value of the cash outflows.

$$\text{Cash outflow} \times \text{Present-value factor} = \text{Cash inflow} \times \text{Present-value factor}$$

	Cash Flow Time Line				Present-Value Computations		
Time	0	1	2	3	Amount	× P.V.F. $S_{\overline{n}\rvert r}$	= Present value
INVESTMENT A							
Cash outflow:							
Initial investment	$(20,000)				$(20,000)	× 1.000 $S_{\overline{0}\rvert}$ 18%	= $(20,000)
Cash inflows:							
Year 1		$11,800			$ 11,800	× .847 $S_{\overline{1}\rvert}$ 18%	= $ 9,995
Year 2			$ 13,240		$ 13,240	× .718 $S_{\overline{2}\rvert}$ 18%	= $ 9,506
Total cash inflows							$ 19,501
Net present value							$ (499)
INVESTMENT B							
Cash outflow:							
Initial investment	$ (9,000)				(9,000)	× 1.000 $S_{\overline{0}\rvert}$ 18%	= $ (9,000)
Cash inflows:							
Year 1		$ 1,200			$ 1,200	× .847 $S_{\overline{1}\rvert}$ 18%	= $ 1,016
Years 2 and 3			$ 6,000	$ 6,000	$ 6,000	× 1.327 $A_{\overline{3-1}\rvert}$ 18%	= $ 7,962
Total cash inflows							$ 8,978
Net present value							$ (22)

EXHIBIT 9-8
Adjusted rate of return for selected investments—Second trial assuming an 18% rate of return

By inserting the known amounts and solving the equation, we compute the present-value factor to equate the two cash flows.

$$\$12{,}000 \times (1.000) = \$4{,}600 \times (\text{P.V.F.})$$
$$\$12{,}000 = \$4{,}600 \times (\text{P.V.F.})$$
$$\text{P.V.F.} = \$12{,}000 \div \$4{,}600$$
$$\text{P.V.F.} = 2.609$$

Time	Cash Flow Time Line: 0	1	2	3	Present-Value Computations: Amount	× P.V.F. $S_{\overline{n}\rvert r}$	= Present value
INVESTMENT A							
Cash outflow:							
Initial investment	$(20,000)				$(20,000) ×	1.000 $S_{\overline{0}\rvert}$ 16%	= $(20,000)
Cash inflows:							
Year 1		$11,800			$ 11,800 ×	.862 $S_{\overline{1}\rvert}$ 16%	= $ 10,172
Year 2			$13,240		$ 13,240 ×	.743 $S_{\overline{2}\rvert}$ 16%	= $ 9,837
Total cash inflows							$ 20,009
Net present value							$ 9

EXHIBIT 9-9
Adjusted rate of return for selected investments—Third trial assuming a 16% rate of return

Referring to the table for the present value of an annuity of $1 (Appendix B), we can find the rate to which the 2.609 present-value factor applies. In the three-year row (Investment C has a three-year life) find the present-value factors nearest to 2.609. The nearest factors are those applicable to 6% and 8%, 2.673 and 2.577 respectively. Interpolating between these values, we find the discounted rate of return for Investment C to be approximately 7.33%.

$$\begin{aligned}\text{Actual rate of return} &= 6\% + 2\% \times \frac{2.673 - 2.609}{2.673 - 2.577}\\ &= 6\% + 2\% \times \frac{.064}{.096}\\ &= 6\% + 1.33\%\\ &= 7.33\%\end{aligned}$$

The ranking of investments based on the criterion of adjusted rate of return ranks Investment B highest, at approximately 18%; Investment A next, at approximately 16%; and Investment C at 7.33%. If we assume a cutoff rate equal to a weighted average cost of capital of 10%, Investments A and B should be accepted and Investment C should be rejected.

Problems of Comparison

Two problems in comparing investment alternatives should be discussed. The first concerns unequal lives; the second, reinvestment of cash as it is recovered. These problems relate only to the methods that use discounted cash-flow techniques.

When the productive lives of investment opportunities differ widely, it may be necessary to set a life span common to all investments being considered. One way is to use the shortest life as the time period for analysis. Investment opportunities with longer lives would be treated as if they were terminated early; a salvage value is used to measure the value at termination. A second way assumes replacement of the short-lived assets and uses the longest life as the time period for analysis. For example, a firm is considering which truck to purchase for making deliveries. One truck has a three-year life and the other, six years. Both will provide the necessary service, but the second truck requires a larger initial investment. We may base the investment on a time frame of three years, treating the resale value of the six-year truck as a cash inflow at the end of the first three years. Another method would be to consider the replacement of the three-year truck with another three-year truck, making the lives equal at six years.

Inherent in discounted cash-flow investment analysis is the assumption that as cash is recovered from an investment, it may be reinvested *at the same rate.* In the net present-value and discounted benefit/cost ratio methods, the assumed rate of reinvestment is the predefined rate of return. Since we will not accept an investment below the predefined rate, this is a reasonable assumption. In the adjusted rate-of-return method it is assumed that cash will be reinvested at the actual rate of return. If the timing of cash flows differs widely among investment alternatives, the adjusted rate-of-return method may lead to inadequate decisions. The firm may not be able to reinvest at the actual rate achieved by the investment being considered.

TECHNIQUES THAT DO NOT CONSIDER THE TIME VALUE OF MONEY

Discounted cash flow is a rather recent concept. It is only in the past decade that it has been taught widely in business schools and used extensively in practice. Two techniques of investment analysis are widely used that do not satisfy the long-range decision rule requiring adjustment for the time value of money—the payback period and unadjusted rate of return. A discussion of these methods follows.

Payback Period

Payback period is a simple technique that asks the question, "How long does it take to recover the initial investment?" Investment opportunities are ranked according to the time, in years, required to recover the initial investment.

INVESTMENT A

			Amount Recovered
Initial investment	$(20,000)		
Cash inflows:			
Year 1	$ 11,800		$11,800
Year 2	13,240	Year of recovery	8,200
Year 3	0		—
			$20,000

Payback period = 1 + ($8,200 ÷ $13,240) = 1.62 years

INVESTMENT B

Initial investment	$ (9,000)		
Cash inflows:			
Year 1	$ 1,200		$ 1,200
Year 2	6,000		6,000
Year 3	6,000	Year of recovery	1,800
			$ 9,000

Payback period = 2 + ($1,800 ÷ $6,000) = 2.30 years

INVESTMENT C

Initial investment	$(12,000)		
Cash inflows:			
Year 1	$ 4,600		$ 4,600
Year 2	4,600		4,600
Year 3	4,600	Year of recovery	2,800
			$12,000

Payback period = 2 + ($2,800 ÷ $4,600) = 2.61 years

Where annual cash inflows are equal payback may be determined by dividing initial investment by the annual cash inflow.

Payback period = $12,000 ÷ $4,600 = 2.61 years

EXHIBIT 9-10
Payback period of selected investments

The payback period for the three investment opportunities considered earlier are presented in Exhibit 9-10. If the cash inflow starts in year 1 and is equal throughout the life of the investment, the initial investment may be divided by the annual cash inflow to determine the payback period. If the cash inflows are not equal or do not begin in the first year, all inflows must be summed in chronological order until the point is reached where cash inflows equal the initial investment. Payback periods for the three investments, computed in

Exhibit 9-10, are: 1.62 years for Investment A, 2.30 years for Investment B, and 2.61 years for Investment C. Investments A, B, and C are ranked in that order.

Although the payback period is very simple to compute, it has serious shortcomings because it does not consider the life or relative profitability beyond the payback period. The following two investments would have the same payback period. Investment Y is clearly the better investment and would be ranked above Investment X by all other techniques of investment analysis.

Investment	*Initial Investment*	*Annual Cash Inflow*	*Productive Life*	*Payback Period*
X	$10,000	$5,000	3 years	2 years
Y	$10,000	$5,000	10 years	2 years

The payback method is a very conservative technique. In a high-risk situation, for example, where threat of nationalization of foreign investments exists, the benefits of the projected long life of the investment might never be enjoyed. In such cases, an investment with a short payback period and low rate of return may be preferable to an investment with a higher rate of return but a longer payback period. Payback period can serve as a supplement to another method. For example, one way to compensate for risk is to set a maximum payback period and use this period as a constraint in conjunction with the net present-value or adjusted rate-of-return methods.

Unadjusted Rate of Return

An **unadjusted rate of return** (not adjusted for the time value of money) is widely used. It is simple to compute and, because it is consistent with the accounting measurements of income, can be computed from the accounting records. This method divides the average income from the investment, as measured by the accounting concept of income, by the initial investment.[1] The income calculation amortizes the initial investment over the life of the project as depreciation. Because average revenue and average costs are used, depreciation must be computed on a straight-line basis.

Using the after-tax cash flows prepared in Exhibit 9-3, the unadjusted rates of return for the three investments are presented in Exhibit 9-11. Investment B ranks highest with a 16% rate of return, followed by A with 13% and C with 5%. For consistency, the data for each investment show average annual revenues as the *net* of cash collections from customers and cash payments for operating expenses.

[1]The investment figure may be measured in several ways. Two of the most common measures are *initial investment* and *average investment.* We have chosen the initial investment for simplicity of calculation.

	INVESTMENT		
	A	B	C
Average annual revenue:			
A. ($13,000 + $15,000) ÷ 2	$ 14,200		
B. ($0 + $8,000 + $8,000) ÷ 3		$ 5,333	
C. ($5,000 + $5,000 + $5,000) ÷ 3			$ 5,000
Average annual depreciation:			
A. $ 20,000 ÷ 2	$(10,000)		
B. $ 9,000 ÷ 3		$ (3,000)	
C. $ 12,000 ÷ 3			$ (4,000)
Average annual taxes:			
A. ($1,200 + $2,160) ÷ 2	$ (1,680)		
B. (−$1,200 + $2,000 + $2,000) ÷ 3		$ (933)	
C. ($400 + $400 + $400) ÷ 3			$ (400)
Average net income	$ 2,520	$ 1,400	$ 600
Initial investment	$ 20,000	$ 9,000	$ 12,000
Unadjusted rate of return (Average net income ÷ Initial investment)	13%	16%	5%

EXHIBIT 9-11
Unadjusted rate of return for selected investments

With the unadjusted rate-of-return method, a dollar of revenue received or cost paid late in the life of the investment will have the same impact as a dollar received or paid initially. This effect can lead to improper decisions. For example, assume the following investment alternatives.

	Investment M	*Investment N*
Initial investment	$10,000	$10,000
Net cash inflows:		
Year 1	$ 7,000	$ 1,000
Year 2	$ 4,000	$ 4,000
Year 3	$ 1,000	$ 7,000
Salvage value	$ 0	$ 0
Net present value (10% rate)	$ 421	$ (526)
Adjusted rate of return	13.1%	7.6%
Payback period	1.75 years	2.71 years
Unadjusted rate of return	6.7%	6.7%

Clearly, Investment M is superior to N, using either the net present-value or adjusted rate-of-return method. However, both investments have the same unadjusted rate of return.

RISK AND UNCERTAINTY

Rarely can the decision maker project all cash flows with certainty. Actual cash flows seldom occur exactly as projected. To the extent that he lacks information to determine the probability of alternative outcomes, the decision maker faces **uncertainty.** A lack of information may be brought into manageable proportions by a search for more complete data or by avoiding the alternatives that carry the possibility of large losses.

The search for better information becomes a question of **information economics.** Information has a cost. Additional data should be sought only to the point where its benefits exceed the cost of obtaining it. Each long-range decision is unique. With the exception of a few recurring long-range decisions, there may be very little relevant information in the accounting data bank. Data must be drawn from sources outside the company, often at a high cost.

Risk, on the other hand, results from conditions over which the firm has no control. For example, a local service firm that contracts with a professional sports team to provide souvenirs and novelties faces the risk of the team moving. The novelty firm has no control over whether the owners will choose to move the team. Even if the team stays, management will be uncertain about how many T-shirts, baseball caps, or other novelties will be sold.

Research in investment decisions has developed decision models that explicitly consider risk. In a recent survey[2] concerning capital-budgeting practices, two-thirds of the responding firms explicitly considered risk and uncertainty in their investment decisions. Use of the following methods of adjusting for risk and uncertainty was indicated by the survey respondents. (Several firms indicated more than one method.)

Method	*Percentage of Respondents Indicating Use*
Requirement of a higher-than-normal index of profitability	54%
Requirement of a shorter-than-normal payback period	40%
Adjustment of estimated cash flows by use of quantitative probability factors	32%
Purely subjective, nonquantitative adjustment	29%
Other methods	8%

[2]J. M. Fremgen, "Capital Budgeting Practices: A Survey," *Management Accounting* (May, 1973), pp. 19–25.

The first method involves the use of a higher desired rate of return for more risky projects. To illustrate, let's assume three classes of risk: high, moderate, and low. By applying higher required rates of return to the moderate- and high-risk classes, the investment decision process places less weight on distant cash inflows as the degree of risk increases. Assume that a 10% rate of return is required for low-risk projects, a 15% rate for moderate-risk projects, and a 20% rate for high-risk projects. Compare the present value of $1 of cash inflows for the three risk classes at points three and five years in the future.

Year	*Low Risk (10%)*	*Moderate Risk (15%)*	*High Risk (20%)*
3	.75	.66	.58
5	.62	.50	.40

The $1 inflow in year 5 from a low-risk investment has a greater present value than the $1 inflow received in year 3 of a high-risk project. A high-risk project must allow recovery of the initial investment sooner and must have a larger cash inflow earlier in the life of the project than does a low-risk project.

The second method, a shorter-than-normal payback, considers only the cash flows in the early life of the project. Commonly, the short payback is used in combination with the net present-value method. The net present-value method determines if an investment will earn at least a desired rate of return; the payback period places a limit on acceptable risk. For example, the novelty firm may be reasonably certain that the professional sports team will remain for two years; it would take at least that long to negotiate and accomplish a move. The firm may choose to accept investment projects with a net present value at the desired rate of return and a two-year-or-less payback.

In the third method, the consideration of risk and uncertainty involves estimating the probabilities of different cash flows. One way, easily applied, is to make three estimates of future cash flows for each investment opportunity: an optimistic estimate, a most likely estimate, and a pessimistic estimate. By assigning subjective probabilities to each of these predictions, the decision maker can decide whether the risk of loss is too great to accept the investment, regardless of the most probable favorable return.

For example, assume that the decision maker expects an optimistic outcome two out of ten times and therefore assigns a probability of .2 to the optimistic cash flow projections. He expects the most likely projection to occur five out of ten times and assigns a probability of .5 to the most likely cash flow projections. Finally, he expects the pessimistic outcome to occur three times out of ten and assigns a probability of .3 to the pessimistic projections. Let's assume that the following after-tax cash flows were projected for our earlier example of Investment B.

	Optimistic	*Most Likely*	*Pessimistic*
First year	$ 1,200	$1,200	$1,200
Second year	$ 9,500	$7,000	$2,000
Third year	$13,500	$6,000	$1,000

The cash projections to be used in investment analysis would be computed as follows:

First year ($1,200 × .2) + ($1,200 × .5) + ($1,200 × .3) = $1,200
Second year ($9,500 × .2) + ($7,000 × .5) + ($2,000 × .3) = $6,000
Third year ($13,500 × .2) + ($6,000 × .5) + ($1,000 × .3) = $6,000

By assigning subjective probabilities to the estimates we have a good picture of the risk facing the company in this investment. Are the probable cash flows worth the risk of a 30% chance that the investment will lose money? Management would pay considerable attention to this question if such a loss would cause the company to fail.

DECISION MAKING IN THE PUBLIC SECTOR: BENEFIT-COST ANALYSIS

In the public sector we are interested in the maximization of welfare and, therefore, use measures of social costs and social benefits in the benefit-cost model. Ideally, all benefits and costs to society of a particular act would enter the analysis. Such measurement, however, is beyond the current state of the art; a more realistic application of the model is necessary.

An illustration of benefit-cost analysis is presented in Exhibit 9-12. Discounted benefits are plotted on the vertical axis and discounted costs on the horizontal axis. The diagonal line, labeled *Benefit-cost decision line,* is a plotting of the proposed long-range decision rule. Any plotting of a benefit-cost ratio that falls on or to the left of the line is favorable; any plotting that falls to the right of the line is unfavorable.

Assume that three proposals for combating a major health problem are proposed. The first proposal involves an educational program and is represented on the chart as a dashed line. This proposal provides a high level of benefits at a low level of cost. However, diminishing returns are encountered as the costs are increased; the benefit-cost ratio drops below one quite soon. The second proposal involves preventive medicine and is plotted as a broken line. It shows a favorable benefit-cost ratio over a larger range of spending levels. The third proposal, medical research, is plotted as a solid line. Research requires a high level of costs before any significant benefits are achieved.

The impact of scale is important in this illustration because the relative ranking of alternatives changes at different spending levels. At cost level 1,

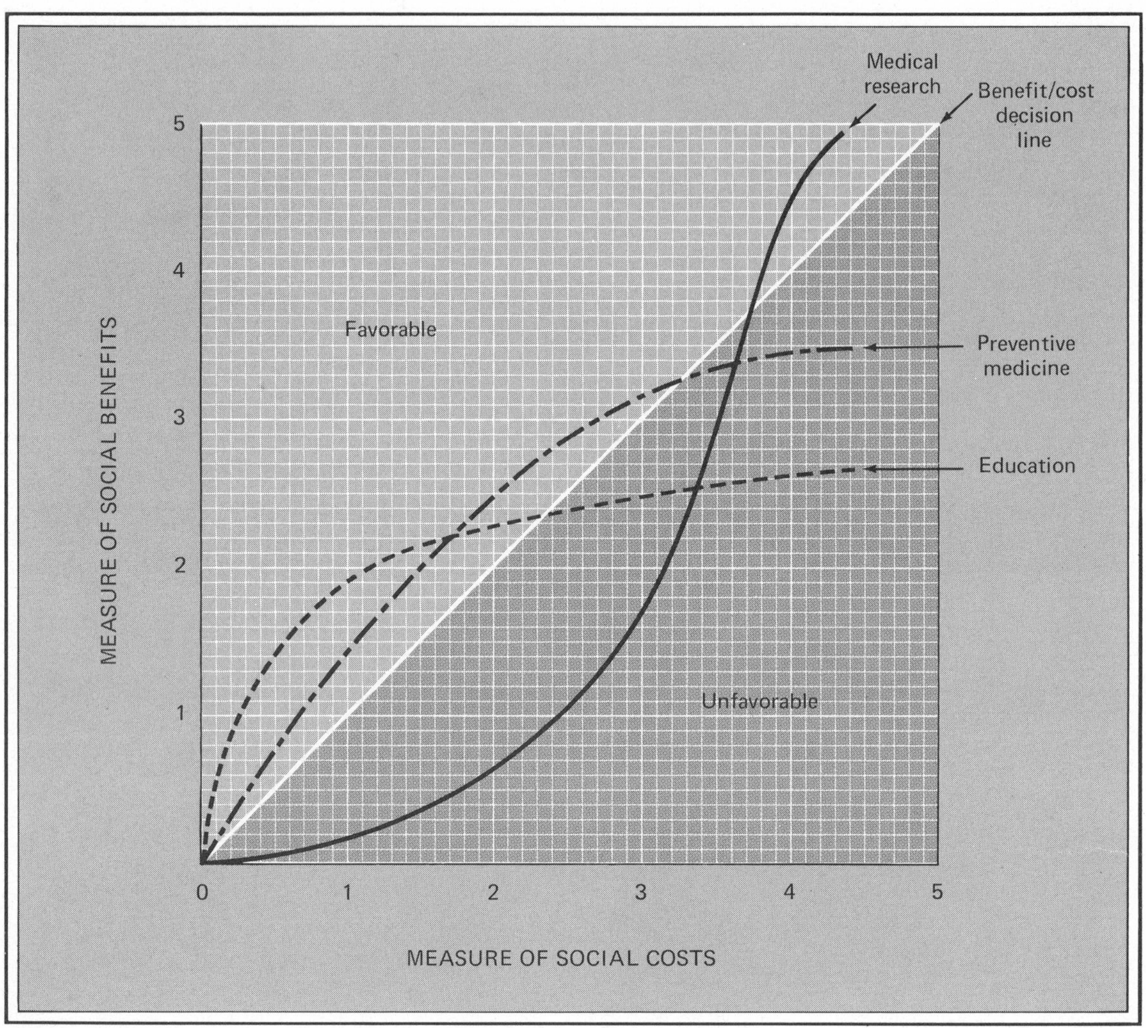

EXHIBIT 9-12
Structure of benefit-cost analysis

education ranks highest; at cost levels 2 and 3, the program of preventive medicine ranks highest; at cost level 4 and above, research is the only favorable alternative. A cutback in funds after the project is approved and started, leading to a curtailment of the project from cost level 4 to level 3 or lower, would result in a very inefficient use of funds.

As a part of benefit-cost analysis, the impact of different spending levels on output should be examined. By comparing the incremental effect of additional expenditures on different programs, a significant increase in benefits may be achieved through a modest trade-off of investment among projects.

Illustration of Benefit-cost Analysis

The benefit-cost analysis chosen for illustration is a study of the Supplemental Food Program (SFP). This study is not offered as an outstanding example of benefit-cost analysis. Rather, it is presented because it includes an interesting measure of economic benefits.

PROGRAM OBJECTIVES

SFP was designed primarily to improve the health of children from low-income families through free food supplements and free professional health care. The real cost associated with malnutrition and lack of medical care is the impaired ability of those who suffered prenatal and infantile brain damage. With medical authorization to secure free food, participating mothers were given an incentive to secure food as well as regular professional health care for themselves and their children.

METHODOLOGY

The study concerns one urban area participating in SFP. Information for the benefit-cost analysis was drawn from medical studies concerning the impact of nutritional deficiencies on mental health, SFP records, and interviews with SFP personnel and residents in the selected neighborhood. A benefit-cost model developed a ratio of discounted benefits to discounted costs for the program.

MEASUREMENT OF ECONOMIC BENEFITS

Significant economic benefits accruing from the program include: (1) the *direct product benefits,* measured by the retail value of the food distributed to the participants ($1,231,465); (2) the *employment opportunities* provided to nonprofessional employees of the program, many of whom had been unemployed ($159,880); and (3) *increased economic contribution* of participants, measured by the present value, in 1970 dollars, of the total additional income expected to be earned over the lifetime of the infants as a result of avoiding permanent brain damage ($237,213).

The number of cases of permanent brain damage avoided was determined by applying the conclusions from other research to this study. Based upon medical studies concerning the incidence of mental retardation in infants due to insufficient prenatal care and nutrition, it was concluded that 10.68 cases of mental retardation were avoided due to SFP. The study assumed that a healthy child would eventually earn the average income of the total population between 18 and 64, whereas the mentally retarded child would eventually earn the average income of those in the age group between 18 and 64 having less than eight years of education. The difference in annual income, based upon census data, is $3,068.26 in 1970 dollars. The following calculation shows the present value of additional lifetime income of each infant (employed during years 18 to 60).[3]

$$\text{Difference in income} \times \text{P.V.F. } A_{\overline{60-18|}}\ 5\% \times \text{Number of cases} = \text{Present value of benefits}$$

$$\$3{,}068.26 \times 7.2389 \times 10.68 = \$237{,}213$$

MEASUREMENT OF ECONOMIC COSTS

The costs included in the analysis were direct expenditures on the project. No side effects or externalities were identified.

CONCLUSIONS

A summary of the analysis is presented in Exhibit 9-13. The benefit-cost analysis indicates that the Supplemental Food Program was desirable from an economic point of view. The dollar value of the benefits was 45% greater than the costs.

The benefit-cost analysis of SFP did not examine and compare alternative ways of achieving the objective of averting brain damage in infants. In this program it was determined only that the benefits exceeded the costs, not that this program was the best that could have been undertaken.

Political and Other Non-efficiency Considerations

The decision processes in this book have used economic efficiency as *the* appropriate decision criterion. If the costs of a decision are purely economic and can be measured in the marketplace, the analysis works well. In the public sector, however, there are political costs as well as economic costs. In fact, the need for political support may assume primary importance. At any level of government one may find cases where politicians choose to support inefficient alternatives because they will produce votes. The economically efficient alternatives may result in a very high political cost when the politician seeks reelection.

The social goal of income redistribution is not given weight in the decision criterion of economic efficiency. One dollar's worth of benefits is equal to any other dollar's worth of benefits. Increments of income to the poor and minorities, for example, are not deemed to be of higher value than increments to the wealthy. For this reason, in most governmental decisions there is a mixture of economic efficiency and political considerations.

[3]The present value factor was found by subtracting the present-value factor for 18 years at 5% from the present-value factor for 60 years at 5%, or 18.9292 − 11.6896 = 7.2396.

SUMMARY OF BENEFITS:		
Direct product benefits: Value of food		$1,231,465
Employment of nonprofessional people		159,880
Incremental economic contribution of participants		237,213
Total benefits		$1,628,558
SUMMARY OF COSTS:		
Personnel costs:		
Doctors and nurses	$ 48,000	
Other personnel	262,469	$ 310,469
Nonpersonnel costs:		
Travel	$ 17,684	
Space rental	11,200	
Supplies and equipment	6,142	
Other costs	38,505	73,531
Cost of food (60% of retail)		738,879
Total costs		1,122,879
NET BENEFITS		$ 505,679
BENEFIT/COST RATIO		$1.45

Source: Terre and Ameiss, "Accounting's Cost/Benefit Analysis for Evaluation of Today's Programs Assisting America's Disadvantage and Low-Income Families," *The National Public Accountant* (May, 1972), pp. 8-18.

EXHIBIT 9-13
Benefit-cost analysis of supplemental food program

INVESTMENT TECHNIQUES IN PRACTICE

We have presented techniques that will result in wise investment decisions if applied with sound judgment. What methods are actually used? The results of a recent survey of investment decision practices are presented in Exhibit 9-14. Most of the firms included in the survey were large corporations that would be expected to use sophisticated techniques.

Three methods were most commonly used: adjusted rate of return (indicated by 71% of responding firms); payback (67%); and unadjusted rate of return (49%). Several firms indicated that more than one method was used. The choice of adjusted rate of return over other discounted cash-flow methods can, in part, be explained by the nature of the measurement criteria provided by the three methods. Most managers think in terms of rate of return and find the adjusted rate of return appealing as profitability criterion.

A firm that used more than one method was asked to indicate the most important method used. The adjusted rate of return stands out clearly as the first choice of 45% of the responding firms. Payback and unadjusted rate of return occupy a much smaller role (17% and 26% respectively) as the first choice. However, as the size of the relevant capital budget declined, and probably the size of the firm as well, the use of the payback as the most important method increased.

Another survey,[4] which compared capital budgeting methods used in 1959 with those in 1970, showed the most sophisticated, primary evaluation method to be:

	Percentage of Respondents	
	1970	*1959*
Discounted cash-flow methods	57%	19%
Unadjusted rate of return	26%	34%
Payback	12%	34%
Other	5%	13%
	100%	100%

This survey and that shown in Exhibit 9-14 yield nearly identical results when the three discounted cash flow techniques in Exhibit 9-14 are combined. It must be kept in mind that the data in both studies represent practices of some of the largest corporations in the country, with annual capital expenditures of millions of dollars. We should expect these firms to use sophisticated techniques. There is no comparable empirical evidence about smaller firms, but we would expect them to favor payback and accounting rate of return over discounted cash-flow techniques today, in much the same proportions indicated by the large corporations in the survey of 1959 practices.

[4]Thomas Klammer, "Empirical Evidence of the Adoption of Sophisticated Capital Budgeting Techniques," *The Journal of Business* (October, 1972), pp. 387–397.

With so many shortcomings, why do the payback and unadjusted rate-of-return methods continue to be used so widely? Several reasons have been advanced to explain the use of inferior investment analysis techniques.

First, business managers of small corporations are not aware of the more sophisticated techniques or do not understand them. Only in the past 10 to 15 years have discounted cash-flow techniques been widely taught in the undergraduate business curricula.

	Techniques Satisfying the Long-Range Decision Rule			Techniques that do not Consider Time Value of Money		
Amount of Annual Capital Budget	Adjusted Rate of Return	Net Present Value	Discounted Benefit/ Cost Ratio	Payback Period	Unadjusted Rate of Return	Other Methods
A. METHODS IN ACTUAL USE*						
Over $100 million	78%	34%	9%	72%	60%	14%
$50-$100 million	79	21	10	62	55	3
$10-$50 million	64	14	2	68	44	11
Under $10 million	67	0	5	52	33	0
No size given	67	33	0	67	0	33
All respondents	71%	20%	6%	67%	49%	10%
B. MOST IMPORTANT METHOD†						
Over $100 million	43%	6%	0%	3%	39%	9%
$50-$100 million	56	10	4	10	20	0
$10-$50 million	45	3	0	26	20	6
Under 10 million	47	0	5	24	24	0
No size given	0	0	0	50	0	50
All respondents	45%	5%	1%	17%	26%	6%

Source: J.M. Fremgen, "Capital Budgeting Practices: A Survey," *Management Accounting* (May, 1973), pp. 19-25.

*Several firms indicated more than one method used.

†Not all firms responded to question; data were adjusted to represent percentage of firms answering question.

EXHIBIT 9-14
Investment analysis techniques in practice

Second, inertia. When a practice has worked in the past and is easily understood, there is great reluctance to accept new methods. Decision making is guided by intuition and experience in many companies. Conservative business managers will use conservative practices such as the payback method. An examination of the mathematical characteristic of the adjusted rate of return has shown that if project lives are at least twice the payback periods, the payback method will provide results similar to the adjusted rate-of-return method. Actually, the payback reciprocal is a close approximation of the discounted rate of return under these conditions. Here an intuitive method gained by experience approximates the theoretically better method.

Third, if the company is evaluated by return on investment and earnings per share computed from accounting income, the decision maker can be expected to favor those investments that maximize the unadjusted (accounting) rate of return. The unadjusted rate of return considers time only through averaging the revenues and costs. Investments that provide for a steadily increasing trend of earnings would be favored over those that lead to wide fluctuations but have a higher time-adjusted rate of return over the life of the project. For this reason, we would expect many decision makers to reject Investment B in our earlier illustration of investment techniques. Investment B would show a loss for accounting purposes in year 1, and equal profits in years 2 and 3. Investment A would be the most highly favored because it provides a short payback, a good overall return, increasing profit, and no loss year. Investment C, which was inferior by all five investment analysis techniques discussed in this chapter, may be favored over Investment B because it provides a steady income rather than a loss followed by larger profits. When management owes its continuation in office to satisfied stockholders, there is a strong tendency to emphasize earning trends and avoid periods of loss.

In the public sector there is very little information available on the extent to which the discounting of benefits and costs is used. The public-sector approach is the ratio of discounted benefits to discounted costs or, if benefits are not measured, a cost-effectiveness model of discounted costs per unit of objective criterion (such as cost per individual trained or cost per death averted). At the federal level, a survey of twenty-three federal agencies[5] indicated that in 1969 eight had used discounting techniques and ten planned to use discounting in the future. At the state and local level, discounting is practically unused. To the extent that economic efficiency is even considered, decisions are often based upon analysis of first-year costs of the project.

[5]Elmer B. Staats, "Survey of Use by Federal Agencies of the Discounting Technique in Evaluating Future Programs," *Program Budgeting and Benefit-Cost Analysis* (Pacific Palisades, Ca.: Goodyear Publishing Company, Inc., 1969), pp. 212–218.

SUMMARY

Five investment analysis techniques were introduced in this chapter. Only the first three—net present-value, discounted benefit/cost ratio, and adjusted rate-of-return techniques—consider the time value of money. The net present-value and discounted benefit/cost ratio methods use a predefined rate of return and base the decision criterion on whether the desired rate is achieved. The adjusted rate-of-return method determines the actual rate of return earned by the investment. The result, in an easily understood percentage form, probably explains the preference for its use over other discounted cash-flow techniques.

The payback-period and unadjusted rate-of-return methods do not consider the time value of money. The payback period measures how long it takes to recover the initial investment. The unadjusted rate-of-return method computes the return achieved by dividing the average income from the investment, as measured by the accounting concept of income, by the initial investment. Methods that do not consider the time value of money should be rejected as deficient. Empirical evidence indicates that, at least among large firms, the use of payback period and unadjusted rate of return is declining.

In the public sector many long-range decisions are still based upon first-year costs and availability of funds rather than economic efficiency. However, the discounted benefit-cost model is gaining acceptance. The ratio of discounted benefits to discounted costs is an easily understood measure. A major advantage of the model is that quantifiable measures of benefits and costs to society can be incorporated.

SUPPLEMENTARY READING

Bierman, H., and C. Smidt. *The Capital Budgeting Decision.* New York: Macmillan and Co., 1971.

Edwards, James B. "Adjusted DCF Rate of Return." *Management Accounting,* January, 1973.

Fremgen, James M. "Capital Budgeting Practices: A Survey." *Management Accounting,* May, 1973.

Hertz, David B. "Investment Policies that Pay Off." *Harvard Business Review,* January–February, 1968.

Klammer, Thomas. "Empirical Evidence of the Adoption of Sophisticated Capital Budgeting Techniques." *The Journal of Business,* October, 1972.

Klammer, Thomas. "The Association of Capital Budgeting Techniques with Firm Performance." *The Accounting Review,* April, 1973.

Meredith, G. G. "Decision Criteria for Investment Strategies." *The Australian Accountant,* November, 1971.

Myers, Ronald E. "Performance Review of Capital Expenditures." *Management Accounting,* December, 1966.

National Association of Accountants. *Financial Analysis Techniques for Equipment Replacement Decisions.* New York: National Association of Accountants, 1965.

Novick, David. "Long Range Planning through Program Budgeting." *Business Horizons,* February, 1969.

Rowley, C. Stevenson. "Methods of Capital Project Selection." *Managerial Planning,* March–April, 1973.

QUESTIONS

9-1 "If the net present value of an investment is zero, the company will show no profit on the project." Do you agree? Discuss.

9-2 Define and explain the following concepts: *time value of money, discounting, payback, adjusted rate of return, predefined discount rate, net present value, discounted benefit/cost ratio,* and *unadjusted rate of return.*

9-3 What are some of the reasons for using one method of depreciation for tax purposes and another for financial accounting purposes?

9-4 Explain how the long-range decision rule may be applied to the selection of a depreciation method for tax purposes.

9-5 In what way do the net present-value and discounted benefit/cost ratio methods differ from the adjusted rate-of-return method of investment analysis?

9-6 How is it possible that the net present-value method and adjusted rate of return may rank acceptable proposals in different orders?

9-7 Payback method has been described as a "conservative" method. Explain why this is true in relation to other methods.

9-8 What are some of the shortcomings of the payback method? Why has it been so widely used for analysis in the past?

9-9 What are the advantages of the payback method?

9-10 How is it possible that an investment project may have an unacceptable unadjusted or accounting rate of return and yet an acceptable adjusted rate of return? Give an example.

9-11 If a firm is evaluated by the stockholders and investing public on accounting rate of return and earnings per share, what probable types of investments will the management desire? Explain. Would this necessarily maximize the "wealth" of the firm? Why or why not?

9-12 Describe the difference between the decision criteria of *maximization of wealth* and *maximization of welfare?*

9-13 Describe some of the methods of dealing with risk and uncertainty in investment analysis.

9-14 State a general rule for long-range decisions. How does this rule differ in the public sector?

9-15 A firm's search for additional information should continue only until the cost of obtaining that information equals the benefits received. Discuss.

PROBLEMS

9-16 Match the following terms and definitions.

1. Cash inflows
2. Benefit-cost analysis
3. Net present value
4. Adjusted rate of return
5. Unadjusted rate of return
6. Payback period
7. Present-value factor
8. Discounted benefit/cost ratio
9. Uncertainty
10. Risk

a. The time it takes to recover an investment.
b. The condition faced when a decision maker lacks information.
c. A general model for measuring economic efficiency.
d. Return on investment based upon discounted cash flows.
e. The relevant measure of benefits in a decision model that meets the long-range decision rule.
f. A number developed to assist in the computation of discounted cash flows.
g. The condition faced when the decision maker has no control over the outcome of an event.
h. Discounted benefits minus discounted costs.
i. Discounted benefits divided by discounted costs.
j. Return on investment based upon accounting income.

9-17 Capital budgeting has received increased attention in recent years. The quantitative techniques employed for capital-budgeting decisions depend largely upon accounting data.

REQUIRED:

A. Distinguish between capital budgeting and budgeting for operations.
B. Three quantitative methods used in making capital-budgeting decisions are (1) payback period, (2) unadjusted accounting rate of return, and (3) discounted cash flow. Discuss the merits of each of these methods.
C. Two variations of the discounted cash-flow method are (1) time-adjusted rate of return and (2) net present value (sometimes referred to as excess present value). Explain and compare these two variations of the discounted cash-flow method.
D. Cost of capital is an important concept in capital budgeting. Define the term *cost of capital* and explain how it is used in capital budgeting.

(CPA adapted)

9-18 At what discount rate do the following alternatives have approximately the same present value? (Compute or estimate the rate to the nearest whole percent.)

A. $1,000 now or $1,000 five years from now
B. $567 now or $1,000 five years from now
C. $2,000 at the end of the next five years or $5,196 at the end of fifteen years

9-19 At what discount rate do the following alternatives have approximately the same present value? (Compute or estimate the rate to the nearest whole percent.)

A. $322 now or $1,000 ten years from now
B. $20,000 now or $1,000,000 thirty years from now
C. $1,000 at the end of each of the next five years or $7,548.39 at the end of ten years

9-20 Black, White, and Gray, three franchised home appliance dealers, have requested short-term financing from Benjamin Industries. The dealers have agreed to repay the loans within three years and to pay Benjamin Industries 5% of net income for the three-year period for the use of the funds. The following table summarizes, by dealer, the financing requested and the total remittances (principal plus 5% of net income) expected at the end of each year.

	Black	White	Gray
Financing requested	$ 80,000	$40,000	$30,000
Remittances expected at end of:			
Year 1	$ 10,000	$25,000	$10,000
Year 2	40,000	30,000	15,000
Year 3	70,000	5,000	15,000
	$120,000	$60,000	$40,000

Management believes these financing requests should be granted only if the annual pre-tax return to the company exceeds the target internal rate of 20% on investment.

REQUIRED:

A. Prepare a schedule to compute the net present value of the investment opportunities of financing Black, White, and Gray.

B. Ignoring any legal problems such as usury, should any of the loans be granted? *(CPA adapted)*

9-21 The following three investments are considered for analysis. (Ignore taxes.)

Investment	*Cost (now)*	*Annual Cash Savings*	*Life*
A	$18,000	$3,000	6 years
B	$12,000	$2,000	8 years
C	$ 6,000	$1,000	10 years

REQUIRED:

A. Compute the payback period for each investment.

B. What are some of the conclusions that can be drawn from this example? Discuss.

C. Suggest a stronger method of analysis.

9-22 You are considering an investment proposal with an initial investment of $17,000, a five-year life, and a $2,000 salvage value. The expected cash inflows before taxes from the investment are:

Year	*Cash Inflow*
1	$8,000
2	$7,000
3	$6,000
4	$5,000
5	$4,000

Assume the company uses straight-line depreciation and is subject to a 40% tax rate.

REQUIRED:

A. If your long-range decision rule limits you to investments with no more than a three-year payback period, will you accept this investment? Show your calculations.

B. Would your decision change if you used sum-of-the-years' digits depreciation? Show your calculations.

9-23 *A.* Compute the net present value of the following investment. Assume an 8% required rate of return. (Ignore taxes.)

Year	*Cash Flow*
0	$(23,115)
1	$ 5,000
2	$ 10,000
3	$ 15,000

B. How much could you pay in addition to the $23,110 and still earn 8% on your investment?

C. What is the approximate adjusted rate of return in part A?

9-24 *A.* Compute the net present value of the following investment. Assume an 8% required rate of return. (Ignore taxes.)

Year	*Cash Flow*
0	$(23,115)
1	$ 15,000
2	$ 10,000
3	$ 5,000

B. What is the approximate adjusted rate of return on this investment?

C. Why is the adjusted rate of return from this investment higher than the rate of return from the investment in problem 9-23, when both have the same total cash flows?

D. Will this investment and the investment in problem 9-23 have the same unadjusted rate of return? Explain.

9-25 Two investments show the following cash flows. (Ignore taxes.)

Period	*Project D*	*Project E*
0	$(12,353)	$(10,588)
1	$ 5,500	$ 3,000
2	$ 5,500	$ 4,000
3	$ 5,500	$ 5,000

REQUIRED:
A. Compute the payback period.
B. Compute the net present value, assuming a 12% required rate of return.
C. Compute the adjusted rate of return.
D. Compute the unadjusted rate of return.

9-26 The Juicy Orange Grove is considering an investment of $40,000 in equipment that will save an estimated $8,000 per year during its eight-year life. The equipment will have no resale value at the end of its useful life. (Ignore taxes.)

REQUIRED:
A. Compute the payback period.
B. Assuming a 10% cost of capital, compute the net present value of the investment.
C. Compute the adjusted rate of return.
D. Should the equipment be purchased?

9-27 Refer to the data for the Juicy Orange Grove in problem 9-26. Assume the following additional information: The tax rate on ordinary income is 40% and on capital gains it is 30%. The equipment qualifies for the 7% investment credit, it will have a $4,000 salvage value, and the company will use sum-of-the-years' digits depreciation.

REQUIRED:
A. Compute the payback period.
B. Compute the unadjusted rate of return.
C. Compute the net present value of the project.
D. Compute the adjusted rate of return of the project.
E. Should the equipment be purchased?

9-28 *A.* Compute the net present value of each of the following investments and rank them according to their desirability. The cost of capital for this company is 10%. (Ignore taxes.)

		Cash Inflows		
Investment	*Initial Investment*	*1*	*2*	*3*
F	$15,000	$9,000	$10,600	0
G	$ 9,000	$3,750	$ 3,750	$3,750
H	$ 6,750	$4,500	0	$4,500

B. Assuming a 40% tax rate and straight-line depreciation, compute the net present value of the investments and rank them according to their desirability.

9-29 Refer to the data in problem 9-28. Assume that the minimum acceptable rate of return is equal to the cost of capital.

REQUIRED:

A. Compute the adjusted rate of return for each investment and rank them according to their desirability. (Ignore taxes.)

B. Assuming a 40% tax rate and straight-line depreciation, compute the adjusted rate of return and rank the investments according to their desirability. The investments do not qualify for the investment credit.

C. Which of the investments should be accepted?

9-30 Two investment opportunities are available to your company. Assume that your company has a cost of capital of 10%. (Ignore taxes.)

Investment	*Initial Investment*	*Annual Cash Inflows*	*Life of Investment*
I	$50,000	$15,000	5 years
J	$35,000	$10,000	4 years

REQUIRED:

A. Compute the net present value of the proposals and rank them according to their desirability.

B. Compute the adjusted rate of return and rank the proposals according to their desirability.

C. What are some considerations, other than the weighted average cost of capital, that might be considered in evaluating this proposal.

9-31 Using the data in problem 9-30, recompute the requirements for each investment, assuming a tax rate of 40%, straight-line depreciation, and that the investments qualify for a 5% investment credit.

9-32 Indicate whether you think each of the following investments would be high risk, medium risk, or low risk.

1. Replacement of a machine with a new and more efficient machine to produce the company's major product. The life of the machine is six years and the patents protecting the product have a ten-year life.

2. Purchase of a contract with an all-American basketball player. He was the unanimous choice of every sportswriter as college player of the year, in spite of missing the last four games because of a knee injury.

3. Investment in a first-mortgage bond issued by Florida Power and Light Company.

4. Purchase of pollution-control equipment necessary to comply with state pollution-control laws. The company is profitable but will probably not receive another waiver for pollution-control compliance.

5. Investment in a new plant layout that radically alters the employee relationships. The new plant layout will allow groups of employees to set their own work assignments, output, and wage scale.
6. Investment in a cattle-feeding venture. The facility will be computer controlled, utilizing the most advanced decision and control models. The price of feed has been rising and the price of fattened beef cattle has been very erratic.
7. Investment of $1,000 in a fund that purchases high-yielding, high-quality certificates of deposit issued by the major banks in the country. The fund will receive a return that is 2% above what an individual investment of $1,000 in certificates will earn. The cost of administration of the fund will be minimal.
8. Purchase of the movie rights to the novel that has headed the best-seller list for the past year.
9. A screening unit for a private medical clinic that will perform standard tests on all patients when they make an appointment. There will be no added charge for the test because it is an extension of the practice of preventive medicine. Added costs of about $3 per patient visit would have to be covered out of additional medical services performed as a result of otherwise undetected problems. If the tests reveal a medical problem and the patient is not informed, there may be liability for malpractice.
10. An investment by a company in refurbishing an old building for a restaurant in the central area of a major city. The investment will be part of an overall plan to develop an area called *Olde City.* It will be several years before the development is complete.

9-33 The Snoopy Electronic Corporation has three investment proposals presented for consideration:

Investment L: An investment of $180,000 that would return $50,000 in cash flows for six years and involve high risk.

Investment M: An investment of $120,000 that would return cash flows of $30,000 per year for five years and involve moderate risk.

Investment N: An investment of $80,000 that would return $45,000 per year for two years and involve only low risk.

Assume the firm uses an 8% cutoff rate for long-term investments. The company adds to the 8% cutoff rate a 6% penalty for moderate-risk projects and a 12% penalty for high-risk ventures.

REQUIRED:

A. Which proposals are acceptable to the firm? Why?

B. If Investment M could obtain $36,000 per year (rather than $30,000) in increased cash flows over a four-year period with the same capital investment, would this change its attractiveness? Why?

9-34 Myrtle and Millie, sisters, are considering the purchase of Ye Olde Donut Shoppe to provide an income until their Social Security and other pension plans will begin payments in five years. An analysis of their personal expenditures determined that Myrtle needed at least $10,000 per year and Millie $16,000 per year (before taxes) to continue their respective life styles. Both women will work in the shop; there will be no other employees. Myrtle will draw $6,000 and Millie $8,000 per year in salaries. Net income (after salaries and taxes) will be distributed evenly to Myrtle and Millie each year in the form of dividends. Ye Olde Donut Shoppe requires an investment of $38,000, which covers the building ($30,000), equipment ($6,000), and additional working capital ($2,000). The building has an expected useful life of ten years and the equipment, five years.

Upon examining the accounting records of the present owner, the sisters found that the net cash inflows from operations (before taxes and salaries) were only $24,000. After talking with the present owner, Myrtle and Millie felt that the business was not well managed and that they could increase cash inflows by at least 25%. The corporation will pay taxes of 25% on the total net income after salaries.

REQUIRED:

A. Prepare a schedule of after-tax cash flows for Ye Olde Donut Shoppe. Your schedule should show cash flows for each of the five years. Use straight-line depreciation and assume that the business can be sold for the book value of the assets at the end of the five years.

B. Will the cash flows allow the owners to meet their personal financial objectives? Explain.

C. What is the adjusted rate of return on their investment after considering salaries and taxes?

9-35 The Loser Company is owned and managed by the grandson of the founder. For several years he has spent the majority of his time on the ski slopes and golf courses. As a result, income has steadily declined until the last two years, when substantial losses were incurred. Income for the past five years (for both tax and financial accounting purposes) was:

Year	*Income or (Loss)*
19X0	$ 300,000
19X1	$ 200,000
19X2	$ 100,000
19X3	$ (600,000)
19X4	$(2,000,000)

Winner Corporation was organized one year ago. After breaking even for its first year of operations, Winner expects to earn $500,000 per year (before taxes) for the next several years. Winner is looking for a tax shield.

If Winner Corporation acquired the stock of Loser Company, it could use the loss carryforward-carryback to offset Winner's income. Operations of Loser Company could be reduced to a breakeven point immediately, and the company would be sold for $100,000 (the value of the land) as soon as the tax carryforward is exhausted.

REQUIRED:

A. What are the cash flows Winner Company may expect from owning Loser? Assume a tax rate of 40%.

B. What is the *maximum* amount Winner should pay the stockholders of Loser in order to return 12% on its investment?

9-36 You manage a large foundation that has a goal of sponsoring research aimed at solving problems in our society. Two research organizations have submitted proposals. Each proposal is to develop certain home appliances in the next four years that will use 50% less power.

Proposal I requires an initial investment of $5,000,000 and annual costs of $1,000,000 for four years.

Proposal II requires an initial investment of $1,000,000 and the following costs during the four years.

Year 1	$2,000,000
Year 2	$5,000,000
Year 3	$1,000,000
Year 4	0

REQUIRED:

Assuming a 10% cost of funds, which proposal is the most attractive? Explain.

9-37 The town of Cowbell, located near an urban area, has been asked to grant a permit for a new shopping center. As the only member of the town council with a knowledge of capital budgeting, you have been asked to develop an analysis of the economic impact on the resources of the town.

Your investigation revealed the following direct benefits and costs to the town over a 20-year period.

A. Incremental direct benefits

1. Sales tax on construction: $20,000 per year for first four years.
2. Sales tax from shopping center sales: $100,000 per year beginning in year 5.
3. Increase in property taxes: $200,000 per year beginning in year 5.
4. Business licenses and permits: $20,000 per year beginning in year 4.
5. Added taxes to the city from new residents attracted because of the shopping center: $30,000 per year beginning in year 5.

B. Incremental Direct Costs

1. Added police protection: $40,000 per year beginning in year 1 with an additional $40,000 per year beginning in year 4.
2. Added street maintenance: $30,000 per year beginning in year 1.
3. Fire protection: $20,000 per year beginning in year 1.
4. Other city government: $30,000 per year beginning in year 1.

REQUIRED:

A. Assuming a 6% cost of capital, compute the discounted benefit/cost ratio for this decision. Based upon this criterion, should the town council approve the permit?

B. Assume that opponents of the shopping center are arguing that 6% is too low and that the appropriate discount rate is 12%. Recompute the discounted benefit/cost ratio using 12%. How does the higher rate affect your recommendation in part A?

C. Discuss the measures of social costs and social benefits requested by the town council. Explain any changes you would like to see.

9-38 Voters of King County approved construction of a King County Multipurpose Domed Stadium. Consultants were hired to recommend locations and develop the data for a benefit-cost study. The report of the consultants identified four sites and estimated the following construction costs.

	Estimated Cost		
Location	*Stadium*	*Parking*	*Total*
King Street	$39,234,200	$ 9,417,900	$48,652,100
Longacres	$38,706,600	$12,040,300	$50,746,900
Riverton	$39,436,000	$11,093,000	$50,529,000
Sicks Stadium	$38,101,100	$26,309,500	$64,410,600

Annual cash flows for the stadium were also projected.

Direct cash inflows to the stadium per year:

From sports activities	$1,157,065
All other events	462,690
Office rental and other	475,412
Annual cash inflows	$2,095,167

Direct cash outflows to the stadium per year:

Management	$ 114,000
Payroll (including fringe benefits)	646,600
Contract services	233,450
Materials and supplies	114,300
Other	220,000
Equipment rental	159,145
Contingencies	266,000
Annual cash outflows	$1,753,495

The consultants attempted to estimate the economic impact of the stadium on the county. They estimated that local and out-of-county fans would spend $6,380,000 on tickets, concessions, food, and lodging while attending events at the stadium. Most of the events, including professional sports, would be new to the county. Based upon other studies, the consultants assumed that for each dollar the sports fan spent on tickets, concessions, food, and lodging, an additional $3.50 of favorable economic impact would be generated in the community.

The county's borrowing cost is 6% and the opportunity cost of capital in the private sector is 12%. Assume a 30-year life for the stadium.

REQUIRED:

A. For each site, prepare a schedule of cash flows for the stadium project.
B. What is the amount of annual economic benefits the stadium should generate?
C. Compute the discounted benefit/cost ratio for each site.
D. What would you recommend to the King County Council? Are there other factors that should be considered?

9-39 The state highway commission is attempting to decide whether to prohibit studded tires on the state's highways. The tires have not been permitted and, for safety reasons, pressure has grown for their use. The results of two studies are presented for evidence.

The first study examined traffic deaths in the state during the past five years. The study found that accidents involving 40 deaths per year would probably have been avoided if studded tires had been used. In addition to deaths, personal property damage and medical costs of $200,000 per year would have also been avoided. The damage and medical cost estimates were drawn from police records and insurance claims. The average age of people killed was 30; their average annual income was $10,000.

The second study was conducted in states that allowed studded tires. Considering the damage to road surfaces, the highway department estimates that annual damage to the streets, highways, and bridges would amount to additional resurfacing costs of $2,000,000 per year, beginning in the fourth year. It is expected that new tires will be developed within 10 years; they will provide all the benefits of studded tires and will not damage road surfaces.

REQUIRED:

A. Assuming that those killed would have earned the average income to age 60, compute the discounted benefit-cost ratio if studded tires are allowed. Is it favorable? Assume a 10% discount rate.
B. Medical researchers at the state university's school of medicine contend that the money should be spent on kidney research. They contend that the cost per death averted in kidney research is about $25,000. How does the cost per death averted in the studded tire program compare?

9-40 The Baxter Company manufactures toys and other short-lived fad type items.

The research and development department came up with an item that would make a good promotional gift for office equipment dealers. Aggressive and effective effort by Baxter's sales personnel has resulted in almost firm commitments for this product for the next three years. It is expected that the product's value will be exhausted by that time.

In order to produce the quantity demanded, Baxter will need to buy additional machinery and rent some additional space. It appears that about 25,000 square feet will be needed. 12,500 square feet of presently unused but leased space is available now. (Baxter's present lease, with 10 years to run, costs $3 a foot.) There are another 12,500 square feet adjoining the Baxter facility, which Baxter will rent for three years at $4 per square foot per year if it decides to make this product.

The equipment will be purchased for about $900,000. It will require $30,000 in modifications, $60,000 for installation, and $90,000 for testing; all of these activities will be done by a firm of engineers hired by Baxter. All of the expenditures will be paid for on January 1, 1973.

The equipment should have a salvage value of about $180,000 at the end of the third year. No additional general overhead costs are expected to be incurred.

The following estimates of revenues and expenses for this product for the three years have been developed.

	1973	*1974*	*1975*
Sales	$1,000,000	$1,600,000	$800,000
Material, labor and factory overhead	$ 400,000	$ 750,000	$350,000
Allocated general expenses	40,000	75,000	35,000
Rent	87,500	87,500	87,500
Depreciation	450,000	300,000	150,000
Total costs	977,500	1,212,500	622,500
Income before tax	$ 22,500	$ 387,500	$177,500
Income tax (40%)	9,000	155,000	71,000
Income after tax	$ 13,500	$ 232,500	$106,500

REQUIRED:

A. Prepare a schedule that shows the incremental after-tax cash flows for this project. (See problem 8-39.)

B. If the company requires a two-year payback period for its investment, would it undertake this project? Show your supporting calculations clearly.

C. Calculate the after-tax accounting rate of return for the project.

D. A newly hired business school graduate recommends that the company consider the use of net present-value analysis to study this project. If the company sets a required rate of return of 20% after taxes, will this project be accepted? Show your supporting calculations clearly. (Assume all operating revenues and expenses occur at the end of the year.)

(CMA adapted)

9-41 The Beta Corporation manufactures office equipment and distributes its products through wholesale distributors.

Beta Corporation recently learned of a patent on the production of a semiautomatic paper collator that can be obtained at a cost of $60,000 cash. The semiautomatic model is vastly superior to the manual model that the corporation now produces. At a cost of $40,000, present equipment could be modified to accommodate the production of the new semiautomatic model. Such modifications would not affect the remaining useful life of four years nor the salvage value of $10,000 that the equipment now has. Variable costs, however, would increase by one dollar per unit. Fixed costs, other than relevant amortization charges, would not be affected. If the equipment is modified, the manual model cannot be produced.

The current income statement relative to the manual collator appears as follows:

Sales (100,000 units @ $4)		$400,000
Variable costs	$180,000	
Fixed costs*	120,000	
Total costs		300,000
Net income before income taxes		$100,000
Income taxes (40%)		40,000
Net income after income taxes		$ 60,000

*All fixed costs are directly allocable to the production of the manual collator and include depreciation on equipment of $20,000, calculated on the straight-line basis with a useful life of 10 years.

Market research has disclosed three important findings relative to the new semiautomatic model. First, a particular competitor will certainly purchase the patent if Beta Corporation does not. If this were to happen, Beta Corporation's sales of the manual collator would fall to 70,000 units per year. Second, if no increase in the selling price is made, Beta Corporation could sell approximately 190,000 units per year of the semiautomatic model. Third, because of the advances being made in this area, the patent will be completely worthless at the end of four years.

Because of the uncertainty of the current situation, the raw materials inventory has been almost completely exhausted. Regardless of the decision reached, substantial and immediate inventory replenishment will be required. The engineering department estimates that if the new model is to be produced, the average monthly raw materials inventory will be $20,000. If the old model is continued, the inventory balance will average $12,000 per month.

REQUIRED:

A. Prepare a schedule that shows the incremental after-tax cash flows for the comparison of the two alternatives. Assume that the corporation will use the sum-of-the-year's-digits method for depreciating the costs of modifying the equipment. (See problem 8-40.)

B. Assuming that the incremental after-tax cash flows calculated in requirement A and the annual incomes for the two alternatives are as given in the following schedule, will Beta Corporation, if it has a cost of capital of 18%, decide to manufacture the semiautomatic collator? Use the net present-value decision rule and assume all operating revenues and expenses occur at the end of the year.

Year	*Incremental Cash Flow (000 Omitted)*	*Annual Income (000 Omitted)*	
		Manual	*Semiautomatic*
1 Beginning	− $110	—	—
1 End	+ $ 40	$24	$39
2 End	+ $ 40	$24	$39
3 End	+ $ 40	$24	$39
4 End	+ $ 50	$24	$39

C. Calculate the accounting rate of return for each project. Using this method, would you recommend Beta manufacture the semiautomatic collator? Explain.

D. Compute the adjusted rate of return realized by modifying the equipment.

E. What additional analytical techniques, if any, would you consider before presenting a recommendation to management? Why?

F. What concerns would you have about using the information, as given in the problem, to reach a decision in this case? *(CMA adapted)*

9-42 The TST Corporation is a family-controlled corporation that has been in business for many years. Recently, profits and the price of common stock have declined. The 400 stockholders (outside the controlling family) are unhappy because they have not achieved a dividend growth rate of 8%. They have criticized the management for poor long-range planning. At the end of 19X1, the capital structure of TST Company consisted of:

4,584 shares of $100 par value preferred stock. Annual dividends on preferred are $8 per share. The market price of preferred has remained at $110 per share, the amount for which the company may repurchase the stock at any time.

12,500 shares of common, par $100. There were 400 shares of common in the treasury (shown at cost) at the end of 19X1 and 2,000 shares in the treasury at the end of 19X2. Market prices at the end of 19X1 were $150 per share, dropping to $130 at the end of 19X2.

Reserve for contingencies of $100,000 was created because of anticipated losses in a foreign contract. The reserve was returned to retained earnings during 19X2.

Reserve for retirement of preferred stock: The treasury stock had a call (repurchase) price of $110. The $10 over par reduced retained earnings when the stock was repurchased in 19X2. The company set up the reserve in 19X1 to segregate the retained earnings equal to the amount paid above par.

Retained earnings:
The following changes occurred during 19X2.

Beginning balance		$1,663,005
Add:		
Net income for 19X2	$370,485	
Reduction of reserve for contingencies	100,000	470,485
Total		$2,133,490
Deduct:		
Preferred dividends	$ 36,672	
Common dividends	100,000	136,672
Retained earnings, December 31, 19X2		$1,996,818

The TST Company is a producer of high-quality equipment for powering manufacturing operations. (In the past its major product was a steam-driven turbine.)

THE TST CORPORATION
STATEMENT OF FINANCIAL POSITION
Assets

	December 31, 19X2	*December 31, 19X1*
Current assets:		
Cash on hand and in banks	$ 391,739	$ 225,551
Accounts receivable—trade	561,689	559,690
Miscellaneous	18,907	13,031
Inventories	831,278	789,224
Marketable securities at cost	1,435,963	2,031,822
Total current assets	$3,239,576	$3,619,318
Plant assets:		
At cost	$1,680,616	$1,675,866
Less: Accumulated depreciation	1,214,999	1,199,699
Net recorded value	465,617	476,167
Total assets	$3,705,193	$4,095,485

Liabilities and Stockholders' Equity

	December 31, 19X2	*December 31, 19X1*
Current liabilities:		
Accounts payable	$ 143,915	$ 134,867
Salaries, wages, and commissions	119,320	119,580
Federal, state, and municipal taxes	390,180	380,754
Pension plan contribution	65,554	3,946
Total current liabilities	$ 718,969	$ 639,147
Stockholders' equity:		
Capital stock—preferred	—	$ 458,400
Capital stock—common	$1,250,000	1,250,000
Reserves	—	145,840
Retained earnings (restricted by cost of stock in treasury)	1,996,818	1,663,005
	$3,246,818	$3,517,245
Less: Common stock in treasury at cost	260,594	60,907
Total stockholders' equity	2,986,224	3,456,338
Total liabilities and stockholders' equity	$3,705,193	$4,095,485

REQUIRED:

A. Based upon the limited information available, including the financial statements, comment upon the charges by the stockholders that long-range planning has been poor.

B. During 19X2, TST Corporation retired the outstanding preferred stock. Was this a wise long-range decision?

C. Prepare a set of recommendations to the company for long-range planning. Your recommendations should include how the company should set up a long-range plan, how the decision rule should be stated, and what criteria the company should use for evaluating long-range decisions.

9-43 The Gercken Corporation sells computer services to its clients. The company completed a feasibility study and decided to obtain an additional computer on January 1, 19X5. Information regarding the new computer follows.

1. The purchase price of the computer is $230,000. Maintenance, property taxes, and insurance will be $20,000 per year. If the computer is rented, the annual rent will be $85,000 plus 5% of annual billings. The rental price includes maintenance.

2. Due to competitive conditions, the company feels it will be necessary to replace the computer at the end of three years with one that is larger and more advanced. It is estimated that the computer will have a resale value of $110,000 at the end of the three years. The computer will be depreciated on a straight-line basis for both financial reporting and income tax purposes.

3. The income tax rate is 50%.

4. The estimated annual billing for the services of the new computer will be $220,000 during the first year and $260,000 during each of the second and third years. The estimated annual expense of operating the computer is $80,000, in addition to the expense mentioned above. An additional $10,000 of start-up expenses will be incurred during the first year.

5. If it decides to purchase the computer, the company will pay cash. If the computer is rented, the $230,000 can be otherwise invested at a 15% rate of return.

6. If the computer is purchased, the amount of the investment recovered during each of the three years can be reinvested immediately at a 15% rate of return. Each year's recovery of investment in the computer will have been reinvested for an average of six months by the end of the year.

7. The present value of $1 due at a constant rate during each year and discounted at 15% is:

Year	*Present Value*
0-1	$.93
1-2	$.80
2-3	$.69

The present value of $1 due at the end of each year and discounted at 15% is:

End of Year	*Present Value*
1	$.87
2	$.76
3	$.66

REQUIRED:

A. Prepare a schedule comparing the estimated annual income from the new computer under the purchase plan and under the rental plan. The comparison should include a provision for the opportunity cost of the average investment in the computer during each year.

B. Prepare a schedule showing the annual cash flows under the purchase plan and under the rental plan.

C. Prepare a schedule comparing the net present values of the cash flows under the purchase plan and under the rental plan.

D. Comment on the results obtained in parts A and C. How should the computer be financed? Why? *(CPA adapted)*

9-44 Use the data from the last requirement of problem 8-36 for the Thorne Transit Company.

A. Compute the following:
   1. Payback period
   2. Net present value
   3. Adjusted rate of return

B. Would you recommend the purchase of the large or small busses? Explain.

PART THREE

Planning and Control Systems for Decision Implementation

10 Budgeting: A Systematic Approach to Planning

THE PLANNING PROCESS
Goals
Objectives
Budgets
THE CONTROL PROCESS
Performance Budget
TIME DIMENSIONS OF BUDGETING
PREREQUISITES OF SUCCESSFUL BUDGETING
Support of Top Management
Clear-cut assignment of Authority and Responsibility
Responsibility Accounting
Types of Responsibility Centers
HUMAN ASPECTS OF BUDGETING
Excessive Pressure
Interdepartmental Conflict
Participation and Motivation
Slack
NEW APPROACHES TO BUDGETING
BUDGETING BY NOT-FOR-PROFIT ORGANIZATIONS
Traditional Budgeting
Program Budgeting
SUMMARY

The first nine chapters concentrated upon decisions that business managers make, both long-range and short-range, and the data relevant to these decisions. A decision involves change—an action in addition to or in place of past actions. Each decision has been treated as a unique, independent activity, but this approach can be misleading. In practice, each decision affects other areas in the operation. A pricing decision will affect the production volume; the production volume in Department A will affect the production volume of Department B; raw material purchases will affect not only the cost of production, but also the cash flow of the firm.

Management has the responsibility of coordinating its plans into an integrated whole. Without coordination the individual managers may actually work at cross-purposes; what seems to be a good decision from one department's point of view can be a bad decision from the standpoint of the total firm. One way to provide coordination is through the budget—a summary of the planned results of individual departmental decisions, expressed in financial terms. This chapter presents an overview of the budgeting process. In the next four chapters we will examine the more detailed aspects of a comprehensive budgeting program.

THE PLANNING PROCESS

The purpose of business planning is to reduce uncertainty about the future and, through coordination of plans, to increase the chances of making a satisfactory profit. Within a planning system is the basic assumption that management can plan its activities and, through these plans, manipulate or control the relevant variables that determine the destiny of the firm. Among the variables subject to control are employee quality and quantity, capital sources, product lines, production methods, and the cost structure of the firm. Other relevant variables affect the operations of the firm but are external to it. These are not subject to manipulation by management. Management can, however, anticipate the direction and magnitude of these variables to maximize their favorable consequences or minimize their unfavorable consequences. Examples of external variables not subject to control are population changes, national economic growth, competitive activities of other firms, and governmental action.

As stated in Chapter 1, the planning process begins with the establishment of the firm's goals. The action management takes to achieve these goals leads to decisions and, in turn, to the development of the budget. An illustration of the planning process and its interrelationship with the control process is presented in Exhibit 10-1. The budget is not only an expression of management's plans, but also a basis of comparison with actual results in the control process.

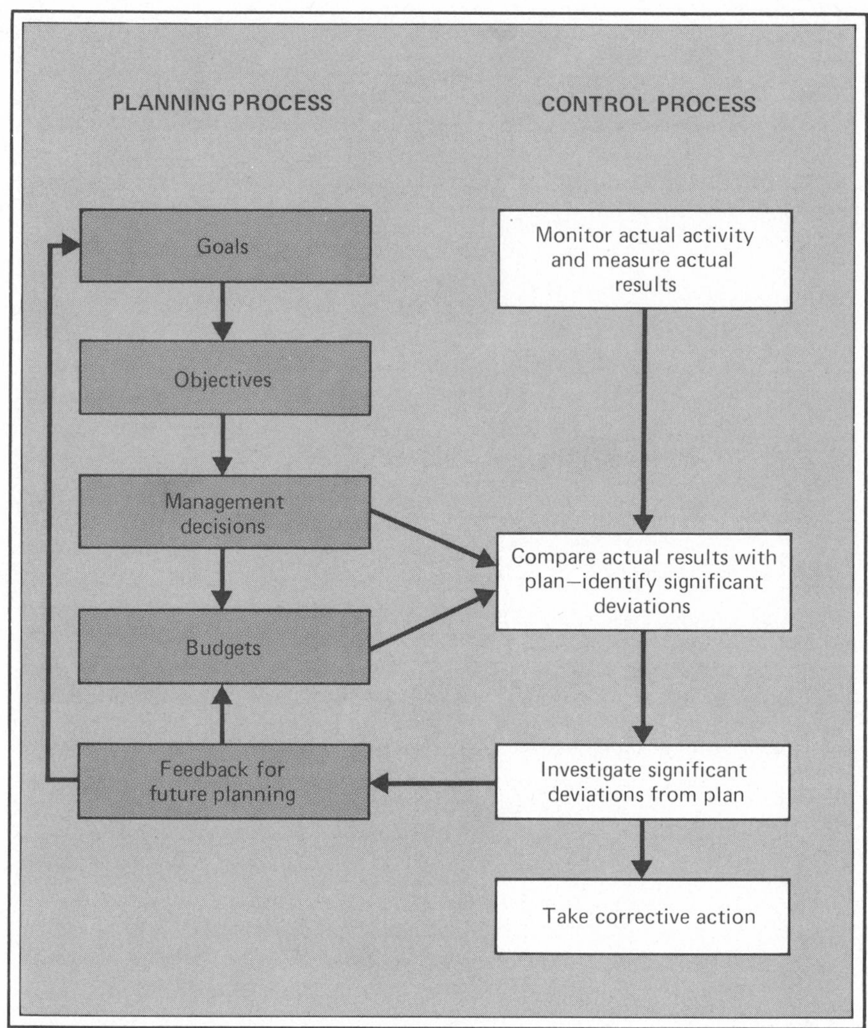

EXHIBIT 10-1
Planning and control process

Goals

Goals are statements of the desired position of the firm in the future. They are directional and motivational in nature and are seldom quantified. Generally, they are statements about the desired direction the relevant variables should take in determining the long-range destiny of the firm. A primary goal is survival of the firm. Survival, however, is dependent upon earning satisfactory profits. Thus, a fundamental goal is often stated as "an adequate profit to sustain the investment in the long run." Subgoals of this profit goal may include desired product lines, competitive position, and organizational structure. Other goals may be less profit-oriented, such as goals of community service, technological advancement, or political influence.

Objectives

Objectives provide a quantitative and time framework to the goals. They are specific performance targets and calendar dates by which desired accomplishments should be attained. For example, the profit *goal* may be to earn satisfactory profits across time so as to increase the value of the firm to the stockholders. The profit *objective,* however, may specify a 20% rate of return on investment, a 6% profit on sales, or, in some cases, a specific dollar amount of profit. Objectives provide targets that, if attained, will achieve the firm's goals.

Budgets

In a business enterprise a **budget** is the formal statement of management's plans and objectives expressed in financial terms for a specific future period of time. The budget permeates every level of activity, integrating revenue plans, expense plans, asset requirements, and financing needs. The comprehensive master budget includes and unifies each manager's activities. This coordinating role is a major, if not *the* major, function of the budget. In most firms there are many decision makers; failure to bring their plans into congruence with the firm's objectives can result in each manager's marching to a different drummer. The budget may be thought of as the network that ties the decisions of the subsystems into a firm-wide system.

BASIC FUNCTIONS OF THE BUDGET

There are five major functions of a budgetary system: forecasting, planning, authorization, performance measurement, and communication.

Forecasting

The budget is based upon an economic forecast of the coming period. **Forecasting** involves projection. Management must forecast the relevant variables that are not subject to the control or manipulation of the firm. By reducing uncertainty about these noncontrollable variables, management may develop plans to take advantage of their favorable consequences or to minimize the impact of their unfavorable consequences. For example, if the sales of the firm depend upon the amount of consumer disposable income, the firm will build its plans upon a forecast of consumer disposable income. If a forecast projects a decrease in consumer disposable income next year, the firm may develop plans to minimize its losses.

Planning

Planning is actively involved in decision making. The final plan expresses the intent to accomplish certain desired results. The plans of action reflected in the budget are management decisions translated into their specific impacts. Since the budget is a financial plan, the activities must be translated into dollars—dollars of resource inputs and outputs. Thus, the budget is a culmination, in dollar terms, of management's proposed decisions.

Authorization

The budget can represent a formal authorization to use or acquire resources or to undertake the activities necessary to accomplish the firm's goals. In governmental planning this function is very important; here the budget sets forth the maximum spending limits that managers may not legally exceed. The authorization role, paramount in governmental budgeting, is less important in business, where the budget provides a target, rather than a legalistic maximum.

Performance measurement

The budget provides a basis for measuring the performance of management. It reflects what management *expects* to accomplish in financial terms and may be compared with actual results. The budget is not the only possible performance measure, however. Many performance objectives, particularly those that cannot be quantified in dollars, are not included in the budget. The budget is a *total* plan of the firm's operations, designed to coordinate activities for the coming time period and provide objectives for performance measurement.

Communication

One of the major functions of the budget is to communicate the goals, objectives, and plans of management throughout the firm. The budget communicates expectations. Then, coupled with feedback reports it provides a basis for comparing actual results with planned results to bring the expectancies into being. The process of preparing and disseminating formal planning and feedback reports can be a major communication vehicle in a firm, as well as a basis for management control.

DEFINITION OF BUDGETING TERMS

Firms differ in their use of budgetary terms; each uses the terms that best communicate to its employees. The terms to be used in this text follow.

Master Budget

The **master budget** is expressed in financial terms and sets out management's plans for the operations and resources of the firm for a given period of time. The term *budget* alone usually refers to the master budget, a comprehensive document with many component schedules or sub-budgets. Exhibit 10-2 presents an illustration of interrelationships of the subcomponents of a master budget. The master budget is usually presented in four parts: a *profit plan* for operations, a *cash budget,* a *projected statement of financial position,* and a *capital expenditures budget.* Supporting schedules or budgets are prepared for all the necessary inputs, such as purchases of material and the costs of the various areas of responsibility. The supporting schedules should present data in as much detail and from as many different dimensions as management considers useful and economically feasible.

Profit Plan

The **profit plan** is the operating plan detailing revenue, expenses, and the resulting net income for a specific period of time. The format is usually a projected income statement. The profit plan reflects the results of the short-range decision models. It is the firm's optimal plan in light of management's expectations of the future. It is a **static budget** because only one level of sales activity is expected; all other plans are based on that level. The profit plan should be detailed by areas of responsibility within the firm and by other significant dimensions, such as product lines and sales territories.

Cash Budget

A critical resource in the firm is cash. Advance knowledge of cash needs allows the firm to provide for optimal liquidity and to find the best way of financing the business. The **cash budget** converts all planned actions into cash inflows and cash outflows. Management can thus see its plans in terms of their cash impact. With knowledge of future cash status, management can plan expense payments, credit policies, the timing of capital additions, and borrowing needs.

Projected Statement of Financial Position

The **projected statement of financial position** is a formal statement of the resources of the firm and their sources at the *end* of the budget period. The interrelationship of profit planning and resource planning is presented in

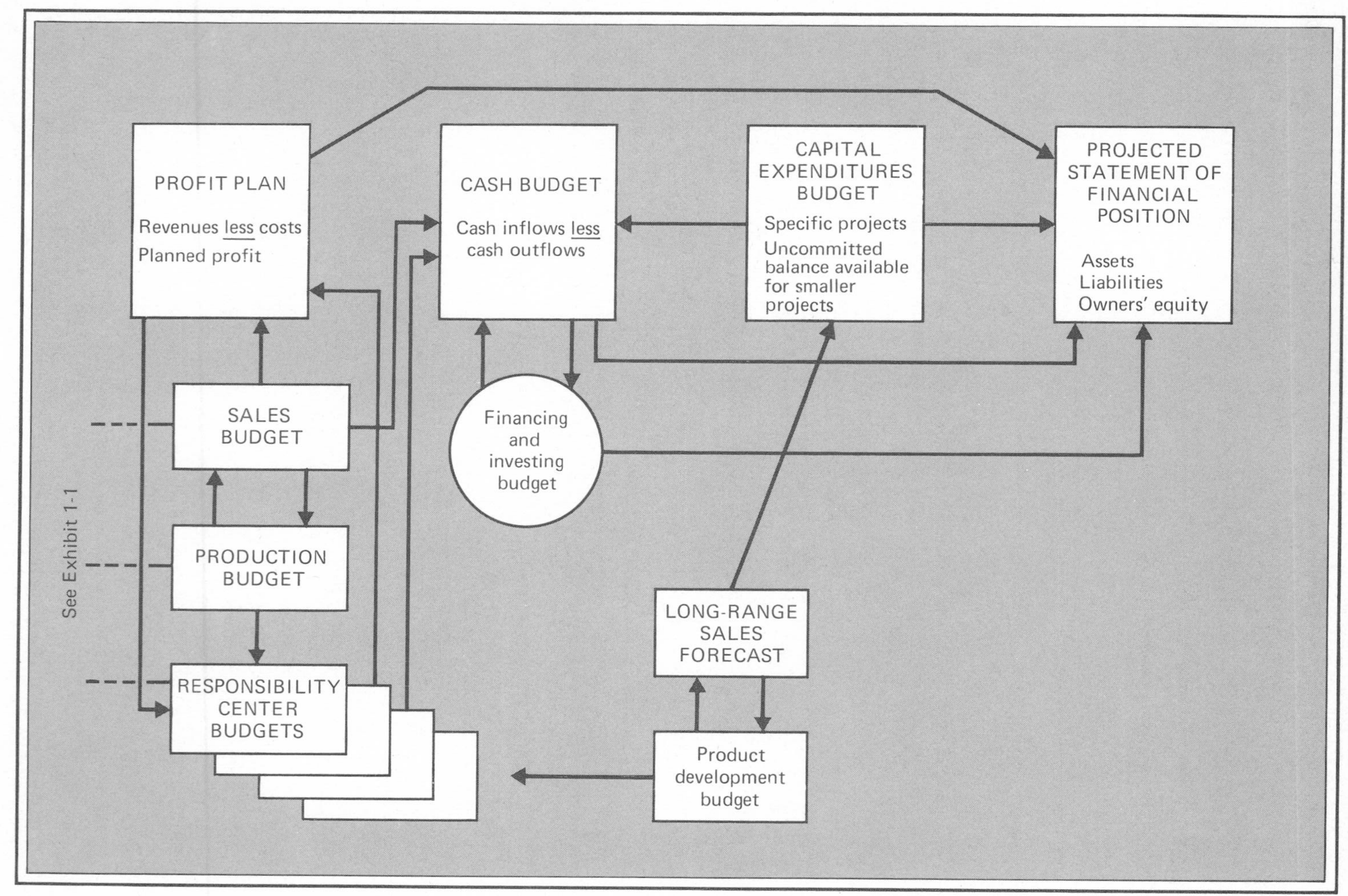

EXHIBIT 10-2
Interrelationships of subcomponents of master budget

Exhibit 10-2. The projected balances of the assets and liabilities for the projected statement of financial position are by-products of the profit plan and cash budget.

Capital Expenditures Budget

The **capital expenditures budget** is a formal list of all approved plans for the procurement or disposition of productive assets. The budgeting process for capital expenditures differs from that of the profit plan and other parts of the master plan. Capital expenditures are approved by *individual project* throughout the year as the need and opportunity arise. As proposals are developed in the organization they are screened; those which meet the long-range decision rules are ranked in order of desirability. Final approval comes from an investment committee, often the board of directors. Many worthwhile projects may not be approved because funds are not available.

Instead of listing all specific projects, the capital expenditures budget may identify only the large projects that require a long lead time, such as a new plant or a large piece of equipment. The remainder of the capital expenditure budget may be presented as a lump sum of funds available for smaller projects. Each manager is then given authorization to approve projects of limited amounts, with an annual maximum. For example, a foreman may approve purchases of tools or small equipment of less than $100, with an annual limit of $1,000, while the plant manager may approve capital expenditures up to $1,000, with an annual limit of $10,000.

THE CONTROL PROCESS

One of the basic functions of budgeting is to provide a benchmark for controlling actual performance, as shown in Exhibit 10-1. The control process involves a number of steps. First, the accounting system monitors actual performance in financial terms. A complete control system will provide actual results for each area of responsibility.

Second, actual performance is compared with the plan and any significant deviations from the plan are identified. The principle of **management by exception** suggests that as long as operations conform with the plan, the activity is in control and no intervention is required. Only exceptional or significant variances require management action. Where possible, control limits that represent the range of normal deviations from plan should be developed for each variable measured.

Third, there must be a feedback mechanism, through reports to management, to inform operating management of deviations from plans. Ideally, feedback is made as soon as possible after the activity is performed.

Fourth, action may be required. Where there is a deviation from the plan, corrective action should be taken to bring all future activities in line with the plan. Action may involve enforcing existing policies, retraining employees, or changing the manufacturing process. If the deviation is a result of a plan that is unrealistic or incorrect, the plan may have to be revised.

Performance Budget

The planned level of activity will seldom be achieved exactly. When the actual level of performance differs from planned performance, the **performance budget** is prepared *after the fact* to show what revenues and costs should have been at the *actual* level of activity. For performance measurement purposes it would be inappropriate to use a profit plan based upon a level of activity that differs from the actual activity level. The performance budget is the flexible budget, as discussed in Chapter 2, adjusted to the actual level attained. For example, if a plant expected to produce 5,000 units per month but, because of declining markets or shortages of materials, produced only 4,000 units, the profit plan with revenues and costs based upon 5,000 units would not be an appropriate measurement base. A performance budget showing the revenues and costs that should have been incurred at 4,000 units is better for evaluating actual performance.

The relationships among the profit plan, the performance budget, and actual results are presented in Exhibit 10-3. The profit plan was based upon planned activity priced at budgeted prices and costs. In Exhibit 10-3, the original profit plan called for selling 5,000 units of finished product at an average selling price of $10 per unit. The budgeted variable cost of production was $4 per unit and fixed costs were budgeted at $20,000. Planned income was therefore $10,000.

A shortage of raw materials developed during the period and the company could only produce 4,000 units. Because of the material shortage, the company incurred an additional $.50 per unit in production costs. The company also increased selling prices by an average of $1 per unit. To modify production processes in order to meet material shortages, the company invested $1,000 in research and development. As a result of the changes, actual income for the period was only $5,000, an unfavorable deviation of $5,000 from the plan.

A performance budget was prepared for the actual 4,000-unit level to aid in measuring performance and to explain the $5,000 deviation in income. The performance budget was based on *planned* selling prices and costs. Income in the performance budget is $4,000. The difference in the contribution margin between the profit plan and the performance budget is an **activity variance.** The unfavorable activity variable is $6,000 (1,000 units below plan × planned contribution margin per unit of $6 = $6,000) and reflects the contribution margin of the lost sales. The difference between the performance budget and the actual results is explained by favorable selling price variances (increased selling price of $1 × 4,000 units sold = $4,000),

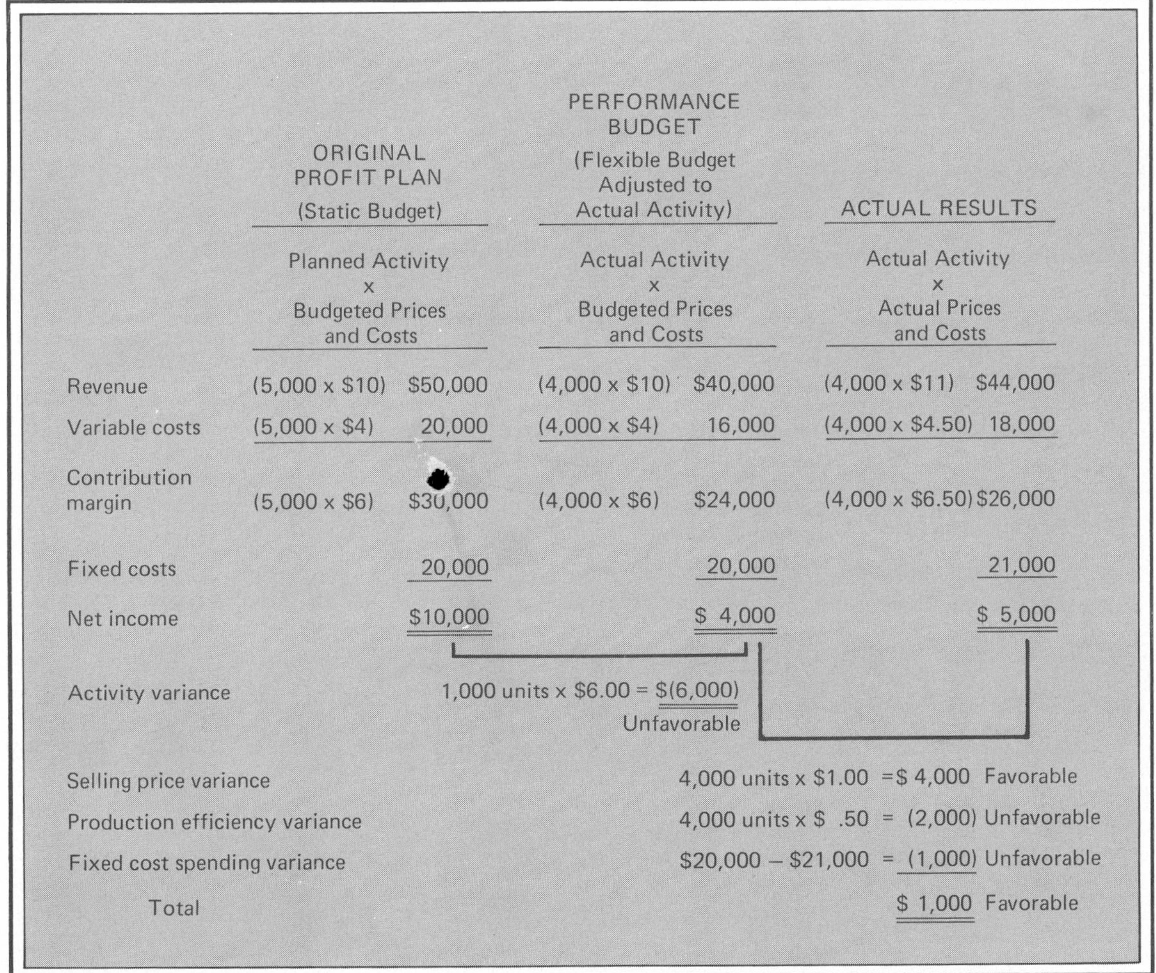

	ORIGINAL PROFIT PLAN (Static Budget)		PERFORMANCE BUDGET (Flexible Budget Adjusted to Actual Activity)		ACTUAL RESULTS	
	Planned Activity x Budgeted Prices and Costs		Actual Activity x Budgeted Prices and Costs		Actual Activity x Actual Prices and Costs	
Revenue	(5,000 x $10)	$50,000	(4,000 x $10)	$40,000	(4,000 x $11)	$44,000
Variable costs	(5,000 x $4)	20,000	(4,000 x $4)	16,000	(4,000 x $4.50)	18,000
Contribution margin	(5,000 x $6)	$30,000	(4,000 x $6)	$24,000	(4,000 x $6.50)	$26,000
Fixed costs		20,000		20,000		21,000
Net income		$10,000		$ 4,000		$ 5,000

Activity variance	1,000 units x $6.00 = $(6,000)	Unfavorable
Selling price variance	4,000 units x $1.00 = $ 4,000	Favorable
Production efficiency variance	4,000 units x $ .50 = (2,000)	Unfavorable
Fixed cost spending variance	$20,000 – $21,000 = (1,000)	Unfavorable
Total	$ 1,000	Favorable

EXHIBIT 10-3
Performance budget for control

unfavorable variable cost variances (increased variable production costs of $.50 × 4,000 units = $2,000), and an unfavorable fixed cost variance (planned fixed costs of $20,000 – actual fixed costs $21,000 = $1,000).

A summary of these variances is presented in Exhibit 10-4, the summary **report on profit plan.** It explains the difference between planned income of $10,000 and actual income of $5,000 by identifying the casual factors and the areas of responsibility. This report is different from the report in Exhibit 10-3 because only the variances are presented.

Planned income (from profit plan)	$10,000
Activity variance (lost contribution margin due to shortage of materials)	(6,000)
Selling price variance (increased selling price of $1 per unit)	4,000
Variable cost variance (increased production costs of $.50 per unit)	(2,000)
Fixed cost variance (new research program to develop raw materials and processes)	(1,000)
Actual income (from income statement)	$ 5,000

EXHIBIT 10-4
Summary report on profit plan

TIME DIMENSIONS OF BUDGETING

Exhibit 10-5 illustrates the time dimension of budgeting. The *vertical* columns relate to particular periods of time (in this case, years) for which operating plans and resource budgets are prepared. The *horizontal* rows relate to long-range decisions for specific projects. The horizontal row entitled *continuing operations* represents the operating activities of completed long-range decisions for sales, production, and distribution. When selected Projects A, B, and C were undertaken in previous years, each became an unidentifiable part of continuing operations. Let's assume these projects involved machines on an assembly line used to manufacture several different products. Once Machine A was installed, separate accountability was lost; its costs and revenues were commingled with other activities. The same was true of Machines B and C. Other projects, such as Project D, maintain their identity and accountability for revenues and costs. An example of a project that would maintain its identity is the acquisition of a separate operating division in another geographic location, intended to provide diversity to the company. In the time-dimensional plan, Project D was added in a previous year and is expected to be replaced by Project F in five years. Project E is included in the capital expenditures budget for next year. The vertical columns represent horizons, in years. The master budget, shown in the year 1 column, includes the profit plan and resources budget for the next year. Typically the master budget will be prepared with month-by-month detail. Many firms also prepare a long-range profit plan and resources budget for the next few years (in our example,

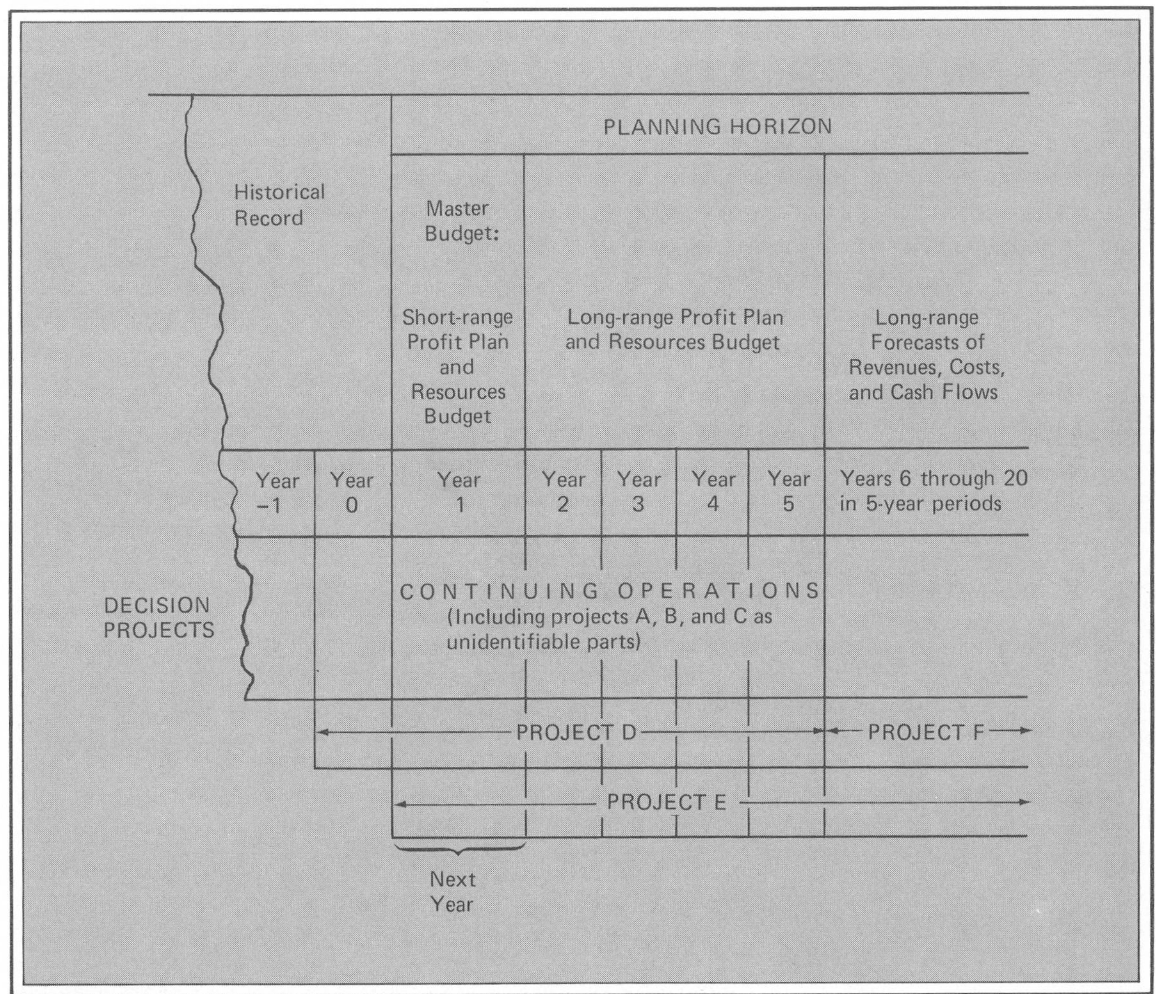

EXHIBIT 10-5
Time dimensions of budgeting

four years), but in considerably less detail than the master budget. Finally, many firms prepare long-range budgets far into the future. These are shown in the last vertical column. In one way these plans represent a broad statement of the firm's objectives in financial terms. They identify the need for new products, new plants, and other changes that may require long lead times. The long-range planning horizon for many companies, such as those involved in natural resources, is very long—often 50 to 100 years.

PREREQUISITES OF SUCCESSFUL BUDGETING

A good budgetary program has many requisites, including the support of top management, a good organizational structure, and a flexible accounting system. In this section we will look at some of these essentials.

Support of Top Management

A successful budgetary system must have the support of top management, whose cost consciousness is fundamental to effective cost control. Behavioral research has shown that the subordinates of a manager who is cost conscious will be approximately three times more cost conscious than the subordinates of a manager who is not.[1]

In addition to developing a positive attitude, management must devote the necessary resources to budget preparation. A designated executive must be held responsible for budget preparation. In most successful budgeting settings, this officer does not prepare the budget. Rather, he coordinates the planning effort with the responsibility of ensuring that managers meet their deadlines and prepare their plans.

Invariably, there will be conflict among the responsibility centers over resource allocations and differences among the goals of individual units and the organization as a whole. A budget committee will often be used to reconcile interdepartmental conflicts and ensure that corporate goals and objectives prevail.

Clear-cut Assignment of Authority and Responsibility

A proper organizational structure is one of the essentials of good management and good budgeting. A definite plan must be established to clearly identify the responsibility and authority of each manager. To be effective, management's plans must be in accordance with assigned responsibilities; performance must be measured in terms of these responsibilities. If the formal budgetary process does not accumulate data that reflects the actual patterns of authority, the planning and control system cannot succeed. Managers would be held accountable for activities over which they had no control.

The particular organizational structure chosen will depend upon the nature of the operation and top management's style of leadership. Some firms select a formal line-staff structure, whereas others choose a more informal pattern. Whatever the arrangement, the planning and control system must be based upon the organizational structure actually in existence.

[1]G. H. Hofstede, *The Game of Budget Control* (New York: Van Nostrand, 1967).

Responsibility Accounting

Effective control systems are structured around the implicit or explicit areas of responsibility within the organization. Responsibility areas may be departments (drilling department or maintenance department), product lines (pickles or mustard), territories (West or South), or any other type of identifiable unit or combination of units. The specific types of responsibility areas will depend upon the nature of the firm and its activities.

Reports are prepared for each level of management, from the departmental foreman up to the company president. Ideally, the reporting system will be tailored to the relevant organization level and the particular individual involved. Budgetary reports should include the specific revenues and costs over which the manager has control. A cost or benefit is controllable by an individual if it is directly affected by his decisions, regardless of how the cost or benefit is actually accounted for within the data system. For example, if a salesperson accepts a rush order that requires exceptional production costs, such as additional setups and overtime, the cost report for his marketing unit should bear the additional production costs. The production department has no control over the delivery date that gave rise to the additional costs. Care must be taken, however; excessive zeal in pinpointing responsibility may lead to interdepartmental conflict that is more detrimental to the company than lack of control over the particular cost. Where control is shared, the assignment of responsibility must be decided by the superior who is responsible for the common activity. One overriding principle is that arbitrary allocations of costs should not enter into a responsibility cost system.

Exhibit 10-6 illustrates cost responsibility. A simplified organization chart shows the organizational relationships; the cost reports show the controllable costs at each level. As the reports are prepared for each higher level in the organization, costs are summarized for the subordinates' areas of responsibility.

Types of Responsibility Centers

In a small firm the manager can personally supervise all decisions and their implementation. He has first-hand knowledge of each activity. However, as the business grows the manager can no longer directly supervise each event and transaction. Growing firms are subdivided into meaningful segments, departments, or divisions. Each subdivision should have responsibility for a specific group of activities and its manager should be responsible for his decisions affecting these activities. One of the requisites for a control system is the development of data relevant to the responsibilities of the individual manager.

We are using the term *responsibility center* in a broad sense. It could be as small as an individual machine or as large as the Chevrolet division of

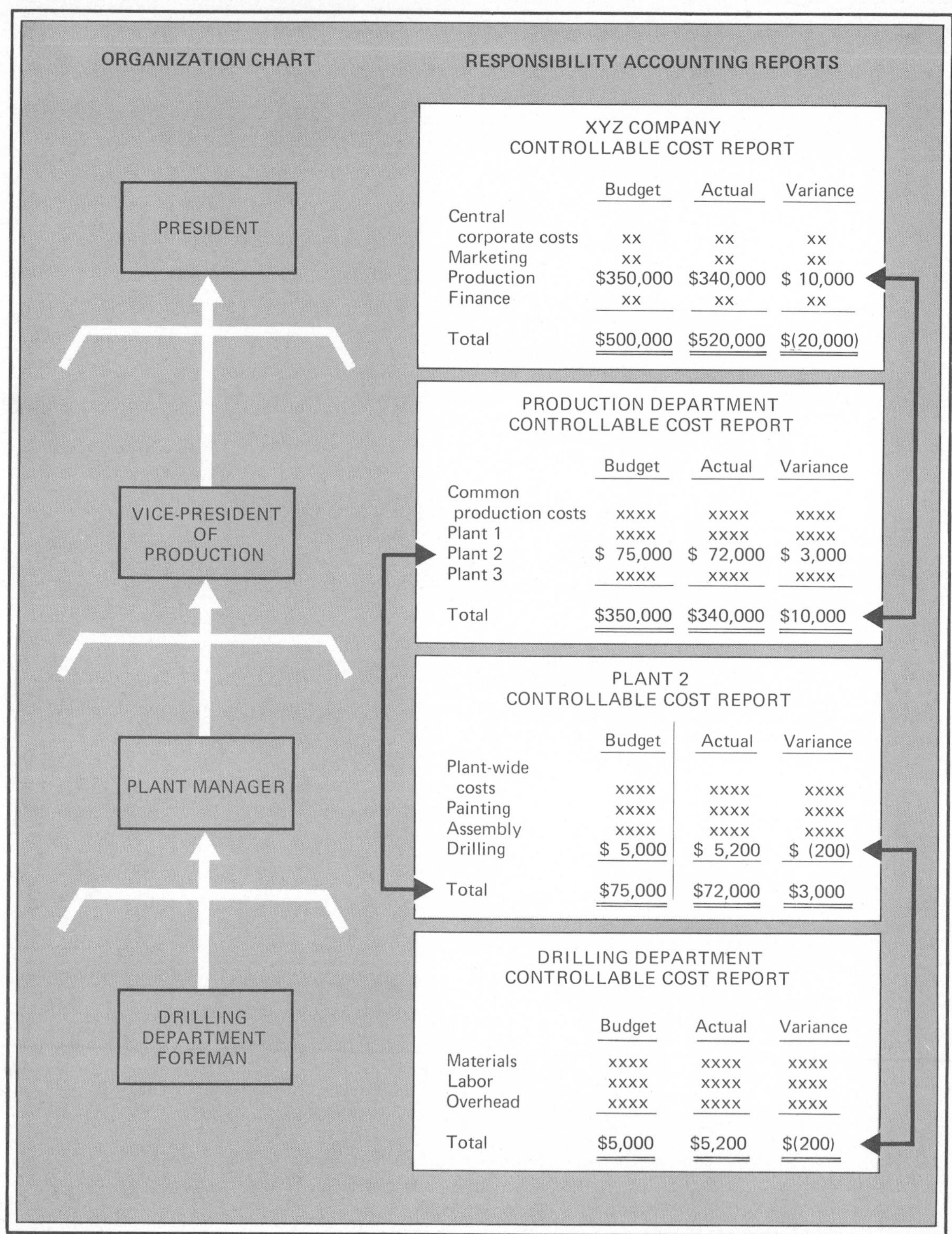

ORGANIZATION CHART
RESPONSIBILITY ACCOUNTING REPORTS
PRESIDENT
VICE-PRESIDENT OF PRODUCTION
PLANT MANAGER
DRILLING DEPARTMENT FOREMAN
XYZ COMPANY
CONTROLLABLE COST REPORT
Budget Actual Variance
Central corporate costs xx xx xx
Marketing xx xx xx
Production $350,000 $340,000 $ 10,000
Finance xx xx xx
Total $500,000 $520,000 $(20,000)
PRODUCTION DEPARTMENT
CONTROLLABLE COST REPORT
Budget Actual Variance
Common production costs xxxx xxxx xxxx
Plant 1 xxxx xxxx xxxx
Plant 2 $ 75,000 $ 72,000 $ 3,000
Plant 3 xxxx xxxx xxxx
Total $350,000 $340,000 $10,000
PLANT 2
CONTROLLABLE COST REPORT
Budget Actual Variance
Plant-wide costs xxxx xxxx xxxx
Painting xxxx xxxx xxxx
Assembly xxxx xxxx xxxx
Drilling $ 5,000 $ 5,200 $ (200)
Total $75,000 $72,000 $3,000
DRILLING DEPARTMENT
CONTROLLABLE COST REPORT
Budget Actual Variance
Materials xxxx xxxx xxxx
Labor xxxx xxxx xxxx
Overhead xxxx xxxx xxxx
Total $5,000 $5,200 $(200)

EXHIBIT 10-6
Responsibility accounting reporting system

General Motors. It could be a sales department in a department store, a service department, a specific production line, a warehouse unit, a group of salesmen, or a tax section in the accounting department. Size is not the criterion for development of a responsibility center. The important criteria are (1) that a subdivision relevant to operating performance is separable and identifiable and (2) that there are relevant measures of performance.

For financial planning and control, accountants usually classify responsibility centers into three classes: cost centers, profit or contribution margin centers, and investment centers. Each class has different characteristics regarding the financial data available for performance assessment.

COST CENTERS

A **cost center** is a responsibility center where costs (expenses) are the principal planning and control data. Performance is assessed by comparing the actual expenses with the performance budget, which shows the expenses the center should have incurred, given their actual activity. Any variances between actual and budgeted expenses are the primary focus of management assessment. In firms where the budgetary process is underdeveloped, the control data may consist of a comparison of current expenses with past expenses.

It is difficult to assess the effectiveness and efficiency of a cost center, even with a budget, because the financial impact of decisions is measured only by costs. There is no corresponding *financial* measure of what the cost center accomplished. If not done carefully, the analysis of a cost center may lead to the assumption that "the best cost center is the one that spends the least." This attitude ignores benefits contributed by the cost center to the overall firm.

Because there are no financial benefits traced to cost centers, most firms mix financial and nonfinancial data in performance assessment. The consumption of the department is measured in financial terms—costs, whereas the benefits are measured in nonfinancial terms—number of units produced, number of customers waited on, or number of invoices processed, for example. It is impossible to determine whether the efficiency of the cost center is acceptable without relating the financial and nonfinancial data. Comparison with the budget will tell whether actual performance conformed with planned expenditures, but it will not tell whether this performance was effective. It is possible that the budget was built upon less than optimal assumptions or that circumstances actually faced were significantly different than budgeted circumstances.

Profit or Contribution Margin Centers

In a **profit center,** or **contribution margin center,** both cost and revenue data are measurable in financial terms, providing greater scope in assessing performance. The profit center is more sophisticated, in terms of management planning and control potential, than a cost center, where only costs are measurable. Outputs as well as inputs may be measured in a profit center, allowing assessment of its ability to earn a "satisfactory profit."

The key to profit-center control systems is the determination of **controllable** and **noncontrollable** activities. Because the manager of a profit center should be held accountable only for the revenues and costs he can control through his decisions, the allocation of indirect costs should be avoided. A department manager has no control over the *costs* of the service departments (although he may have control over the quantity of services consumed). The inclusion of an allocated portion of service department costs will only confuse the issue. Accordingly, many firms prefer to think in terms of contribution margin centers rather than profit centers. In a contribution margin center the manager's controllable costs are deducted from his controllable revenue. The resulting contribution margin is his contribution to the firm's joint costs and, ultimately, net income.

Implicit to the profit center concept is the assumption that a manager's economic decisions affect the profits of his division. Thus, there can be an effective assignment of responsibility for both costs and revenues. Second, it is assumed that an increase in the profit center's net income will act to increase the net income of the firm. Without this implied relationship, a manager could optimize his division's net income to the detriment of the firm's net income. Third, and very important, is the assumption that the profit center's activities are not significantly dependent upon the actions of the other divisions. There must be some autonomy. In a sense, the profit center is viewed as a separate, identifiable firm. Finally, it is important that divisional profits be a fair measure of each center's contribution to the firm's net income. For this reason, the allocation of noncontrollable joint costs would be detrimental.

INVESTMENT CENTERS

In an **investment center,** performance is measured not only by net income, but also by relating this net income to the asset investment. The investment center concept allows an assessment of the efficiency of investment utilization; the rate of return on investment may be used in performance evaluation. Investment centers are treated as individual businesses where the manager is responsible for all activities—costs, revenues, and investments.

In Chapters 12, 13, and 14 are examples of budgeting and control reporting for cost centers and profit centers. In Chapter 15 investment centers are studied more closely.

HUMAN ASPECTS OF BUDGETING

There is a tendency to overemphasize the mechanical aspects of the budgetary system and expect it to work without regard to the interpersonal relationships implied therein. However, goals and objectives are achieved through people. It is important that we examine the effects of budgets on people and the effects of people on the budget. The human element is an extremely complex issue; oversimplification is easy in our brief discussion. A review of behavioral research literature reveals that the studies have raised more questions regarding human behavior than they have answered.

Early budgetary literature adopted a mechanical and materialistic view of human behavior. This view of the behavior of workers and managers was based upon a number of assumptions:

1. Employees are primarily motivated by monetary rewards.
2. Work is an unpleasant task and people avoid work whenever possible.
3. Human beings are ordinarily inefficient and wasteful.
4. There is one best way of behaving and this can be discovered through research and taught to individuals.[2]

These assumptions led to the belief that responsibility had to be established and external pressure applied to achieve the desired results. In practice, a high level of performance through budgets has often been accompanied by several unfavorable consequences, including excessive pressure on employees, hostility toward the budget, and conflict among departments.[3]

Excessive Pressure

Behavioral research has provided some information on the effects of pressure in the management process. It appears that individuals and groups work best with some kind of pressure. One researcher[4] found that when benchmarks are too loose, motivation diminishes; as they are tightened, motivation increases. However, when a benchmark becomes too tight, motivation is poor. Another researcher[5] found the results of empirical findings to indicate that established performance requirements should be achievable not more than 40% of the time, but not less than 25% of the time. It would be inappropriate to treat these percentages as irrefutable facts, but it is clear that the degree of difficulty encountered by workers to attain the planned activity level will have a motivational impact.

Responsibility accounting identifies individual responsibility for budgeted costs and deviations from plan. Management by exception implies

[2]E. H. Caplan, *Management Accounting and Behavioral Science* (Reading, Mass.: Addison-Wesley, 1971).

[3]Chris Argyris, "Human Problems with Budgets," *Harvard Business Review* (January–February, 1953.).

[4]Hofstede, *Game of Budget Control.*

[5]R. L. M. Dunbar, "Budgeting for Control," *Administrative Science Quarterly* (March, 1971), pp. 88–96.

that significant deviations from the plan will cause the superior to exert pressure for correction. Excessive pressure can effect growing antagonism toward the budget. It is possible for a firm to create a situation where budgetary success means failure for worker and managers. This state can completely negate the planning and coordinating function of the budget; the budget becomes something to be feared.

Interdepartmental conflict

Responsibility accounting focuses attention upon limited areas of responsibility and tends to cause managers to overemphasize departmental goals. The lower-line managers may attempt to direct budgetary pressure away from themselves by shifting the blame to other departments. This departmental overemphasis can operate against the organization's goals and objectives.

Participation and Motivation

Participation by the managers in preparing the budget has been advocated as a way to increase employee motivation and reduce organizational conflict. The call for such participation is widespread in accounting literature. Most current management theorists and management accountants believe that employee initiative, performance, and morale are increased with employee participation. The value of participation rapidly becomes interwoven with the theory of organizational structures.

Caplan[6] classified the types of organizational structures and their effects upon accounting into two extremes. The "classical" organization emphasizes profit maximization, formal and hierarchical structure, economic rewards, and the inherent laziness and inefficiency of employees. The "modern" organization is characterized by coalitions of individuals who are adaptive problem-solvers, motivated by a variety of psychological, social, and economic drives and needs. The modern organization certainly appears to be more conducive to true employee participation.

One indication of an organization encouraging active employee participation is the existence of good superior-subordinate relationships fostered by (1) frequent person-to-person contacts; (2) the use of results in performance appraisal; (3) the use of departmental meetings to review actual results; and (4) the creation of a "game" spirit (margin for error, tolerance, and slack).[7]

[6]Caplan, *Management Accounting and Behavioral Science.*

[7]Hofstede, *Game of Budget Control.*

A closer look at this list provides further insights into the planning and control process. First, participation is achieved on a personal basis. A formal, indirect mode of communication creates the danger of pseudoparticipation. Pseudoparticipation, which pretends to be participation but it is not, is a form of deceit; the result can be a decrease in motivation. Second, the achievement of the goal or budget should bear directly upon the reward received by the employee. Further, direct, clear feedback allows the employee to adjust his aspiration level and strive to achieve his desired reward. Finally, a certain amount of leeway, termed *slack,* gives the employee some freedom of movement and action. It keeps employee pressure at an accepted level.

Slack

An individual in an organization is motivated to achieve two sets of goals: personal and organizational. A manager's personal goals within the organization may relate to his income, status, size of staff, or discretionary control over the allocation of resources. Where a budget serves to measure performance, a manager will strive to set his budget at a level that allows him an excellent chance of attainment and still meets top management's objectives. As a means of avoiding the stigma attached to failure, a manager will attempt to introduce a cushion, or slack.

Slack can be thought of as a budgetary lubricant. Some slack is necessary to reduce friction between individual and organizational goals and to give managers room to perform. It has been shown that success causes people to raise their levels of aspiration and that aspirations are lowered by failure. The provision of slack is one way employees attempt to avoid failure.

Every firm operates with slack; perfection of the traditional economic model is not possible. Resources cannot be perfectly allocated. The treasurer introduces slack by maintaining excessive cash balances; division management understates sales projections; line management requests employee positons that will be filled only as budgetary expectations are met; and manufacturing costs are based on estimates that do not reflect improvements. Slack tends to grow in good years, when satisfactory profits are easily attainable; in bad years slack is voluntarily decreased throughout the firm. Cost-cutting campaigns are attempts to reduce the excessive slack that will jeopardize long-run profit objectives of the firm through inefficiency. Too much pressure to reduce slack will create conflict in the system and may result in system failure. The solution is to find a level of slack that maintains efficiency and avoids the conflict caused by excessive pressure.

NEW APPROACHES TO BUDGETING

This overview and the four chapters that follow use an **iterative** (sequence of steps) approach to budgeting. Tentative projections made by operating divisions undergo any necessary revision as the budget is coordinated and resource needs are compared with available resources. For example, a change in the sales estimate or product mix will require revision of many budget schedules. A pervasive change is a costly process.

Recent advancements in firm modeling have provided mathematical techniques for budgeting, including linear programming. Introduced in Chapter 7 as a solution to product mix problems, linear programming may also be used to develop a model of the budgetary process. For example, in setting the budget subsystem for production, the inventory and financing decisions would provide constraints to the linear programming model. The model provides an optimal set of resource levels, given management's objectives. The set of resource levels may then be translated into a master budget. A real advantage of linear programming is that, as a by-product of the model, we can see the impact upon the resources when we vary the constraints. The use of a linear programming model requires mathematical skills and computer capabilities not possessed by many companies and is beyond the scope of this text.

Another modeling advancement that is rapidly gaining popularity is the computerized simulation of a firm. **Simulation** is a natural extension of the traditional budgeting process. First, a mathematical statement of the interrelationship of accounts is developed. Then, a simulation model is used to incorporate the relationships among the variables affecting the budget. As an example, a food-processing firm developed a successful profit planning system using a computerized simulation model. The firm's major product was pickles. After testing several different combinations of cucumber sizes on costs and profit to determine the best product mix, it was then able to contract growers to produce the sizes and varieties that provided the optimal input. After the profit plan was adopted, the impact of any changes in the relevant variables, such as crop shortages due to bad weather, rising costs, or changes in consumer demand, could be tested quickly. It is not economically possible to determine the impact of similar changes in a traditional, manually prepared profit plan.

Further discussion of these mathematical approaches to budgeting is beyond the scope of this book. It should be clear, however, that a computerized model of the budgetary process can improve the planning process. By including more variables and examining more alternatives, the firm should not only reach a better plan, but should also be better able to react to external changes.

BUDGETING BY NOT-FOR-PROFIT ORGANIZATIONS

All organizations in both private and public sectors must plan their activities and make decisions about how to allocate resources. The objective of accounting data collection is to provide economic information useful to decision makers; the objective of budget preparation is to integrate these decisions. Historically, the accounting and budgeting systems used by not-for-profit organizations have focused upon administrative control of funds and have provided little, if any, information useful to decision makers. Recently, changes in budgeting and accounting have taken place, particularly at the state and local level, with the development and implementation of program budgeting. In this section we will examine budgeting practices for not-for-profit organizations, principally local governmental units.

Traditional Budgeting

All goverment acts must be authorized by law. The collection of cash must conform with constitutional and statutory authority and the expenditure of cash must be specifically authorized through an approved budget. In the public sector the budget is not only an expression of the decision process. Once approved, it is also the legal ceiling of expenditures. In a profit-oriented firm the budget is a guide, not a law.

Not-for-profit organizations and, in particular, governments utilize an entity concept in administrative controls. A separate entity, called a *fund,* is created for each type of activity. For example, the city motor pool may be treated as a separate entity for accounting purposes. It has its own budget, separate accounting records, often a separate bank account, and independent financial statements. The number and nature of funds will depend upon the law and upon administrative needs for control, but it is not uncommon for small cities to have eight to ten separate funds nor for large cities to have funds numbering in the hundreds.

The traditional budget and accounting system presents information in two dimensions. First, expenditures are accumulated by the object of expenditure; that is, the input for which the expenditure was made. Personnel, travel, supplies, and contractual services are a few examples of objects of expenditure. The second dimension involves the organizational units of the government. Examples include the fire department, the police department, and the parks department.

Program Budgeting

Prior to the early 1960s, evaluation of the benefits and costs of governmental programs was unusual. Capital expenditure decisions were often based on the first-year costs, with no consideration of subsequent operating costs. During the 1960s a new approach to budgeting in the public sector was developed. The new system, called *Planning, Programming, Budgeting System,* or **program budgeting** for short, focuses upon the output of the organization rather than specific inputs.

At the local level, program budgets have enjoyed widespread public acceptance because they focus on services and outputs that are meaningful to the average citizen, rather than on organizations and inputs. Decision makers at the local government level can compare alternative programs and allocate resources to those programs that will produce the greatest return for the funds invested. Before the emergence of program budgeting, budget deliberations often centered upon the number of additional personnel to be added to the payroll or the type of machinery to be purchased. With program budgeting, the discussion has moved to consideration of a service at a cost that can be afforded.

Program budgeting cuts across organizational lines and requires three dimensions of information: information on output (important for decisions); information on organizational activities (important for control—responsibility accounting); and information on inputs (salaries, materials, etc.). Industry has long dealt with these three dimensions. The public sector has not previously addressed itself to the output dimension and it has been necessary to establish new patterns of thinking about efficiency.

Program budgeting has several distinguishing characteristics:

1. Development of a program structure with a statement of goals and objectives for each program
2. Multiyear costing
3. Evaluation criteria and output measurement
4. Zero-based budgeting
5. Quantitative analysis of alternatives

DEVELOPMENT OF THE PROGRAM STRUCTURE

A good program structure may be the only way the private citizen can gain an overview of the benefits and services provided by his local government. The development of a program structure starts with an identification of goals and major desired outputs of the organization. A government entity must identify the goods and services it distributes to the citizen it serves. The second step is to group these services into broad categories, called *programs* or *program categories.* Program categories should be few in number, probably less than 10, and represent the major goals of the society served.

A typical program structure for a city follows:

I. Personal safety
II. Health
III. Intellectual development
IV. Satisfactory home and community environment
V. Economic satisfaction and satisfactory work opportunities for individuals
VI. Leisure-time opportunities
VII. Transportation and communication

A statement of goals is then prepared, setting out the benefits or outputs for each program category. A goal for category I, *Personal safety,* might be: "To reduce the amount and effects of external harm to individuals and, in general, to maintain an atmosphere of personal security from such external events."

Each program category is then expanded to identify the specific goods and services necessary to achieve its goals. For example, a subprogram of *Personal safety* would be *Law enforcement,* which carries its own set of goals and may be further expanded into program elements.

A. Law enforcement (Goal: To reduce the amount and effects of crime and, in general, to maintain an atmosphere of personal security from criminals.)
   1. Crime prevention
   2. Crime investigation
   3. Judging and assignment of punishment
   4. Detention and supervision of offenders
   5. Rehabilitation of offenders

In practice, the development of a program structure and statement of goals is the most difficult part of program budgeting. There is no prescribed number of program categories nor a "right" way to express the organization's goals. For agencies that have developed a program structure, the process of program development and goal formulation has been a healthy experience and worth the effort, even when the planning process stopped at that point.

EVALUATION CRITERIA AND OUTPUT MEASUREMENT

After the goals of the organization are identified and the complete program structure is developed, it is necessary to identify a specific set of criteria that can be used to evaluate actual performance. Each of the objectives explicit in the goal statement should have criteria for measurement. To continue with our previous example, under the crime prevention program are the following criteria for evaluation.

1. Annual number of each category of offense
2. Crime rate per thousand of inhabitants
3. Number and percentage of population committing criminal acts
4. Annual cost to the population by type of crime

For each evaluation criterion a specific target or objective should be set. The objective may state a level or a change expected for the year.

MULTIYEAR COSTING

A significant contribution of program budgeting is the perspective given to view the total costs of a program, not for just one year but for several years ahead. In addition to showing past costs, program budgeting estimates costs for the current year and for future years. A five-year period has evolved in practice and apparently is a sufficiently long planning horizon for most needs. At times, special analyses require projections of costs and benefits over the entire life of a project. Understandably, when the projections exceed a five-year time frame they become more vague and subject to greater error.

For the first time, decision makers in the not-for-profit sector are required to take a long-range outlook in their planning. Proposals with relatively low initial expenditures but large operating and maintenance costs will be examined more closely in this system.

ZERO-BASED BUDGETING

A distinguishing feature of program budgeting is the method used to review and defend both existing and new projects. Traditionally, the previous year's expenditures were considered a base; only changes in the base were defended. In other words: "This is where we are, where do we go from here?" Zero-based budgeting begins with the objectives and requires that old programs compete on an equal footing with new programs. Priorities are established each year; changes in the budget necessitate a realignment of resources in accordance with changing priorities. In a period of cutback and retrenchment, budget cutting would take place in lowest-priority programs rather than across the board.

One can expect different budgetary outcomes from program budgeting than from the traditional approach. Traditional budgeting practices typically repeat existing programs with minor variations. Zero-based budgeting should produce radical changes as old programs are supplanted by new ones. In practice, an annual in-depth defense of all activities may be too costly. But a periodic review, perhaps every two or three years, would serve to hold down assessment costs and, at the same time, ensure no program continuing beyond its productive life.

QUANTITATIVE EVALUATION OF ALTERNATIVES

The major purpose of program budgeting is to improve decisions. Program budgeting provides the information system for benefit-cost analysis. Integral to this budgeting process are statements of objectives for each program and alternative ways of achieving the objectives. Consideration of the alternatives through benefit-cost analysis (if both costs and benefits of each alternative may be determined) or cost-effectiveness analysis (if benefits cannot be measured in financial terms) will provide the basis for efficient choice.

RELATIONSHIPS BETWEEN INDUSTRY AND NOT-FOR-PROFIT ORGANIZATIONS

It would be shortsighted to believe that there is no cross-pollination between the profit-oriented and the not-for-profit segments of society. Each has unique problems and answers. Yet the need for data in the planning and control process brings them to some common solutions.

Since the early 1900s governmental agencies have been actively involved in budgeting their activities. This emphasis upon a formalized budgetary program preceded most business budgeting efforts. Although the benefit of experience has been a positive influence, there have also been negative effects. Because the government has used budgeting as a compliance accounting vehicle rather than for coordinating and planning, severe negative attitudes toward budgeting have developed. In the governmental sphere a budget is an authorization to spend, founded in law. If an unusual occurrence causes activities to increase, the funding may be inadequate. If the activities fall below planned levels, there is an abundance of funds. The not-for-profit budget does not change as activity levels change.

There is another detrimental effect of the static (nonflexible) budgets used by the not-for-profit area. An agency that does not expend all its budgeted funds may receive a smaller appropriation the following year. This practice leads many governmental managers into spending frenzy at the end of the fiscal year; the result is wasted resources.

A manager's inability to obtain more resources easily as his activities increase also has a negative effect. Because he is funded only once per year and cannot count on obtaining additional resources, he must try to build slack into his budget, often padding his request to anticipate all possible variances. These budgeting games destroy the public's faith in the process and create a situation where the manager may lie to ensure his department's continuing function.

Businesses can learn from these negative experiences of not-for-profit organizations. First, they can strive to maintain flexible budgets where a manager's resources are related directly to his activities. This practice would help avoid the unfavorable results of budget padding, across-the-board cuts, and last-minute expenditures to use the resources before expiration of the budget.

Second, the typical business firm does not attempt to commit its objectives to writing because they are often vague and difficult to specify. The goal orientation implicit in a program-budgeting attitude could bring about a concerted effort to state the organizations' objectives more concretely.

The control of research and development costs and advertising costs are two excellent examples of areas where the program-budgeting approach would be constructive. It is very difficult to plan and control these expenses because the costs are not directly related to a volume measure. Planning and control could be facilitated by the establishment of a program approach where specific objectives are stated and funds are appropriated on the basis of the program outline.

SUMMARY

The master budget is management's principal vehicle for coordinating the firm's plans. Without the integrating features of the budget there is a danger that the various responsibility centers will act to optimize their own performance to the detriment of the total firm. To achieve its long-run goals and objectives, management must plan and control actual operations. The budget serves as a focus of the planning process, as an integrative tool for the many plans, and as a reference for control. By comparing actual results with plans on a timely basis, management can ensure that actual performance is congruent with the plans.

The master budget is composed of four separate subcomponents. The profit plan is the operating plan detailing revenues, expenses, and net income in the form of a projected income statement. The projected statement of financial position includes the planned asset, liability, and equity levels. The cash budget shows the effects of management's plans on cash inflows and outflows. The capital expenditures budget details planned procurements and disposals of the major production assets.

There are many requisites in the development of a successful budgetary program. A workable budget rests upon a realistic approach to the human factors involved. Top management should support the budgetary program and take a flexible, participative attitude. Responsibility centers must be defined, and the managers in charge of the responsibility centers must have some freedom in establishing and achieving their performance targets. This freedom is attained through budgetary slack. It is through participation and slack that those affected by the budget can accept the firm's goals.

Budgeting for not-for-profit organizations differs from budgeting for profit-oriented organizations in at least two ways. First, the budget, particularly in governmental units, becomes a law. The approval of the budget represents an authorization to act with a constraint of an upper spending limit. In the profit area the budget serves more as a coordinating vehicle and a guide to action. Second, it is difficult to match costs with benefits in the not-for-profit area because there is no open-market measure of benefits. One approach to this problem has been program planning, which focuses upon the output of the organization.

SUPPLEMENTARY READING

Argyris, Chris. "Human Problems with Budgets." *Harvard Business Review,* January–February, 1953.

Becker, S., and D. Green, Jr. "Budgeting and Employee Behavior." *Journal of Business,* October, 1962.

Black, Thomas N., and Donald J. Modenbach. "Profit Planning for Action and Results." *Management Accounting,* January, 1971.

Bruns, William J. Jr., and Don T. DeCoster. *Accounting and Its Behavioral Implications.* New York: McGraw-Hill Book Company, 1969.

Caplan, E. H. "Behavioral Assumptions of Management Accounting." *The Accounting Review,* July, 1966.

Caplan, E. H. "Behavioral Assumptions of Management Accounting—Report of a Field Study." *The Accounting Review,* April, 1968.

Horngren, Charles T. "Motivation and Coordination in Management Costing Systems." *Management Accounting,* May, 1967.

Khoury, E. N., and H. Wayne Nelson. "Simulation in Financial Planning." *Management Services,* March—April, 1965.

Sawatsky, J. C. "What are the Motivations for Work?" *The Canadian Chartered Accountant,* January, 1967.

Schiff, Michael, and Arie Y. Lewin. "Where Traditional Budgeting Fails." *Financial Executive,* May, 1968.

Schiff, Michael, and Arie Y. Lewin, *Behavioral Aspects of Accounting.* Englewood Cliffs, N.J.: Prentice-Hall, Inc., 1974.

QUESTIONS

10-1 What is the primary purpose of planning?

10-2 What basic assumptions make planning relevant?

10-3 What is the interaction between the budget and planning? The budget and control?

10-4 List the major functions of a budgetary system and explain each.

10-5 Define *goals, objectives,* and *budgets.* What are the interrelationships among them?

10-6 Define *master budget, profit plan, performance budget,* and *cash budget.* What is the primary purpose of each?

10-7 Explain the concept *management by exception.* Explain the use of management by exception in both quantitative and nonquantitative areas?

10-8 What is the link between planning and the control process? Explain.

10-9 The control process may be illustrated through a number of steps. List the steps of the control process and indicate the importance of each.

10-10 The planning and control system is a tool for management and does not, by itself, control. How then is control achieved? Discuss.

10-11 "People control through other people." Discuss the implications this statement holds for an accounting control system.

10-12 "The attitude of top management is crucial to the success or failure of the budgetary system." Do you agree? Discuss.

10-13 In addition to other roles the budget may serve, it may be described as a formal communication system. What does the system communicate?

10-14 The traditional view of human behavior was based upon a number of assumptions. List as many as you can. Are these assumptions still valid? Explain.

10-15 "Responsibility accounting has the tendency to make the line manager's position very visible." Do you agree? Explain.

10-16 While responsibility accounting is a useful tool for performance evaluation, it has a weakness that may lead to suboptimization of the firm's goals and objectives. Explain.

10-17 One author described the budgetary process as "the game of the budget control." How may budget control be considered a game? Explain.

10-18 Distinguish among *cost centers, profit centers,* and *investment centers.*

10-19 Contrast traditional not-for-profit budgeting with program budgeting.

10-20 What relationship does the program structure have to decision making in a program budgeting system?

PROBLEMS

10-21 Indicate whether the following statements are *true* or *false.*

1. Research studies have shown that cost consciousness by management has very little effect on subordinates.

2. In order to succeed, the planning and control system must reflect only the formal organizational structure. Informal patterns of authority and responsibility must be ignored in the system.

3. The nature of the firm's operations and the attitude of top management will, to a large extent, define the organizational structure of a particular firm.

4. In practice, a high level of motivation through budgets eliminates excessive pressure on employees and tends to remove unfavorable attitudes toward the budget.

5. Proper operation of a system of budgetary control requires that the larger the deviation from budget, the greater the amount of pressure that must be applied by management.

6. A cost is controllable by an individual if his decision will directly affect the cost, regardless of where the cost is actually incurred.

7. For control purposes, the budget used to measure performance must be based upon the expected level of activity, regardless of the actual activity level.

8. The sales activity variance is usually caused by some variable outside the firm and is a measure of the firm's efficiency.

9. The performance budget is based on the desired level of activity priced at budgeted prices and costs.

10. A program budget for the not-for-profit sector serves the same role as the profit plan in the private sector.

10-22 Match the following terms and definitions.

1. Goals
2. Master budget
3. Profit plan
4. Program budget
5. Capital expenditures budget
6. Forecast
7. Objective
8. Flexible budget
9. Performance budget
10. Slack

a. A statement of cost behavior patterns from which a budget may be prepared for any level of activity.
b. An operating budget for a specific future period of time.
c. A budget prepared after the fact, showing what costs should have been at the actual level of activity.
d. A budget reflecting long-range decisions of the company.
e. A set of statements providing broad direction for the firm.
f. An inefficiency introduced into the budget to allow an individual manager to achieve his personal goals.
g. A quantitative benchmark for measuring company achievement.
h. A quantitative statement of management's plans for a specific future period of time.
i. A projection of a relevant variable.
j. A budget for a not-for-profit organization that relates resources to organizational goals.

10-23 Match the following terms and definitions.

1. Master budget
2. Responsiblity accounting
3. Cost center
4. Management by exception
5. Participation
6. Contribution margin
7. Activity variance
8. Sales forecast
9. Profit center
10. Investment center

a. An active involvement by an individual manager.
b. A system that relates costs to organizational structure.
c. An integrated plan of action for the firm as a whole, expressed in financial terms.
d. A measure of incremental income that is the criterion for evaluating short-range decisions.

(This problem is continued on the next page.)

e. The difference between the profit plan and the performance budget.
f. The most important input for budget preparation. All estimates of activity depend upon this information.
g. An organizational unit where costs, revenues, and resources are controllable.
h. An organizational unit where costs are controllable.
i. The practice of focusing attention on those activities where the actual performance differs significantly from planned performance.
j. A responsibility center where controllable costs are deducted from controllable revenue.

10-24 Participation has long been advanced as a way to increase motivation and reduce conflict. However, there is a tendency to substitute pseudoparticipation for real participation. Explain both types of participation, the benefits of one and the weaknesses of the other. In what way does goal congruence interact with real participation?

10-25 Management at all levels tend to introduce slack into the control system. Define the term *slack* and list both the advantages and disadvantages associated with the introduction of slack into the system. Give examples of slack at the lowest management level, at the middle management level, and at the top management level.

10-26 For several years some outstanding people in the field of accounting have advocated the inclusion of budgets in corporate and annual reports.

Fuqua Industries' 1972 annual report included actual financial statements for 1972 and a budget for 1973. The president stated:

> We have not determined whether making public the forecasts used for internal management purposes will be of real interest or value. Continuation of this practice will depend upon the response we receive from our shareholders and the investment community. However, as a shareholder you should know that we place the greatest importance on forward planning and on the accuracy of our financial analysis. We just don't know any other way to properly operate a business.*

*Fuqua Industries, Inc. *1972 Annual Report,* p. 2.

REQUIRED:
What are some of the advantages to the stockholders of publishing the corporation's profit plan in the annual report? To potential investors? To the company itself? Is this practice likely to gain wide acceptance in the United States? Why or why not?

10-27 After two years of poor profits, the top management of Gregory Nuts and Bolts Company has decided to implement a budgeting system. You have been asked to supervise the installation.

REQUIRED:

A. Before beginning the preparation of the first budget, you call a meeting of the managers of the various cost centers to explain the advantages of a budgeting system to them. What are the advantages you present?
B. What information will you request of the sales manager, the factory manager, and the controller of the company?
C. How will the new budgetary system change the information presented to Mr. Gregory, president of the company.

10-28 In a not-for-profit setting it is very common to implement budget reductions through an across-the-board budget cut. If projected expenditures are 5% above projected revenues, all agencies are ordered to reduce projected expenditures by 5%.

REQUIRED:

A. Discuss the wisdom of this kind of resource-allocation process.
B. What would you suggest as an alternative to reduce projected expenditures to the desired level?
C. Would a similar across-the-board budget cut work in an industrial setting? Explain.

10-29 The development of a program structure is a critical step in implementation of a program budget. Two different program structures were proposed for the U.S. Post Office.

PROPOSAL I

1. Collection and delivery of mail
   a. Collection
   b. Processing
   c. Transportation
   d. Delivery
   e. Special services
2. Non-mail service
3. Supporting activities

PROPOSAL II

1. First class mail
2. Second class mail
3. Third class mail
4. Fourth class mail
5. Support programs
6. Construction of facilities
7. Research and development

REQUIRED:

A. Why is the development of a program structure so important to program budgeting?

B. Which of the two proposals do you favor? Why?

C. How will your choice in part B assist in decision making?

10-30 Tom Nelson is a young and aggressive management accountant employed by Essex, Inc., a highly decentralized corporation with plants throughout the United States. Nelson was promoted to controller of the Burns Plant last year, after only two years with the company. His salary provides his family with a comfortable living, including an attractive home in one of the city's nicer subdivisions.

Essex encourages employees to continue their education and reimburses them for tuition and fees as part of their benefit program. Nelson has been enrolled in the night MBA program at a local university for the past two years and hopes to receive his degree next year. He is the only employee on the financial staff of the Burns Plant to take advantage of this employee benefit.

Nelson regularly has sent memoranda to his superiors indicating potential improvements in the operations of the controller's department and in other aspects of the plant's operations. A recent memorandum sent to the plant manager and the corporate controller included recommendations to improve the reporting systems used to communicate with corporate headquarters. The ideas embodied in the recommendation resulted from knowledge acquired in the MBA program. During the recent salary review the corporate controller complimented Nelson on the fine ideas contained in his recommendations. Nelson was disappointed to learn that none had yet been implemented or even scheduled for implementation but guessed that the delay was due to the fact that his memorandum had not recommended either implementation steps or further study.

Earlier this year Nelson presented the plant manager (who had previously served as plant controller) with proposals to revise the plant's production scheduling and cost accounting system. The plant manager agreed that the proposals were good, although they did not describe implementation procedures. He has not yet submitted the proposals for corporate review, although he said he would do so. Nelson has not asked about the proposals since he introduced them.

Nelson is the newest and youngest member of the plant top management; the others have been with Burns Plant for five to ten years. When the plant management meets, Nelson's ideas appear to be well conceived and presented and are seldom criticized. However, the other members of the plant management tend to view and refer to Nelson as "the new head bookkeeper" and "idea man."

Nelson has been offered a similar position by another firm. He is seriously considering the position even though the salary and employee benefits are not as attractive as in his present employment.

REQUIRED:

A. Explain the needs that serve as motivating factors for individuals in their work.

B. Identify and explain the problems and factors that influence Tom Nelson to consider seriously changing jobs.

C. Is there goal congruence with this firm? Explain. *(CMA adapted)*

10-31 In an analysis of company expenses, the management of the Jumping Jack Company compared this year's expenses against last year's.

	This Year	*Last Year*	*Difference (Increase) Decrease*
Direct labor	$ 50,000	$ 65,000	$15,000
Supervisory salaries	31,000	30,000	(1,000)
Indirect labor	35,000	40,000	5,000
Maintenance	7,000	5,000	(2,000)
Power	18,000	13,000	(5,000)
Depreciation	8,000	6,500	(1,500)
Insurance	2,400	1,700	(700)
Total	$151,400	$161,200	$ 9,800

REQUIRED:

A. Comment upon the expense comparison as a tool for analyzing company performance. What are the advantages and disadvantages of the above comparison?

B. What other information would you consider necessary? Explain.

10-32 Monthly departmental performance reports are prepared by the Minervia Manufacturing Corporation. A manager of the month award is given to the manager who has performed best in relation to his budget. A bonus is paid to any department manager whose performance is better than budget or whose unfavorable deviations do not exceed 1% of the budget. Two departmental reports for the month of May follow.

MARKETING-PRODUCT B
PERFORMANCE REPORT FOR MAY

	Master Budget	*Performance Budget*	*Actual*
Sales revenue	$450,000	$500,000	$505,000
Variable costs	270,000	300,000	300,000
Contribution margin	$180,000	$200,000	$205,000
Departmental fixed costs	50,000	50,000	50,000
Departmental income	$130,000	$150,000	$155,000

PRODUCTION-ASSEMBLY
PERFORMANCE REPORT FOR MAY

	Master Budget	*Performance Budget*	*Actual*
Subassemblies (material)	$300,000	$315,000	$308,700
Labor	200,000	210,000	230,000
Variable factory overhead	100,000	105,000	125,000
Total variable costs	$600,000	$630,000	$663,700
Departmental fixed costs	80,000	80,000	75,000
Total departmental costs	$680,000	$710,000	$738,700

One of the goals of the company is customer satisfaction. The marketing manager for Product B received the manager of the month award for exceptional customer service. He had received several new orders and was commended by many customers for filling rush orders when competitors refused to do so.

The manager of the production-assembly department is extremely unhappy with the company's accounting system. His department operated near capacity and completed all orders within the promised delivery schedule but had excessive labor and variable factory overhead costs. He can show that the entire unfavorable deviation was caused by changing production schedules for rush orders and that without the rush orders his overall performance would be about the same as his performance on materials.

REQUIRED:

A. Did the manager of the production-assembly department receive a bonus in May? Explain.

B. Why should the manager of the production-assembly department be so unhappy with the accounting system?

C, If identical conditions continued the following month, what would you do if you were the manager of the production-assembly department? Why?

D. Does this firm have goal congruence? Explain.

10-33 Departmental performance reports for the Minervia Manufacturing Company are presented in problem 10-32.

REQUIRED:

A. Recast the two reports for the month of May to conform with sound responsibility accounting.

B. Which managers are entitled to bonuses? Explain.

C. Would your responsibility accounting reports in part A provide any assistance to the sales manager making the decision to accept rush orders? Explain.

10-34 The operating budget is a very common instrument used by many businesses. While it usually is thought to be an important and necessary tool for management, it has been subject to some criticism from managers and researchers studying organizations and human behavior.

REQUIRED:

A. Describe and discuss the benefits of budgeting from the behavioral point of view.

B. Describe and discuss the criticisms levelled at the budgeting processes from the behavioral point of view.

C. What solutions are recommended to overcome the criticism described in part B? *(CMA adapted)*

10-35 An important concept in management accounting is that of responsibility accounting.

REQUIRED:

A. Define the term *responsibility accounting.*

B. What are the conditions that must exist for there to be effective responsibility accounting?

C. What benefits are said to result from responsibility accounting?

D. Listed below are three charges found on the monthly report of a division that manufactures and sells products primarily to outside companies. This division is an investment center and is evaluated by the use of return on investment. You are to state which, if any, of the following expenses are consistent with the responsibility accounting concept. Support each answer with a brief explanation.

   1. An expense for a general corporation administration at 10% of division sales.

   2. An expense for the use of the corporate computer facility. The expense is determined by taking actual annual computer department costs and allocating an amount to each user on the ratio of its use to total corporation use.

   3. An expense for goods purchased from another division. The expense is based upon the competitive market price for the goods.

(CMA adapted)

10-36 The Parsons Co. compensates its field sales force on a commission and year-end bonus basis. The commission is 20% of standard gross margin (planned selling price less standard cost of goods sold on a full-absorption basis) contingent upon collection of the account. Customer credit is approved by the company's credit department. Price concessions are granted on occasion by the top sales management, but sales commissions are not reduced by the discount. A year-end bonus of 15% of commissions earned is paid to salespeople who equal or exceed their annual sales target. The annual sales target is usually established by applying approximately a 5% increase to the prior year's sales.

REQUIRED:

A. What features of this compensation plan would seem to be effective in motivating the salespeople to accomplish company goals of higher profits and return on investment. Explain why.

B. What features of this compensation plan would seem to be counter-effective in motivating the salespeople to accomplish the company goals of higher profits and return on investment. Explain why. *(CMA adapted)*

10-37 Two women who had been working in pottery as a hobby received so many requests for stoneware dishes that they decided to produce the sets commercially. They formed a company, withdrew their savings, refinanced their homes, purchased equipment, rented an old barn, and started business as The Crockery Barn. They need additional financing from the bank and came to you for assistance in financial planning. Upon formation, the company has the following assets:

Cash	$ 2,000
Equipment	$20,000

The women expect to sell 500 sets of dishes at $100 per set during the first six months. They believe an inventory of 20 finished sets is needed to fill rush orders. Because of drying time required there will always be 20 half-finished sets in production. Costs (except depreciation and interest) for the first six months should be:

Production	$10,000 plus $50 per set produced
Selling and administration	$5,000 plus $10 per set sold

Purchases and sales will be on account, with average balances of $20,000 for accounts receivable and $4,000 for accounts payable. Other payments will be made in the month the costs are incurred. A minimum cash balance of $2,000 is necessary.

The bank is willing to grant a two-year loan of up to $25,000 with 10% interest payable at maturity. Equipment is to be depreciated by the straight-line method over an estimated useful life of five years.

REQUIRED:

A. Prepare a one-paragraph statement of goals for this company.

B. Prepare a master budget for the first six months of operations. Your master budget should include a profit plan, a cash budget, and a projected statement of financial position. The contribution margin approach is to be used.

C. Prepare a breakeven chart for the company.

10-38 At the end of the first six months of operations The Crockery Barn (in problem 10-37) asked you to continue your financial consultation. The owners of the business had expected to sell 500 sets of stoneware at $100 each. They expected the following costs: production, $10,000 plus $50 per set produced; selling and administration, $5,000 plus $10 per set sold. For purposes of this problem, assume that depreciation was planned at $2,000 and interest at $1,250.

Orders for the first six months exceeded expectations and the women actually sold 600 sets of dishes at an average price of $110. Inventory levels were maintained at 20 finished sets and 10 half-finished sets.

Actual costs were as follows:

Production	
Variable	$ 60 per set
Fixed	$11,000
Selling and administration	
Variable	$ 8 per set
Fixed	$ 5,500
Interest expense	$ 1,500
Depreciation of equipment	$ 2,000

REQUIRED:

A. Prepare an income statement showing profit plan, performance budget, actual results, and variances.

B. Prepare a report on profit plan that explains the difference between planned net income and actual net income.

C. Comment upon the performance of The Crockery Barn.

10-39 The KD Toy Company had the following assets and equities upon formation.

Assets		*Equities*	
Cash	$ 50,000	Capital Stock	$150,000
Equipment	100,000		
	$150,000		

The company was formed to produce a plastic doll that market tests have shown to have immediate consumer acceptance. On the basis of future earnings potential, the bank approved a loan of $100,000. However, before the company can receive any cash from the loan it must submit a profit plan, a cash budget, and a projected statement of financial position.

The sales forecast for the first year estimated sales of 250,000 dolls at $5 each. The company wants an inventory of 50,000 dolls by year-end. An inventory of raw materials (plastic) for 20,000 dolls must be maintained.

The following costs are expected for the first year.

Plastic for production of dolls	$1.00 per doll
Direct labor	$ .50 per doll
Factory overhead	$20,000 per month plus $.50 per doll produced
General and selling	$10,000 per month plus $.50 per doll sold

Depreciation of equipment will be computed on a straight-line basis with a five-year life.

All doll sales and material purchases will be on credit. At the end of the year, sales of 50,000 dolls and purchases of $60,000 of plastic will not be paid. Other cash payments will be made as the cost is incurred. Interest of 9% will be paid annually.

REQUIRED:

Prepare the following:

A. Profit plan for the year, using variable costing.
B. Cash budget for the year.
C. Projected statement of financial position.
D. Profit-volume chart for the company. What is the margin of safety?
E. What is the role of each of the requirements (A through D) in the master budget?

10-40 The KD Toy Company (in Problem 10-39) had planned to sell 250,000 dolls at $5 each. The following costs were expected for the year.

Plastic	$1.00 per doll
Direct labor	$ .50 per doll
Factory overhead	$20,000 per month plus $.50 per doll produced
General and selling	$10,000 per month plus $.50 per doll sold
Depreciation of equipment	$20,000
Interest expense	$ 9,000

Actual sales did not reach management's expectations; 220,000 dolls were produced and 200,000 sold. The selling price was reduced to $4.80. Actual costs follow.

Plastic used in production	$198,000
Direct labor	$110,000
Factory overhead ($244,000 fixed)	$355,000
General and selling ($90,000 fixed)	$200,000
Depreciation of equipment	$ 20,000
Interest expense	$ 9,000

REQUIRED:

A. Prepare an income statement for the year showing profit plan, performance budget, actual results, and variances.

B. Prepare a report on profit plan that explains the difference between planned net income and actual net income.

10-41 Rears, Soebuck and Company is a medium-sized manufacturing firm that is interested in implementing a responsibility accounting system. Factory overhead data generated by a full-absorption accounting system and other cost behavior data for one department for the past month follow.

Factory Overhead Costs	*Actual*	*Flexible Budget for Planning (x) = Direct labor hours*
Supervision	$1,000	$1,000 + $0(*x*)
Indirect labor	3,400	$3,000 + $.20(*x*)
Supplies	800	$ 0 + $1.00(*x*)
Depreciation of equipment	2,000	$2,000 + $0(*x*)
Rent (includes building repairs)	960	Budgeted allocation: 4,000 sq. ft. @ $.20
Factory administration	1,300	Budgeted allocation: 12 employees @ $100
Cafeteria (loss)	240	No loss budgeted
	$9,700	

REQUIRED:

A. Assuming 1,000 direct labor hours were worked, prepare a departmental cost report applying responsibility accounting concepts.

B. Comment on the ability of this department manager to control the cost generated by the accounting system.

10-42 Clarkson Company is a large multidivision firm with several plants in each division. A comprehensive budgeting system is used for planning operations and measuring performance. The annual budgeting process commences in August, five months prior to the beginning of the fiscal year. At this time the division managers submit proposed budgets for sales, production and inventory levels, and expenses. Capital expenditure requests also are formalized at this time. The expense budgets include direct labor and all overhead items, which are separated into fixed and variable components. Direct materials are budgeted separately in developing the production and inventory schedules.

The expense budgets for each division are developed from its plants' results, as measured by the percent variation from an adjusted budget in the first six months of the current year and a target expense reduction percentage established by the corporation.

To determine plant percentages, the plant budget for the just completed half-year period is revised to recognize changes in operating procedures and costs outside the control of plant management (e.g. labor wage-rate changes, product style changes, etc.). The difference between this revised budget and the actual expenses is the controllable variance, and is expressed as a percentage of the actual expenses. This percentage is added (if unfavorable) to the corporate target expense reduction percentage. A favorable plant variance percentage is subtracted from the corporate target. If a plant had a 2% unfavorable controllable variance and the corporate target reduction was 4%, the plant's budget for next year should reflect costs approximately 6% below this year's actual costs.

Next year's final budgets for the corporation, the divisions, and the plants are adopted after corporate analysis of the proposed budgets and a careful review with each division manager of the changes made by corporate management. Division profit budgets include allocated corporate costs; plant profit budgets include allocated division and corporate costs.

Return on assets is used to measure the performance of divisions and plants. The asset base for a division consists of all assets assigned to the division, including its working capital, and an allocated share of corporate assets. Recommendations for promotions and salary increases for the executives of the divisions and plants are influenced by how well the actual return on assets compares with the budgeted return on assets.

The plant managers exercise control only over the cost portion of the plant profit budget because the divisions are responsible for sales. Only limited control over the plant assets is exercised at the plant level.

The manager of the Dexter Plant, a major plant in the Huron division, carefully controls his costs during the first six months so that any improvement appears after the target reduction of expenses is established. He accomplishes this by careful planning and timing of his discretionary expenditures.

During 1973 the property adjacent to the Dexter Plant was purchased by Clarkson Company. This expenditure was not included in the 1973 capital expenditure budget. Corporate management decided to divert funds from a project at another plant since the property appeared to be a better long-term investment.

Also during 1973 Clarkson Company experienced depressed sales. In an attempt to achieve budgeted profit, corporate management announced in August that all plants were to cut their annual expenses by 6%. In order to accomplish this expense reduction, the Dexter Plant manager reduced preventive maintenance and postponed needed major repairs. Employees who quit were not replaced unless absolutely necessary. Employee training was postponed whenever possible. The raw materials, supplies, and finished goods inventories were reduced below normal levels.

REQUIRED:
Evaluate the budget procedure of Clarkson Company with respect to its effectiveness for planning and controlling operations. *(CMA adapted)*

11 Cost Efficiency through Standard Costs

TYPES OF STANDARD COSTS
THE SETTING OF STANDARDS
Standards for Motivation
Establishing Technical Standards
Acceptance of Standards
Revision of Standards
THE STANDARD COST SYSTEM
Illustration of Absorption Standard Cost System
Illustration of Variable Standard Cost System
SELECTION OF A STANDARD COST SYSTEM
SUMMARY

Management needs criteria for judging the results of day-to-day operating decisions. Production decisions are repetitive, recurring activities that are too small and discrete for the application of an overall measure such as return on investment. A different type of benchmark is needed to measure satisfactory production performance. If management can assume that the sales price per unit of product is relatively constant within the relevant range of activity, profits will be maximized within that range if costs are minimized. Standard costs are an efficient way to plan and control the costs of repetitive activities such as production.

A **standard** is a precise measure of what *should* occur if performance is efficient. Par is a standard for the golf course; 80 words per minute is a standard for typists; and a four-minute mile is a difficult standard for runners. In management decisions a **standard cost** is a measure of acceptable cost performance based on scientifically predetermined costs. The term *scientifically predetermined* implies that considerable thought and energy have been used to decide how a task should be accomplished and how many resources (costs) should be consumed. Although there are many different tasks and activities performed in a business firm, standard costs are usually focused on the costs of manufacturing the product—raw materials, direct labor, and factory overhead costs. The focus upon manufacturing activities is deliberate. These activities are repetitive and hence susceptible to the establishment of standards. Standards can be set for any repetitive task—selling and administrative duties as well as production tasks—but most firms concentrate on the control of their production activities through the standard-setting process.

There are many benefits in using standard costs. First, a standard cost system, once instituted, can be cheaper to maintain than an historical cost system because it eliminates some of the inventory bookkeeping and paperwork. Second, the time and energy expended in developing standards will likely highlight possible production inefficiencies *before* actual production begins. The potential benefits of these efforts are cost savings and, as a result, higher profits. Third, standard costs assist management in formally constructing its plans and budgets. Fourth, standards allow management to maintain operational control.

The difference between actual cost and standard cost is called a **variance.** By frequently comparing actual results with standard costs via the variances, management can determine whether actual performance is under control. If the actual exceeds the standard, the variance is unfavorable, indicating the need for management action. The variance is favorable if the actual is less than the standard, implying the firm's costs are under control. A comparison of this period's costs with those of a previous period will not assure management of proper control over its operation. This month's activities could be just as inefficient as those of a previous month. It is the ability to create meaningful variances by comparing actual results with a measure of what *should* happen that makes the standard cost system a potent management tool.

TYPES OF STANDARD COSTS

There is more than one philosophical approach to the scientific determination of a performance standard. One approach is to set an **ideal standard** that estimates what should happen if all conditions are perfect—no waste, no scrap, no idle time, no rest periods, and no machine breakdowns. Over any extended period of time it would be impossible for the actual activities to equal the ideal standard.

A normal, or average, standard is a widely used philosophy in establishing standard costs. **Normal standards** are achievable, but attainment requires that activities be efficient. They allow for normal workers performing in normal settings. In a production firm, allowances would be made for normal scrap and waste, normal fatigue and breaks, normal machine breakdowns and maintenance, and normal mistakes in production.

Another concept of a standard is used by some firms. The **expected standard** is based upon the most likely attainable result. Technically, this is not a standard cost because it has no inherent provision for efficiency, although many people call it a standard. It is an estimate of what *will* happen, not what *should* happen.

The difference between ideal, normal, and expected standards is a philosophical one. The mental approach to the setting of standards determines the philosophy. If the standard is so tight that very few can attain it, it is an ideal standard; if based upon an estimate of what will happen, it is an expected standard; and if tight but attainable, it is a normal standard. The method of establishing the standard does *not* determine whether it is ideal, normal, or expected. All may be set by past experience, by work measurement and time-and-motion studies, by engineering estimates, or by a combination of these. It is the intent that determines the type of standard.

THE SETTING OF STANDARDS

The primary purpose of a standard cost system is to keep the unit cost of production as low as possible, given the current state of the industry. The standard cost per se does not keep the unit cost of production at a minimum. The system is made efficient by the achievements of the workers in using no more than the standard amount of materials, labor, and factory overhead to produce the product. Thus, in a real way the standard cost is a motivational system. Its goal is to provide a benchmark of good performance that workers will strive to achieve.

Standards for Motivation

When a standard is set at the ideal or perfect level, the worker will almost always fail to achieve the standard, and variances will be unfavorable. In the long run, this failure can frustrate the worker and cause a feeling of hopelessness. When the standards are too loose, the worker has no need to perform efficiently; his performance may or may not be satisfactory. The observance that motivational factors seem to increase with tightening standards up to a point, and then drop off, has led most standard costers to believe that a tight, but attainable, standard is most useful in motivating efficient performance. The normal, or **currently attainable,** standard aims for this motivational level.

The role of standards in motivating employees is a complicated subject. There are definite interactions among the tightness of the standards, employee attitudes, organizational structure, performance feedback, and employee reward systems. At this time we know far too little about these interactions. An area of research called **behavioral accounting** offers the possibility of further insights and understanding. Current beliefs seem to be that standards motivate best when there is valid participation in their establishment, when they are tight but reasonable, when the organizational structure is more democratic than authoritarian, when there is rapid performance feedback, and when the employee's rewards are tied to his success in achieving the standard.

Establishing Technical Standards

At the heart of a standard cost system is the **standard cost card,** the scientifically predetermined estimate of what one unit of product should cost if produced efficiently. It includes detailed estimates of material quantities and prices, labor quantities and prices, and factory overhead quantities and rates. These details serve as the benchmarks of efficiency against which actual quantities and costs are compared. This focus upon the efficient cost of producing one unit requires a reemphasis of the relevant range of activity concept. When standards for material, labor, and factory overhead are established, there is an implicit assumption that the actual production volume will be within a relevant range of activity.

MATERIAL STANDARDS

In most companies the material quantities are determined by the industrial engineers who design the product and determine the production process. Typically, the prices paid for raw materials are the responsibility of the purchasing agent. If the quantity of raw material consumed results in price discounts, the material prices must be set through cooperation between the purchasing department and the production schedulers. For a new product management cannot rely upon past experience; the parts list must be taken from blueprints and the material prices obtained from suppliers' quotations and bids.

LABOR STANDARDS

Labor time standards are often established from work measurement and time-and-motion studies. Performed by the industrial engineering department, these studies are often a source of conflict between the workers and management. The industrial engineer usually observes a worker in actual working conditions and then suggests ways of increasing worker efficiency. The methods of measuring labor time standards require special training and a considerable amount of professional judgment. Based on a certain amount of subjectivity, the labor time standards are often less certain and more open to variation than material standards.

In industries with a high proportion of hand-work labor, the **learning curve** has been useful in estimating labor time. The learning curve, which shows that workers have a constant rate of improvement, is a mathematical expression of the well-known adage, Practice makes perfect. Everyone, at some point, has performed a repetitive task over a long period of time. With each repetition one becomes more proficient and requires less time. A machinist, as a result of his accumulated skills, knows how to lay out his work and choose his tools in an efficient way. Accrued skills and familiarity, orderly work layout and tooling, and better selection of suitable designs and materials are sources of improvement with experience.

The airframe industries, beginning in the 1930s, found that this improvement was regular and predictable. In general terms, empirical studies have shown that the improvement was a constant percentage over doubled quantities. For example, if the second unit consumes 90% of the labor hours required by the first unit, then the fourth unit will consume 90% as much as the second, and the eighth unit will consume 90% as much as the fourth. A learning curve indicates that the *rate* of improvement is constant. It does not imply that all production activities have the same rate of improvement. For most aircraft fabrication and assembly-line labor, the *average* improvement rate for all labor used on an airplane during World War II was about 80%. However, it was found that a welder improves at a different rate than a riveter. The quantification of the learning-curve rate for any given activity can only be found empirically.

Let's illustrate the impact of the learning curve with the Mason Company, a manufacturer of hand-assembled television cabinets. Past experience indicates that a 69% learning curve is applicable to cabinet production and that the first unit of the new product took 100 hours to manufacture. Exhibit 11-1 shows the projected labor hours plotted on graph paper. The second unit would require 69% of 100 hours; the four unit, 69% of 69 hours, or 48 hours; and the eighth unit, 69% of 48 hours, or 33 hours. Notice that production of the sixteenth unit should require only 22.7% as many hours as the first unit. This difference represents a significant savings in labor.

In an industry with a large production volume, the learning curve becomes less significant over time. Exhibit 11-1 shows why. At first the curve slopes downward rapidly; then it decreases slowly. Firms with a large volume

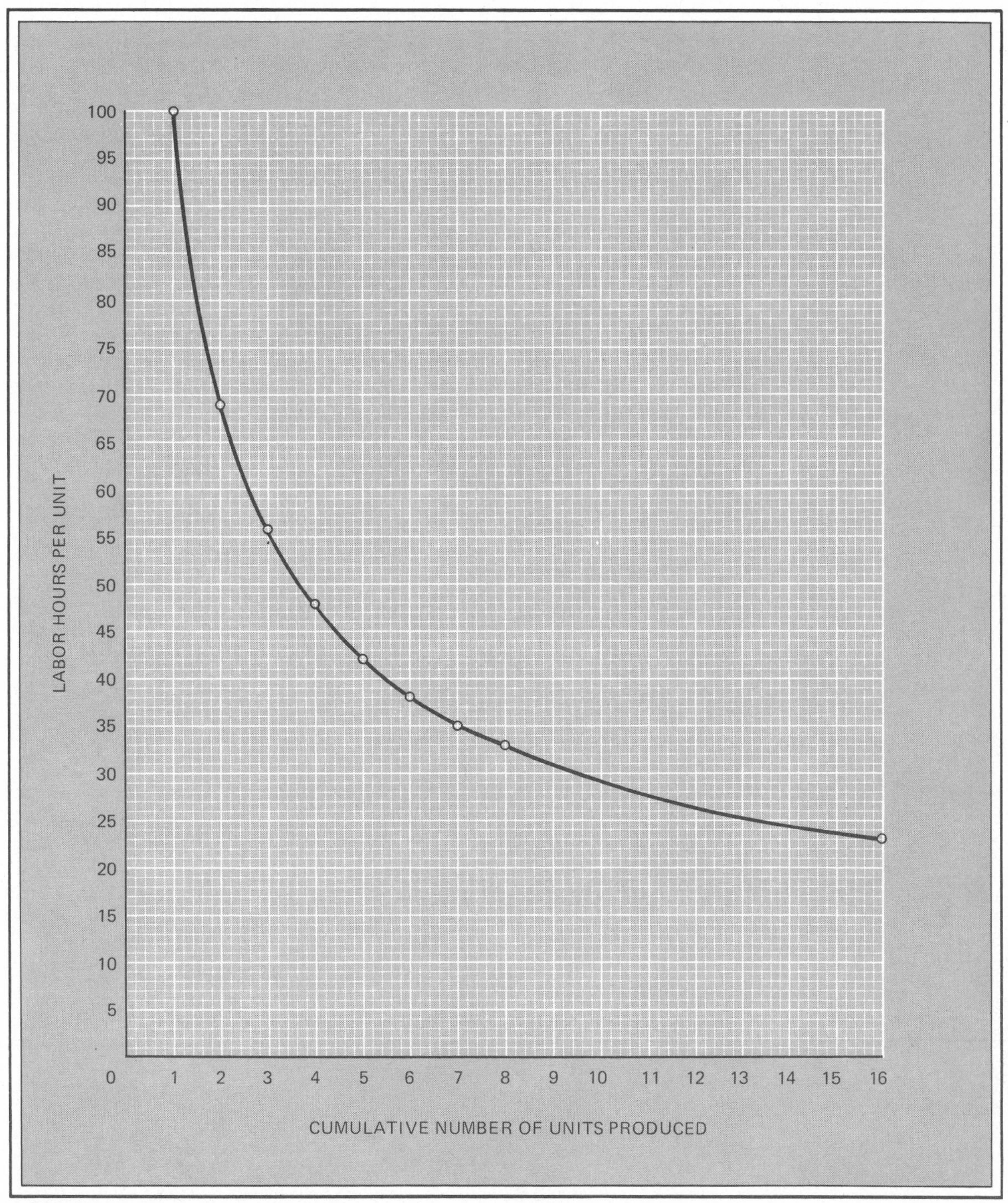

EXHIBIT 11-1
Illustration of learning curve

of repetitive operations move quickly down the learning curve, soon operating at a volume where the curve is relatively flat. The learning curve is still operative, but the results are not as spectacular.

In some production activities the learning curve is not useful. For instance, where an automated production line exists, the speed of the line, not the workers' individual learning capabilities, determines their time. Some firms segregate production tasks into many small, uncomplicated activities. Employees learn the simple tasks rapidly, and the firm soon reaches the relatively flat portion of the curve.

Standard labor quantities for a product require a single, average estimate. The data from the empirically determined curve must be averaged to provide a standard. Suppose that the Mason Company produced four television cabinets the previous year, and that during the coming year it plans to produce four more units. The direct labor hours required for each of these units, as shown in Exhibit 11-1, would be:

Units	*Direct Labor Hours*
1	100
2	69
3	56
4	48
5	42
6	38
7	35
8	33

For the fifth through eighth units, the total labor should be 148 hours (42 + 38 + 35 + 33). On the average, these four units should take 37 hours (148 ÷ 4). If 37 hours is selected as the standard, the workers will be unable to meet it during early production, but in later production they will use fewer labor hours than the standard. At the beginning of the learning curve a firm will have to revise its labor time standards often. As it moves down the learning curve, it will have to revise standards less often. In our example there are very few units involved. An increase from four to eight units is still at the beginning of the curve. In this case the addition of a few units has a large effect upon the planned labor times. If, instead, the firm had produced 5,000 units previously, a four-unit increase in output would contribute very little to learning and would have a small impact upon labor times.

Standard wage rates are often the result of collective bargaining agreements. Where union contracts exist, they can be used as the basis for establishing wage standards. In unionized plants the responsibility for wage rate standards rests with those involved in contract negotiations. In nonunion plants this responsibility often lies with the departmental managers or the personnel department. Although the wage rate for each skill level may be determined by contract negotiations, the establishment of standard costs can be complicated if the manager is able to mix worker skill levels. The standard wage rate is usually a composite of many wage rates, assuming a specific mix of employee skills.

FACTORY OVERHEAD STANDARDS

The development of standard factory overhead costs begins with cost-volume analysis. The separation of factory overhead costs into fixed and variable components allows not only the prediction of costs, but also a detailed examination of *how* costs behave relative to volume. With this understanding management can undertake a study of what costs *should* be at different volumes of output.

The flexible budget based upon past experience cannot automatically be considered a standard. It becomes a standard only when energy and thought have been applied to see if these are what costs *should* be. Only when management is satisfied that the flexible budget expresses what costs should be if operations are efficient can it serve as a standard for overhead.

Acceptance of Standards

The advocates of standard costing see it as a way to achieve efficient operations through its planning and control influences on managers and workers. The operation of a good standard cost system—with currently attainable, yet tight, standards—is not an easy task. It requires considerable thought, effort, and commitment. The value of the system may be negated if the standards set are constantly under attack by the managers and workers.

Acceptance of the standards is necessary for at least two reasons. First, the workers must believe that they are reasonable. If the standards set are considered unfair, the workers may not attempt to achieve them. More likely, they will try to subvert the standard cost system. The results are misdirected energy and, ultimately, misused resources—the antithesis of the goal of standard costs.

Second, the standards must be accepted if the variances are to have meaning. Standard cost minus actual cost equals variance. If the standards are open to question, then so are the variances. When the workers consider the standard cost to be "incorrect," the automatic implication is that actual cost is "correct" and the variance becomes a measure of the inaccuracy of the standard cost. Thus, there is no attitude of measuring or correcting inefficiencies. Let's look at the nature of the variance if the standard cost is accepted as "correct" by the workers. Here, the actual cost is "incorrect." (It is not necessarily incorrect in terms of its measurement. We assume the actual cost has been accounted for correctly. It is "incorrect" because it is not what it *should* be.) It is not efficient. The unfavorable variance is the measure of resources wasted through inefficiency; the favorable variance is a measure of resources saved through efficiency.

Revision of Standards

Standards must be revised whenever the conditions upon which they are based change. Most firms find that a continual program of revision is necessary. A typical policy is to revise the standards whenever quantity or prices change significantly, but at least once per year. Failure to revise them periodically can result in the standards' becoming unfair for evaluating performance.

Typically, price standards are more subject to change than quantity standards. New contracts and inflation are regular occurrences in most firms. With each incidence, the price standards must be adjusted. Changes in the quantity standards are required only when there are improvements in performance, new production specifications or methods, or changes in product mixes. If a long-range decision results in the purchase of new production equipment, the quantity standards may have to be modified.

Many firms trace the direction of variance details to glean information about production efficiency and about the existing standards. If the variances are continually unfavorable, employees may begin to reduce their effort, believing that the standards are unattainable. If, on the other hand, the variances are always favorable, the standards may be too loose and thus ineffective in stimulating efficient performance. The amount and the direction of the variances can point to the need for revising the standard costs.

THE STANDARD COST SYSTEM

The process of establishing standards is a valuable activity in itself. The strengths and weaknesses of the production system are highlighted along with opportunities for cost reduction. In addition, the benchmarks established allow a day-to-day comparison of actual results with the standard. Through this comparison production costs can be controlled.

The standard cost system is not only a method of controlling operating efficiency by the reporting of variances; it is also a system for income determination purposes. When it is used as an inventory costing system, each unit in the Work-in-Process Inventory, Finished Goods Inventory, or Cost of Goods Sold is carried at *standard cost.* Of course, the resources actually used will be recorded at their actual cost. The differences between standard and actual—the variances—are typically treated as period costs for income determination purposes.

In the context of historical costing (Chapter 5), we presented two systems of determining the product cost for income determination and management decision making: absorption costing and variable costing. The same two costing systems can be used with standard costing. In a variable standard cost system only the variable production costs would be used to cost the inventory, whereas in an absorption standard cost system both variable and fixed production costs would be absorbed into the inventory. Exhibit 11-2 summarizes the flow of costs for a variable standard costing system; Exhibit 11-3 summarizes the flow of costs for an absorption standard costing system.

The arguments presented in Chapter 5, for and against absorption and variable costing, are applicable to standard costing. Variable standard costing provides the cost-volume-profit information needed for differential production decisions but is unacceptable for external reporting purposes. Absorption standard costing does not allow management to perform cost-volume-profit analysis, but it is acceptable for external reporting purposes, provided the variances are not so material as to distort net income. (Refer to Chapter 5 for a review of the benefits and weaknesses of each costing system.)

Illustration of Absorption Standard Cost System

In this and the following section we will look at the way standard costs are used in an ongoing accounting system to isolate timely variances and simultaneously measure inventory values.

Let's assume the workers and management of the Forddon Furniture Company scientifically established the standard cost cards in Exhibit 11-4 for its two products before the beginning of the accounting period. These standards represent the best estimates of what production costs *should* be during the coming accounting period.

When the standards were set, management anticipated producing 575 style 10A bookcases and 1,000 style 11A bookcases each month. In additon to the variable standard costs per product for material and labor, management also prepared the following flexible budgets.

Total factory overhead = \$9,600 per month + \$1.50 per direct labor hour
Total selling expenses = \$2,400 per month + \$2.00 per unit sold
Total administrative expenses = \$3,000 per month

The standard factory overhead rates were determined using the flexible budget. The first step was the estimation of the normal activity hours. Plans called for 575 style 10A bookcases at eight hours each, or a total of 4,600 direct labor hours; and 1,000 style 11A bookcases at five hours each, or a total of 5,000 direct labor hours. The total normal activity level was 9,600 direct labor hours (4,600 + 5,000). The second step, using the flexible budget adjusted to the normal hours, was the calculation of the standard factory overhead rates. These rates were determined by:

$$\text{Variable factory overhead rate} = \frac{\$1.50(9{,}600)}{9{,}600 \text{ hours}} = \$1.50 \text{ per direct labor hour}$$

$$\text{Fixed factory overhead rate} = \frac{\$9{,}600}{9{,}600 \text{ hours}} = \$1.00 \text{ per direct labor hour}$$

These factory overhead rates are the source of the standard overhead costs shown on the standard cost cards. Because selling and administrative expenses are treated as period costs rather than product costs, no standard rate is prepared for them.

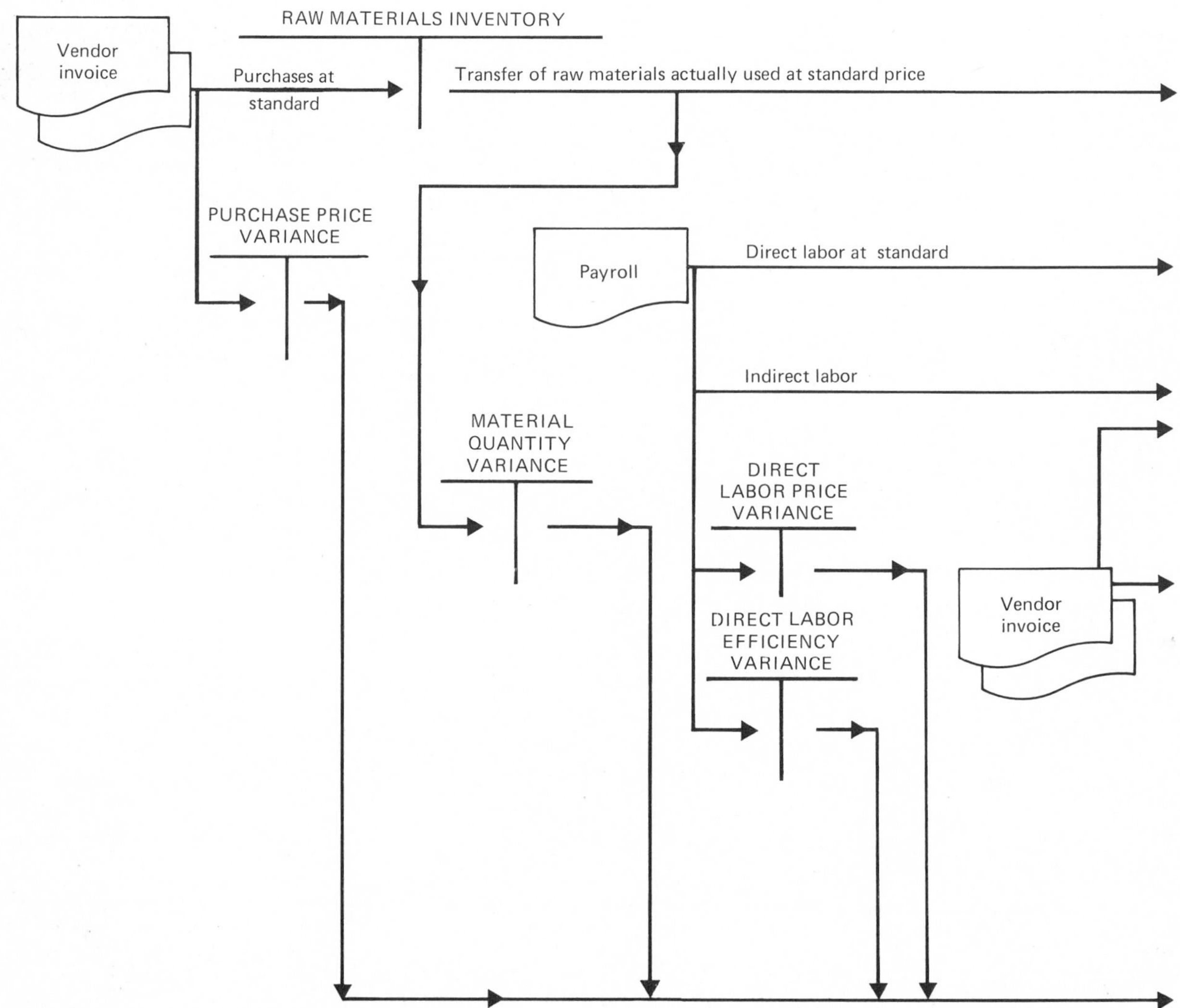

EXHIBIT 11-2
Variable standard cost system

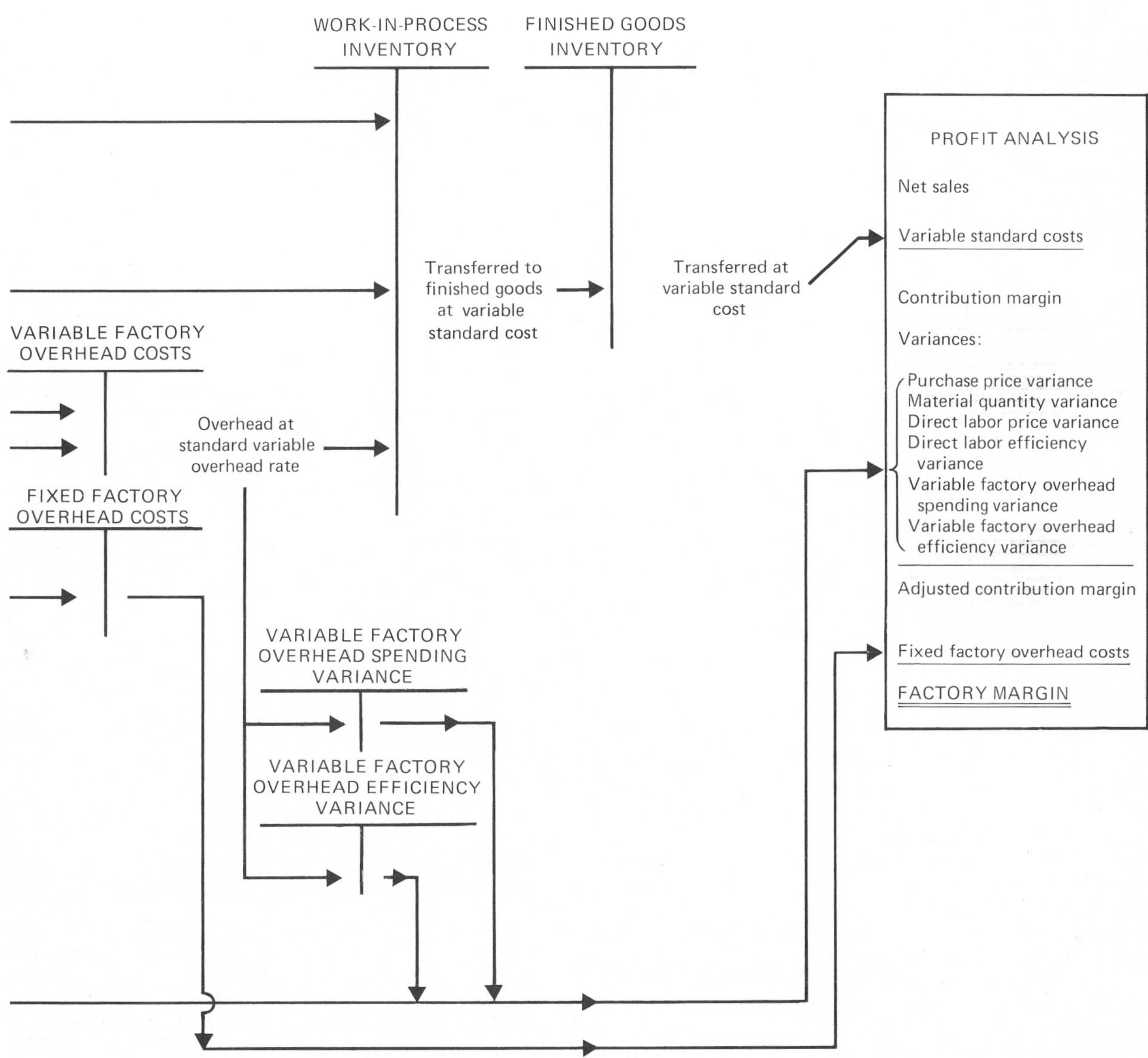
WORK-IN-PROCESS INVENTORY
FINISHED GOODS INVENTORY
Transferred to finished goods at variable standard cost
Transferred at variable standard cost
VARIABLE FACTORY OVERHEAD COSTS
Overhead at standard variable overhead rate
FIXED FACTORY OVERHEAD COSTS
VARIABLE FACTORY OVERHEAD SPENDING VARIANCE
VARIABLE FACTORY OVERHEAD EFFICIENCY VARIANCE
PROFIT ANALYSIS
Net sales
Variable standard costs
Contribution margin
Variances:
Purchase price variance
Material quantity variance
Direct labor price variance
Direct labor efficiency variance
Variable factory overhead spending variance
Variable factory overhead efficiency variance
Adjusted contribution margin
Fixed factory overhead costs
FACTORY MARGIN

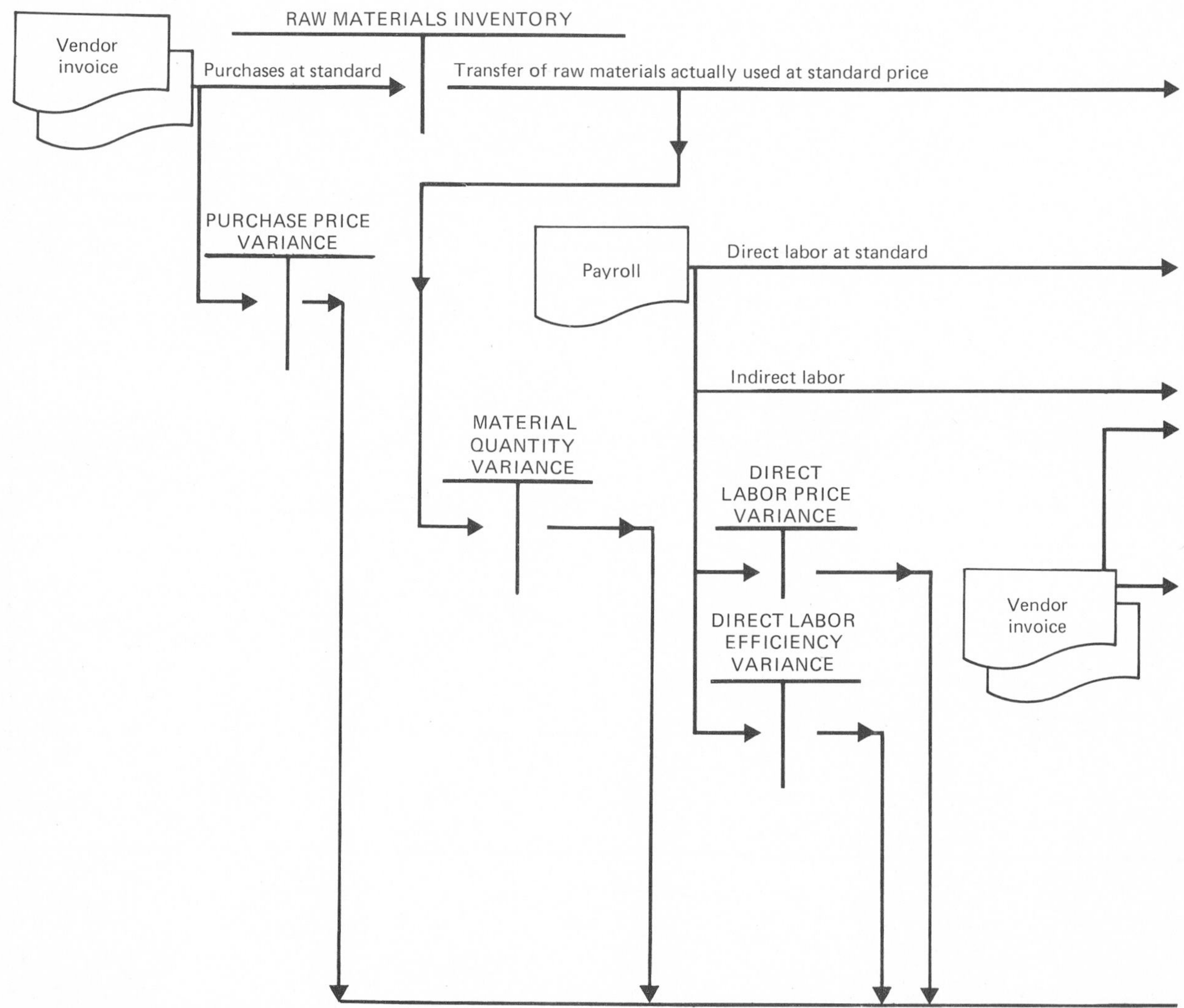

EXHIBIT 11-3
Absorption standard cost system

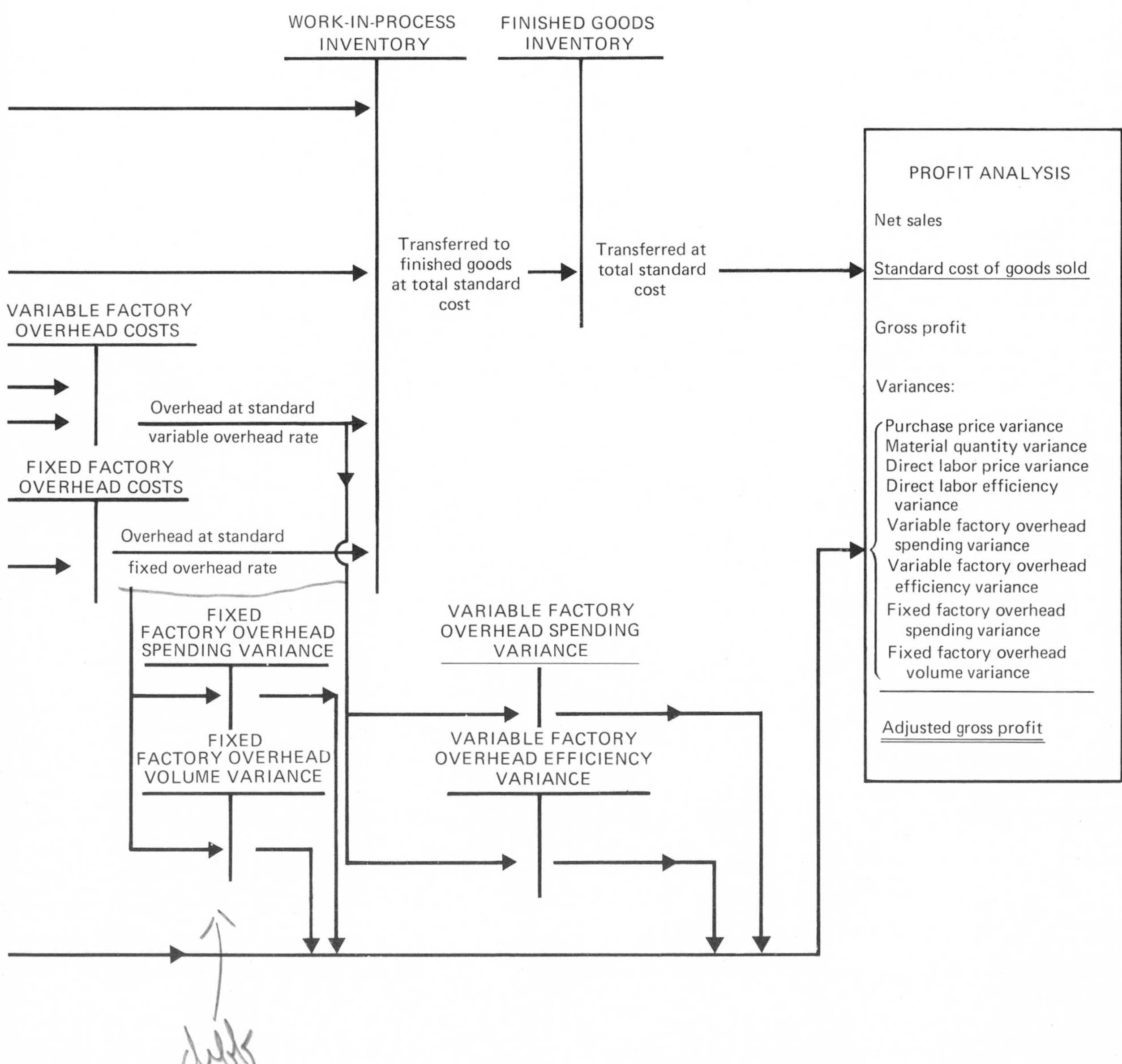
WORK-IN-PROCESS INVENTORY
FINISHED GOODS INVENTORY
Transferred to finished goods at total standard cost
Transferred at total standard cost
PROFIT ANALYSIS
Net sales
Standard cost of goods sold
Gross profit
Variances:
Purchase price variance
Material quantity variance
Direct labor price variance
Direct labor efficiency variance
Variable factory overhead spending variance
Variable factory overhead efficiency variance
Fixed factory overhead spending variance
Fixed factory overhead volume variance
Adjusted gross profit
VARIABLE FACTORY OVERHEAD COSTS
Overhead at standard variable overhead rate
FIXED FACTORY OVERHEAD COSTS
Overhead at standard fixed overhead rate
FIXED FACTORY OVERHEAD SPENDING VARIANCE
FIXED FACTORY OVERHEAD VOLUME VARIANCE
VARIABLE FACTORY OVERHEAD SPENDING VARIANCE
VARIABLE FACTORY OVERHEAD EFFICIENCY VARIANCE

BOOKCASE 10A – LARGE
STANDARD COST CARD

Direct materials	
100 feet @ $.30	$30.00
Direct labor	
8 hours @ $4.00	32.00
Variable factory overhead	
8 hours @ $1.50	12.00
Total variable standard cost	$74.00
Fixed factory overhead	
8 hours @ $1.00	8.00
Total standard cost	$82.00

BOOKCASE 11A – SMALL
STANDARD COST CARD

Direct materials	
50 feet @ $.30	$15.00
Direct labor	
5 hours @ $4.00	20.00
Variable factory overhead	
5 hours @ $1.50	7.50
Total variable standard cost	$42.50
Fixed factory overhead	
5 hours @ $1.00	5.00
Total standard cost	$47.50

EXHIBIT 11-4
Standard cost cards for Forddon Furniture Company

During January production began on 550 style 10A bookcases and 1,200 style 11A bookcases. Raw materials were purchased in two batches. The first batch was 70,000 feet at a price of $.27 per foot. The second batch was 50,000 feet at $.32 per foot. During the month 118,000 feet of direct materials were issued to the factory. Production employees spent 10,400 direct labor hours on the bookcases, at $4.10 per hour. Actual factory overhead incurred was $24,400, of which $9,000 was fixed and $15,400 was variable. At the end of the accounting period, 50 of the style 10A bookcases were incomplete and remained in the factory. These 50 units had all materials issued, but no other work had been accomplished on them. The completed bookcases (500 of 10A and 1,200 of 11A) were placed in the finished goods storeroom. Customers purchased 450 of the 10A bookcases at $125 each and 1,100 of the 11A bookcases at $60 each. Actual selling expenses were $2,000 fixed and $2,800 variable. The actual administrative expenses were $3,500. There were no beginning inventories in the Work-in-Process Inventory or Finished Goods Inventory.

MATERIALS PURCHASES

The following two journal entries record the purchases of materials.[1]

Raw Materials Inventory	$21,000	
Material Price Variance		$ 2,100
Accounts Payable		$18,900

Raw Materials Inventory	$15,000	
Material Price Variance	$ 1,000	
Accounts Payable		$16,000

The Raw Materials Inventory account is a control account. There would be a subsidiary ledger for each type of material showing the quantities purchased, the quantities issued, and the quantities on hand. By recording the inventory at standard price ($70,000 \times \$.30 = \$21,000$), there are no complications such as LIFO, FIFO, or average costing because all materials will be carried at their standard cost. The credit to Accounts Payable must, of course, be recorded at the actual price suppliers are paid ($70,000 \times \$.27 = \$18,900$).

The **material price variance** is the difference between the actual price and the standard price, times the actual quantity of materials purchased. Perhaps a more accurate title would be the *material purchased price variance.* The price variance may be expressed in formula form.

$$\text{Material price variance} = \left[\text{Standard price per unit of material} - \text{Actual price per unit of material}\right] \times \text{Actual quantity of materials purchased}$$

[1]We will omit all explanations on all journal entries in this chapter.

When actual costs exceed standard costs, the variance is unfavorable. Thus, a Material Price Variance account with a debit balance is unfavorable. With a credit balance it is favorable.

In the Forddon Company the material price variance is computed as:

First purchase:

Material price variance $= [\$.30 - \$.27] \times 70{,}000$ feet

$= \$2{,}100$ Favorable

Second purchase:

Material price variance $= [\$.30 - \$.32] \times 50{,}000$ feet

$= \$(1{,}000)$ Unfavorable

The aggregate material price variance is favorable in the amount of $1,100.

Ideally, the material price variance should be isolated at the time the purchase invoice is recorded. It is then possible to sum all the invoices on a particular day by raw material class, by supplier, or by purchasing agent. Purchasing management can receive daily reports on the price variance for the previous day's purchases.

Responsibility for analyzing the price variance lies with the purchasing officers. Because purchases are made continuously, it is important to report the variances regularly. There may be many causal factors for the price variance. A sudden change in the production volume can force the purchasing agent to buy uneconomic quantities, inflation can force the prices upward, material shortages can modify the supplier's pricing structure, or the purchasing department may simply fail to find the most desirable supplier. Obviously, the responsibility for some of these factors, such as the sudden change in production schedule, rests with someone other than the purchasing agent. It would be naive to automatically assign all results directly to the purchasing officer without a detailed analysis. It is generally true, however, that the causes rest with the purchasing agent and that it is his responsibility to explain unusual circumstances.

ISSUE OF MATERIALS

The following journal entry records the issue of raw materials to the factory.

Work-in-Process Inventory	$34,500	
Material Quantity Variance	$ 900	
Raw Materials Inventory		$35,400

Each unit of product in the Work-in-Process Inventory is costed at the cost shown on the standard cost card. Because materials for 550 large bookcases and 1,200 small bookcases were issued to production, the Work-in-Process Inventory should be charged for (550 × $30) + (1,200 × $15), or $34,500. The Raw Materials Inventory must be credited for the actual quantity issued, costed at the standard material price. Since 118,000 feet were actually used and the Raw Materials Inventory is costed at standard cost ($.30), the credit to the inventory is $35,400.

The **material quantity variance,** or **material usage variance,** measures how well the physical resources were utilized. It is computed by multiplying the standard cost per unit by the difference between the actual materials used and the amount of materials that should have been used to produce the units. In formula form the material quantity variance is:

$$\begin{array}{l}\text{Material}\\ \text{quantity}\\ \text{variance}\end{array} = \left[\left(\begin{array}{l}\text{Actual}\\ \text{units}\\ \text{produced}\end{array} \times \begin{array}{l}\text{Standard}\\ \text{quantity}\\ \text{per unit}\end{array}\right) - \begin{array}{l}\text{Actual quantity}\\ \text{of}\\ \text{materials used}\end{array}\right] \times \begin{array}{l}\text{Standard price}\\ \text{per unit of}\\ \text{raw materials}\end{array}$$

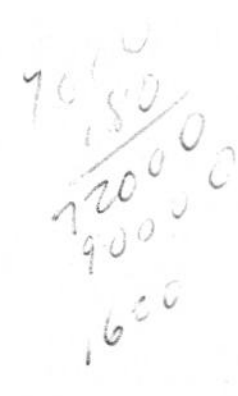

In the Forddon Company the material quantity variance is computed as:

$$\begin{aligned}\text{Material quantity variance} &= [(550 \times 100) + (1{,}200 \times 50) - 118{,}000] \times \$.30 \\ &= [55{,}000 + 60{,}000 - 118{,}000] \times \$.30 \\ &= \$(900) \text{ Unfavorable}\end{aligned}$$

The company used 3,000 feet of materials in excess of standard; the result is an unfavorable material quantity variance of $900.

The material quantity variance can be isolated any time output is measured (in some cases on an hourly or daily basis), by department, by worker, or by responsibility center. Some firms find a two-stage issue procedure works best. When a worker receives management's instructions (production releases) to produce a unit of product, he presents the work order to the raw materials storeroom. The storekeeper will issue exactly the standard quantity of materials on a materials requisition. At that time the entry would be:

Work-in-Process Inventory	$34,500	
Raw Materials Inventory		$34,500

If the worker needs more materials to finish, having failed to meet standard, he is issued the needed materials on an excess materials requisition. The issue of these excess materials would be recorded as:

Material Quantity Variance	$900	
Raw Materials Inventory		$900

This method works well if the standards are tight. If the standards are too loose, more materials than are necessary for production will be issued the first time. Unless the company controls the handling of materials in the factory, the workers may try to stockpile any excess materials as a hedge against a time when the standard cannot be met. If the worker is not encouraged to return excess materials to the storeroom, there will be no favorable quantity variance. The goal of the standard cost system is negated, and the possibilities for materials theft and loss are increased.

There can be many reasons for a material quantity variance. Excess usage may be the result of carelessness by the workers using the material, improper machine adjustment, or the substitution of substandard material. Also, employees could be taking materials home or squirreling them throughout the factory. Another possible cause is a modification of quality control standards during a period. Less-than-standard usage could result from the substitution of higher-quality materials than the standard, improvements in the production process, or extra care by the workers in laying out their jobs.

Examination of some of the causal factors for the material quantity variance indicates that overall responsibility for the variance lies with the production personnel. As with all variances, however, this premise should not be accepted without further investigation. For example, assume that a close examination showed the principal cause of a favorable material quantity variance to be the substitution of above-standard materials. This higher-quality material should result in less waste than was anticipated when the standard quantity was set, and could account for a favorable quantity variance. It could also help account for an unfavorable material price variance; above-standard materials would probably cost more. Both variances would have been unavoidable if the materials specified in developing the standard costs were not available, and the purchasing agent bought what he could.

DIRECT LABOR PURCHASED AND CONSUMED

The following journal entry records the direct labor.

Work-in-Process Inventory	$40,000	
Labor Price Variance	$ 1,040	
Labor Quantity Variance	$ 1,600	
Wages Payable		$42,640

The debit to Work-in-Process Inventory is for the actual units produced times standard hours per unit times the standard wage rate per hour. The company produced 500 of the 10A bookcases and 1,200 of style 11A. (Note: Materials were issued for 550 style 10A bookcases, but no labor or overhead was expended on 50 of them. They are still in the Work-in-Process Inventory.) The production of 500 of the 10A style *should* consume 4,000 labor hours (500 units × 8 hours), and the 1,200 style 11A bookcases *should* consume 6,000 hours (1,200 units × 5 hours). Thus, the debit to Work-in-Process

Inventory would be 10,000 standard hours times the $4 standard wage rate. The credit to Wages Payable is for the actual wages paid (10,400 × $4.10).

The **labor price variance** parallels the material price variance. Often called the **wage rate variance,** it is the difference between the standard wage rate and the actual wage, multiplied by the actual hours worked. The labor price variance may be expressed as a formula.

$$\text{Labor price variance} = \left[\text{Standard wage rate per hour} - \text{Actual wage rate per hour}\right] \times \text{Actual hours worked}$$

For the Forddon Company the labor price variance is computed as:

$$\text{Labor price variance} = [\$4.00 - \$4.10] \times 10{,}400 \text{ hours}$$

$$= \$(1{,}040) \text{ Unfavorable}$$

An actual wage rate of $.10 above the standard rate, times the 10,400 hours worked, resulted in an unfavorable labor price variance of $1,040.

One possible cause of a favorable wage rate variance is that management was able to obtain a better worker mix than predicted when the standard was developed. By hiring more workers with lower wage rates, management can affect the wage rate variance. If these workers are less skilled than the skill level planned in the standard wage rate, their employment could have an unfavorable effect on both the material quantity variance and the labor quantity variance. Unskilled workers probably waste more material and time than do skilled workers. Also, a labor-mix problem may arise because of failures in production control to properly schedule the workers' activities.

Just as the labor price variance parallels the material price variance, the **labor quantity variance** is built upon the same theory as the material quantity variance. Also called the **labor efficiency variance,** it is the difference between the hours workers should have consumed in actual production and the actual hours worked, multiplied by the standard hourly wage rate. This variance may be expressed in formula form.

$$\text{Labor quantity variance} = \left[\left(\text{Actual units produced} \times \text{Standard hours per unit}\right) - \text{Actual hours worked}\right] \times \text{Standard wage rate}$$

For the Forddon Company the labor quantity variance is computed as:

$$\text{Labor quantity variance} = [(500 \times 8) + (1{,}200 \times 5) - 10{,}400 \text{ hours}] \times \$4$$

$$= [4{,}000 + 6{,}000 - 10{,}400] \times \$4$$

$$= \$(1{,}600) \text{ Unfavorable}$$

Bookcase 10A required 4,000 standard hours (500 × 8) and Bookcase 11A required 6,000 hours (1,200 × 5). The excess of actual hours (10,400) over the standard hours allowed (10,000) times the standard wage rate resulted in an unfavorable labor quantity variance of $1,600.

This variance is of prime significance to the production managers. It measures how well they use their workers' time. Many causes of the variance stem from the work itself. Poor production planning may have created idle time, machine breakdowns could have occurred, changes in planned volumes could have affected the learning-curve estimates, blueprints and designs could have had errors, or failures to receive raw materials on time could have created worker inactivity. The individual worker and group foreman should be aware of the labor efficiency variances, in hours or units of output, on a daily basis. The *real* control takes place at this point. The statement of the variance in dollar terms at the end of the month is less valuable to the foreman than is the variance stated in hours; his actual planning and controlling activities are in hours.

To make the variances as timely as possible, some firms prefer to separate the entry into two parts. Since the work done in the factory and the workers' actual time can be measured daily, each day an entry would be made to segregate the labor quantity variance. The following entry summarizes the daily entries for the month.

Work-in-Process Inventory	$40,000	
Labor Quantity Variance	$ 1,600	
Payroll to be Distributed		$41,600

Often this data is accumulated by clerks who work at night. The following morning the manager receives a report showing the labor quantity variance of the preceding day. If something is amiss, this timely feedback allows a rapid adjustment. When the payroll is calculated in the payroll department, often weekly or biweekly, the following entry would be made:

Payroll to be Distributed	$41,600	
Labor Price Variance	$ 1,040	
Wages Payable		$42,640

The balance of the Payroll to be Distributed account will be zero at the end of the accounting period. There will be no labor inventory, since workers' time is not stored and workers are paid *after* they work. This method provides additional control over the labor cost. The payroll department computes actual pay and the labor rate variance from the employees' clock cards. The cost accounting department computes the standard cost to be charged to Work-in-Process Inventory and Labor Quantity Variance. The records of the two departments must reconcile through the Payroll to be Distributed account. In a large organization this procedure makes the padding of hours and other fraudulent acts more difficult.

INCURRENCE OF ACTUAL FACTORY OVERHEAD COSTS

The following journal entry records the actual factory overhead costs.

Variable Factory Overhead Control	$15,400	
Fixed Factory Overhead Control	$ 9,000	
Various Accounts		$24,400

The Variable Factory Overhead Control and Fixed Factory Overhead Control accounts will have subsidiary ledgers where the details are classified. Some firms have a *natural* classification of factory overhead. They record factory overhead detail by the nature of the invoice. Separate records are kept for indirect materials, indirect labor, maintenance, heat-light-power, insurance, depreciation of factory buildings, depreciation of factory machinery, and so forth. Other firms prefer a *functional* classification of costs. In these firms the costs are recorded by the function they perform. Examples of functional classifications are departments, cost centers, and factory operations such as materials handling and storage, purchasing, production engineering, and quality control.

Many accounts would be credited to record actual factory overhead. Raw Materials Inventory would be credited for indirect materials; Wages Payable, for indirect labor; Accumulated Depreciation, for depreciation charges; Prepaid Expenses, for such things as prepaid insurance; and Payables, for invoices to be paid.

APPLICATION OF VARIABLE FACTORY OVERHEAD TO WORK-IN-PROCESS INVENTORY

The following journal entry records the assignment of variable factory overhead to the units produced.

Work-in-Process Inventory	$15,000	
Variable Factory Overhead Applied		$15,000

Work-in-Process Inventory is charged for the actual units produced times the standard hours allowed per unit times the standard *variable* overhead hourly rate (10,000 hours × $1.50). The 10,000 hours are the same 10,000 hours used in the charge to Work-in-Process Inventory for standard labor. The Variable Factory Overhead Applied account accumulates the amount of variable overhead charged to Work-in-Process Inventory.

DETERMINATION AND ISOLATION OF VARIABLE OVERHEAD VARIANCES

The difference between Variable Factory Overhead Applied and Variable Factory Overhead Control is Under- or Overapplied Variable Factory Overhead, which can be separated into the variable factory overhead spending variance and the variable factory overhead efficiency variance.

When the volume base of the flexible budget is direct labor hours, it is implied that every hour the workers save or waste has a direct impact upon overhead expenditures. Since variable costs should change with changes in volume, and volume is measured by direct labor hours, a savings in labor hours also results in a savings of variable factory overhead costs. Labor hours saved means overhead dollars saved and labor hours wasted means overhead dollars wasted. The **variable factory overhead efficiency variance** measures the cost impact upon variable factory overhead caused by the labor efficiency. This may be expressed as a formula.

$$\text{Variable factory overhead efficiency variance} = \left[\left(\text{Actual units produced} \times \text{Standard labor hours per unit}\right) - \text{Actual labor hours worked}\right] \times \text{Standard variable factory overhead rate per hour}$$

For the Forddon Company the variable factory overhead efficiency variance would be:

$$\begin{aligned}\text{Variable factory overhead efficiency variance} &= [10{,}000 \text{ hours} - 10{,}400 \text{ hours}] \times \$1.50 \\ &= \$(600) \text{ Unfavorable}\end{aligned}$$

This variance is unfavorable because the actual hours exceeded the standard hours per unit times actual production. The company wasted $600 on overhead because the workers were not efficient. Note that the overhead efficiency variance is equal to the labor efficiency variance in hours times the standard variable overhead rate (400 hours × $1.50).

The causal factors for the variable factory overhead efficiency variance would be identical with the causes for the labor quantity (efficiency) variance. For this reason, some firms combine the labor efficiency and the factory overhead efficiency variances in their management reports. In formula form this variance is:

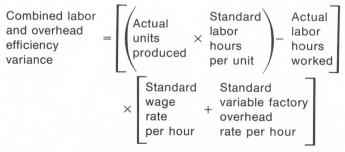

$$\text{Combined labor and overhead efficiency variance} = \left[\left(\text{Actual units produced} \times \text{Standard labor hours per unit}\right) - \text{Actual labor hours worked}\right] \times \left[\text{Standard wage rate per hour} + \text{Standard variable factory overhead rate per hour}\right]$$

The overhead efficiency variance will not be directly related to the labor quantity (efficiency) variance if the company does not use direct labor hours as a volume base for determining the flexible budget. What if the company uses machine hours as a basis of measuring cost variability? The following formula would express the efficiency variance.

$$\begin{array}{l}\text{Variable}\\\text{factory}\\\text{overhead}\\\text{efficiency}\\\text{variance}\end{array} = \left[\left(\begin{array}{l}\text{Actual}\\\text{units}\\\text{produced}\end{array} \times \begin{array}{l}\text{Standard}\\\text{machine hours}\\\text{per unit}\end{array}\right) - \begin{array}{l}\text{Actual}\\\text{machine hours}\\\text{used}\end{array}\right] \times \begin{array}{l}\text{Standard variable}\\\text{factory overhead rate}\\\text{per machine hour}\end{array}$$

The theory of this variance is the same as that of the variance based upon labor hours, but the causal factors are different. Causes for an unfavorable overhead efficiency variance based upon machine hours could include improper maintenance schedules, unscheduled and random machine breakdowns, or human failures in the use of the machines.

As stated earlier, the best method of establishing factory overhead standards begins with developing a flexible budget. The flexible budget in a standard-cost setting states the cost behavior patterns for overhead that the company *should* experience if operations are efficient. It is a standard of performance. The **variable factory overhead spending variance** is the difference between the actual overhead costs incurred and the amount that the flexible budget indicates should be spent on variable costs for the actual volume worked. It is the difference between actual costs and the flexible budget allowance computed for actual hours worked. In formula form the variable factory overhead spending variance is:

$$\begin{array}{l}\text{Variable factory}\\\text{overhead}\\\text{spending variance}\end{array} = \left(\begin{array}{l}\text{Standard variable}\\\text{rate per hour}\\\text{from flexible budget}\end{array} \times \begin{array}{l}\text{Actual}\\\text{hours}\\\text{worked}\end{array}\right) - \begin{array}{l}\text{Actual}\\\text{variable factory}\\\text{overhead costs}\end{array}$$

For the Forddon Furniture Company the standard flexible overhead budget developed before production began was:

$$\begin{array}{l}\text{Standard factory}\\\text{overhead flexible}\\\text{budget}\end{array} = \$9{,}600 + \$1.50 \text{ per direct labor hour}$$

The variable factory overhead spending variance would be:

$$\begin{array}{l}\text{Variable factory}\\\text{overhead spending}\\\text{variance}\end{array} = [\$1.50 \times 10{,}400 \text{ hours}] - \$15{,}400$$

$$= \$200 \text{ Favorable}$$

The calculation of the two variances for variable factory overhead can be summarized into the following schedule.

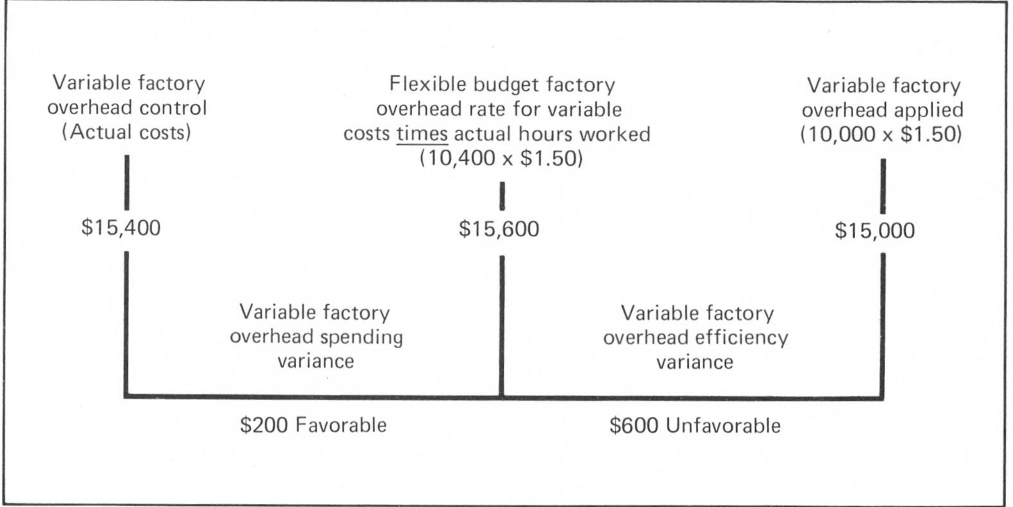

To isolate these variances within the accounting system, the following entry is made.

Variable Factory Overhead Applied	$15,000	
Variable Factory Overhead Efficiency Variance	$ 600	
Variable Factory Overhead Spending Variance		$ 200
Variable Factory Overhead Control		$15,400

This entry closes the Variable Factory Overhead Applied and the Variable Factory Overhead Control accounts, transferring the differences between these accounts into two variance accounts. The algebraic sum of the two variances is $400, which is the Underapplied Variable Factory Overhead.

APPLICATION OF FIXED OVERHEAD TO WORK-IN-PROCESS INVENTORY

If the company uses absorption standard costing, the fixed factory overhead is applied to Work-in-Process Inventory with the following entry.

Work-in-Process Inventory	$10,000	
Fixed Factory Overhead Applied		$10,000

Work-in-Process Inventory is charged for the actual units produced times the standard hours allowed per unit times the standard *fixed* overhead rate per hours. The 10,000 hours are the same as the hours used to charge labor and variable factory overhead to the Work-in-Process Inventory.

DETERMINATION AND ISOLATION OF FIXED FACTORY OVERHEAD VARIANCES

A comparison of the balances of Fixed Factory Overhead Control ($9,000) and Fixed Factory Overhead Applied ($10,000) shows that fixed factory overhead is overapplied by $1,000. The overapplied fixed factory overhead can be divided into two variances: a spending variance and a volume variance.

First, we can see that the Forddon Company originally planned to spend $9,600 for fixed overhead. It actually spent $9,000. The difference of $600 between the planned level of expenditure and the actual level is the fixed factory overhead spending variance. Expressed in formula form:

$$\text{Fixed factory overhead spending variance} = \left(\text{Actual fixed overhead costs} - \text{Fixed costs from standard flexible budget}\right)$$

For the Forddon Company this variance is:

$$\text{Fixed factory overhead spending variance} = [\$9{,}600 - \$9{,}000] = \$600 \text{ Favorable}$$

Second, since the Forddon Company actually produced more than the number of units planned, the fixed factory overhead costs were overapplied. If only the production planned for the period were produced, the Forddon Company would have had 9,600 standard direct labor hours. Instead, actual production required 10,000 standard direct labor hours, or 400 hours above plan. The 400 extra hours times the fixed overhead application rate of $1 per standard direct labor hour resulted in a favorable volume variance of $400 (400 × $1), as shown in the following computation.

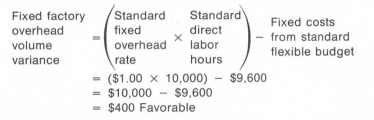

$$\begin{aligned}\text{Fixed factory overhead volume variance} &= \left(\text{Standard fixed overhead rate} \times \text{Standard direct labor hours}\right) - \text{Fixed costs from standard flexible budget}\\ &= (\$1.00 \times 10{,}000) - \$9{,}600\\ &= \$10{,}000 - \$9{,}600\\ &= \$400 \text{ Favorable}\end{aligned}$$

The volume variance is favorable because the company applied more fixed costs than it had planned.

By coincidence, the variable factory overhead efficiency variance is also based upon a variance of 400 labor hours. These are *not* the same 400 labor hours. The Forddon Company used 10,400 actual hours to produce units that should have taken 10,000 hours. This difference is due to labor inefficiency. The company had *planned* to use 9,600 standard hours and actually used 10,000 standard hours, the result of overutilization of the productive capacity measured by the volume variance. It is *not* the result of efficiency or inefficiency.

The **fixed factory overhead volume variance** results from the application of fixed factory overhead costs to the products through a predetermined overhead rate. The standard fixed factory overhead rate is determined by dividing budgeted fixed factory overhead by the planned level of direct labor hours. Unless the planned number of hours is actually attained during the period, a volume variance will occur. The volume variance is favorable (overabsorbed) if more hours are worked (and therefore more fixed factory overhead applied) than planned. If the volume used to apply fixed factory overhead is less than the standard normal hours, the volume variance is unfavorable (underabsorbed).

The volume variance can be appreciated through a graph. The Fordon Furniture Company budgeted fixed factory overhead at $9,600 per month. Since production was planned at 9,600 standard normal hours for the month, the standard fixed factory overhead rate is $1 ($9,600 ÷ 9,600 hours) per standard direct labor hour. The accompanying graph shows the volume variances.

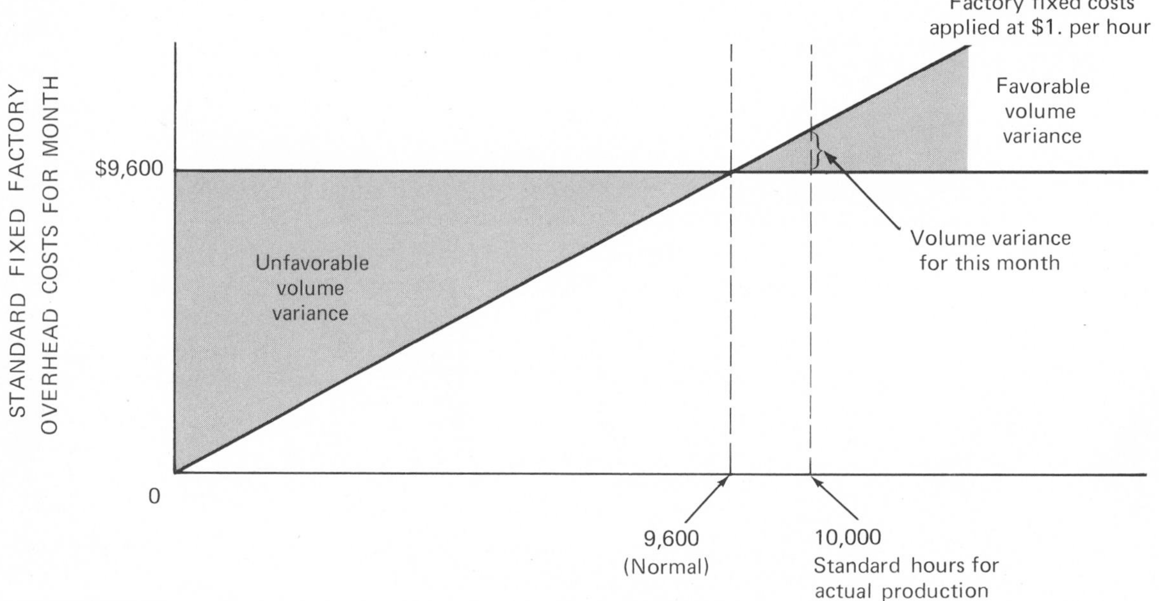

In our example the $9,600 of fixed factory overhead costs are assumed to remain constant over the entire production range. At the same time, the fixed factory overhead costs assume the characteristics of a variable cost when they are applied to work in process through the overhead rate. The application of fixed factory overhead is represented by a straight line from the zero cost and activity point through $9,600 of cost at the 9,600-hour level.

Short of the 9,600-hour level, an unfavorable volume variance results from an insufficient amount of fixed factory overhead costs being applied to the products. Beyond the 9,600-hour level, more fixed factory overhead costs are applied than budgeted.

The calculation of the two fixed factory overhead variances can be summarized into the following schedule.

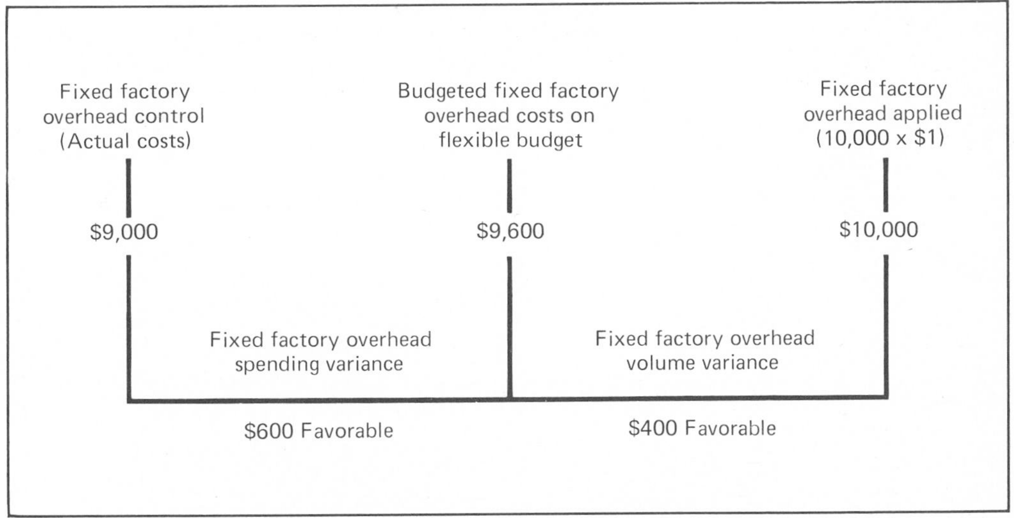

Under absorption standard costing, the following entry closes the Fixed Factory Overhead Applied and Control accounts and establishes the fixed factory overhead volume variance and the fixed factory overhead spending variance for the Forddon Company.

Fixed Factory Overhead Applied	$10,000	
Fixed Factory Overhead Volume Variance		$ 400
Fixed Factory Overhead Spending Variance		$ 600
Fixed Factory Overhead Control		$9,000

The algebraic sum of the two fixed factory overhead variances ($1,000) is the overapplied fixed factory overhead.

COMPLETION AND TRANSFER TO FINISHED GOODS INVENTORY

When the finished product is transferred from the factory to the finished goods warehouse, the following entry is made under absorption standard costing.

Finished Goods Inventory	$98,000	
Work-in-Process Inventory		$98,000

There were 500 style 10A bookcases at the total standard cost of $82.00 per unit (see the standard cost card) and 1,200 of the 11A bookcases at a total standard cost of $47.50 per unit completed this period. The total transferred to Finished Goods Inventory is $98,000 [(500 × $82.00) + (1,200 × $47.50)]. Since Work-in-Process Inventory is charged only for the total standard costs of actual production, the transfer from Work-in-Process Inventory to Finished Goods Inventory will be at total standard cost.

The following T-account shows the Work-in-Process Inventory general ledger account after all transactions are posted.

Work-in-Process Inventory (Absorption Costing)

Beginning Inventory	$ 0	Transferred to	
Materials	34,500	Finished Goods	$98,000
Labor	40,000	Ending Inventory	1,500
Variable Overhead	15,000		$99,500
Fixed Overhead	10,000		
	$99,500		
Inventory	$ 1,500		

The end-of-the-period inventory is $1,500. The correctness of this inventory can be tested with a physical count. You will remember that materials were issued for 550 style 10A bookcases, but only 500 were completed, leaving a final inventory of 50 units consisting only of raw materials. The standard cost of material for the 10A style is $30 and the final inventory is (50 × $30), or $1,500.

SALES TO CUSTOMERS

The following journal entry records the sales revenue.

Accounts Receivable	$122,250	
Sales		$122,250

The source of this entry is the individual sales invoice, which is completely independent of the standard cost system. Total sales were $122,250 [(450 × $125) + (1,100 × $60)].

COST OF GOODS SOLD RECOGNITION

The following journal entry records the transfer from the Finished Goods Inventory to Cost of Goods Sold under absorption costing.

Cost of Goods Sold	$89,150	
Finished Goods Inventory		$89,150

Because the Finished Goods Inventory is carried at total standard cost, the transfer to Cost of Goods Sold will be at total standard cost [(450 × $82) + (1,100 × $47.50)]. To see the Finished Goods account, let's post all transactions to the general ledger account.

Finished Goods Inventory (Absorption Costing)

Beginning Inventory	$ 0	Units Sold	$89,150
Units Completed	98,000	Ending Inventory	8,850
	$98,000		$98,000
Inventory	$ 8,850		

A physical count of the units in the final finished goods inventory should show 50 units of style 10A (500 completed less 450 sold) and 100 units of style 11A (1,200 completed less 1,100 sold). At the standard cost, the final balance of Finished Goods Inventory is:

Style 10A	50 × $82.00	=	$4,100
Style 11A	100 × $47.50	=	4,750
Total Ending Inventory			$8,850

RECORDING SELLING AND ADMINISTRATIVE EXPENSES

The following summary entry records the selling and administrative expenses.

Fixed Selling Expense Control	$2,000	
Variable Selling Expense Control	$2,800	
Administrative Expense Control	$3,500	
Various Accounts		$8,300

At this point managerial reports for the nonproduction costs can be prepared. These reports should contrast the planned level of expenditures with the actual performance. The accompanying tabulation shows such a report for the Forddon Company.

	Flexible Budget Allowances	*Actual Expenditures*	*Spending Variance*
Fixed selling expenses	$2,400	$2,000	$ 400
Variable selling expenses	3,100	2,800	300
Administrative expenses	3,000	3,500	(500)
Total	$8,500	$8,300	$ 200

Variable selling expenses should be $2 times the actual units sold. The company sold 450 plus 1,100 units for a total of 1,550. Thus, planned variable expenses are 1,550 × $2, or $3,100.

DISPOSITION OF VARIANCES

At the end of the accounting period the variance accounts must be closed. In the majority of cases the variances are closed directly to Cost of Goods Sold or Income Summary for the current period. With absorption standard costing, this entry would be:

Cost of Goods Sold (or Income Summary)	$1,840	
Variable Factory Overhead Spending Variance	$ 200	
Material Price Variance	$1,100	
Fixed Factory Overhead Volume Variance	$ 400	
Fixed Factory Overhead Spending Variance	$ 600	
Material Quantity Variance		$ 900
Labor Price Variance		$1,040
Labor Quantity Variance		$1,600
Variable Factory Overhead Efficiency Variance		$ 600

This entry treats the variances as period costs rather than product costs. This treatment is generally accepted if the standards are based upon the philosophical approach of tight but attainable goals, i.e. the normal standard. If the standards are so tight or so loose that they are not valid measures of what costs should be with efficient operations, most accountants believe that the variances should be allocated among Work-in-Process Inventory, Finished Goods Inventory, and Cost of Goods Sold, proportionate to the locations of produced inventory. This method is used only when the variances are so material in amount as to distort the purposes of the standard cost system and hence net income.

PREPARATION OF INCOME STATEMENT

The final step is the reporting process via the preparation of the end-of-the-period income statement. Exhibit 11-5 shows an absorption standard costing income statement for the Forddon Furniture Company.

Illustration of Variable Standard Cost System

As shown in Exhibits 11-2 and 11-3, the only difference between variable and absorption standard costing lies in the handling of the fixed factory overhead costs. With absorption standard costing they are applied to the Work-in-Process Inventory and treated as product costs. With variable standard costing the fixed factory overhead costs are *not* applied to work in process; rather, they are treated as period costs.

In this section we will continue with our illustration of the Forddon Furniture Company, using variable standard costing. The inventory values per unit of product with variable standard costing would be $74.00 for the style 10A bookcase and $42.50 for the style 11A bookcase. Under absorption

THE FORDDON FURNITURE COMPANY
ABSORPTION COSTING INCOME STATEMENT
For the Month of January, 19X7

Sales		$122,250
Less: Standard cost of goods sold		89,150
Gross margin		$ 33,100
Adjustments for variances		
Material price variance	$ 1,100	
Material quantity variance	(900)	
Labor price variance	(1,040)	
Labor quantity variance	(1,600)	
Variable factory overhead spending variance	200	
Variable factory overhead efficiency variance	(600)	
Fixed factory overhead spending variance	400	
Fixed factory overhead volume variance	600	(1,840)
Adjusted gross margin		$ 31,260
Less		
Fixed selling expenses	$ 2,000	
Variable selling expenses	2,800	
Administrative expenses	3,500	8,300
Net income		$ 22,960

EXHIBIT 11-5
Income statement using absorption standard costing

standard costing they were $82.00 and $47.50 respectively. The difference is the amount of apportioned fixed factory overhead, as shown in Exhibit 11-4. Since the only difference between the two costing systems lies in the fixed factory overhead area, the following entries would be the same under either costing assumption.

1. Material Purchases
2. Issue of Materials
3. Direct Labor Purchased and Consumed
4. Incurrence of Actual Factory Overhead Costs
5. Application of Variable Factory Overhead to Work-in-Process Inventory
6. Determination and Isolation of Variable Factory Overhead Variances
7. Sales to Customers
8. Recording Selling and Administrative Expenses

With the following entries, however, there would be differences.

1. Application of Fixed Factory Overhead
2. Completion and Transfer to Finished Goods Inventory
3. Cost of Goods Sold Recognition
4. Disposition of Variances
5. Preparation of Income Statement

A discussion of these differences follows.

APPLICATION OF FIXED FACTORY OVERHEAD AND DETERMINATION OF VARIANCES

There is no entry to apply fixed factory overhead costs in a variable standard cost system because they are treated as period costs. The actual fixed factory overhead costs shown in the Fixed Factory Overhead Control account are closed directly to Income Summary at the end of the accounting period. There would, of course, be no volume variance with variable standard costing, but there would be a fixed factory overhead spending variance. This variance, however, is seldom recorded in a specific variance account in the books of account. Instead, most firms show the detail of the fixed factory overhead spending variance in a supplementary management report.

COMPLETION AND TRANSFER TO FINISHED GOODS INVENTORY

The following journal entry under variable standard costing transfers the goods from Work-in-Process Inventory to the Finished Goods Inventory.

Finished Goods Inventory	$88,000	
Work-in-Process Inventory		$88,000

The amount of the transfer was determined as [(500 × $74) + (1200 × $42.50)], or $88,000. The Work-in-Process Inventory account, after posting, would be as shown in the following T-account.

Work-in-Process Inventory (Variable Costing)

Beginning Inventory	$ 0	Transferred to Finished Goods	$88,000
Materials	34,500	Ending Inventory	1,500
Labor	40,000		$89,500
Variable Overhead	15,000		
	$89,500		
Inventory	$ 1,500		

The final Work-in-Process Inventory is the same for absorption and variable costing in our example because there are no overhead costs in the ending Work-in-Process Inventory. The only costs associated with the 50 units in Work-in-Process Inventory were raw materials. Materials were issued, but no other work had been performed.

COST OF GOODS SOLD RECOGNITION

The following journal entry records the transfer from Finished Goods Inventory to Cost of Goods Sold under variable standard costing.

Cost of Goods Sold	$80,050	
Finished Goods Inventory		$80,050

Since the Finished Goods Inventory is carried at variable standard cost, the transfer to Cost of Goods Sold will be at variable standard cost [(450 × $74) + (1,100 × $42.50)]. The Finished Goods Inventory account, after posting, would be:

Finished Goods Inventory (Variable Costing)

Beginning Inventory	$ 0	Units Sold	$80,050
Units Completed	88,000	Ending Inventory	7,950
	$88,000		$88,000
Inventory	$ 7,950		

The final Finished Goods Inventory, based upon the physical count, can be reconciled as:

Style 10A	50 × $74.00	=	$3,700
Style 11A	100 × $42.50	=	4,250
Total ending inventory			$7,950

DISPOSITION OF VARIANCES

With variable standard costing, the following entry closes the variances to Cost of Goods Sold.

Cost of Goods Sold (or Income Summary)	$2,840	
Variable Factory Overhead Spending Variance	$ 200	
Material Price Variance	$1,100	
Material Quantity Variance		$ 900
Labor Price Variance		$1,040
Labor Quantity Variance		$1,600
Variable Factory Overhead Efficiency Variance		$ 600

PREPARATION OF INCOME STATEMENT

Exhibit 11-6 shows the income statement prepared with variable standard costs. There is a $900 difference in net income between variable standard costing ($22,060) and absorption standard costing ($22,960). This is accounted for by the difference in the inventory values. Variable costing charged all fixed production costs to the current period, whereas absorption costing held $900 of these fixed costs in the inventory.

THE FORDDON FURNITURE COMPANY
CONTRIBUTION MARGIN INCOME STATEMENT
For the Month of January, 19X7

Sales		$122,250	100%
Less: Standard variable cost of goods sold		80,050	65%
Standard contribution from production		$ 42,200	35%
Adjustments for variances			
Material price variance	$ 1,100		
Material quantity variance	(900)		
Labor price variance	(1,040)		
Labor quantity variance	(1,600)		
Variable factory overhead spending variance	200		
Variable factory overhead efficiency variance	(600)	(2,840)	
Adjusted contribution margin from production		$ 39,360	
Variable selling costs		2,800	
Contribution margin		$ 36,560	
Less fixed costs			
Fixed factory overhead expense	$ 9,000		
Fixed selling expenses	2,000		
Administrative expenses	3,500		
Total fixed costs		14,500	
Net income		$ 22,060	

EXHIBIT 11-6
Income statement using variable standard costing

SELECTION OF A STANDARD COST SYSTEM

Management's selection of accounting policies is influenced by many factors. Some of these factors include the need for planning and control information within the firm, the requirements for external and compliance reporting, and the provisions of the IRS tax code. In this chapter we have contrasted an absorption standard costing system with a variable standard costing system—a specific application of the broader discussion of absorption and variable costing in Chapter 5.

On the whole, a variable standard costing system is more consistent with the planning process because it allows management to use variable costs in several decision models without adjustment. The unit cost under absorption standard costing cannot be used directly as a measure of incremental costs because it includes an element of fixed factory overhead. However, the absorption standard costing system is consistent with external reporting and income tax requirements. If the standard costs represent currently attainable performance standards, the inventory values under absorption standard costing are acceptable under generally accepted accounting principles. The inventory values under variable standard costing are not acceptable for external reporting because they exclude fixed factory costs.

Control is achieved through developing accounting data by responsibility centers. Under a responsibility accounting system, revenues and costs are charged to the responsibility center that controls them. Responsibility for costs does not follow the fixed-variable cost distinction stressed in variable costing. In this chapter the impression was given that the standard cost variances were computed only in total for the firm. Variances should be computed by responsibility centers as well. Of course, the total of the responsibility centers' variances will equal the total variances shown here. Only the volume variance under absorption costing is inconsistent with responsibility accounting.

By maintaining both variable- and full-cost data as we have done in the absorption costing system in this chapter, the firm is able to draw out variable-cost data for planning and control purposes and full-cost data for external reporting requirement.

SUMMARY

Standard cost systems are intended to aid management in the planning and control of costs. Standard costs are scientific determinations of what costs *should* be if production is efficient. Standards must be established for each material, labor, and factory overhead cost. They are set by examining production processes, material usage patterns, work measurement and time studies, learning curves, and the development of a flexible budget for overhead.

There are numerous approaches to the setting of standards. The most useful in planning and controlling costs are normal standards, sometimes called *currently attainable standards.* These costs are achievable. They are useful in providing realistic benchmarks for workers' activities and represent reasonable goals for performance.

The value of a standard cost system is predicated upon the ability to extract meaningful variances by developing standard costs for one unit of product. Then, by comparing actual activity with standards, it is possible to assess performance. There are two types of variances applicable to all variable costs: the price variance and the quantity variance. The price variance is:

(Standard price − Actual price) × Actual quantity

The quantity variance is:

(Standard quantity − Actual quantity) × Standard price

These variances act as direction finders. They indicate when actual performance differs from standard performance but do not give the causal factors for these differences. In this sense, the variances could be looked upon as the starting point of investigation, rather than as the terminal point. Management must use the variances as attention-directing devices, and then follow up with a more detailed analysis of the causes and their effects.

To achieve the maximum benefits from standard costs, they should be blended into the accounting system. In this way standard costs become both planning and control vehicles and inventory costing values. In accounting for the inventories, a firm may use, internally, either variable standard costing or absorption standard costing.

SUPPLEMENTARY READING

Claydon, Henry L. "Setting Standards and Evaluating Performance." *Cost and Management,* May, 1965.

Kravitz, Bernard J. "The Standard Cost Review." *Management Controls,* November, 1968.

Miles, Raymond E., and Roger C. Vergin. "Behavioral Properties of Variance Controls." *California Management Review,* Spring, 1966.

National Association of Accountants. *How Standard Costs are Used Currently.* New York: National Association of Accountants, 1948.

Rayburn, L. Gayle. "Setting Standards for Distribution Costs." *Management Services,* March–April, 1967.

Solomons, David. "Flexible Budgets and the Analysis of Overhead Variances." *Management International,* 1961.

Summers, Edward L., and Glenn A. Welsch. "How Learning Curve Models can be Applied to Profit Planning." *Management Services,* March–April, 1970.

Wright, Wilmer. *Direct Standard Costs for Decision Making and Control.* New York: McGraw-Hill Book Company, 1962.

Wright, Wilmer. "Use of Standard Direct Costing." *Management Accounting,* January, 1967.

Zannetos, Zenon S. "On the Mathematics of Variance Analysis." *The Accounting Review,* July, 1963.

QUESTIONS

11-1 Define the term *standard* as it is used in accounting.

11-2 What are some of the benefits of using standard costs? What are some of the costs?

11-3 Is a standard cost system suitable for all types of firms? Explain. What types of businesses could make the most effective use of a standard cost system? In what types of businesses would a standard cost system be least effective?

11-4 Does the method of establishing the standard determine the type of standard it is? Explain and describe three types of standards.

11-5 "A standard cost system is a motivational system." Do you agree? Why or why not? Discuss.

11-6 Explain the advantages and disadvantages of using an ideal standard, a normal standard, and an expected actual standard. Which would you recommend for most situations? Why?

11-7 What is a standard cost card? What items should be included on a standard cost card?

11-8 In using standards as a motivating tool, who should be responsible for setting:

a. Material quantities
b. Material prices
c. Labor times
d. Standard wage rate
e. Standard variable factory overhead rate
f. Standard fixed factory overhead rate

11-9 What is a learning curve? Why does it exist?

11-10 What are the principal sources of improvement shown in a learning curve? Can the quantification of the learning-curve rate be found by other than an empirical approach? Explain.

11-11 Explain how the establishment of standard labor costs can be complicated by the mix of labor skills used. Would a schedule of wage rates for each skill level help? Explain.

11-12 A flexible budget based upon past experience cannot automatically be considered a standard. Explain.

11-13 Define and explain the significance of the following:

a. Material price variance
b. Material usage variance
c. Labor rate variance
d. Labor efficiency variance

11-14 What is the relationship between the labor efficiency variance and the overhead efficiency variance?

11-15 Explain the volume variance and its usefulness to management in controlling operations.

11-16 What differences exist in the variances for an absorption costing system and a variable costing system?

PROBLEMS

11-17 Match the following terms and definitions.

1. Ideal standard
2. Normal standard
3. Expected actual standard
4. Material price variance
5. Material usage variance
6. Labor rate variance
7. Labor efficiency variance
8. Variable overhead spending variance
9. Overhead efficiency variance
10. Total variable overhead variance

a. The difference between the actual price and the standard price, times the actual quantity of materials purchased.
b. What should be achieved with normal workers in a normal setting.
c. The difference between actual hours worked and the hours that should have been worked at the level of production, times the standard wage rate.
d. The difference between actual hours worked and the hours that should have been worked at the level of production, times the standard variable overhead rate.
e. What should be achieved if all conditions are perfect.
f. The sum of the variable overhead spending variance and the variable overhead efficiency variance.
g. A measure of how well materials were utilized in the production process.

(This problem is continued on the next page.)

h. The difference between the actual variable overhead incurred and a performance budget for variable overhead.
i. An estimate of what will happen.
j. The difference between the actual hours worked times the standard wage rate and the actual payroll.

11-18 The Ace Manufacturing Company, Ltd. is a medium-sized manufacturing concern producing a variety of regular stock items. The present accounting system is designed primarily for purposes of preparing the financial statements of the business and does not include any formal cost system. The general manager has relied upon periodic statements of profit and loss to indicate the efficiency of operations.

R. Jones, recently appointed as cost accountant, has suggested to the general manager that a standard cost system be installed because it would provide more effective control over the operations of the various plant departments.

REQUIRED:
The general manager has had little experience with cost accounting systems and has asked you to explain briefly each of the following points.
A. The basic principles and theory of standard costing.
B. How standard costs are established.
C. The changes or additions that would have to be made to the present accounting system.
D. How standard costing could be used to effectively control the operations of the various plant departments. *(Canada SIA adapted)*

11-19 The following information is available for the Sunshine Brick Company.

Standard quantity per unit	2 pounds of raw material
Standard cost per pound of raw material	$.75
Direct materials used	210,000 pounds
Units produced	100,000
Actual cost of materials used	$168,000

Assume no beginning or ending inventories.

REQUIRED:
A. Compute the material price variance.
B. Compute the material quantity variance.
C. Assuming that the normal variation from standard for material quantity is approximately plus and minus 2%, should the quantity variance be investigated? Explain.

11-20 The Moonshine Block Company presented the following information for labor.

Standard direct labor	1 hour per unit
Standard direct labor rate	$4.50 per hour
Actual wages paid	$189,200
Actual direct labor hours	44,000
Units produced	40,000

Assume no beginning or ending inventories.

REQUIRED:

A. Compute the labor price variance.
B. Compute the labor quantity variance.
C. Assuming that the normal variation from standard for labor efficiency is approximately plus and minus 2%, should the quantity variance be investigated? Explain.
D. To the extent the information permits, comment upon the control of labor cost.

11-21 The Starshine Bat Company expected to spend $75,000 on variable factory overhead (the standard for variable factory overhead is $1 per direct labor hour) based upon standard direct labor of one hour per unit and $50,000 for fixed factory overhead. During the month the company actually spent $89,000 on variable factory overhead and $55,000 on fixed factory overhead. Actual hours worked were 80,000 to produce 75,000 units. Past experience has shown normal variation in variable overhead to be plus and minus 5% from the standard.

REQUIRED:

A. Compute the variable factory overhead efficiency variance. What does this variance tell management?
B. Compute the variable factory overhead spending variance.
C. Comment upon the control of factory overhead costs. Should you investigate further, or were the costs within reasonable control?

11-22 Blue Waters, Inc., a producer of glass bottles, established the following material standards for its product, #62 blue glass.

3 pounds @ $.60 = $1.80

During the year the company purchased 30,000 pounds of direct materials at a total cost of $19,500 and produced 9,000 units using 28,000 pounds of materials.

REQUIRED:

A. Compute the material price variance.
B. Compute the material usage variance.
C. Are the variances favorable or unfavorable?
D. What will be the inventory cost of the 2,000 pounds of raw material in the ending inventory?

11-23 Blue Waters, Inc. (from problem 11-22) also established labor standards for its product #62 as follows:

2 direct labor hours @ $4.80 = $9.60 per unit

The employees worked 18,500 actual hours to produce the 9,000 units and were paid an average wage rate of $4.85 per hour.

REQUIRED:
A. Compute the labor rate variance.
B. Compute the labor efficiency variance.
C. Are the variances favorable or unfavorable?

11-24 Blue Waters, Inc. (from problems 11-22 and 11-23) established the following standards for variable factory overhead for product #62:

2 hours @ $1.50 = $3.00 per unit

Direct labor hours were used as the measure of volume in developing the flexible budget.

During the year the company produced 9,000 units, employees worked 18,500 hours, and actual variable factory overhead of $30,000 was incurred.

REQUIRED:
A. Utilizing the relevant facts from the three problems, compute the variable factory overhead efficiency variance and the variable factory overhead spending variance. Are they favorable or unfavorable?
B. What is the relationship between the variable factory overhead efficiency variance and the labor efficiency variance?
C. What is the total inventory cost of one unit of product #62 in the finished goods inventory? Use the necessary information from all three problems.

11-25 The Merry S. Company has just completed 100 units of a new product. Production of the 100 units required 1,000 hours of labor at $5 per hour. The company has been asked to produce 300 additional units on a cost-plus-fixed-fee contract. Production of these units involves a complicated machining operation requiring skilled labor. In the past the company has experienced a learning rate of 70% on other complex machining operations.

REQUIRED:
A. What labor cost should the company incur in the production of the 300 units?
B. Assuming the company uses a standard cost system, what labor standard would you use for the 300 units?

11-26 The factory manager of the Robert Springer Company was severely criticized by the vice-president of operations for overspending at a time when sales (and production) had dropped unexpectedly. The vice-president had studied the cost reports of every responsibility center for excessive costs. In the factory cost report he found the following data concerning factory overhead expenses.

FACTORY OVERHEAD EXPENSES
September 19X6

	Actual	*Budget*	*Variance*
Direct labor hours	22,000	30,000	8,000 Unfavorable
Factory overhead	$80,000	$90,000	$10,000 Favorable
Factory overhead applied	66,000	90,000	24,000 Unfavorable
Underapplied overhead	$14,000	0	$14,000 Unfavorable

The factory manager was confused. Labor hours were exactly at standard, and he was certain that he had controlled the factory overhead costs to the best of his ability. He reviewed the previous cost reports and noticed that the budgeted amounts were the same since January 1, 19X6. He came to you for assistance.

You found that the predetermined overhead rate would have been $4 if the expected level of production for the year had been 240,000 units.

REQUIRED:

A. Compute the overhead variances for September, 19X6.

B. Prepare a report to the vice-president of operations explaining the cause of the "overspending." Explain fully, using your analysis from part A above.

11-27 The following standard and actual unit-cost data are for the Shaw Company.

	Standard Cost per Unit	*Actual Cost per Unit*
Direct materials	10 pounds @ $ .50 = $ 5.00	11 pounds @ $ .40 = $ 4.40
Direct labor	2 hours @ $3.00 = 6.00	1.9 hours @ $3.10 = 5.89
Variable factory overhead (based upon direct labor hours)	2 hours @ $2.00 = 4.00	1.9 hours @ $2.20 = 4.18
Total	$15.00	$14.47

During the month Shaw Company produced 10,000 of this product. There were no beginning or ending inventories.

REQUIRED:

A. Compute each of the following variances and indicate whether they are favorable or unfavorable.

1. Material price variance
2. Labor rate variance

3. Material usage variance
4. Labor efficiency variance
5. Variable factory overhead efficiency variance
6. Variable factory overhead spending variance

B. What additional information do you need to tell if costs are out of control?

11-28 The Standard Company has developed standards for its variable costs of manufacturing. The following data relate to February.

Direct material:
 Standard quantity allowed: 3 pounds per unit
 Standard cost allowed: $2 per pound
 Quantity purchased: 260 pounds (Total cost: $532)
 Quantity used: 230 pounds
Direct labor:
 Standard hours allowed: 2 hours per unit
 Standard wage allowed: $4 per hour
 Actual direct labor: 165 hours (Total cost: $644)
Variable factory overhead:
 Standard cost allowed: $3 per direct labor hour
 Actual overhead incurred: $518

During February 90 units were scheduled for production, but only 80 units were actually produced.

1. The material price variance was
 a. $12 favorable
 b. $12 unfavorable
 c. $72 favorable
 d. $72 unfavorable
 e. None of the above

2. The material usage variance was
 a. $20 favorable
 b. $40 favorable
 c. $40 unfavorable
 d. $80 favorable
 e. None of the above

3. The direct labor rate variance was
 a. $4 favorable
 b. $4 unfavorable
 c. $16 favorable
 d. $16 unfavorable
 e. None of the above

(This problem is continued on the next page.)

4. The direct labor efficiency variance was
  a. $16 unfavorable
  b. $20 favorable
  c. $20 unfavorable
  d. $60 unfavorable
  e. None of the above

5. The variable factory overhead spending variance was
  a. $15 unfavorable
  b. $23 unfavorable
  c. $38 favorable
  d. $38 unfavorable
  e. None of the above

6. The variable factory overhead efficiency variance was
  a. $15 unfavorable
  b. $23 unfavorable
  c. $38 favorable
  d. $38 unfavorable
  e. None of the above

(Canada SIA adapted)

11-29 The High Plains Company produces a range of products. Normal activity for a month is 50,000 direct labor hours. Budgeted fixed factory overhead is $100,000, and the standard fixed factory overhead rate is $2 per hour ($100,000 ÷ 50,000 hours = $2).

REQUIRED:
Compute the fixed factory overhead spending variance and fixed factory overhead volume variance under each of the following independent conditions. Indicate whether the variances are favorable or unfavorable.

A. Assume actual activity for July was 41,000 hours and actual fixed costs were $96,000.
B. Assume actual activity for July was 63,000 hours and actual fixed costs were $104,000.
C. Assume actual activity for August was 50,000 hours and actual fixed costs were $108,000.
D. Assume actual activity for September was 80,000 hours and actual fixed costs were $110,000.

11-30 The Westside Community Health Center has established standards for some routine activities including certain lab tests. The standards for performing a particular lab test are:

Lab technician	.8 hours @ $5	=	$4
Materials	2 ounces @ $1	=	$2

During 19X7, 2,000 tests were performed. The tests used 1,750 hours and 3,800 ounces of material. Actual costs were:

Lab technician	$9,100
Material	$5,700

REQUIRED:

A. Compute the price (rate) variance and the efficiency (usage) variance for both the technicians and the material. Indicate whether the variances were favorable or unfavorable.

B. The lab technicians maintained the records of their time by type of tests performed. There are no independent checks on their time. Overall the tests show a small unfavorable technician efficiency variance. None of the tests shows a large favorable or large unfavorable variance for the year. The health center is trying to decide whether to hire another lab technician or contract outside for some of the tests. How useful will be the technician efficiency variance by type of test for this decision? Explain.

11-31 The Meadowdale General Hospital has established standards to control costs for several repetitive operations. The standards for one X-ray are .5 hours at $5 per hour, plus one plate at $2 per plate. During 19X5, 8,000 X-rays were taken. Actual costs were:

Labor ($5.20 per hour)	$21,840
Plates ($2.25 per plate)	$18,675

REQUIRED:

A. How many hours were used in 19X5?

B. How many plates were used in 19X5?

C. Compute the price (rate) variance and efficiency (usage) variance for labor and plates. Indicate whether the variances were favorable or unfavorable.

11-32 The Ontario Company entered a labor contract containing a guaranteed annual wage clause providing a minimum wage of $600 per month for plant employees with at least ten years service. A total of 100 employees qualify for coverage under the guaranteed annual wage clause. All plant employees receive wages at the rate of $5.50 per hour.

Annual budgeted labor costs were based on the usage of 400,000 hours and totalled $2,200,000. Because of the guaranteed annual wage clause, $720,000 of the budgeted labor costs were regarded as fixed.

The following results for the first three months of the budget period were submitted to the plant manager.

	Month 1	*Month 2*	*Month 3*
Actual hours worked	20,000	30,000	40,000
Budgeted labor costs	$134,000	$171,000	$208,000
Actual labor costs	110,000	165,000	220,000
Variance: Favorable	$ 24,000	$ 6,000	—
Unfavorable	—	—	$ (12,000)

The plant manager was perplexed by the fact that the results showed a favorable variance when production was low and an unfavorable variance when production was high. In the opinion of the plant manager, his control over labor costs was consistently good, regardless of volume fluctuations.

REQUIRED:

A. With supporting computations, explain the labor variances submitted to the plant manager.

B. Should the method of measuring the labor variance be changed? If so, how? Be specific. *(Canada SIA adapted)*

11-33 The Hamilton Gadget Company produces only one product. During November the following production variances were shown.

Material price variance	$5,000 Unfavorable
Material quantity variance	$3,000 Unfavorable
Labor rate variance	$2,000 Unfavorable
Labor efficiency variance	$4,000 Favorable
Variable factory overhead spending variance	$1,000 Unfavorable
Variable factory overhead efficiency variance	$2,000 Favorable

During November, production consisted of 10,000 purple gadgets. There were no inventories at the beginning or end of the month. Selling price of the product was $20 per unit. Fixed manufacturing costs amounted to $30,000, and selling and administrative costs were $40,000. The standard variable cost per purple gadget is:

Material	$ 4
Labor	4
Variable factory overhead	2
	$10

REQUIRED:

A. Reconstruct the journal entries for the month.

B. Prepare an income statement for the month using the contribution margin approach.

11-34 The Buzy Donnie Knitting Factory produces a line of mohair sweaters for distribution to wholesalers. Standards for their costs are:

Direct material: 5 skeins @ 4 ounces	$7.50
Direct labor: 2 hours @ $2.50	$5.00
Factory overhead: $23,400 + $1.10 per direct labor hour	
Selling expenses: $15,300 + $1.00 per unit sold	
Administrative expenses: $21,986 + $0 per unit sold	

Normal capacity is 9,000 units, or 18,000 direct labor hours per month. There were no beginning inventories in the Raw Materials, Work-in-Process, or Finished Goods Inventories.

Actual data for the month were:

Sales: 9,100 units at $24 per unit
Production: Materials were issued for 9,500 units; labor and overhead were added for 9,400 units; 9,300 units were completed and transferred to Finished Goods Inventory.
Raw materials:
Purchases: 2,000 boxes of yarn (24 skeins per box) at $37.20 per box
Issues: 1,990 boxes of yarn
Direct labor: 18,950 actual hours at $2.60 per hour
Factory overhead:

Variable	$21,160
Fixed	$26,320

Selling expenses:

Variable	$ 9,300
Fixed	$15,345

Administrative expenses: $23,500

REQUIRED:

A. Prepare journal entries for the Buzy Donnie Knitting Factory, assuming the firm uses variable standard costing.

B. Prepare an income statement for the month. Treat all variances as period costs.

11-35 REQUIRED:

A. Using the information in problem 11-34, prepare journal entries for the Buzy Donnie Knitting Factory, assuming the firm uses absorption standard costing.

B. Prepare an income statement for the month. Treat all variances as period costs.

11-36 Troy Manufacturing Company has decided to branch into the production of fiberglass swimming pools. Early in 19X7 the first pool was completed at the following cost.

Material	$ 500
Direct labor (240 hours @ $4)	$ 960
Variable factory overhead (applied at $1 per direct labor hour)	$ 240
Forms (molds and forms that have a 100-pool life)	$1,000

Troy Manufacturing Company plans to produce a total of 16 pools during the year. Research by the trade association for the swimming pool industry found a learning curve of 75% for the production of fiberglass pools.

REQUIRED:

A. Which of the costs for the first pool are subject to an improvement in learning?

B. What is the cost of the second pool produced?

C. Calculate the cost of the last pool produced in 19X7.

D. How would you set standard costs for the pool division?

11-37 The Alton Company is going to expand its punch press department. It is about to purchase three new punch presses from Equipment Manufacturers, Inc. Equipment Studies indicate that for Alton's intended use, the output rate for one press should be 1,000 pieces per hour. Alton has very similar presses now in operation. At the present time, production from these presses averages 600 pieces per hour.

A study of the Alton experience shows the average is derived from the following individual outputs.

Worker	*Daily Output*
L. Jones	750
J. Green	750
R. Smith	600
H. Brown	500
R. Alters	550
G. Hoag	450
Total	3600
Average	600

Alton management also plans to institute a standard cost accounting system in the very near future. The company engineers are supporting a standard based upon 1,000 pieces per hour, the accounting department is arguing for 750 pieces per hour, and the department foreman is arguing for 600 pieces per hour.

REQUIRED:

A. What arguments would each proponent be likely to use to support his case?

B. Which alternative best reconciles the needs of cost control and the motivation of improved performance? Explain. *(CMA adapted)*

11-38 The management of Bobbi Jo Wholesale Food Company was displeased with the return on investment the company was earning. The company hired a consultant to study the business and make recommendations for changes that would result in an improved return on investment. After extensive study the consultant assured the company that it would increase profits by more than the desired amount if it accepted his recommendations. One of the recommendations was a system of labor standards for repetitive operations (filling orders, packing cases, etc.). Employee morale was high and the workers regarded the company as a good place to work.

Company management accepted the consultant's recommendations and took great pains to have genuine participation in establishing the standards. The foremen and workers involved in each operation assisted in developing the standards. In every operation the employees accepted the standard as attainable by the average employee with reasonable effort. The standard for each operation was tested before formal implementation. A minimum acceptable performance was established at 85% of the labor standard.

By the end of the first year under the standards, income of the company exceeded the consultant's predictions. During the year average performance was about 90% of standard with an average deviation of approximately 2%. Employees whose performance fell below 85% of standard were first counseled, then warned. Of the approximately 250 employees working under the standard only one was terminated for substandard performance. Others were terminated for reasons other than performance capabilities. The terminated employee was not well liked and most employees were pleased to see him go. Not only was his work substandard, he caused many problems and no one liked to work with him.

Union representatives protested the termination on the grounds that the contract with the union listed only three acceptable reasons for dismissal: conduct (primarily missing work and being late), drunkenness, and refusal to obey a proper order. The union argued that quality of performance on the job was not a dismissable offense. A vote of the employees was taken and they unanimously backed the union, giving the union the authority to call a strike.

By the end of the year employee morale was low and labor turnover was high. Most employees were working just above the level of minimum performance. The employees were willing to strike over an action by the company which individually they approved but collectively they opposed.

REQUIRED:

A. What do you think of the manner in which the standards were established?
B. The company achieved its profit objective, but what went wrong?
C. What level of performance could be expected in the future?
D. Is the possibility of termination for poor performance necessary to ensure employee compliance?
E. What would you recommend at this time?

11-39 The Dearborn Company manufactures Product X in standard batches of 100 units. A full-absorption standard cost system is used. The standard costs for one batch of X follow.

Raw materials (60 pounds @ \$.45)	\$ 27.00
Direct labor (36 hours @ \$3.00)	108.00
Factory overhead (36 hours @ \$2.75)	99.00
	\$234.00

The factory overhead rate was based upon normal output of 240 batches. The flexible budget for factory overhead is:

Budgeted factory overhead per month = \$15,120 + \$1 per direct labor hour

Production for April amounted to 210 batches. There were no beginning or ending inventories. Actual data for April are:

Raw materials used	13,000 pounds
Cost of raw materials used	\$ 6,110
Direct labor cost	\$23,364
Actual factory overhead (of which \$14,544 is fixed)	\$20,592
Average actual factory overhead rate per hour	\$ 2.60

REQUIRED:

Prepare a schedule that contains a detailed explanation of the variances between actual costs and standard costs. Indicate whether they are favorable or unfavorable. (The number of actual direct labor hours are not stated in the problem but can be computed from the data. Remember that overhead is applied on the basis of direct labor hours.) *(CPA adapted)*

11-40 The Jones Furniture Company uses a variable standard cost system in accounting for its production costs. The standard cost of a unit of furniture follows.

Lumber (100 feet at \$150 per 1,000 feet)	\$15.00
Direct labor (4 hours at \$2.50 per hour)	10.00
Variable factory overhead (60% of standard direct labor)	6.00
Total unit cost	\$31.00

Standard variable factory overhead was determined from the following factory overhead costs at different levels of activity.

Direct Labor Hours	*Factory Overhead*
5,200	$10,800
4,800	$10,200
4,400	$ 9,600
4,000 (normal capacity)	$ 9,000
3,600	$ 8,400

The actual unit costs for one month were as follows:

Lumber used (110 feet at $120 per 1,000 feet)		$13.20
Direct labor ($4\frac{1}{4}$ hours at $2.60 per hour)		11.05
Variable factory overhead ($7,500 ÷ 1,200 units)		6.25
Total actual unit cost		$30.50
Actual fixed factory overhead	$3,060	

REQUIRED:

A. From the overhead data, develop the linear equation for the flexible budget.

B. Determine the variable factory overhead rate per direct labor hour.

C. Compute the following variances and indicate whether they were favorable or unfavorable.

1. Material price variance
2. Material usage variance
3. Labor rate variance
4. Labor efficiency variance
5. Variable factory overhead efficiency variance
6. Variable factory overhead spending variance
7. Fixed factory overhead spending variance

D. Revise the standard cost card to show the standard cost of production assuming the Jones Furniture Company used standard absorption costing. Calculate the volume variance. *(CPA adapted)*

11-41 Harden Company has experienced increased production costs. The primary area of concern identified by management is direct labor. The company is considering adopting a standard cost system to help control labor and other costs. Useful historical data are not available because detailed production records have not been maintained.

Harden Company has retained Finch & Associates, an engineering consulting firm, to establish labor standards. After a complete study of the work process, the engineers recommended a labor standard of one unit of production every 30 minutes or 16 units per day for each worker. Finch further advised that Harden's wage rates were below the prevailing rate of $3 per hour.

Harden's production vice-president thought this labor standard was too tight and the employees would be unable to attain it. From his experience with the labor force, he believed a labor standard of 40 minutes per unit or 12 units per day for each worker would be more reasonable.

The president of Harden Company believed the standard should be set at a high level to motivate the workers, but he also recognized the standard should be set at a level to provide adequate information for control and reasonable cost comparisons. After much discussion, management decided to use a dual standard. The labor standard recommended by the engineering firm of one unit every 30 minutes would be employed in the plant as a motivation device, and a cost standard of 40 minutes per unit would be used in reporting. Management also concluded that the workers would not be informed of the cost standard used for reporting purposes. The production vice-president conducted several sessions prior to implementation in the plant informing the workers of the new standard cost system and answering questions. The new standards were not related to incentive pay but were introduced at the time wages were increased to $3 per hour.

The new standard cost system was implemented on January 1, 19X4. At the end of six months of operation, the following statistics on labor performance were presented to top management. (*U* designates an unfavorable variance; *F,* a favorable variance.)

	Jan.	*Feb.*	*Mar.*	*Apr.*	*May*	*June*
Production (units)	5100	5000	4700	4500	4300	4400
Direct labor hours	3000	2900	2900	3000	3000	3100
Variance from labor standard	$1350 U	$1200 U	$1650 U	$2250 U	$2550 U	$2700 U
Variance from cost standard	$1200 F	$1300 F	$ 700 F	$ 0	$ 400 U	$ 500 U

Raw material quality, labor mix, and plant facilities and conditions have not changed to any great extent during the six-month period.

REQUIRED:

A. Discuss the impact of different types of standards on motivation, and specifically discuss the effect on motivation in Harden Company's plant of adopting the labor standard recommended by the engineering firm.

B. Evaluate Harden Company's decision to employ dual standards in its standard cost system. *(CMA adapted)*

12 Budgeting: The Profit Plan

SALES FORECASTING

Basic Approaches to Sales Forecasting

ILLUSTRATION OF A COMPREHENSIVE MASTER BUDGET

Company Background

Organization of the Company

Steps in Development of Profit Plan

SUMMARY

In this and the next two chapters, a single firm will be used to illustrate the budgeting process. After an examination of sales forecasting methods, the profit plan for the company will be discussed in this chapter. In Chapter 13 we will develop the cash budget and projected statement of financial position. The planning for profits and the planning for financial resources are thus separated into manageable proportions. However, they are interdependent plans and should be considered as such. Exhibit 10-2 may be used as a reference for an overview of the many parts of the master budget. In Chapter 14 we will complete the discussion of the budgetary process with an illustration of the reporting system and an examination of deviations from the budget.

SALES FORECASTING

A budgeting system must start with an estimate of the output demanded from the organization. In the private sector this output is measured by sales of goods and services. The amount of goods and services to be sold by a firm is a combination of what the market will absorb (*demand*) and what the productive capacity and cost structure of the firm will allow (*supply*). The sales forecast, or demand curve (a continuous curve showing a forecast of sales at different prices), provides an estimate of the potential sales market.

Sales for a particular company depend upon many factors. Too often the price factor is overemphasized. Nonprice factors, such as customer service and promotion, may have a greater impact on sales volume than price. In order to plan its sales a firm must have knowledge of the market in which it operates. Ideally, it knows the impact of each relevant variable on product sales, including the effect of price, customer service, and promotion. More likely, a firm has only partial information and turns to market research to supply the needed market data.

Basic Approaches to Sales Forecasting

There are two approaches to sales forecasting. One, which we will term a *macro* approach, develops a model to forecast total sales. The other projects sales by product, customer, territory, or salesperson, and then groups these individual estimates into an overall sales forecast. We will call this system a *micro* approach.

MACRO APPROACH

Where a firm is fortunate enough to have both a picture of its demand curve and a knowledge of its own cost structure, the optimum sales level may be determined by economic analysis. The demand curve is a graphic statement of the impact of only one variable, price on sales. In Chapter 6 we examined the demand curves for each type of market and the economic approach to pricing. Unfortunately, the demand curve is difficult, if not impossible, to determine in practice. Seldom will a firm have reliable knowledge of more than a very small segment of the demand curve. Market research is one way to develop information about the market so that a picture of demand may be drawn.

Another method used in estimating total sales is the development of a mathematical model that describes the relationship between relevant variables and company sales. Simple regression analysis, demonstrated in Chapter 2 to measure the relationship between costs and volume, may be used to measure the relationship between sales of the firm (the dependent variable) and some relevant variable upon which sales depend (the independent variable). Ideally, changes in the independent variable will lead (precede) changes in the company sales. For example, for a company selling a product used in home construction the number of residential building permits issued in the market area may be closely related to potential sales. If there is a good relationship between sales and building permits issued, and permits lead sales by one period, then regression analysis will provide an estimate of the *next* period's sales based upon housing starts in *this* period. Seldom, however, does one find such a clear relationship.

An advantage of least squares regression is that measures of the expected amount of deviation from the regression line may be computed in probabilistic terms. These measures indicate the reliability of the sales estimate and provide a way to estimate the probability of any deviation from the estimate. Simple regression analysis uses straight-line relationships and requires that a number of conditions be present if it is to provide reliable estimates of the sales. Those conditions were discussed in Chapter 2.

Where sales are influenced by more than one variable, multiple regression provides a mathematical statement of the relationship between sales and several variables. Instead of using only building permits, as in our earlier example, the firm might also use consumer disposable income and the availability of mortgage money in a multiple regression model. We have limited our discussion in this text to simple regression.

Another approach to forecasting total sales is market-share analysis. By applying a company's expected share of the market to economic forecasts of an entire market or industry, a projection of that firm's sales is obtained. For example, assume that one pharmaceutical firm's share of all drug sales in the country is 10%. Further, assume that all legitimate drug sales may be positively related to 1% of personal disposable income. The firm can use government forecasts of personal disposable income, to estimate total drug sales and forecast its share of these sales. One of the goals of many large businesses is to maintain or increase their share of the market. Because government antitrust action is usually based upon market concentration, market-share data is often maintained.

Economic data on markets are compiled, analyzed, and projected by governments, trade associations, and research bureaus. The *Survey of Current Business* published by the U.S. Department of Commerce is one good source of overall market information.

MICRO APPROACH

A company's sales force is a good source of information about future sales. Salespeople can vary from order-takers with very little knowledge of the market to technical specialists who may have a better knowledge of customer needs than the customers themselves. A salesperson with good customer relationships and a knowledge of the market can often project sales with a high degree of accuracy. Total sales projections for the company can be constructed by compiling the salespeople's projections of sales by product or territory.

One possible weakness of these forecasts is that a salesperson's own goals may influence his projection. Where the projection serves as a performance measurement, he may attempt to set an easily attainable sales level with low quotas so that he will look successful. On the other hand, if the sales projection is not a performance measurement, a salesperson's optimistic projections may reflect his hopes rather than his objective opinion of the marketplace.

If at all possible, the sales forecast should be based upon more than one projection. A projection of total sales, through regression analysis or share of the market for instance, should be compared with a composite estimate such as an aggregate of the sales staff's forecasts. If the projections differ significantly, further investigation may be needed.

Many companies use several sales forecasting methods, which may actually constitute separate steps in the overall forecast. Let's assume that the Bobbi Jo Company, a cosmetics firm, uses the following methods of projecting sales to produce a composite that may be called "executive opinion."

1. Each territory sales manager makes an estimate of expected sales in his area; these estimates are grouped into a composite forecast.
2. The product-line managers create a forecast by product groups. These estimates are also combined into a composite forecast.
3. The market research staff prepares a trend analysis, fitting a line to past data and projecting the line for the next five years.
4. The market research staff also uses multiple correlation by considering disposable income, growth trends in the cosmetics industry, and forecasts of the company's share of industry sales.

Each of the preliminary forecasts is studied by the executive committee and a composite final forecast is established. The estimates for the next year by each method were:

	Millions
Sales force composite	$20
Product-line analysis	$17
Trend-line estimate	$19
Multiple correlation projection	$18
Executive committee's final forecast	$18

The final forecast of the Bobbi Jo Company, as determined by "executive opinion," is $18,000,000.

ILLUSTRATION OF A COMPREHENSIVE MASTER BUDGET

The remainder of this chapter is devoted to an illustration of a profit plan for the DeFord Company. It is patterned after a real company, but simplified for purposes of illustration. To keep our example simple we have chosen to limit monthly examples to the first three months of the year and to the total for the year. In its actual budget the firm also prepares monthly budgets for the other nine months. Through this extended illustration we have developed the budget from the firm's basic assumptions, through the various budget schedules, and into the annual profit plan, cash budget, capital expenditures budget, and projected statement of financial position.

Company Background

The DeFord Company is a small manufacturing firm that has been in business for a number of years. It has about 400 stockholders, but a majority of the stock is owned by Mr. DeFord, president of the company and son of its founder. Mr. DeFord is concerned about the firm's future profitability and has decided to develop and implement a formal planning and control system.

The company produces hand tools, which have had good customer acceptance. Two models are produced: Product A is used in the construction industry; Product B is used in the home. Production takes place in a rented plant that has been adequate for the company's needs.

In the past, the major purpose of the accounting system has been to provide inventory costs and financial statements for tax and credit purposes. Internal reports were limited to monthly income statements and statements of financial position. Mr. DeFord wants to implement a comprehensive planning and control system that integrates technical standards for production material and labor, a standard variable cost system, and a comprehensive budget for the entire company. As a first step, technical standards for material and labor were developed by the producing departments. The standards are tight, but the employees accept them as attainable.

Business planning, as discussed in Chapter 10, should include a set of goals that give broad direction. A set of subgoals or objectives can then be developed to provide a time frame and quantity dimension. Objectives furnish the standard for the question, "How much is enough?" As a second step in the planning process, Mr. DeFord developed a set of goals and objectives for the company with the help of his functional managers. The objectives were divided into three groups as follows:

Profit objectives:
1. Achieve a net income after tax of 25% of reported owners' equity at the beginning of the year.
2. Achieve a net income after tax of 10% on net sales.
3. Increase earnings per share by 10% over previous year.

Market objectives:
1. Increase dollar sales of Product A by 5%.
2. Increase dollar sales of Product B by 5%.

Manpower objective:
1. Maintain a stable work force with no more than 5% turnover through layoffs.

Organization of the Company

A simple organization chart for the company is presented in Exhibit 12-1. The marketing department is organized along product lines. Sales to the construction market are made to independent manufacturers' representatives. Sales to the home market are made to wholesalers.

In the shaping department, a machining process shapes the raw material, called a *blank,* into a tool. In the heat-treating department, a hardening compound is placed on a portion of the tool. It is this special hardening process that gives the tool its competitive advantage. The materials handling department has the responsibility for purchasing, handling, and control of the inventories.

Steps in Development of Profit Plan

Development of a profit plan is most clearly illustrated through a series of steps. Each step is preceded by the accumulation of background data. Although they are discussed sequentially, some of the steps could take place concurrently.

Step 1. Sales forecast by product
Step 2. Product mix by product
Step 3. Sales budget by product
Step 4. Production budget by department and by product
Step 5. Purchasing budget by raw material type
Step 6. Departmental budgets by responsibility area
Step 7. Compilation of departmental budgets into profit plan
Step 8. Comparison of profit plan with corporate objectives

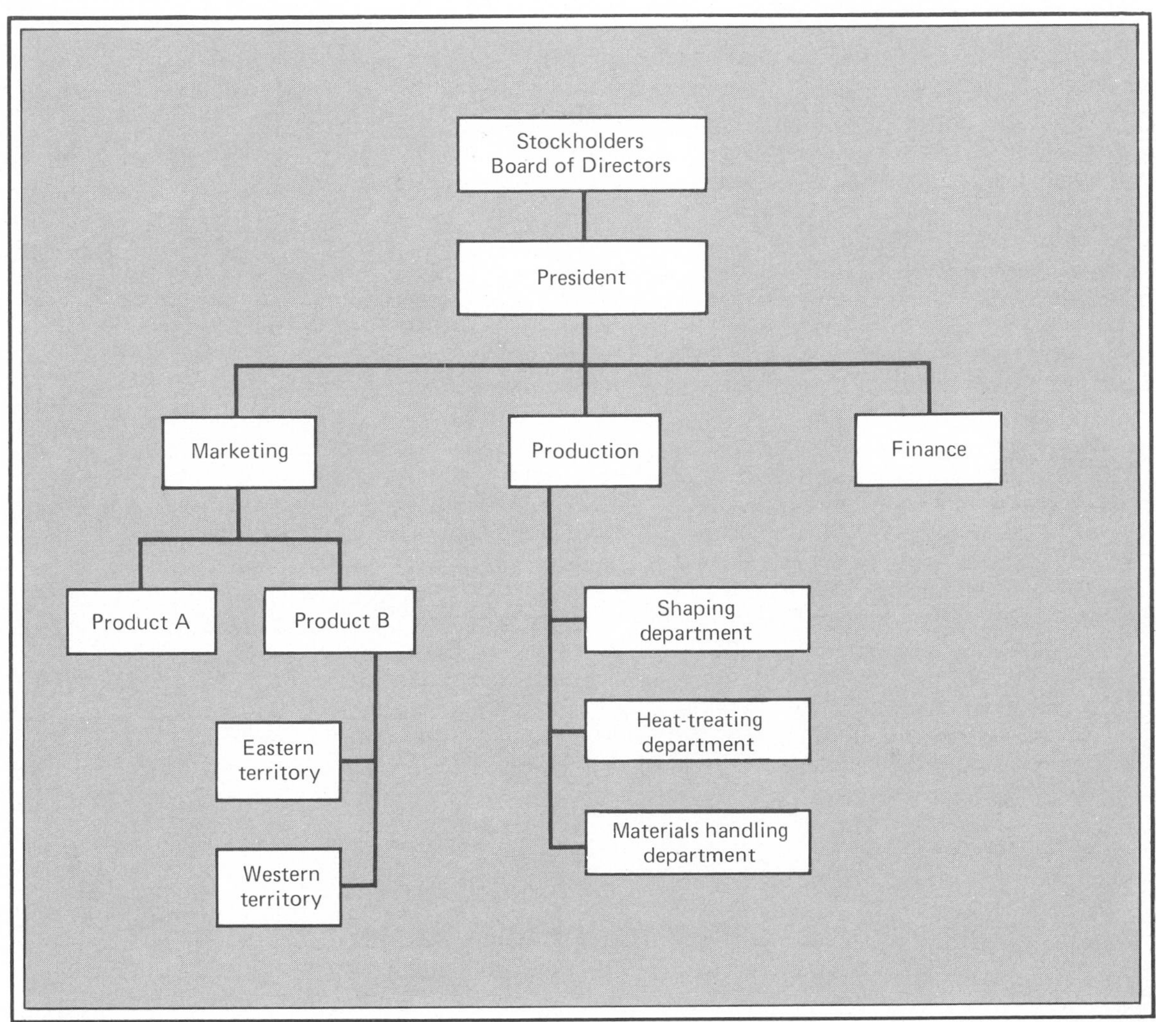

EXHIBIT 12-1
Organization chart for DeFord Company

STEP 1: SALES FORECAST BY PRODUCT

Product A

Product A is sold to the construction market. Mr. DeFord has been following a published summary of construction awards for the market area. He believes these awards may be used to project sales. A scattergraph relating sales of Product A with construction awards for a 12-year period is presented in Exhibit 12-2. Construction awards are rounded to millions of dollars and

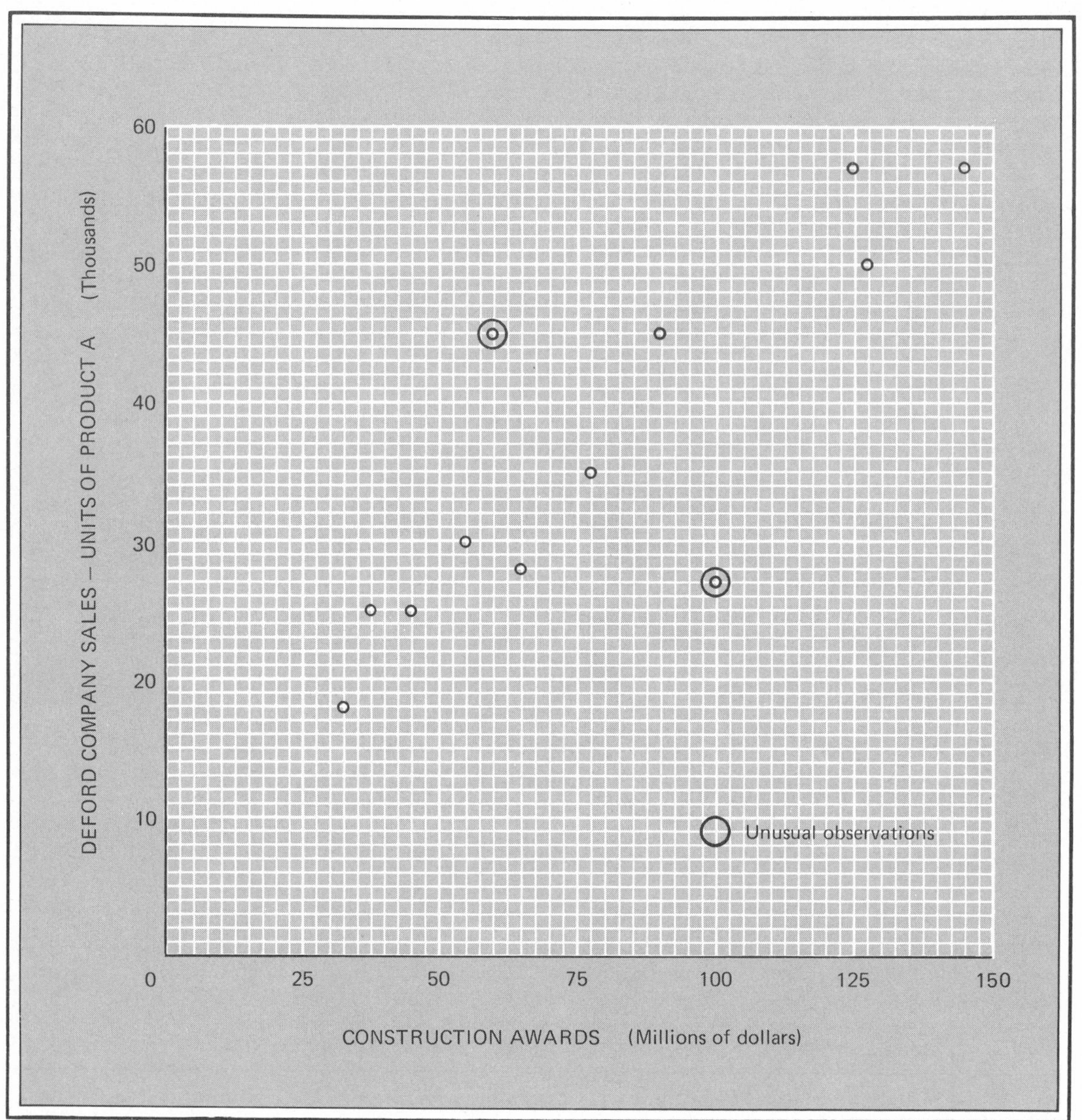

EXHIBIT 12-2
Scattergraph showing relationship between DeFord Company sales and nonresidential construction awards for 12-year period ending 19X9

sales of Product A to thousands of units. Because awards are in dollars and sales are in units, it was necessary to adjust the award data for price-level changes during the 12-year period under study. The scattergraph allows a visual examination of the data for patterns of relationship and for unusual data before regression analysis is performed. This inspection is important because least squares regression will fit a straight line to the data whether or not the actual data falls in a straight line. The data for two of the years seemed unusual and were investigated further. (They are circled on the scattergraph.) In one of the two years employees of the company were on strike and sales were unusually low. In the other year a large government contract included an unusual amount of construction work that did not require Product A. The unusual observations were dropped from further analysis, reducing the number of years of data from 12 to 10.

By visual inspection, a strong positive relationship between sales and construction awards is apparent. The data fall in a straight-line pattern, and a straight line should provide a good measure of relationship. A least squares regression line is computed in Exhibit 12-3 and plotted on the scattergraph in Exhibit 12-4. After omitting the abnormal data, the regression line determined from the 10 years of data is:

$$\tilde{y} = 9.25 + .346\,(x)$$

where x is the amount of construction awards and $\tilde{y}$ is the estimate of sales of Product A in thousands of units. Mr. DeFord subscribes to a data service for the construction industry that has projected construction awards in the DeFord Company's market area for 19X1 to be $147,000,000. Using this estimate in the regression equation, the sales of Product A for 19X1 may be projected as follows:

$$\tilde{y} = 9.25 + .346\,(x)$$
$$\tilde{y} = 9.25 + .346\,(147)$$
$$\tilde{y} = 60.11 \text{ thousand units of Product A}$$

How much variation can we expect from this forecast of approximately 60,000 units of Product A? Standard error of the estimate provides a measure of the deviation of data from the regression line. From Exhibit 12-3 the standard error is computed to be 3.18. Remember that units of Product A were rounded to thousands of units in Exhibit 12-4. Therefore, one standard error is equal to 3,180 units. We may now state that sales of Product A in 19X1 should fall between 56,930 (60,110 − 3,180) and 63,290 ($60,110 + 3,180) units two out of three times. It is assumed that past relationships will continue.

Product A is sold in a very competitive market with an established price of $12 per unit. The Product A sales manager does not believe that the present markets can be maintained if the price is raised. Based upon his knowledge of the market and the customers, he believes that 60,000 units is an attainable level of sales for Product A in 19X1. The sales forecast for Product A is established at 60,000 units at $12 per unit.

Product B

Product B is sold to home craftsmen in a competitive marketplace. Past experience has shown that product sales in the industry are sensitive to price changes and, to a lesser extent, promotion. The trade association's study of the market and an examination of past industry sales data provided the information for the industry's demand curve for Product B, as shown in Exhibit

Construction Awards	Product A Sales						
x	y	xy	x^2	y^2	$\tilde{y}$	$(y-\tilde{y})$	$(y-\tilde{y})^2$
33	18	594	1,089	324	21	−3	9
38	25	950	1,444	625	22	3	9
45	25	1,125	2,025	625	25	0	0
56	30	1,680	3,136	900	29	1	1
77	35	2,695	5,929	1,225	36	−1	1
66	28	1,848	4,356	784	32	−4	16
91	45	4,095	8,281	2,025	41	4	16
127	50	6,350	16,129	2,500	53	−3	9
144	57	8,208	20,736	3,249	59	−2	4
125	57	7,125	15,625	3,249	53	4	16
802	370	34,670	78,750	15,506			81

Computation of regression equation:

(1) $\Sigma xy = a\Sigma x + b\Sigma x^2$	$34{,}670 = 802a + 78{,}750b$
(2) $\Sigma y = na + b\Sigma x$	$370 = 10a + 802b$
(3) Equation (1)	$34{,}670 = 802a + 78{,}750b$
(4) Equation (2) x 80.2	$29{,}674 = 802a + 64{,}320.4b$
(5) (3) − (4)	$4{,}996 = 0 + 14{,}429.6b$
(6) Solve for b	$b = .346$
(7) Insert .346 in (2)	$370 = 10a + 277.5$
(8) Solve for a	$a = 9.25$
(9) State the formal equation	$\tilde{y} = 9.25 + .346(x)$

Computation of standard error of the estimate:

(1) $SE_{y \cdot x} = \sqrt{\frac{(y-\tilde{y})^2}{n-2}}$

(2) $= \sqrt{\frac{81}{10-2}}$

(3) $= \sqrt{\frac{81}{8}}$

(4) $= \sqrt{10.13}$

(5) $= 3.18$

EXHIBIT 12-3
Computation of regression line for sales forecast for DeFord Company

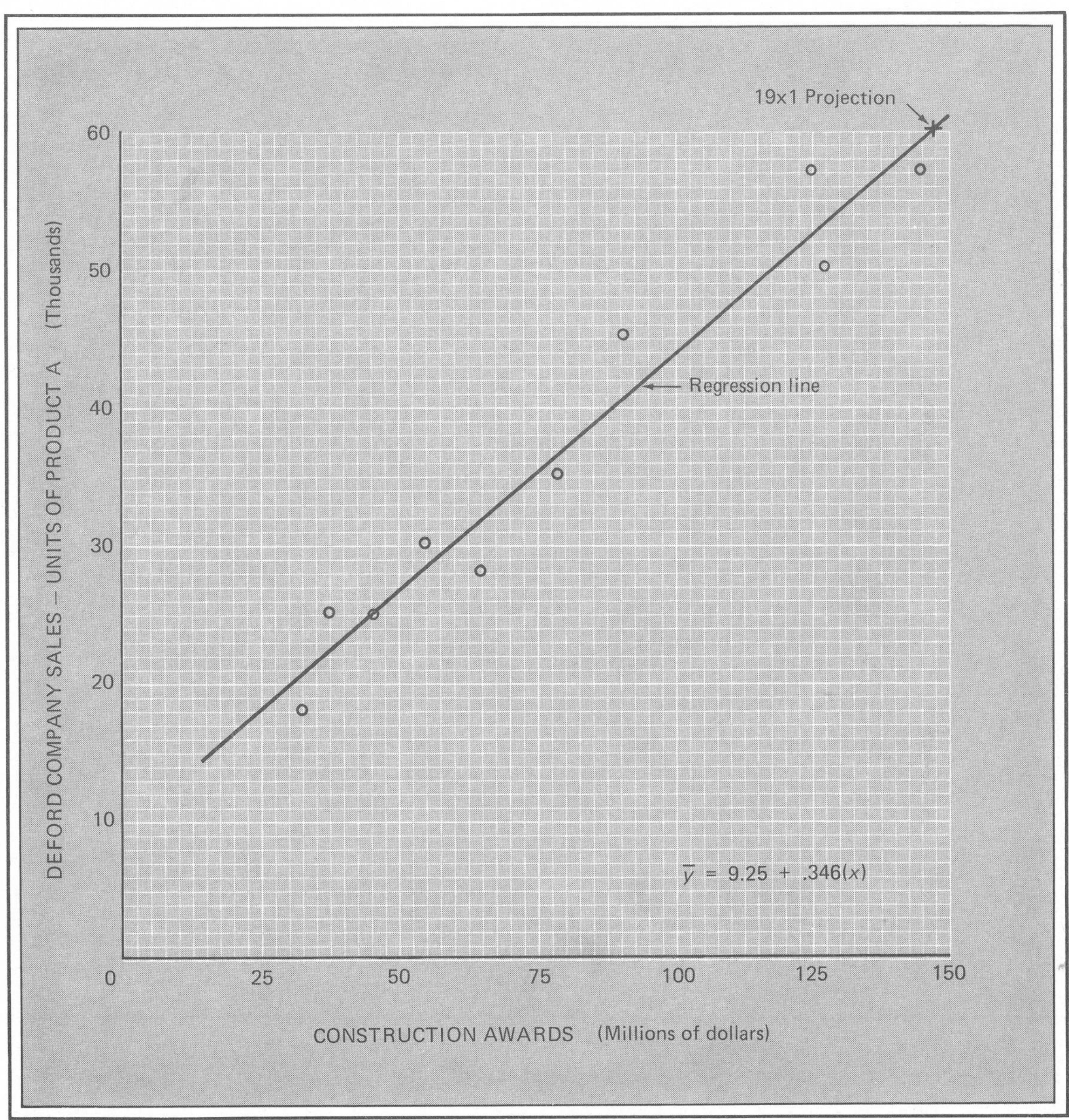

EXHIBIT 12-4
Regression line showing relationship between DeFord Company sales and nonresidential construction awards for 10-year period

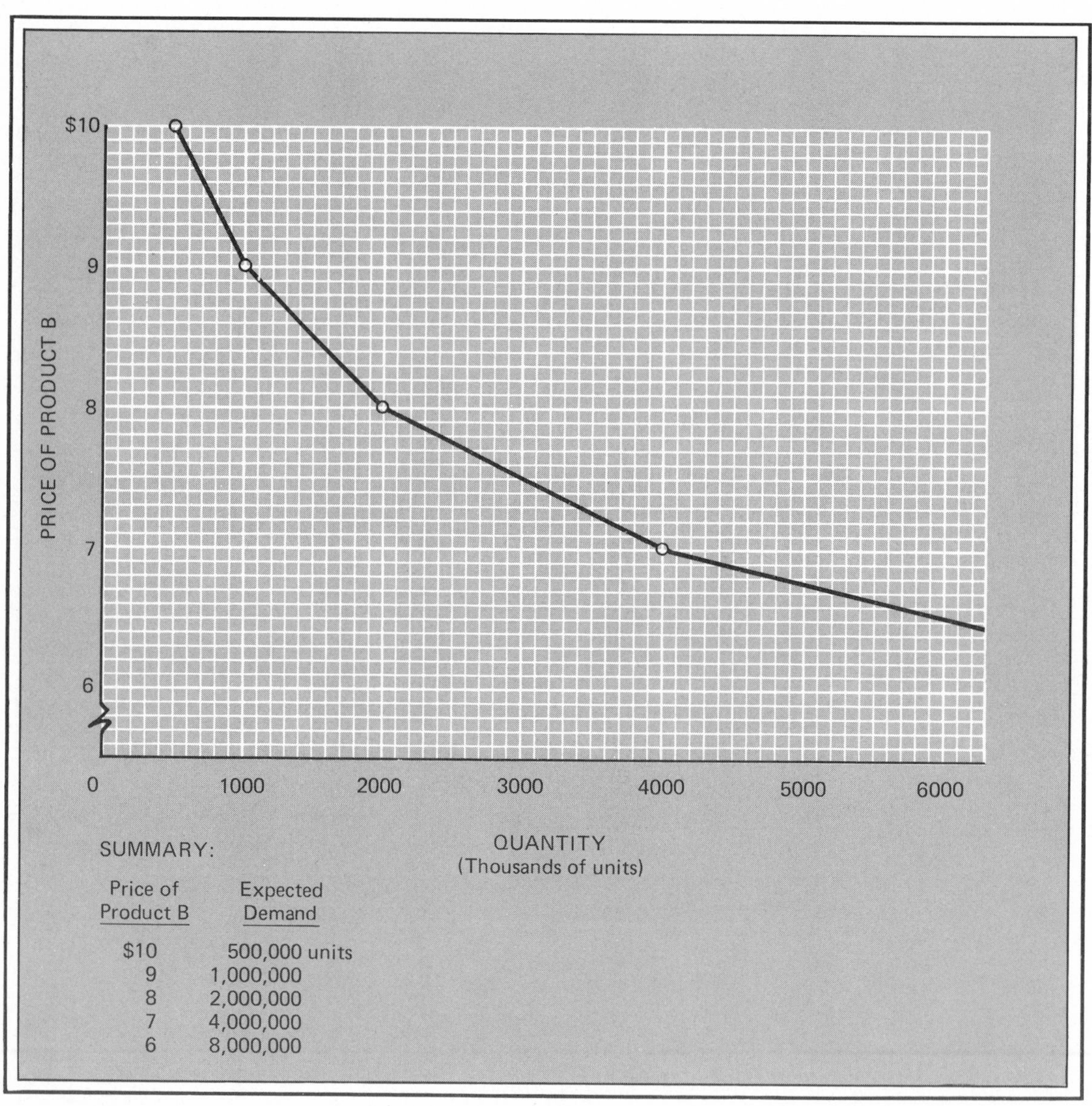

Price of Product B	Expected Demand
$10	500,000 units
9	1,000,000
8	2,000,000
7	4,000,000
6	8,000,000

EXHIBIT 12-5
Industry demand curve for Product B

12-5. The estimated demand curve provides a number of possible industry-wide forecasts, depending upon the price charged. The trade association forecasts that customers will demand approximately 2,000,000 units next year. The industry price will average about $8 per unit.

For the past few years the DeFord Company has achieved about 10% of the total industry market. It has spent about $36,000 in each of the past two years on promotion of Product B. Mr. DeFord believes that because of the competitive market, advertising expenditures would have to be increased substantially to boost his firm's share of the market significantly. He believes that this extra promotion is beyond the financial capacity of the firm. Based upon the trade association's demand curve (shown in Exhibit 12-5), the industry forecast based upon the demand curve, and the DeFord Company's market-share studies, the company can expect to sell about 200,000 units of Product B at $8 per unit.

In addition to the market-share study, the sales manager of each territory totaled the sales projections made by each salesperson and provided the following range of expected sales.

Eastern territory	58,000 to 62,000 units of Product B
Western territory	120,000 to 140,000 units of Product B

Totaling the sales projections of the territories, sales of Product B should be between 178,000 and 202,000 units. An average of the two would provide a projection of 190,000 units. The two projections, 200,000 units from a macro approach and 190,000 from a micro approach, are close. However, before the firm can decide upon the number of units it can sell, it will have to determine the productive capacity of the firm and the level of inventory.

STEP 2: PRODUCT MIX BY PRODUCT

Capacity

Mr. DeFord has defined capacity in terms of one-shift operations. He does not believe that the company has the managerial talent to operate multiple shifts. Practical capacity, the maximum level of output that can be maintained over a long period of time, is measured in labor hours and is limited by the number of machines in each producing department. The shaping department has the practical capacity to operate at a level of 3,000 hours per month, or 36,000 hours per year. The heat-treating department has the productive capacity to operate 2,000 hours per month, or 24,000 hours per year.

The technical standards for labor indicate that Product A can be shaped at the rate of 5 units per hour and heat-treated at the rate of 10 units per hour. Shaping and heat-treating of Product B are each performed at the rate of 10 units per hour. The following tabulation shows practical capacity for the DeFord Company.

	Shaping Department (36,000 hours)	*Heat-treating Department (24,000 hours)*
Product A	180,000 units	240,000 units
Product B	360,000 units	240,000 units

The shaping department can turn out either 180,000 units of A (5 per hour for 36,000 hours) or 360,000 units of B (10 per hour for 36,000 hours) or any combination that does not exceed 36,000 hours. The heat-treating department can produce 240,000 units of either product or any combination that does not exceed 240,000 units.

The practical capacity constraints are illustrated in Exhibit 12-6. Feasible combinations lie inside the dark area bounded by points *a, b, c, d.* A portion of the capacity in the heat-treating department will be idle if only Product A is produced, and a portion of the capacity in the shaping department will be idle if only Product B is produced. In Exhibit 12-7 the market constraints developed by the sales forecast are superimposed over the production constraints, limiting the feasible combinations of products to the number that can be produced *and* sold. Feasible combinations now lie within the dark area bounded by points *a, e, f, g, h.* The following tabulation shows the quantities at each point.

Point	*Units of A*	*Units of B*
a	0	0
e	0	200,000
f	40,000	200,000
g	60,000	180,000
h	60,000	0

Product mix

In Chapter 7 a short-range decision model for product mix was introduced. The short-range decision rule requires the selection of the feasible combination of products that will maximize total contribution margin. In the short range, fixed costs are not relevant to the decision of what to produce or sell. The combination of products that will maximize total contribution margin should be produced and sold.

Standard variable costs have been developed for each product. The standard cost cards are shown in Exhibit 12-13. At this point we will use these standard variable costs to determine contribution margin and discuss their development later. The following tabulation shows contribution margins for the two products.

	Product A	*Product B*
Selling price per unit	$12	$8
Standard variable costs per unit	7	4
Contribution margin per unit	$ 5	$4

Referring to Exhibit 12-7 and the discussion of feasible production combinations, it should be obvious that combinations at points *a, e,* and *h* would be rejected. Combination *f* must provide a higher total contribution

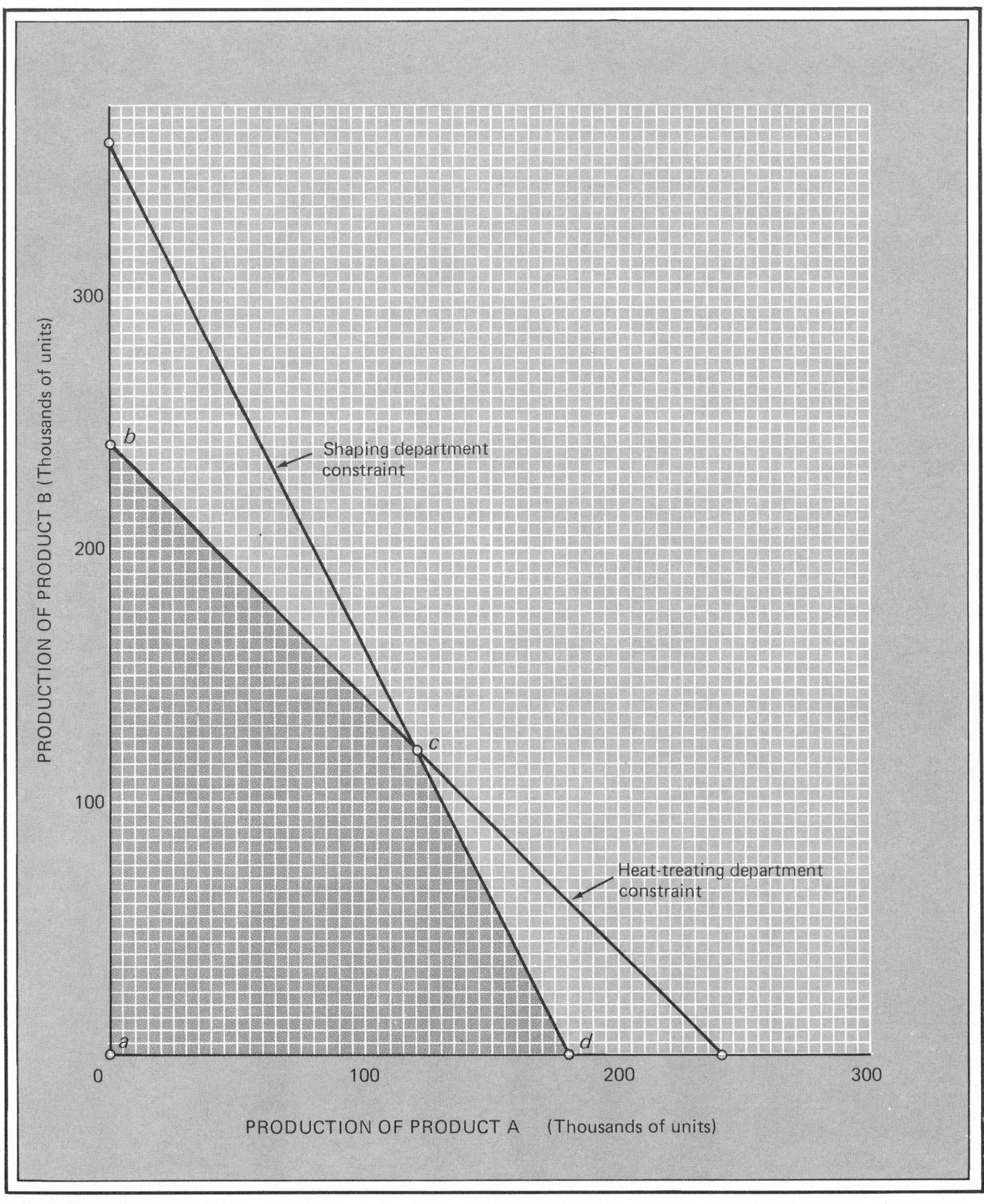

EXHIBIT 12-6
Capacity constraints for DeFord Company

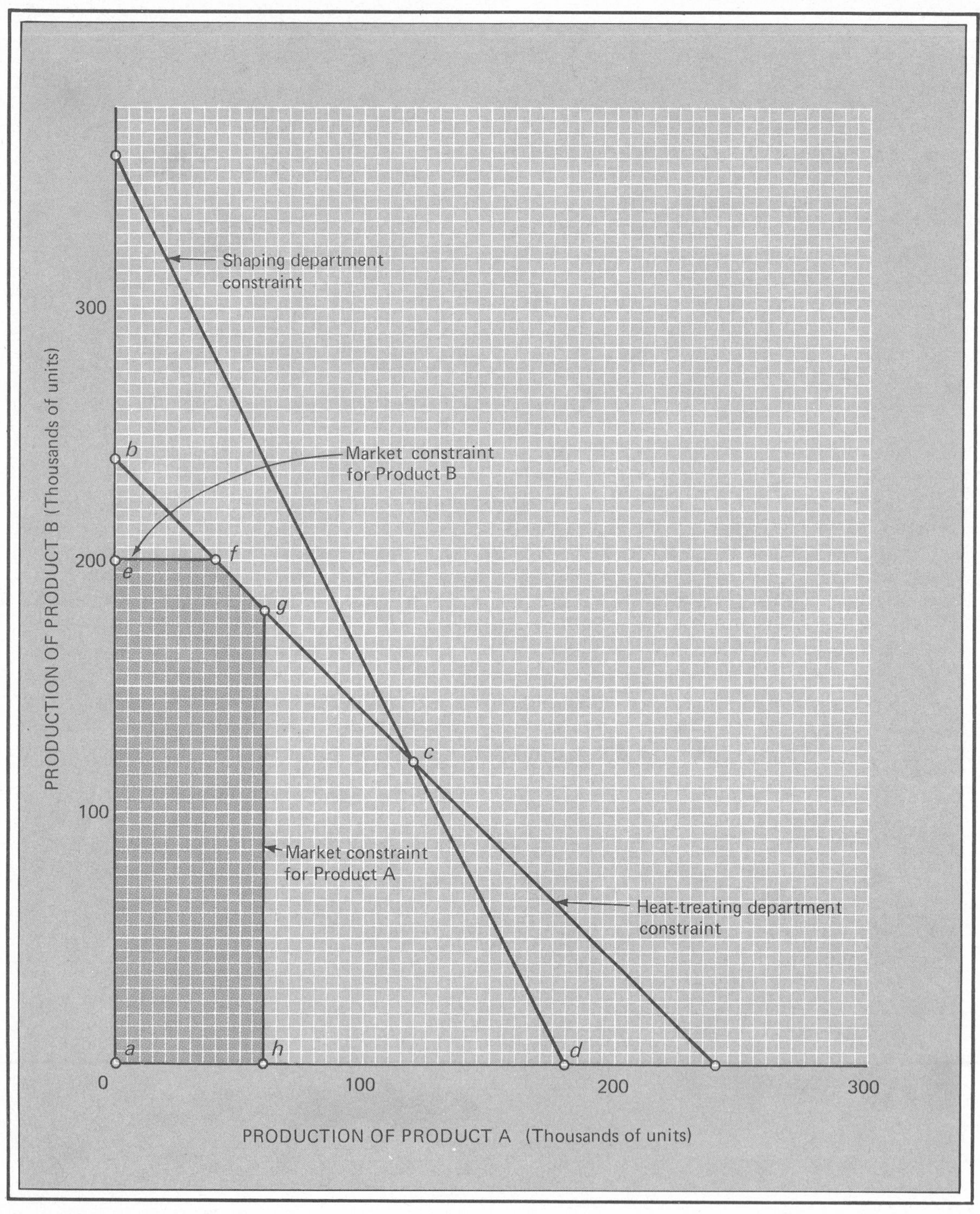

EXHIBIT 12-7
Product mix decision for DeFord Company

margin than point *e* because in addition to the 200,000 units of Product B at point *e*, 40,000 units of Product A would be produced and sold at point *f*. Likewise, production and sales at point *g* would be superior to point *h*. The optimal product mix must be either combination *f* or *g*. Only if the contribution margin were equal at the two points *f* and *g* would any (*and every*) point on the line between the two points provide an optimal product mix. The total contribution margin at each feasible combination is presented in Exhibit 12-8. The optimal product mix is therefore at point *g*, requiring production and sale of 60,000 units of Product A and 180,000 units of Product B.

Referring to the demand curve for Product B in Exhibit 12-5, we can see that at 180,000 units the firm may be able to charge slightly more than $8 per unit for B. It is possible that a higher price for Product B may provide a higher contribution margin at point *h*. One of the assumptions inherent in linear programming is linearity of the objective function; in this case, the contribution margin. If in fact linearity does not exist, as suggested by a downward-sloping demand curve, our solution may not be optimal. One advantage of the mathematical solution to linear programming is that it provides information on what impact movements from an optimal solution will have upon the objective function.

Although the demand curve indicates that a higher price could be charged, Mr. DeFord wants to maintain the price of Product B at $8. He has, therefore, introduced slack by not pricing at what the market will bear.

	PRODUCT A			PRODUCT B			TOTAL
Point	Units	Contribution Margin Per Unit	Total Contribution Margin	Units	Contribution Margin Per Unit	Total Contribution Margin	Company Contribution Margin
a	0	$5.00	0	0	$4.00	0	0
e	0	$5.00	0	200,000	$4.00	$800,000	$ 800,000
f	40,000	$5.00	$200,000	200,000	$4.00	$800,000	$1,000,000
g	60,000	$5.00	$300,000	180,000	$4.00	$720,000	$1,020,000
h	60,000	$5.00	$300,000	0	$4.00	0	$ 300,000

EXHIBIT 12-8
Selection of optimal product mix for DeFord Company

STEP 3: SALES BUDGET BY PRODUCT

The sales budget represents what management believes it will sell. For the marketing areas, it represents the sales target upon which performance measures are based. Budgeted sales are determined by three factors: potential sales as determined by the sales forecast, feasible production as determined by the production model, and inventory levels. If potential sales are less than productive capacity, the sales budget will use the sales forecast, and production capacity will not act as a constraint.

In the DeFord Company the sales forecast exceeded production capacity. The extra sales cannot be made up from the finished goods inventory because the present inventory levels are at the minimum level necessary to maintain customer service.

The management of DeFord Company settled on a sales budget of 60,000 units of Product A and 180,000 units of Product B. The sales projection made by the sales manager of the Western territory was the least certain of the aggregated forecasts. By accepting his lowest estimate of 120,000 units of Product B, the total sales budget of Product B is equal to remaining productive capacity to manufacture Product B. Budgeted sales by month, product, and territory are presented in Exhibit 12-9. Product A shows wide fluctuations in sales to the construction industry, with most of the sales in the summer months. Sales of Product B have a similar seasonal pattern, but the seasonal variations are much smaller. This finalized sales budget now becomes the basis for the remainder of the master budget.

STEP 4: PRODUCTION BUDGET BY DEPARTMENT AND BY PRODUCT

The production budget expresses management's plan for factory operations for the year. It provides each department with an activity base for planning. Normally, the production budget would follow an approach such as:

Planned sales	$xxx
Less: Beginning inventory of finished goods	xxx
Total production needed to meet sales	$xxx
Plus: Desired ending inventory	xxx
Required production for period	$xxx

This step is not necessary in the DeFord Company. In order to meet the sales budget, the DeFord Company must operate at practical capacity each month of the year. Production will be constant in each month and will not vary seasonally with sales variations.

Exhibit 12-10 presents the production budget by department and product. Projected finished goods inventory levels are important because of the wide fluctuations in sales. The fact that planned levels of production and sales are equal for the year as a whole does not mean that finished goods inventory will be sufficient to meet sales during the months when sales exceed production.

	SALES IN UNITS				SALES IN DOLLARS				
		PRODUCT B				PRODUCT B			
	Product	TERRITORY			Product	TERRITORY			Company
Month	A	Eastern	Western	Total	A	Eastern	Western	Total	Total
January	1,000	4,000	8,000	12,000	$ 12,000	$ 32,000	$ 64,000	$ 96,000	$ 108,000
February	2,000	4,000	8,000	12,000	24,000	32,000	64,000	96,000	120,000
March	3,000	4,000	10,000	14,000	36,000	32,000	80,000	112,000	148,000
April	5,000	4,000	10,000	14,000	60,000	32,000	80,000	112,000	172,000
May	10,000	6,000	12,000	18,000	120,000	48,000	96,000	144,000	264,000
June	10,000	6,000	12,000	18,000	120,000	48,000	96,000	144,000	264,000
July	10,000	6,000	12,000	18,000	120,000	48,000	96,000	144,000	264,000
August	10,000	6,000	10,000	16,000	120,000	48,000	80,000	128,000	248,000
September	5,000	6,000	10,000	16,000	60,000	48,000	80,000	128,000	188,000
October	2,000	6,000	10,000	16,000	24,000	48,000	80,000	128,000	152,000
November	1,000	4,000	10,000	14,000	12,000	32,000	80,000	112,000	124,000
December	1,000	4,000	8,000	12,000	12,000	32,000	64,000	96,000	108,000
Total for year	60,000	60,000	120,000	180,000	$720,000	$480,000	$960,000	$1,440,000	$2,160,000

EXHIBIT 12-9
Sales budget by product for DeFord Company

STEP 5: PURCHASING BUDGET BY RAW MATERIAL TYPE

Technical standards for materials usage are applied to the production budget to determine the amount of materials required for production during the year. The following tabulation shows the technical standards for material for each product.

Type of material	*Product A*	*Product B*
Blank A	1 blank	
Blank B		1 blank
Hardening compound	2 pounds	1 pound

These standards are drawn from the standard cost cards in Exhibit 12-13.

The DeFord Company established a desired raw materials inventory level of four-weeks' usage. Required purchases for the DeFord Company are determined in Exhibit 12-11. Computation of required purchases starts with the materials needed for production (from the production budget), then deducts the beginning materials inventory, and finally adds the desired ending materials inventory. In Exhibit 12-11 the company expects the desired inventory levels to be attained by the end of February. For the remainder of the

	JANUARY	FEBRUARY	MARCH	TOTAL FOR YEAR 19X1
PRODUCTION BY DEPARTMENT				
Shaping department (83% of practical capacity)				
Product A (units)	5,000	5,000	5,000	60,000
Product B (units)	15,000	15,000	15,000	180,000
Heating-treating department (100% of practical capacity)				
Product A (units)	5,000	5,000	5,000	60,000
Product B (units)	15,000	15,000	15,000	180,000
FINISHED GOODS INVENTORY LEVEL				
Product A				
Units produced	5,000	5,000	5,000	60,000
Beginning inventory	15,000	19,000	22,000	15,000
Total	20,000	24,000	27,000	75,000
Units sold	1,000	2,000	3,000	60,000
Ending inventory	19,000	22,000	24,000	15,000
Product B				
Units produced	15,000	15,000	15,000	180,000
Beginning inventory	10,000	13,000	16,000	10,000
Total	25,000	28,000	31,000	190,000
Units sold	12,000	12,000	14,000	180,000
Ending inventory	13,000	16,000	17,000	10,000

EXHIBIT 12-10
Production budget for DeFord Company

year, purchases will be equal to production. The actual quantity to be purchased on any one purchase order will depend upon the size of an *economic order quantity*. The decision of optimal order size is examined in the next chapter.

STEP 6: DEPARTMENTAL BUDGETS BY RESPONSIBILITY AREA

In Chapter 10 we stressed the need for coordination or congruence among goals of the manager and goals of the company. The foreman must not only

	JANUARY	FEBRUARY	MARCH	TOTAL FOR YEAR 19X1
Blank A:				
Units required for production	5,000	5,000	5,000	60,000
Add: Desired ending inventory	10,000	10,000	10,000	10,000
Total	15,000	15,000	15,000	70,000
Deduct: Beginning inventory	5,000	10,000	10,000	5,000
Required purchases (units)	10,000	5,000	5,000	65,000
Standard purchase price	x $2	x $2	x $2	x $2
Required purchases	$20,000	$10,000	$10,000	$130,000
Blank B:				
Units required for production	15,000	15,000	15,000	180,000
Add: Desired ending inventory	20,000	20,000	20,000	20,000
Total	35,000	35,000	35,000	200,000
Deduct: Beginning inventory	40,000	25,000	20,000	40,000
Required purchases (units)	0	10,000	15,000	160,000
Standard purchase price	x $1	x $1	x $1	x $1
Required purchases	$ 0	$10,000	$15,000	$160,000
Hardening compound:				
Units required for production	25,000	25,000	25,000	300,000
Add: Desired ending inventory	40,000	40,000	40,000	40,000
Total	65,000	65,000	65,000	340,000
Deduct: Beginning inventory	30,000	40,000	40,000	30,000
Required purchases (units)	35,000	25,000	25,000	310,000
Standard purchase price	x $1	x $1	x $1	x $1
Required purchases	$35,000	$25,000	$25,000	$310,000
Summary:				
Blank A	$20,000	$10,000	$10,000	$130,000
Blank B	0	10,000	15,000	160,000
Hardening compound	35,000	25,000	25,000	310,000
Total	$55,000	$45,000	$50,000	$600,000

EXHIBIT 12-11
Purchasing budget for DeFord Company

be a participant in the budgetary process, he must consider the departmental budget to be *his* budget. As such, it should include only those costs over which he has control—those which he can influence or change. In the DeFord Company all costs have been related to the lowest level of management with the authority to influence or change them. This system was introduced in Chapter 10 as a prerequisite to successful budgeting and was called *responsibility accounting.*

Cost structure

The accounting staff of the DeFord Company examined the cost behavior patterns of *all* costs in the company and obtained projections from the various responsibility areas. The results of the study are summarized in Exhibit 12-12 by the responsibility areas indicated in the organization chart (Exhibit 12-1).

Cost standards

A standard cost system was discussed in Chapter 11. The controller of DeFord Company developed standard costs for each product by pricing the technical standards for materials and labor that had been utilized in the factory. Variable overhead rates were developed as a part of the analysis of costs described under cost structure and presented in Exhibit 12-12.

Variable standard cost cards for Product A and B are presented in Exhibit 12-13. Factory wage rates are expected to average $5 per hour. Material prices are based upon the price the company expects to pay during the next year.

Standard costs play a key role in the planning and control system. For planning purposes, the firm wants to know what costs *will be;* for control purposes, what costs *should be.* Ideally, costs will be what they should be, but in practice this is seldom the case. For planning purposes, management must be certain that resources are available in sufficient quantity to meet production needs, including any inefficiencies that may arise. Thus, the budget must show the amount of material that is expected to be used. If the material usage rate is expected to run above standard, then an unfavorable material usage variance should be budgeted. For control purposes, however, management uses the standard and works toward reducing the variance.

Departmental budgets

The organization chart in Exhibit 12-1 identifies the factory departmental foremen and the marketing product-line managers as the lowest level of

MANUFACTURING COSTS

		FACTORY RESPONSIBILITY AREAS				
		Total Cost	Shaping	Heat-Treating	Materials Handling	Factory Management
Variable factory costs (per direct labor hour)						
(1) Supplies	ⓑ *		$ .40	$ 1.00		
(2) Payroll fringe	ⓓ		1.00	1.00		
(3) Power	ⓑ		.60	3.00		
Variable rate per DLH			$ 2.00	$ 5.00		
Fixed factory costs (per month)						
(4) Salaries	ⓐ	$12,000	$3,000	$2,000	$3,000	$ 4,000
(5) Payroll fringe	ⓓ	2,400	600	400	600	800
(6) Factory rent	ⓕ	4,000				4,000
(7) Utilities	ⓑ	1,000				1,000
(8) Depreciation of equipment	ⓘ	9,000	4,000	3,000	2,000	
(9) Other	ⓐ	1,600	400	600	400	200
Total		$30,000	$8,000	$6,000	$6,000	$10,000

MARKETING COSTS

		MARKETING RESPONSIBILITY AREAS				
				Product B		
		Total Cost	Product A	Eastern	Western	Marketing Management
Variable marketing costs (per unit sold)						
(10) Travel, etc.	ⓑ		$ .60	$ .30	$ .30	
Fixed marketing costs (per month)						
(11) Salaries	ⓐ	$ 8,000	$1,000	$2,000	$2,000	$ 3,000
(12) Payroll fringe	ⓓ	1,600	200	400	400	600
(13) Product promotion	ⓒ	4,000	1,000	2,000	1,000	
(14) Other	ⓐ	2,400	800	600	600	400
		$16,000	$3,000	$5,000	$4,000	$ 4,000

GENERAL

		GENERAL RESPONSIBILITY AREA		
		Total Cost	Treasurer	General Mgmt.
Fixed general costs (per month)				
(15) Salaries	ⓐ	$ 7,500	$2,500	$5,000
(16) Payroll fringe	ⓓ	1,500	500	1,000
(17) Rent	ⓕ	1,000		1,000
(18) Research	ⓒ	1,000		1,000
(19) Other	ⓐ	2,000	1,000	1,000
		$13,000	$4,000	$9,000
Financing rates				
(20) Investment income	ⓗ	.5% per month		
(21) Interest, short-term	ⓖ	1% per month		
(22) Interest, long-term	ⓔ	9% per year		
(23) Dividends	ⓔ	$1 per share, semiannual dividends		

*Payment schedule

- ⓐ Paid in month of expense
- ⓑ Paid in following month
- ⓒ Paid every other month
- ⓓ Paid 80% monthly, 20% in June, July, and August
- ⓔ Paid semiannually, January and July
- ⓕ Paid annually, January
- ⓖ Paid at maturity
- ⓗ Collected monthly
- ⓘ No cash flow

EXHIBIT 12-12
Cost structure for DeFord Company

PRODUCT A

STANDARD COST CARD

Effective 1/1/X1

Shaping process			
Material	1 blank A	@ $2.00	$2.00
Labor	.2 hours	@ $5.00	1.00
Variable overhead	.2 hours	@ $2.00	.40
Total shaping costs			$3.40
Heat-treating process			
Material (hardening compound)	2 pounds	@ $1.00	$2.00
Labor	.1 hours	@ $5.00	.50
Variable overhead	.1 hours	@ $5.00	.50
Total heat-treating costs			3.00
Total variable Product A costs			$6.40

PRODUCT B

STANDARD COST CARD

Effective 1/1/X1

Shaping process			
Material	1 blank B	@ $1.00	$1.00
Labor	.1 hours	@ $5.00	.50
Variable overhead	.1 hours	@ $2.00	.20
Total shaping costs			$1.70
Heat-treating process			
Material (hardening compound)	1 pound	@ $1.00	$1.00
Labor	.1 hours	@ $5.00	.50
Variable overhead	.1 hours	@ $5.00	.50
Total heat-treating costs			2.00
Total variable Product B costs			$3.70

EXHIBIT 12-13 Standard cost cards for Products A and B for DeFord Company

management. A portion of the organization chart follows, with two departments highlighted. To simplify our illustrations we will emphasize these areas.

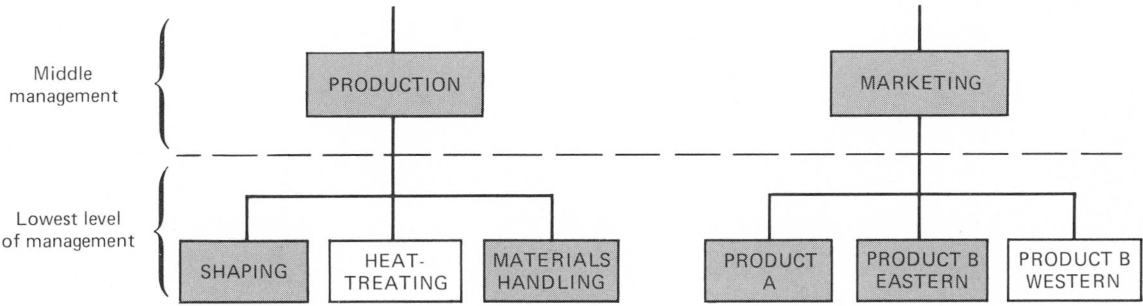

The standard cost cards (Exhibit 12-13) and the detailed flexible budget (Exhibit 12-12) provide the cost behavior patterns of the various departments or cost centers of the company. By applying the sales levels from the sales budget (Exhibit 12-9) for the marketing department, and the production levels from the production budget (Exhibit 12-10) for the factory departments, each department manager can use the flexible budget (Exhibit 12-12) to prepare his own budget. Where the individual department manager believes that conditions are unusual, as in the case of low efficiency because of newly hired unskilled workers, or that unusual expenditures should be made, for such needs as extensive repairs, his initial budget should reflect the added costs. He would have to defend his budget at the time of budget compilation and coordination at the factory level.

From the six departments in the previous illustration we have selected the heat-treating department from manufacturing and the Western territory of Product B from marketing as the bases for our departmental budget illustrations. Data relating to these departments are highlighted in the several exhibits that follow.

The heat-treating department foreman is responsible for the costs incurred in his department, including materials (hardening compound), direct labor, variable overhead, and those fixed factory overhead costs directly related to his operation (departmental indirect labor and related fringe benefits, depreciation of heat-treating equipment, and other departmental fixed costs). No portion of the factory rent or insurance, the plant manager's salary, or other plant-wide costs is included in the heat-treating department foreman's budget. The departmental budget for heat-treating is presented in Exhibit 12-14. Total departmental costs of $612,000 for the year 19X1 are proposed by the departmental manager. When approved, they are carried to the factory manager's budget as a cost controllable by a subordinate department.

The marketing area is responsible for both costs and revenue. Each of the three product-line managers has a responsibility to meet the revenue target as accepted in the sales budget (Exhibit 12-10) and the costs necessary to generate that revenue. Note that the activity base is in terms of *units sold.*

	JANUARY	FEBRUARY	MARCH	TOTAL FOR YEAR 19X1
Material				
Hardening compound	$25,000	$25,000	$25,000	$300,000
Direct labor	10,000	10,000	10,000	120,000
Variable overhead				
Supplies	$ 2,000	$ 2,000	$ 2,000	$ 24,000
Payroll fringe	2,000	2,000	2,000	24,000
Power	6,000	6,000	6,000	72,000
Total	10,000	10,000	10,000	120,000
Total variable product costs	$45,000	$45,000	$45,000	$540,000
Departmental fixed costs				
Departmental fixed labor	$ 2,000	$ 2,000	$ 2,000	$ 24,000
Fringe benefits	400	400	400	4,800
Depreciation of equipment	3,000	3,000	3,000	36,000
Other	600	600	600	7,200
Total	6,000	6,000	6,000	72,000
Total departmental costs	$51,000	$51,000	$51,000	$612,000
Physical data				
Scheduled production of A (units)	5,000	5,000	5,000	60,000
Scheduled production of B (units)	15,000	15,000	15,000	180,000
Hardening compound used (pounds)	25,000	25,000	25,000	300,000
Direct labor hours	2,000	2,000	2,000	24,000
Percentage of capacity	100%	100%	100%	100%

EXHIBIT 12-14
Heat-treating department budget for DeFord Company

Sales of the Western territory were projected for the year at 120,000 units of Product B.

Because the marketing area is responsible for both revenue and cost, the budget will show **product contribution;** that is, the amount the product contributes toward company fixed costs and net income. Product contribution is computed by deducting standard variable manufacturing costs, variable marketing costs, and fixed costs incurred in the Western territory from the sales of the Western territory. None of the company-wide marketing or general costs are included in the departmental budget. The Western territory expects to generate product contributions of $432,000 for the year 19X1, as shown in Exhibit 12-15.

	JANUARY	FEBRUARY	MARCH	TOTAL FOR YEAR 19X1
Sales	$64,000	$64,000	$80,000	$960,000
Variable costs				
Manufacturing	$29,600	$29,600	$37,000	$444,000
Marketing	2,400	2,400	3,000	36,000
Total	32,000	32,000	40,000	480,000
Contribution margin	$32,000	$32,000	$40,000	$480,000
Fixed costs related to Product B				
Salaries	$ 2,000	$ 2,000	$ 2,000	$ 24,000
Payroll fringe	400	400	400	4,800
Product promotion	1,000	1,000	1,000	12,000
Other	600	600	600	7,200
Total	4,000	4,000	4,000	48,000
Product contribution	$28,000	$28,000	$36,000	$432,000

EXHIBIT 12-15
Product line budget for DeFord Company—Product B Western territory

STEP 7: COMPILATION OF DEPARTMENTAL BUDGETS INTO THE PROFIT PLAN

After a downward flow of information through the sales budget and production budget that determined departmental volume levels, departmental budgets provide an upward flow of information for compilation at the factory and marketing level. Budgets by these functional areas are compiled into a company-wide cost budget and then into the profit plan. At each level, review and feedback take place. This process of budget compilation is illustrated in Exhibit 12-16. The upward compilation is illustrated by a solid line and the process of review and feedback by a broken line. At this point the goals of the lower levels of management are compared with the firm's goals.

The first level of budget compilation for the DeFord Company is illustrated in Exhibits 12-17 and 12-18. The factory cost budget (Exhibit 12-17) includes a one-line cost summary for each subordinate factory department. The total of the heat-treating budget from Exhibit 12-14 can be traced into the factory cost budget in Exhibit 12-17. Total budgeted costs for the heat-treating department are highlighted for emphasis in the factory cost budget.

A responsibility accounting system groups accounting data by responsibility area. In so doing, other possible aggregations, such as by cost element, are lost; they must be presented as supplementary information. A summary by cost element is presented at the bottom of Exhibit 12-17.

The marketing budget (Exhibit 12-18) also includes a one-line summary of each subordinate area budget. The total from the budget for the

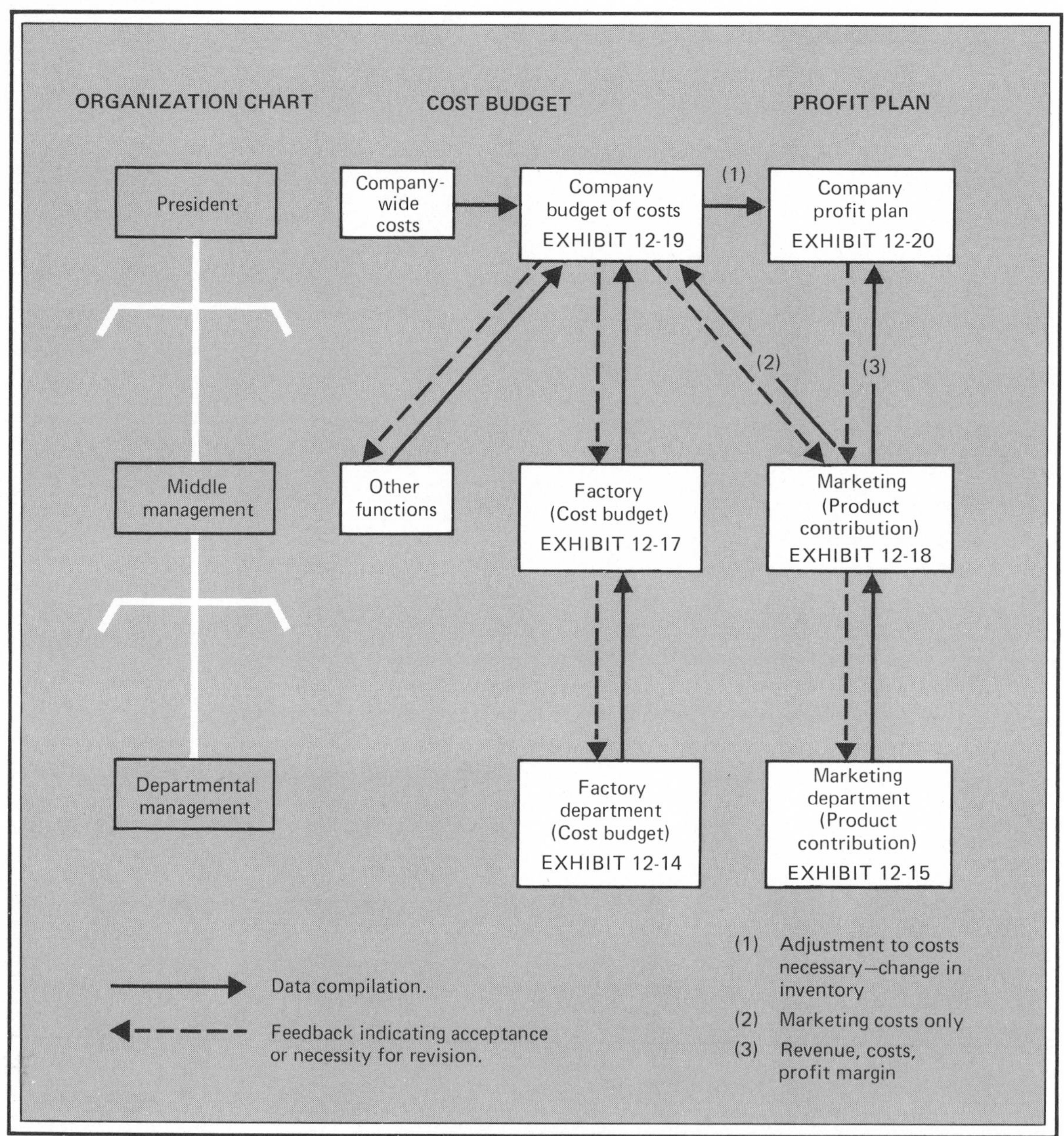

EXHIBIT 12-16
Illustration of compilation of departmental budgets into profit plan for DeFord Company

Western territory (Exhibit 12-15) may be traced into the marketing budget. The summary of the Western territory budget is highlighted for emphasis in Exhibit 12-18. Since the marketing budget shows product margin (contribution margin less fixed costs of the particular responsibility area) for each subordinate area, the amount of costs for the entire marketing area is lost.

	JANUARY	FEBRUARY	MARCH	TOTAL FOR YEAR 19X1
Costs controllable by subordinate department				
Shaping department	$ 50,500	$ 50,500	$ 50,500	$ 606,000
Heat-treating department	51,000	51,000	51,000	612,000
Materials handling department	6,000	6,000	6,000	72,000
Total	$107,500	$107,500	$107,500	$1,290,000
Fixed costs common to factory				
Salaries	$ 4,000	$ 4,000	4,000	$ 48,000
Fringe benefits	800	800	800	9,600
Factory rent	4,000	4,000	4,000	48,000
Utilities	1,000	1,000	1,000	12,000
Other	200	200	200	2,400
Total	10,000	10,000	10,000	120,000
Total factory costs	$117,500	$117,500	$117,500	$1,410,000
Summary of costs				
Standard product costs				
Material	$ 50,000	$ 50,000	$ 50,000	$ 600,000
Direct labor	22,500	22,500	22,500	270,000
Variable overhead	15,000	15,000	15,000	180,000
Total product costs to inventory	$ 87,500	$ 87,500	$ 87,500	$1,050,000
Fixed costs	30,000	30,000	30,000	360,000
Total factory costs	$117,500	$117,500	$117,500	$1,410,000
Physical data				
Units produced				
Product A	5,000	5,000	5,000	60,000
Product B	15,000	15,000	15,000	180,000
Direct labor hours	4,500	4,500	4,500	4,500
Percentage of usable capacity	100%	100%	100%	100%

EXHIBIT 12-17
Factory cost budget for DeFord Company

A summary of budgeted marketing costs is presented at the bottom of the budget.

The cost budget for DeFord Company (Exhibit 12-19) provides an overall picture of budgeted costs. This budget is the responsibility of the president and, as such, shows subordinate areas' costs in total and costs

	JANUARY	FEBRUARY	MARCH	TOTAL FOR YEAR 19X1
Product contribution				
Product A	$ 2,000	$ 7,000	$12,000	$264,000
Product B – Eastern	$11,000	$11,000	$11,000	$180,000
Product B – Western	28,000	28,000	36,000	432,000
Total Product B	39,000	39,000	47,000	612,000
Total product contribution	$41,000	$46,000	$59,000	$876,000
Fixed costs				
Salaries	$ 3,000	$ 3,000	$ 3,000	$ 36,000
Payroll fringe	600	600	600	7,200
Other	400	400	400	4,800
Total	4,000	4,000	4,000	48,000
Contribution to common fixed costs and profit	$37,000	$42,000	$55,000	$828,000
Summary of marketing costs				
Product A	$ 3,600	$ 4,200	$ 4,800	$ 72,000
Product B – Eastern	6,200	6,200	6,200	78,000
Product B – Western	6,400	6,400	7,000	84,000
Product managers' costs	$16,200	$16,800	$18,000	$234,000
Sales management	4,000	4,000	4,000	48,000
Total marketing costs	$20,200	$20,800	$22,000	$282,000

EXHIBIT 12-18
Marketing budget for DeFord Company

under the direct responsibility of the president in detail. Note that the total of the factory cost budget ($1,410,000 from Exhibit 12-17) is carried as one line into the cost budget for the company. This overall budget shows *incurrence* of costs. No distinction is made between product and period costs. It is not important in the *control* of costs. Differentiation between product and period costs is important, however, in the profit plan. Budgeted costs in the profit plan include the variable manufacturing costs attributable to the products sold (product costs), variable selling costs, and all constant costs (period costs). Increases or decreases in inventories will cause differences between the total factory costs *incurred* in the factory budget and factory

	JANUARY	FEBRUARY	MARCH	TOTAL FOR YEAR 19X1
Cost by subordinate responsibility area				
Manufacturing	$117,500	$117,500	$117,500	$1,410,000
Marketing	20,200	20,800	22,000	282,000
Finance	4,000	4,000	4,000	48,000
Total	$141,700	$142,300	$143,500	$1,740,000
Costs under direct supervision of president				
Salaries	$ 5,000	$ 5,000	$ 5,000	$ 60,000
Payroll fringe	1,000	1,000	1,000	12,000
Office rent	1,000	1,000	1,000	12,000
Research program	1,000	1,000	1,000	12,000
Other	1,000	1,000	1,000	12,000
Total	9,000	9,000	9,000	108,000
Total budgeted costs	$150,700	$151,300	$152,500	$1,848,000
Total budgeted costs	$150,700	$151,300	$152,500	$1,848,000
Deduct change in finished goods inventory:				
Increase in Product A	$ 25,600	$ 19,200	$ 12,800	0
Increase in Product B	11,100	11,100	3,700	0
Total increase	36,700	30,300	16,500	0
Total costs in profit plan	$114,000	$121,000	$136,000	$1,848,000
Summary of costs in profit plan				
Variable costs	$ 55,000	$ 62,000	$ 77,000	$1,140,000
Fixed costs related to products	12,000	12,000	12,000	144,000
Common fixed costs	47,000	47,000	47,000	564,000
Total	$114,000	$121,000	$136,000	$1,848,000

EXHIBIT 12-19
Cost budget for DeFord Company

DEFORD COMPANY
PROFIT PLAN
For the Year 19X1

	JANUARY	FEBRUARY	MARCH	TOTAL FOR YEAR 19X1
Sales	$108,000	$120,000	$148,000	$2,160,000
Variable costs				
Manufacturing	$ 50,800	$ 57,200	$ 71,000	$1,050,000
Marketing	4,200	4,800	6,000	90,000
Total variable costs	55,000	62,000	77,000	1,140,000
Contribution margin	$ 53,000	$ 58,000	$ 71,000	$1,020,000
Fixed marketing costs related to products	12,000	12,000	12,000	144,000
Product contribution	$ 41,000	$ 46,000	$ 59,000	$ 876,000
Common fixed costs				
Manufacturing	$ 30,000	$ 30,000	$ 30,000	$ 360,000
Marketing	4,000	4,000	4,000	48,000
General	13,000	13,000	13,000	156,000
Total fixed costs	47,000	47,000	47,000	564,000
Net operating income (loss)	$ (6,000)	$ (1,000)	$ 12,000	$ 312,000
Investment income	1,000	200		7,900
Interest expense	(4,500)			(10,500)
Net income before taxes (loss)	$ (9,500)	$ (800)	$ 12,000	$ 309,400
Income taxes (40%)				123,800
Net income after taxes				$ 185,600

EXHIBIT 12-20
Profit plan for DeFord Company

costs *expensed* in the profit plan. A summary of costs at the bottom of the factory budget accounts for the change in inventories and reconciles the factory budget with the profit plan.

The profit plan is presented in Exhibit 12-20. It is the consolidation of decisions made to allocate the firm's resources in the short run. All the effort to project sales, determine optimum product mix, and project costs for the firm was necessary to develop the profit plan. The goals of the individual managers are brought together and may now be related to company goals, and the profit plan can be compared with company objectives. If profit is not sufficient, the company must restudy the planning effort and perhaps prepare a revised profit plan.

PROFIT OBJECTIVES	19X1 PROFIT PLAN PROJECTION
1. Achieve a net income after tax of:	
a. 25% of reported owners' equity at the beginning of the year	28% on reported owners' equity ($185,600 ÷ $660,300)
b. 10% on net sales	9% on net sales ($185,600 ÷ $2,160,000)
2. Increase earnings per share by 10% over previous year	11% increase in earnings per share 19X0 $5.60 19X1 $6.19 ($.59 increase ÷ $5.60)
MARKET OBJECTIVE	
1. Increase dollar sales of Product A by 5%	5% increase in Product A sales 19X0 sales $ 684,000 19X1 projected sales $ 720,000 ($36,000 increase ÷ $684,000)
2. Increase dollar sales of Product B by 5%	6% increase in Product B sales 19X0 sales $1,360,000 19X1 projected sales $1,440,000 ($80,000 increase ÷ $1,360,000)
MANPOWER OBJECTIVE	
Stable work force with no more than 5% turnover through layoffs	Of necessity, 0% turnover through layoffs is projected. Production scheduled for 100% of effective capacity. If problems develop it will be necessary to work overtime.

EXHIBIT 12-21
Comparison of profit plan with DeFord Company objectives

STEP 8: COMPARISON OF PROFIT PLAN WITH CORPORATE OBJECTIVES

The profit plan is the focal point of the master budget. It shows the profit management can expect to earn, given the resources and facilities committed. Is the planned profit of $185,600 enough? Earlier we presented a set of company goals and objectives developed by Mr. DeFord in consultation with his functional managers. A comparison of these objectives and the profit plan are presented in Exhibit 12-21. The profit plan has met or exceeded all company objectives, with the exception of percentage of profit on sales. Mr. DeFord was pleased with the planning process and the profit plan was accepted.

SUMMARY

There are two basic approaches to sales forecasting: (1) a macro, or total sales, approach, where a model is used to project total sales and (2) a micro, or sales aggregation, approach, where sales are projected by product or customer and grouped into total sales.

The development of a profit plan, illustrated in this chapter with a single case—the DeFord Company, is a sequential-step process.

Step 1. A sales forecast is developed for the company using simple regression for one product and a demand curve for the other.

Step 2. An optimal product mix is developed for the two products using a graphic linear-programming approach.

Step 3. The sales budget by product is developed. The company cannot produce all the products that could be sold. The sales budget reflects sales the company expects to make and provides direction to the marketing departments.

Step 4. The production budget is determined to provide a volume level.

Step 5. Based upon the quantity to be produced in step 4, a materials purchases budget is prepared.

Step 6. Departmental budgets reflect the departmental managers' cost expectations. By applying the flexible budget to the volume level from the production budget, a departmental cost budget is prepared.

Step 7. The many responsibility area budgets are compiled into a single profit plan.

Step 8. The final profit plan is compared to company objectives to resolve the question: "How much is enough?"

SUPPLEMENTARY READING

Copulsky, William. *Practical Sales Forecasting.* New York: American Management Association, 1970.

DeCoster, Don T. "The Budget Director and PERT." *Business Budgeting,* March, 1964.

Hall, William K. "Forecasting Techniques for use in the Corporate Planning Process." *Managerial Planning,* November–December, 1972.

Irvine, V. Bruce. "Budgeting: Functional Analysis and Behavioral Implications." *Cost and Management,* March–April, 1970.

Malcom, R. E. "Improving Forecast Effectiveness." *Managerial Planning,* July–August, 1970.

Pryor, LeRoy J. "Simulation: Budgeting for a 'What if . . . .'." *The Journal of Accountancy,* November, 1970.

Sandbulte, Arend J. "Sales and Revenue Forecasting." *Management Accounting,* December, 1969.

Wallace, M. E. "Behavioral Consideration in Budgeting." *Management Accounting,* August, 1966.

Welsch, Glenn A. "Budgeting for Management Planning and Control." *The Journal of Accountancy,* October, 1961.

Welsch, Glenn A. *Budgeting: Profit Planning and Control.* Englewood Cliffs, N.J.: Prentice-Hall, Inc., 1971.

QUESTIONS

12-1 What is the relationship between the profit plan and the cash budget?

12-2 What is the role of the sales forecast in the budgeting process?

12-3 Distinguish between macro and micro approaches to sales forecasting. Give examples of techniques used in each.

12-4 How may a demand curve be used in sales forecasting?

12-5 List at least three specific techniques used to develop a sales forecast. What are the sources of information for each?

12-6 What behavioral aspects may influence the aggregation of estimates by the company's salespeople? What can be done to lessen any distortion of the sales forecast caused by these behavioral aspects?

12-7 List the steps necessary to develop a profit plan. Is the order of the steps critical? Explain.

12-8 What is the difference between a sales forecast and a sales budget? Will they always be the same? Why or why not?

12-9 In determining product mix, what factors must be taken into consideration? Explain. Would these factors differ between industrial products and consumer products? Why?

12-10 What effect does a downward-sloping demand curve have on the optimality of a production output solution derived by linear programming? Explain.

12-11 Variable costs are controlled by the lowest level of management. Discuss why this is so. What is the importance of this statement as far as participation in the budgetary process is concerned?

12-12 Fixed, or nonvariable, costs are usually planned on a monthly or yearly basis. Control over fixed costs is exercised at widely differing times and points in the firm. Explain why and give examples.

12-13 If there is to be congruence between the goals of the company and the goals of subordinate management levels, there must be real participation in the budgetary process. Explain what is meant by real participation? How may it be achieved?

12-14 For planning purposes it is necessary to know what costs *will be*. What does this mean?

12-15 For control purposes it is necessary to know what costs *should be.* What does this mean?

12-16 Discuss the differences between the use of costs for planning purposes and the use of costs for control purposes.

12-17 Seasonal sales variations when production for the year is near plant capacity presents several problems. List these problems and explain how management might deal with them.

PROBLEMS

12-18 Match the following terms and definitions.

1. Profit plan
2. Sales forecast
3. Micro approach
4. Macro approach
5. Constraint
6. Sales budget
7. Production budget
8. Product contribution
9. Constant costs
10. Responsibility accounting system

a. Another name for fixed costs.
b. A sales forecasting technique to arrive at total sales.
c. A statement setting forth what management believes it will sell.
d. The income a product will generate to cover common fixed costs and provide a profit.
e. A sales forecasting technique that aggregates forecasts for individual products or territories.
f. A projected income statement.
g. A statement setting forth management's plan for factory operations for the year.
h. An accounting system that aggregates accounting data by organizational structure.
i. An estimate of the potential sales market.
j. A restriction of production or sales of a product.

12-19 Taurus Trinkets Company undertook a thorough research of the market for the company's single product. Data concerning demand for the company's product is as follows:

Price	*Quantity Demanded (Units)*
$5.00	200,000
$4.00	500,000
$3.00	1,000,000
$2.50	1,250,000
$2.00	1,500,000
$1.50	2,000,000
$1.00	4,000,000

Plant capacity is two million units. Fixed costs are $1,000,000; variable costs are $.75 per unit.

REQUIRED:

A. Determine the optimum level of production and sales.

B. Prepare a profit plan for the company at the optimum level using a contribution margin approach.

12-20 The advertising manager of the Taurus Trinket Company (problem 12-19) has studied the impact of advertising on demand for the company's product. He believes that a $1,500,000 advertising campaign will cause the demand curve to shift as follows:

Price	*Quantity Demanded (Units)*
$5.00	500,000
$4.00	1,000,000
$3.25	1,500,000
$3.00	1,750,000
$2.75	2,000,000
$2.50	4,000,000

Plant capacity is two million units. Fixed costs are $1,000,000; variable costs are $.75 per unit.

REQUIRED:

A. Assuming the company will be within its relevant range as to costs, determine the optimum level of production and sales.

B. Prepare a revised profit plan for the company at the optimum level using a contribution margin approach.

C. Should the advertising campaign be undertaken? Explain. (Note: Refer to problem 12-19.)

12-21 The Handy Dandy Home Products Company is about to introduce a new product. Most of the company's products have four-year sales lives. Sales peak in year 3 and decline dramatically in year 4.

The marketing department has developed the following data for the new product.

Probability of Occurrence		**Estimated Sales**			
		Year 1	*Year 2*	*Year 3*	*Year 4*
Most optimistic estimate	25%	$200,000	$600,000	$1,200,000	$200,000
Most likely estimate	60%	$100,000	$400,000	$ 800,000	$100,000
Most pessimistic estimate	15%	$ 50,000	$100,000	$ 50,000	$ 10,000

REQUIRED:

Prepare a sales budget by year for this new product, taking into account the probability of the most optimistic, most likely, and most pessimistic sales levels occurring. (Note: An expected value for sales may be determined by multiplying amount of estimated sales times the probability of occurrence.)

12-22 The management of the Late Hours Light Company is attempting to develop a forecast of the company's sales for 19X7. The following estimates were derived independently.

Trend-line estimate (projection of past sales trend)	$4,700,000
Composite of salesmen's estimates	$4,500,000
Sales manager's planned sales quota	$5,100,000
Share of the market (Late Hours' share of the market for lights has been 8%. The total market for lights has been estimated at $62,500,000 by the State University business research department.)	?
Simple regression of sales with disposable income: (Regression equation: $y = \$1,000,000 + .01(x)$, where (x) is disposable income in the market area. Standard error: $100,000. Disposable income in the market area was estimated by the Department of Commerce at $380,000,000.)	?

The salesmen expect their estimates to be used as sales quotas and the sales manager expects his estimate to be a maximum for bonus purposes.

REQUIRED:
Prepare a sales forecast from the five projections. Explain how you considered or weighted the various projections.

12-23 The sales manager of the Barker Brothers Company, a producer of adult games, believes that there is a strong relationship between personal income and sales of the company's products. The following data show personal income and product sales in the market area served by the company for a 10-year period.

Year	*Personal Income (Millions) (x)*	*Company Sales (Thousands) (y)*
19X0	\$200	\$380
19X1	\$210	\$420
19X2	\$260	\$480
19X3	\$280	\$460
19X4	\$280	\$480
19X5	\$325	\$520
19X6	\$360	\$580
19X7	\$380	\$580
19X8	\$390	\$600
19X9	\$440	\$640

The company wants to use regression analysis to project sales and computed the following totals from the given amounts.

$$\begin{aligned} \Sigma x &= \$\ \ \ \ 3{,}125 \\ \Sigma y &= \$\ \ \ \ 5{,}140 \\ \Sigma xy &= \$1{,}666{,}000 \\ \Sigma x^2 &= \$1{,}033{,}825 \end{aligned}$$

REQUIRED:

A. Compute the variables for the straight-line [$y = a + b(x)$] relationship between company sales and personal income.

B. Economists have projected personal income for the next year (19Y0) at \$460. Assuming the relationship continues, what should be the company's forecast of sales next year?

C. Can you say anything about the reliability of the forecast from the calculation above? Would observing the relationship with a scattergraph improve your confidence in the forecast? Explain.

12-24 The Blue Streakers, a local hockey team, were contemplating upgrading the quality of their team. It appears that the more games the team won, the higher were the total gate receipts for the year. You have been given the following information and asked to verify the accuracy of this statement.

Year	*Games Won*	*Total Yearly Receipts*
1	21	$410,000
2	18	$330,000
3	26	$510,000
4	23	$430,000
5	18	$370,000
6	31	$650,000
7	28	$590,000
8	15	$270,000
9	24	$530,000
10	36	$690,000

Assume that all data have been adjusted for price level changes.

REQUIRED:

A. Using simple regression analysis, state the relationship in a linear equation.

B. Assume that contemplated improvements in the team require an increase in annual fixed costs of $80,000 but should raise the games won to 40 in year 11. What would be your forecast of revenues for year 11? If variable costs have been 20% of revenue and annual fixed costs $320,000, what would be your recommendations to management?

C. What other variables, besides games won, might have some effect on annual receipts?

12-25 The Locked Box Company produces two types of storage boxes. The following are standard costs for the products.

	Chest		*Trunk*	
Material	30 feet @ $ .10	= $ 3	50 feet @ $ .10	= $ 5
Labor	2 hours @ $5	= 10	3 hours @ $5	= 15
Variable factory overhead	2 hours @ $2	= 4	3 hours @ $2	= 6
Fixed factory overhead	2 hours @ $3	= 6	3 hours @ $3	= 9
		$23		$35

The standards are set at an efficient but attainable level. The factory overhead budget is based upon working 2,000 direct labor hours per quarter. The following variances from standard were recorded during 19X5. Parentheses indicate unfavorable variances.

Quarter	Standard Hours Worked	Material Price	Material Usage	Labor Efficiency	Variable Overhead Efficiency	Variable Overhead Spending	Overhead Volume
First	1,000	0	$(100)	$ (500)	$(200)	$ 200	$(3,000)
Second	2,000	$ (300)	$(300)	$(1,000)	$(400)	$ 300	0
Third	3,000	$ (800)	$ 100	$ 400	$ 160	$ 800	$ 3,000
Fourth	4,000	$(1,800)	$ 300	$ (500)	$(200)	$1,000	$ 6,000

During 19X5 the variances were not recorded by product. The labor rate variance was zero in all four quarters.

Sales are expected to level off during 19X6 to a constant production level of 5,000 hours per quarter. Only the fixed portion of the standard is to be revised. Management does not want to change the variable cost standards. It plans to budget expected variances.

REQUIRED:

A. Assuming that fixed production costs will not change in total amount, revise the standard cost for fixed overhead.

B. Based upon a production budget for a quarter in 19X6 requiring 5,000 hours (2,000 hours for production of chests and 3,000 hours for trunks) and your knowledge of variances in 19X5, prepare a factory cost budget for 19X6 setting out expected variances from standard.

12-26 Sooper Slippery Sales Corporation manufactures and sells two products. To meet sales needs, the company often shifts production from one product to another on short notice. The production manager decided this practice was inefficient and came to you with the following information in the hope that you could assist him in preparing a production budget for the company's profit plan.

	Product 1	Product 2	Production Constraints
Department A	2 hours	2 hours	20 hours
Department B	4 hours	6 hours	48 hours
Material	7 pounds	20 pounds	140 pounds
Selling price	$24	$40	
Variable costs	$14	$28	

REQUIRED:

A. Show the constraints graphically, and indicate the feasible regions.

B. Determine the optimum production quantities of each product.

C. Prepare a production budget for the next period.

12-27 Cox Tool Company expects sales of its major product to be 300,000 units during the first quarter of 19X4. There are 20,000 units of finished goods on hand at the beginning of the quarter. Because of rising demand, the company wants to increase the inventory level to 50,000 units by the end of the quarter.

Each finished unit requires one-third hour of direct labor, two feet of Material X, and three pounds of Material Y. At the beginning of the quarter the company has 200,000 feet of Material X and no Material Y on hand. The company wants to maintain a minimum inventory level of 140,000 feet of Material X and 210,000 pounds of Material Y. Standard rates and prices are: $6 per direct labor hour, $.40 per foot for Material X, and $.10 per pound for Material Y.

Other costs of the company are:

Manufacturing overhead: $440,000 per year plus $3 per direct labor hour

Marketing costs: $400,000 per year plus $2 per unit sold

Administrative costs: $280,000 per year

All fixed costs are incurred uniformly throughout the year. The income tax rate is 40%. The company expects to sell the product at $10 per unit.

REQUIRED:

A. Prepare a production budget for the quarter.

B. Prepare a purchasing budget for the quarter.

C. Prepare a factory cost budget for the quarter.

D. Prepare a profit plan for the quarter, using absorption standard costing.

E. Prepare a profit plan for the quarter, using variable standard costing.

12-28 Summer Sports, Inc. produces a product for summer use. As a result, sales show a strong seasonal pattern.

Quarter	*Percentage of Annual Sales*
1	10%
2	25%
3	50%
4	15%

Demand for the company's product has grown to the point where 1,000,000 units should be sold in both 19X7 and 19X8. The company has established an inventory policy that requires the ending inventory to be equal to 25% of the next quarter's sales. A total of 25,000 finished units are on hand at the beginning of 19X7. Practical capacity of the company's plant is 1,200,000 units per year (300,000 per quarter). The management of the company has not permitted overtime in the past.

REQUIRED:

A. Prepare a production budget by quarter for 19X7.

B. If Summer Sports, Inc. could not replace skilled employees laid off during slack seasons, how would your production budget and inventory policy change? What information would you need to establish a production budget that optimizes production and storage costs?

12-29 The product produced by Summer Sports, Inc. in problem 12-28 requires two types of raw material. Each finished unit requires two pounds of Material A and four units of Material B. Raw materials equal to one-fourth of the following quarter's production are to be on hand at the end of each quarter. The January 1, 19X7, inventory meets this requirement. The standard costs of the raw materials are $2 per pound for Material A and $1 per unit for Material B.

REQUIRED:

A. Prepare a purchases budget for the two raw materials, by the quarter and for the year.

B. What changes in the purchasing budget would you recommend if the per-quarter inventory holding costs were equal to 7% of the units held, and you expected a 25% increase in the price of Material B in quarter 3?

12-30 The Benji Joe Corporation manufactures two types of swings: high swings and low swings. Manufacturing facilities include two departments: fabrication, with a maximum capacity of 800 machine hours, and assembly, with a maximum of 1,200 man hours. Production time per swing is:

	Fabrication	*Assembly*
High swings	3 machine hours	5 man hours
Low swings	5 machine hours	2 man hours

REQUIRED:

A. Illustrate graphically the feasible combination of production.

B. Assume the company has forecast maximum sales to be 100 high swings at $350 each and 200 low swings at $200 each. Plot these market constraints on your graph from part A above. Indicate the feasible combinations on your graph.

C. Assuming the following cost structure, determine the optimum product mix.

High swings	$150 per unit (variable costs)
Low swings	$100 per unit (variable costs)
Fixed costs per period	$25,000

D. Prepare a profit plan for the period, showing contribution margin by product and for the company as a whole.

12-31 The Marcia Company has asked your assistance in preparing a profit plan for an economical sales and production mix of its products for 19X4. The company manufactures a line of dolls and a doll-dress sewing kit. The following sales forecast was made by the sales department.

Product	*Estimated Demand for 19X4 ·(Units)*	*Established Net Price (Units)*
Laurie	50,000	$5.20
Debbie	42,000	$2.40
Sarah	35,000	$8.50
Kathy	40,000	$4.00
Sewing kit	325,000	$3.00

To promote sales of the sewing kit, there is a 15% reduction in the established net price for a kit purchased at the same time that a Marcia Company doll is purchased. The sales department expects kits to be sold with approximately 50% of the dolls.

From the accounting records you develop the following:

1. Production standards per unit:

Item	*Material*	*Labor*
Laurie	$1.40	$ .80
Debbie	$ .70	$ .50
Sarah	$2.69	$1.40
Kathy	$1.00	$1.00
Sewing kit	$ .60	$ .40

2. The labor rate of $2 per hour is expected to continue without change in 19X4. The plant has an effective capacity of 130,000 labor hours per year on a single-shift basis.
3. The total fixed costs for 19X4 will be $100,000. Variable factory overhead costs will be equivalent to 50% of direct labor costs. There are no variable selling or administration costs.
4. There are no beginning or ending inventories.

REQUIRED:

A. Prepare a sales budget by product for the Marcia Company.
B. Prepare a production budget by product that can be attained within the productive capacity of the company.
C. Prepare a profit plan showing product margin by product and net income for the company. *(CPA adapted)*

12-32 Gemini Gadgets, Inc. produces and sells a single product. The 19X7 sales budget by quarter, in number of gadgets, was:

First quarter	21,000 gadgets
Second quarter	24,000 gadgets
Third quarter	30,000 gadgets
Fourth quarter	36,000 gadgets

The long-range sales forecast shows expected sales for 19X8 at approximately 3,000 gadgets per month above the 19X7 expected sales level.

The established inventory policy of the company is to maintain a supply of raw materials equal to 50% of the next quarter's needs and a supply of finished goods equal to one-third of the next quarter's budgeted sales. On January 1, 19X8, inventories consisted of 20,000 units of finished goods and 80,000 pounds of raw materials.

Standard costs for material and labor and a flexible budget for other costs are as follows:

Materials	(5 pounds @ $2)	=	$10
Labor	(2 hours @ $4)	=	$8
Factory overhead			$60,000 per month plus $3 per direct labor hour
Marketing and administrative costs			$25,000 per month plus 10% of sales

The established selling price is $40 per gadget.

REQUIRED:

A. Prepare the following budgets for the first two quarters of 19X8.

1. Sales budget
2. Production budget
3. Purchasing budget
4. Factory cost budget
5. Profit plan

B. The executive committee of top management officers has established a profit objective of at least breakeven operations in each quarter and an overall rate of profit of 10% of sales. What is the breakeven point per quarter? If budgeted net income is $456,000 for the year, does the profit plan meet company objectives?

12-33 A condensed income statement for the Circle M Company for 19X5 follows.

Sales (25,000 units)		$600,000
Variable cost of goods sold	$300,000	
Variable selling costs	100,000	400,000
Contribution margin		$200,000
Fixed Costs:		
Manufacturing	$ 60,000	
Selling	40,000	
Administrative	60,000	160,000
Net income before taxes		$ 40,000

The following changes in income and costs are projected by the budget committee for 19X2.

40% increase in number of units sold
20% increase in the price of materials
15% increase in direct labor wage rates
10% increase in variable factory overhead cost per unit
15% increase in constant selling costs
5% increase in other constant costs

The company produces a single product. There are no beginning or ending inventories. The composition of the cost of a unit of finished goods in the 19X5 income statement for direct materials, direct labor, and variable overhead respectively was in the ratio of 3 to 2 to 1. There are no other changes contemplated by the company.

REQUIRED:

A. Compute the unit sales price (to the nearest cent) that the company must charge for its product in 19 × 6 to earn a budgeted profit of $60,000.
B. Prepare the profit plan for 19X6.
C. Do you see any shortcomings in preparing a profit plan in this manner? *(CPA adapted)*

12-34 The Sno-King Manufacturing Company anticipates a sales volume of $500,000 (25,000 units) for the coming year. The beginning inventory level is 1,200 units. Objectives of the company include a growth rate of 15% per year.

REQUIRED:

A. Assuming the following seasonal sales pattern, prepare a sales budget by quarter for the next year.

First quarter	10%
Second quarter	30%
Third quarter	50%
Fourth quarter	10%

B. Assume that productive capacity is 9,000 units per quarter (3,000 units per month). Assume also that the product is perishable and cannot be stored for more than one-half quarter. Prepare a production budget by quarter for the next year.

C. Assume that the product is not perishable and that one of the company's goals is a stable work force. Prepare a new production budget by quarter for the next year. Will the revision of the production budget have any impact upon the sales budget? Other than timing of variable production costs, what changes in costs will arise because of your change in the production schedule?

12-35 The Yello Straw Basket Company produces a line of three straw products: a hamper, a chest, and a large basket. The company does not have a formal budgetary system. Management has described its planning and control system as "experience and good judgment."

Sales during the current year were $640,000. The sales manager believes that sales will increase by about 10% each year, and projects sales at $704,000 for the coming year. The production manager is planning to increase production by about 10%. Planned production by product would be:

Hamper	12,000 units
Chest	500 units
Basket	42,000 units

The controller compiled the following information.

	Last Year's Sales		Ending Inventory
	Amount	*Unit Price*	
Hamper	$300,000	$20	1,500 units
Chest	60,000	$25	3,000 units
Basket	280,000	$ 7	3,000 units
	$640,000		

In addition, the controller found that with the exception of the last quarter, when sales were about 40% of the annual total, sales were fairly uniform throughout the year. The controller believes the inventory policy should require an ending level of one-half of the next quarter's sales.

REQUIRED:

A. Prepare a sales budget and production budget by quarter and in total for the year.

B. Write a brief recommendation to top management detailing your reasons for recommending implementation of the budget process for all departments.

C. If you could have any two specific pieces of additional information to help persuade management to adopt a budgeting system, what would you request? Why?

12-36 The Melcher Company produces farm equipment at several plants. The business is seasonal and cyclical in nature. The company has attempted to use budgeting for planning and controlling activities, but the variable nature of the business has caused some company officials to be skeptical about the usefulness of budgeting. The accountant for the Adrian plant has been using a system he calls *flexible budgeting* to help his plant management control operations.

The company president asks him to explain what the term means, how he applies the system at the Adrian plant, and how it can be applied to the company as a whole. The accountant presents the following data as part of his explanation.

Budget data for 19X3:

Normal monthly capacity of the plant in direct labor hours		10,000 hours
Material costs	(6 pounds @ $1.50)	$9 per unit
Direct labor costs	(2 hours @ $3.00)	$6 per unit
Overhead estimate at normal monthly capacity:		
Variable (controllable):		
Indirect labor		$ 6,650
Indirect materials		600
Repairs		750
Total variable		$ 8,000
Fixed (noncontrollable):		
Depreciation		$ 3,250
Supervision		3,000
Total fixed		6,250
Total fixed and variable		$14,250

Planned units for January, 19X3	4,000
Planned units for February, 19X3	6,000

REQUIRED:

A. Prepare a cost budget for the Melcher Company for January, 19X3.

B. During January, 19X3, the company worked 8,400 hours and produced 3,800 units. Can you use your budget in part A to evaluate performance? Explain.

C. Prepare a performance budget to evaluate the performance of the Melcher Company for January, 19X3.

D. Explain the term *flexible budgeting* to the company president.

(CMA adapted)

12-37 The Metropolitan News, a daily newspaper, services a community of 100,000. The paper has a circulation of 40,000, with 32,000 copies delivered directly to subscribers. The rate schedule for the paper is as follows.

	Daily	*Sunday*
Single issue price	$0.15	$0.30
Weekly subscription		
(Includes daily and Sunday)	$1.00	

The paper has experienced profitable operations as can be seen from the Income Statement for the Year Ended September 30, 19X4 (000 omitted).

Revenue		
Newspaper sales	$2,163	
Advertising sales	1,800	$3,963
Costs and expenses		
Personnel costs		
Commissions		
Carriers and sales	$ 365	
Advertising	48	
Salaries		
Administration	250	
Advertising	100	
Equipment operators	500	
Newsroom	400	
Employee benefits	188	$1,851
Newsprint		834
Other supplies		417
Repairs		25
Depreciation		180
Property taxes		120
Building rental		80
Automobile leases		10
Other		90
Total costs and expenses		3,607
Income before income taxes		$ 356
Income taxes		142
Net income		$ 214

The Sunday edition usually has twice as many pages as the daily editions. Analysis of direct edition variable costs for 19X3–X4 is shown in the following schedule.

	Cost per Issue	
	Daily	*Sunday*
Paper	$0.050	$0.100
Other supplies	0.025	0.050
Carrier and sales commissions	0.025	0.025
	$0.100	$0.175

Several changes in operations are scheduled for the next year, and there is a need to recognize increasing costs.

1. The building lease expired on September 30, 19X4, and has been renewed with a change in the rental fee provisions from a straight fee to a fixed fee of $60,000 plus 1% of newspaper sales.
2. The advertising department will eliminate the payment of a 4% advertising commission on contracts sold by its employees. An average of two-thirds of the advertising has been sold on a contract basis in the past. The individual salaries of the four who solicited advertising will be raised from $7,500 to $14,000. Other advertising salaries will be increased by 6%.
3. Automobiles will no longer be leased. Employees whose jobs require automobiles will use their own and be reimbursed at $0.15 per mile. The leased cars were driven 80,000 miles in 19X3–X4, and it is estimated that the employees will drive some 84,000 miles next year on company business.
4. Cost increases estimated for next year:
   a. Newsprint: $0.01 per daily issue and $0.02 for the Sunday paper
   b. Salaries:
      (1) Equipment operators 8%
      (2) Other employees 6%
   c. Employee benefits (from 15% of personnel costs, excluding all commissions, to 20%) 5%
5. Circulation increases of 5% in newsstand and home delivery are anticipated.
6. Advertising revenue is estimated at $1,890,000, with $1,260,000 from employee-solicited contracts.

REQUIRED:

A. Prepare a projected income statement for the Metropolitan News for the 19X4–X5 fiscal year using a format that shows the total variable costs and total fixed costs for the newspaper. (Round calculations to the nearest thousand dollars.)

B. The management of Metropolitan News is contemplating one additional proposal for the 19X4–X5 fiscal year—raising the rates for its newspaper to the amounts as computed.

	Daily	*Sunday*
Single issue price	$0.20	$0.40
Weekly subscription (includes daily and Sunday)	$1.25	

It is estimated that the newspaper's circulation would decline to 90% of the currently anticipated 19X4–X5 level for both newsstand and home delivery sales if this change is initiated. Advertising revenue will not be affected by the change. Calculate the effect on the projected 19X4–X5 income if this proposed rate change is implemented. *(CMA adapted)*

12-38 Patterson Company has projected demand for its product sufficient to use its full productive capacity during 19X7. Planning data follow.

Productive capacity 30,000 units
Flexible budget equations:
Material $0 + $2.95 per unit
Labor $0 + $1.25 per unit
Factory overhead $21,000 + $1.20 per unit produced
General and administrative costs $30,000 + $0 per unit sold
Other:
Sales commissions are 10% of sales.
Desired profit is $1 per unit.
Ignore taxes.

REQUIRED:

A. Assuming that the company will produce at capacity, what should be the selling price to achieve the planned profit?
B. What is the breakeven point both in units and in dollars?
C. Using your selling price from part A, prepare a profit plan for 19X7.

12-39 Doctors' Clinic is a private medical clinic operated by a group of doctors. The executive committee has asked you to prepare a budget for 19X8.

The clinic serves a suburban community of about 24,000 population, of which 25% are expected to become patients of the clinic. Each patient is expected to average five visits per year. A billing rate of $12 per patient visit was established. Normally about 5% of billings are not collected.

Each doctor can accommodate about 600 patient visits per month. One nurse is required for each 500 patient visits per month. On the average, a doctor's salary is $4,000 per month and a nurse's salary is $1,000 per month. Doctors may be hired on a half-time basis. All other employees are full-time. Operating costs for the clinic include:

Administration	$5,000 per month
Medical supplies	$1.50 per patient visit
Lab and X-ray technicians	$4,000 per month
Rent	$24,000 per year
Medical and financial records	$1,000 per month plus $.25 per patient visit
Other expenses	$500 per month plus $.15 per patient visit

REQUIRED:

A. Assuming that patient visits occur evenly throughout the year, prepare a profit plan for Doctors' Clinic for an average month.

B. The primary goal of Doctors' Clinic is to provide quality health care to a limited segment of the population at a fee structure sufficient to meet the personal goals of the practicing doctors. The doctors' personal goals require an average individual income of $4,000 per month. What fee must be charged to allow the doctors to accomplish their goals?

12-40 Vernon Enterprises designs and manufactures toys. Past experience indicates that the product life cycle of a toy is three years. Promotional advertising produces large sales in the early years, but there is a substantial sales decline in the final year of a toy's life.

Consumer demand for new toys placed on the market tends to fall into three classes. About 30% of the new toys sell well above expectations, 60% sell as anticipated, and 10% have poor consumer acceptance.

The management of Vernon Enterprises has decided to produce a new toy. The following sales projections were made after carefully evaluating consumer demand for the new toy.

Consumer Demand for New Toy	*Chance of Occurring*	**Estimated Sales** *Year 19X7*	*Year 19X8*	*Year 19X9*
Above average	30%	$1,200,000	$2,500,000	$600,000
Average	60%	$ 700,000	$1,700,000	$400,000
Below average	10%	$ 200,000	$ 900,000	$150,000

Variable production costs are estimated at 30% of sales. Fixed production expenses, excluding depreciation, related to the new toy are estimated at $50,000 per year. New machinery costing $860,000 will be installed by January 1, 19X7, to produce the new toy. The new machinery will be depreciated by the sum-of-the-years'-digits method. There is no other use anticipated for the equipment. It will be sold at the end of the third year at its salvage value, expected to be $110,000. A vacant portion of the plant that has no other prospect for use will be used to produce the toy. Rent expense apportioned to this space is $20,000 per year.

Advertising and promotional expenses are expected to be $100,000 the first year, $150,000 the second year, and $50,000 the third year. Assume that state and federal taxes will total 60% of income.

REQUIRED:

A. Prepare a sales budget for this new toy in each of the three years, taking into account the probability of above-average, average, and below-average sales occurring.

B. Prepare a profit plan for the new toy for each of the three years of its life.

(CPA adapted)

12-41 The administrator of Wright Hospital has asked you to prepare an operating budget (profit plan) for the next year ending June 30, 19X2, and presented you with a number of service projections for the year. The following are estimated room requirements for inpatients by type of service.

Type of Patient	*Total Patients Expected*	*Average Number of Days in Hospital*	**Percentage of Regular Patients Selecting Types of Service**		
			Private	*Semiprivate*	*Ward*
Medical	2,100	7	10%	60%	30%
Surgical	2,400	10	15%	75%	10%

Daily rentals per patient are $40 for a private room, $35 for a semi-private room, and $25 for a ward.

Operating-room charges are based on man-minutes (number of minutes the operating room is in use multiplied by number of personnel assisting in the operation). The per-man-minute charges are $.13 for inpatients and $.22 for outpatients. Studies for the current year show that operations are divided by type as follows:

Type of Operation	*Number of Operations*	*Average Number of Minutes Per Operation*	*Average Number of Personnel Required*
A	800	30	4
B	700	45	5
C	300	90	6
D	200	120	8
	2,000		
Outpatient	180	20	3

The following is a budget of direct costs for the year ending June 30, 19X2, by departments.

Service departments:	
Maintenance of plant	$ 50,000
Operation of plant	27,500
Administration	97,500
All others	192,000
Revenue-producing departments:	
Operating room	68,440
All others	700,000
Total direct costs	$1,135,440

All service department costs are to be allocated to the revenue-producing departments. The following information is provided for cost-allocation purposes.

	Square Feet	*Salaries*
General services:		
Maintenance of plant	12,000	$ 40,000
Operation of plant	28,000	25,000
Administration	10,000	55,000
All others	36,250	102,500
Revenue-producing departments:		
Operating room	17,500	15,000
All others	86,250	302,500
	190,000	$540,000

Bases of allocations:
- Maintenance of plant—salaries
- Operation of plant—square feet
- Administration—salaries
- All others—8% to operating room
  92% to other revenue-producing services

REQUIRED:
Prepare schedules showing the computation of:

A. The number of patient days (number of patients multiplied by average stay in hospital) expected by type of patients (medical or surgical) and type of room service (private, semiprivate, or ward).
B. Expected gross revenue from room service.
C. The total number of man-minutes expected for operating-room services for inpatients and outpatients. For inpatients, show the breakdown of total operating-room man-minutes by type of operation.
D. Expected gross revenue from operating-room services.

E. Cost per man-minute for operating-room services, assuming that the step-down method of cost allocation is used. (Costs of the general services departments are allocated first to the general services departments that they serve and then to the revenue-producing departments.)

F. Operating budget (profit plan) showing the budget for each revenue-producing center and the entire hospital. *(CPA adapted)*

12-42 Modern Products Corporation, a manufacturer of molded plastic containers, determined in October 19X8 that it needed cash to continue operations. The corporation began negotiating for a one-month bank loan of $100,000 that would be discounted at 6% per annum on November 1; that is, the interest would be deducted in advance and the corporation would pay $100,000 on December 1. In considering the loan, the bank requested a projected income statement and a cash budget for the month of November. (Note: The cash budget will be required as part of problem 13-42.)

The following information is available.

1. Sales were budgeted at 120,000 units per month in October 19X8, December 19X8, and January 19X9 and at 90,000 units in November 19X8. The selling price is $2 per unit. Sales are billed on the fifteenth and last day of each month on terms of 1/10, net 30. Past experience indicates sales are even throughout the month, and 50% of the customers pay the billed amount within the discount period. The remainder pay at the end of 30 days, except for bad debts, which average 1% of gross sales.

2. The inventory of finished goods on October 1 was 24,000 units. The finished goods inventory at the end of each month is to be maintained at 20% of the sales anticipated for the following month. No Work-in-Process Inventory remains at the end of any month.

3. The inventory of raw materials on October 1 was 22,800 pounds. At the end of each month the raw materials inventory is to be maintained at not less than 40% of the production requirements for the following month. Materials are purchased as needed in minimum quantities of 25,000 pounds per shipment. Raw material purchases for each month are paid in the succeeding month on terms of net 30 days.

4. All salaries and wages are paid on the fifteenth and last day of each month for the period ending on the date of payment.

5. All manufacturing overhead, selling, and administrative expenses are paid on the tenth of the month following the month in which they were incurred. Selling expenses are 10% of gross sales. Administrative expenses, which include depreciation of $500 per month on office furniture and fixtures, total $33,000 per month.

6. The standard cost of a molded plastic container, based on normal production of 100,000 units per month, is as follows:

Materials ($\frac{1}{2}$ pound)	$ .50
Labor	.40
Variable factory overhead	.20
Fixed factory overhead	.10
Total	$1.20

Fixed factory overhead includes depreciation on factory equipment of $4,000 per month.

REQUIRED:

A. Prepare a sales budget for October, November, and December.
B. Prepare a production budget for October, November, and December.
C. Prepare a purchases budget for October and November.
D. Prepare a projected income statement (profit plan) for November.

(CPA adapted)

12-43 Chapter 12 presented a comprehensive budgeting illustration for the DeFord Company. The sales budget for the DeFord Company by month for 19X1 is presented in Exhibit 12-9. The budget schedules leading to the profit plan are developed for the first three months of 19X1.

REQUIRED:

Continue the budget illustration for the DeFord Company for April. Remember that production is at practical capacity of 5,000 units of Product A and 15,000 units of Product B per month. Exhibit 12-12 presents the cost structure for *each* responsibility area of the company.

A. Prepare a production budget.
B. Prepare a purchasing budget.
C. Prepare a budget for the heat-treating department.
D. Prepare a product line budget for the Western territory of Product B.
E. Prepare a factory cost budget. (It is necessary to determine the total costs for the shaping department and the materials handling department for April. Exhibits 12-12 and 12-13 provide the necessary data.)
F. Prepare a marketing budget. (It will be necessary to prepare summary data for Product A and for the Eastern territory of Product B.)
G. Prepare a profit plan.

13 Budgeting for Resource Planning

THE STATEMENT OF FINANCIAL POSITION
PLANNING AND BUDGETING FOR SHORT-TERM RESOURCE NEEDS
The Cash Budget
Planning Liquidity
PLANNING AND BUDGETING FOR LONG-TERM RESOURCE NEEDS
Capital Expenditures Budget
Planning Long-Term Sources of Funds
PROJECTED STATEMENT OF FINANCIAL POSITION
SUMMARY

A company cannot undertake the activities necessary to achieve its profit plan without adequate financial resources. The interrelationship of profit planning and resource planning should become clear as the cash budget is prepared in this chapter.

The purpose of decision making is to allocate resources in an optimal manner. The term *resources* encompasses financial resources, such as cash and assets to be converted into cash; human resources; physical resources, such as inventory, land, buildings, and equipment; and intangibles such as patent rights and the position of the firm in the marketplace. All these resources are important to firm management, but some cannot be measured in financial terms. The management accountant is primarily concerned with those resources that can be measured in financial terms.

THE STATEMENT OF FINANCIAL POSITION

The statement of financial position (balance sheet) is the starting and ending point in planning financial resources. It provides a statement of the composition and sources of a firm's financial resources at a given point in time. The statement of financial position at the beginning of 19X1 for the DeFord Company, our continuing illustration, is presented in Exhibit 13-1. The assets listed in the position statement are the financial resources at the company's disposal at the beginning of the period. These assets are separated into current and fixed.

If the existing current assets are insufficient to meet the projected cash outflows, the company may meet its short-term needs for funds by borrowing from the bank. If the company projects a long-term need for funds, it may borrow by issuing long-term notes or bonds or by selling additional stock. The question of how and where additional funds will be raised is beyond the scope of this book.

Resource planning involves a projection of both short- and long-term needs. We usually call the short-term, or current, resources **working capital.** The amount of working capital is measured by deducting current liabilities from current assets. Working capital is often called *circulating capital* because of its constant turnover from cash to inventory to accounts receivable and back into cash. Working capital for the DeFord Company at the beginning of the year is $420,300 ($562,000 of current assets − $141,700 of current liabilities).

The remainder of the statement of financial position shows the resources committed to long-term purposes and the capital structure of the firm (long-term sources of funds).

DEFORD COMPANY
STATEMENT OF FINANCIAL POSITION FOR MANAGEMENT
December 31, 19X0

ASSETS		
Current assets		
Cash	$ 35,000	
Marketable securities	200,000	
Accounts receivable	114,000	
Inventories		
Raw materials	80,000	
Finished goods	133,000	$562,000
Fixed assets		
Equipment	$540,000	
Accumulated depreciation	200,000	340,000
Total assets		$902,000
LIABILITIES AND STOCKHOLDERS' EQUITY		
Current liabilities		
Accounts payable	$ 70,000	
Accrued expenses	16,700	
Dividends payable	30,000	
Income taxes payable	25,000	$141,700
Long-term liabilities		
Note payable, 9%, due 6/1/X2		100,000
Total liabilities		$241,700
Stockholders' equity		
Capital stock, $10 par, 50,000 shares authorized, 30,000 issued and outstanding	$300,000	
Retained earnings	360,300	660,300
Total liabilities and stockholders' equity		$902,000

EXHIBIT 13-1
Beginning statement of financial position for management of DeFord Company

PLANNING AND BUDGETING FOR SHORT-TERM RESOURCE NEEDS

Short-range resource planning is concerned with liquidity and solvency. **Liquidity** describes the amount and composition of the assets. **Solvency** represents the ability of the firm to pay its debts as they become due. We are primarily concerned with liquidity. By maintaining sufficient cash and other liquid assets, and budgeting the timing and magnitude of the cash inflows and cash outflows, the firm should remain solvent.[1]

How liquid does the firm need to be to finance its operations? With too much liquidity the firm incurs an excessive capital cost and subjects itself to greater risk through mismanagement and embezzlement. Too little liquidity subjects the firm to excessive costs (inability to take quantity and cash discounts for example), lost sales, and the risk of insolvency.

In planning for liquidity we are concerned with the circulation of liquid resources during an operating cycle. An **operating cycle** is the period of time required for the cash invested in inventories to be returned to the firm through the collection of cash from the sale of its products. In Exhibit 13-2 the operating cycle is illustrated as a circle that begins and ends with cash. The first step in the cycle is the purchase of raw materials. The next step is production, where labor and overhead costs are incurred to convert the raw materials into a salable product. The third step is the sale of the product and incurrence of selling and administrative expenses. In the final step cash is collected from the customer and becomes available to start another cycle. New cash enters working capital through the issuance of capital stock, long-term and short-term borrowing, and the sale of assets. Cash exits in the form of investments in productive assets, repayments of loans and interest, and distributions to stockholders.

The amount of working capital needed depends upon the size of the business (illustrated by the size of the circle) and the length of the operating cycle (illustrated by the speed or velocity of movement around the circle). Changes in the size of the circle may be due to growth of the business or seasonal variation. As sales increase, additional working capital is needed and the circle grows. Velocity may be increased by delaying payments to materials suppliers, shortening the time required in the production process, and speeding up collections from customers.

In this chapter we are interested in two aspects of planning for short-term resource needs. The first involves the timing of cash flows. Cash is the focal point of resource planning; it begins with the investment of cash and ends with the recovery of cash. The cash budget projects the cash inflows and outflows necessary to carry out the operating decisions on which the profit plan is based and the long-range decisions on which the capital expenditures budget is based.

[1]The term *insolvent* also has a technical meaning. A firm is technically insolvent when its liabilities exceed its assets.

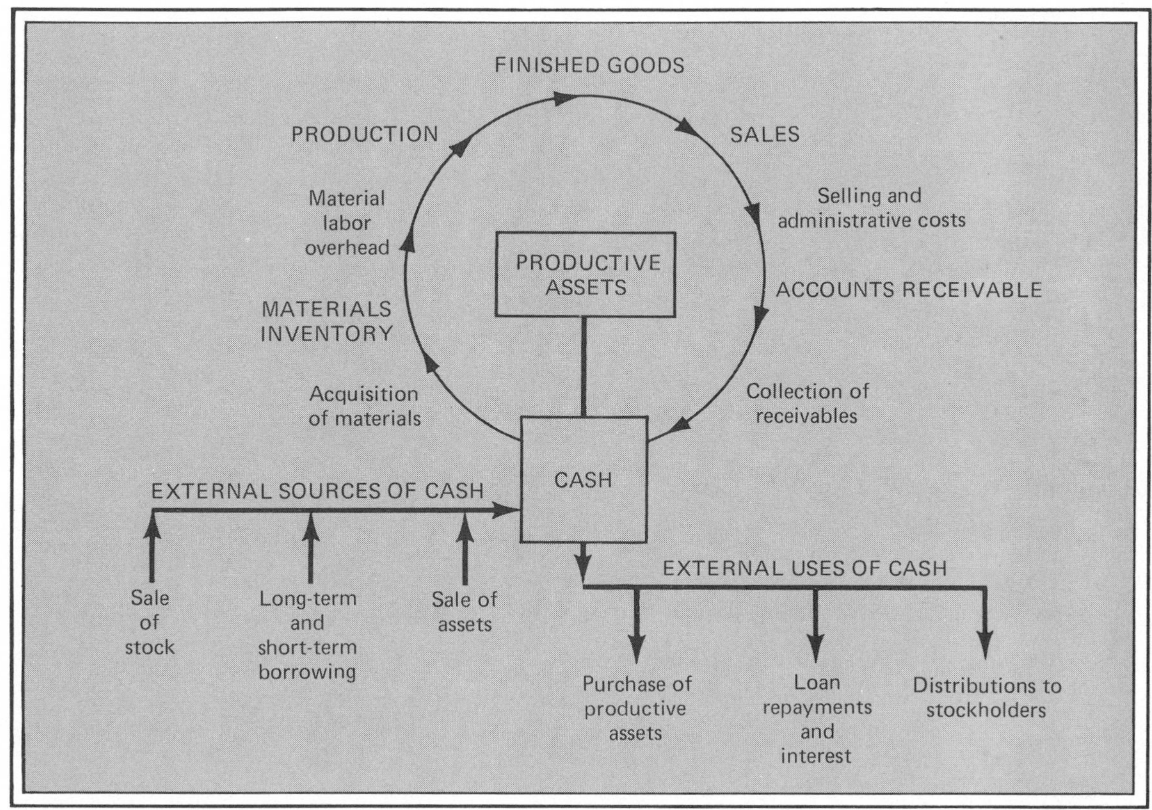

EXHIBIT 13-2
Cash flows—operating cycle

The second aspect of planning for short-term resource needs involves an answer to the question, "How much working capital is enough?" Each step in the operating cycle requires planning and establishing the objectives and policies of the particular financial resource involved at that point: cash, accounts receivable, or inventory.

The Cash Budget

In this section the cash budget for the DeFord Company will be developed. We will present the finished cash budget first and then examine the supporting schedules that were required to prepare it. The particular form of the cash budget is not important so long as cash flows from operations—the continuing source of funds—are separated from other cash flows. It is essential that the firm have a clear picture of operating cash flows.

A condensed monthly cash budget for the DeFord Company, for the year 19X1, is presented in Exhibit 13-3 to emphasize the seasonality of cash flows from operations. Looking only at *total* operating cash flows for the year,

DEFORD COMPANY
SUMMARY CASH BUDGET
For the Year 19X1, by Month

	EXPECTED CASH INFLOW FROM OPERATIONS	EXPECTED CASH (OUTFLOWS) FROM OPERATIONS	NET CASH FLOWS FROM OPERATIONS	OTHER SOURCES OF CASH	OTHER (USES) OF CASH	NET CASH SOURCES (USES)
January	$ 102,000	$ (239,700)	$(137,700)	$161,000	$ (34,500)	$(11,200)
February	108,000	(136,700)	(28,700)	40,200	—	11,500
March	108,000	(133,300)	(25,300)	50,000	(20,000)	4,700
April	136,000	(163,500)	(27,500)	20,100	—	(7,400)
May	148,000	(140,700)	7,300	—	—	7,300
June	204,000	(146,900)	57,100	—	(71,500)	(14,400)
July	264,000	(182,900)	81,100	100	(74,500)	6,700
August	264,000	(146,900)	117,100	300	(120,000)	(2,600)
September	248,000	(144,300)	103,700	900	(100,000)	4,600
October	248,000	(165,300)	82,700	1,400	(80,000)	4,100
November	188,000	(139,500)	48,500	1,800	(60,000)	(9,700)
December	136,000	(132,300)	3,700	102,100	(100,000)	5,800
19X1	$2,154,000	$(1,872,000)	$ 282,000	$377,900	$(660,500)	$ (600)

EXHIBIT 13-3
Summary cash budget for DeFord Company

there appears to be no problem of liquidity. Cash inflows from operations are expected to be $2,154,000, providing an increase in cash of $282,000. The seasonal pattern in sales, however, is different from the seasonal pattern for production, resulting in uneven cash flows over months. A short-term cash shortage will exist if planning is not detailed by month.

During the first four months of the year, operations of the DeFord Company will require more cash than will be collected from customers. In January the largest cash payments will be coupled with the smallest cash collections of the year. The DeFord Company will be operating at practical capacity with stable production throughout the year. Therefore, with the exception of a very few significant payments, such as annual rent and income taxes (both payable in January), cash payments for operations will also be stable. The seasonal pattern for sales, however, causes cash timing problems. The smallest cash collections are during the winter and early spring, and the largest cash collections are during the summer and early fall. When cash payments exceed cash collections, the company sells marketable securities or, if necessary, takes out short-term loans from the bank. When collections exceed payments, the firm repays loans or purchases securities.

	(*)	JANUARY	FEBRUARY	MARCH	TOTAL FOR YEAR
Expected cash flow from operations					
Sources of cash					
Collections from customers-A	A	$ 12,000	$ 12,000	$ 12,000	$ 720,000
Collections from customers-B	A	90,000	96,000	96,000	1,434,000
Total		$ 102,000	$108,000	$108,000	$2,154,000
Uses of cash					
Payments to suppliers	B	$ 70,000	$ 58,000	$ 48,000	$ 653,000
Payroll	C	50,000	50,000	50,000	600,000
Payroll fringe	D	8,000	8,000	8,000	120,000
Power and utilities	E	8,500	8,500	8,500	102,000
Rent	F	60,000			60,000
Variable marketing expense	G	4,200	4,200	4,800	90,000
Product promotion	H	8,000		8,000	48,000
Research	I		2,000		12,000
Other	J	6,000	6,000	6,000	72,000
Income taxes	K	25,000			115,000
Total		239,700	136,700	133,300	1,872,000
Net flow of cash from operations		$(137,700)	$ (28,700)	$ (25,300)	$ 282,000
Other sources of cash					
Sale of investments		160,000	40,000		320,000
Short-term borrowing				50,000	50,000
Investment income	O	1,000	200		7,900
Other uses of cash					
Purchase of investments				(20,000)	(440,000)
Repayment of short-term borrowing					(50,000)
Interest on short-term borrowing					(1,500)
Interest on long-term borrowing	L	(4,500)			(9,000)
Dividends	M	(30,000)			(60,000)
Capital expenditures					(100,000)
Net cash sources (uses)		$ (11,200)	$ 11,500	$ 4,700	(600)
Add: beginning balance of cash		35,000	23,800	35,300	35,000
Ending balance of cash		$ 23,800	$ 35,300	$ 40,000	$ 34,400

(*) Reference to supporting schedule in text

EXHIBIT 13-4
Cash budget for DeFord Company

A detailed cash budget for the DeFord Company is presented in Exhibit 13-4. Each cash flow (except those involving short-term investments and short-term borrowings) is referenced to the schedules presented later in this chapter. Like the exhibits in Chapter 12, the cash budget and related schedules are presented for the first three months of 19X1 and in total for the year.

SOURCES OF CASH FROM OPERATIONS

A. *Collections from customers* were determined by applying the terms of sale to the monthly sales from the sales budget (Exhibit 12-9). Product A customers (construction contractors) are allowed 60 days to pay, whereas Product B customers (wholesalers) are allowed only 30 days.

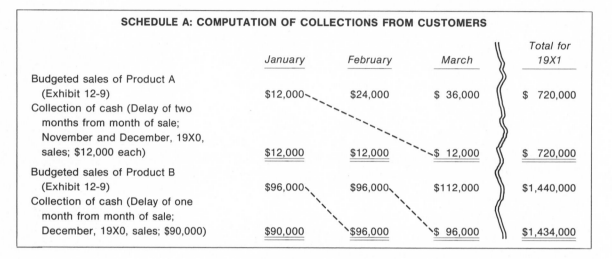

SCHEDULE A: COMPUTATION OF COLLECTIONS FROM CUSTOMERS

	January	*February*	*March*	*Total for 19X1*
Budgeted sales of Product A (Exhibit 12-9)	$12,000	$24,000	$ 36,000	$ 720,000
Collection of cash (Delay of two months from month of sale; November and December, 19X0, sales; $12,000 each)	$12,000	$12,000	$ 12,000	$ 720,000
Budgeted sales of Product B (Exhibit 12-9)	$96,000	$96,000	$112,000	$1,440,000
Collection of cash (Delay of one month from month of sale; December, 19X0, sales; $90,000)	$90,000	$96,000	$ 96,000	$1,434,000

For simplicity we have assumed that all payments are made on schedule and that there are no bad-debt losses. In reality most firms will have late collections and bad debts. Rather than collecting 100% of the sales of Product A in the second month after sale (as we may expect from 60-day credit terms), we may find an actual collection experience similar to the following:

5%	in month of sale
15%	in month following sale
60%	in second month following sale (expected month of collection with 60-day terms)
10%	in third month following sale
8%	collected over next six months
98%	total amount collected
2%	bad debts
100%	

This collection schedule would affect the timing of the cash collections but not the technique of budgeting.

B. *Payments to suppliers* include payments for purchases of materials and factory supplies. Material purchases were presented in the purchases budget (Exhibit 12-11). Where factory supplies are not included in the material purchases budget, as in the DeFord Company, it is necessary to summarize the supplies used from departmental cost reports (Exhibit 12-17, as an example). Payments to suppliers in the cash budget are determined in Schedule B.

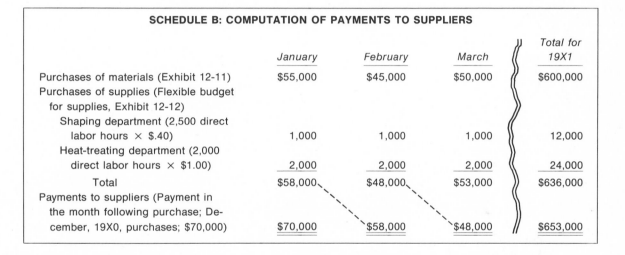

SCHEDULE B: COMPUTATION OF PAYMENTS TO SUPPLIERS

	January	*February*	*March*	*Total for 19X1*
Purchases of materials (Exhibit 12-11)	$55,000	$45,000	$50,000	$600,000
Purchases of supplies (Flexible budget for supplies, Exhibit 12-12)				
Shaping department (2,500 direct labor hours × $.40)	1,000	1,000	1,000	12,000
Heat-treating department (2,000 direct labor hours × $1.00)	2,000	2,000	2,000	24,000
Total	$58,000	$48,000	$53,000	$636,000
Payments to suppliers (Payment in the month following purchase; December, 19X0, purchases; $70,000)	$70,000	$58,000	$48,000	$653,000

Unlike the cash inflows from accounts receivable, where the customer decides when he will make a payment, the timing of the cash outflows can be controlled by the firm in order to take full advantage of credit terms.

C. *Payroll* is paid in the same month employees work. In a responsibility accounting system, such as that used by the DeFord Company, costs are summarized by responsibility area rather than natural expense classification (such as direct labor, indirect labor, supervision). Therefore payroll costs must be summarized from the departmental budgets (Exhibits 12-14, -15, -17, -18, and -19) throughout the company. Monthly salaries other than direct labor are $27,500 (factory $12,000, marketing $8,000, and general $7,500). For the DeFord Company we may refer to the cost structure of the company in Exhibit 12-12. Cash payments for payroll are determined in Schedule C.

SCHEDULE C: COMPUTATION OF PAYMENTS FOR PAYROLL

	January	*February*	*March*	*Total for 19X1*
Direct labor (From departmental budgets, Exhibit 12-14, for example) (4,500 direct labor hours × $5 per hour)	$22,500	$22,500	$22,500	$270,000
Other salaries (Exhibit 12-12) ($12,000 + $8,000 + $7,500)	27,500	27,500	27,500	330,000
Cash payment	$50,000	$50,000	$50,000	$600,000

D. *Payroll fringe* is the package of employee benefits estimated to cost 20% of total payroll. Timing of the expense varies from the timing of cash payments. The portion related to insurance premiums and payroll taxes, estimated to be 80% of the fringe benefits, is remitted monthly. The balance of payroll fringe is vacation pay, which will be paid in equal amounts during the months of June, July, and August.

SCHEDULE D: COMPUTATION OF PAYMENTS FOR FRINGE BENEFITS

	January	*February*	*March*	*Total for 19X1*
Payroll from Schedule C	$50,000	$50,000	$50,000	$600,000
Payroll fringe (20% of total payroll)	$10,000	$10,000	$10,000	$120,000
Payment schedule:				
80% in month of cost	$ 8,000	$ 8,000	$ 8,000	$ 96,000
20% of total, one-third in June, July, and August	—	—	—	24,000
Total	$ 8,000	$ 8,000	$ 8,000	$120,000

E. *Power and utilities* cash outflows are delayed one month from the expense recognition in the profit plan. Power costs are included in the profit plan at $.60 per direct labor hour in shaping and $3.00 per direct labor hour in heat treating. Production is scheduled at 2,500 hours in shaping and 2,000 hours in heat treating. Utilities for the company were budgeted at $1,000 per month.

SCHEDULE E: COMPUTATION OF PAYMENT FOR POWER AND UTILITIES

	January	*February*	*March*	*Total for 19X1*
Power (Exhibit 12-12)				
Shaping department (2,500 direct labor hours × $.60)	$1,500	$1,500	$1,500	$ 18,000
Heat-treating department (2,000 direct labor hours × $3.00)	6,000	6,000	6,000	72,000
Total power	$7,500	$7,500	$7,500	$ 90,000
Utilities (Exhibit 12-12)	1,000	1,000	1,000	12,000
Total power and utilities	$8,500	$8,500	$8,500	$102,000
Cash payment (Delay of one month; December, 19X0, amount; $8,500)	$8,500	$8,500	$8,500	$102,000

F. *Rent* for the factory and general office totals $60,000 for the year, payable on January 1.

G. *Variable marketing costs* are variable costs based upon units sold. The cost for Product A is $.60 per unit sold and for Product B, $.30 per unit sold. Payment is delayed one month.

SCHEDULE G: COMPUTATION OF PAYMENT FOR VARIABLE MARKETING COSTS

	January	*Feburary*	*March*	*Total for 19X1*
Units of Product A sold (Exhibit 12-9)	1,000	2,000	3,000	60,000
Units of Product B sold (Exhibit 12-9)	12,000	12,000	14,000	180,000
Variable marketing for Product A $.60 (Exhibit 12-12)	$ 600	$1,200	$1,800	$36,000
Variable marketing for Product B $.30 (Exhibit 12-12)	3,600	3,600	4,200	54,000
Total variable marketing costs	$4,200	$4,800	$6,000	$90,000
Cash payment (Delay of one month; December cost; $4,200)	$4,200	$4,200	$4,800	$90,000

H. *Product promotion* is paid every other month. In the marketing cost budgets (and Exhibit 12-12) product promotion totals $4,000 per month. Cash payments are $8,000 every other month, beginning in January.

I. *Research* costs were projected at $1,000 per month by Mr. DeFord. Payment is projected for every other month. The last payment was in December, 19X0. Therefore, payments will be $2,000 every other month, beginning in February.

J. *Other costs* total $6,000 [Exhibit 12-12 ($1,600 + $2,400 + $2,000)] and are payable monthly.

K. *Income taxes* are payable quarterly and are based upon the company's estimate of taxes payable for the year. The final quarterly payment makes up any difference between actual taxes for the year and estimated taxes paid during the year. The final payment of $25,000 for 19X0 taxes is to be made in January, 19X1. The company has estimated 19X1 income tax at $123,800 (Exhibit 12-20), with payments of $30,000 in April, July, and October. The final payment for 19X1 of $33,800 [$123,800 ÷ ($30,000 × 3)] will be paid in January, 19X2.

All cash flows from operations have now been projected. The first three months show expected payments in excess of expected receipts.

January	$(137,700)
February	$ (28,700)
March	$ (25,300)
Cumulative excess of payments over receipts	$(191,700)

For the entire year, however, cash receipts from operations are expected to exceed cash payments for operations by $282,000.

OTHER CASH FLOWS

Other planned cash flows include capital expenditures, transactions in the capital stock of the company, cash dividends, and issuance and repayment of long-term debt.

L. *Interest on long-term debt* is payable semiannually, in January and July. Outstanding long-term debt is $100,000 with annual interest of 9%. Interest of $4,500 ($100,000 × 9% × $\frac{1}{2}$ year) will be paid on January 1 and July 1.

M. *Dividends* of $2 per share (30,000 shares outstanding) will be declared during 19X1 and will be payable at the rate of $1 per share on July 1, 19X1, and January 1, 19X2. Payments during 19X1 will include the $30,000 of dividends declared late in 19X0 but payable on January 1, 19X1, and the July 1 dividend.

N. *Capital expenditures* are the result of long-range decisions. The capital expenditures budget is a separate part of the master budget. The cash payments must be included in the cash budget. During 19X1 the only cash outflow is $100,000. Payment is to be made upon delivery and installation of the new equipment in December. The capital expenditures budget will be presented later in this chapter.

SHORT-TERM INVESTMENTS AND SHORT-TERM BORROWING

The DeFord Company has a policy of investing idle cash in marketable securities. Mr. DeFord insists on maintaining a cash balance of at least $20,000, but not in excess of $40,000. Company policy is to invest excess cash in U.S. Treasury Bills that have a 30-day maturity date. Since the securities mature often, the interest on the investment is collected monthly. At the beginning of January the DeFord Company has $200,000 of marketable securities. The amount of cash needed in January is determined in the following tabulation.

Net outflow of cash for operations	$(137,700)
Add: Interest payments on long-term debt	(4,500)
Add: Dividends	(30,000)
Deduct: Investment income	1,000
Total cash decline	$(171,200)
Beginning cash balance	35,000
Subtotal	$(136,200)
Minimum ending cash balance	20,000
Amount of cash needed	$(156,200)

In order to meet the cash requirements, Mr. DeFord decided to sell $160,000 of marketable securities in January and the balance of $40,000 in February.

By March it will be necessary for the company to borrow money from the bank by issuing short-term notes. Because Mr. DeFord does not want to go back to the bank again in the following month or two, he plans to borrow $50,000 in March. This amount is sufficient to carry the firm until operating cash inflows increase. A part of the cash obtained from the loan ($20,000) will be invested in marketable securities until needed. The loan will be repaid later in the year as cash is generated from operations.

By planning cash flows as completely as possible, the firm will be able to reduce borrowing costs and keep idle cash invested. Some cash management systems determine the probable needs for cash on a daily basis and invest any balance that will not be needed for as little as three days.

Planning Liquidity

Earlier we asked, "How much working capital is enough?" The discussions that follow should answer this question.

RATIO ANALYSIS

One way to examine the adequacy of working capital is through ratio analysis. Over many years a set of ratios has evolved to measure liquidity. Ratios measure the average position and movement of working capital. While they are widely used by credit-granting agencies, they provide only general relationships and are deficient for day-to-day planning. The most common ratios for analysis of working capital are current ratio, liquidity ratio, receivables turnover, and inventory turnover. They deal with the major steps in the operating cycle.

The **current ratio** is current assets divided by current liabilities, showing the ability to meet current obligations. Most long-term debt agreements require some minimum current ratio. An old banking rule required that the minimum be 2 to 1. Unfortunately, the current ratio says nothing about composition of the working capital or about timing of payments. There is no assurance that a firm with $150,000 of current assets and $50,000 of current liabilities, and therefore a current ratio of 3 to 1, will be able to pay its creditors. For example, most of the $150,000 could be in slow-moving inventories.

The use of **liquid assets** (cash, marketable securities, and receivables), rather than total current assets, provides a better measure of liquidity. If $75,000 of the $150,000 current assets in the previous illustration were in liquid assets, the **liquidity ratio** would be 1.5 to 1 ($75,000 of liquid assets ÷ $50,000 of current liabilities). An old banking rule placed the minimum acceptable liquidity ratio at 1 to 1.

The current and liquidity ratios are subject to important limitations. First, they relate to positions at a single point in time. Unless that particular time is representative of the continuing financial position of the firm, the ratios may be misleading. Second, they relate only to current, or liquid, assets and current liabilities as measured under generally accepted accounting principles. Thus, only *existing* assets and liabilities are measured. Yet the projected cash flows may be as important as the items present among the current assets and current liabilities.

The **accounts receivable turnover** relates the balance of accounts receivable to credit sales. It is computed by dividing accounts receivable into credit sales. If a firm has annual credit sales of $120,000 and an average accounts receivable balance of $20,000, the accounts receivable turnover is six times. A refinement of the ratio computes the number of days' sales outstanding. A turnover of six times a year would be stated as "60 days of sales outstanding" (360 days ÷ 6 turnovers). In a seasonal business the number of days' sales outstanding will depend on when the ratio is computed. If the ratio is computed at a time when sales activity is very high and, as a result, accounts receivable are very high, the turnover will be low. If computed when activity is low, the turnover figure will be high.

Inventory turnover is determined by dividing cost of goods sold by the finished goods inventory. If cost of goods sold is $72,000 and the inventory is $24,000, the inventory turnover is three times. Unfortunately, there is no basis for evaluating whether three, four, or some other number of inventory turns is appropriate. We must consider the lead time required to replace the inventory and the risk or cost of running short.

Ratios for the DeFord Company follow. Computations were made using data from the 19X0 statement of financial position, the 19X1 projected statement of financial position, and the 19X1 profit plan (Exhibits 13-1, 13-10, and 12-20 respectively).

	Actual 19X0 Statement	*Projected 19X1 Statements*
Current assets	$562,000	$ 687,400
Current liabilities	$141,700	$ 233,500
Current ratio	4.0 to 1	2.9 to 1
Liquid assets	$349,000	$ 474,400
Liquidity ratio	2.5 to 1	2.0 to 1
Accounts receivable		$ 120,000
Sales		$2,160,000
Accounts receivable turnover		18.0 times
Days in receivables		20 days
Cost of goods sold		$1,050,000
Inventory (finished goods)		$ 133,000
Inventory turnover		7.9 times

By traditional standards for a firm in light manufacturing, the ratios are favorable. The projected statement of financial position shows a decline in the current ratio and liquidity ratio. However, the decline is due primarily to a reclassification of maturing notes payable from long-term to short-term liabilities.

The accounts receivable turnover is deceptively high with only 20 days of sales outstanding. Credit terms are 60 days for Product A and 30 days for Product B. The figure of 20 days for the DeFord Company does not indicate that customers are paying early. Accounts receivable at the end of the year were low because sales are normally low in November and December. When a smaller-than-average balance of accounts receivable is related to total sales for the year, the resulting days in receivables is misleading. To avoid this problem, an average of several month-end balances during the year may be computed or the actual age of the receivables may be determined from the records. An aging of accounts receivable classifies the balances of accounts receivable by the amount of time outstanding. Age categories should relate to credit and collection actions. For example, balances up to 60 days are current with only usual billings; balances 60 to 120 days are past due and past due notices have been sent; balances 120 to 180 days are delinquent and require strong follow-up action; balances of 180 to 365 days may be in the hands of a collection agent; and all balances over 365 days may be written off as uncollectible. The aging schedule provides feedback on the effectiveness of various steps in the collection process. It may also act as a basis for the provision for bad debts.

The inventory turnover (cost of goods sold divided by finished goods inventory) is approximately eight times, or about 45 days of goods on hand. Mr. DeFord planned for 60 days of finished goods inventory on hand (a turnover of six times). When compared with the monthly sales budget, there are 90 days of finished goods for Product A and 20 days of finished goods for Product B on hand.

Ratio analysis is useful to analysts outside the firm and as an overall view, but it provides little guidance for specific management decisions. In order to plan liquidity, management needs information concerning expected resource inflows and outflows. A better method for management decision making is the development of planning models that balance the costs of holding too much of the resource with the costs of holding too little. A discussion of some of these models follows.

PLANNING CASH

A firm holds cash for two reasons: transactions and contingencies. Because there are timing differences between the transactions creating cash inflows and cash outflows, a balance of cash must be maintained to meet the day-to-day needs of normal transactions. This amount must increase as the level of economic activity in the firm increases.

The contingency reason for holding cash is best described by the old adage, Set a little aside for a rainy day. Because budgeted cash inflows and outflows are projections of the future, a degree of uncertainty exists. There must be some provision for uncertainties and for unplanned or unexpected occurrences such as a major equipment breakdown.

Often the amount of cash needed for transactions may be projected with a high degree of accuracy. For example, if daily cash flows are plotted for past periods, a pattern will usually develop. In Exhibit 13-5, examples of daily cash inflows and cash outflows are plotted for one month. The weekly payroll caused cash outflows to peak on Wednesday and drop off to minimum flows for the remainder of the week. Normal purchase terms in the example are *n*/10, EOM (payable within 10 days after the end of the month), causing a peak cash outflow on the eighth and ninth days of the month. Cash inflows peaked just prior to the twentieth because the normal sales terms were *n*/20, EOM. With different terms for purchases and sales, the timing of the cash flows varies, and the company must maintain a relatively high cash balance.

Net daily cash flows are shown in Exhibit 13-6. For the first 11 days of the month the cash outflows exceeded cash inflows and the cash balance declined. By the eleventh of the month the cumulative cash outflow reached $37,000, after which the cash inflows exceeded cash outflows and the cash balance grew. From the twenty-fourth to the end of the month cash inflows and cash outflows were nearly identical.

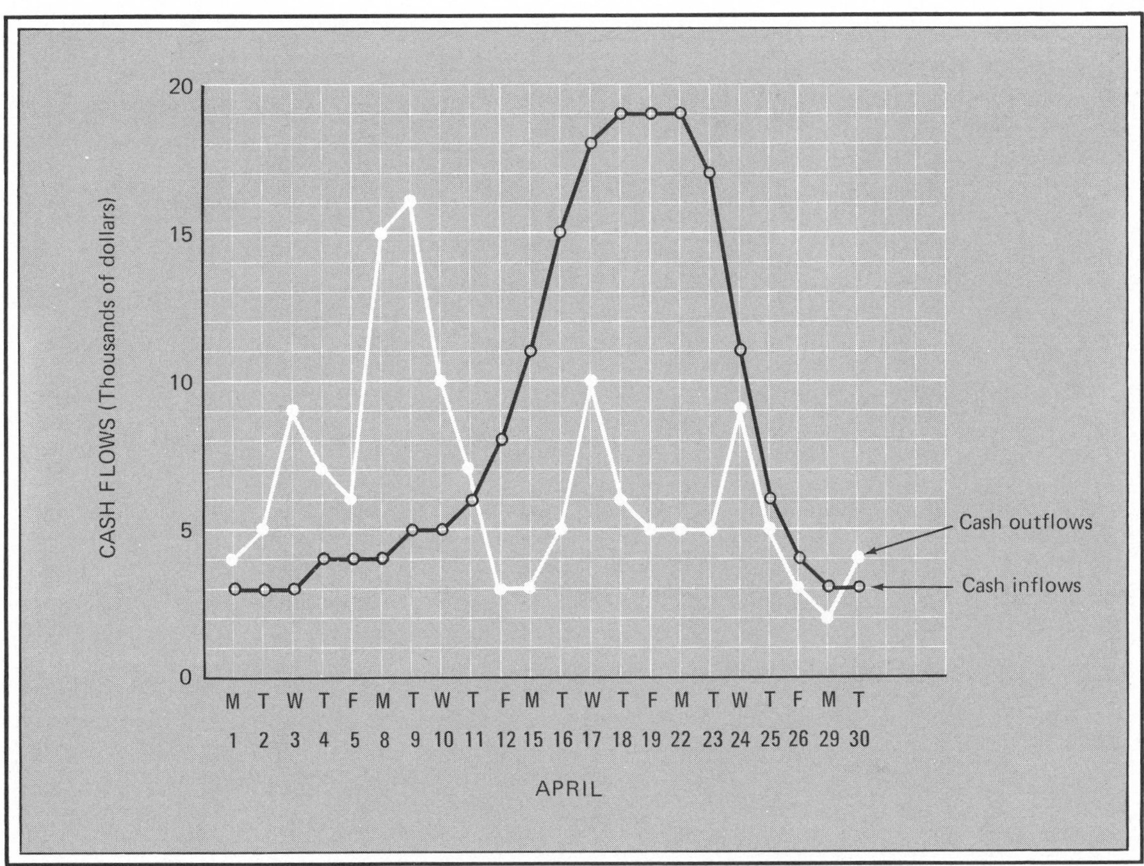

EXHIBIT 13-5
Daily timing of cash flows

By plotting net cash flows for several months, the strength of the cash flow pattern and deviations can be determined. The firm can establish the necessary cash balance for normal transactions and then, by studying the deviations and considering nonroutine payments such as dividends, can establish the balance for contingency purposes.

The contingency balance may be reduced by maintaining short-term borrowing authority, called a *line of credit,* at a bank. Maintenance may cost .5% to 1% of the credit line, but this is considerably below the cost of capital incurred by the firm. Each dollar of cash balance freed means another dollar that may be invested in productive assets.

PLANNING ACCOUNTS RECEIVABLE

The firm manages its accounts receivable by establishing policies on credit length, cash discounts, credit-granting criteria, and the nature of the collection effort. For resource planning it is necessary to know the timing and magnitude of collections from sales. The firm's credit and collection policies

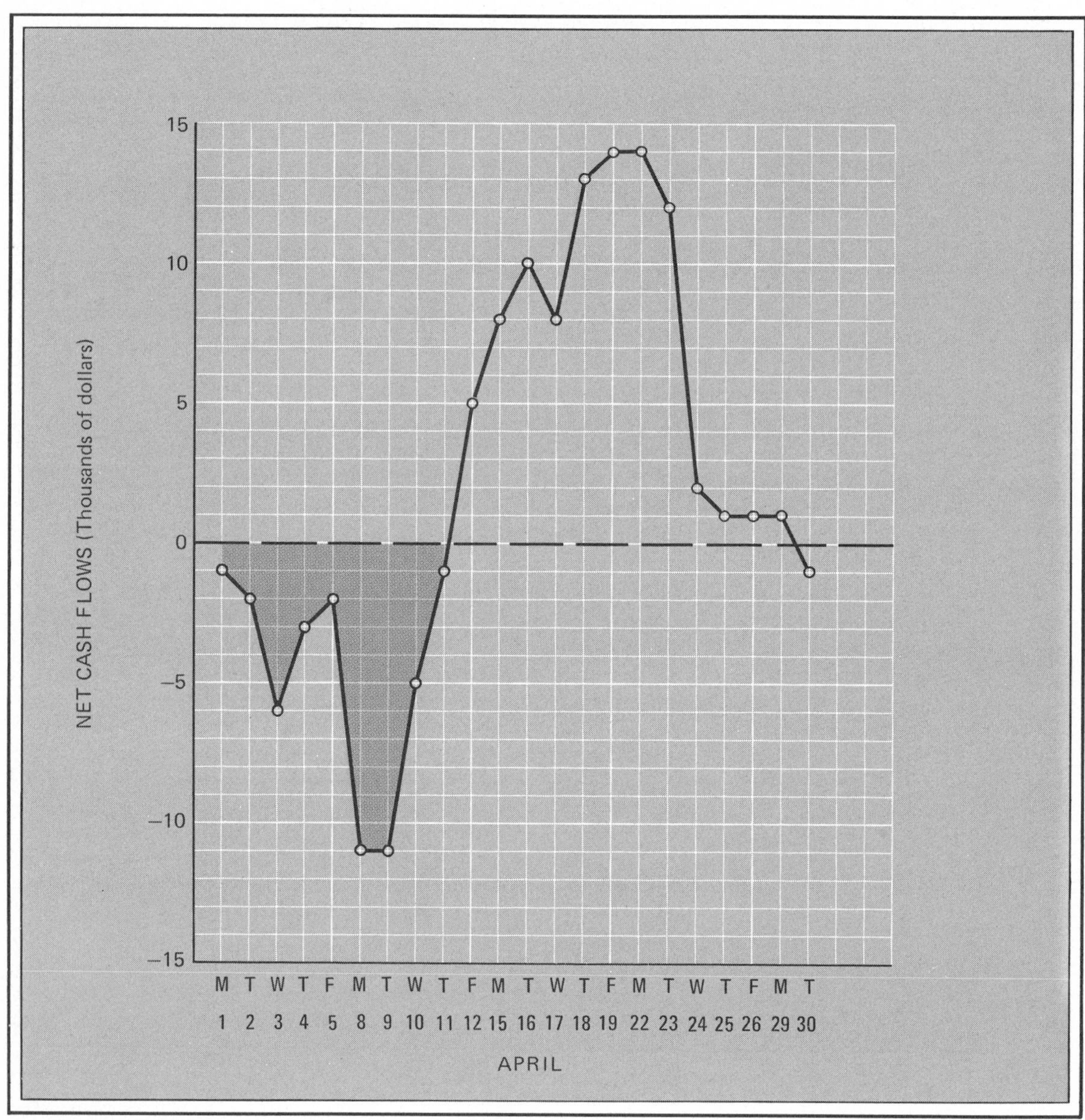

EXHIBIT 13-6
Daily net cash flows

determine the timing and magnitude of cash flows from receivables. Any policy that extends credit terms will postpone the collection of cash. The granting of cash discounts or increases in collection expenses will reduce the magnitude of net cash inflows.

In most lines of business there are established trade practices concerning cash discounts and the length of credit. To offer shorter credit periods and smaller cash discounts than competitors may drastically reduce sales. To offer longer credit periods and larger cash discounts could provide a competitive advantage that should increase sales; at the same time it will negatively affect the timing of cash and the magnitude of cash collections. A firm must balance the benefits of added sales with the costs of a decreased cash flow per dollar of sales.

PLANNING INVENTORIES

Firms hold inventories for the same two basic reasons they hold cash: transactions and contingencies.[2] In some ways, planning for an inventory of cash is much like planning for an inventory of raw materials or finished goods. The firm must hold a minimum amount of inventory to satisfy production and sales demands. If the rate of usage and delivery dates could be predicted with certainty, the firm would need to hold only the minimum inventory level necessary for the known transactions. However, business activity is not certain, and provision must be made for contingencies as well as for expected transactions.

Models have been developed to determine inventory levels necessary for inventory transactions and contingencies. Once the expected usage or sale of goods is determined, inventory models may be used to determine the most economic order size, or **economic order quantity** (EOQ). By considering probable variations in delivery dates and usage rates, a minimum inventory level necessary to provide for contingencies can also be determined.

Exhibit 13-7 shows the fluctuation of the raw materials inventory level over a period of time. The cycle begins when goods are received at the **replenishment point.** As goods are withdrawn from inventory, a level is reached—the **reorder point**—where an order must be placed to provide a **lead time** adequate to ensure delivery when needed. The **safety stock,** or contingency level, makes provision for uncertainties in usage rate and lead time. If we are certain of the usage rate and lead time, there is no need for a safety stock.

Economic order quantity (EOQ) was discussed in Chapter 7 in the context of deciding how much the firm should produce. The same theory is applicable to determining the amount of goods to buy on a particular purchase order. As shown in the following chart, ordering costs increase as the

[2]A third reason, speculation, is often advanced for holding inventories. The motives behind speculation differ, and a discussion of inventory speculation is beyond the scope of this text.

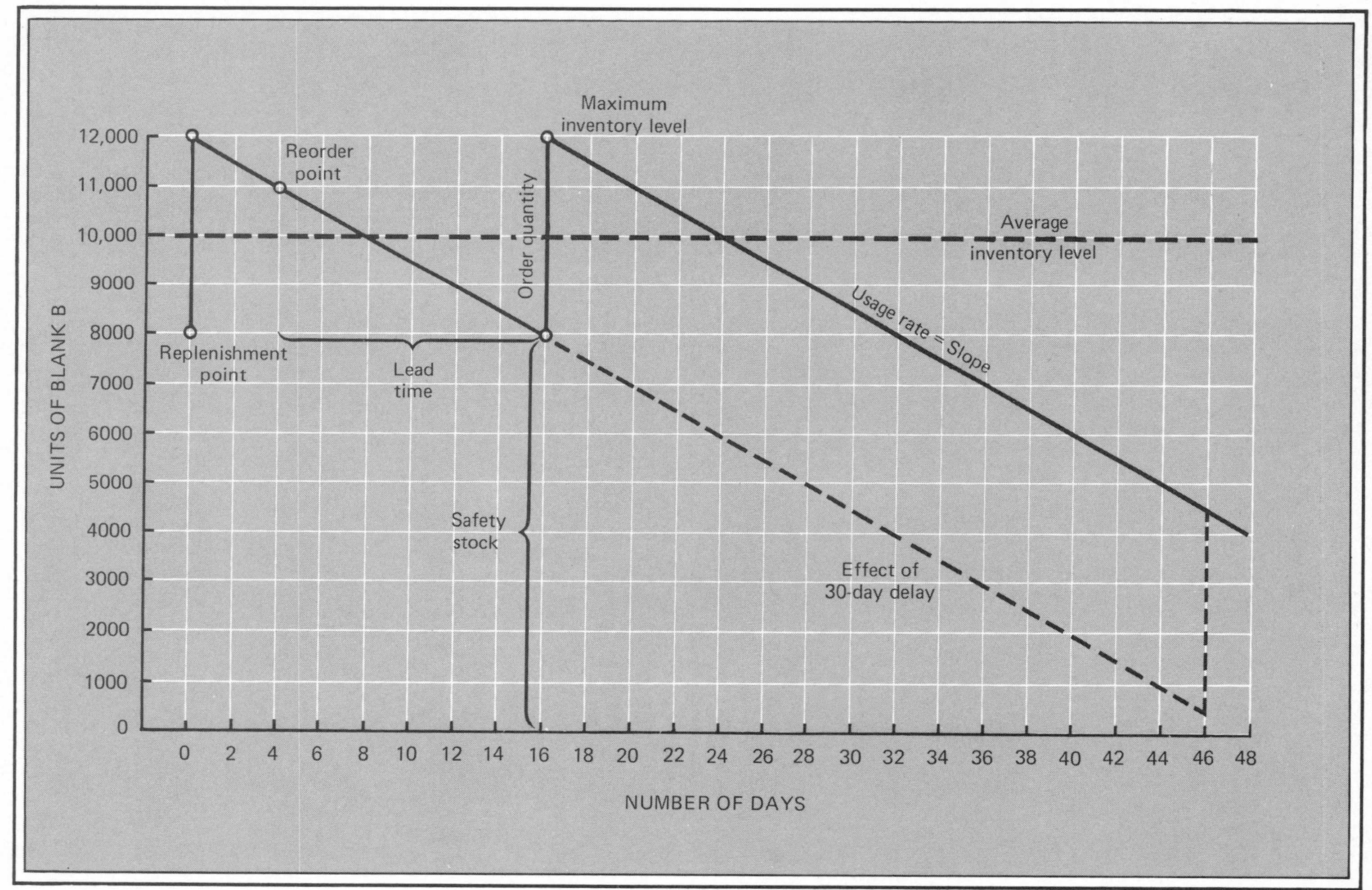

EXHIBIT 13-7
Illustration of inventory model for DeFord Company

number of orders increases. On the other hand, as the number of orders tory declines. the EOQ model determines the point at which total inventory costs are lowest.

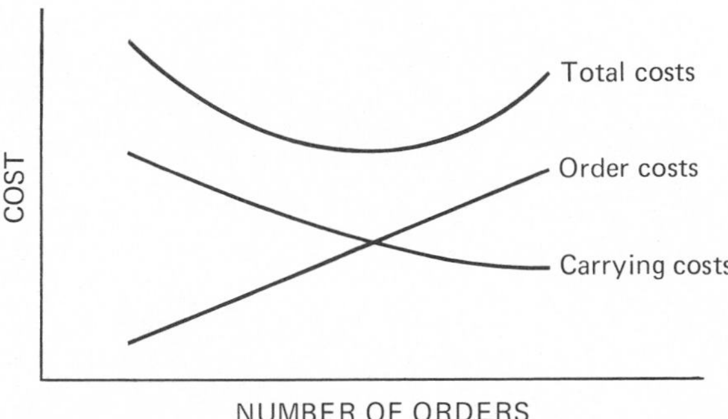

The following data relates to the planned purchase of materials for Product A by the DeFord Company and illustrates the calculation of EOQ.

$$\text{EOQ} = \sqrt{\frac{A \times C}{2 \times S}}$$

A = Annual purchases of inventory = 60,000 units at \$2 per unit
C = Inventory carrying cost = 10% of cost of inventory
S = Cost of an order = \$25 per order

$$\text{Number of orders} = \sqrt{\frac{\$120{,}000 \times 10\%}{2 \times \$25}}$$

$$= \sqrt{\frac{\$12{,}000}{\$50}}$$

$$= \$240$$

$$\text{EOQ} = 15 \text{ orders}$$

$$\text{Units per order} = \frac{60{,}000 \text{ total units}}{15 \text{ orders}} = 4{,}000 \text{ units}$$

With an economic order quantity of 4,000 units, the average in-tory (assuming constant usage) to maintain production would be 2,000 (4,000 ÷ 2). The safety stock, or contingency level, must provide for different rates of usage, late deliveries, and other variations in inventory transactions. In the past, orders for the DeFord Company have been delayed as long as 30 working days. At a daily usage rate of 250 units, a 30-day delay in receiving an order would force the firm to draw 7,500 units from the safety stock. The effect of a 30-day delay in receiving an order is shown by the dotted line on Exhibit 13-7.

Mr. DeFord established an average inventory level of 10,000 units based upon a desired inventory turnover of six times (annual usage 60,000 ÷ 6 times). This level provides a safety stock of 8,000 units and an average working stock of 2,000. Production for the next year is planned at practical capacity. Therefore, raw materials usage should be stable throughout the year. The only uncertainty is the delivery schedule. If no delay greater than 30 days is expected, an average inventory level of 10,000 units should be a sufficient level to provide for normal inventory transactions and contingencies.

PLANNING AND BUDGETING FOR LONG-TERM RESOURCE NEEDS

Long-range decisions involve individual projects to replace or expand the productive or service potential of the firm. Each project is unique and may require large amounts of money; benefits of the project are realized over a long period of time.

Capital Expenditures Budget

The capital expenditures budget differs significantly from the profit plan, in both the nature of the budget and the budgeting process. A capital expenditures budget is an **appropriation budget.** That is, a specific amount is approved or appropriated for expenditures. The amount approved cannot be exceeded without additional approval.

The budgeting process for capital expenditures is an ongoing process throughout the year. New projects may be proposed at any time and, if attractive, accepted by the investment committee to the extent that funds are available. If a large proposal is sufficiently attractive, additional financing may be arranged. The capital expenditures budget will include (1) individual projects previously approved; (2) an amount to be expended in small amounts at various levels in the firm (for example, up to $1,000 by a cost-center manager); and (3) a lump sum for additional projects to be approved later.

For the DeFord Company, the capital expenditures budget involves a proposal to purchase new equipment for the heat-treating department. The budget is presented in Exhibits 13-8 and 13-9. There are no other capital expenditures planned.

Planning Long-term Sources of Funds

In addition to planning the best use of their resources, both current and long-term, firms must plan how to use these resources. Options include short-term and long-term borrowing and the issuance of additional shares of stock. In this text we will not examine the question of how a firm can obtain financing. We leave this subject to texts in corporate finance.

DEFORD COMPANY
CAPITAL EXPENDITURES BUDGET
For the Year 19X1

PROJECT

Replacement of equipment in heat-treating department

Cost

Down payment	$100,000
Value of old equipment*	100,000
Balance in 3 years	300,000
Total	$500,000

Financing

Down payment from marketable securities.
Expected balance of marketable securities on 12/1/X1: $420,000.
Balance due in single payment of $300,000 12/1/X4 with annual interest payment at 8% of balance.

Investment analysis

Analysis in Exhibit 13-9. Return (after taxes) exceeds corporate objective of 12%.

*Value approximates undepreciated cost. Original cost $180,000; accumulated depreciation at 1/1/X1: $80,000.

EXHIBIT 13-8
Capital expenditures budget for DeFord Company

PROJECTED STATEMENT OF FINANCIAL POSITION

The master budget is completed with the preparation of a projected statement of financial position, which shows the consequences of planned actions on the financial resources of the firm. Its usefulness as a planning or control tool is limited, however. Planning and control of the various financial resources are interwoven through the various planning steps in developing the profit plan, cash budget, and capital expenditures budget. The statement of financial position merely consolidates the results.

DEFORD COMPANY
CAPITAL EXPENDITURE ANALYSIS

PROPOSAL:

To replace equipment in heat-treating department with new equipment. Power use by old equipment is excessive and additional capacity is needed. Investment proposal exceeds 12% on investment with minimum net present value of $9,646. Financing is included in the proposal and additional production and sales can be accommodated in present cost structure.

Benefits (After tax of 40%)		
1. Decrease power cost by $5,000 per month. ($60,000 annual savings x 60% after taxes)		$ 36,000
2. Increase heat-treating capacity by 50%. (Present unfilled demand of 20,000 units x contribution margin $4.25 x 60% after taxes)		51,000
3. Tax savings from depreciation deduction. (Cost of new asset $500,000 ÷ 5-year life x 40% tax effect)		40,000
Total annual benefits		$ 127,000
Present value of benefits ($127,000 x 3.605) $A_{\overline{5}\rceil 12\%}$		$ 457,835
Costs (After tax)		
1. Down payment: 12/1/X1 [($100,000) x 1.000]	$(100,000)	
2. Value of equipment in trade [($100,000) x 1.000]	(100,000)	
3. Deferred payment (12/1/X4) [($300,000) x .712] $S_{\overline{3}\rceil 12\%}$	(213,600)	
4. Annual interest (8%) [($24,000) x 60% after tax = ($14,400)] [($14,400) x 2.402] $A_{\overline{3}\rceil 12\%}$	(34,589)	(448,189)
Net present value		$ 9,646

EXHIBIT 13-9
Analysis of investment proposal for DeFord Company

The projected statement of financial position for the DeFord Company is presented in Exhibit 13-10. Balances of assets, liabilities, and owners' equities were generated through the development of the profit plan, the cash budget, and the capital expenditures budget.

The source of each amount in the projected statement of financial position is explained by reference to the exhibits and schedules in which the balances were developed. Since the exhibits in Chapters 12 and 13 were condensed to show data for January, February, March, and the year in total, some amounts cannot be traced to the source exhibit. In these cases the balance is explained by reference to the cost structure and activity level from which the profit plan and cash budget were prepared.

DEFORD COMPANY
PROJECTED STATEMENT OF FINANCIAL POSITION
FOR MANAGEMENT
December 31, 19X1

ASSETS			
Current assets			
Cash		$ 34,400	
Marketable securities		320,000	
Accounts receivable		120,000	
Inventories			
Raw materials		80,000	
Finished goods		133,000	$ 687,400
Fixed assets			
Equipment		$860,000	
Accumulated depreciation		228,000	632,000
Total assets			$1,319,400
LIABILITIES AND STOCKHOLDERS' EQUITY			
Current liabilities			
Accounts payable		$ 53,000	
Accrued expenses		16,700	
Dividends payable		30,000	
Income taxes payable		33,800	
Note payable, 9%, due 7/1/X2		100,000	$ 233,500
Long-term liabilities			
Note payable, 8%, 3-year note due 12/1/X4			300,000
			$ 533,500
Stockholders' equity			
Common stock, $10 par, 50,000 authorized, 30,000 issued		$300,000	
Retained earnings			
Beginning balance	$360,300		
Add: Net income	185,600		
	$545,900		
Deduct: Dividends	60,000	485,900	785,900
Total liabilities and stockholders' equity			$1,319,400

EXHIBIT 13-10 Projected statement of financial position for management of DeFord Company

Cash, $34,400, is the ending cash balance from the cash budget (Exhibit 13-4).

Marketable securities, $320,000, is determined from the investment transactions necessary to maintain the desired cash balance as shown in the following tabulation.

Beginning balance (Exhibit 13-1)	$200,000
Purchase of marketable securities during the year (Exhibit 13-4	440,000
Total	$640,000
Sale of marketable securities during the year (Exhibit 13-4)	320,000
Ending balance	$320,000

Accounts receivable, $120,000, is determined from Schedule A—Computation of collections from customers, a schedule supporting the cash budget. The condensed schedule does not detail the balances for November and December. The balance of accounts receivable includes sales for Nc-vember and December for Product A (60-day terms) and only December sales for Product B (30-day terms). Reference to the sales budget (Exhibit 12-9) shows sales for each month. The balance of accounts receivable is shown in the following table.

	November Sales Uncollected	*December Sales Uncollected*	*Total*
Product A	$12,000	$12,000	$ 24,000
Product B	—	$96,000	96,000
Balance of accounts receivable, 12/31/19X1			$120,000

Inventory—Raw Materials, $80,000, is determined from the purchasing budget (Exhibit 12-11), where estimated ending inventories were projected as shown in the following table.

Material	*Number of Units*	×	*Standard Cost*	=	*Inventory*
Blank A	10,000		$2		$20,000
Blank B	20,000		$1		20,000
Hardening compound	40,000		$1		40,000
Total inventory of raw materials					$80,000

Inventory—Finished Goods, $133,000, is determined from the production budget (Exhibit 12-10), where ending inventory of finished goods was planned. The unit costs of the products were taken from the standard cost cards, Exhibit 12-13.

Products	Number of Units	×	Variable Standard Cost	=	Inventory Cost
Product A	15,000		$6.40		$ 96,000
Product B	10,000		$3.70		37,000
Total inventory of finished goods					$133,000

Equipment, $860,000, includes the total of the beginning balance of equipment (Exhibit 13-1) and changes in equipment proposed in the capital expenditures budget (Exhibit 13-8).

Beginning balance of equipment (Exhibit 13-1)	$540,000
Less: Cost of equipment traded in (Exhibit 13-8)	(180,000)
Plus: Cost of equipment purchased (Exhibit 13-8)	500,000
Ending balance of equipment	$860,000

Accumulated Depreciation, $228,000, includes the beginning balance from Exhibit 13-1, a reduction from trade-in of used equipment (Exhibit 13-8), and depreciation for the year (Exhibit 12-12).

Beginning balance of accumulated depreciation (Exhibit 13-1)	$200,000
Deduct: Accumulated depreciation on equipment traded in (Exhibit 13-8)	(80,000)
Add: Depreciation for the year (Exhibit 12-12) ($9,000 per month × 12)	108,000
Ending balance of accumulated depreciation	$228,000

Accounts Payable, $53,000, is determined from Schedule B—Payments to suppliers. Since the exhibits are condensed, December 19X0, purchases of materials and supplies of $70,000 are not shown. However, monthly purchases during 19X1 are constant at $53,000, beginning in March. Purchases are paid in the month following sale.

Accrued Expenses, $16,700, include the expenses accrued at the end of 19X1 in the various schedules: Schedule I—Power and utilities; Schedule F—Variable marketing expenses; and Schedule H—Product promotion. These costs are paid in the month following incurrence. Since December data are not detailed, it is necessary to refer back to the cost structure (Exhibit 12-12). These costs for December 19X1 are shown in the following computation.

Power (Exhibit 12-12)		
Shaping department (2,500 hours × $.60)	$1,500	
Heat-treating department (2,000 hours × $3.00)	6,000	$ 7,500
Utilities (Exhibit 12-12)		1,000
Variable marketing cost (Exhibits 12-12 and 12-9)		
Product A (1,000 units × $.60)	$ 600	
Product B (12,000 units × $.30)	3,600	4,200
Product promotion (Exhibit 12-12)		4,000
Ending balance of accrued expenses		$16,700

Dividends payable, $30,000, represents the semiannual dividend of $1 per share declared in December, payable in January (Schedule M—Dividends).

Income taxes payable, $33,800, is determined in Schedule K—Income taxes. This amount includes the payment for the final quarter of 19X1, payable in January.

Note payable 9%, $100,000, is reclassified from long-term liabilities in Exhibit 13-1 to current liabilities. There is no change in the balance.

Note payable 8%, $300,000, is taken from the capital expenditures budget (Exhibit 13-8). The note is the result of the purchase of new equipment.

Common stock, $300,000, remains unchanged from the beginning statement of financial position (Exhibit 13-1).

Retained earnings, $485,900, is detailed in the projected statement of financial position. The beginning balance is carried forward from the beginning statement of financial position (Exhibit 13-1), the net income is from the profit plan (Exhibit 12-20), and dividends from Schedule M—Dividends.

The completed development of the master budget shows the interrelationship of its various parts. In the next chapter we will discuss the control side of the planning and control system for the DeFord Company.

SUMMARY

There are two aspects of planning for short-term resource needs. The first involves the timing of cash flows through preparation of a cash budget. The development of a cash budget illustrates the projection of cash flows from the planned transactions for the year. The second aspect involves the development of planning models for each step in the operating cycle to determine optimum resource levels. Most short-term resources are held for two reasons: (1) to provide sufficient resources to service the firm's normal transactions and (2) to provide for contingencies. Planning and budgeting for short-term resource needs involves the determination of the proper level of liquidity for the company. With too much liquidity the firm incurs excessive costs. With too little liquidity the firm is unable to carry out its objectives.

The budgeting process for capital expenditures is an ongoing process throughout the year. The statement of financial position is the starting and ending point in planning for financial resources.

SUPPLEMENTARY READING

Baer, Wilmer. "A Cash Flow Model." *Managerial Planning,* March–April, 1972.

Kellogg, Martin N. "Analysis and Control of a Cash Flow System." *The Controller,* October, 1957.

Krueger, Donald A., and John M. Kohlmeier. "Financial Modeling and 'What if' Budgeting." *Management Accounting,* May, 1972.

National Association of Accountants. *Techniques of Inventory Management.* New York: National Association of Accountants, 1964.

Prater, George I. "Accounting and Inventory Decisions." *Managerial Planning,* November–December, 1968.

Rinehart, Jack R. "Economic Purchase Quantity Calculations." *Management Accounting,* September, 1970.

Smith, Ephraim P., and Raymond G. Laverdiere. "Cash Management." *Managerial Planning,* July–August, 1973.

QUESTIONS

13-1 What is the purpose of the statement of financial position?

13-2 What is meant by the term *liquidity? Solvency?*

13-3 How is working capital measured?

13-4 Describe an *operating cycle.*

13-5 What determines the amount of working capital required by a firm? Is the amount required constant? What effect will too much or too little working capital have on a firm?

13-6 What purpose does the cash budget serve?

13-7 What types of circumstances will cause uneven cash flows during the year? What can be done to compensate for them?

13-8 How does the cash budget differ from the profit plan? Give specific examples.

13-9 What types of cash flows are uncontrollable by the firm? Which ones lend themselves to cash planning?

13-10 How great should the various ratios concerning working capital be, according to traditional standards? Are these ratios adequate for all firms? Explain and indicate how each should be used.

13-11 What circumstances cause variations in the inventory and receivables turnover? What can be done to obtain a more representative turnover figure?

13-12 How are contingency cash requirements usually determined?

13-13 Define *reorder point, lead time,* and *safety stock.* How do these relate to the economic order quantity computations?

13-14 How does the capital expenditures budget differ from the profit plan? What is included in the capital expenditures budget?

13-15 What is the final step in the master budgeting process? Of what use is it? To whom?

PROBLEMS

13-16 Match the following terms and definitions.

1. Working capital
2. Liquidity
3. Statement of financial position
4. Solvency
5. Operating cycle
6. Transactions balance
7. Inventory turnover
8. Current ratio
9. Liquidity ratio
10. Capital expenditures budget

a. The period of time between which cash is invested in operations and recovered from operations.
b. Cost of goods sold divided by finished goods inventory.
c. Concerned with the ability of a firm to pay its debts as they become due.
d. Short-term, or current, resources.
e. Current assets divided by current liabilities.
f. The amount of a current resource required to maintain the normal level of activities.
g. Cash, receivables, and marketable securities divided by current liabilities.
h. Balance sheet.
i. A list of approved investment projects.
j. Concerned with the amount and composition of assets.

13-17 Match the following terms and definitions.

1. Liquid resources
2. Contingency balance
3. Safety stock
4. Lead time
5. Cash budget
6. Accounts receivable turnover
7. Economic order quantity
8. Reorder point
9. Replenishment point
10. Appropriation

a. Accounts receivable divided into credit sales.
b. Amount of liquid resources maintained because of uncertainty.
c. Contingency balance for inventories.
d. The amount of purchases made at one time to minimize total inventory costs.
e. Approval for a specific amount that cannot be exceeded without additional approval.
f. A formalized plan of receipts and expenditures.
g. Decision point for issuing purchasing order.
h. Time needed to ensure delivery on schedule.
i. Cash and assets to be converted to cash.
j. Time of delivery.

13-18 The Northshore Hospital began 19X6 with accounts receivable of $300,000. Patients were billed for services of $1,800,000 of which 10% is not expected to be collected. During 19X6 uncollectible accounts of $150,000 were written off. At the end of the year accounts receivable were $400,000.

REQUIRED:
How much cash was collected from patients during 19X6?

13-19 All sales by the Reeve Company are made on account. The following data relate to credit transactions during 19X5.

Credit sales	$250,000
Accounts receivable, Jan. 1, 19X5	$ 40,000
Accounts receivable, Dec. 31, 19X5	$ 30,000
Allowance for uncollectible accounts, Jan. 1, 19X5	$ 2,000
Allowance for uncollectible accounts, Dec. 31, 19X5	$ 3,000
Write-off of uncollectible accounts	$ 1,000

REQUIRED:
Determine the amount of cash collected from customers during 19X5.

13-20 The sales budget for the Gamma Wholesale Company for the first quarter of 19X4 is:

January	$40,000
February	$20,000
March	$60,000

All sales are on credit and the company's collection pattern shows:

In month of sale	60%
In following month	37%
Uncollectible	3%

A 2% cash discount is allowed on collections in the month of sale.

REQUIRED:

A. How much cash will be collected from customers in February?
B. How much cash will be collected from customers in March?
C. What is the balance of accounts receivable at the end of March?

13-21 The purchases budget for the Bearse Company for the third quarter of 19X8 follows.

July	$50,000
August	$80,000
September	$40,000

All purchases are made on terms of 2/10, *n*/60. (A 2% discount is allowed if payment is made within 10 days; the balance is due within 60 days.) One of the company's financial objectives is to take advantage of all discounts offered. Normally 70% of the payments are made in the month of purchase and 30% are paid during the first 10 days of the following month. Purchases were $30,000 in June.

REQUIRED:

A. Determine the amount of cash to be paid to suppliers during each month of the quarter.
B. What is the balance of accounts payable at the beginning of July? At the end of September?

13-22 Theta Wholesale Company distributes specialty food products. The company has serious cash flow problems and came to you for assistance. The sales budget for the first six months of 19X7 follows.

January	$100,000	April	$240,000
February	$120,000	May	$180,000
March	$200,000	June	$150,000

The inventory policy of the firm is to maintain an inventory equal to sales for the next one and one-half months. The beginning inventory was in conformity with this policy. Purchases are subject to terms of 2/10, *n*/60.

(A 2% discount is allowed on payments within 10 days of the purchase; the balance is due within 60 days.) Fifty percent of all purchases are made during the last 10 days of each month. It is the policy of the firm to take full advantage of credit terms but never to miss a discount. Purchases during December were $110,000 and sales were $100,000.

The company has a gross margin of 40%. Operating expenses are $20,000 per month plus 10% of sales, including depreciation of $4,000 per month. Sixty percent of expenses are paid in the month of the expense; the balance is paid in the following month.

REQUIRED:

A. Prepare a purchases budget for the first three months of 19X7.

B. Determine the cash payments to suppliers and the cash payments for expenses during the first three months of 19X7.

13-23 You have just been elected treasurer of the Golden Hills Racquet Club for the year 19X8. The accounting records are limited to a checkbook and a desk drawer full of invoices and receipts. The board of governors has asked you to prepare a financial plan for the next year. It was disturbed by the decline in cash during the past year and must consider a dues increase. The present cash balance is $3,000; the board wants a cash balance of $5,000 by year-end.

An examination of the records produced the following information. There are 200 members who have paid dues of $50 per year and $3 per hour for use of the tennis courts. The club owns four courts, each of which is used an average of five hours per day for approximately 300 days per year.

In addition to the $3,000 in the bank, club assets consist of receivables from members of $2,000, half of which apply to members who have moved away and should be written off, and land and tennis courts worth $50,000. The club owes $600 for maintenance performed in 19X7.

For managing the club a tennis pro is paid one-third of the court fees billed. The pro also gives lessons and sells equipment. Cash payments last year, in addition to the payment to the tennis pro, were: maintenance $12,000, utilities $3,000, property taxes $2,000, new playing surface $10,000, and miscellaneous $1,000. During 19X8, taxes and utilities are expected to increase by 50%, new surfaces will cost $4,900, and miscellaneous expenses will be $1,100. Maintenance costs and the contract with the pro are expected to remain unchanged. At the end of the year 5% of 19X8 court fees are expected to be outstanding; and unpaid maintenance expenses should be $1,000.

The board does not want you to consider depreciation.

REQUIRED:

A. Prepare a statement of financial position at the beginning of 19X8.

B. Prepare a cash budget for 19X8 that will achieve the cash flow objectives of the board. How much will dues have to be increased?

C. Assuming that dues are increased, prepare a projected statement of financial position at December 31, 19X8.

13-24 Pier Two Imports, Inc. was organized to import unusual gift items. The statement of financial position on April 1, 19X6, the date the company was organized, follows.

PIER TWO IMPORTS, INC.
STATEMENT OF FINANCIAL POSITION
April 1, 19X6

Assets		*Equities*	
Cash	$ 30,000	Capital stock	$100,000
Land	20,000		
Buildings and equipment	50,000		
	$100,000		$100,000

Sales for the first six months are expected to be as follows:

April	$ 30,000	July	$200,000
May	$ 60,000	August	$250,000
June	$120,000	September	$100,000

The owners are worried about the cash position of the company for the first three months of operations. They believe cash flows will be favorable after June. The company plans to borrow any amount needed to carry it through the first quarter as soon as a minimum cash balance of $10,000 is reached. A line of credit has been arranged at the bank requiring interest of 1% per month on the money borrowed. Interest will be paid at the time the loan is repaid.

The gross margin on sales is expected to be 60%. The company plans to carry an inventory equal to expected sales for the next two months. Purchases are paid in the following month.

Variable selling expenses are expected to equal 20% of sales. Fixed selling and administrative expenses are expected to be $25,000 per month, including $1,000 of depreciation. Two-thirds of the expenses will be paid in the month of expense, the balance will be paid in the following month.

Sixty percent of sales are expected to be cash sales. The balance of sales will be credit card sales with 25% collected in the month of sale and 75% in the following month.

REQUIRED:

A. Prepare a profit plan by month for the first three months of operations.

B. Prepare a cash budget by month for the first three months of operations. How much does the company have to borrow to maintain a minimum cash balance of $10,000? How soon?

C. Prepare a projected statement of financial position at June 30, 19X6.

D. Compute the breakeven point in sales dollars, ignoring any interest cost. Does it appear that the problems of liquidity will be solved and that the firm will be profitable after June?

13-25 The Dilly Company marks up all merchandise at 25% of gross purchase price. All purchases are made on account with terms of 1/10, net/60 (1% discount if paid in 10 days, balance due in 60 days). Purchase discounts are always taken. Normally, 60% of each month's purchases are paid for in the month of purchase; the other 40% are paid during the first 10 days of the first month after purchase. Inventories of merchandise at the end of each month are kept at 30% of the next month's projected cost of goods sold.

Terms for sales on account are 2/10, net/30 (2% discount if paid in 10 days, balance due in 30 days). Cash sales are not subject to discount. Fifty percent of each month's sales on account are collected during the month of sale, 45% are collected in the succeeding month, and the remainder are usually uncollectible. Seventy percent of the collections in the month of sale are subject to discount; 10% of the collections in the succeeding month are subject to discount.

Projected sales data for selected months follow.

	Sales on Account—Gross	*Cash Sales*
December	$1,900,000	$400,000
January	$1,500,000	$250,000
February	$1,700,000	$350,000
March	$1,600,000	$300,000

1. Projected gross purchases for January are
a. $1,400,000
b. $1,470,000
c. $1,472,000
d. $1,248,000
e. None of the above

2. Projected inventory at the end of December is
a. $420,000
b. $441,600
c. $552,000
d. $393,750
e. None of the above

3. Projected payments to suppliers during February are
a. $1,551,200
b. $1,535,688
c. $1,528,560
d. $1,509,552
e. None of the above

4. Projected sales discounts to be taken by customers making remittances during February are
   a. $12,210
   b. $15,925
   c. $13,250
   d. $11,900
   e. None of the above

5. Projected total collections from customers during February are
   a. $1,875,000
   b. $1,861,750
   c. $1,511,750
   d. $1,188,100
   e. None of the above *(CPA adapted)*

13-26 Tomlinson Retail Company seeks your assistance to develop cash and other budget information for May, June, and July 19X3. On April 30, 19X3, the company had cash of $5,500, accounts receivable of $437,000, inventories of $309,400, and accounts payable of $133,055.

The budget is to be based on the following assumptions.

1. Sales
   a. Each month's sales are billed on the last day of the month.
   b. Customers are allowed a 3% discount if payment is made within 10 days after the billing date. Receivables are recorded at the full amount.
   c. Sixty percent of the billings are collected within the discount period, 25% are collected by the end of the month, 9% are collected by the end of the second month, and 6% prove uncollectible.

2. Purchases
   a. Fifty-four percent of all purchases of material and selling, general, and administrative expenses are paid in the month purchased and the remainder in the following month.
   b. Each month's units of ending inventory is equal to 130% of the next month's units of sales.
   c. The cost of each unit of inventory is $20.
   d. Selling, general, and administrative expenses, of which $2,000 is depreciation, are equal to 15% of the current month's sales.

Actual and projected sales are as follows:

19X3	*Dollars*	*Units*
March	$354,000	11,800
April	$363,000	12,100
May	$357,000	11,900
June	$342,000	11,400
July	$360,000	12,000
August	$366,000	12,200

REQUIRED:

1. Budgeted cash collections during May are
a. $333,876
b. $355,116
c. $340,410
d. $355,656

2. The amount of sales discounts taken by customers during June are
a. $6,426
b. $6,534
c. $10,260
d. $10,710

3. The balance of accounts receivable at the end of May, assuming no uncollectible accounts are written off during May, is
a. $357,000
b. $417,984
c. $453,590
d. $460,124

4. The budgeted number of units of inventory to be purchased during May is
a. 14,820
b. 11,250
c. 11,900
d. 15,470

5. The budgeted payments to suppliers during May for purchases of merchandise are
a. $225,000
b. $230,428
c. $236,800
d. $240,020

6. The budgeted selling, general, and administrative expenses during June are
a. $26,622
b. $49,300
c. $50,335
d. $51,300

7. Budgeted cash payments during May are
   a. $278,550
   b. $281,978
   c. $282,392
   d. $283,978
8. The projected balance of accounts payable at the end of May is
   a. $103,500
   b. $127,213
   c. $127,627
   d. $225,000
9. The projected balance of cash at the end of May is
   a. $5,500
   b. $51,484
   c. $56,984
   d. $108,948
10. The budgeted net income for May is
   a. $51,484
   b. $65,450
   c. $67,030
   d. $78,450

(CPA adapted)

13-27 Using the data from problem 13-26 for the Tomlinson Retail Company, prepare a cash budget by month for May, June, and July, 19X3.

13-28 Joel Warner, a student at Therrell University, is planning his program for his junior year. Joel has saved $2,000 from summer work with a construction company. He has arranged for a part-time job at $3 per hour. He must carry five three-hour courses each term and cannot work more than 20 hours per week.

Joel will share an apartment near campus with a friend. The rent is $150 per month, and food is expected to cost each roommate $125 per month. Tuition is $52 per credit-hour; books and supplies, $18 per course; and other fees and organization dues, $50 per term.

His two trips home, between terms and at spring break, will cost approximately $50 each. Joel's parents will cover any costs while at home. They are not financially able to assist his educational expenses, however.

Joel expects to spend an average of $15 per week on social activities. He does not own a car and is able to walk or bicycle to work and campus. His roommate has a car and Joel will help with gas when he shares the car. He will have to use his social activities budget to cover this expense.

REQUIRED:

A. Assumming a nine-month academic year and two terms, prepare a cash budget for expenses.
B. How many hours per week must Joel work in order to cover his expenses? If he works 20 hours per week, how much extra money will he have?

13-29 Judy Holding graduated three years ago from State University with a major in accounting. Since graduation she has been working for a large CPA firm in Urbanville. She has had excellent training and challenging assignments from the CPA firm, but wants to live in a smaller city. One of the CPA's in her home town wants to retire at the end of June and will sell his practice.

For the past few years he has withdrawn about $20,000 per year. Judy may purchase the practice for $20,000, payable 25% down and one-fourth at the end of each of the next three years without interest. His billings to clients last year, by quarter, were: January through March, $15,000; April through June, $9,000; July through September, $6,000; and October through December, $9,000. Of a quarter's billings, 5% are uncollectible and 20% of the balance are collected in the next quarter. Because of the change in ownership, Ms. Holding can expect her billings to be only half the previous billings for the first quarter she owns the practice (July through September), two-thirds in the next quarter, and equal to his billings for the remainder of the year. She expects his pattern of cash collections to continue.

Office rent, telephone expense, and secretarial expense will be $600 per month. Part-time help will be used after business increases and will cost $500 during October through December, $1,800 during January through March, and $800 during April through June. Automobile expenses will be $40 per month plus 2% of billings to clients. The state recently enacted continuing education requirements. Judy will spend $400 in the first quarter and $800 in the second quarter she owns the business to meet these requirements. Other expenses will be 8% of billings. Automobile and other expenses will be paid in the month following the expense. The remaining expenses will be paid in the month the expense is incurred.

The $20,000 purchase price includes $2,000 of equipment, $2,000 of accounts receivable, and $16,000 for the clients' files. The equipment is old and is to be depreciated over two years; the amount allocated to clients' files will be amortized over four years.

Judy Holding has accumulated $6,000 in savings and will invest the entire amount in the practice. She believes she must withdraw at least $600 per month for personal living expenses for the first year.

REQUIRED:

A. Assuming Judy Holding purchases the accounting practice on July 1, prepare a profit plan by quarter for the first year she owns the business.
B. Prepare a cash budget by quarter for the first year.
C. How much revenue is needed each quarter to break even?

13-30 The Raymond Company has adopted a four-week, 28-day month for internal planning and reporting. The following data on operating cash inflows and outflows may be regarded as normal for one month. (Saturdays and Sundays are omitted.)

Day	Cash Inflow	Cash Outflow	Day	Cash Inflow	Cash Outflow
1	5,000	3,000	15	4,000	3,000
2	5,000	10,000	16	4,000	3,000
3	4,000	10,000	17	3,000	10,000
4	4,000	3,000	18	4,000	3,000
5	5,000	2,000	19	5,000	3,000
8	8,000	8,000	22	4,000	3,000
9	15,000	8,000	23	4,000	3,000
10	20,000	10,000	24	3,000	15,000
11	20,000	2,000	25	3,000	4,000
12	8,000	2,000	26	5,000	5,000

REQUIRED:

A. Disregarding cash flows from other than operations (i.e. borrowing, repayment, purchase or sale of assets), what minimum cash balance would you recommend for transaction purposes at the beginning of the month?

B. What is the largest cash payment that could be made on the fifteenth day of the month to maintain an ending cash balance at least equal to the beginning cash balance?

13-31 The accounting department for Butler Corporation has furnished the credit manager with the following selected data.

Cash sales	\$ 750,000
Credit sales	1,750,000
Gross sales	\$2,500,000
Accounts receivable (December 31, 19X5)	\$ 250,000

REQUIRED:

A. Compute the accounts receivable turnover and number of days' sales in receivables at the end of the year.

B. If the credit department has a policy of extending credit for 60 days, what does the information in part A indicate?

C. The Butler Corporation's slack season occurs during the winter months. What effect would this have on the receivables turnover?

13-32 From the diagram shown, answer the questions that follow.

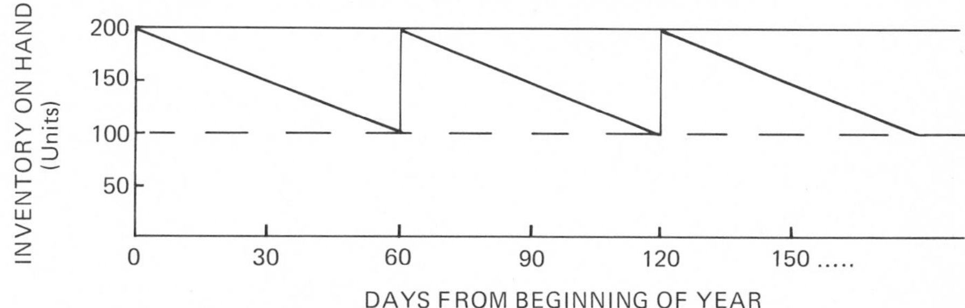

REQUIRED:

A. What is the maximum inventory?
B. What is the safety stock?
C. How long is the turnover cycle?
D. What is the economic order quantity?
E. How many orders will be placed this year?
F. Assuming an order takes 10 days to receive, at what level of inventory should the order be placed so as to maintain the safety stock?

13-33 Seaswirl Boats computes its cost of goods sold in the following manner.

Beginning inventory	$ 50,000
Plus: Purchases	800,000
Goods available for sale	$850,000
Less: Ending inventory	25,000
Cost of goods sold	$825,000

REQUIRED:

A. From this information compute
  1. Inventory turnover
  2. Days of inventory on hand
B. The information shown was computed at the end of the fiscal year, June 30. Seaswirl's busiest season is the summer. What difference would it make if Seaswirl's year-end was December 31?

13-34 The following list of expenses relates to inventory.

a. Acquisition cost
b. Storage cost
c. Breakage and pilferage cost
d. Cost of shortages
e. Spoilage cost
f. Cost of placing an order
g. Freight fees
h. Stockroom personnel wages

REQUIRED:

A. Which costs are directly used in computing the economic order quantity?

B. Which costs might be affected by the use of EOQ? Which would not? Explain.

C. Can the costs for determining EOQ be taken directly from normal accounting records? What information beyond the accounting records is needed?

13-35 Bekington Industries has revised its procedures to control raw materials and plans to purchase in economic order quantities. The following data relate to inventories.

Annual requirement	1,200,000 pounds
Purchase price	$3 per pound
Ordering cost	$50 per order
Carrying cost of inventory	10% of cost
Safety stock requirements	20,000 pounds

REQUIRED:

A. Compute the economic order quantity for Bekington Industries.

B. Graph the flow of raw materials for the year, showing number of units on the vertical axis and time on the horizontal axis. Assume that the inventory is at the maximum level on the first day of the year. Assume that the lead time is approximately two days. Label the following on the graph: replenishment point, reorder point, lead time, safety stock, and economic order quantity.

13-36 The Alpha Company has the following ratios and other financial measures.

Current ratio	3 times
Liquidity ratio	1.5 times
Working capital	$6,000
Inventory turnover	6 times

REQUIRED:

Assuming there are no supplies or prepaid expenses, determine the following:

A. Current assets

B. Current liabilities

C. Inventory

D. Cost of goods sold

E. Total of cash, receivables, and marketable securities

13-37 Financial statements for the Snowball Company follow.

SNOWBALL COMPANY
STATEMENT OF FINANCIAL POSITION
December 31, 19X6

Assets		Equities	
Cash	$ 50,000	Accounts payable	$ 80,000
Accounts receivable (net)	100,000	Short-term notes payable	50,000
Inventories	200,000	Income tax payable	20,000
Marketable securities	90,000	Mortgage payable	200,000
Prepaid expenses	20,000	Reserve for contingencies	50,000
Investment in subsidiary	150,000	Capital stock	250,000
Land	50,000	Retained earnings	350,000
Building and equipment (net)	300,000		
Patents	40,000		
	$1,000,000		$1,000,000

SNOWBALL COMPANY
INCOME STATEMENT
For the Year Ended December 31, 19X6

Sales	$2,000,000
Cost of goods sold	1,200,000
Gross margin	$ 800,000
Operating expenses	500,000
Net income	$ 300,000

REQUIRED:

A. From the financial statements determine the following:
   1. Current assets
   2. Current liabilities
   3. Fixed assets
   4. Working capital
   5. Stockholders' equity
   6. Total assets

B. Compute the following ratios:
   1. Current ratio
   2. Liquidity ratio
   3. Days in accounts receivable
   4. Days in inventory

C. What role does the statement of financial position play in the planning process?

13-38 Financial ratios are often used to project balances as well as to test the soundness of a balance or its relationship with an industry position. The Rag Tag Mill End Carpet Shop is being formed. There are no similar shops for remnants of quality carpeting, and the promoters predict immediate success. A prospective creditor will loan the shop $10,000 to start, but he insists that by the end of the first year of business the financial statements of the shop must meet or exceed normal ratios and other financial measures for this type of firm. The following are ratios the creditor expects the firm to meet or exceed.

Current ratio	2 to 1
Liquidity ratio	1 to 1
Inventory turnover	3.6 times per year
Accounts receivable turnover	12 times per year
Ratio of long-term debt to working capital	1 to 1
Ratio of total debt to owners' equity	1 to 1
Cash as a percentage of liquid assets	50%
Gross margin on sales	60%
Net income on sales	10%

Other data:

The note will be payable in two years. Interest at 10% will be paid annually.

Fixed assets will be depreciated on a straight-line basis over 10 years.

The following accounts should be used.

Statement of financial position:	Income statement:
Cash	Sales
Accounts receivable	Cost of goods sold
Inventory	Operating expenses
Fixed assets	Depreciation expenses
Accounts payable	Interest expense
Long-term note payable	
Owners' equity	

REQUIRED:

A. Using the ratios required by the potential creditor, prepare an income statement for the year and a statement of financial position at the end of the first year of operations for the Rag Tag Mill End Carpet Shop. Assume that any amount required to reach the desired ending balance in owners' equity will be invested by the owners. Ignore taxes.

B. How much will the owners be required to invest in order to achieve the desired financial position at the end of the year?

13-39 After studying the profit plan prepared for Doctors' Clinic (in problem 12-39), the executive committee decided to raise patient fees to $17 per visit. You are asked to prepare a new profit plan, a cash budget, and a projected statement of financial position. (Note: While the background provided by problem 12-39 is helpful, it is not necessary for the solution of this problem. All data needed are provided here.)

Doctors' Clinic serves a suburban community of about 24,000 population, of which 25% are expected to become patients of the clinic. Each patient is expected to average five visits per year. You may assume that patient visits occur evenly throughout the year. Normally about 5% of billings to patients are not collected. Accounts receivable at the end of the year is expected to be equal to an average month's billings.

Each doctor can serve about 600 patient visits per month. A half-time consulting physician is available if the patient load requires less than a full-time doctor. (For example, if 3,750 patient visits require $6\frac{1}{4}$ doctors, one half-time and six full-time doctors would be hired.) One nurse is required for each 500 patient visits per month. The average individual doctor's salary is $4,000 per month; a nurse's average salary is $1,000 per month. Doctors are paid in the following month; all other personnel are paid in the month service is performed.

Operating costs for the clinic include:

Administrative salaries	$5,000 per month
Lab and X-ray technicians	$4,000 per month
Medical supplies	$1.50 per patient visit
Rent	$24,000 per year
Medical and financial records	$1,000 per month plus $.25 per patient visit
Other operating costs	$500 per month plus $.15 per patient visit

Medical supplies are purchased monthly on 30-day terms. The medical and financial records are maintained by a computer service bureau. Payment is made in the month following service. All other operating costs are paid in the month of service.

The statement of financial position at the end of 19X7 follows.

DOCTORS' CLINIC
STATEMENT OF FINANCIAL POSITION
December 31, 19X7

Assets		Equities	
Cash	$10,000	Accounts payable	$12,500
Accounts receivable	25,000	Salaries payable	4,000
Supplies	2,000	Owners' equity	20,500
	$37,000		$37,000

REQUIRED:

A. Prepare a profit plan for 19X8.

B. Prepare a cash budget for 19X8. Assume a desired minimum cash balance of $5,000. A line of credit is available if needed.

C. Prepare a projected statement of financial position at the end of 19X8.

13-40 The Kirkpatrick Pharmacy has completed its first year of business in a new shopping center. The owners are very optimistic about the future and plan a number of changes that will expand the business. They plan to develop a budgetary system for planning and control of operations. The following data were accumulated.

1. Sales and merchandise costs for 19X8:

Department	*Sales*	*Gross Profit*	*Inventory Turnover (Ending Inventory)*
Prescription drugs	$ 60,000	60%	4 times
Patent medicine	$100,000	40%	6 times
Cosmetics	$ 50,000	20%	10 times
Sundries	$ 90,000	30%	7 times

2. Operating expenses for 19X8:

Expense	*Amount*	*Traceable to Department*	*Cost Behavior Pattern Fixed and Variable*
Salaries	$40,000	40% prescriptions 20% patent medicine	$40,000 + $0
Advertising	$12,000	50% cosmetics	$12,000 + $0
Rent	$18,000		$0 + 6% of sales
Depreciation of fixtures	$10,000		$10,000 + $0
Miscellaneous	$15,000		$ 6,000 + 3% of sales

3. Statement of Financial Position at the end of 19X8:

Statement of Financial Position

Cash	$ 3,500	Accounts payable	$15,000
Accounts receivable	12,500	Accrued expenses	12,000
Inventory	29,000		
Fixtures and equipment	50,000	Capital stock	40,000
Accumulated depreciation	(10,000)	Retained earnings	18,000
	$ 85,000		$85,000

4. A number of policy changes have been made that will change the character of the store. The following results are expected.

Department	*Percentage Increase in Sales*	*New Gross Margin Percentage*	*New Inventory Turnover (End of Year)*
Prescription drugs	100%	60%	4 times
Patent medicine	50%	40%	6 times
Cosmetics	100%	25%	15 times
Sundries	300%	20%	8 times

5. Other information:

At the end of 19X9 accounts receivable are expected to be $25,000, accounts payable $60,000, and accrued expenses $20,000. Salaries will be increased to $50,000 and miscellaneous expense will become $10,000 + 4% of sales. All other cost-volume relationships will be maintained. The stockholders expect the maximum cash dividend possible that will leave a balance of $10,000 in cash.

REQUIRED:

A. Prepare a profit plan for 19X9 following a contribution margin approach.
B. Prepare a cash budget for 19X9.
C. Prepare a projected statement of financial position at the end of 19X9.
D. Did the changes improve the profitability of the company? Explain.

13-41 Therrel University is developing its budget for the coming academic year. You are supplied with the following information.

1. Statistics for the *current* academic year:

Average number of students per class	25
Average number of credit-hours carried per student per year	32
Present enrollment	3,100
Average faculty teaching load in credit-hours per year (6 classes of 4 credit-hours each)	24
Average salary of faculty members	$12,000
Scholarships (tuition-free scholarships)	35
Tuition (per credit-hour)	$ 50

2. Projected enrollment data for 19X1–19X3:

Student enrollment is expected to increase by 10%. Therrel University expects to add five new tuition-free scholarships.

3. Budgeted revenue for 19X1–19X2:

Intercollegiate athletics	$200,000
Net income from food services, dormitories, and bookstore	$250,000
Income from endowments	$105,000

The board of regents approved a tuition increase of $2 per credit-hour.

4. Budgeted expenditures for 19X1–19X2:

Faculty salaries are to be increased by 5%	
Additional merit increases for faculty members	$ 150,000
Faculty retirement and benefits—20% of faculty salaries	
Eight faculty members will be on leave with full pay	
Administration and general operation	$ 380,000
Academic department direct costs (secretarial, grading, supplies, etc.) $5 per credit-hour	
Athletics	$ 180,000
Library	$ 250,000
Intramural sports	$ 200,000
Building and grounds (maintenance and operation of physical facilities)	$ 500,000
Interest and principal payment on long-term debt (Long-term debt at the beginning of 19X1–19X2 consisted of a 6%, $900,000 debt that requires annual payments of $100,000 plus interest at the end of each year.)	$ 154,000
Building construction	$1,000,000

5. An annual contribution campaign is held each year to "balance the budget."

REQUIRED:

A. Determine the amount of
   1. Expected enrollment
   2. Total credit-hours to be carried
   3. The number of faculty needed

B. Prepare a cash budget for 19X1–19X2. Your budget should include direct cost per student-hour and should separate operating expenses from capital expenditures and reduction of debt.

13-42 Modern Products Corporation (in problem 12-42) was requested to submit a cash budget as one of the requirements for a loan. A projected income statement (profit plan) and several related budgets were prepared as a requirement in problem 12-42. The profit plan is helpful but not critical to preparation of the cash budget.

REQUIRED:
Prepare a cash budget for November and December for the Modern Products Corporation. It will be necessary to refer to problem 12-42 for the necessary data. The cash balance on November 1, before the loan is granted, is expected to be $10,000.

13-43 This problem is a continuation of the DeFord Company illustration in Chapters 12, 13, and 14 of the text and in problem 12-43. In problem 12-43 you were asked to prepare the profit plan and supporting budgets for production, purchasing, and selected responsibility centers.

REQUIRED:
Prepare a cash budget for April. You should continue the budget illustration in the text for April. Draw upon the text and your solution to problem 12-43.

14 Budgetary Reporting and Responsibility Accounting

BASIC REQUIREMENTS FOR A GOOD REPORTING SYSTEM
- *Relevancy*
- *Timeliness*
- *Accuracy*

ILLUSTRATION OF A FORMAL REPORTING SYSTEM
- *Departmental Cost Report—Manufacturing*
- *Departmental Report—Marketing*
- *Factory Cost Report*
- *Marketing Report*
- *Reports to Top Management*
- *Comparison of Actual Results with Objectives*

COMPARISON OF INTERNAL AND EXTERNAL REPORTING NEEDS

SUMMARY

The control process begins after the planning process is completed and as the decisions are being implemented. The accounting system performs a monitoring role by accumulating actual performance data, comparing the actual results with the plans, and communicating the results to management. To the extent that relevant data are accumulated accurately and reporting is timely, accounting reports will be useful for control. In this chapter we will present the reporting system for our continuing illustration, the DeFord Company. In Chapter 12 a profit plan was developed for the DeFord Company. In Chapter 13 the cash budget and projected statement of financial position were prepared. We will now compare the actual results of operations with those plans and illustrate reports for each management level.

The discussion in this chapter begins with an examination of the requirements for a good reporting system, then presents a set of reports for the DeFord Company, and, finally, compares the year-end reporting procedure for internal and external needs.

BASIC REQUIREMENTS FOR A GOOD REPORTING SYSTEM

In Chapter 10 the prerequisites of successful budgeting were discussed. The same prerequisites underlie a good reporting system. Any deviations from the course of action planned in the budget must be identified so that corrective action can be taken. The budget is an integral part of the reporting system. Qualitative standards for good reporting are relevancy, timeliness, and accuracy.

Relevancy

Accounting's role is to provide information relevant to user needs. To be relevant for the needs of management, a reporting system must reflect the factors over which each manager has control and must identify the areas that need management attention. Responsibility accounting and management by exception are ways of stressing relevant data.

RESPONSIBILITY ACCOUNTING

The reporting function of accounting requires the **feedback** of information to management so that performance can be evaluated and, if necessary, actions altered. The reporting function also provides a base of information about the activities over which an individual manager has responsibility. In preparing the budgets in Chapter 12, we included only the costs over which the particular manager had control.

Some accountants have suggested that reports should include information beyond a manager's present scope of responsibility in order to prepare him for broader managerial responsibilities in the future. However, performance evaluation is too important to the individual manager to use the report for professional development. There are many other ways to develop the interests of a departmental manager in firm-wide activities. These could include training programs, committee memberships, staff meetings, and participative management.

Exhibit 14-1 summarizes the types of continuing information needs at the various levels of a firm. At the lower levels in the organization, emphasis is almost exclusively on nonfinancial information. Group leaders and individual workers are measured in nonfinancial terms: How many hours must they work? How many units must they produce? How much scrap is allowed? The

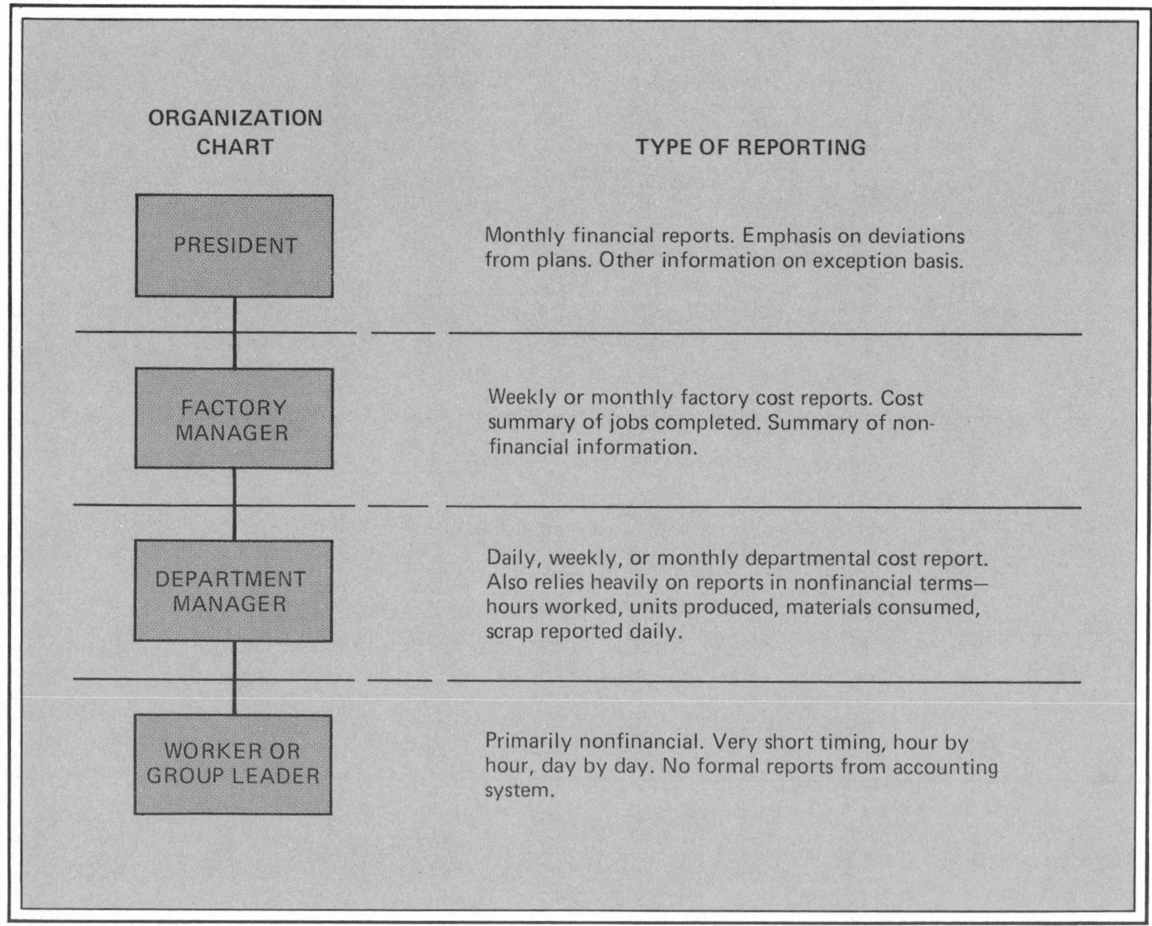

ORGANIZATION CHART
TYPE OF REPORTING
PRESIDENT
Monthly financial reports. Emphasis on deviations from plans. Other information on exception basis.
FACTORY MANAGER
Weekly or monthly factory cost reports. Cost summary of jobs completed. Summary of nonfinancial information.
DEPARTMENT MANAGER
Daily, weekly, or monthly departmental cost report. Also relies heavily on reports in nonfinancial terms—hours worked, units produced, materials consumed, scrap reported daily.
WORKER OR GROUP LEADER
Primarily nonfinancial. Very short timing, hour by hour, day by day. No formal reports from accounting system.

EXHIBIT 14-1
Reporting to different levels of management

individual worker is not involved with accounting reports. His information needs are met by nonfinancial data accumulated in the factory, and his performance is evaluated in nonfinancial terms when actual results are compared to the standards. The time frame of information at this level is very short. Most information is concerned with hour-by-hour or day-by-day activities.

At the department manager level there is concern over costs. The department is identified as a cost center, and costs for which the manager is responsible are accumulated for his department. However, the department manager also deals in physical quantities on a day-to-day basis. Many of the objectives of the department are expressed in physical terms, and the technical standards, in physical terms, provide guides for performance measurements. From the summaries of labor tickets the manager should know roughly what the labor efficiency variance will be before it is computed and reported by the accounting department. Having approved any excess materials requisitions for material usage beyond standard, he would know if the material usage variance were unfavorable and would know its approximate amount. The accounting system should later verify what the department manager already knows. The time horizon of the department manager will be limited to a relatively short period, probably the time covered by a production schedule.

At the level of vice-president for manufacturing (factory manager in our case), the concern of the manager has moved from physical (nonfinancial) measures to financial measures. He is not responsible for profit, but he is involved in a wide range of decisions that are measurable in financial terms. Although the factory manager will receive information in physical terms, most of the data will also have been converted to financial terms to allow summarization.

At the level of top management, the president is concerned with the attainment of objectives and plans for the future. The amount of information he needs will depend upon his style of management. If decisions are decentralized, he will establish company goals and objectives and look to his subordinates for administering the continuing activities of the company. As long as subordinates are meeting their objectives, he will deal only in summary information. If decisions are centralized, the president will need more information, in greater depth, about the operations of the company.

Similar levels of reporting exist in the marketing area. At the lowest level, the salespeople are interested in quantity sold, number of calls, number of customers, and other data related to the selling effort. The product or territory manager's interests are restricted to his product, his territory, and his customers. The sales manager is interested in demand for the company's product, the actions of competitors, and income or contribution margin. However, there is a basic difference between the information concerns of the marketing and manufacturing areas. The marketing area is a profit center where the manager has responsibility for both revenues and costs. In the manufacturing area, the manager has responsibility only for costs.

MANAGEMENT BY EXCEPTION

Another aspect of relevancy is the concept of management by exception. To be relevant for management, reports must emphasize exceptional deviations from plan. The system should provide some basis for the manager to separate significant deviations, which should be investigated further, from those that are insignificant. Ideally, the reporting system would report deviations from plans based upon the probability of their occurrence. Then, if a deviation from the plan is within the accepted probability level, based on past experiences and the nature of the cost, it would not be treated as exceptional. For example, in a particular firm a 10% deviation may be more likely to occur in the use of supplies than in employee fringe benefits, and little variation would be expected in many of the fixed costs such as depreciation. Accounting, however, has not progressed to the point where a control system reports both the actual results and the probability of these results occurring. Accounting data reports only the actual results and variances from budget; in most firms the individual manager decides what is significant.

Timeliness

One dimension of timeliness is the date a report is received. A major criticism of accounting reports is that they are often delayed until the information content is no longer useful. To be useful for a decision, a report must be received before the decision is made. If information is to be useful for control, it must be received as soon as possible after the measured action takes place. A cost report for the month of May that arrives in the middle or latter part of June is not useful to management for operational control. A delay of several days to improve the precision of a report is seldom worthwhile. Out-of-date information is not useful, regardless of how precise it may be.

Another dimension is the period of time covered by the reports. Out of tradition, reports are issued weekly, monthly, or for some other set period of time. A fixed reporting schedule is adequate only if the planning and control process fits naturally into the time periods used. Where there are special problems, such as an unusual production quantity decision or a capital expenditures decision, the regular reports will be inadequate. For nonroutine decisions special reports must be prepared.

Accuracy

Accounting reports may have an aura of precision that is not warranted. It is taken for granted by most managers that the accounting system will produce information in an objective manner. The accuracy of the data, however, is dependent upon many factors, including the nature of the accounting classification system, the reliability of the source documents, and the interpretations given to events and transactions.

One possibility for error that may be largely overlooked stems from errors in the data input that originate elsewhere in the firm. Labor records are a good example. If excessive pressure is applied on foremen to have their subordinates meet time standards, the employees may falsify their records by averaging the time spent on several activities in order to hide large deviations from standard. This action may even be condoned or encouraged by the foremen.

As an example, consider the following two activities:

	Process A	*Process B*
Standard labor	1,000 hours	1,000 hours
Actual labor	940 hours	1,150 hours

If we assume that any deviation over 5% will result in an investigation and pressure for improved future performance, employee time tickets may be falsified to show approximately 1,045 hours on each process, both safely within the 5% limit. The accountant using the data may be completely unaware of the smoothing of labor deviations. Unfortunately, this kind of error can have a significant impact upon subsequent decisions because the decision maker is mislead about the facts.

Empirical research on the accuracy of labor data has revealed errors of 20% to 25% in the recording of labor hours on particular jobs.[1] The management accountant must take pains to ensure that his data sources provide accurate information.

ILLUSTRATION OF A FORMAL REPORTING SYSTEM

The remainder of this chapter is devoted to an illustration of the formal reporting system for the DeFord Company. Included are monthly reports prepared for a department manager, a marketing territory manager, the vice-president for manufacturing, and the vice-president for marketing. Reports to top management include activities for the entire year. The chapter will conclude with a conversion of the data from the internal reporting system to financial statements for external reporting in conformity with the generally accepted accounting principles.

Departmental Cost Report—Manufacturing

The departmental budget for the DeFord Company's heat-treating department was developed in Exhibit 12-14 as a part of the profit plan. Our reporting example continues with the same department. The departmental budget in the profit plan was a *static* budget; only one level of activity was planned.

[1]Sam E. Scharff, "The Industrial Engineer and the Cost Accountant," *N.A.A. Bulletin* (March, 1961), pp. 17–18.

When reported, the budget is adjusted to a performance budget, showing what the costs should be at the *actual level* of activity. The departmental budget in the profit plan and the performance budget in the cost report will seldom be the same. Only if actual activity is equal to planned activity will the two budgets match.

A departmental cost report for the heat-treating department is illustrated for the month of March and year-to-date in Exhibit 14-2. Each part of the report contains three cost columns: a performance budget, actual costs for the month or year-to-date, and variances in actual costs from the performance budget. We will develop the report for March in detail and briefly examine the year-to-date portion.

The March performance budget is based upon the actual production of 5,000 units of Product A and 15,000 units of Product B. Because this was also the planned level of production, the performance budget for March in Exhibit 14-2 is identical to the departmental budget in Exhibit 12-14. In other illustrations in this chapter actual activity differs from planned activity, and the two budgets differ.

The performance budget was developed from the company's standard cost cards (Exhibit 12-13) and flexible budget (Exhibit 12-12). Material and labor costs in the performance budget were developed as shown in the following computations.

Materials

Product	*Quantity Standard for Material per Unit*	×	*Actual Units Produced*	=	*Standard Materials*
A	2 pounds hardening compound		5,000 units		10,000 pounds
B	1 pound hardening compound		15,000 units		15,000 pounds
	Standard material in actual production				25,000 pounds
	Standard cost of material in performance budget ($1 per pound)				$25,000

Labor

Product	*Quantity Standard for Labor per Unit*	×	*Actual Units Produced*	=	*Standard Labor*
A	.1 hour		5,000 units		500 hours
B	.1 hour		15,000 units		1,500 hours
	Standard hours in actual production				2,000 hours
	Standard cost of labor in performance budget ($5 per hour)				$10,000

	MARCH			YEAR-TO-DATE		
	Performance Budget	Actual	Variance	Performance Budget	Actual	Variance
Material— hardening compound	$ 25,000	$ 24,000		$ 75,000	$ 78,000	
Material usage variance			$ 1,000			$(3,000)
Direct labor	10,000	10,800		30,000	31,100	
Labor rate variance			200			(600)
Labor efficiency variance			(1,000)			(500)
Variable overhead						
Variable overhead spending variance						
Overtime premium	$ 0	$ 300	(300)	$ 0	$ 500	(500)
Supplies	2,200	2,600	(400)	6,100	6,200	(100)
Fringe benefits	2,200	2,260	(60)	6,100	6,200	(100)
Power	6,600	6,840	(240)	18,300	19,100	(800)
Total	11,000	12,000	(1,000)	30,500	32,000	(1,500)
Variable overhead efficiency variance	(1,000)		(1,000)	(500)		(500)
Total variable overhead	10,000	12,000	(2,000)	30,000	32,000	(2,000)
Total variable costs	$ 45,000	$ 46,800	$(1,800)	$135,000	$141,100	$(6,100)
Fixed costs of department						
Fixed overhead spending variance						
Salaries	$ 2,000	$ 2,200	$ (200)	$ 6,000	$ 6,200	$ (200)
Fringe benefits	400	440	(40)	1,200	1,240	(40)
Depreciation of equipment	3,000	3,000	0	9,000	9,000	0
Other	600	560	40	1,800	1,760	40
Total	6,000	6,200	(200)	18,000	18,200	(200)
Total departmental costs	$ 51,000	$ 53,000	$(2,000)	$153,000	$159,300	$(6,300)
Physical data						
Units produced: A		5,000			15,000	
B		15,000			45,000	
Material used (pounds)	25,000	24,000	1,000	75,000	78,000	(3,000)
Direct labor hours	2,000	2,200	(200)	6,000	6,100	(100)

EXHIBIT 14-2
Heat-treating department cost report for DeFord Company

Variable overhead is incurred in relation to *actual hours worked.* Therefore, the performance budget for variable overhead must be developed from actual hours worked (2,200). The following tabulation shows how budgeted variable overhead amounts were determined.

	Variable Overhead Rate from Flexible Budget (Exhibit 12-2)	×	*Actual Hours Worked*	=	*Performance Budget*
Overtime premium	$0		2,200		$ .0
Supplies	1		2,200		2,200
Fringe benefits	1		2,200		2,200
Power	3		2,200		6,600
Total	$5				$11,000

Since the performance budget for variable overhead is based upon actual direct labor of 2,200 hours, and the cost of units produced included only standard overhead based upon 2,000 standard direct labor hours, the difference must appear in the cost report as a variable overhead efficiency variance. It is actually a variance in variable overhead caused by labor efficiency. The variance of $1,000 was determined by multiplying the hours above standard times the variable overhead rate (200 hours × $5 = $1,000). If fewer than the standard labor hours had been used, a favorable variable overhead efficiency variance would have been included in the cost report.

Fixed overhead costs of the department do not change because of activity changes and, therefore, are at the budgeted amounts in the performance budget each month.

The *Actual* column shows the actual costs incurred in *this* department. Materials used are priced at the standard cost of $1 per pound. Any price variance arises from the purchasing activity and should not be charged against the using department unless that department manager participated in the purchasing decisions.

Variances from standard are presented in the third column of the departmental cost report. The following computations show how each of the six variances were calculated for the DeFord Company.

Material usage variance:

$$\left[\left(\begin{array}{c}\text{Standard}\\ \text{quantity}\end{array} - \begin{array}{c}\text{Actual}\\ \text{quantity}\end{array}\right) \times \begin{array}{c}\text{Standard}\\ \text{price}\end{array}\right]$$

[(25,000 pounds − 24,000 pounds) × $1] = $1,000 Favorable

Labor rate variance:

$$\left[\left(\begin{array}{l}\text{Actual}\\ \text{hours}\\ \text{worked}\end{array} \times \begin{array}{l}\text{Standard}\\ \text{wage}\\ \text{rate}\end{array}\right) - \begin{array}{l}\text{Actual direct}\\ \text{labor payroll}\end{array}\right]$$

[(2,200 × $5) − $10,800] = $200 Favorable

Labor efficiency variance:

$$\left[\left(\begin{matrix}\text{Actual}\\ \text{units}\\ \text{produced}\end{matrix} \times \begin{matrix}\text{Standard}\\ \text{hours}\\ \text{per unit}\end{matrix}\right) - \begin{matrix}\text{Actual}\\ \text{hours}\\ \text{worked}\end{matrix}\right] \times \begin{matrix}\text{Standard}\\ \text{wage}\\ \text{rate}\end{matrix} =$$

[(20,000 units × .1 hour) − 2,200 hours] × $5 per hour =
200 hours × $5 per hour = $(1,000) Unfavorable

Variable overhead spending variance:

$$\left(\begin{matrix}\text{Standard}\\ \text{variable}\\ \text{overhead}\\ \text{rate per}\\ \text{hour}\end{matrix} \times \begin{matrix}\text{Actual}\\ \text{hours}\\ \text{work}\end{matrix}\right) - \begin{matrix}\text{Actual}\\ \text{variable}\\ \text{overhead}\end{matrix} =$$

($5 × 2,200 hours) − $12,000 =
$11,000 − $12,000 = $(1,000) Unfavorable

Variable overhead efficiency variance:

$$\left[\left(\begin{matrix}\text{Actual}\\ \text{units}\\ \text{produced}\end{matrix} \times \begin{matrix}\text{Standard}\\ \text{hours}\\ \text{per unit}\end{matrix}\right) - \begin{matrix}\text{Actual}\\ \text{hours}\\ \text{worked}\end{matrix}\right] \times \begin{matrix}\text{Standard}\\ \text{variable}\\ \text{overhead rate}\end{matrix} =$$

200 hours* × $5 per hour† = $(1,000) Unfavorable

*Refer to labor efficiency variance.
†Note that the wage rate and variable overhead rate are identical in this illustration. This will seldom be the case.

Fixed overhead spending variance:

$$\begin{matrix}\text{Performance}\\ \text{budget for}\\ \text{fixed overhead}\end{matrix} - \begin{matrix}\text{Actual}\\ \text{fixed}\\ \text{overhead}\end{matrix} =$$

$6,000 − $6,200 = $(200) Unfavorable

The departmental cost report in Exhibit 14-2 could be simplified by presenting only the variances. In some firms the individual manager specifies the amount of information he wants in his departmental cost report. He may request only the variances that exceed a given percentage or, if control limits were established, those variances that exceed the control limits. The essence of management by exception is that there is no need for intervention when activities are progressing according to plan.

Departmental Report—Marketing

The marketing departments are profit centers. Selling more or fewer units than planned will affect the income of the period. The difference between planned and actual sales is called an **activity variance;** it should be separated from the price, efficiency, and spending variances in the reports. The activity variance is the increased contribution margin from the sale of more units than predicted in the profit plan or the reduced contribution margin from selling fewer than planned.

Because of the possible activity variance, reports for marketing areas must show the profit plan, the performance budget, and the actual results. Exhibit 14-3 illustrates a report prepared for the marketing manager of the Western territory for March and the year-to-date. The first column in the report, headed *Profit Plan,* is the budget developed for this department in Chapter 12 as part of the total profit plan (Exhibit 12-15). At that time the sales manager of the Western territory expected to sell 10,000 units of Product B and prepared his budget for that sales volume. During March 12,000 units were actually sold, and the performance budget was prepared for the higher level. Standard prices and cost behavior patterns from the flexible budget were used in developing the performance budget. The profit plan and performance budget would be identical only if the same number of units planned were actually sold. The activity variance is the difference between the two budgets and shows the contribution margin of the extra 2,000 units sold.

At a standard selling price of \$8 per unit and standard variable cost per unit of \$4 (including variable marketing costs), the standard contribution margin of Product B is \$4 per unit. The activity variance is computed as follows:

$$\left(\begin{array}{l}\text{Actual sales}\\ \text{in units}\end{array} - \begin{array}{l}\text{Planned sales}\\ \text{in units}\end{array}\right) \times \begin{array}{l}\text{Standard}\\ \text{contribution}\\ \text{margin}\end{array}$$

$$(12{,}000 - 10{,}000) \times \$4 = \$8{,}000 \text{ Favorable}$$

The column headed *Actual* shows the actual results for March. Differences between the performance budget and actual results are caused by selling price variances and spending variances. During March there were no selling price variances and no variances in variable costs. There should be no variance in manufacturing costs in the reports for the marketing area since it has no responsibility for manufacturing costs. Any variances in production costs are isolated in the factory cost reports. The only spending variances were in *Product Promotion* (\$200 unfavorable) and *Other* (\$800 unfavorable).

For the year-to-date, the activity variance is \$16,000 (4,000 units above the profit plan × \$4 standard contribution margin.) All but \$200 of the year-to-date spending variance was explained by the March spending variance. It appears that demand in this territory is running well above plan and the firm will soon exhaust the finished goods inventory unless the factory increases production through overtime.

MARCH 19X1	Profit Plan	Performance Budget	Actual	Variance: Activity	Variance: Price Efficiency Spending
Units sold	10,000	12,000	12,000		
Sales	$ 80,000	$ 96,000	$ 96,000	$16,000	
Variable costs					
Manufacturing	$ 37,000	$ 44,400	$ 44,400	$ (7,400)	
Marketing	3,000	3,600	3,600	(600)	
Total	40,000	48,000	48,000	(8,000)	
Contribution margin	$ 40,000	$ 48,000	$ 48,000	$ 8,000	
Fixed costs related to territory					
Salaries	$ 2,000	$ 2,000	$ 2,000		$ 0
Fringe benefits	400	400	400		0
Product promotion	1,000	1,000	1,200		(200)
Other	600	600	1,400		(800)
Total	4,000	4,000	5,000		(1,000)
Product contribution	$ 36,000	$ 44,000	$ 43,000	$ 8,000	$ (1,000)

YEAR-TO-DATE	Profit Plan	Performance Budget	Actual	Variance: Activity	Variance: Price Efficiency Spending
Units sold	26,000	30,000	30,000		
Sales	$208,000	$240,000	$240,000	$32,000	
Variable costs					
Manufacturing	$ 96,200	$111,000	$111,000	$(14,800)	
Marketing	7,800	9,000	9,000	(1,200)	
Total	104,000	120,000	120,000	(16,000)	
Contribution margin	$104,000	$120,000	$120,000	$ 16,000	
Fixed costs related to territory					
Salaries	$ 6,000	$ 6,000	$ 6,000		$ 0
Fringe benefits	1,200	1,200	1,200		0
Product promotion	3,000	3,000	3,200		(200)
Other	1,800	1,800	2,800		(1,000)
Total	12,000	12,000	13,200		(1,200)
Product contribution	$ 92,000	$108,000	$106,800	$ 16,000	$ (1,200)

EXHIBIT 14-3
Product manager's monthly report for DeFord Company

Factory Cost Report

The factory cost report focuses on the control of manufacturing costs. Therefore, the costs of each subordinate department are shown as a single-line summary. If more information is desired by the factory manager, he can examine the individual cost report for any subordinate department.

The factory cost report is presented in Exhibit 14-4, where actual costs are compared with the performance budget. As in other cost center reports,

	MARCH			YEAR-TO-DATE		
	Performance Budget	Actual	Variance	Performance Budget	Actual	Variance
Costs controllable by subordinate departments						
Shaping	$ 50,500	$ 49,200	$ 1,300	$151,500	$151,100	$ 400
Heat-treating	51,000	53,000	(2,000)	153,000	159,300	(6,300)
Materials handling	6,000	6,000	0	18,000	18,000	0
Total	$107,500	$108,200	$ (700)	$322,500	$328,400	$(5,900)
Purchasing – Material price variance	$ 0	$ (3,000)	$ 3,000	$ 0	$ (7,900)	$ 7,900
Fixed costs common to factory						
Salaries	$ 4,000	$ 4,000	$ 0	$ 12,000	$ 12,000	$ 0
Payroll fringe	800	800	0	2,400	2,400	0
Factory rent	4,000	4,000	0	12,000	12,000	0
Utilities	1,000	1,200	(200)	3,000	3,300	(300)
Other	200	200	0	600	600	0
Total	10,000	10,200	(200)	30,000	30,300	(300)
Total factory costs	$117,500	$115,400	$ 2,100	$352,500	$350,800	$ 1,700
Summary of variances						
Material price variance			$ 3,000			$ 7,900
Material usage variance			500			(4,000)
Labor rate variance			(200)			(2,000)
Labor efficiency variance			500			1,500
Variable overhead spending variance			(800)			(1,200)
Variable overhead efficiency variance			(400)			300
Fixed overhead spending variance			(500)			(800)
			$ 2,100			$ 1,700

EXHIBIT 14-4
Factory cost report for DeFord Company

inclusion of the profit plan is not necessary. The performance budget is prepared by applying the flexible budget to the actual level of production in the plant as a whole. In this case the budget figures for the subordinate departments come from the summary of their departmental reports. Only the costs under direct control of the plant manager are detailed in this report.

A summary of the variances from budget is presented as a part of the report. Since control is exercised over most of the variances in subordinate departments, the summary gives the factory manager an overview of cost control. There may be overall patterns that cannot be determined from individual reports. For example, the price variances may be largely due to external factors, whereas the efficiency variances may be due to factors under the company's control.

Marketing Report

The report to the marketing manager (Exhibit 14-5) summarizes the product or territory reports as one-line entries. All marketing areas have responsibility for revenue as well as costs. The activity variance shows the difference between the profit plan and the performance budget. In March the sales of Product A were under plan (1,000 units × $5 contribution margin = $5,000 unfavorable activity variance). The report for the Western territory had previously shown that sales of Product B were above plan in that area (2,000 units × $4 contribution margin = $8,000 favorable activity variance). Price and spending variances in the report are very small.

Reports to Top Management

The reports to top management concentrate upon explaining the difference between planned profit and actual profit. Traditionally, the reports include an income statement and a statement of financial position. We are also presenting a cash flow statement and report on profit plan. These reports are illustrated for the year as a whole.

The income statement (Exhibit 14-6) is prepared in a variable-costing format. Both the profit plan (from Exhibit 12-20) and a performance budget are included with the income statement. Actual net income exceeded the profit plan by $29,340 ($214,940 − $185,600). Actual earnings per share were $7.16 versus a planned earnings per share of $6.19. In the income statement the activity variance (resulting from sales above plan) is separated from the price, efficiency, and spending variances.

The report on profit plan (Exhibit 14-7) shows all variances from plan. The purpose of the report is to show, as simply as possible, the causes for a difference between planned and actual *operating income.* The marketing area accounted for $118,600 of additional operating income through additional sales (shown by the activity variance of $54,000) and a price increase (shown by the price variance of $72,000), less increased marketing costs of

MARCH	Profit Plan	Performance Budget	Actual	Variances: Activity	Variances: Price Efficiency Spending
Product contribution					
Product A	$ 12,000	$ 7,000	$ 7,100	$ (5,000)	$ 100
Product B — Eastern territory	$ 11,000	$ 11,000	$ 11,200	$ 0	$ 200
Western territory	36,000	44,000	43,000	8,000	(1,000)
Total Product B	47,000	55,000	54,200	8,000	(800)
Total product contribution	$ 59,000	$ 62,000	$ 61,300	$ 3,000	$ (700)
Fixed marketing costs					
Salaries	$ 3,000	$ 3,000	$ 3,000		0
Fringe benefits	600	600	600		0
Other	400	400	600		(200)
Total fixed marketing costs	4,000	4,000	4,200		(200)
Contribution toward common fixed costs and profit	$ 55,000	$ 58,000	$ 57,100	$ 3,000	$ (900)

YEAR-TO-DATE	Profit Plan	Performance Budget	Actual	Variances: Activity	Variances: Price Efficiency Spending
Product contribution					
Product A	$ 21,000	$ 16,000	$ 16,400	$ (5,000)	$ 400
Product B — Eastern territory	$ 33,000	$ 33,000	$ 33,300	$ 0	$ 300
Western territory	92,000	108,000	106,800	16,000	(1,200)
Total Product B	125,000	141,000	140,100	16,000	(900)
Total product Contribution	$146,000	$157,000	$156,500	$11,000	$ (500)
Fixed marketing costs					
Salaries	$ 9,000	$ 9,000	$ 9,000		$ 0
Fringe benefits	1,800	1,800	1,800		0
Other	1,200	1,200	1,400		(200)
Total fixed marketing costs	12,000	12,000	12,200		(200)
Contribution toward common fixed costs and profit	$134,000	$145,000	$144,300	$11,000	$ (700)

EXHIBIT 14-5
Marketing manager's monthly report for DeFord Company

DEFORD COMPANY
INCOME STATEMENT FOR MANAGEMENT
For the Year Ended December 31, 19X1

	Profit Plan	Performance Budget	Actual	Variances: Activity	Variances: Price Efficiency Spending
Sales	$2,160,000	$2,264,000	$2,336,000	$104,000	$ 72,000
Variable costs					
Manufacturing	$1,050,000	$1,096,400	$1,096,400	$ (46,400)	
Selling	90,000	93,600	93,600	(3,600)	
Total	1,140,000	1,190,000	1,190,000	(50,000)	
Contribution margin (standard)	$1,020,000	$1,074,000	$1,146,000	$ 54,000	
Variances from standard costs	0	0	(60,200)		(60,200)
Contribution margin (adjusted)	$1,020,000	$1,074,000	$1,085,800	$ 54,000	$ 11,800
Fixed marketing costs related to products	144,000	144,000	150,400		(6,400)
Product margin	$ 876,000	$ 930,000	$ 935,400	$ 54,000	$ 5,400
Common fixed costs					
Manufacturing	$ 360,000	$ 360,000	$ 376,000		$(16,000)
Marketing	48,000	48,000	49,000		(1,000)
General	156,000	156,000	152,000		4,000
Total	564,000	564,000	577,000		(13,000)
Net operating income	$ 312,000	$ 366,000	$ 358,400	$ 54,000	$ (7,600)
Interest income	7,900	7,900	9,020		1,120
Interest expense	(10,500)	(10,500)	(9,200)		1,300
Net income before taxes	$ 309,400	$ 363,400	$ 358,220	$ 54,000	$ (5,180)
Income taxes (40%)	123,800	145,400	143,280	21,600	2,120
Net income after taxes	$ 185,600	$ 218,000	$ 214,940	$ 32,400	$ (3,060)
Earnings per share	$ 6.19	$ 7.27	$ 7.16		

EXHIBIT 14-6
Income statement for management of DeFord Company

DEFORD COMPANY
REPORT ON PROFIT PLAN
For the Year Ended December 31, 19X1

Planned operating profit		$ 312,000
Marketing variances		
Activity variance — Product A	$ (10,000)	
Activity variance — Product B	64,000	
Total	$ 54,000	
Selling price variance	72,000	
Marketing cost variance	(7,400)	
Total variance from planned profit due to marketing variances		118,600
Manufacturing variances		
Material price variance	$ (13,000)	
Material usage variance	(21,000)	
Labor rate variance	1,800	
Labor efficiency variance	(5,500)	
Variable overhead efficiency variance	(5,200)	
Variable overhead spending variance	(17,300)	
Total variances in variable costs	$ (60,200)	
Fixed overhead spending variance	(16,000)	
Total variance from planned profit due to manufacturing variances		(76,200)
General variances		
Spending variances — treasurer	$ 1,000	
Spending variances — president	3,000	
Total variance from planned profit due to general variances		4,000
Actual operating profit		$ 358,400

EXHIBIT 14-7
Report on profit plan for DeFord Company

$7,400. With the exception of the labor rate variance, all variances in the manufacturing area are unfavorable and accounted for $76,200 of the variations from plan. The factory worked beyond the normally defined practical capacity. By going into overtime the firm was less efficient, as shown by the usage and efficiency variances. In addition, there was a substantial increase in material prices and usage during the year.

To identify the entire benefit of additional sales volume with the marketing area and all the inefficiencies of additional production with the factory may be misleading and could create intrafirm hostility. The unfavorable variances that arose from operations above the defined practical capacity were necessary to accomplish the extra sales. The manager of the factory may question why the feedback to the factory should be so negative, whereas the feedback to the marketing area is so positive. A special study may be necessary to determine the proportion of variances that resulted from the extra sales. Certainly, it would be inappropriate to castigate the factory manager without further investigation.

The cash flow statement (Exhibit 14-8) compares actual cash flows with planned cash flows and serves more of a score-keeping function than an attention-directing function. In cash planning, unlike profit planning, the firm cannot fall short of its objectives without serious problems. A loss from operations may be sustained, but the firm cannot have an overdraft without immediate action.

The statement of financial position is presented in Exhibit 14-9. It is the starting and ending point in the financial planning and control effort, although it is not a particularly useful statement in the planning and control of daily decisions. The statement of financial position serves as a still photograph of a firm's financial standing. Its role in providing useful information on financial strength is greatest to those outside the firm, such as creditors and stockholders.

Comparison of Actual Results with Objectives

As the last step in the budgetary cycle, Mr. DeFord compared the actual achievements of the year with the objectives he had prepared at the beginning of the year. Exhibit 14-10 shows this comparison. Overall, the results were on target and Mr. DeFord was pleased with the outcome of the first year using a budget.

COMPARISON OF INTERNAL AND EXTERNAL REPORTING NEEDS

Internal reporting has no specific requirements other than those established by the firm itself. Income, assets, and liabilities may be measured for internal reporting in any manner that is relevant and useful to management. Of course, the accounting system must provide objective, verifiable evidence for external reporting.

DEFORD COMPANY
CASH FLOW STATEMENT FOR MANAGEMENT
For the Year Ended December 31, 19X1

	Cash Budget	19X1 Actual
Cash flows from operations		
Sources		
Collections from customers	$2,154,000	$2,322,000
Uses of cash		
Payments to suppliers	$ 653,000	$ 682,100
Payroll and fringe benefits	720,000	749,400
Power and utilities	102,000	113,600
Rent	60,000	60,000
Marketing costs	138,000	145,100
Research	12,000	11,100
Other	72,000	77,100
Income taxes	115,000	115,000
Total	1,872,000	1,953,400
Net flow of cash from operations	$ 282,000	$ 368,600
Other sources of cash		
Sale of investments	320,000	260,000
Investment income	7,900	9,020
Short-term borrowing	50,000	20,000
Other (uses) of cash		
Purchase of investments	(440,000)	(470,000)
Repayment of debt	(50,000)	(20,000)
Interest on debt	(10,500)	(9,200)
Capital expenditures	(100,000)	(110,000)
Dividends	(60,000)	(60,000)
Net cash sources (uses)	$ (600)	$ (11,580)

EXHIBIT 14-8
Cash flow statement for management of DeFord Company

DEFORD COMPANY
STATEMENT OF FINANCIAL POSITION FOR MANAGEMENT
December 31, 19X1

ASSETS

Current assets		
Cash		$ 23,420
Marketable securities		410,000
Accounts receivable		128,000
Inventories:		
Raw materials	$ 89,000	
Finished goods	78,100	167,100
Total current assets		$ 728,520
Fixed assets		
Equipment	$ 870,000	
Less: Accumulated depreciation	228,000	642,000
Total assets		$1,370,520

LIABILITIES AND STOCKHOLDERS' EQUITY

Current liabilities		
Accounts payable		$ 59,500
Accrued expenses		12,500
Dividends payable		30,000
Income taxes payable		53,280
Notes payable, 9%, due 7/1/X1		100,000
Total		$ 255,280
Long-term liabilities		
Note payable, 8%, due 12/1/X4		300,000
Total liabilities		$ 555,280
Stockholders' equity		
Common stock, $10 par, 50,000 shares authorized, 30,000 issued and outstanding	$ 300,000	
Retained earnings	515,240	815,240
Total liabilities and stockholders' equity		$1,370,520

EXHIBIT 14-9
Statement of financial position for management of DeFord Company

PROFIT OBJECTIVES	19X1 RESULTS
1. Achieve a net income after tax of:	
a. 25% on reported owners' equity at the beginning of the year	33% on reported owners' equity ($214,940 ÷ $660,300)
b. 10% on net sales	9% on net sales ($214,940 ÷ $2,336,000)
2. Increase earnings per share by 10% over previous year	28% increase in earnings per share 19X0 EPS $5.60 19X1 EPS $7.16 ($1.56 increase ÷ $5.60)
MARKET OBJECTIVE	
1. Increase dollar sales of Product A by 5%	2% increase in Product A sales 19X0 sales $ 684,000 19X1 sales $ 696,000 ($12,000 increase ÷ $684,000)
2. Increase dollar sales of Product B by 5%	21% increase in Product B sales 19X0 sales $1,360,000 19X1 sales $1,640,000 ($280,000 increase ÷ $1,360,000)
MANPOWER OBJECTIVE	
Stable work force with no more than 5% turnover through layoffs	No layoffs in basis work force. Above practical capacity production for several months resulted in some temporary hiring.

EXHIBIT 14-10
Comparison of actual results with company objectives for DeFord Company

The DeFord Company, in our extended illustration, chose to use a standard variable costing system. The standard costs provide targets for control of operations as well as a measure of future costs for planning. Variable costing and the contribution margin approach allows management to anticipate the impact of change simply and react quickly when decisions are needed to resolve pricing and production problems. All variances from plan are regarded as efficiencies or inefficiencies of the period and written off in the period during which they arise.

External reporting is constrained by a set of guidelines, generally accepted accounting principles, that have been developed over several decades of public reporting. These principles are aimed at providing a full and fair disclosure of the *past* events of the company to investors. They require an income statement, a statement of financial position, and a statement of changes in financial position. All assets and liabilities must be carried at cost. The inventories must be costed at the *full* cost of production. To conform to generally accepted accounting principles, the DeFord Company must allocate a part of the fixed factory overhead of $376,000 to the ending inventory of finished goods in the statement of financial position. Because *both* the beginning and ending inventories of finished goods must be adjusted, the effect on income is minimized.

A separate issue in external reporting is the $60,200 production variances incurred by the DeFord Company in 19X1. To the extent that they represent efficiencies or inefficiencies that should not have occurred, they may be written off to income of the period and not apportioned to ending inventories and cost of goods sold. To the extent that the variances resulted from incorrect standards, such as a standard that does not reflect an increase in material prices, the variances should be apportioned. In Exhibit 14-7, where the variances are reported, the largest variances were in material usage and variable overhead spending, both of which were traced to the addition of new employees and overtime work. You may recall that Mr. DeFord defined capacity as a one-shift operation because the firm lacked the supervisory talent to expand into two shifts. With new equipment that will increase capacity, these variances are not expected to continue. The material price variance of $13,000 is insignificant when compared with over $600,000 of purchases. Therefore, none of the production variances are apportioned to inventories; they are included in cost of goods sold.

The apportionment of fixed costs to the beginning and ending inventories of finished goods (there are no units in process) is done simply by computing an actual blanket factory overhead rate for the entire factory. Adjustment of the beginning inventory requires data for the year 19X0 that we have not presented in our example. Therefore, let's assume that fixed factory overhead was $360,000 in 19X0 and that the company worked 48,000 hours. The fixed factory overhead rate for the beginning inventory is therefore $7.50 per direct labor hour ($360,000 ÷ 48,000 hours). Each unit of Product A required .3 hours of direct labor and each unit of Product B required .2 hours. The beginning inventory of finished goods on a full-absorption basis is revised as shown in the following tabulation.

	Product A	*Product B*
Standard variable unit cost (Exhibit 12-13)	$ 6.40	$ 3.70
Fixed factory overhead rate times standard labor:		
Product A $7.50 × .3 hours	2.25	
Product B $7.50 × .2 hours		1.50
Absorption unit cost	$ 8.65	$ 5.20
Number of units in beginning inventory of finished goods	15,000	10,000
Revised inventory	$129,750	$52,000

The ending inventory of finished goods is revised in a similar manner. During 19X1, fixed factory overhead amounted to $376,000 and the standard direct labor hours were 54,000. The fixed factory overhead rate for 19X1 is $6.96 ($376,000 ÷ 54,000 hours). The ending inventory of finished goods for external reporting is computed as shown in the following tabulation.

	Product A	*Product B*
Standard variable unit cost	$ 6.40	$ 3.70
Fixed factory overhead rate:		
Product A $6.96 × .3	2.09	
Product B $6.96 × .2		1.39
Absorption unit cost	$ 8.49	$ 5.09
Number of units in ending inventory of finished goods	7,000	9,000
Revised inventory	$59,430	$45,810

The adjustment to cost of goods sold must reflect the difference in both beginning and ending inventories. The income statement for management includes variable cost of goods sold of $1,096,400, fixed factory overhead of $376,000, and production variances of $60,200. The following computation of cost of goods sold would be used for external reporting.

Variable cost of goods sold		$1,096,400
Add: Fixed factory overhead for 19X1		376,000
Production variances for 19X1		60,200
Total		$1,532,600
Add: Difference (increase) in beginning inventory of finished goods:		
Inventory as reported	$133,000	
Revised inventory	181,750	48,750
Total		$1,581,350
Deduct: Difference (increase) in ending inventory of finished goods:		
Inventory as reported	$ 78,100	
Revised inventory	105,240	27,140
Cost of goods sold for external reporting		$1,554,210

The adjustment caused income before taxes to decline by $21,610. In Chapter 5 we concluded that, when compared with income under variable costing, income under absorption costing will decline when sales exceed production. During 19X1, Product A inventory declined by 8,000 units and Product B inventory declined by 1,000 units.

The amount of taxes is determined by the accounting methods used in the tax return. Although different accounting methods may be used to postpone payment of taxes, the DeFord Company uses the same methods in its tax return as on external financial statements. The decrease in income of $21,610 results in a decrease of $8,636 in income tax expense in the income statement and taxes payable in the statement of financial position. If we assume that sales and production were equal in 19X0, the change from variable to absorption costing in the beginning inventory did not affect income in 19X0 and, therefore, did not affect taxes payable at the beginning of 19X1.

The conversion from standard variable costing for management to absorption costing for external reporting purposes for the DeFord Company may be summarized as follows:

1. Beginning statement of financial position (Exhibit 14-11): Inventories and retained earnings are increased by $48,750, the amount of fixed factory overhead added to the inventory.

2. Ending statement of financial position (Exhibit 14-11): Inventories are increased by $27,140 and taxes payable decreased by $8,636. Retained earnings reflects the cumulative increase of $35,784, the sum of the changes in the beginning inventory as well as the changes in 19X1.

DEFORD COMPANY
STATEMENT OF FINANCIAL POSITION
December 31, 19X0 and 19X1

	19X1	19X0
ASSETS		
Current assets		
Cash	$ 23,420	$ 35,000
Marketable securities	410,000	200,000
Accounts receivable	128,000	114,000
Inventories	194,240	261,750
Total	$ 755,660	$ 610,750
Fixed assets		
Equipment	$ 870,000	$ 540,000
Less: Accumulated depreciation	228,000	200,000
Total	642,000	340,000
Total assets	$1,397,660	$ 950,750
LIABILITIES AND STOCKHOLDERS' EQUITY		
Current liabilities		
Accounts payable	$ 59,500	$ 70,000
Accrued expenses	12,500	16,700
Dividends payable	30,000	30,000
Income taxes payable	44,644	25,000
Note payable, 9%, due July 1, 19X2	100,000	—
Total	$ 246,644	$ 141,700
Long-term notes payable		
Note payable, 9%, due July 1, 19X2		$ 100,000
Note payable, 8%, due December 1, 19X4	$ 300,000	
Total liabilities	$ 546,644	$ 241,700
Stockholders' equity		
Common stock, $10 par, 50,000 shares authorized, 30,000 issued and outstanding	$ 300,000	$ 300,000
Retained earnings	551,016	409,050
Total	851,016	709,050
Total liabilities and stockholders' equity	$1,397,660	$ 950,750

NOTE: SUMMARY OF SIGNIFICANT ACCOUNTING POLICIES

INVENTORIES: Inventories are maintained at average cost, which approximates market. Composition of inventories.

	19X1	19X0
Raw materials	$ 89,000	$ 80,000
Finished goods	105,240	181,750
	$194,240	$261,750

DEPRECIATION: Fixed assets consist of equipment that is depreciated on a straight-line basis over a five-year life. Depreciation for 19X1 amounted to $108,000.

LEASE: The company rents a building on a noncancellable lease. Five years remain on the lease. Annual rental is $60,000 for the life of the lease. The company may renew the lease, but there is no option to purchase.

EXHIBIT 14-11
Statement of financial position for stockholders of DeFord Company

DEFORD COMPANY INCOME STATEMENT For the Year Ended December 31, 19X1		
Revenues		
Sales		$2,336,000
Interest revenue		9,020
Total revenue		$2,345,020
Expenses		
Cost of goods sold	$1,554,210	
Operating expenses	445,000	
Interest expense	9,200	
Income taxes	134,644	2,143,054
Net income		$ 201,966
Retained earnings, January 1, 19X1		409,050
Total		$ 611,016
Dividends		60,000
Retained earnings, December 31, 19X1		$ 551,016

EXHIBIT 14-12
Income statement for stockholders of DeFord Company

3. Income statement (Exhibit 14-12): The format of the income statement is condensed and revised to the absorption costing format. Costs increase by $21,610, tax expense decreases by $8,636, and net income decreases by $12,974.

4. Statement of changes in financial position (Exhibit 14-13): Since the adjustments did not involve changes in cash flows, the statement of changes in financial position, using the cash flow method, is not affected by the change in accounting method.

The financial statements for external reporting are presented in Exhibits 14-11, 14-12, and 14-13. The notes to the financial statements provide disclosure of the significant accounting policies.

DEFORD COMPANY
STATEMENT OF CHANGES IN FINANCIAL POSITION
For the Year Ended December 31, 19X1

Sources of cash		
From operations		
Collections from customers		$2,322,000
Payments to suppliers	$ 682,100	
Payment of expenses	1,156,480	
Payment of income taxes	115,000	1,953,580
Net from operations		$ 368,420
From other sources		
Sale of investments	$ 260,000	
Short-term borrowing	20,000	280,000
Other changes not involving cash:		
Issuance of note for equipment		300,000
Total sources of cash		$ 948,420
Uses of cash		
Purchase of investments	$ 470,000	
Repayment of debt	20,000	
Payment of dividends	60,000	
Purchase of equipment	110,000	
Total	$ 660,000	
Other changes not involving cash:		
Acquisition of equipment for note	300,000	960,000
Decrease in cash		$ (11,580)

EXHIBIT 14-13
Statement of changes in financial position for stockholders of DeFord Company

SUMMARY

To be effective, reports must be relevant to management needs. Two dimensions of relevancy exist: First, the concept of responsibility accounting requires that costs and revenues be identified with the manager responsible for their incurrence. Second, the concept of management by exception requires that significant deviations from plan be identified so that the cause may be determined and action taken, if necessary, to prevent future variances. To ensure their effectiveness, reports to management must also be timely and accurate.

At the bottom of the chart of organization, the information needs are primarily nonfinancial and involve a limited time horizon. Moving upward through the chart, there is increasing emphasis upon financial planning. At the top, the reporting process serves to explain deviations from plan.

Internal reporting has no specific requirements except those imposed by management. In our illustration the DeFord Company chose to use a variable standard costing system for internal purposes. External reporting is constrained by generally accepted accounting principles. To conform to these principles, the adjustment of the variable standard costing system to an absorption standard costing system involves the application of fixed factory overhead to the inventories.

SUPPLEMENTARY READING

Calas, Robert. "Variance Analysis in Profit Planning" *Management Accounting,* July, 1971.

Higgins, John A. "Responsibility Accounting." *The Arthur Anderson Chronicle,* April, 1952.

Holmes, Robert W. "An Executive Views Responsibility Reporting." *Financial Executive,* August, 1968.

Kellogg, Martin N. "Fundamentals of Responsibility Accounting." *N.A.A. Bulletin,* April, 1962.

Kiessling, J. R. "Profit Planning and Responsibility Accounting." *Financial Executive,* July, 1963.

Koehler, Robert W. "Statistical Variance Control: Through Performance Reports and On-the-Spot Observation." *Management Accounting,* December, 1969.

Morris, R. D. F. "Budgetary Control is Obsolete." *The Accountant,* May 18, 1968.

Netten, E. W. "Responsibility Accounting for Better Management." *The Canadian Chartered Accountant,* September, 1963.

Pick, John. "Is Responsibility Accounting Irresponsible?" *The New York Certified Public Accountant,* July, 1971.

Walker, Charles W. "Profitability and Responsibility Accounting." *Management Accounting,* December, 1971.

QUESTIONS

14-1 What qualitative factors go into the development of standards for good reporting?

14-2 What ideas underlie the concept of management by exception?

14-3 At what levels in the organization are accounting data most useful? Why? What types of information are used at other levels?

14-4 Of what significance is timing to good reporting?

14-5 What are some causes of inaccuracy in accounting reports? How can they be guarded against?

14-6 Discuss the trade-off between timeliness and accuracy in good reporting. How do these two concepts relate to relevancy in reporting for control purposes?

14-7 Why does the profit plan for a department usually differ from the performance budget? When will they become the same?

14-8 From what sources is the performance budget developed?

14-9 What are the two general reasons for variable overhead variances when overhead rates are based on direct labor hours?

14-10 How is the absorption costing fixed overhead rate used in performance budgeting?

14-11 What is control limit? How is it used by management?

14-12 How do reports for cost centers differ from reports for profit centers? Give an example of each type of center.

14-13 How does the activity variance affect net income? What types of departments have activity variances?

14-14 What is the emphasis in reports to top management? What is included in these reports?

14-15 What changes must be made in the report to top management for external reporting? Why?

PROBLEMS

14-16 Match the following terms and definitions.

1. Control
2. Planning
3. Responsibility accounting
4. Management by exception
5. Feedback
6. Activity variance
7. Material usage variance
8. Report on profit plan
9. Generally accepted accounting principles
10. Relevancy

a. A step in the control process that informs of progress.
b. Meaningful and usable.
c. Variance arising from volume of material used.
d. Variance arising from volume of goods sold.
e. A system of reporting that conveys information about the activities over which an individual manager has control.
f. External constraints imposed upon financial reporting outside the firm.
g. Leaving well enough alone.
h. Process of measuring and correcting actual performance to ensure that a firm's objectives and plans are accomplished.
i. Explanation of differences between planned net income and actual net income.
j. Process of selecting goals, objectives, and the actions required to attain them.

14-17 The following income statement was prepared for the president of Burr Saddle Company.

				Variances	
	Profit Plan	*Performance Budget*	*Actual*	*Activity*	*Price Efficiency Spending*
Sales	$30,000	$27,000	$31,500	$(3,000)	$ 4,500
Variable production costs	20,000	18,000	18,000	2,000	—
Contribution margin	$10,000	$ 9,000	$13,500	$(1,000)	$ 4,500
Production variances:					
Material price			(2,500)		(2,500)
Material usage			500		500
Labor rate			(200)		(200)
Labor efficiency			800		800
Variable overhead spending			(1,000)		(1,000)
Variable overhead efficiency			200		200
Contribution margin adjusted	$10,000	$ 9,000	$11,300	$(1,000)	$ 2,300
Fixed costs:					
Manufacturing	3,000	3,000	3,200		(200)
Administration	2,000	2,000	2,100		(100)
Net income	$ 5,000	$ 4,000	$ 6,000	$(1,000)	$ 2,000
Saddles sold	100	90	90		

The Burr Saddle Company has been in business for many years. Production is to order, primarily from repeat customers, so there are no significant marketing costs. A standard variable costing system was implemented, and Mr. Burr is confused with the first report. He wants a simple explanation of why net income is $1,000 higher than planned.

REQUIRED:
Prepare a simple report for Mr. Burr that explains, by area of responsibility, why actual net income exceeded planned net income.

14-18 The following financial statements were prepared for the president of Collins Company.

INCOME STATEMENT

Sales (15,000 @ $5)			$75,000
Variable costs:			
Production (15,000 @ $2)	$30,000		
Selling (15,000 @ $1)	15,000		45,000
Contribution margin—standard			$30,000
Production variances			(3,000)
Contribution margin—adjusted			$27,000
Fixed costs:			
Manufacturing		$18,000	
Selling and administration		5,000	23,000
Net income			$ 4,000

STATEMENT OF FINANCIAL POSITION

Assets	Beginning	Ending
Cash	$ 8,000	$ 4,000
Accounts receivable	12,000	15,000
Inventories:		
Raw materials	5,000	4,000
Finished goods (3,000 and 6,000)	6,000	12,000
Fixed assets (net)	15,000	12,000
	$46,000	$47,000
Equities		
Current liabilities	$10,000	$ 7,000
Capital stock	30,000	30,000
Retained earnings	6,000	10,000
	$46,000	$47,000

The company has the following cost structure.

Production	$18,000 fixed and $2 variable per unit produced
Selling and Administration	$ 5,000 fixed and $1 variable per unit sold

In each of the past two years 18,000 units were produced. Inventories are costed at standard variable production cost. Variances represent inefficiencies that are not expected to reoccur. Beginning and ending inventories included:

	Beginning	*Ending*
Raw materials	10,000 pounds @ $ .50	8,000 pounds @ $ .50
Finished goods	3,000 units @ $2.00	6,000 @ $2.00

The company is applying to the bank for a loan. The bank has asked for financial statements prepared in conformity with generally accepted accounting principles.

REQUIRED:

A. Recast the financial statements to comply with generally accepted accounting principles. Explain your inventory values.

B. Compute the following ratios for both the internal and external statements.

1. Current ratio (times)
2. Liquidity ratio (times)
3. Accounts receivable turnover (times)
4. Inventory turnover (times)
5. Net income on sales (percentage)
6. Net income on beginning owners equity (percentage)

Did any of the ratios improve? Why?

14-19 The literature concerning cost analysis for decision making may be characterized by the numerous generalizations it contains.

a. No technique for the allocation of joint manufacturing costs should be used for deciding whether a product should be sold at the split-off point or processed further.

b. The undepreciated book value of existing equipment must be recognized as being irrelevant to the equipment replacement decision.

c. In decisions that primarily concern activity levels, it may be generalized that variable costs are always relevant and that fixed costs are always irrelevant.

d. Relating to format, cost reports to management for decision-making purposes may concentrate on relevant items only or, alternatively, may incorporate a *Difference* column and include the items that remain unchanged.

For each of the above statements, indicate whether you agree or disagree and briefly explain your reasons for agreement or disagreement.

(Canada SIA adapted)

14-20 Travel and entertainment expenses for the Shaw Company were $10,000 when sales were $200,000, and $15,000 when sales were $400,000.

REQUIRED:
During 19X1 sales were $300,000 and travel and entertainment expenses were $13,200. Using past sales as a basis for establishing a performance budget for travel and entertainment expenses, compute the variance from budget for 19X1.

14-21 Below is the organization chart for Pillow Furniture, Inc. and a list of costs incurred by the company. What area would be held responsible for each of these costs?

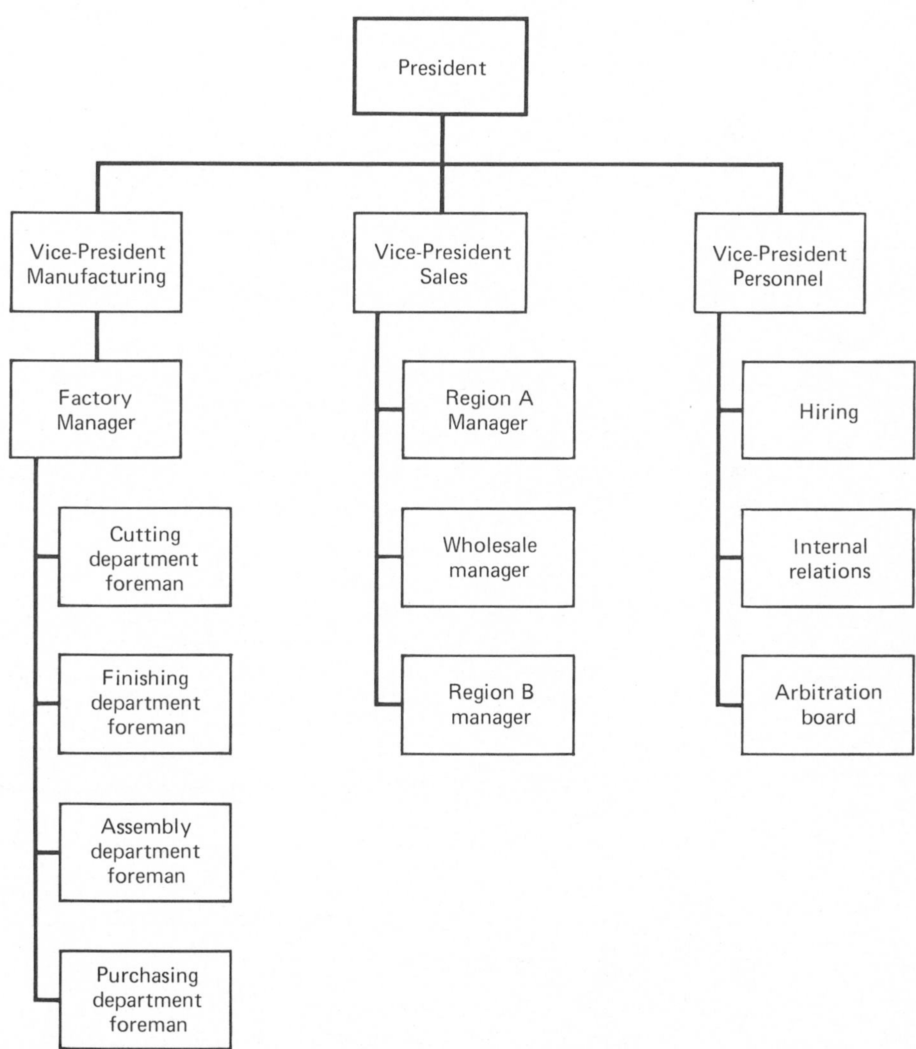

1. Cost of pillow-covering material
2. Salespeople's salaries for Region B
3. Clerical wages in hiring department
4. Costs of lost sales to a large wholesale customer
5. Salespeople's travel expense for Region A
6. Differential costs of customer order from wholesale customers
7. Cost of factory medical services
8. Employee recruiting expense
9. Depreciation on factory building
10. Nationwide advertising
11. Rush order setup costs
12. Factory utilities
13. Bad-debt expense for wholesale customer in Region B
14. Scrap losses
15. Janitorial services contracted by firm allocated to internal relations department

14-22 The results for the Marborough Company, which uses absorption costing, for the month of March, 19X6, show that total factory overhead was $201,170 and applied factory overhead was $157,280. From the operating budget, the overhead estimated for the capacity attained was $190,000. This is the third consecutive month in which factory overhead has not been fully absorbed. Company management is extremely concerned, and a directive has been issued to the chief accountant to investigate and report the results that have been responsible for this condition.

REQUIRED:

A. Briefly state five reasons that could contribute to this unfavorable operating position.

B. Because an unfavorable balance has occurred, the resulting difference must be analyzed under two separate variances. Define these two variances.

C. Indicate how the variances should be disposed of.

(Canada SIA adapted)

14-23 The president of Taylor School Supply Company, a wholesaler, presents you with a comparison of distribution costs for two salesmen and wants to know if you think the salesmen's compensation plan is working to the detriment of the company. He supplies you with the following data.

	Salesmen	
	McKinney	*Sim*
Gross sales	$247,000	$142,000
Sales returns	$ 17,000	$ 2,000
Cost of goods sold	$180,000	$ 85,000
Reimbursed expenses (e.g. entertainment)	$ 5,500	$ 2,100
Other direct charges (e.g. samples distributed)	$ 4,000	$ 450
Commission rate on gross sales dollars	5%	5%

REQUIRED:

A. The salesmen's compensation plan encourages a salesman to work to increase the measure of performance to which his compensation is related. List the questionable sales practices by a salesman that might be encouraged by basing commissions on gross sales.

B. What evidence that the compensation plan may be working to the detriment of the company can be found in the data?

C. What other information should the president obtain before reaching definite conclusions about this particular situation? Why?

(CPA adapted)

14-24 Rollie Bauman, president of Conspicuous Cabinets, has just received a request for an additional 700 special-order kitchen cabinets from Ramsey Construction. After reviewing Job 52, a recently completed job for the same type of cabinet, he accepted the order. Data from Job 52 follow.

	Job 52		
	Standard	*Actual*	*Efficiency Variance*
Sales	$15,000	$15,000	
Variable costs:			
Material	$ 2,000	$ 1,950	$ 50
Labor	8,000	8,400	(400)
Variable factory overhead*	2,000	2,100	(100)
Total variable costs	12,000	12,450	$(450)
Contribution margin	$ 3,000	$ 2,550	
Traceable fixed costs	2,000	1,050	
Net income	$ 1,000	$ 1,500	

*Applied on the basis of labor hours. Standard wage rate is $8 per hour.

Rollie was not concerned about the $400 variance in labor because Job 52 was a new job. He reasoned that performance should improve on the second job.

While walking through the factory on the way to his office, he overheard Ollie Ajax, the group leader for special cabinet construction, talking to another group leader. ". . . those work tickets on Job 52," Ajax was saying. The other man answered, "You mean you plugged the labor hours too?" "Of course," replied Ajax, "Johnson [the foreman] hits the roof if the variances are over 50 hours on any job. We just keep them under 50 hours and everyone is happy. Saves having to explain to the boss and get chewed out. Why, I bet we were at least 25% over standard on that Ramsey job. There is no way we can make standard on that type of job. We loaded the hours on other jobs."

REQUIRED:

A. Assuming the 25% estimate of labor variance on Job 52, correct the report that was presented to Mr. Bauman.
B. Were any costs other than labor affected?
C. How would the additional information have affected his decision?
D. What suggestions do you have concerning the control system and reporting to management?

14-25 The Kramer Bag Company recently completed an analysis of overhead cost behavior patterns. The linear equation for each overhead item follows.

	Best Fit Line $y = a + b(x)$*		*Standard Error of*
	a	*b*	*Estimate*
Overtime premium	$ 0	$1.00	$ 25
Supplies	$ 0	$ .2	$ 75
Fringe benefits	$1,000	$ 0	$ 10
Power	$1,000	$8.40	$400
Utilities	$ 500	$ .50	$ 25
Contracted janitorial service	$ 600	$ 0	$ 0
Supervisory salaries	$1,200	$ 0	$ 20
Repairs	$ 250	$ .50	$ 25
Miscellaneous	$ 100	$2.80	$200

*(x) is direct labor hours.

The profit plan for September called for 500 direct labor hours. The actual direct labor hours were 700, however, and the following actual costs were incurred.

Overtime premium	$ 500
Supplies	$ 325
Fringe benefits	$1,000
Power	$5,800
Utilities	$ 765
Janitorial service	$ 600
Supervisory salaries	$1,200
Repairs	$1,300
Miscellaneous	$1,800

REQUIRED:

A. Which overhead costs are fixed? Which are variable? Which are mixed?

B. Prepare a report to the departmental manager on overhead costs for September. Which variances bear further investigation?

14-26 Within the same company, there are numerous instances where manufacturing costs are maintained and controlled to a fine degree. However, when it comes to distribution costs, a great laxity seems to prevail. There is a lack of control when the distribution dollar is not spent where it will do the most good.

REQUIRED:

A. List the considerations that should be taken into account when classifying distribution expenses for the purpose of control.

B. How would you control order-getting costs and order-filling costs?

(Canada SIA adapted)

14-27 As part of your on-the-job training for Slalom Water Skis, you have been assigned the task of assisting in preparation of monthly performance reports. You are given the following data for the finishing department for May.

Standard Cost per Unit		*Actual Total Costs*	
Labor: Sanding (2 hours @ $3)	$ 6.00	Labor: Sanding	$12,000
Coating (1 hour @ $5)	5.00	Coating	8,500
Material ($\frac{1}{2}$ pound @ $25 per pound)	12.50	Material	30,000
Variable overhead (3 hours @ $4)	12.00	Variable overhead	27,000
		Rejects	3,000
Total	$35.50		$80,500

Any variance due to fluctuations in material price is isolated and reported as purchased. Variances in labor rates are isolated by the payroll department. Fixed costs were $10,000 and did not vary from budget.

Slalom Water Skis had planned to produce 2,000 pairs of skis this month. However, only 1,800 were produced and an additional 100 had to be scrapped because one batch of material was allowed to harden before it was applied to the skis. Several of the 1,800 pairs of skis had to be reworked, using overtime and dropping actual performance below budget. The cost of rejects includes the standard costs of prior departments.

REQUIRED:

A. Prepare a report on this month's operations for the finishing department manager. It should be accompanied by a narrative explaining the variances.

B. How much of this information should be presented in the factory cost report to the manager?

14-28 The following is a report to the manager of the classified ad department of the Fresno Bee, a daily newspaper, on his performance for the month of April.

				VARIANCE		
					Price Efficiency Spending	
	Profit Plan	*Performance Budget*	*Actual*	*Activity*	*Amount*	*Percentage*
Lines sold	25,000	20,000	20,000			
Sales	$50,000	$40,000	$41,000			
Variable costs:						
Original sales	$25,000	$20,000	$23,000			
Corrections	5,000	4,000	4,000			
Write off due to printing error	2,500	2,000	3,000			
Total	32,500	26,000	30,000			
Contribution margin	$17,500	$14,000	$11,000			
Fixed costs:						
Salaries	$10,000	$10,000	$10,000			
Fringe benefits	500	500	500			
Advertising	1,000	1,000	1,100			
Other	1,000	1,000	1,200			
Total	12,500	12,500	12,800			
Departmental contribution	$ 5,000	$ 1,500	$ (1,800)			

REQUIRED:

A. Compute the variances for April.

B. Management has a policy of investigating only those variances that exceed budget by 10% or more. Which variances should be looked into? What might be the causes of some of the variances?

C. Is 10% an appropriate level for all expenses? Explain.

14-29 At the beginning of 19X6, the Delta Company, a small specialty retail shop, developed the following planning data.

Sales	12,000 units @ $15	
Cost of goods sold	$10.50 per unit	
Operating expenses:		
	Fixed	*Variable*
Salaries	$ 6,000	10.5% of sales
Depreciation	$10,000	—
Supplies	—	2% of sales
Utilities	$ 500	$\frac{1}{2}$% of sales
Advertising	$ 500	1% of sales

The income statement prepared at the end of 19X6 follows.

DELTA COMPANY
INCOME STATEMENT
For the Year 19X6

Sales (8500 units)		$130,900
Cost of goods sold		91,800
Gross margin		$ 39,100
Operating expenses:		
Salaries	$23,000	
Depreciation	10,000	
Supplies	3,600	
Utilities	1,200	
Advertising	2,500	40,300
Net loss		$ (1,200)

Ms. Delta does not believe she should have shown a loss for the year. The cost of merchandise increased by $.30 and she raised her price by a larger amount. Many of her customers have suffered economic setbacks, resulting in a lower demand for her products. However, she believes her activity level should be above the breakeven point.

REQUIRED:

A. Based on planning data, what was Ms. Delta's breakeven point in dollars of sales?

B. Considering only the changes in the cost of merchandise and her selling price, what is her new breakeven point?

C. Prepare a report to Ms. Delta explaining the performance for the period.

14-30 The Bixby Company manufactures a single product with the following standard costs and selling price per unit.

Raw material	$0.20
Direct labor	.60
Variable overhead	.20
Fixed overhead*	.50
Total cost	$1.50
Selling price	2.00
Profit	$0.50

*Based on standard volume of 10,000 units per month.

During the first three months of the year, production, sales, and profits were:

	Month		
	1	*2*	*3*
Production in units	10,000	15,000	5,000
Sales in units	10,000	5,000	15,000
Profit in dollars	$ 5,000	$ 5,000	$ 5,000

Inventories and cost of goods sold are accounted for at standard cost. There have been no variances except for those due to volume of goods produced, and those variances have been charged in total to cost of goods sold each month.

Management is unable to understand why profits have been the same each month despite substantial changes in sales volume. Pointing to the indicated profit of $.50 per unit, the president questions the correctness of the third-period profit of $5,000, when 15,000 units were sold.

REQUIRED:
Prepare a presentation for management to explain what has happened. Comment on your presentation. *(Canada SIA adapted)*

14-31 You have recently been appointed the controller of a medium-sized manufacturing company. During your first month as controller it becomes apparent to you that the company's absorption costing system may be dysfunctional. To the extent that the system induces people to act in a way that does not contribute to the goals of the organization, the system may be termed dysfunctional. As controller you suspect that either a variable costing system or responsibility accounting may be less dysfunctional in respect to planning and control.

REQUIRED:

A. Compare and contrast variable costing and responsibility accounting.

B. Select *one* of these methods and draft what you would include in a brief memorandum to the executive committee of the company explaining the advantages of the method selected. Indicate why the method selected might be less dysfunctional than the company's absorption costing system.

(Canada SIA adapted)

14-32 The Brite Lite Company has just introduced the concept of control by responsibility and has decided to use the winding department for the test application. The variable overhead absorption rate for the winding department is $1 per hour and was based on a forecast level of activity of 30,000 hours as follows:

	Fixed	*Variable per Hour*
Forecasted overhead costs:		
Supervision	$16,000	$ —
Materials handling	5,000	.15
Quality inspection	10,000	.10
Overtime premium	—	.08
Clerical	6,000	—
Fringe benefits	3,000	.12
Supplies	7,000	.40
Repairs and maintenance	3,000	.10
Rework	—	.05
Depreciation of machinery	2,500	—
Allocated general plant	7,500	—
Total	$60,000	$1.00

During April the winding department actually worked 28,000 hours and incurred the following actual overhead costs.

Supervision	$15,000
Materials handling	10,700
Quality inspection	13,400
Overtime premium	1,600
Clerical	6,200
Fringe benefits	6,100
Idle time	800
Supplies	16,400
Repairs and maintenance	7,400
Depreciation of machinery	2,600
Allocated general plant	6,900
Total	$87,100

REQUIRED:

A. Prepare a detailed overhead control report for the manager of the winding department recording the favorable or unfavorable variances.

B. Comment briefly regarding the performance of the manager of the winding department in controlling overhead. *(Canada SIA adapted)*

14-33 The Clark Company has a labor union contract that guarantees a minimum wage of $500 per month to each direct labor employee with at least 12 years of service. A total of 100 employees currently qualify for coverage. All direct labor employees are paid $5 per hour.

The direct labor budget for 19X7 was based on the annual usage of 400,000 hours of direct labor × $5, or a total of $2,000,000. Of this amount, $50,000 (100 employees × $500) per month (or $600,000 for the year) was regarded as fixed. Thus, the budget for any given month was determined by the formula, $50,000 + $3.50 × Direct labor hours worked.

Data on performance for the first three months of 19X7 follow. (*U* means unfavorable; *F* means favorable.)

	January	*February*	*March*
Direct labor hours worked	22,000	32,000	42,000
Direct labor costs budgeted	$127,000	$162,000	$197,000
Direct labor costs incurred	110,000	160,000	210,000
Variance	$ 17,000 F	$ 2,000 F	$ 13,000 U

The factory manager was perplexed by the results showing favorable variances when production was low and unfavorable variances when production was high; the employees output per hour of work was constant throughout the three months. He expected little or no labor variance during these three months.

REQUIRED:

A. Why did the variances arise? Explain.

B. Prepare a graph with labor costs on the vertical axis and labor hours on the horizontal axis. Plot one line for budgeted labor costs and another for actual labor costs. Determine the flexible budget equation for each line.

C. Does this direct labor budget provide a basis for controlling direct labor cost? Explain, indicating any changes you think should be implemented to facilitate performance evaluation of direct labor employees.

D. For inventory valuation purposes, how should per-unit standard costs for direct labor be determined in a situation such as this? Explain, assuming that in some months fewer than 10,000 hours are expected to be utilized. *(CPA adapted)*

14-34 Honkey Tonk Piano Company manufactures an average of 50 pianos per month. Data on the manufacturing process includes:

Standard prime costs	
Standard labor	25 hours @ $5
Standard material	$100 per piano
Variable factory overhead	
Supplies	$500 per month
Power	$400 per month
Other	$75 per month
Fixed factory overhead	
Supervision	$1,000 per month

The February plan called for 50 pianos. However, only 45 were produced. Actual costs for the month were:

Labor (1,000 hours)	$5,700
Material, including favorable price variance of $200	$4,000
Supplies	$ 485
Power	$ 305
Other	$ 300
Fixed costs	$1,050

In the past, variations that could not be explained by unusual events seldom exceeded 5%.

REQUIRED:

A. Compute the standard unit cost under variable costing.
B. Prepare a performance report for the factory under variable costing.
C. What variances need further study?

14-35 Klastorin Metal Products Company has three different plants in its manufacturing operations. Each plant performs a different step on the product.

The foundry plant has two producing and two service departments. Costs of the maintenance and administration cost centers are reallocated to the producing departments. Data for May for the foundry plant, by department, are in the accompanying report.

The foundry plant incurred no variances in labor rates during the month; the only variance in material price was an unfavorable price variance of $1,000 in the casting department. All budgets were prepared from flexible budget data for the company at the actual level of operation.

The two other plants are the grinding plant and the finishing plant. Summary data from the cost reports of these two plants are:

	Budget	*Actual*
Grinding plant	$40,000	$38,000
Finishing plant	$50,000	$55,000

Costs incurred by the vice-president of manufacturing for the month were:

	Budget	*Actual*
Salaries	$6,000	$5,800
Supplies	300	280
Depreciation	1,000	1,000
	$7,300	$7,080

FOUNDRY PLANT
COST REPORT

	PRODUCING DEPARTMENTS			
	Casting		**Burring**	
	Budget	*Actual*	*Budget*	*Actual*
Materials used	$ 8,000	$ 8,800	$ 3,000	$ 3,100
Direct labor	6,000	4,800	15,000	15,800
Indirect labor	4,000	4,400	2,000	2,200
Supplies	1,000	800	2,000	2,400
Depreciation	7,000	7,000	5,000	5,000
Allocation of maintenance	4,500	5,500	4,500	5,000
Allocation of administration	1,800	1,500	4,500	5,100
	$32,300	$32,800	$36,000	$38,600

	SERVICE DEPARTMENTS			
	Maintenance		**Administration**	
	Budget	*Actual*	*Budget*	*Actual*
Indirect labor	$ 4,000	$ 5,000	$ 5,000	$ 5,400
Supplies	3,000	3,500	300	200
Depreciation	2,000	2,000	1,000	1,000
Allocation to producing departments	(9,000)	(10,500)		
Allocation to producing departments			(6,300)	(6,600)
	$ 0	$ 0	$ 0	$ 0

REQUIRED:

A. Prepare departmental cost reports for the supervisors of the casting and maintenance departments. Your reports should isolate variations from plans that are clearly under their responsibility.

B. Prepare a factory cost report for the manager of the foundry plant.

C. Prepare a cost report for the vice-president of manufacturing.

14-36 This problem is a continuation of problem 12-36. The budget requirements are repeated from problem 12-36 and reporting requirements are added.

The Melcher Company produces farm equipment at several plants. The business is seasonal and cyclical in nature. The company has attempted to use budgeting for planning and controlling activities, but the variable nature of the business has caused some company officials to be skeptical about the usefulness of budgeting. The accountant for the Adrian plant has been using a system he calls *flexible budgeting* to help his plant management control operations.

The company president asks him to explain what the term means, how he applies the system at the Adrian plant, and how it can be applied to the company as a whole. The accountant presents the following data as part of his explanation.

Budget data for 19X3		Actual data for January, 19X3	
Normal monthly capacity of the plant in direct labor hours	10,000 hours	Hours worked	8,400
Material costs (6 pounds @ $1.50)	$9.00 per unit	Units produced	3,800
Direct labor costs (2 hours @ $3.00)	$6.00 per unit	Costs incurred:	
Overhead estimate at normal monthly capacity		Material (24,000 pounds)	$36,000
Variable (controllable):		Direct labor (8,000 hours)	25,200
Indirect labor	$ 6,650	Indirect labor	6,000
Indirect materials	600	Indirect materials	600
Repairs	750	Repairs	1,800
Total variable	$ 8,000	Depreciation	3,250
Fixed (noncontrollable):		Supervision	3,000
Depreciation	$ 3,250	Total	$75,850
Supervision	3,000		
Total fixed	6,250		
Total fixed and variable	$14,250		
Planned units for January, 19X3	4,000		
Planned units for February, 19X3	6,000		

A. Prepare a budget for January (This requirement is repeated from problem 12-36.)
B. Prepare a report for January, comparing actual and budgeted costs for the actual activity for the month.
C. Can flexible budgeting be applied to the nonmanufacturing activities of the company? Explain your answer. *(CMA adapted)*

14-37 The Arsco Co. makes three grades of indoor-outdoor carpets. The sales volume for the annual budget is determined by estimating the total market volume for indoor-outdoor carpet and then applying the company's prior year market share, adjusted for planned changes due to company programs for the coming year. The volume is apportioned between the three grades based upon the prior year's product mix, again adjusted for planned changes due to company programs for the coming year.

The company budget for 19X3 and the results of operations for 19X3 follow.

	Budget (000 omitted from dollar amounts)			
	Grade 1	*Grade 2*	*Grade 3*	*Total*
Sales (units)	1,000 rolls	1,000 rolls	2,000 rolls	4,000 rolls
Sales	$1,000	$2,000	$3,000	$6,000
Variable expense	700	1,600	2,300	4,600
Variable margin	$ 300	$ 400	$ 700	$1,400
Traceable fixed expense	200	200	300	700
Traceable margin	$ 100	$ 200	$ 400	$ 700
Selling and administrative expense				250
Net income				$ 450

	Actual (000 omitted from dollar amount)			
	Grade 1	*Grade 2*	*Grade 3*	*Total*
Sales (units)	800 rolls	1,000 rolls	2,100 rolls	3,900 rolls
Sales	$810	$2,000	$3,000	$5,810
Variable expenses	560	1,610	2,320	4,490
Variable margin	$250	$ 390	$ 680	$1,320
Traceable fixed expense	210	220	315	745
Traceable margin	$ 40	$ 170	$ 365	$ 575
Selling and administrative expense				275
Net income				$ 300

Industry volume was estimated at 40,000 rolls for budgeting purposes. Actual industry volume for 19X3 was 38,000 rolls.

REQUIRED:

A. Calculate the profit impact of the unit sales activity variance for 19X3 using budgeted variable margins.

B. What portion of the variance, if any, can be attributed to the state of the carpet market?

C. What is the dollar impact on profits (using budgeted variable margins) of the shift in product mix from the budgeted mix? *(CMA adapted)*

14-38 In recent years distribution expenses of the Avey Company have increased more than other expenditures. For more effective control the company plans to provide each local manager with an income statement for his territory showing monthly and year-to-date amounts for the current and the previous year. Each sales office is supervised by a local manager; sales orders are forwarded to the main office and filled from a central warehouse; billing and collections are also centrally processed. Expenses are first classified by function and then allocated to each territory in the following ways.

Function	*Basis*
Sales salaries	Actual
Other selling expenses	Relative sales dollars
Warehousing	Relative sales dollars
Packing and shipping	Weight of package
Billing and collections	Number of billings
General administration	Equally

REQUIRED:

A. Explain responsibility accounting and the classification of revenues and expenses under this concept.

B. What are the objectives of profit analysis by sales territories in income statements?

C. Discuss the effectiveness of Avey Company's comparative income statements by sales territories as a tool for planning and control. Include in your answer additional factors that should be considered and changes that might be desirable for effective planning by management and evaluation of the local sales managers.

D. Compare the degree of control that can be achieved over production costs and distribution costs and explain why the degree of control differs.

E. Criticize Avey Company's allocation and/or inclusion of (1) other selling expenses, (2) warehousing expense, and (3) general administration expense. *(CPA adapted)*

14-39 This problem is a continuation of problem 13-39. In problem 13-39 a profit plan, a cash budget, and a projected statement of financial position were prepared. In this problem you are asked to prepare the financial statements for the year, comparing the actual results to the plan you established in problem 13-39. It will be necessary to refer to problem 13-39 for data.

During 19X8 the following actual events were recorded.

1. Patient visits amounted to 28,000 in 19X8. The billing rate through the year was $17 per patient visit. The collection rate was better than anticipated. Only 3% of 19X8 billings were considered uncollectible.
2. Costs for 19X8:

Doctors' salaries (December salaries $14,000)	$200,000
Nurses' salaries	$ 60,000
Administrative salaries	$ 60,000
Lab and X-ray technicians' salaries	$ 45,000
Medical supplies	$ 39,200
Rent	$ 24,000
Medical and financial records	$ 19,000
Other costs	$ 11,000

3. Other information:
During the last month of 19X8 there were 2,000 patient visits. Supplies of $2,800 were purchased, and the bill for medical and financial records was $1,500. The inventory of supplies at the end of 19X8 was $2,000.

REQUIRED:

A. Prepare an income statement for 19X8 for the Doctors' Clinic. Your income statement should compare actual results with plans and identify variances.
B. Prepare a cash flow statement for the year.
C. Prepare a statement of financial position at the end of 19X8.

14-40 The Expo Manufacturing Co. Ltd. produces a single product and uses a standard cost system. The standards for cost and price for each unit are shown in the following tabulation.

Material: 4 yards of Cloth X @ $2.88	$11.52	
3 yards of Cloth Q @ $2.16	6.48	$18.00
Direct labor: 5 hours @ $2.00		10.00
Factory overhead: Based on direct labor hours (1/3 fixed)		7.50
Cost to manufacture		$35.50
Selling and administrative expense (2/3 fixed)		7.20
Total cost		$42.70
Net profit		5.30
Selling price		$48.00

Materials are recorded in the Raw Materials Inventory account at standard cost, and any variance therefrom, as well as all variances, are assigned to the operations of the current year as period costs.

For the year ended March 31, 19X8, budgeted production and sales were 12,000 units. Actual sales for the year were 12,000 units.

An examination of the accounts discloses the following:

1. During the year, 180,000 feet of Cloth X were purchased at $1.00 per foot, and 120,000 feet of Cloth Q were purchased at $.70 per foot. There was no inventory at the beginning of the year. Materials issued were 148,500 feet of X and 111,000 feet of Q.
2. Direct labor cost was $121,056. Hourly wage rates averaged 3% less than standard.
3. Actual factory overhead was $112,800, of which $35,000 was fixed.
4. Selling and administrative expenses totalled $100,880, of which $60,000 was fixed.
5. A special sale of 1,000 finished units was made at a price of $44 each.

REQUIRED:

A. Prepare a profit plan for the year ended March 31, 19X8.

B. Prepare an income statement for the year, comparing it with the profit plan and a performance budget.

C. Prepare a report on profit plan. *(Canada SIA adapted)*

14-41 The Argon County Hospital is located in the county seat. Argon County is a well-known summer resort area. Its population doubles during the vacation months (May–August), and hospital activity more than doubles during these months. The hospital is organized into several departments. Although it is relatively small, its pleasant surroundings have attracted a well-trained and competent medical staff.

An administrator was hired a year ago to improve the business activities of the hospital. Among the new ideas he has introduced is responsibility accounting. This program was announced along with quarterly cost reports supplied to department heads. Previously cost data were presented to department heads infrequently. Excerpts from the announcement and the report received by the laundry superivsor follow.

> The hospital has adopted a responsibility accounting system. From now on you will receive quarterly reports comparing the costs of operating your department with budgeted costs. The reports will highlight the differences (variations) so you can zero in on the departure from budgeted costs (This is called *management by exception*). Responsibility accounting means you are accountable for keeping the costs in your department within the budget. The variations from the budget will help you identify what costs are out of line and the size of the variation will indicate which ones are the most important. Your first such report accompanies this announcement.

ARGON COUNTY HOSPITAL
PERFORMANCE REPORT—LAUNDRY DEPARTMENT
July–September 19X3

	Budget	*Actual*	*(Over) Under Budget*	*Percentage (Over) Under Budget*
Patient days	9,500	11,900	(2,400)	(25)
Pounds of laundry processed	125,000	156,000	(31,000)	(25)
Costs				
Laundry labor	$ 9,000	$12,500	$(3,500)	(39)
Supplies	1,100	1,875	(775)	(70)
Water and water heating and softening	1,700	2,500	(800)	(47)
Maintenance	1,400	2,200	(800)	(57)
Supervisor's salary	3,150	3,750	(600)	(19)
Allocated administration costs	4,000	5,000	(1,000)	(25)
Equipment depreciation	1,200	1,250	(50)	(4)
	$21,550	$29,075	$(7,525)	(35)

Administrator's comments: Costs are significantly above budget for the quarter. Particular attention needs to be paid to labor, supplies, and maintenance.

The annual budget for 19X3 was constructed by the new administrator. Quarterly budgets were computed as one-fourth of the annual budget. The administrator compiled the budget from analysis of the prior three years' costs. The analysis showed that all costs increased each year, with more rapid increases between the second and third year. He considered establishing the budget at an average of the prior three years' costs hoping that the installation of the system would reduce costs to this level. However, in view of the rapidly increasing prices, he finally chose 19X2 costs less 3% for the 19X3 budget. The activity level measured by patient days and pounds of laundry processed was set at 19X2 volume, which was approximately equal to the volume of each of the past three years.

REQUIRED:

A. Comment on the method used to construct the budget.
B. What information should be communicated by variations from budgets?
C. Recast the budget to reflect responsibility accounting assuming the following:
   1. Laundry labor, supplies, water and water heating and softening, and maintenance are variable costs. The remaining costs are fixed.
   2. Actual prices are expected to be approximately 20% above the levels in the budget prepared by the hospital administrator. *(CMA adapted)*

14-42 The Carberg Corporation manufactures and sells a single product. The company uses a variable cost system. The standard variable cost for one unit of product follows.

Material (1 pound plastic @ $2.00)	$ 2.00
Direct labor (1.6 hours @ $4.00)	6.40
Variable factory overhead	3.00
Total	$11.40

The Carberg Corporation prepares budgets by responsibility center. The 19X6 budget was based upon producing and selling 60,000 units. Production was scheduled evenly throughout the year. Overhead costs for the manufacturing department were planned at $267,000.

MANUFACTURING DEPARTMENT Budgeted Overhead for 19X6	
Variable overhead cost	
Indirect labor (30,000 hours @ $4.00)	$120,000
Supplies—Oil (60,000 gallons @ $.50)	30,000
Allocated variable service department costs	30,000
Total variable overhead cost	$180,000
Fixed overhead cost	
Supervision	$ 27,000
Depreciation	45,000
Other fixed costs	15,000
Total fixed overhead cost	87,000
Total budgeted annual overhead cost at 60,000 Units	$267,000

During the month of November, 19X6, 5,000 units were produced. Actual costs for the month were:

Material (5,300 pounds @ $2.00)	$10,600
Direct labor (8,200 hours @ $4.10)	33,620
Indirect labor (2,400 hours @ $4.10)	9,840
Supplies—Oil (6,000 gallons @ $0.55)	3,300
Allocated variable service department costs	3,200
Supervision	2,475
Depreciation	3,750
Other	1,250
Total	$68,035

The purchasing department is responsible for buying materials and supplies. Normally, the purchasing agent buys about the same quantity of material as is used in production during the previous month. In November 5,200 pounds were purchased at a price of $2.10 per pound.

REQUIRED:

A. Calculate the price variance under the responsibility of the purchasing agent. The company has divided its responsibilities such that the purchasing department is responsible for the price at which materials and supplies are purchased. The manufacturing department is responsible for the quantities of materials used. Does this division of responsibilities solve the conflict between price and quantity variances? Explain your answer.

B. Prepare a report for the November activities of the manufacturing department. The report, which will be given to the manufacturing department manager, should highlight the information in ways that would be useful to the manager in evaluating departmental performance and when considering corrective action.

C. Assume that the department manager performs the timekeeping function for this manufacturing department. From time to time, analysis of overhead and direct labor variances have shown that the department manager has deliberately misclassified labor hours (e.g. listed direct labor hours as indirect labor hours and vice versa) so that only one of the two labor variances is unfavorable. It is not feasible, economically, to hire a separate timekeeper. What should the company do, if anything, to resolve this problem? *(CMA adapted)*

14-43 This problem is a continuation of the DeFord Company illustration in Chapters 12, 13, and 14 of the text and problems 12-43 and 13-43. Previous problems required a profit plan and a cash budget. Actual transactions and costs for the month of April follow.

FACTORY

Shaping Department

	Budget	*Actual*	*Variance*
Variable costs	$45,900	$ 47,100	
Material usage			$(1,200)
Labor rate			$ 300
Labor efficiency			$ (500)
Variable overhead efficiency			$ (200)
Variable overhead spending			$ 400
Fixed costs	$ 8,000	$ 7,900	

Heat-treating Department

Units produced	
Product A	5,000
Product B	17,000
Materials used (hardening compound)	29,000 pounds
Direct labor (@ $4.70)	2,500 hours
Variable overhead	
Overtime premium	$ 1,500
Supplies	$ 2,700
Payroll fringe	$ 2,800
Power	$ 8,000
Fixed overhead	
Salaries	$ 2,500
Payroll fringe	$ 500
Depreciation	$ 3,000
Other	$ 1,000

Materials Handling Department		
Fixed costs	$ 6,000	$ 5,900

Factory Management	
Fixed costs	
Salaries	$ 4,200
Fringe benefits	$ 840
Factory rent	$ 4,000
Utilities	$ 1,080
Other	$ 280

MARKETING

Product A	
Units sold (8,000 @ $12)	$ 96,000
Variable selling costs	$ 4,800
Territory fixed costs	$ 3,000

Product B—Eastern Territory	
Units sold (6,000 @ $8)	$ 96,000
Variable selling costs	$ 1,600
Territory fixed costs	$ 5,000

Product B—Western Territory	
Units sold (12,000 @ $9)	$108,000
Variable selling costs	$ 4,000
Territory fixed costs	
Salaries	$ 2,500
Payroll fringe	$ 500
Product promotion	$ 800
Other	$ 1,200

Marketing Management	
Fixed costs	
Salaries	$ 3,000
Payroll fringe	$ 600
Other	$ 700

GENERAL	
Treasurer	$ 4,200
General Administration	$ 8,900
Other	
Investment income	$ 100
Do not accrue interest expense	

REQUIRED:

Prepare the following reports for the DeFord Company for the month of April. Your reports should be in good form and apply the concepts of responsibility accounting and management by exception.

A. Cost report for the month of April for the manager of the heat-treating department.

B. Cost report for the vice-president of manufacturing for the month of April.

C. Report for the manager of the Western territory for Product B showing the performance of his territory.

D. Report to the vice-president of marketing for the month of April.

E. Income statement and report on profit plan for Mr. DeFord for the month of April.

15 Measurement of Divisional Performance

DIVISIONALIZATION
RETURN ON INVESTMENT
- *Measurement of Return on Investment Components*
- *Performance Assessment through Return on Investment Analysis*
- *Overemphasis upon Return on Investment Analysis*

RESIDUAL INCOME
INTRAFIRM TRANSFER PRICING
- *Transfer Pricing for Measuring Management Performance*
- *Transfer Prices for Decisions*
- *Transfer Prices for External Reporting*
- *Transfer Pricing Case*

MULTIPLE PERFORMANCE MEASURES
SUMMARY

Throughout this text we have stressed management's role in making decisions that allocate the firm's resources. In evaluating the results of those decisions, we stressed the importance of establishing responsibility centers and the use of responsibility accounting. Under responsibility accounting, costs, revenues, and, in some cases, investment in resources are assigned to the manager who exercised control over them. Our illustrations in the previous chapters have concerned only cost centers and profit centers; that is, those units of the firm in which responsibility extended only over costs or, in some units, costs and revenue. An entirely different dimension is added when management's responsibility is extended to cover resource investment, as is the case in an investment center.

DIVISIONALIZATION

A **division** (investment center) is a responsibility center where the manager is held accountable for both production and marketing operating decisions as well as decisions involving investments in the resources necessary to carry them out. Division management is concerned not only with *how* operations are carried on, but also *what* operations are to be carried on. All the conditions for overall evaluation of a company are present in a division. Corporate goals and objectives provide constraints on the divisions. However, within those broad constraints, a division may operate as a separate company. It may be identified along geographic lines, as Eastern and Western divisions, along product lines, as Chevrolet and Cadillac divisions, or along separate industry lines, as in food products and leisure-time products divisions.

Firms form separate divisions for several reasons. The most important is to provide a natural separation of activities that allows decentralization. Decentralization provides a climate of individual management responsibility in decision making, as well as in the administration of the decisions. Complementing decentralization is the ability to measure a division's performance in terms of corporate objectives, principally through the measurement of return on investment. Because the performance measure is compatible with overall corporate objectives, division management may be given a high degree of freedom in the management of resources.

Beginning with the concept of planning for decisions, we stressed decision rules that allow management to select from among the available alternatives those that allocate the resources so as to provide a satisfactory rate of return on the investment. This principle was the guiding force in long-range decisions and the basis for the use of the contribution margin in short-range production, pricing, and distribution decisions. The ultimate test of the effectiveness of management decisions is whether they provide the firm with a satisfactory overall rate of return on the assets committed. It is the ability to measure return on investment that makes decentralized administration attractive.

Several conditions must be present, however, for divisionalization to operate successfully.[1] First, each division must be independent of other divisions. Unless separation is possible, performance measurement as an individual division is illusory. The more difficulty encountered in separating profit and investment measures, the lower is the probability of independent decision making. Interdivisional transactions may cause measurement problems but do not preclude separate divisional status. Second, the decisions of one division to increase its own income must not be allowed to reduce corporate income. It would be dysfunctional to allow a division to compete with other divisions or deal with other divisions in such a way as to cause overall corporate income to decline. This situation may arise if division boundaries are poorly drawn or corporate goals and objectives are not clearly stated. Finally, it is important to decentralization that corporate management refrain from making decisions for the divisions; divisions must be free to make their own. Corporate management should step in only as an emergency measure.

RETURN ON INVESTMENT

Simply stated, **return on investment** (ROI) is found by dividing net income by some measure of investment. The major purpose of return on investment analysis is the measurement, both absolutely and relatively, of the success of the company or its subdivisions. Return on investment analysis relates the net income, as determined on the income statement, to the resources, as measured on the statement of financial position. There are two components to the return on investment calculation: profit margin and investment turnover. **Profit margin,** sometimes called *profit as a percentage of sales,* is found by dividing net income by sales. **Investment turnover** is sales divided by investment in assets. Return on investment is the product of two components:

$$\text{Return on investment} = \text{Profit margin} \times \text{Investment turnover}$$

Stated in formula form, return on investment is as follows:

$$\text{Return on investment} = \frac{\text{Net income}}{\text{Investment}} = \frac{\text{Net income}}{\text{Sales}} \times \frac{\text{Sales}}{\text{Investment in assets}}$$

The return on investment may be increased by increasing the profit margin, by increasing the investment turnover, or by some combination of the two. Planning and evaluation of operations is enhanced by the ability to examine each component separately. To illustrate the components of return on investment, let's assume that a firm has budgeted sales of $500,000,

[1] David Solomons, *Divisional Performance, Measurement and Control* (Homewood, Ill.: Richard D. Irwin, Inc., 1965).

costs of $400,000, net income of $100,000, and investment in assets of $250,000. The return on investment is computed as:

$$\text{Return on investment} = \frac{\text{Net income}}{\text{Investment}} = \frac{\text{Net income}}{\text{Sales}} \times \frac{\text{Sales}}{\text{Investment}}$$
$$= \frac{\$100{,}000}{\$250{,}000} = \frac{\$100{,}000}{\$500{,}000} \times \frac{\$500{,}000}{\$250{,}000}$$
$$= 40\% = 20\% \times 2 \text{ times}$$

If, through cost reduction, the firm is able to increase the net income as a percentage of sales by 3%, the return on investment will increase by 6%. The investment turnover acts as a multiplier.

$$\text{Return on investment} = 46\% = 23\% \times 2 \text{ times}$$

Suppose instead that the firm is able to speed up collection of receivables and reduce inventories through better planning. The turnover component of the return on investment calculation would be increased. If working capital could be decreased by $25,000, the total investment in assets would decrease and the investment turnover would increase to 2.2 times. The return on investment would increase to 44%.

$$\text{Return on investment} = \frac{\text{Net income}}{\text{Sales}} \times \frac{\text{Sales}}{\text{Investment in assets}}$$
$$= \frac{\$100{,}000}{\$500{,}000} \times \frac{\$500{,}000}{\$225{,}000}$$
$$= 20\% \times 2.2 \text{ times}$$
$$= 44\%$$

Measurement of Return on Investment Components

To use return on investment analysis in management assessment, it is important that measures of net income and investment be clearly understood by all concerned. There are some variations in practice in both the measurement of net income and the measurement of investment.

The net income figure used in calculating return on investment is usually taken directly from the financial statements. Generally accepted accounting principles guide the determination of income for external reporting. To the extent that these principles are followed for internal income measurements, internally reported income will be consistent with income for external reporting. In this case, inventories will be costed under full-absorption costing, and all assets and liabilities will be recorded at historical cost.

Net income for internal reports used in measuring divisional performance can differ from generally accepted accounting principles in two important respects. First, when products or other assets are transferred between divisions of the company, proper evaluation of the divisions may require that transfer prices be based upon market prices or other values. The use of a transfer price based upon some measure other than historical cost will result in intercompany profit in divisional inventories or other assets acquired from other divisions. Transfer pricing will be discussed later in this chapter.

Second, because of its usefulness in short-range decisions, variable costing may be used for internal profit measurement. This should not be troublesome to management. The income principles used in calculating divisional rates of return may or may not conform to generally accepted accounting principles. It is more important that the net income measure be understood and used consistently throughout the firm.

The measurement of investment is even less standardized than the net income measure. The most readily available measure of investment is the book value of assets shown on the statement of financial position.[2] However, this measure has an inherent weakness. Over time, the carrying value of the assets decreases through depreciation charges. As long as the net income remains relatively constant, the return on investment will increase because of the declining investment base. If a manager holds net income reasonably constant and makes no new investments, his rate of return will show improving performance. The ultimate result is a decline in the firm's productive capacity as the plant wears out.

There are several ways to overcome this defect in return on investment analysis. One approach is to use the original cost of the asset before any deduction for depreciation, providing a constant return on investment if earnings are constant. Another approach is to use a method of depreciation with increasing charges over the life of the asset. The result is a constant rate of return on investment; each year a lower income is related to a smaller asset base.

To illustrate increasing-charge depreciation, called the **sinking fund method of depreciation,** let's assume that a firm paid $5,000 for an asset with an estimated three-year life and an estimated cash inflow of $2,010 each year. If we ignore taxes for simplification, the time-value adjusted rate of return is 10%. This rate was determined in the following computation.

$$\$5{,}000 = \$2{,}011\ (\text{P.V.F.})_{A\overline{3|}\,?}$$

$$\text{P.V.F.} = \frac{\$5{,}000}{\$2{,}011}$$

$$\text{P.V.F.} = 2.486$$

(In Appendix B, Present value of an annuity of $1, the present-value factor of 2.486 is found in the three-year row of 10% column.) Because we *know* that the actual rate of return is 10%, we may compute the net income *first* and allow the balance of the annual cash inflow (revenue) to recover a part of the cost of the asset (depreciation) each year. The asset will be fully depreciated

[2]**Book value** is original cost less the accumulated depreciation to date.

at the end of the third year, and the company will have earned a 10% rate of return on the investment.

Year	*Investment at Beginning of Year*	*Net Income (10%)**	*Depreciation (Cash flow − Income)*	*Investment at End of Year (Beginning Investment Less Accumulated Depreciation)*
1	\$5,000	\$500	(\$2,011 − \$500) \$1,511	\$3,489
2	\$3,489	\$349	(\$2,011 − \$349) \$1,662	\$1,827
3	\$1,827	\$183	(\$2,011 − \$183) \$1,828	\$ 1†

*Note that the net income (column 3) is *always* 10% of the investment at the beginning of the year (column 2).

†Rounding error

This method is not widely used for computing depreciation. However, it is used in preparing loan amortization schedules that allow the creditor to earn a constant rate of return over the life of the loan. If you have an installment loan or home mortgage with equal monthly payments, study the schedule of loan balances over the life of the loan. You will find most of the early payments are interest, with very little going to reduce the loan balance. Near the end of the loan most of the payment goes to reduce the loan balance; the interest portion is very small. These schedules are based upon the same notion as the depreciation method where depreciation is very small early in the life of the asset and increases throughout the life of the asset.

Some firms use only **productive assets** in their investment base. Under this method, assets not currently committed to productive use are excluded from the investment base. Assets such as idle plants, land held for possible plant expansion or for speculative purposes, and obsolete inventories are examples of nonproductive assets. If any assets are removed from the base, earnings related to them should be excluded from the net income. This definition of the investment base is not particularly useful. If the firm has nonproductive resources, it has capital invested that is not earning a satisfactory return. The mere existence of idle resources implies that management may not be using its resources wisely; exclusion of these assets from the investment base may serve as a disguise.

Any return on investment calculation that uses historical cost to measure the investment base may be overstating the return in a period of inflation. As the asset base increases in value because of a change in the price level, the company may be misled about the rate of return being achieved. As an example, assume that Stagnation, Inc. has reported assets of \$100,000 and income of \$20,000 in its most recent financial statements. The return on investment, based upon depreciated cost, is 20% (\$20,000 ÷ \$100,000).

Let's assume that since the assets were acquired, their replacement cost has doubled, primarily because of an increase in construction costs. A more meaningful rate of return can be found by restating the value of the assets on the statement of financial position and the depreciation expense on the income statement to reflect their current replacement costs. The following comparison shows return on investment for assets at original cost and at replacement cost.

	Original Cost		*Replacement Cost*	
Assets	$100,000		$200,000	
Operating income	$ 30,000		$ 30,000	
Depreciation	10,000		20,000	
Net income	$ 20,000		$ 10,000	
Return on investment	$\left(\frac{\$20{,}000}{\$100{,}000}\right)$	= 20%	$\left(\frac{\$10{,}000}{\$200{,}000}\right)$	= 5%

To the management of Stagnation, Inc. it appears that a satisfactory rate of return on investment of 20% is being earned. In reality, the return is only 5% when replacement costs are considered. If the replacement costs had been higher than $200,000 and if accelerated depreciation had been used, the company could show a loss when replacement costs are used.

The rates of return among divisions within the same company may not be comparable if their asset bases were acquired at different times. The carrying costs of recently acquired assets will be relatively close to replacement costs, whereas the carrying costs of old assets may be substantially different. For a proper comparison of two different divisions it may be necessary to restate each unit's assets and depreciation expenses at current replacement costs.

In many companies with decentralized divisions, the home office will centralize some corporate activities, such as cash management or billing and collection of receivables. In cases where corporate assets are pooled or where assets are shared among divisions, the common, or jointly-shared, assets must be allocated to the benefiting divisions for the proper measurement of their individual investments. Difficulty in indentification of assets with separate divisions may indicate that the responsibility center should be identified as a cost or profit center rather than an investment center.

The most commonly apportioned assets include cash, receivables, and inventories.

Cash. To provide better control and use of this resource, cash is often managed by the central office. Only the cash balance necessary to cover local transactions should be allocated to a particular division. As a result, many divisions will include a smaller amount of cash in their asset base than would be necessary if they were truly separate businesses.

Receivables. Where the division maintains its own receivables, there is no need for allocation. The investment base would simply include the ending balances of accounts receivable held by that division. Where receivables are maintained by the central office, the allocation is often based upon receivables turnover. The investment base would include the amount of receivables generated by the firm's credit and collection policies applied to the division's sales.

Inventories. Inventories are usually maintained and controlled by the individual division. Where this is the case, there is no need for apportionment. If the inventories and their levels are centrally controlled, they can be apportioned by applying an inventory turnover to actual sales volume or material consumption.

Performance Assessment through Return on Investment Analysis

Return on investment analysis can be used to provide information about specific aspects of a manager's decisions. Separation of the overall rate of return into profit margin and investment turnover allows a manager to see the overall effects of his decisions. To illustrate this point, let's assume a corporation has three independent divisions and that top management's overall goal is a total return on investment of 24%. This goal is illustrated in graphic form in Exhibit 15-1. The vertical scale measures investment turnover (Sales ÷ Investment). Profit margin (Net income ÷ Sales) is shown on the horizontal scale. The desired rate of 24% may be attained by any combination of investment turnover and profit margin shown on the curve. For example, a 24% return could be achieved with an investment turnover of twelve and a profit margin of 2%; it could also be obtained with an investment turnover of six and a profit margin of 4%.

Actual rates of return on investment for the three divisions are shown on Exhibit 15-1. Division A shows a rate of return of 36%. The investment turnover is six times per year and the profit margin is 6%. Division A achieved results above the desired rate.

The manager of Division B did not achieve the desired rate of return. He obtained an 18% return with an investment turnover of two and a profit margin of 9%. On the surface, the 9% margin seems satisfactory, but the turnover seems low. If the investment turnover had been increased to three, the division would have earned a satisfactory rate of return of 27%. The low

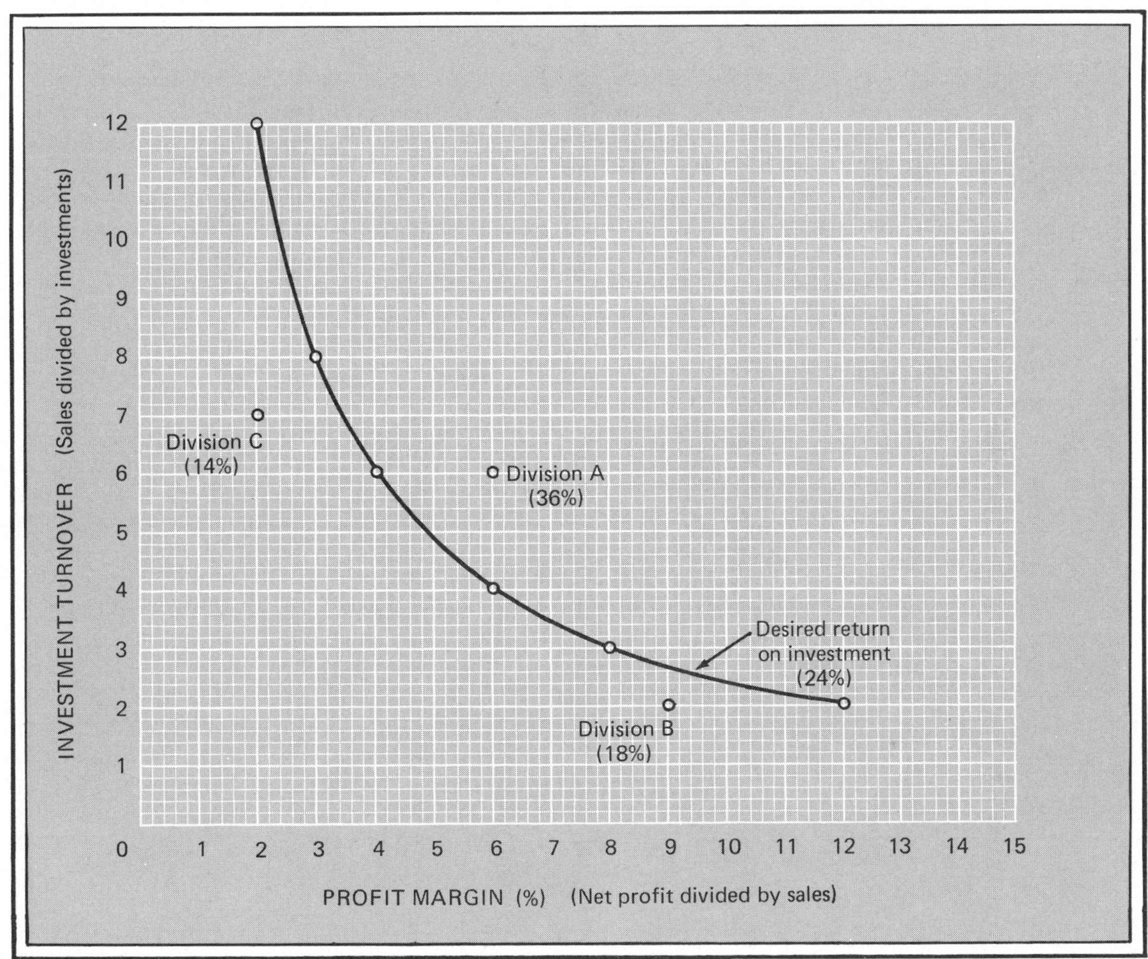

EXHIBIT 15-1
Divisional performance assessment through return on investment analysis

turnover indicates that the manager did not properly utilize his assets relative to sales. He should begin his assessment by studying his asset structure to see if nonproductive assets are excessive. Perhaps he has excess inventory, idle cash, or unused plant capacity. It is also possible that he has misinterpreted the demand for the product or has not actively pursued additional sales.

Division C's 14% rate of return also did not achieve the desired rate. The investment turnover of seven seems to be adequate, indicating good utilization of the assets. The profit margin of 2% seems low, however. It could perhaps be improved by a study of the cost structure; a low profit margin may be indicative of poor cost control. The manager should assess the production facilities in an attempt to lower manufacturing costs, and he should test other costs, particularly those such as advertising, to ensure that they are being incurred wisely.

This type of anaysis is useful in directing the manager's attention toward broad areas for improvement, but it does not determine what should be done. The ability to interpret the profit margin and investment turnover will depend upon the specific business or industry involved. For example, a retail grocery store typically has a low profit margin and a high investment turnover. A steel mill, on the other hand, would have a relatively high profit margin and, with a heavy investment in plant and equipment, a relatively low investment turnover. The manager must relate rate of return analysis to the specific situation.

Overemphasis upon Return on Investment Analysis

There is no question that the rate of return on investment is a valuable measure of *overall firm or divisional performance.* It relates the resources to their utilization better than any other single measure. It also allows the comparison of one firm with another, or one division with another. If a given firm consistently earns a rate of return of 5% while another firm earns 25%, we would expect investors to prefer the firm with a 25% return. In the long run, capital investment will flow away from firms with low rates of return toward those with higher return rates.

There are many advantages in using investment centers and return on investment to measure performance. First, return on investment is a generally accepted measure of overall performance. As a measure of divisional performance, it is compatible with firm-wide rate of return analysis. In addition, it corresponds to the intuitive view that investments are made with the goal of achieving a desired rate of return.

Second, return on investment analysis, since it is a ratio, provides a common denominator allowing comparisons of different activities. Retailing activities can be compared with wholesaling activities, steel companies can be compared with fabrication companies, and one company can be compared with other companies in the same industry.

Third, rate of return can be easily understood and interpreted. Managers can understand and accept it as a valid indicator of their performance.

Finally, return on investment analysis can provide a solid incentive for optimal utilization of the firm's assets. It encourages managers to obtain assets that will provide a satisfactory return on investment and to dispose of assets that are not providing an acceptable return. In this sense, the return on investment analysis of divisions corresponds and integrates well with the way long-range capital investment decisions are made.

It would be simplistic, however, to assume that return on investment is always the best method of measuring performance. Its limitations must be considered. First, many subjective judgments contribute to a measurement of the investment base. In most firms there must be some allocation of the centrally controlled assets; any apportionment is subject to arbitrary interpretation.

Second, the rate of return represents a single control point that can be manipulated by the manager. Earlier we pointed out that one way to increase the rate of return is to make no new capital investments. Because book values decline due to depreciation, the investment base will continually decrease in value, causing the rate of return to increase. This effect could lead to a situation where the manager's favorable performance assessment is jeopardizing the long-range profit potential of the firm.

A third shortcoming of overemphasis upon divisional rate of return in evaluating performance is that it can distort the overall allocation of firm resources. To illustrate, let's assume that a firm is currently earning an overall rate of return of 15%, but that Division A is earning a net income of $20,000 on capital investments of $100,000. Division A's 20% return ($20,000 ÷ $100,000) exceeds the 15% corporate rate of return. Assume that the manager of Division A has the opportunity to purchase a new asset that would earn $1,800 on an investment of $10,000. The firm has the needed $10,000 to purchase the asset. Investment in the new asset would yield an 18% return on investment ($1,800 ÷ $10,000), which is greater than the overall company return of 15%. However, if the new project is undertaken by Division A, its rate of return will fall to 19.8% ($21,800 ÷ $110,000). Further assume that the next best alternative use of the $10,000 is a project desired by Division C, whose operations are currently earning only 10%. If Division C can earn 14% on the new investment, it will increase its rate of return but reduce the overall corporate rate of return. Thus, what is good for Division C will be bad for the company as a whole, and what is bad for Division A will be good for the company as a whole. For reasons shown in this example, many firms use a firm-wide capital investment committee to oversee major investments.

RESIDUAL INCOME

As an alternative to the rate of return, General Electric Company developed the concept of residual income to measure divisional performance. **Residual income** is the incremental income of a division after deducting an interest charge based upon the value of the division's investment in assets. The company's weighted average cost of capital is usually used as a measure of the interest charges. For example, assume Division S has a budgeted net income of $100,000 this year, with a budgeted investment of $500,000. The weighted average cost of capital for the corporation is 15%. The income objective for the division, in terms of residual income, is:

Divisional income	$100,000
Cost of capital used by division (15% × $500,000)	75,000
Residual income of Division S	$ 25,000

A principal advantage of residual income is that it encourages capital investment any time the manager can exceed the firm's cost of capital. Any new investment will increase the division's residual income if it yields an income higher than the cutoff (required) percentage. A second advantage is that it allows different rates of return for different assets. For example, a manager can use a different cost of capital for risky projects than for stable, relatively certain projects. In this way the performance measure can be made consistent with the decision rules employed in capital investment decisions.

Residual income as a performance measure overcomes some of the shortcomings of return on investment analysis. It is not a perfect measure, however. Most of the problems in measuring divisional income and divisional investment discussed earlier in this chapter are present in the measurement of residual income. There is an additional problem of deriving a fair and equitable measure of cost of capital. (Calculation of the weighted average cost of capital was discussed in Chapter 8.)

Setting a residual income target is a unique challenge. The target must be set in dollars. The division manager is then evaluated by his success in meeting or bettering the target. Exhibit 15-2 shows why residual income may be a better measure of divisional performance than return on investment. As the capital investment increases, the divisional income curve first increases at a rate reflecting an increasing return on investment, then slows to a constant rate of return, and, finally, flattens out to reflect a declining rate of return. The cost of capital, line K, and three different rates of return, lines R_1, R_2, and R_3, are shown as straight lines. Residual income is the dark area between divisional income and cost of capital. Residual income peaks at point E_2 and remains fairly constant between points E_2 and E_3.

A division manager could earn an equal or larger rate of return at any investment level between I_1 and I_2 than at any other level of investment, although this higher rate of return would not result in higher income for his division. In this illustration the highest rate of return (R_1) can be achieved at only investment level I_1. Yet, a higher level of divisional income and residual income can be achieved with the larger investment level at I_2. In this case the target residual income should be set between points E_2 and E_3, even though the rate of return is lower. It is only within this range that the residual income available to cover home office expenses and profits is highest.

INTRAFIRM TRANSFER PRICING

Divisional income as a control measure is based upon the view that the divisions operate much like independent companies. It is assumed that a division buys its resources in one market and sells its products or services in another. Yet products and services are often exchanged between divisions. For this practice it is necessary to establish a **transfer price,** the price at which goods and services are transferred among divisions. *Any price* can be a transfer price, whether based upon a price that would exist in an independent market, the cost to the producing division, or an arbitrarily established price.

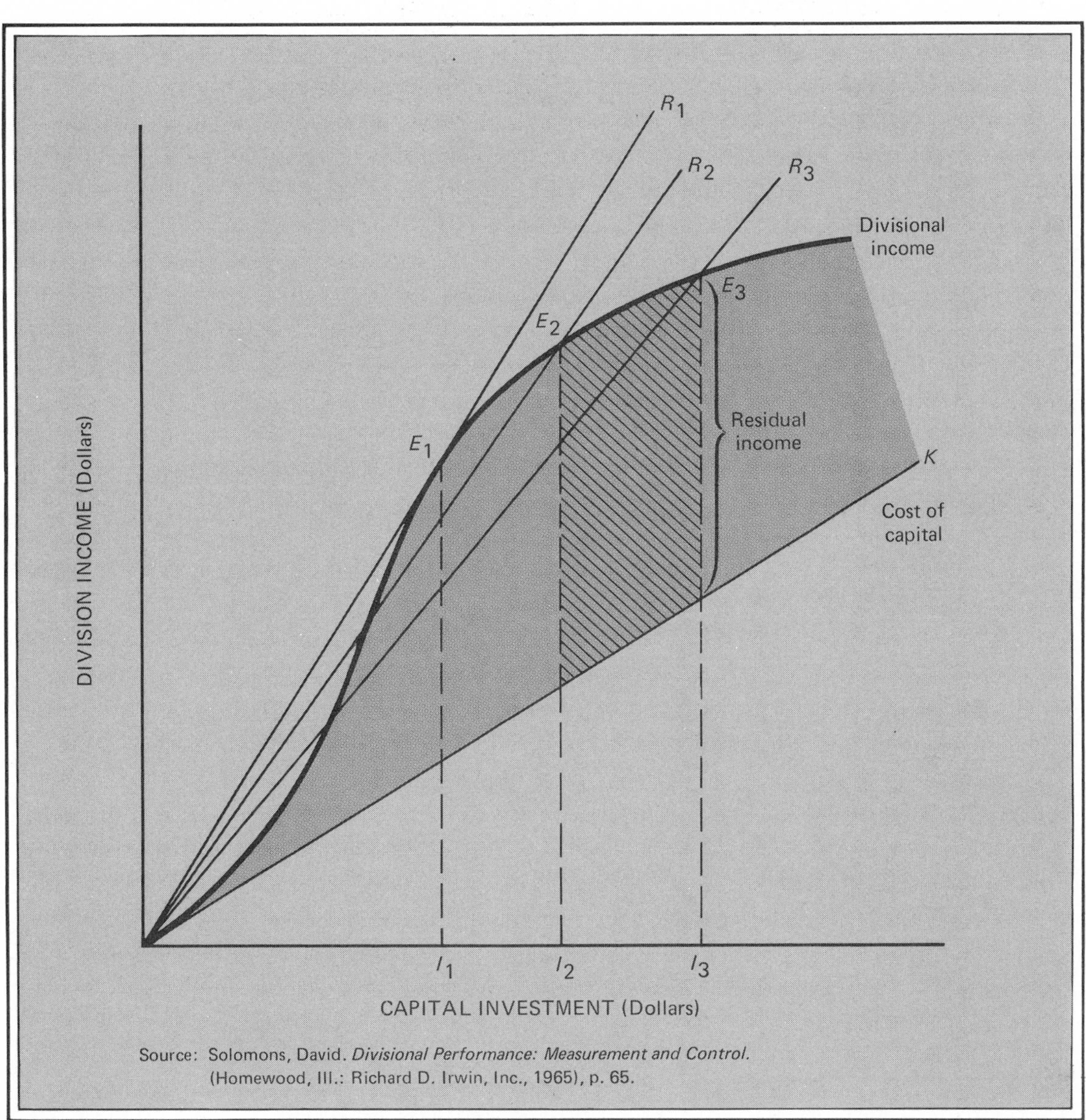

Source: Solomons, David. *Divisional Performance: Measurement and Control.* (Homewood, Ill.: Richard D. Irwin, Inc., 1965), p. 65.

EXHIBIT 15-2
Residual income and return on investment

There is no simple measure of transfer price that can meet all the needs of a decentralized firm. Obviously the transfer price of goods and services between divisions has an important impact upon the income of both the selling and purchasing divisions, as well as on the differential costs used in short-range decisions. Any transfer price that is not the price a division would pay in the open marketplace results in an arbitrary allocation of income among the divisions and weakens the measurement of divisional performance. The task of management is to develop a transfer pricing system that

(1) allows a measure of performance to reflect the division's use of resources and (2) allows the optimal allocation of the firm's resources.

Where there is an intermediate market that is competitive and the divisions are independent (a division may either buy or sell externally if it is more profitable), these open-market prices provide the best transfer price. However, when corporate policy requires trading among the company's divisions, a portion of the control over resource utilization is removed from the divisions and their profit responsibility is blurred. For decentralization to work in these cases, there must be an arbitration procedure to settle any disputes regarding transfer prices and the subsequent assessment of management performance.

Transfer Pricing for Measuring Management Performance

The best transfer price for measuring management performance is one that reflects the price in an open, competitive market. Where such a market exists for the products being transferred, it provides a value for the inputs used and a value for the outputs produced. These market prices are the best measure of revenue for the selling division and of cost inputs for the buying division. A major drawback in the use of market prices is that few markets are perfectly competitive. In many instances no intermediate market exists for the products or services being transferred. One way to establish market prices is through bids from outside firms. However, unless the divisions actually purchase from these external suppliers occasionally, the bids may not be representative. If the supplier is aware that the bid is simply to establish an internal transfer price and will probably not result in an order, the quoted price may be unrealistic.

For market prices to have maximum effectiveness in management performance measurement, both the buying and selling divisions must be able to act independently. The divisions must be free to buy or sell their products in any market. If there is no intermediate market for the products or services, or if corporate policy requires interdivisional trading, negotiated market prices may be necessary. Here, a price is negotiated between the buying and selling units, often with the aid of a corporate arbitrator. Without some external market for comparison, these negotiated market prices are artificial, just as the cost-plus-fixed-markup transfer price is artificial. Too great a reliance upon arbitration tends to centralize decisions and weaken the ability to measure divisional performance.

In circumstances where there are no competitive market prices and a negotiated transfer price cannot be established, the company cannot establish profit or investment centers. It can only use cost centers for management performance evaluation. By using standard costs as the transfer prices for cost centers, the selling divisions are encouraged to have good cost control. The manager of a selling division would be evaluated as the manager of any other cost center. His performance would be measured by the question, "How well did he control costs subsequent to the transfer?"

In responsibility accounting, a division's performance should reflect only revenues and costs subject to the control of the division. Artificial prices, such as a constant markup on cost or departmentally negotiated prices, allow divisional income to be measured and therefore give an appearance of a profit center. An artificial transfer price with an arbitrary markup does not fit the requisite of controllability. Control over revenue is not present and the divisions are not true profit centers. Therefore, artificial prices are not useful in assessing managerial performance. The measure of a specific division's performance should also be independent of performance measurements used to assess other divisions in the company. This independence is not possible if negotiated prices are used.

Transfer Prices for Decisions

The ideal transfer price for management decision making is the price that would be used by the corporation if it were not organized into divisions. Such a price would emphasize the well-being of the company as a whole, rather than of the individual divisions. For decision-making purposes, the transfer price should reflect the opportunity cost of the goods or services transferred between the divisions. An optimal allocation of resources takes place only if the goods or services are priced on transfer at the opportunity cost that would be incurred to obtain the goods or services elsewhere when they are needed. Where an intermediate market exists, the goods and services are available from external sources and the open-market price is the best measure of opportunity cost.

Where no intermediate market exists, only top management may be in a position to know the opportunity costs of a particular exchange. It may be necessary for top management to prescribe a transfer price or arbitrate in the negotiations so that decisions reflect corporate objectives and coordinate the activities of all divisions. Economic analysis has shown that a good surrogate measure of the opportunity cost for firm-wide decisions is to use the variable costs incurred by the selling division as the transfer price charged to the buying division. The use of variable costs allows each divisional manager to assess his differential costs more accurately. When used as a transfer price, standard variable costs, representing what costs should be, are preferred over actual variable costs. The selling division is thus prevented from passing inefficiencies onto the buying division.

Although economic analysis shows that the variable cost is the appropriate transfer price where no intermediate market exists, the manager of the selling division cannot be expected to accept a price as a performance measure that will produce a large loss for his division even if it is best for the firm as a whole. In fact, if variable costs are used as the transfer price, and there is no intermediate market, the manager of the selling division should be indifferent between selling to another division of the company or closing down. In either case the selling division's loss would be equal to the fixed costs of the division.

Top management support is essential in negotiations between divisions to show each division the effect of the transfer pricing policy on firm-wide profits. The transfer prices used must recognize the economic reality of the division's environment for decision making and at the same time be fair to division managers for performance evaluation.

Transfer Prices for External Reporting

Under generally accepted accounting principles, assets must be stated at cost, and revenue is not recognized until a sale is completed with an outside party. The only transfer price appropriate for external reporting is an actual cost based upon full-absorption costing. In this way the inventory is stated at the full cost required to bring the goods to the condition for resale.

When divisional financial statements are consolidated into financial statements for the firm as a whole, all interdivisional profits resulting from transfer prices must be eliminated from assets on hand. All interdivisional payables, receivables, purchases, and sales must also be eliminated.

Transfer Pricing Case

To illustrate the problems of transfer prices, let's assume that the Rex Company produces industrial chemicals. Three divisions are evaluated on the basis of their divisional income and return on investment. Division R extracts material from animal by-products. The resulting product, Product R, is sold to Division E, as well as to outside customers, for $100 per barrel. Division R has been operating at 80% of capacity and has a contribution margin ratio of 40%. Division E processes Product R into a number of other products. One of these products, Product E, is sold primarily to Division X. Product E requires $110 of variable costs, in addition to the cost of one barrel of Product R. Division E has been operating at about 60% of capacity and has a contribution margin ratio of 30%. Division X combines one unit of Product E with other ingredients in a process that incurs $100 in variable costs. The result is an industrial cleaner, Product X, which is sold to outsiders for $500 per unit. A diagram of the product flow follows.

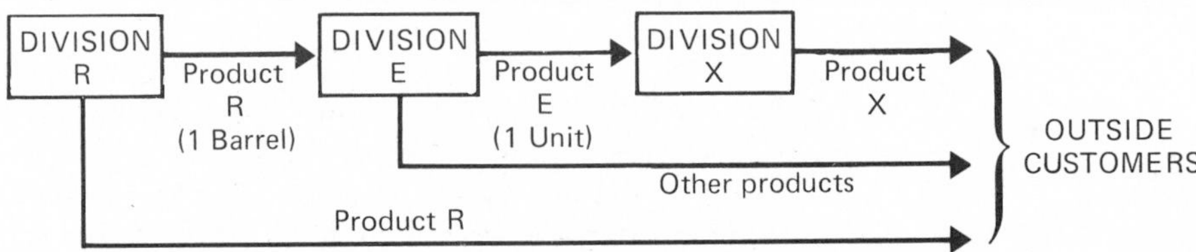

Each division buys and sells externally in addition to interdivisional transactions.

Division X's purchasing agent requested bids from Division E and two outside companies that also make Product E. The bids were $300 per unit from Division E, $250 per unit from Mohawk Chemical Company, and $270 per unit from Yucca Flats Chemical Company. Yucca Flats will purchase $80 of its materials from Division R, allowing Division R its normal contribution margin ratio. The manager of Division E refuses to match either of these competing prices and has requested that corporate top management require Division X to purchase Product E from him at the bid price of $300.

From a *decision-making standpoint,* the purchase should clearly be made internally, thus maximizing the total contribution margin of the firm. From a company-wide standpoint, the three alternatives are shown in the following tabulation.

	Buy Internally	*Buy from Mohawk*	*Buy from Yucca Flats*
Selling price of Product X	$500	$500	$500
Variable costs:			
Division R	$ 60	$ 0	$ 48
Division E	110	0	0
Division X	100	100	100
External purchase price	0	250	190*
Total variable costs	270	350	338
Contribution margin	$230	$150	$162

*Price of $270 includes $80 of material from Division R. Variable costs of this material are $48 ($80 × 60%).

If we assume that the decision is made to purchase internally, what transfer price should be used for Products R and E? No single transfer price will satisfy each division for the evaluation of its performance. Division X will object to a purchase price of $300 and insist upon a price of $250. Division E will object to a selling price of $250 and insist upon a price of $300. Any price selected will be debatable and will affect performance measures. One solution is to use different prices in the different divisions. Since each division is evaluated as a separate company, the transfer prices need not be the same. Each division could be allowed to use the transfer price determined by the best market price available. If this practice were followed, the resulting divisional contribution margins would be as shown in the following tabulation.

	Division		
	R	*E*	*X*
Selling price	$92*	$270†	$500
Materials transferred from another division	$ 0	$ 92	$250§
Divisional variable costs	60	110	100
Total variable costs	60	202	350
Divisional contribution margin	$32	$ 68	$150

*If the bid by Yucca Flats is accepted by Division X, Division R is permitted to earn a contribution margin of only $32, therefore a transfer price of $92 ($60 variable cost plus $32 contribution margin).

†The price quoted by Yucca Flats is the best measure of market price for Division E.

§Division X is in the strongest negotiating position and should have a transfer price of $250, the best market price available.

This case illustrates that the question of suitable transfer prices for the two functions of managerial performance assessment and decision optimization does not have an easy answer. The firm must give serious consideration to its goals and objectives in using transfer prices before adopting a particular measure. There are obviously many implications that permeate management's decisions and assessments.

MULTIPLE PERFORMANCE MEASURES

Throughout the entire text we have stressed financially quantifiable data for judging the effectiveness of management decision making. Financial measures such as the rate of return on investment are valid and useful, but they are not the only suitable measures. Many nonfinancial measures are also valuable.

When a method of assessment emphasizes a small number of financial measures to the exclusion of others, the system can be more easily manipulated. This is true even though the measure is inherently valid. There is no question that rate of return on investment and net income for the period, as examples, are valid measures of performance. However, reliance upon a single control tool can distort the decision-making process. The manager who maximized his rate of return by delaying potentially profitable capital investment is an example.

Many firms prefer multiple goals and multiple performance measures, both financial and nonfinancial. General Electric Company is an example of a firm that has developed a series of multiple goals for assessing management performance. Goals are stated for each of the following areas.

1. Profitability
2. Market position
3. Productivity
4. Product leadership
5. Personnel development
6. Employee attitudes
7. Public responsibility
8. Balance between long-range and short-range goals

Three observations may be made from a close examination of these eight goals. First, the measures to assess performance are both financial and nonfinancial. Profitability and productivity may be financial measures. Employee morale and personnel development measures are certainly nonfinancial and highly subjective. The mixture of subjective and objective assessment measures taxes the measurement skill of the accountant and the evaluation skills of management.

Second, the goals are somewhat contradictory. For example, increasing profitability through increasing employee productivity may lower employee morale. Also, maintaining product leadership may call for research and development costs that lower short-range profitability. The manager should not emphasize one goal by jeopardizing another; he must seek an optimal balance.

Third, multiple goals will increase pressure upon the managers. An attempt to meet many criteria simultaneously can be frustrating and confusing. The proper balance of goals and performance measures is difficult to set. While many of the concepts presented in this text appear highly quantitative and objective, we can never overlook the fact that the setting of goals, the evaluation of actual performance, and the development of a system to measure management decisions are highly subjective. Management accounting relies upon scientific methods, but it is now and will always be an art.

SUMMARY

A widely used test of the effectiveness of management's decisions is the rate of return on investment. The return on investment is:

$$\text{Return on investment} = \frac{\text{Net income}}{\text{Investment}} = \frac{\text{Sales}}{\text{Investment}} \times \frac{\text{Net income}}{\text{Sales}}$$

where (Sales ÷ Investment = Investment turnover) and (Net income ÷ Sales = Profit margin).

While conceptually sound and easy to determine, the rate of return on investment has limitations. It focuses management's attention upon a single measure and can result in optimizing the measure rather than optimizing the decisions. For example, failure to make new capital investments will increase the rate of return and simultaneously reduce the company's long-range profit potential. The use of residual profit as a measure of divisional performance is one way of overcoming some of the shortcomings of return on investment analysis.

Where there are responsibility centers that rely upon each other for their production inputs, the problems of interdivisional transfer pricing exist. With profit centers or investment centers, a firm must develop transfer prices when the divisions exchange goods or services. There are many possible transfer prices. To obtain optimum utilization of company resources, transfer prices based upon variable costs seem best. For management performance assessment, transfer prices based upon current market prices or standard costs seem best. For external reporting purposes, transfer prices based upon full cost with no added profit margin conform to generally accepted accounting principles.

There is no single performance measure that can fulfill all management's needs. Overemphasis upon one measure, although that measure seems appropriate, can be detrimental. The best control system includes many performance measures, such as budgets, cost standards, product leadership, and technical standards; and many nonquantifiable measures, such as personnel attitudes and public responsibility. If a firm is to achieve a goal of long-run profitability and stability, it must consider *all* the relevant factors.

SUPPLEMENTARY READING

Bierman, Harold, Jr. "Pricing Intracompany Transfer." *The Accounting Review,* July, 1959.

Clayden, Roger. "A New Way to Measure and Control Divisional Performance." *Management Services,* September–October, 1970.

Dearden, J. "Interdivisional Pricing." *Harvard Business Review,* January–February, 1960.

Dearden, J. "Limits on Decentralized Profit Responsibility." *Harvard Business Review,* July–August, 1962.

Dearden, J. "The Case Against ROI Control." *Harvard Business Review,* May–June, 1969.

Fremgen, James M. "Transfer Pricing and Management Goals." *Management Accounting,* December, 1970.

Ma, Ronald. "Project Appraisal in a Decentralized Company." *Abacus,* December, 1969.

Mauriel, John J., and Robert N. Anthony. "Misevaluation of Investment Center Performance." *Harvard Business Review,* March–April, 1966.

National Association of Accountants. *Accounting for Intra-Company Transfers.* New York: National Association of Accountants, 1956.

Shillinglaw, Gordon. "Problems in Divisional Profit Measurement." *N.A.A. Bulletin,* March, 1961.

Solomons, David. *Divisional Performance: Measurement and Control.* Homewood, Ill.: Richard D. Irwin, Inc., 1965.

QUESTIONS

15-1 What does *decentralization* mean? What are its advantages and disadvantages?

15-2 What are some of the disadvantages of using division profit as the measure of performance?

15-3 What are the weaknesses of using *book value* as a measure of investment in calculating return on investment? How can these weaknesses be overcome?

15-4 "The rate of return on investment is the best measure of overall firm performance." Do you agree? Explain.

15-5 "One of the more difficult tasks in return on investment analysis is the evaluation of profit." Explain. What are some of the problems of measuring profit for this purpose?

15-6 Explain the concepts:

Current replacement cost of assets as a measure of investment
Productive assets as an investment base
Gross book value as an investment base

15-7 What are the two components of return on investment? Explain how they interact.

15-8 Relate the concept of responsibility accounting to the evaluation of responsibility centers.

15-9 The development of a profit center requires four conditions, or assumptions, on the part of the firm. List and explain why each is necessary to a profit center.

15-10 "The investment center provides greater control than a profit center." Explain.

15-11 Explain how the following centrally controlled assets may be allocated to investment center divisions.

Cash
Accounts receivable
Inventories

15-12 Define *residual income*. What are the advantages of using residual income for performance evaluation? The disadvantages?

15-13 What is a *transfer price?* Under what conditions are transfer prices necessary?

15-14 If a market-based transfer price can be determined, why is it usually considered the best transfer price to use?

15-15 What is the best transfer price to be used for evaluating divisional performance? Explain.

15-16 What is the best transfer price to be used for decisions such as output levels and product pricing? Explain.

15-17 If cost is used as a transfer price for a service center such as maintenance, why is standard cost usually considered better than actual cost?

PROBLEMS

15-18 Match the following terms and definitions.

1. Division
2. Return on investment
3. Profit margin
4. Investment turnover
5. Sinking fund method of depreciation
6. Residual income
7. Replacement cost
8. Transfer price
9. Investment center
10. Historical cost

a. Allocation of cost of asset over its life through increasing charges to income.
b. Division contribution less an interest charge for cost of capital.
c. Consideration actually given for an asset.
d. Net income divided by investment.
e. Sales divided by investment.
f. Net income divided by sales.
g. Interdivisional sales price.
h. Another name for decentralized investment center.
i. Consideration that would be given to purchase an asset now.
j. Responsibility center with control over resources as well as revenues and costs.

15-19 Individuals at several levels in the organizational structure of a firm are listed below. Match the reporting concept on the right with the appropriate individual. A particular concept may apply to more than one individual.

1. Stockholder
2. Member of board of directors
3. President
4. Vice-president (marketing or manufacturing)
5. Factory manager or marketing product manager
6. Factory department foreman
7. Group leader
8. Worker or salesperson

a. Primary information for planning and control is financial.
b. Primary information for planning and control is nonfinancial.
c. Information must meet externally imposed requirements.
d. If a good control system is present, user is more concerned with planning information.
e. Practices management by exception in use of information.
f. Time frame is very short, perhaps daily or hourly.
g. Receives no formal reports from accounting system.
h. Receives monthly reports and additional reports for shorter periods on an exception basis.
i. Receives only historical information and the most general projections.
j. All planning and control information may be received orally.

15-20 In the following four cases, determine the amounts where (?) appears.

	A	*B*	*C*	*D*
Net income	$100	$?	$?	$ 600
Cost of capital	$ 40	$?	$ 540	$ 300
Sales	$400	$1000	$ 900	$?
Investment base	$200	$?	$2700	$1500
Profit margin	?%	20%	$33\frac{1}{3}$%	?%
Investment turnover	? time(s)	1 time	? time(s)	4 times
Return on investment	?%	?%	11%	?%
Residual income	$?	$ 0	$?	$ 300

15-21 Two divisions of the Decentralized Company, Inc. are attempting to establish a transfer price for intercompany transfers. Selling division provided the following data.

Income Statement	
Sales	$100,000
Variable costs	30,000
Fixed costs	60,000
Net income	$ 10,000

Units	
Capacity in units	15,000
Units produced	10,000
Units sold to buying division	6,000
Units sold to others	4,000
	10,000

Buying division is expanding production to a level that will require 12,000 units. An outside company has offered to provide the units at $9 each. Buying division asked selling division for a price quote.

REQUIRED:

A. What price should selling division charge to achieve the same amount of net income?

B. What price should selling division charge to maintain a 10% rate of profit?

C. What transfer price should be used in evaluating the performance of buying division? Selling division?

D. What transfer price should the top management of Decentralized, Inc. use in deciding whether to have selling division make the product or buy it outside?

15-22 The drilling equipment division of Biel Company has prepared the following profit plan for 19X7.

Sales	$10,000,000
Variable costs	$ 5,000,000
Fixed costs	3,000,000
Total costs	8,000,000
Income	$ 2,000,000
Assets employed by the division	$ 8,000,000

The entire company has projected a rate of return of 15%. The cost of capital for the company is 12%.

The drilling equipment division is considering the following investment in new equipment for a new product.

Cost of equipment	$200,000
Expected annual sales	$300,000
Variable costs	40% of sales
Annual fixed costs	$140,000

Other divisions have submitted proposals for new projects that will provide a return on investment of approximately 15%.

REQUIRED:

A. As manager of the drilling equipment division, would you accept or reject the proposal? Explain.

B. As president of Biel Company, would you want the division to accept or reject the proposal? Explain.

C. What would you recommend to avoid problems of this nature in the future?

15-23 The Long Fiber Products Company (LFP Company) has several divisions that produce a number of packaging products. The bag division purchases processed fibers for the production of bags from the finished fibers division of LFP Company, as well as several outside companies. In May the bag division received an order for one million bags at $10 per thousand and requested bids for finished fiber from a number of companies, as well as from the finished fibers division. Three bids were considered:

1. The finished fibers division bid will result in a materials cost of $5 per thousand bags based upon full cost. Finished fibers is operating at 65% of capacity and earning a contribution margin ratio of 40%.

2. A bid resulting in a materials cost of $4.50 per thousand bags was received from the Himalayas Company. This company will buy its raw materials from the import division of LFP Company. Raw materials account for $1.00 of the $4.50 price. The import division earns a contribution margin ratio of 50%.

3. The lowest bid, resulting in a materials cost of $4.25 per thousand, was received from the Andes Company, a completely independent company.

REQUIRED:

A. From whom should the bag division manager buy if he acts in conformity with his division's goals?

B. From whom should the bag division manager buy if he acts in conformity with corporate goals?

C. If you were the president of Long Fiber Products Company, what would you do to maximize the corporation's net income and yet maintain decentralization?

15-24 The Gold Bracelet Custom Manufacturing Company desired a return on investment of 36%. The following were actual results by sales outlet.

	Investment Turnover	*Profit Margin*
Outlet A	4 times	6%
Outlet B	9 times	5%
Outlet C	6 times	6%

REQUIRED:

A. Compute the return on investment for each outlet.

B. Illustrate graphically each outlet's return on investment and the company's desired return on investment.

C. List some possible reasons for the performance of Outlets A and B.

15-25 The Hirtal Corporation was in the process of reviewing the previous year's performance. The following information was drawn from the accounting records.

Sales	$1,500,000
Costs	$1,300,000
Investment in assets	$ 500,000

REQUIRED:

A. Compute the corporation's investment turnover, profit margin, and return on investment.

B. What other information might be helpful as an aid in evaluating the company's performance? Explain.

15-26 The Blackhawk Manufacturing Company, a decentralized producer of building materials, has a firm-wide goal of 18% return on investment and a cost of capital of 15%. The following data relate to the operating divisions.

	Income	*Investment*
Division D	$15,000	$100,000
Division E	$25,000	$125,000
Division F	$10,000	$ 40,000

REQUIRED:

A. Compute the return on investment for each division.

B. Compute the residual income for each division.

C. Rank the divisions according to performance.

15-27 The Blackhawk Manufacturing Company (from problem 15-26) is considering the purchase of a new venture that would be placed in one of the existing operating divisions. The project will have assets of $15,000 and earn $3,000 per year.

A. What will the new project do to each of the performance measures in problem 15-26?

B. If the asset is acquired, in which division should it be placed?

15-28 The Kenneth-Harley Farming Corporation produces wheat and soybeans. When the crops are harvested they are transferred from the Harley producing division to the Kenneth selling division where they are dried and stored for sale at the best price.

During 19X8, 90,000 bushels of wheat and 60,000 bushels of soybeans were produced. At the time of harvest, wheat was selling at $3 per bushel and soybeans at $4 per bushel. The entire crop was sold before the end of the fiscal year, at $4 per bushel of wheat and $7 per bushel of soybeans. At the end of fiscal year 19X8, the prices were $4.50 for wheat and $7.50 for soybeans.

The income statement for the fiscal year follows.

Sales		$780,000
Operating expenses:		
Variable production costs	$300,000	
Variable selling costs	30,000	
Fixed production costs	100,000	
Fixed selling costs	10,000	440,000
Net income		$340,000

REQUIRED:

A. The president of the corporation, Mr. Vern, wants to see how each division performed. Prepare separate income statements for each division. Explain the transfer price you used.

B. Explain how your income statements will assist in the following roles.
   1. Evaluation of performance
   2. Awarding of bonuses
   3. Decision of when to sell the grain (sell or store longer)

15-29 The Hadden Company uses rates of return on investment for performance evaluation. Other firms in the industry earn a return on assets invested of 20%. The Hadden Company earned $100,000 on sales of $800,000. Capital invested is $400,000.

REQUIRED:

A. Calculate the profit margin, investment turnover, and rate of return.

B. How does the Hadden Company compare with the industry? What inter-firm comparison problems do you see?

15-30 A. R. Oma, Inc. manufactures a line of men's perfumes and after-shaving lotions. The manufacturing process is basically a series of mixing operations with the addition of certain aromatic and coloring ingredients; the finished product is packaged in a company-produced glass bottle and packed in cases containing six bottles.

A. R. Oma feels that the sale of its product is heavily influenced by the appearance and appeal of the bottle and has, therefore, devoted considerable managerial effort to the bottle production process. This has resulted in the development of certain unique bottle production processes in which management takes considerable pride.

The two areas (perfume production and bottle manufacture) have evolved over the years in an almost independent manner; in fact, a rivalry has developed between management personnel as to which division is the more important to A. R. Oma. This attitude is probably intensified because the bottle manufacturing plant was purchased intact 10 years ago and no real interchange of management personnel or ideas (except at the top corporate level) has taken place.

Since the acquisition, all bottle production has been absorbed by the perfume manufacturing plant. Each area is considered a separate profit center and evaluated as such. As the new corporate controller you are responsible for the definition of a proper transfer value to use in crediting the bottle production profit center and in debiting the packaging profit center.

At your request, the bottle division general manager has asked certain other bottle manufacturers to quote a price for the quantity and sizes demanded by the perfume division. These competitive prices are:

Volume	*Total Price*	*Price per Case*
2,000,000 eq. cases*	$ 4,000,000	$2.00
4,000,000	$ 7,000,000	$1.75
6,000,000	$10,000,000	$1.67

*An *equivalent case* represents 6 bottles each.

A cost analysis of the internal bottle plant indicates that it can produce bottles at the following costs.

Volume	*Total Price*	*Cost per Case*
2,000,000 eq. cases	$3,200,000	$1.60
4,000,000	$5,200,000	$1.30
6,000,000	$7,200,000	$1.20

(Your cost analysts point out that these costs represent fixed costs of $1,200,000 and variable costs of $1 per equivalent case.)

These figures have given rise to considerable corporate discussion as to the proper value to use in the transfer of bottles to the perfume division. This interest is heightened because a significant portion of a division manager's income is an incentive bonus based on profit center results.

The perfume production division has the following costs in addition to the bottle costs.

Volume	*Total Cost*	*Cost per Case*
2,000,000 cases	$16,400,000	$8.20
4,000,000	$32,400,000	$8.10
6,000,000	$48,400,000	$8.07

After considerable analysis, the marketing research department has furnished you with the following price-demand relationship for the finished product.

Sales Volume	*Total Sales Revenue*	*Sales Price per Case*
2,000,000 cases	$25,000,000	$12.50
4,000,000	$45,600,000	$11.40
6,000,000	$63,900,000	$10.65

REQUIRED:

A. The A. R. Oma Company has used market-price transfer prices in the past. Using the current market prices and costs, and assuming a volume of 6,000,000 cases, calculate the income for the bottle division, the perfume division, and the corporation.

B. Is this production and sales level the most profitable volume for the bottle division? The perfume division? The corporation? Explain your answer.

C. The A. R. Oma Company uses the profit center concept for divisional operation.

1. Define *profit center.*

2. What conditions should exist for a profit center to be established?

3. Should the two divisions of the A. R. Oma Company be organized as profit centers? *(CMA adapted)*

15-31 Two identical small companies, A and B, manufacture cleaning compounds under identical franchises from a larger company. Their franchises give each an exclusive right to sell anywhere within 300 miles of its factory and require each to show substantial increases in sales until a volume is reached that indicates satisfactory cultivation of its entire franchised territory. Each has 10 salesmen, and each president estimates that 100 salesmen would provide optimal coverage (measured by return on investment) of his allotted territory.

At the beginning of year 2 each company had $10,000 cash available for investment. The companies considered various methods of utilizing the $10,000 available cash to improve their operations. Each company adopted a different plan.

Company A

The president of Company A investigated his costs of raw materials and discovered that his company bought liquid raw materials in carload lots. He estimated a prospective saving of $8,000 per year on raw materials costs if such liquids were purchased in tank cars instead of boxcars, and that an investment of $10,000 would be needed in underground storage tanks to make use of tank cars feasible.

Company A acquired the storage tanks. Liquid raw materials were purchased in tank cars and the predicted $8,000 annual saving on purchased raw materials was realized in all subsequent years.

Company B

Company B, on the other hand, decided to expand its sales force. The $10,000 cash available at the beginning of year 2 would be used during the year to recruit and train five additional salesmen. Since the entire $10,000 would be written off as an expense in year 2, the after-tax profits would be reduced by $5,000. However, in year 3 and subsequent years, this 50% increase in salesmen would increase sales by 50%, and annual sales could be expected to go to $300,000. Furthermore, since breakeven volume was $100,000 and the company made a $10,000 profit on $200,000 sales, it could be expected to make a $20,000 profit on $300,000 sales. This would defend its territorial rights under its franchise.

The results for both companies are condensed in the following schedule.

	Year 1		Year 2		Year 3	
	A	*B*	*A*	*B*	*A*	*B*
Sales	$200,000	$200,000	$200,000	$200,000	$200,000	$300,000
Net income						
Before taxes	$ 20,000	$ 20,000	$ 27,000*	$ 10,000†	$ 27,000	$ 40,000
After taxes	$ 10,000	$ 10,000	$ 13,500	$ 5,000	$ 13,500	$ 20,000
Total assets	$ 50,000	$ 50,000	$ 59,000	$ 50,000	$ 58,000	$ 50,000
Return on investment	20.0%	20.0%	22.9%	10.0%	23.2%	40.0%
Cash flow (to be paid in dividends)			$ 14,500	$ 15,000	$ 14,500	$ 20,000

Calculation of figures:

*Net income of A in year 1	$20,000
Add: Reduction in raw materials costs	8,000
	$28,000
Deduct: Depreciation, 10% of $10,000	1,000
Net income of A in year 2	$27,000
†Net income of B in year 1	$20,000
Deduct: Expense of training salesmen	10,000
Net income of B in year 2	$10,000

(Training expenses entirely written off in year 2)

REQUIRED:
Is the return on investment a good measure of the relative performance of Companies A and B in year 2 and 3? Discuss fully. *(Canada SIA adapted)*

15-32 The Woolley Company has several divisions that have interdivisional sales of components. The company is fully decentralized. Individual divisions may purchase or sell in any market consistent with the division's goals. The electronics division purchases most of its wire from the metal products division. The two divisions are in the process of negotiating the price for the wire the electronics division will purchase next quarter. The following information was accumulated for the decision.

1. Costs of metal products division (per spool for 6,000 spools, 60% of capacity):

Material	$ 80
Direct labor	20
Variable factory overhead	20
Fixed factory overhead	40
Fixed selling and administration costs	20
Fixed central corporate costs	4
	$184

2. The metal products division has a net income objective of 8% of sales. Pricing has been consistent with this rule.

3. The current market price for the wire has dropped to $150 per spool.

REQUIRED:

A. Determine the selling price that would allow the metal products division to achieve its income objective.

B. What price should the electronics division offer to pay for wire to maximize its income?

C. What is the minimum price the metal products division could charge and be no worse off than if the electronics division purchased from the outside?

D. What price should top corporate management use in evaluating whether to have the wire made by the metal products division or purchase it from the outside?

15-33 A common measure of a manager's performance is return on net worth. This is a particularly important measure from the shareholder's point of view. This ratio can be expressed as the product of three other ratios as shown below:

$$\frac{\text{Return on}}{\text{net worth}} = \frac{\text{Net income}}{\text{Net worth}} = \underset{1}{\frac{\text{Net income}}{\text{Sales}}} \times \underset{2}{\frac{\text{Sales}}{\text{Assets}}} \times \underset{3}{\frac{\text{Assets}}{\text{Net worth}}}$$

REQUIRED:

A. Discuss the return on net worth as a management goal and as a measurement of management performance.

B. What management activities are measured by each of the ratios 1, 2, and 3?

C. Would separation of the return on net worth into the three ratios and use of these ratios for planning targets and performance measures result in goal congruence (or improvement toward goal congruence) among the responsible managers? Explain your answer.

(CMA adapted)

15-34 George Johnson was hired on July 1, 1969, as assistant general manager of the Botel Division of Staple, Inc. It was understood that he would be elevated to general manager of the division on January 1, 1971, when the current general manager retired; this was duly done. In addition to becoming acquainted with the division and the general manager's duties, Mr. Johnson was specifically charged with the responsibility for development of the 1970 and 1971 budgets. As general manager in 1971, he was, obviously, responsible for the 1972 budget.

The Staple Company is a multiproduct company that is highly decentralized. Each division is quite autonomous. The corporation staff approves division-prepared operating budgets but seldom makes major changes in them. The corporate staff actively participates in decisions requiring capital investment (for expansion or replacement) and makes the final decisions. The division management is responsible for implementing the capital program. The major method used by the Staple Corporation to measure division performance is contribution return on division net investment. The budgets that follow were approved by the corporation. Revision of the 1972 budget is not considered necessary, even though 1971 actual departed from the approved 1971 budget.

BOTEL DIVISION (000 Omitted)

Accounts	**Actual**			**Budget**	
	1969	*1970*	*1971*	*1971*	*1972*
Sales	$1,000	$1,500	$1,800	$2,000	$2,400
Less division variable costs:					
Material and labor	$ 250	$ 375	$ 450	$ 500	$ 600
Repairs	50	75	50	100	120
Supplies	20	30	36	40	48
Less division managed costs:					
Employee training	30	35	25	40	45
Maintenance	50	55	40	60	70
Less division committed costs:					
Depreciation	120	160	160	200	200
Rent	80	100	110	140	140
Total	600	830	871	1,080	1,223
Division net contribution	$ 400	$ 670	$ 929	$ 920	$1,177
Division investment:					
Accounts receivable	$ 100	$ 150	$ 180	$ 200	$ 240
Inventory	200	300	270	400	480
Fixed assets	1,590	2,565	2,800	3,380	4,000
Less: Accounts and wages payable	(150)	(225)	(350)	(300)	(360)
Net investment	$1,740	$2,790	$2,900	$3,680	$4,360
Contribution return on net investment	23%	24%	32%	25%	27%

REQUIRED:

A. Identify Mr. Johnson's responsibilities under the management and measurement program previously described.

B. Appraise the performance of Mr. Johnson in 1971.

C. Recommend to the president any changes in the responsibilities assigned to managers or in the measurement methods used to evaluate division management based upon your analysis. *(CMA adapted)*

15-35 Birch Paper Company*

"If I were to price these boxes any lower than $480 a thousand," said James Brunner, manager of Birch Paper Company's Thompson division, "I'd be countermanding my order of last month for our salesmen to stop shaving their bids and to bid full-cost quotations. I've been trying for weeks to improve the quality of our business, and if I turn around now and accept this job at $430 or $450 or something less than $480, I'll be tearing down this program I've been working so hard to build up. The division can't very well show a profit by putting in bids that don't even cover a fair share of overhead costs, let alone give us a profit."

Birch Paper Company was a medium-size, partly integrated paper company, producing white and kraft papers and paperboard. A portion of its paperboard output was converted into corrugated boxes by the Thompson division, which also printed and colored the outside surface of the boxes. Including Thompson, the company had four producing divisions and a timberland division, which supplied part of the company's pulp requirements.

For several years, each division had been judged independently on the basis of its profit and return on investment. Top management had been working to gain effective results from a policy of decentralizing responsibility and authority for all decisions except those relating to overall company policy. The company's top officials believed that in the past few years the concept of decentralization had been successfully applied and that the company's profits and competitive position had definitely improved.

Early in 1957, the Northern division designed a special display box for one of its papers in conjunction with the Thompson division, which was equipped to make the box. Thompson's staff for package design and development spent several months perfecting the design, production methods, and materials to be used. Because of the unusual color and shape, these were far from standard. According to an agreement between the two divisions, the Thompson division was reimbursed by the Northern division for the cost of its design and development work.

When all the specifications were prepared, the Northern division asked for bids on the box from the Thompson division and from two outside companies. Each division manager was normally free to buy from whatever supplier he wished; and even on sales within the company, divisions were expected to meet the going market price if they wanted the business.

In 1957, the profit margins of converters such as the Thompson division were being squeezed. Thompson, as did many other similar converters, bought its paperboard, and its function was to print, cut, and shape it into boxes. Though it bought most of its materials from other Birch divisions, most of Thompson's sales were made to outside customers. If Thompson got the order from Northern, it probably would buy its linerboard and corrugating medium from the Southern division of Birch. The walls of a corrugated box consist of outside and inside sheets of linerboard sandwiching the fluted corrugating medium. About 70 percent of Thompson's out-of-pocket cost of $400 for the order represented the cost of linerboard and corrugating medium. Though Southern had been running below capacity and had excess inventory, it quoted the market price, which had not noticeably weakened as a result of the oversupply. Its out-of-pocket costs on both liner and corrugating medium were about 60 percent of the selling price.

The Northern division received bids on the boxes of $480 a thousand from the Thompson division, $430 a thousand from West Paper Company, and $432 a thousand from Eire Papers, Ltd. Eire Papers offered to buy from Birch the outside linerboard with the special printing already on it, but would supply its own inside liner and corrugating medium. The outside liner would be supplied by the Southern division at a price equivalent of $90 a thousand boxes, and it would be printed for $30 a thousand by the Thompson division. Of the $30, about $25 would be out-of-pocket costs.

Since this situation appeared to be a little unusual, William Kenton, manager of the Northern division, discussed the wide discrepancy of bids with Birch's commercial vice-president. He told the vice-president: "We sell in a very competitive market, where higher costs cannot be passed on. How can we be expected to show a decent profit and return on investment if we have to buy our supplies at more than 10 percent over the going market?"

Knowing that Mr. Brunner had on occasion in the past few months been unable to operate the Thompson division at capacity, it seemed odd to the vice-president that Mr. Brunner would add the full 20 percent overhead and profit charge to his out-of-pocket costs. When asked about this, Mr. Brunner's answer was the statement that appears at the beginning of the case. He went on to say that having done the developmental work on the box, and having received no profit on that, he felt entitled to a good markup on the production of the box itself.

The vice-president explored further the cost structures of the various divisions. He remembered a comment that the controller had made at a meeting the week before to the effect that costs which were variable for one division could be largely fixed for the company as a whole. He knew that in the absence of specific orders from top management Mr. Kenton would accept the lowest bid, which was that of the West Paper Company for $430. However, it would be possible for top management to order the acceptance of another bid if the situation warranted such action. And though the volume represented by the transactions in question was less than 5 percent of the volume of any of the divisions involved, other transactions could conceivably raise similar problems later.

Questions

1. In the controversy described, how, if at all, is the transfer price system dysfunctional?
2. Describe other types of decisions in the Birch Paper Company in which the transfer price system would be dysfunctional.

Glossary

A

Absorption Costing A system of measuring inventory costs that assigns a fair share of production costs of material, labor, variable factory overhead, and fixed factory overhead to the product. Nonproduction costs are treated as period costs. Also called *Full Costing.*

Accountability (A) The responsibility of management to protect and increase the assets of the firm for the stockholders. (B) The assignment of delegated duties to individual managers for the development of responsibility accounting.

Accounting Method (see *Unadjusted Rate of Return.*)

Accounts Receivable Turnover Credit sales divided by average balance of accounts receivable.

Activity Accounting Recording data by a specific organizational segment; (See *Responsibility Accounting.*)

Activity Base A measure of an operating activity within a department, division, plant, or company; used to allocate indirect costs.

Activity Variance A measure of the ability of the firm to meet budgeted sales volume; the difference between the period's planned activity in the master budget and the actual volume attained. The variance may be measured in number of units or in dollars of contribution margin.

Actual Costs (A) Historical costs measured by their cash equivalent value on an after-the-fact, arms-length transaction basis. Also called *Incurred Costs* and *Historical Costs.* (B) Costs measured by consideration given to acquire the resource.

Adjusted Rate of Return The rate of return on a long-term project computed by adjusting cash flows for the time value of money. Also called *Discounted Rate of Return.*

Administrative Costs Costs that are not directly associated with production, selling, or distribution.

Allocation The process of distributing or apportioning costs or revenues to products, departments, divisions, or other organization units on the basis of benefits received or resources used.

Annuity A series of equal payments or receipts to be paid or received at the end of successive periods of equal time.

Appropriation An expenditure authorization with specific limits as to amount, purpose, or time period.

Asset Turnover Sales divided by total assets available.

Assets The resources currently available to a firm for the benefit of future activities.

Attained Volume The level of production or sales activity actually reached during the accounting period. Also called *Actual Volume.*

Attention Directing The accountant's task of supplying information that focuses upon those activities of a firm needing corrective action.

Attest Function The action of the independent CPA who audits the financial records of a firm to reduce uncertainty regarding the accuracy and fairness of reported financial statements.

Average Cost Fixed costs plus variable costs divided by the units produced.

Average Cost Pricing (See *Cost-based Pricing.*)

Average Costing (See *Weighted Average Costing.*)

Average Revenue Total revenue earned in a particular accounting period divided by the total units sold during the period.

Avoidable Costs Costs that would not be incurred if a particular activity were discontinued.

B

Balance Sheet A formal statement of the resources of a firm and their sources at a particular point in time. Also called *Statement of Financial Position.*

Behavioral Accounting An area of accounting that studies the interactions among individuals, organizations, and the accounting process.

Benefit-Cost Analysis An evaluation of the relationship between the benefits and the costs of a particular project.

Bill of Materials A statement of the quantity of raw materials allowed for manufacturing a specific quantity of units.

Blanket Overhead Rate A method of apportioning factory overhead to work in process that uses only one rate for the entire factory.

Book Value The carrying value of a resource measured at cost less accumulated depreciation.

Book Value Method (See *Unadjusted Rate of Return.*)

Breakeven Graph A graphic presentation of cost-volume-profit relationships over the relevant range with special emphasis upon the point at which total costs equal total revenue.

Breakeven Point The activity level where total sales equal total costs. Graphically the breakeven point is where the sales line intersects the total cost line.

Budget An integrated plan of action expressed in financial terms.

Budget Variance The difference between actual costs incurred and the flexible budget adjusted to actual activity level.

Budgeted Capacity (See *Expected Capacity.*)

Budgeted Costs Future costs (predictions, estimates, forecasts) that are formally combined into an integrated plan of action.

C

Capacity Costs (A) Another term for fixed costs. (B) Costs necessary to provide organization and operating facilities to produce and sell at the budgeted volume level.

Capacity Decisions (See *Long-range Decisions.*)

Capacity Variance A variance computed in an absorption costing system showing the overapplication or underapplication of fixed manufacturing costs to products. It is measured as the difference between planned fixed manufacturing costs and applied fixed manufacturing costs. Also called *Volume Variance or Fixed Factory Overhead Volume Variance.*

Capital Budgeting (A) The process of long-range planning involved with adding or reducing the productive facilities of a firm. (B) The process of long-range planning for specific projects and their financing.

Capital Expenditure Budget A formal plan involving the procurement or disposition of productive resources.

Capital Gains Gains on the sale of assets that are not held for resale as inventory and are usually taxed at a lower rate than ordinary income.

Capital Rationing A necessary ranking of investment proposals for a firm with a shortage of capital to invest.

Carryback and Carryforward An IRS tax code provision in which an operating loss may be carried back to each of the previous three years and forward to each of the succeeding five years as an offset to operating income in those years.

Carrying Costs Costs incurred in maintaining an inventory, including storage and warehousing, insurance, and cost of money invested in inventory.

Cash Budget A formal, integrated plan of cash inflows, outflows, and balances.

Clock Card A record of an employee's work time; used in determining an employee's pay.

Committed Costs (A) Fixed costs incurred by the productive facilities and organization maintained to provide a firm's output capacity. (B) Costs treated as fixed costs because they cannot be separated into their fixed and variable components.

Common Costs (A) In multiple product firms, costs that are not inherently traceable to individual products or product lines (*Joint Product Costs*). (B) Costs applicable to more than one costing objective; they cannot be traced to the objective without using an allocation base. Also called *Joint Costs* and *Indirect Costs.*

Comprehensive Budget (See *Master Budget.*)

Comptroller (See *Controller.*)

Conservatism The practice of undervaluing assets and revenues and overvaluing liabilities and expenses so that financial position is never overstated.

Constant Costs (See *Fixed Costs.*)

Constraint A restriction on the production process limiting the amount of resources that can be committed.

Continuous Budget A technique of budget preparation that adds a new period (such as a month) in the future as the period just ended is completed.

Contribution Center (See *Profit Center.*)

Contribution Margin Selling price per unit less the variable cost per unit. Also called *Marginal Income.* The contribution margin may be expressed on a per-unit basis, as a total, or as a ratio.

Contribution Margin Approach Income statements that separate costs into fixed and variable components and measure the contribution margin by deducting all variable costs from sales.

Contribution Margin from Operations Sales revenue less all variable costs.

Contribution Margin from Production Sales revenue less variable production costs.

Contribution Margin Ratio Sales percentage (100%) minus the variable cost ratio. That portion of each sales dollar that provides the contribution margin. Contribution margin divided by sales.

Control The process of measuring and correcting actual performance to ensure that a firm's objectives and plans are accomplished.

Control Limit An acceptable range within which costs may deviate from standard or budget. Beyond this limit costs are "out of control."

Controllable Cost A cost that can be regulated by a given manager in either the short run or the long run. A cost that is the responsibility of a specific manager.

Controller A firm's principal accounting officer responsible for planning and controlling the firm's financial data base. Also called *Comptroller.*

Conversion Costs The sum of direct labor and manufacturing overhead costs, including both fixed and variable costs.

Cost (A) The cash or the cash equivalent value of the resource obtained or the resource committed, whichever can be measured most objectively. (B) Value foregone to achieve an economic benefit.

Cost Accounting Standards Board (CASB) A federal agency established by Congress to assist governmental agencies as buyers of goods and services in understanding and negotiating cost-based prices.

Cost-based Pricing The process of determining a selling price by calculating the cost of a unit of product and adding a markup. An addition for profit is made to some suitable cost base. Also called *Cost-Plus Pricing* and *Average Cost Pricing.*

Cost Centers Organizational units where costs naturally come together. A natural clustering of costs by functional areas.

Cost Effectiveness Analysis The measure of the relationship between the incurrence of costs and a nonfinancial criterion.

Cost of Capital The cost of providing financial resources for the firm, including interest on borrowed money and costs of maintaining adequate owner's equity.

Cost of Goods Sold Costs released from the inventory and matched with revenue in the period the products are sold.

Cost-Plus-Fixed-Fee Contract A sales contract in which the seller is reimbursed for all reasonable (allowable) costs incurred in fulfilling the contract plus an agreed upon fee.

Cost-Plus-Percentage Contract A sales contract in which the seller is reimbursed for all reasonable (allowable) costs incurred in fulfilling the contract plus a profit determined as a negotiated percentage of the actual costs.

Cost-Plus Pricing (See *Cost-based Pricing.*)

Cost Reimburseable Contract A sales contract in which the seller is reimbursed for all costs incurred in fulfilling the contract. (See *Cost-Plus-Fixed-Fee, Cost-Plus-Percentage,* and *Cost Renegotiable Contracts.*)

Cost Renegotiable Contracts A sales contract in which the buyer and the seller have opportunities to redefine certain aspects of the contract after production has begun.

Current Assets Cash plus those assets that are expected to be converted into cash or consumed during the coming year or normal operating cycle.

Current Liabilities Liabilities that will mature and require payment within the coming year or operating cycle.

Current Ratio The ratio of current assets divided by current liabilities; used as a measure of liquidity.

Currently Attainable Standards Standards of performance that can be attained in the actual operations with skilled, efficient effort. Also called *Normal Standards* and *Average Standards.*

D

Data Base Information available to management for planning, decision making, and control functions.

Demand Curve A graphic curve showing the product quantity that will be sold at different prices. The curve normally slopes downward and to the right showing that as the selling price increases, customer demand decreases and that as price decreases, customer demand increases.

Depreciation The allocation of the original cost of plant and equipment to the time periods benefitted by the use of the asset.

Differential Benefit The difference in total benefits between any two acceptable alternatives. Also called *Incremental Benefit.*

Differential Cost The difference in total costs between any two acceptable alternatives. Also called *Incremental Cost.*

Differentiality The concept that only costs or benefits that differ between alternatives are relevant to decisions.

Diminishing Returns The economic concept that increased usage of production facilities requires more productive energy per unit to produce one additional unit.

Direct Costing (See *Variable Costing*.)

Direct Costs Costs that are capable of being traced and logically associated with a particular objective such as product, time period, or organizational unit.

Direct Labor Labor that is expended directly on the final product and traced directly to the product by the accounting system.

Direct Materials Materials used in the production of the final product and traced directly to the product by the accounting system.

Discounted Benefit/Cost Ratio A method of capital budgeting that applies a predetermined discount rate to cash inflows and outflows and ranks the alternatives by their ratio of discounted benefits to discounted costs.

Discounted Cash Flow Any capital investment decision process that adjusts cash flows over the life of the investment for the time value of money. (See *Adjusted Rate of Return, Discounted Benefit/Cost Ratio,* and *Net Present Value*.)

Discounted Rate of Return (See *Adjusted Rate of Return*.)

Discounting The process of adjusting cash flows for the time value of money. Also called *Present Value Analysis.*

Discretionary Costs Fixed costs that arise from specific management decisions to appropriate a specific sum. Also called *Managed Costs* and *Programmed Costs*.

Distribution Costs Nonproduction costs that arise from ensuring that the proper goods are in the proper place, ready to sell. Also called *Order-Filling Costs*.

Division A responsibility center where the manager is held responsible for both production and marketing operating decisions and for decisions involving investments in the resources necessary to implement plans.

E

Economic Income (A) A concept that no income exists until all who provided resources are paid for the cost of their resources. (B) The maximum amount that can be paid in dividends and leave the firm with the same economic wealth at the end of a period that it had at the beginning of the period.

Economic Order Quantity The amount of purchases (or production) that should be made at any one time to minimize the carrying costs and the procurement (or setup) costs.

Economies of Scale Gains in operating efficiencies due to increases in volume.

Effectiveness The accomplishment of a desired objective, goal, or action.

Efficiency The accomplishment of a desired objective, goal, or action with the minimum resources necessary.

Efficiency Variance (A) A quantity variance for labor determined by the difference between the actual hours worked and the standard hours times the labor wage rate. (B) A variance for overhead determined by the difference between the actual hours worked and the standard hours times the variable overhead rate.

Elasticity of Demand The responsiveness of consumers to price changes. If consumers are sensitive to price changes, demand is elastic. If consumers are unresponsive to price changes, demand is inelastic.

Engineering Cost Estimates A method of separating costs into their fixed and variable components by direct estimates based upon technical expertise.

Equilibrium Point The intersection point of the supply and demand curve. At this point the amount that producers provide equals the amount that customers demand and the market is in balance.

Equivalent Production The number of whole units of product for which a department or cost center is accountable during the time period.

Excess Material Requisition A form used to request needed production materials in excess of the standard amount of materials allowed for the output.

Excess Present Value A technique of discounted cash flow analysis that determines whether the present value of future cash inflows at the desired rate of return is greater or less than the present value of the future cash outflows. Also called *Net Present Value*.

Expected Actual Standard A standard based upon the most likely attainable results; an estimate of what will happen, not what should happen.

Expected Capacity The anticipated level of activity for the coming year. Also called *Budgeted Capacity*.

Expense (A) A cost that has been consumed in the production of revenue. (B) An expired cost.

Expired Costs (A) A cost that has no future revenue-producing potential. (B) An expense.

Externalities Indirect side effects of a decision in the public sector.

F

Factory Burden (See *Factory Overhead*.)

Factory Overhead All costs of operating the factory except those designated as direct labor and direct material costs. Also called *Factory Burden, Manufacturing Expense, Indirect Factory Costs, Manufacturing Overhead, Indirect Expense, Indirect Manufacturing Costs*.

Factory Overhead Rate A method of allocating the indirect factory costs to the products, creating an average overhead cost per unit of production activity.

Favorable Variance (A) A variance where actual costs are less than budgeted or standard costs. (B) A variance where actual revenue exceeds budgeted revenue.

Feedback The reporting function of accounting concerned with providing information to management so that performance may be evaluated and, if necessary, actions altered.

Financial Accounting Focus of accounting data for interfirm allocations and for the generation and maintenance of the capital structure of a firm.

Financial Accounting Standards Board (F.A.S.B.) An independent group of accountants concerned with establishing policy for external reporting practices.

Financial Costs Costs of obtaining financing for an organization's capital requirements.

Finished Goods Inventory The cost of unsold but completed goods that are held in inventory awaiting sale.

First In, First Out (FIFO) An inventory costing method where the first costs received are the first costs transferred out.

Fixed Budget A plan that expresses only one level of estimated activity or volume. Also called *Static Budget*.

Fixed Costs Costs that in total do not change with changes in output volume. On a per-unit basis, the cost per unit of output will vary inversely with changes in volume.

Fixed Factory Overhead Spending Variance The difference between actual fixed production costs incurred and budgeted fixed production costs shown in the flexible budget.

Fixed Factory Overhead Volume Variance The difference between budgeted fixed costs and fixed costs applied to Work-in-Process Inventory.

Fixed Price Contract Agreement to a price that remains unchanged over the life of a contract. Willingness to enter into this contract is dependent upon low risk to both buyer and seller.

Flexible Budget A statement of how costs change with changes in the activity level; often expressed as the formula $y = a + b(x)$ where a is the fixed costs, b the variable rate, and x a measure of the activity level. May refer to any specific cost or grouping of costs. Also called *Variable Budget*.

Forecast A projection of variables, both controllable and noncontrollable, that is used in the development of plans and budgets.

Full Costing (See *Absorption Costing*.)

Functional Classification (A) Classification of costs by the department or the responsibility center affected. (B) Allocation of costs to functions performed, such as office expense, warehouse expense, order-filling costs, etc.

Future Benefits Benefits that are expected to be gained at some future time, based on predictions, estimates, and forecasts.

Future Costs Costs that are expected to be incurred at some future time, based on predictions, estimates, and forecasts.

Future Value of Money The value to which an invested sum will grow by the end of a certain period if compounded at a given annual rate of interest.

Futurity A time or event that is yet to come.

G

General Costs (See *Administrative Costs.*)

Goal The basic plan or direction of a decision maker. The direction toward which all decisions and activities are focused.

Goal Congruence The process of combining the many diverse, separate goals of firm subcomponents into a unified whole.

H

Heuristic (A) A trial and error approach to problem solving. (B) Methods of investigation that lead to further investigation.

High-Low Method A method of determining fixed and variable costs that utilizes the highest and lowest activity levels and their related costs.

Historical Costs (See *Actual Costs.*)

Historical Overhead Rate A method of apportioning overhead costs to work in process after production for the period is completed.

I

Ideal Capacity The maximum plant output (in units) that can be achieved in the short run, with no allowances for repairs, maintenance, or rest periods.

Ideal Standard A standard that can be achieved only if all conditions are perfect.

Identifiable Costs Costs that can be associated with a particular product or department.

Idle Time (A) Labor time not involved in productive effort; usually treated as indirect labor. (B) Unused plant capacity.

Incentive Contract A contract based on a cost-plus-fixed-fee if the seller meets or exceeds the budgeted costs. In addition, there is a bonus incentive if costs are below the budgeted amount. In some cases a penalty is assessed if costs exceed the budgeted amount.

Income Statement A statement that evaluates operating performance by comparing revenues (accomplishments) with costs (efforts).

Incremental Analysis (A) The process of measuring the additional costs or benefits of one alternative chosen over another. (B) A method of comparing alternative plans of action by calculating the present values of the differences between *net* cash inflows.

Incremental Cost The total additional cost that will be incurred if a particular alternative is chosen. The difference in total costs between two alternatives. (See *Differential Cost.*)

Incurred Costs (See *Actual Costs.*)

Indirect Costs Costs that cannot be logically assigned to an objective without allocation. (See *Common* or *Joint Costs.*)

Indirect Expenses (See *Factory Overhead.*)

Indirect Factory Costs (See *Factory Overhead.*)

Indirect Labor Labor included in factory overhead because it cannot be traced directly to the units of output or to a department.

Indirect Manufacturing Costs (See *Factory Overhead.*)

Indirect Materials Minor materials included in factory overhead because they are not directly traceable to the finished products.

Information Economics The study of the costs and benefits of data in the belief that the benefits from using data should exceed the costs of gathering it.

Insolvency The inability of a firm to meet its debts when they are due.

Inspection of Contracts A method of separating costs into their fixed and variable components by examining existing production activities and contracts.

Interfirm Allocations Allocation of resources among firms in the economy, usually through the capital (stock and bond) markets.

Intrafirm Allocations Allocation of resources within a firm to the various departments or responsibility centers.

Inventory Turnover Cost of goods sold or Cost of Goods Consumed divided by inventory value.

Investment Centers Large segments of a firm where resources, revenues, and costs are traced and the rate of return on investment is used as a control measure.

Investment Decisions (See *Long-range Decisions;* also see *Capital Budgeting.*)

Investment Tax Credit A special tax provision that allows direct reductions of income taxes for the acquisition of certain depreciable assets.

Investment Turnover Sales divided by investment in assets. One component of return on investment. A measure of activity that shows how assets have generated revenue.

Invoice A form sent by a supplier billing a firm for materials purchased; serves as a source document for the purchases entry.

Iterative Process An approach to budgeting where the budget is developed through a sequential series of steps.

J

Job Cost Sheet A basic record for the accumulation of product costs in a job-costing system. Also called *Work Order* or *Job Order*.

Job Costing A system of determining production costs that traces the materials, labor, and other factory costs to specific units or batches.

Joint Costs (See *Common Costs*.)

Joint Process A production process in which a single input results in more than one output.

Joint Product Cost (See *Common Costs*.)

L

Labor (See *Direct Labor* and *Indirect Labor*.)

Labor Efficiency (Quantity) Variance The variance that measures the efficient or inefficient use of labor; the difference between standard hours in actual production and actual hours worked priced at the standard wage rate.

Labor Rate (Price) Variance The variance that measures the ability to control wage rates and labor mix; the difference between actual wage rate and standard wage rate multiplied by the actual hours worked.

Last In, First Out (LIFO) An inventory costing method where the last costs received are the first costs transferred out.

Lead Time The interval between the time a purchase order is placed and the time materials are received and available for use.

Learning Curve A mathematical expression of the fact that labor time will decrease at a constant percentage over doubled output quantities.

Least Squares Regression A statistical tool for fitting a straight line to data, providing a systematic and reliable method of estimating fixed and variable costs. Can also be used in projecting sales. Also called *Statistical Regression Analysis* or *Regression Analysis*.

Leverage (See *Trading on the Equity*.)

Liabilities Economic obligations of a firm to outsiders.

Linear Programming A mathematical method used in a number of business decisions, (including optimum product mix problems), where many interacting variables are combined to use limited resources to maximize profits or minimize losses.

Liquidity The amount and composition of a firm's assets with emphasis upon their conversion to cash.

Liquidity Ratio A ratio of liquid assets to current liabilities, computed as: (Cash + Marketable securities + Receivables) ÷ Current liabilities.

Long-range Decisions Decisions adding to or reducing the productive capability of a firm. These decisions affect the cash flows of more than one accounting period so that the time value of money is a significant variable.

Long-range Excess Capacity A measure of capacity held in reserve to meet fluctuations in demand; long-term growth determined in units as the difference between practical capacity and normal capacity.

Loss A cost that has been consumed without providing a benefit or revenue.

M

Managed Costs Fixed costs whose amounts are determined by management, not by their direct relationship to production output. (See *Discretionary Costs.*)

Management Accounting The focus of accounting data for intrafirm allocations through the planning and control process.

Management by Exception The practice of focusing attention only on those activities where actual performance differs significantly from planned performance.

Manufacturing Expenses (See *Factory Overhead.*)

Manufacturing Overhead (See *Factory Overhead.*)

Margin of Safety The amount (or ratio) by which the current volume exceeds the breakeven volume, either in units or dollars.

Margin on Sales Net profit divided by net sales. Also called *Profit Margin.*

Marginal Costing (See *Variable Costing.*)

Marginal Costs The cost of one additional unit of output. The cost incurred to move from output n to output $n + 1$.

Marginal Income (See *Contribution Margin.*)

Marginal Revenue The increment in total revenue obtained when output is increased by one additional unit.

Marketing Activity Variance A measure of the sales staff's ability to generate budgeted sales; determined in units by the difference between the sales orders received and the budgeted capacity. This variance is a part of the activity variance.

Master Budget An integrated plan of action for a firm as a whole, expressed in financial terms.

Matching The accounting process of comparing costs and revenues for the determination of net income.

Material Price Variance A measure of the ability to control material prices incurred; the difference between the actual material cost and the standard material cost multiplied by the actual quantity purchased. Also called *Material Purchases Variance.*

Material Purchased Price Variance (See *Material Price Variance.*)

Material Quantity Variance (See *Material Usage Variance.*)

Material Requisition A request for release of material held in the storeroom to authorized personnel. The source document to record raw material issues.

Material Usage Variance A measure of the efficient or inefficient use of materials; the difference between the standard quantity in actual production and the actual quantity used priced at the standard cost per unit of material.

Materials Physical commodities consumed to make the final product.

Mixed Cost A cost that has both fixed and variable cost attributes.

Monopolistic Competition An economic marketplace where there is a large number of firms. Each firm has little control over price except to create product differentiation.

Monopoly An economic marketplace characterized by a single firm as the sole producer of a product for which there are no close substitutes.

Motivation The internal and external factors that influence an individual to act.

Multiple Correlation Analysis A mathematical method of measuring the change in the dependent variable (cost) with changes in two or more different independent variables (measures of volume).

N

Natural Classification Classification of overhead costs by the nature of the expense, i.e. utilities, insurance, depreciation, rent, or taxes.

Negotiated Market Price A transfer price negotiated between the buying and selling divisions where there is no open market price established.

Net Book Value The unexpired cost of an asset carried on the financial records of the firm. Historical cost of an asset less accumulated depreciation to date.

Net Present Value A method of selecting capital investment projects. Proposals are ranked by the difference between discounted cash inflows and discounted cash outflows using a desired rate of return. (See *Present Value.*)

Net Working Capital The excess of current assets over current liabilities. Also called *Working Capital.*

Noncontrollable Costs Costs that a given manager cannot affect by his decisions.

Nonproduction Costs The costs of selling and distributing the final product and of general administration.

Nonrelevant Benefits Benefits that are not affected by a decision and will not change as a result of the decision.

Nonrelevant Costs Costs that are not affected by a decision and will not change as a result of the decision.

Normal Activity The level of output necessary to meet sales demands over a span of years (usually three to five), encompassing seasonal and cyclical variations.

Normal Overhead An overhead rate based upon normal capacity.

Normal Standard A standard that can be achieved if activities are efficient.

O

Objective Function A mathematical statement used in linear programming that relates production output to profit.

Objectives Specific quantitative and time-performance targets to achieve a firm's goals.

Oligopoly An economic marketplace where a few firms control a significant share of the market. Firms are mutually interdependent and often follow the dominant firm in pricing and production volume decisions.

Operating Cycle The period involved from the time cash is invested in inventory until the time cash is recovered from sale of the goods.

Operating Decisions (See *Short-range Decisions.*)

Opportunity Cost (A) Benefit that would have been obtained from an alternative if that alternative had been accepted. (B) The cost of foregone revenue by choosing a particular alternative.

Order-Filling Costs (See *Distribution Costs.*)

Order-Getting Costs (See *Selling Costs.*)

Out-of-Pocket Costs Costs that will require an expenditure of cash as a result of an anticipated decision.

Overabsorbed Overhead The excess of overhead cost applied to the product over the actual overhead costs incurred. Also called *Overapplied Overhead.*

Overapplied Overhead (See *Overabsorbed Overhead.*)

Overhead Efficiency Variance (See *Variable Factory Overhead Efficiency Variance.*)

P

Payback Period The length of time necessary to recover the initial investment of a project; investment cost divided by planned annual revenue.

Performance Budget An adjusted budget prepared *after* operations to compare actual results with costs that *should* have been incurred at the actual level attained.

Performance Report A report to a manager comparing actual results with planned results in his area of responsibility.

Period Costs Costs that are not inventoried and are treated as an expense in the period in which they are incurred.

Planning The process of selecting goals and objectives and the actions required to attain them.

Planning Budget (See *Master Budget.*)

Plant-wide Overhead Rate (See *Blanket Overhead Rate.*)

Practical Capacity (A) The most efficient operating level if fixed costs remain constant and output levels per unit of effort do not diminish; ideal capacity less allowances for repairs, maintenance, and rest periods. (B) Maximum sustainable long-run capacity.

Predetermined Overhead Rate An overhead rate determined in advance of production by dividing estimated (budgeted) factory overhead costs by an estimated (budgeted) volume base.

Preferred Stock Capital stock with priority over other shares in the areas of dividends and distribution of assets upon liquidation.

Present Value The concept that a sum invested today will earn interest and be worth more at a later date; a dollar in the hand today is worth more today than a dollar to be received (or spent) in the future.

Present Value of Money The amount that must be invested now to reach a given amount at some future given point of time, assuming it is compounded annually at a given rate of interest.

Price Variance A measure of how well actual prices agreed with planned prices; the difference between the actual prices and the standard (budgeted) prices multiplied by the actual quantity purchased.

Prime Costs The sum of direct material and direct labor.

Procedures Detailed instructions specifying how certain activities are to be accomplished.

Process Costing A method of determining the unit cost of manufacturing where production costs are divided by units produced during a given time period.

Producing Departments Departments or organizational units that contribute directly to the conversion of raw materials into finished products. Departments that come in physical contact with the products.

Product Costs Costs that attach to the unit of output and remain as an asset in the inventory until the goods to which they are attached are sold.

Product Margin The contribution margin of a particular product less directly identifiable fixed costs.

Production Activity Variance A measure of a factory's effectiveness in meeting production demand; the difference, in units, between sales orders received and actual capacity worked. A component of the activity variance.

Production Base A common denominator that equates all units produced. The most common measures of production base are units of product, machine hours, labor hours, and labor cost.

Production Budget A component of the master budget that establishes the level of production planned for some future period.

Production Costs Costs that are necessary to produce a finished product. Also called *Manufacturing Costs.*

Productive Assets Assets committed to production, storage, or distribution of a firm's products or services.

Profit Centers Organizational units where both revenue and costs naturally come together and net profit or net contribution to profit are used as control measures.

Profit Margin Percentage of profit on sales. One component of the return on investment calculation. Profit divided by sales.

Profit Plan A budgeted income statement.

Profit-Planning Chart (See *Breakeven Graph.*)

Profit-Volume Chart A graphic technique that shows breakeven analysis by plotting only the contribution margin on the chart.

Pro-Forma Statements Financial statements prepared before actual occurrence of events. Also called *Budgeted Statements.*

Profitability Accounting (See *Responsibility Accounting.*)

Program Budgeting A budgetary system used in the public sector that focuses upon the output of the organization rather than on specific inputs. Also called *Planning, Programming, Budgeting System.*

Programmed Costs (See *Discretionary Costs.*)

Projected Statement of Financial Position A projected balance sheet prepared to reflect expected financial position at the end of the planning period.

Purchase Order A form sent to a supplier by the purchasing department requesting the shipment of material.

Purchase Requisition A form issued by the storeroom requesting the purchasing department to procure some specific material.

Purchasing Budget A component of the master budget showing planned purchases for some future period.

Pure Competition An economic marketplace where a large number of independent firms produce a standardized product. No single firm can influence the market price; the price equals marginal revenue; a firm's demand schedule is horizontal.

Q

Quantity Variance A measure of how well actual quantities agreed with planned quantities; the difference between the actual quantities used and the standard (budgeted) quantities for actual production, multiplied by the standard price.

R

Rated Capacity Equipment capacity determined by its designers.

Rate Variance (See *Price Variance.*)

Raw Materials Inventory Production materials on hand but not yet processed.

Regression Analysis (See *Least Squares Regression.*)

Regression Method (See *Least Squares Regression.*)

Relevant Benefit A benefit that is cogent to the alternative being considered and will be affected by the decision.

Relevant Cost A cost that is cogent to the alternatives being considered and will be affected by the decision.

Relevant Data for Decision Making Future differential costs or benefits related to a particular decision.

Relevant Range The span of volume over which the cost behavior (or management plans) can be expected to remain valid.

Reorder Point The inventory level where an order must be placed to provide adequate lead time to ensure delivery when needed.

Replenishment Point The point in time when the physical inventory is restocked by deliveries.

Report on Profit Plan A financial statement explaining the differences between the profit plan and the income statement for a particular time period.

Residual Income A measure of divisional performance; the cost of capital deducted from divisional net income or contribution.

Residual Sum of Squares The sum of the variation of each *y* value from the corresponding predicted value given by the regression equation.

Responsibility Accounting (A) A system of recording costs and revenues where each manager is assigned only those factors that he can affect by his decisions. (B) A system that attempts to assign and match authority and responsibility.

Responsibility Centers A broad term that implies the development of an organizational structure where there is identifiable responsibility for each cost, revenue, and resource.

Return on Investment (ROI) The most widely used single measure of an operation's performance; (1) profits divided by assets committed or (2) margin on sales times asset turnover.

Revenue The inflow of economic values from company operations. Also called *Sales* or *Sales Revenue*.

Revenue Center Responsibility centers where only revenues are traced directly.

Risk An exposure to loss because of inability to control conditions upon which the firm is dependent.

Rolling or Moving Average A method of calculating an average; the oldest data is dropped and the newest data added each time the average is calculated.

S

Safety Stock The minimum inventory level that provides a cushion against running out of stock because of changes in demand or changes in lead time.

Sales Forecast A projection of sales for a particular future period of time.

Sales Mix The relative combination of the quantities of each type of product sold in a multiproduct firm.

Scattergraph A graphic representation showing the general relationship of cost to some base of activity; used in segregating costs into their fixed and variable components.

Scattergraph Method A method of segregating fixed and variable costs by plotting cost and activity data on a graph and then fitting a line by visual inspection so that half the plots lie above the line and half lie below the line.

Scheduled Production A production plan that identifies the specific quantity and type of goods to be produced in the next period.

Segment A subcomponent of a firm; a responsibility center.

Segment Margin The contribution margin of a subcomponent, segment, or division of a firm less all separable, identifiable fixed costs.

Selling Costs Nonproduction costs that result from marketing activities. Also called *Order-Getting-Costs*.

Semifixed Costs (See *Semivariable Costs*.)

Semivariable Costs Costs that are neither completely fixed nor completely variable, changing with changes in production volume, but not in direct proportion. They may be stepped, mixed, or curvilinear.

Separable Costs (A) Costs that can be identified with a specific segment of the firm, (B) Costs that would be avoided if a product line or segment of the firm were dropped.

Service Department A department that supports the producing departments in their activities but is not directly in contact with converting the raw materials into finished products.

Setup Costs Costs incurred to prepare a factory for a production run.

Short-range Decisions Decisions involving production output, pricing, product mix, and distribution of profit. They are concerned with the optimum use of existing resources and typically the time value of money is not considered significant.

Short-range Excess Capacity A measure of the difference between the current period and short-range expectancies; the difference, in units, between normal capacity and budgeted capacity.

Simplex Method A mathematical method of solving simultaneous equations which, because of bulk and size, would be impractical to solve graphically or manually.

Simulation A method—usually computerized—that uses a mathematical statement of the interrelationships of variables to test the effects of changes.

Sinking-Fund Method of Depreciation A method of depreciation with increasing charges over the life of the asset; there is a constant rate of return in each year.

Solvency Ability of a firm to pay its debts when due.

Source Document A form that serves as a basis for an accounting entry; an original record.

Specific Cost of Capital The cost of a specific source of capital.

Spending Variance The difference between actual factory overhead and budgeted factory overhead in the performance budget for the actual level of operations. Also called *Budget Variance*.

Split-off Point The point in the production process where products with joint costs are separated and become individual products.

Stairstepped Cost A semivariable cost that increases in discrete intervals.

Standard A precise measure of what should occur if performance is efficient.

Standard Absorption Costing A system of product costing that focuses upon management planning and control; product cost is determined by the sum of the standard costs for materials, labor, and both variable and fixed factory overhead. The variances between actual and standard are treated as period costs.

Standard Cost A scientific predetermination of what a unit of product *should* cost; a planning and control reference.

Standard Error of the Estimate A measure of how well a regression line fits the actual data when using least squares regression analysis. The further the observations from the regression line, the larger will be the standard error.

Standard Overhead Rate A scientific predetermination of what overhead *should* cost per unit of output.

Standard Variable Costing A system of product costing that focuses upon management planning and control; product cost is determined by the sum of the standard costs for materials, labor, and variable factory overhead. The fixed factory overhead costs and the variances between actual and standard costs are treated as period costs.

Statement of Financial Position (See *Balance Sheet.*)

Static Budget (See *Fixed Budget.*)

Statistical Regression Analysis (See *Least Squares Regression.*)

Sunk Cost A cost that has already been incurred and will not require a future expenditure of cash.

Supplementary Fixed Factory Overhead Rate An overhead rate calculated at the end of the accounting period to adjust the inventories from variable costing to absorption costing.

Supply Curve An economic concept that relates market prices to the quantity of product that suppliers or producers are willing to supply.

T

Tax Shield Recognition that a cost shields income of future years against tax to the extent that the cost may be deducted against income. The most common example is a depreciable asset.

Time-adjusted Rate of Return The rate of interest at which the present value of budgeted cash inflows for a project equals the present value of budgeted cash outflows for the project.

Time Ticket A factory record of how the employee spends his time.

Time Value of Money The difference between the value of a dollar today and its value at some future point in time if invested.

Total Contribution Margin The contribution margin per unit times the number of units sold.

Total Cost The sum of all fixed costs and all variable costs.

Total Revenue The quantity sold times the price per unit.

Traceable Cost (See *Controllable Cost.*)

Trading on the Equity Using borrowed money with a fixed interest cost to invest in a project with a higher rate of return so that the return on the stockholder's equity is increased.

Transfer Price The price charged by one segment of an organization when it supplies a product or service to another segment of the same organization.

U

Unadjusted Rate of Return A rate of return that has not been adjusted for the time value of money.

Uncertainty A lack of information about the probability of alternative results.

Underapplied Overhead The amount by which overhead incurred exceeds overhead applied to the products.

Unexpired Costs Assets; costs carried forward to future periods where they have the potential of contributing to future revenues.

Unfavorable Variance (A) A variance where the actual costs are greater than the budgeted or standard costs. (B) A variance where actual revenue is less than planned or budgeted revenue.

Usage Variance (See *Quantity Variance.*)

V

Variable Budget (See *Flexible Budget.*)

Variable Costs Costs that vary in total dollar amount in direct proportion to changes in production volume. The cost per unit of output is constant over the relevant range of activity.

Variable Cost Ratio Variable costs divided by sales.

Variable Costing A system of measuring inventory costs that assigns variable production costs of material, labor, and variable factory overhead to the product unit cost. Fixed factory overhead costs and nonproduction costs are treated as period costs. Also called *Marginal Costing* and *Direct Costing.*

Variable Factory Overhead Efficiency Variance The variance that measures the effect of inefficient or efficient use of labor on variable overhead costs; the difference between standard hours in actual production and actual hours worked, priced at the variable overhead rate.

Variable Factory Overhead Spending Variance The difference between actual variable costs incurred and the amount that the flexible budget allows for variable costs for the actual volume worked.

Variable Profit Ratio (See *Contribution Margin Ratio.*)

Variance The difference between actual results and planned results.

Volume Variance (See *Fixed Factory Overhead Volume Variance.*)

W

Weighted Average Inventory A method of inventory costing where total dollars of goods available during the period are summed and divided by the total units available.

Work-in-Process Inventory The cost of uncompleted products still in the factory.

Working Capital The excess of current assets over current liabilities.

Z

Zero-based Budgeting A method used in programmed budgeting where old programs already instituted are required to compete on an equal footing with new programs each year.

Appendix A

Present Value of $1 $PV = (1 + r)^{-n} = \frac{1}{(1 + r)^n}$

Period	2%	4%	6%	8%	10%	12%	14%	16%	18%
1	.980	.962	.943	.926	.909	.893	.877	.862	.847
2	.961	.925	.890	.857	.826	.797	.769	.743	.718
3	.942	.889	.840	.794	.751	.712	.675	.641	.609
4	.924	.855	.792	.735	.683	.636	.592	.552	.516
5	.906	.822	.747	.681	.621	.567	.519	.476	.437
6	.888	.790	.705	.630	.564	.507	.456	.410	.370
7	.871	.760	.665	.583	.513	.452	.400	.354	.314
8	.853	.731	.627	.540	.467	.404	.351	.305	.266
9	.837	.703	.592	.500	.424	.361	.308	.263	.225
10	.820	.676	.558	.463	.386	.322	.270	.227	.191
11	.804	.650	.527	.429	.350	.287	.237	.195	.162
12	.788	.625	.497	.397	.319	.257	.208	.168	.137
13	.773	.601	.469	.368	.290	.229	.182	.145	.116
14	.758	.577	.442	.340	.263	.205	.160	.125	.099
15	.743	.555	.417	.315	.239	.183	.140	.108	.084
16	.728	.534	.394	.292	.218	.163	.123	.093	.071
17	.714	.513	.371	.270	.198	.146	.108	.080	.060
18	.700	.494	.350	.250	.180	.130	.095	.069	.051
19	.686	.475	.331	.232	.164	.116	.083	.060	.043
20	.673	.456	.312	.215	.149	.104	.073	.051	.037
21	.660	.439	.294	.199	.135	.093	.064	.044	.031
22	.647	.422	.278	.184	.123	.083	.056	.038	.026
23	.634	.406	.262	.170	.112	.074	.049	.033	.022
24	.622	.390	.247	.158	.102	.066	.043	.028	.019
25	.610	.375	.233	.146	.092	.059	.038	.024	.016
30	.552	.308	.174	.099	.057	.033	.020	.012	.007
35	.500	.253	.130	.068	.036	.019	.010	.006	.003
40	.453	.208	.097	.046	.022	.011	.005	.003	.001
45	.410	.171	.073	.031	.014	.006	.003	.001	.001
50	.372	.141	.054	.021	.009	.003	.001	.001	

20%	22%	24%	26%	28%	30%	35%	40%	45%	50%
.833	.820	.806	.794	.781	.769	.741	.714	.690	.667
.694	.672	.650	.630	.610	.592	.549	.510	.476	.444
.579	.551	.524	.500	.477	.455	.406	.364	.328	.296
.482	.451	.423	.397	.373	.350	.301	.260	.226	.198
.402	.370	.341	.315	.291	.269	.223	.186	.156	.132
.335	.303	.275	.250	.227	.207	.165	.133	.108	.088
.279	.249	.222	.198	.178	.159	.122	.095	.074	.059
.233	.204	.179	.157	.139	.123	.091	.068	.051	.039
.194	.167	.144	.125	.108	.094	.067	.048	.035	.026
.162	.137	.116	.099	.085	.073	.050	.035	.024	.017
.135	.112	.094	.079	.066	.056	.037	.025	.017	.012
.112	.092	.076	.062	.052	.043	.027	.018	.012	.008
.093	.075	.061	.050	.040	.033	.020	.013	.008	.005
.078	.062	.049	.039	.032	.025	.015	.009	.006	.003
.065	.051	.040	.031	.025	.020	.011	.006	.004	.002
.054	.042	.032	.025	.019	.015	.008	.005	.003	.002
.045	.034	.026	.020	.015	.012	.006	.003	.002	.001
.038	.028	.021	.016	.012	.009	.005	.002	.001	.001
.031	.023	.017	.012	.009	.007	.003	.002	.001	
.026	.019	.014	.010	.007	.005	.002	.001	.001	
.022	.015	.011	.008	.006	.004	.002	.001		
.018	.013	.009	.006	.004	.003	.001	.001		
.015	.010	.007	.005	.003	.002	.001			
.013	.008	.006	.004	.003	.002	.001			
.010	.007	.005	.003	.002	.001	.001			
.004	.003	.002	.001	.001					
.002	.001	.001							
.001									

Appendix B

Present Value of an Annuity of $1 $PV = \frac{1 - (1 + r)^{-n}}{r}$

Period	2%	4%	6%	8%	10%	12%	14%	16%	18%
1	0.980	0.962	0.943	0.926	0.909	0.893	0.877	0.862	0.847
2	1.942	1.886	1.833	1.783	1.736	1.690	1.647	1.605	1.566
3	2.884	2.775	2.673	2.577	2.486	2.402	2.322	2.246	2.174
4	3.808	3.630	3.465	3.312	3.170	3.037	2.914	2.798	2.690
5	4.713	4.452	4.212	3.993	3.791	3.605	3.433	3.274	3.127
6	5.601	5.242	4.917	4.623	4.355	4.111	3.889	3.685	3.498
7	6.472	6.002	5.582	5.206	4.868	4.564	4.288	4.039	3.812
8	7.325	6.733	6.210	5.747	5.335	4.968	4.639	4.344	4.078
9	8.162	7.435	6.802	6.247	5.759	5.328	4.946	4.607	4.303
10	8.983	8.111	7.360	6.710	6.145	5.650	5.216	4.833	4.494
11	9.787	8.760	7.887	7.139	6.495	5.938	5.453	5.029	4.656
12	10.575	9.385	8.384	7.536	6.814	6.194	5.660	5.197	4.793
13	11.348	9.986	8.853	7.904	7.103	6.424	5.842	5.342	4.910
14	12.106	10.563	9.295	8.244	7.367	6.628	6.002	5.468	5.008
15	12.849	11.118	9.712	8.559	7.606	6.811	6.142	5.575	5.092
16	13.578	11.652	10.106	8.851	7.824	6.974	6.265	5.668	5.162
17	14.292	12.166	10.477	9.122	8.022	7.120	6.373	5.749	5.222
18	14.992	12.659	10.828	9.372	8.201	7.250	6.467	5.818	5.273
19	15.678	13.134	11.158	9.604	8.365	7.366	6.550	5.877	5.316
20	16.351	13.590	11.470	9.818	8.514	7.469	6.623	5.929	5.353
21	17.011	14.029	11.764	10.017	8.649	7.562	6.687	5.973	5.384
22	17.658	14.451	12.042	10.201	8.772	7.645	6.743	6.011	5.410
23	18.292	14.857	12.303	10.371	8.883	7.718	6.792	6.044	5.432
24	18.914	15.247	12.550	10.529	8.985	7.784	6.835	6.073	5.451
25	19.523	15.622	12.783	10.675	9.077	7.843	6.873	6.097	5.467
30	22.396	17.292	13.765	11.258	9.427	8.055	7.003	6.177	5.517
35	24.999	18.665	14.498	11.655	9.644	8.176	7.070	6.215	5.539
40	27.355	19.793	15.046	11.925	9.779	8.244	7.105	6.233	5.548
45	29.490	20.720	15.456	12.108	9.863	8.283	7.123	6.242	5.552
50	31.424	21.482	15.762	12.233	9.915	8.304	7.133	6.246	5.554

20%	22%	24%	26%	28%	30%	35%	40%	45%	50%
0.833	0.820	0.806	0.794	0.781	0.769	0.741	0.714	0.690	0.667
1.528	1.492	1.457	1.424	1.392	1.361	1.289	1.224	1.165	1.111
2.106	2.042	1.981	1.923	1.868	1.816	1.696	1.589	1.493	1.407
2.589	2.494	2.404	2.320	2.241	2.166	1.997	1.849	1.720	1.605
2.991	2.864	2.745	2.635	2.532	2.436	2.220	2.035	1.876	1.737
3.326	3.167	3.020	2.885	2.759	2.643	2.385	2.168	1.983	1.824
3.605	3.416	3.242	3.083	2.937	2.802	2.508	2.263	2.057	1.883
3.837	3.619	3.421	3.241	3.076	2.925	2.598	2.331	2.109	1.922
4.031	3.786	3.566	3.366	3.184	3.019	2.665	2.379	2.144	1.948
4.192	3.923	3.682	3.465	3.269	3.092	2.715	2.414	2.168	1.965
4.327	4.035	3.776	3.543	3.335	3.147	2.752	2.438	2.185	1.977
4.439	4.127	3.851	3.606	3.387	3.190	2.779	2.456	2.196	1.985
4.533	4.203	3.912	3.656	3.427	3.223	2.799	2.469	2.204	1.990
4.611	4.265	3.962	3.695	3.459	3.249	2.814	2.478	2.210	1.993
4.675	4.315	4.001	3.726	3.483	3.268	2.825	2.484	2.214	1.995
4.730	4.357	4.033	3.751	3.503	3.283	2.834	2.489	2.216	1.997
4.775	4.391	4.059	3.771	3.518	3.295	2.840	2.492	2.218	1.998
4.812	4.419	4.080	3.786	3.529	3.304	2.844	2.494	2.219	1.999
4.843	4.442	4.097	3.799	3.539	3.311	2.848	2.496	2.220	1.999
4.870	4.460	4.110	3.808	3.546	3.316	2.850	2.497	2.221	1.999
4.891	4.476	4.121	3.816	3.551	3.320	2.852	2.498	2.221	2.000
4.909	4.488	4.130	3.822	3.556	3.323	2.853	2.498	2.222	2.000
4.925	4.499	4.137	3.827	3.559	3.325	2.854	2.499	2.222	2.000
4.937	4.507	4.143	3.831	3.562	3.327	2.855	2.499	2.222	2.000
4.948	4.514	4.147	3.834	3.564	3.329	2.856	2.499	2.222	2.000
4.979	4.534	4.160	3.842	3.569	3.332	2.857	2.500	2.222	2.000
4.992	4.541	4.164	3.845	3.571	3.333	2.857	2.500	2.222	2.000
4.997	4.544	4.166	3.846	3.571	3.333	2.857	2.500	2.222	2.000
4.999	4.545	4.166	3.846	3.571	3.333	2.857	2.500	2.222	2.000
4.999	4.545	4.167	3.846	3.571	3.333	2.857	2.500	2.222	2.000

Index

Absorption costing:
- compared with variable costing, 192–93, 196–200
- cost flow diagram, 108, 194, 474–75
- defined, 107, 710
- income statement illustrated, 121, 197
- role of activity level, 154–55
- selection of activity base, 152
- and standard costing, 471

Accountability, 433, 446, 710
Accountant:
- controller, 32
- financial vs. managerial duties, 3–5, 32
- management, 32, 572
- responsibilities of, 32

Accounting:
- for compliance reporting, 4
- for control, 427
- defined, 3
- financial, 3
- managerial, 3, 5
- responsibility, 433, 621
- role of, 3

Accounting rate of return. *See* unadjusted rate of return
Accounts receivable planning, 587
Accounts receivable turnover, 584, 710
Activity accounting, 710
Activity base, 152, 710
Activity variance, 165, 428, 626, 710
Actual costs, 710
Actual volume, 153, 164–65
Adjusted rate of return:
- defined, 382, 710
- illustrated, 383
- interpolation to measure, 384
- unequal cash flows, 382
- uses in industry, 395–97

Administrative costs, 111, 710
Alex, Marcus, 33
Allocation, 710
Allocation of costs:
- to departments, 150–51
- to joint products, 255
- to products, 151–52, 290–91
- to time periods, 150

Ameiss, Albert P., 395
American Accounting Association (AAA), 201
American Institute of Certified Public Accountants (AICPA), 200–201
Analysis of variances:
- for cost control, 463
- timing, 478, 479, 482, 484
- when to investigate, 470

Annuity:
- defined, 350, 710
- table of, Appendix B, 736

Anthony, Robert N., 33, 130, 694
Application of overhead, 118
Apportioned fixed costs, 213, 216, 254
Appropriation, 445, 711
Appropriation budget, 592
Archer, Stephen H., 33
Argyris, Chris, 437, 446
Armed Services Procurement Regulations, 258
Asset, allocations of, 681
Assets, 711
Assets, expiration of, 106
Asset turnover, 711. *See also* investment turnover
Attained volume. *See* actual volume
Attention directing, 711
Attestation, 4, 711
Authority, of management, 432
Authorization in budgeting, 424, 441, 445
Average collection period, 584
Average cost, 711
Average costing. *See* weighted average
Average cost pricing, 253, 711
Average investment, 387
Average rate of return. *See* unadjusted rate of return
Average revenue, 711
Average total cost, 23
Avoidable costs, 213, 711

Baer, Wilmer, 599
Balance sheet, 711. *See also* statement of financial position
Baxter, William T., 264
Becker, S., 446
Beckett, John A., 174

Behavioral accounting, 465, 711
Bell, Albert L., 80
Benefit-cost analysis, 351, 391–94, 711
Benefits:
  differential, 11, 284
  relevant, 10, 284
Benninger, L. J., 130
Berezi, Andrew, 354
Bergquist, Richard E., 174
Bierman, H., Jr., 399, 694
Bill of materials, 711
Black, Thomas N., 446
Blanket overhead rate, 171, 711
Book value, 679, 711
Book value rate of return. *See* unadjusted rate of return
Breakeven analysis:
  and the contribution margin, 68–69
  defined, 65
  economic vs. accounting approaches, 26–28
  effects of changing factors, 69–73
  equation technique, 67–68
  graphical technique, 65
Breakeven graph:
  accounting, 28, 66, 209, 711
  economic, 28, 75
Breakeven point, 65, 712. *See also* cost-volume-profit analysis
Brenner, Vincent C., 264
Broster, E. J., 218
Bruns, William J., Jr., 33, 446
Budgeted capacity, 157, 165, 712
Budgeted costs, 712
Budgeting:
  committee, 432
  comparison of profit and not-for-profit budgets, 444–45
  functions of, 423
  human aspects of, 436–37
  prerequisites of successful, 432
  relationship to planning and control, 30–31, 421–22
  time dimensions of, 430–31
Budgets:
  appropriation, 592
  capital expenditures, 427, 592
  cash, 425
  communication, 424
  control by, 30–31
  coordination, role of, 423
  defined, 30, 423, 712
  departmental, 534, 536
  flexible, 63–64
  forecasting in, 423–24
  in formalized planning, 29–30
  human aspects of, 436–37
  illustrated, 519–47
  master, 30, 425
  in not-for-profit organizations, 440–41
  performance, 30, 424
  production, 532–34
  profit plan, 425
  purchasing, 533–35
  sales, 532–33
  sales forecasting for, 516
  simulation, 440
  statement of financial position, 425
  static, 445
  tentative, 29–30
  time span, 430–31
  variable. *See* flexible budget
  variance, 712

Calas, Robert, 647
Capacity:
  actual, 153, 164–65
  budgeted, 157, 165
  defined, 155
  expected, 157
  ideal, 162
  interrelationship of long-range and short-range, 162–65
  normal, 155
  practical, 155
  rated, 162
Capacity costs, 712. *See also* fixed costs
Capacity decisions, 9, 26, 29, 333, 712. *See also* capital budgeting
Capacity variance, 712. *See also* activity variance; volume variance
Capital budgeting:
  adjusted rate of return method, 382
  capital rationing, 373
  cash flow measurement, 335–36
  cost of capital, 342–45
  decision rule, 27–29, 333
  defined, 333, 712
  depreciation in, 337–39
  discounted benefit-cost ratio, 378, 381
  discounted cash flow, 333–36
  income tax considerations, 336–42
  net present value method, 373–78
  payback method, 385–87
  project selection:
    reinvestment of cash flows, 385
    unequal lives, 385
  public sector, 391
  risk and uncertainty, 345, 389–91
  time adjusted rate of return, 382
  time value of money, 345
  unadjusted rate of return, 387–89
  uses in industry, 395–98
Capital, cost of, 342, 344, 373
Capital expenditures budget, 427, 592, 712
Capital gains and losses, 341, 712
Capital rationing, 373, 712

Caplan, E. H., 437, 438, 446
Carroll, Lewis, 6
Carryback and carryforward, 339, 712
Carrying costs, 306, 712
Cartels, 252
Cash budgets, 575, 712
Cash flow:
  budgets, 425, 575–77
  in capital budgeting, 336
  discounted, 333
  income taxes and, 336–42
Cash planning, 586
Certified Public Accountant, 4
Chapin, Wayne R., 310
Circulating capital, 572
Clark, J. Maurice, 9
Clayden, Roger, 694
Claydon, Henry L., 498
Clayton Act, 262
Clock cards, 118, 713
Closing overhead accounts, 120–21, 492
Colbert, Bertram A., 130
Combined labor and overhead efficiency variance, 484
Committed costs, 713
Common costs, 150, 713
Communication in budgeting, 424
Competitive marketplace, 250
Compliance reporting, 4, 445
Comprehensive budget, 713
Comptroller, 713
Conflict in budgeting, 438
Conservatism, 713
Constant costs, 713
Constraint:
  defined, 297, 713
  in linear programming, 301–9
Contingency balance, 586, 587, 589
Continuous budget, 713
Contribution center, 713
Contribution margin:
  in breakeven analysis, 68–69
  defined, 18–19, 713
  income statement, 197, 205, 210, 212, 259, 260, 261
  ratio:
    defined, 18–19, 68, 713
    from production, 204
    from total operations, 204
  total:
    defined, 18–19
    from production, 203, 713
    from total operations, 203, 713
  unit:
    defined, 18–19
    from production, 204
    from total operations, 204
  in variable costing, 203
Contribution margin approach:
  assumptions, 205
  compared with absorption costing, 192–93
  compared with variable costing, 203–4
  cost allocation and, 289
  to cost-volume-profit analysis, 68, 205–6, 713
  and differential analysis, 284
  dropping or adding a product line, 285, 294
  limitations of, 214–15
  in make-or-buy decisions, 292
  in nonmanufacturing activities, 209
  in performance measurement, 164, 203, 428
  in pricing decisions, 259
  and production decisions, 285
  product line contributions, 213–14
  and product mix decisions, 298
  and sell or process further decisions, 286–92
Contribution margin centers, 435–36
Control:
  accounting, 31, 427
  budgets for, 30–31, 421–27
  decentralization and, 676
  defined, 30, 427, 713
  flow diagram of process, 31, 422
  goal congruence, 8
  human aspects of, 436–39
  inventory, 589
  limit, 714
  nonfinancial, 31–32
  organizational structure and, 433
  planning related to, 30–31, 422
  physical measures for, 31
  reporting systems for, 621
  responsibility accounting for, 30–31, 433, 621
  service department, 171–72
  standard costs for, 463–69
  variances for, 31, 463
Controllability, 436
Controllable costs, 151, 436, 714
Controller, 32, 714
Conventional costing. *See* absorption costing
Conversion cost, 122, 714
Conversion from variable to absorption costing, 216
    641
Copeland, Ben R., 174
Copulsky, William, 548
Correlation, 63, 521–23
Cost, 714
Cost absorption, 107
Cost Accounting Standards Board, 202, 258, 714
Cost allocations:
  cost object, 150–51
  direct and indirect costs, 109–10
  motivation for 290–91
  overhead, 166–71
  relevancy for decisions, 171, 290–91

- selection of a base, 49
  - ability to bear, 167
  - benefits received, 167
  - facilities provided, 167
  - relative sales-value basis, 291
  - services used, 167
- service departments, 166–69

Cost application, 107
Cost-based pricing, 253, 714
Cost behavior patterns:
- linearity assumptions, 51
- methods of determination:
  - analysis of accounts, 50
  - choosing an independent variable, 49–50
  - choosing a relevant range, 64–65
  - engineering cost estimates, 50
  - high-low point estimates, 55–56
  - inspection of contracts, 50
  - inspection of past, 50–53
  - least squares regression estimates, 56–63
  - multiple regression, 63
  - scattergraph analysis, 53–54
  - statistical regression analysis, 56–63
  - visual fit, 53–54
- nonlinearity assumptions, 16–17, 63
- types of:
  - fixed, 12–14, 19
  - semivariable, 14–18
  - variable, 11–12, 19

Cost-benefit analysis, 351, 391–93
Cost of capital:
- common stock, 343
- computation, 342
- defined, 714
- long-term debt, 343–44
- risk, 345
- specific, 342
- uncertainty, 389
- weighted average, 342, 344, 373

Cost center, 151, 435, 714
Cost effectiveness analysis, 714
Cost of goods sold, 107, 714
Cost incentive pricing contracts, 258
Costing systems:
- absorption, 107
- direct, 192
- job, 111
- marginal, 192
- overhead, 117–21
- process, 111
- product, 106–11
- standard, 470
- variable, 192

Cost-plus-fixed-fee pricing, 258, 714
Cost-plus-percentage pricing, 257, 714
Cost-plus pricing, 253, 714
Cost reapportionment, 166–69
Cost reimbursable pricing, 257, 714
Cost renegotiable pricing, 258, 715
Costs:
- apportioned fixed costs, 213
- average total, 22–24
- avoidable, 213
- behavior patterns, 11–18
- capacity. *See* fixed costs
- carrying, 306, 591
- classification of, 11–18, 106–7, 192–93
- common, 150
- controllable, 151, 436
- conversion, 122
- departmental, 166–71
- differential, 11, 284
- direct, 109, 150, 166
- discretionary, 63
- distribution, 110
- expired, 106
- financial, 111
- fixed, 12, 19, 49
- future, 10, 284
- general and administrative, 111
- incremental, 11
- indirect, 109, 150, 166
- inventoriable, 107
- joint, 150, 255, 289
- labor, 107, 109
- least squares approach to, 56–63
- manufacturing, 107
- marginal, 22–23
- material, 107, 109
- mixed, 16
- noncontrollable, 151
- nonlinear, 16–17
- nonproduction, 107
- opportunity, 10, 284
- order-filling, 110
- order-getting, 110
- ordering, 589
- out-of-pocket, 29
- overhead, 107, 109–10
- past, 10
- period, 106
- prime, 192
- product, 106
- production, 107
- relevant, 10, 284
- semivariable, 14
- separable, 213
- setup, 304
- stairstep, 15
- standard, 463
- sunk, 29
- total, 19

traceable, 151
unexpired, 106
unit, 111
variable, 11, 19, 49
Cost standards, 464–69
Cost-volume-profit analysis:
applications, 69–73
assumptions, 74
breakeven point:
comparison of fixed and variable costs, 11–14, 49
contribution margin technique, 68
curvilinear approach, 74–75
defined, 65
economics vs. accounting, 74
effects of changing factors, 69–73
equation technique, 67
fixed costs changes, 71
graphical technique, 65
illustrated, 65–73
multiple department situations, 78
multiple product situations, 75–78
product line evaluation, 75–78
relevant range, 64
sales mix, 75
selling price changes, 69
and taxes, 72
variable cost changes, 71
volume to achieve desired income, 72
Credit policies, 587
Current assets, 572, 715
Current liabilities, 572, 715
Currently attainable standards, 465, 715
Current ratio, 584, 715

Data base, 3, 32, 715
Davidson, H. Justin, 130
Dearden, J., 694
Decentralization:
benefits of, 677
cost center in, 435
defined, 676
defining income, 678
defining investment, 679
division, 676
investment center, 436, 676
performance measurement, 682
profit center in, 435
rate of return, 676–77
responsibility accounting, 433
transfer pricing, 686
Decision making:
capacity decisions:
accounting rate of return, 387
defined, 26–29, 333
net present value, 373
payback period, 385
time adjusted rate of return, 382
cost-volume-profit analysis, 69–73
intrafirm vs. interfirm, 4–5
long-range vs. short-range 9–10, 333
operating decisions:
accounting approach, 11–18
defined, 11
economic approach, 19–26
pricing:
contribution margin approach, 259
economic approach, 244–49
full-cost approach, 253
production, 285
role of book value, 284, 335
role of uncertainty, 389
DeCoster, Don T., 33, 174, 446, 548
Demand curve:
defined, 715
illustrated, 246, 247, 249, 251, 526
shift in, 247–49
Departmental cost sheet, 169
Departmentalization of costs, 166
Depreciation, 14, 337, 679, 715
Depreciation and capital budgeting, 337
Depreciation and cost behavior, 14
Depreciation and return on investment, 679
Differential benefit, 715
Differential cost, 715
Differentiality, 284, 715
Diminishing return, 715
Direct cost, 109, 150, 715
Direct costing, 192, 715. *See also* variable costing
Direct labor:
clock card, 116
defined, 109, 715
general ledger, 114
standards for, 466
time ticket, 116
variances, 480–81
Direct labor cost base, 152
Direct labor hour base, 153
Direct material:
defined, 109, 715
general ledger, 114
material requisition, 115
standards for, 465
variances, 478–79
Discounted benefit-cost ratio:
defined, 378, 716
illustrated, 381
limitations of, 381
Discounted cash flow:
defined, 716
depreciation considerations, 337
time adjusted rate of return, 382
time value of money, 345
Discounted present value, 333
Discounted rate of return, 333, 382, 716
Discounting, 333, 716

Discretionary costs, 63, 716
Distribution costs, 110, 716
Division, 676, 716
Divisional performance assessment, 683
Doney, Lloyd D., 310
Double-declining balance depreciation, 337
Dow, Alice S., 80
Dunbar, R. L. M., 437

Economic approach:
- to breakeven analysis, 26–28, 74–75
- to operating decisions, 19–26
- to product pricing, 245–52
- to transfer pricing, 689

Economic income, 716
Economic order (production) quantity, 308, 589, 716
Economies of scale, 19, 716
Edwards, James B., 399
Edwards, James W., 354
Effectiveness defined, 6, 716
Efficiency defined, 6, 716
Efficiency variances, 481, 484, 716
Elasticity of demand, 249, 717
Engineering cost estimates, 50, 717
Environmental Protection Agency, 4
Equilibrium point, 246, 247, 717
Equivalent production, 717
Estes, Ralph W., 354
Excess materials requisition, 479, 717
Excess present value, 717. *See also* net present value
Expected activity rates, 157–58
Expected capacity, 157, 717
Expected standards, 464, 717
Expenses:
- defined, 106, 717
- measurement of, 106–7, 192–93

Expired costs, 106, 717
Externalities, 351, 717

Factory burden, 110, 717
Factory cost reports, 625–30
Factory ledgers, 114–17
Factory overhead:
- defined, 109–10, 717
- fixed, 154
- historical vs. predetermined, 153
- job order costing, 117–19
- ledger entries for, 117–19
- nature of, 118, 152
- process costing and, 122
- production bases for, 152
- under- or overapplied, 120–21
- variable, 154
- variances, 159–65

Factory overhead rates:
- average rates, 155
- budgeted capacity, 157
- defined, 118, 717
- expected, 157
- fixed, 154, 158
- function of, 111
- historical, 153
- illustrated, 118, 158
- labor bases, 153
- machine hour base, 152
- normal, 155
- plant wide (blanket), 171
- practical, 155
- predetermined, 154
- rolling (or moving) average, 156
- selection of activity level, 152
- variable, 154

Favorable variance, 717
Federal Trade Commission, 262
Feedback, 30, 424, 427, 621, 718
Financial accounting, 3–4, 106, 718
Financial Accounting Standards Board, 5, 718
Financial costs, 111, 718
Financial leverage, 344
Financial statements:
- changes in financial position, 4, 573, 593, 638
- financial position, 4, 425, 572–73, 639, 644
- funds statement, 4, 638
- income statement, 4, 635, 645
- retained earnings, 4

Finished goods inventory, 107, 718
First-in, first-out, 198, 718
Fixed budget, 718. *See also* static budget
Fixed costs:
- accounting approach, 12–13, 718
- economic approach, 19

Fixed factory overhead:
- development of rate, 154, 158
- supplementary rate, 218
- variances:
  - activity, 162–65, 428, 630
  - analysis, 159–65
  - spending, 160–63, 487, 629, 718
  - volume, 160–63, 488, 718

Fixed price contracts, 257, 718
Flexible budgets, 63, 718. *See also* contribution margin approach
Forecasting, 423, 718
Fremgen, James H., 218, 389, 397, 399, 694
Frye, Delbert J., 218
Full absorption costing, 106
Full costing, 106, 718
Functional cost classification, 117, 718
Fund accounting, 441
Funds flow statement. *See* statement of changes in financial position
Future benefits, 719

Future costs, 719
Future value of money, 346, 719
Futurity, 284, 719

GAAP (generally accepted accounting principles), 5, 192, 200–1
General and administrative costs, 111, 719
General Electric Company, 685, 692
General ledger:
  for job order costing, 114
  for process costing, 129
  for standard costing, 472–75
Goals:
  congruence of, 8, 438, 719
  defined, 8, 422, 719
  multiple, 692–93
  organizational, 6, 422
Green, David, Jr., 446
Gross margin, 121, 209
Gross profit, 121
Gunn, Sanford C., 355
Gynther, R. S., 80

Hall, William K., 548
Harris, William T., Jr., 310
Haseman, Wilber C., 130, 220
Hekimian, James S., 130
Herson, Richard J. L., 264
Hertz, David B., 355, 399
Hertz, Ronald S., 264
Heuristic, 719
Heuristic pricing, 253
Higgins, John A., 647
High-low point method, 55, 719
Historical costs, 719
Historical factory overhead rate, 153, 719
Hofstede, G. H., 432, 437, 438
Holmes, Robert W., 647
Horberger, Arnold C., 354
Horngren, Charles T., 164, 174, 446
Human aspects of budgeting, 436

Ideal capacity, 719
Ideal standards, 464, 719
Identifiable costs, 719
Idle time, 719
Ijiri, Yuji, 33
Imperfect competition, 245, 250
Incentive contracts, 258, 719
Income:
  absorption costing, 193–96
  absorption vs. variable across time periods, 196
  variable costing, 192–96
Income statement:
  absorption form of, 121, 197, 209, 211, 493, 645
  budgeted, 546
  contribution form of, 197, 205, 210, 212, 259, 260, 261, 496, 546, 635
  defined, 719
  of manufacturing firm, 121, 197
  of not-for-profit concern, 211, 212
  by product line, 77, 214
  of service concern, 209, 210
  with standard costs, 493, 496
Income taxes:
  and breakeven analysis, 72
  and capital budgeting, 336–42
  capital gains and losses, 341
  and cash flow, 336
  depreciation, effects of, 337–38
  investment tax credit, 340–42
  operating loss carryback and carryforward, 339
  tax shields, 337
Incremental analysis, 11, 720
Incremental costs, 11, 720
Incurred costs, 720
Indirect costs, 109, 150, 166, 720
Indirect expenses, 110, 720
Indirect factory expenses, 110, 720
Indirect labor costs, 109, 720
Indirect manufacturing costs, 110, 720
Indirect material costs, 109, 720
Information economics, 32, 389, 720
Initial investment, 387
Insolvency, 574, 720
Inspection of contracts, 50, 720
Inspection of past behavior patterns, 50
Interest:
  compound, 345–50
  tables of:
    present value of an ordinary annuity of $1, Appendix B, 736
    present value of $1, Appendix A, 734
Interfirm decisions, 3–4, 720
Internal rate of return. *See* time adjusted rate of return
Internal revenue code, 337
Internal Revenue Service, 202
Interstate Commerce Commission, 4
Intracompany transfers, 686
Intrafirm decisions, 3, 5, 720
Inventoriable cost, 107
Inventory:
  economic order quantity, 589–91
  finished goods, 106
  lead time, 589
  in manufacturing concerns, 107
  raw materials, 106
  reorder point, 589
  replenishment point, 589
  safety stocks, 589
  turnover, 584, 720

valuation:
absorption vs. variable costing, 192–200
average methods, 125
Fifo, 198
Lifo, 198
when to order, 589
work-in-process, 106
Inventory turnover, 584
Investment:
comparison of bases, 679–81
defined, 679
possible bases, 679–81
unadjusted rate of return and, 387
Investment center, 151, 436, 676, 720
Investment decisions, 718. *See also* capital budgeting
Investment tax credit, 341–42, 720
Investment turnover, 677, 721
Invoice, 115, 721
Irvine, V. Bruce, 548
Iterative budgeting, 439, 721

Jaedicke, Robert K., 33, 310
Jenkins, David, 80
Job cost sheet:
defined, 111, 112, 721
illustrated, 113
Job order costing:
defined, 111, 721
documents for, 115–20
example of, 112–21
general ledger for, 114
overhead application in, 118
and process costing, 111–12
uses of, 111
Johnson, Orace, 80
Joint costs:
defined, 150, 721
nonrelevance in decision making, 289–91
and pricing decisions, 153
Joint processes, 289, 721
Joint products:
cost apportionment by:
physical measures, 255
relative sales value method, 291
defined, 255, 721
and pricing decisions, 255

Kellogg, Martin N., 599, 647
Kemp, Patrick S., 33
Khoury, E. N., 446
Kiessling, J. R., 647
Killough, Larry N., 33
King, Barry G., 355
Klammer, Thomas, 396, 399
Knight, Kenneth E., 33
Koehler, Robert W., 80, 647
Kohlmeier, John M., 599
Kravitz, Bernard J., 498
Krueger, Donald A., 599

Labor:
cost of, 109, 721
ledger entries for, 116–17
mix, 481
standards for, 466
variances, 481
Labor dollar base, 152
Labor hour base, 152
Labor variances:
efficiency, 481, 721
price, 481, 721
wage rate. *See* price
Largay, James, 218
Last-in, first-out, 198, 721
Lead time, 589, 721
Learning curve, 466, 721
Least squares regression method, 56–63, 721
Leverage, 344, 721
Lewin, Arie Y., 446
Liabilities, 721
Linearity of costs, 17, 26, 63
Linear programming:
algebraic method, 305–6
assumptions of, 299–300
in budgeting, 440
defined, 299, 722
graphic method, 300–304
in sales budgeting, 527
simplex method, 306
Liquid assets, 584
Liquidity, 574, 722
Liquidity ratio, 584, 722
Livingstone, John Leslie, 355
Long-range decisions, 722. *See also* capacity decisions
Long-range excess capacity, 165, 722
Loss, 106, 722

Machine hour base, 152
Macro sales forecasting, 516–17
Make or buy decisions, 292–94
Malcom, R. E., 548
Managed costs, 722
Management:
budgetary support by, 432
functions, 6, 421
goals, 422
objectives, 423, 520
organization structure of, 432
participation, 438

Management accounting, 3, 722
Management by exception, 427, 624, 722
Manufacturing costs:
  defined, 106–7
  direct labor, 109
  direct material, 109
  factory overhead, 109–10
  indirect, 152
Manufacturing expenses, 110, 722
Manufacturing overhead, 110, 722
Marginal cost, 22, 24, 722
Marginal costing, 192, 722
Marginal income, 722. *See also* contribution margin
Marginal revenue, 23, 722
Margin of safety, 79, 722
Margin on sales, 722. *See also* profit margin
Marketing activity variance, 165, 633–34, 723
Marketplaces:
  monopolistic competition, 250
  oligopoly, 251–52
  pure competition, 250
  pure monopoly, 250
Markup on cost, 253
Ma, Ronald, 694
Marple, Raymond P., 218
Master budget, 30, 425–26, 723
Matching, 723
Material:
  cost of, 109
  defined, 723
  direct, 109
  indirect, 109
  ledger entries for, 115–16
  standards for, 465
Material requisitions, 115, 723
Material variances:
  price, 477, 723
  quantity (usage), 479, 723
Mauriel, John J., 694
Meredith, G. G., 399
Method of least squares regression, 56, 517
Micro sales forecasting, 518
Miles, Raymond E., 498
Minimum desired rate of return. *See* cost of capital
Mixed costs:
  described, 16, 723
  illustrated, 17
  methods of separating, 50–63
Modenbach, Donald J., 446
Monopolistic competition, 250, 723
Monopoly, 250, 723
Morris, R. D. F., 647
Moss, Morton F., 218
Motivation:
  in budgeting, 438
  defined, 723
Moving average for overhead, 156
Multiple correlation, 63, 517, 723
Multiple performance measures, 692–93
Multiyear costing, 443
Myers, Ronald E., 399

National Association of Accountants (NAA):
  research reports, 80, 130, 174, 218, 264, 310, 355, 400, 498, 599, 694
  and variable costing, 202
Natural cost classification, 117, 723
Negotiated market price, 723
Nelson, H. Wayne, 446
Net book value, 724
Net income, 121, 333
Net present value:
  comparison of alternative projects, 377–78
  defined, 373, 724
  illustrated, 374–77
  ranking by, 377–78
  use in industry, 395–97
Netten, E. W., 647
Net working capital, 724
Neyhart, Charles A., Jr., 80
Noncontrollable costs, 151, 724
Nonproduction costs, 106, 110, 724
Nonrelevant benefits, 724
Nonrelevant costs, 724
Normal activity, 155, 724
Normal capacity, 155
Normal equations for least squares, 57
Normal overhead, 724
Normal standards, 464, 724
Normal statistical distribution, 60
Normal volume, 155
Not-for-profit organizations:
  benefit-cost analysis, 391
  budgeting for, 440
  decisions in, 391
Novick, David, 400

Objective function, 300, 724
Objectives, 423, 520, 724
Oligopoly, 251–52, 724
Open market pricing, 245
Operating cycle, 574–75, 724
Operating decisions:
  and the accounting approach, 11, 284
  assumptions, 24
  comparison of accounting and economic approaches, 26–27
  defined, 10, 724
  and the economic approach, 19
Opportunity costs, 10, 284, 724
Order-filling costs, 110, 724

Order-getting costs, 110, 725
Ordering costs, 589
Organization structure:
  and budgeting, 432
  controllability, 436
  decentralization, 676
  goals of, 6
  illustrated, 521
  types of, 438
Out-of-pocket costs, 29, 725
Overapplied overhead, 120, 159–62, 483, 487, 725
Overhead. *See* factory overhead
Overhead variances:
  efficiency, 484, 718, 725
  spending, 160–63, 487, 718
  volume, 160–63, 488, 718
Oxenfeldt, Alfred R., 264

Palmer, B. Thomas, 310
Participation in budgeting, 438
Past costs and decision making, 10
Payback method:
  calculation, 385–86
  defined, 725
  illustrated, 386
  nonuniform cash flows, 386
  uses in industry, 395–97
Payback period, 725
Payback reciprocal, 398
Performance budget, 428–29, 725. *See also* flexible budget
Performance data, 30, 682
Performance reports, 30–31, 725
Period budget. *See* static budget
Period cost, 106, 193, 725
Pick, John, 647
Planning:
  budget, 725
  defined, 6, 424, 725
  diagram of, 7,
  process, 421
  relationship to control, 29–31, 427
  role of, 5–6
Planning and control process:
  budgets, 29–31
  diagram of, 422
  framework for, 7, 31
  management by exception, 427
  performance reports, 427
Planning Programming Budgetary Systems (PPBS), 441
Plant-wide overhead rate, 171, 725
Political factors, 394
Practical capacity, 155, 162–65, 725
Prater, George I., 599
Predetermined overhead rate, 725
Preferred stock, 725
Present value:
  of annuity, Appendix B, 736
  defined, 333, 347, 725
  of a single sum, Appendix A, 734
  tables of, Appendixes A and B, 734–37
  See also discounted present value; net present value; rate of return
Pressure in budgeting, 437
Price variance, 477, 481, 726
Pricing:
  and apportioned fixed costs, 254
  contribution margin approach, 259
  cost-based, 253
  cost-plus, 257
  economic approach, 245
  heuristic approach, 253
  influential factors, 245
  and multiple products, 255
  Robinson-Patman Act, 262
  supply and demand approach, 245–52
  target, 356–57
  transfer, 686
Prime cost, 192, 726
Prior department costs, 123–24
Procedures, 726
Process costing:
  defined, 111–12, 726
  equivalent units in, 125
  example of, 122–29
  and job order costing, 111–12
  ledger entries for, 129
  uses of, 111
  weighted average method of, 125
Product contribution, 540
Product cost, 106, 193, 726
Product costing:
  absorption costing, 107
  direct costing. *See* variable costing
  job order costing, 111, 112–21
  joint products, 291
  objectives of, 111
  process costing, 111, 122–29
  standard costing, 470
Product cost sheet, 216
Production activity variance, 165, 726
Production base, 213, 726
Production budget, 726
Production costs, 106, 109, 726
Production decisions, 285
Production departments, 166, 726
Production lot sizes, 306
Productive assets, 680, 726
Product margin, 213, 286, 726
Profitability accounting, 727. *See also* responsibility accounting
Profit center, 151, 435, 726
Profit margin, 677, 726

Profit plan:
- defined, 425, 726
- illustrated, 546
- steps in, 520

Profit planning chart, 73, 207, 726
Profit volume chart, 70, 208, 726
Pro-forma statements, 729
Program budgeting:
- defined, 441, 726
- multiyear costing, 443
- program structure, 442
- zero-based budgeting, 444

Programmed costs, 727
Projected statement of financial position, 727
Project selection. *See* capital budgeting
Pryor, LeRoy J., 548
Pseudoparticipation, 439
Public sector investment decisions, 391
Purchase invoice, 115
Purchase order, 115, 727
Purchase requisition, 115, 727
Purchasing budget, 727
Pure competition, 250, 727

Quantity report, 122
Quantity variance, 727
Quick ratio. *See* liquidity ratio

Ramanathan, K. V., 33
Rated capacity, 727
Rate of return:
- accounting. *See* unadjusted rate of return
- under decentralization, 676–77
- for decisions, 3
- minimum desired, 342
- target, 345
- time adjusted, 382
- and time value of money, 345–51
- unadjusted, 387
- unequal project lives, 385
- *See also* return on investment

Rates for overhead, 118, 152–58, 166–71
Rate variance, 727
Ratios:
- accounts receivable turnover, 584
- average collection period, 584
- current ratio, 584
- inventory turnover, 584
- investment turnover, 677
- liquidity, 584
- margin percentage on sales, 677
- trading on the equity, 344

Raw materials inventory, 727
Rayburn, L. Gayle, 498

Regression analysis:
- assumptions, 57
- correlation, 63
- multiple regression, 63, 517
- normal equations, 57
- simple regression, 56, 517, 727
- standard error of the estimate, 59

Relative sales-value basis, 291
Relevant benefits, 10, 284, 727
Relevant costs:
- book value, 284, 335
- and capacity decisions, 10, 333–34
- defined, 10, 284, 727
- fixed costs, 285
- and operating decisions, 10, 284
- opportunity costs, 284
- product line, 288

Relevant data for decision making, 727
Relevant range, 17, 26, 64, 727
Reorder point, 587, 728
Replenishment point, 589, 728
Reporting system:
- accuracy, 624–25
- external vs. internal, 637
- feedback, 621
- illustrated, 625
- relevancy, 621
- requirements for, 621
- timeliness, 624
- for top management, 633

Report on profit plan, 430, 636, 728
Residual income, 685, 728
Residual sum of squares, 59, 728
Residual variance, 59
Resource allocations, 8
Responsibility accounting:
- characteristics of, 433
- controllable costs, 150–51, 171, 436
- cost allocation, 150–51, 171
- defined, 433, 621, 728
- feedback, 621
- human aspects, 436
- illustrated, 172, 622
- participation, 438

Responsiblity center, 5, 150, 433, 728
Return on investment:
- composition of, 677–78
- defined, 3, 677, 728
- divisional, 683
- example of, 682
- limitations of, 684–85

Revenue:
- average, 23–25
- marginal, 23–25
- total, 22, 728

Revenue center, 151, 728

Rinehard, Jack R., 310, 599
Risk, 389, 728
Robinson-Patman Act, 262
Rolling (or moving) average, 728
Rowley, C. Stevenson, 400

Safety stock, 589, 728
Sales budget, 532–33
Sales for cost allocations, 291
Sales forecasting, 516, 521–23, 729
Sales invoice, 119
Sales mix, 75, 729
Sandbulte, Arend J., 548
Sawatsky, J. C., 446
Scattergraph estimates, 53–54, 729
Scharff, Sam E., 625
Scheduled production, 729
Schiff, Michael, 446
Schuba, Kenneth E., 310
Securities and Exchange Commission (SEC), 4, 202
Segment, 729
Segment margin, 729
Selling costs, 110, 729
Semifixed costs, 14, 729
Semivariable costs, 14, 729
Separable costs, 213, 729
Service departments, 166, 729
Setup costs, 306, 729
Sharp, Harold E., 174
Shillinglaw, Gordon, 694
Short-range decisions, 10, 729. *See also* operating decisions
Short-range excess capacity, 165, 729
Short-term credit analysis, 587–89
Shwayder, K., 174
Simple regression. *See* statistical regression analysis
Simplex method, 306, 730
Simulation in budgeting, 440, 730
Sinking fund depreciation, 679, 730
Slack, 439
Smidt, C., 399
Smith, Ephraim P., 599
Social benefits, 352
Social costs, 351
Soldosky, Robert M., 80
Solomons, David, 498, 677, 694
Solvency, 574, 730
Source documents, 115–19, 730
Specific cost of capital, 342, 730
Spending variance 160–63, 730
Split-off point, 289, 730
Staats, Elmer B., 398
Stairstep cost, 15, 730
Standard, 463, 730
Standard activity. *See* normal activity
Standard cost:
  for cost control, 463
  defined, 463, 730
  setting of, 464
  types of:
    expected, 464
    ideal, 464
    normal, 464
Standard cost card, 465, 476, 538
Standard costing:
  absorption, 474–75, 730
  benefits of, 463
  purpose of, 497
  variable, 472–73, 730
Standard deviation, 60
Standard error of the estimate, 59–61, 730
Standard overhead rate, 730
Standards:
  acceptance of, 469
  currently attainable, 465
  defined, 463
  expected, 464
  ideal, 464
  labor, 466
  material, 465
  normal, 464
  overhead, 469
  responsibility for variances, 480–82
  revision of, 470
  setting of, 465
Statement of changes in financial position, 4, 573, 593, 638
Statement of financial position, 4, 425, 572–73, 639, 644, 731
Static budget, 445, 731
Statistical regression analysis:
  advantages of, 56
  assumptions of, 57
  defined, 731
  least squares method, 56–57
  in sales forecasting, 517
  standard error of estimate, 59
Step costs. *See* stairstep costs
Stores card, 117
Straight line depreciation, 14, 337
Structure of organization, 6, 432
Suboptimization, 689
Subsidiary ledgers, 115
Summers, Edward L., 498
Sum-of-the-years' digits depreciation, 14, 337
Sundem, Gary L., 33
Sunk cost, 29, 731
Supplemental food program, 393
Supplementary fixed factory overhead rate, 216, 728

Supply curve, 246–48, 731
Supply and demand analysis, 245–49, 516
Swalley, Richard W., 220

Target rate of return, 345
Taylor, Otto F., 264
Tax shield, 337, 731
Tentative budget, 29
Terre, Norbert C., 395
Tersine, Richard J., 33
Time adjusted rate of return:
  calculation of, 382–83
  compared to accounting rate of return, 388
  compared to net present value, 385
  defined, 382, 731
  trial and error methods, 382
  See also adjusted rate of return
Time standards, 466
Time tickets, 116, 731
Time value of money, 9, 29, 345, 731
Top management objectives, 422–23
Total asset turnover. *See* investment turnover
Total contribution margin, 18–19, 203, 731
Total cost, 19–20, 731
Total income, 22
Total revenue, 21–22, 731
Traceable costs, 151, 731
Trading on the equity, 344, 731
Transaction balance, 586–87, 589
Transfer pricing:
  cost-plus, 689
  for decision making, 689
  defined, 686, 731
  dual pricing, 690–92
  for external reporting, 690
  full cost bases, 689
  illustrated, 690
  market prices, 688
  need for, 686
  negotiated, 688
  no intermediate market, 689
  objectives of, 686
  as a performance measure, 688
  standard costs, 688
  variable cost, 689
Trueblood, Robert M., 130

Unadjusted rate of return:
  defined, 387, 732
  illustrated, 388
  uses in industry, 395–97
Uncertainty:
  in capital budgeting, 389
  in decision making, 421
  defined, 732
Uncontrollable costs. *See* noncontrollable costs
Underapplied factory overhead, 120, 159–62, 732
Under- or overapplied factory overhead:
  analysis of, 159–62
  illustrated, 163
Unexpired costs, 106, 732
Unfavorable variance, 732
Unit costs, 111
U.S. Department of Commerce, 4, 517
Usage variance, 479, 481, 732

Variable budget, 732. *See also* flexible budget
Variable cost:
  accounting definition of, 11, 732
  economic definition of, 19
  graph, 12
  types of:
    curvilinear, 16–17
    mixed, 16
    pure variable, 11
    stairstep, 15
Variable costing:
  comparison with absorption costing, 192–200
  and the contribution margin approach, 203
  cost flow diagram, 195, 472–73
  defined, 193, 732
  for external reporting, 200–202
  income statement illustrated, 197
  and pricing decisions, 259
  and production decisions, 285
  and standard costing, 470–73
Variable cost ratio, 68, 732
Variable overhead efficiency variance, 484, 732
Variable overhead spending variance, 160, 163, 485, 732
Variable profit ratio, 68, 732
Variances:
  activity, 165, 464, 630
  causes of, 480, 481, 484–85, 487–88
  defined, 463, 732
  disposition of, 492
  fixed overhead:
    spending, 160–63, 487, 629
    volume, 160–63, 488, 732
  labor:
    efficiency, 481, 629
    price (wage rate), 481, 628
  marketing activity, 165
  material:
    price, 477
    quantity (usage), 479, 628
  need to isolate, 463
  overhead. *See* fixed overhead; variable overhead

- production activity, 165
- variable overhead:
  - efficiency, 484
  - spending, 160, 163, 485

Ventura, Jose, 354
Vergin, Roger C., 498
Vickers, D., 80
Volume:
- and cost behavior patterns, 49
- definitions of:
  - actual 153, 164–65
  - budgeted, 157
  - expected, 157
  - ideal, 162
  - normal, 155
  - practical, 155
  - rated, 162

Volume measure, 49
Volume variance, 160–63

Walker, Charles W., 647
Wallace, M. E., 548
Weighted average cost of capital, 342, 373
Weighted average inventory method, 125, 732
Weiser, Herbert J., 80
Welsch, Glenn A., 498, 548
Wilson, Charles Z., 33
Working capital, 335, 572, 733
Work-in-process inventory, 107, 733
Work measurement, 464
Work ticket. *See* time ticket
Wright, Howard W., 264
Wright, Wilmer, 498

Zannetos, Zenon S., 498
Zero-based budgeting, 444, 733